CW01025321

THE MODERN CRUISER

THE MODERN CRUISER

The evolution of the ships that fought the Second World War

ROBERT C STERN

Seaforth
PUBLISHING

Dedication

To the many kind and generous individuals who have helped make this and my previous books so much better out of a shared passion for naval history, I dedicate this book. It is a curious quality of 21st-century communications that I have physically met few of the gentlefolk who make up my particular 'support community', but I hope that through the process of sharing knowledge and resources, we have become friends.

This edition first published in Great Britain in 2020 by
Seaforth Publishing,
An imprint of Pen & Sword Books Ltd,
47 Church Street,
Barnsley
South Yorkshire S70 2AS

www.seaforthpublishing.com
Email: info@seaforthpublishing.com

British Library Cataloguing in Publication Data
A catalogue record for this book is available from the British Library

ISBN 978 1 5267 3791 5 (Hardback)
ISBN 978 1 5267 3792 2 (ePub)
ISBN 978 1 5267 3793 9 (Kindle)

Pen & Sword Books Limited incorporates the imprints of Atlas, Archaeology, Aviation, Discovery, Family History, Fiction, History, Maritime, Military, Military Classics, Politics, Select, Transport, True Crime, Air World, Frontline Publishing, Leo Cooper, Remember When, Seaforth Publishing, The Praetorian Press, Wharncliffe Local History, Wharncliffe Transport, Wharncliffe True Crime and White Owl.

Typeset and designed by Mousemat Design Limited
Printed and bound in India by Replika Press Pvt. Ltd

Frontispiece: The ultimate expression of Royal Navy wartime cruiser design was the 'colonial cruiser' idea developed as the *Hawkins* class, of which HMS *Frobisher* (D81) was an example, seen here soon after completion in 1924, flying the flag of the Rear Admiral commanding the 1st Cruiser Squadron, Mediterranean Fleet. Three of her 7.5in/45 Mk VI single-mount guns can be seen. To accommodate seven of these large guns, *Frobisher* was big – more than 2200 tons heavier than the 'E' class – with a short forecastle with almost no sheer. This proved to be a feature with unfortunate side-effects; these ships were very wet forward in any weather. *Frobisher* was completed with a new larger two-level bridge, which became the early model for the bridge layout for the new cruisers built between the wars. (NHHC)

Contents

Acknowledgements

Having just completed *The Battleship Holiday*, a book of similar scope and style, I was fortunate enough to have already gathered many of the necessary resources, both human and historical, needed to write and review this work. Still, this is a different work and much new material had to be gathered. I have attempted to list below all who helped in that effort. To any I have failed to mention, please accept my thanks and my apologies.

- William Jurens, for his deep knowledge of naval history and technology, his invaluable advice and assistance and for his excellent drawings reproducing in black and white the complex war damage diagrams of the cruisers that fought at the Battle of Savo Island – for all of these I am eternally grateful;
- My brother Richard and my wife Beth, who have read over my manuscripts, often in very rough form, and have given me myriad helpful suggestions;
- John Jordan, for his sharing of his knowledge of the French Navy of this period, for several excellent photographs and for his permission to reproduce drawings he originally created for the seminal work he co-wrote with Jean Moulin, *French Cruisers: 1922-1956*;
- Enrico Cernuschi, for his generosity with his time and deep knowledge of the *Regia Marina*;
- Anthony Tully and Allyn Nevitt, for reading over the sections covering Japanese cruisers and their helpful comments;
- David Doyle, for providing photographs;
- Troy Valos, of the Sargeant Memorial Collection, Norfolk (VA) Public Library, for his great assistance in making photographs available from the excellent Virginian-Pilot Collection;
- Randy Stone, for timely comments on the Battle of Savo Island;
- Vince O'Hara, as ever, for his gracious assistance in providing help when my resources seemed to reach a dead-end; and
- The ever-patient staff at the Modern Military Branch at the US National Archives (officially, the National Archives and Records Administration (NARA)), College Park, MD.

All of these generous folks have my undying gratitude. They have helped make this book much better than it would otherwise have been. They bear no responsibility for any defects that may show up here. Responsibility for those is mine alone.

Photo Credits

All photographs for which I have recorded the source are credited at the end of each caption. Unfortunately, I have been collecting naval photographs since long before digitization and Adobe Lightroom made organising and record-keeping easy, and, in the early day of my collecting, my notes were haphazard at best. The sad fact is that I am unable to recover the source of some of the images I have used here, which is why a few of the images in this book are uncredited. I apologise to the generous anonymous people who allowed me to copy their photographs, whose names I failed to record, and can only hope they approve of my use of them here.

The following abbreviations have been used in crediting photographs:

AWM	Australian War Memorial
DoD	Department of Defense (US)
LOC/BNS	US Library of Congress/Bain News Service Collection
LOC/HEC	US Library of Congress/Harris & Ewing Collection
MoD	Ministry of Defence (UK)
NA	National Archives (UK)
NARA	National Archives & Records Administration (US)
NHHC	Naval History & Heritage Command (US)
NPL/VPC	Norfolk (VA) Public Library/ Virginian-Pilot Collection
RNSM	Royal Navy Staff Monographs
SLV/AGC	State Library of Victoria (Australia)/Allen C Green Collection
TSNA&ME	Transactions of the Society of Naval Architects & Marine Engineers (US)
USAF	US Air Force
USMM	*Ufficio Storico della Marina Militare* (Italy)
USN	US Navy

A Note on Nomenclature and Units, etc

Names of geographical locations mentioned in this book are those that would have been used by an educated English-speaker of the first half of the twentieth century. Where those differ from the current name or spelling of a place, the current usage is given in parentheses when first encountered. Ranks and rates for the men of navies other than the US Navy, excepting only the Royal Navy, are translated to the closest USN equivalent.

Mention should be made of the fact that, as the reader probably has already noticed, the author is American; for the most part, this should make no difference to the British reader. However, there is one point of terminology on which the Americans and British differ that should be pointed out lest confusion result. To the Americans, the highest continuous deck in a ship is the Main Deck; to the British, it is the Upper Deck. To the Americans, the next lower deck is the Second Deck; to the British, this is the Main Deck. The author uses American terminology throughout, except that quotes from British sources retain British terminology.

When first referenced, US Navy ships are identified by their hull number (e.g., USS *Baltimore* (CA68)) in which the letters designate hull type (CA – heavy cruiser) and the number is a one-up counter of hulls of that type as ordered.[1] For Royal Navy ships of the treaty era, pennant numbers are given when they are first mentioned (e.g., HMS *Kent* (54)).[2] Warship prefix designators, such as 'USS', 'HMS' or 'RN', are also used only the first time a ship is mentioned. Some nations, such as Imperial Japan, used no such designator and none is used in this book.

Dimensions of ships are given in feet (12in/304.8mm/abbreviated 'ft') and inches (25.375mm/abbreviated 'in'). Distances are given in feet and yards (3ft/0.9144m/abbreviated 'yd') and nautical miles (2025.37yd/1.853km/abbreviated 'nm'). These are the units used by most seamen in this time period and remain in use in America and, to a lesser extent, Great Britain. Gun calibres are given in the system used by the nation to which a ship belonged. Radar wavelengths are given in metric units. Weights are given in those units used by the nation whose weapon or craft is being described. For the US and UK, this was the English system of pounds and ounces; for the rest of the world, this was the metric system (1kg = 2.205lb; 1lb = 16oz = 453.6g). One has to be careful when speaking of tons. This tripped up experts at the time and can confuse modern readers as well. When the Americans and British navies spoke of tons, they meant 'long tons', which equalled 2240lb; the rest of the world meant 'metric tonnes', which equalled 1000kg or 2204.6lb. (To confuse matters even more, there was also the 'short ton', used in commerce, which equalled 2000lb, but was never used in regard to ship characteristics.)

To aid any readers unfamiliar with the conversion of gun calibres between 'pounders', inches and metric measures, the following crib is provided. The reader should always remember that nations felt no obligation to hew exactly to the precise diameters to which their guns were labelled. The German 28cm (11in) gun, throughout its development history from 1890 until 1934, was always actually 28.3cm (11.1in) in bore diameter. Sometimes guns were mislabelled to mislead an enemy, as in the case of the Japanese 46cm (18.1in) guns developed for the *Yamato* class. These guns were labelled as 40cm (15.7in) to deceive American intelligence. Also, some conversions from old-style 'pounder' designations to inch or metric calibres were far from exact; the ones given here are simply the most common and should be taken as representative rather than necessarily exact for any given gun:

.50cal	=	12.7mm	4.7in	=	120mm/12cm	7.5in	=	190mm/19cm
0.79in	=	20mm/2cm	5in	=	127mm/12.7cm	7.6in	=	194mm/19.4cm
1.1in	=	28mm/2.8cm	5.1in	=	130mm/13cm	7.87in	=	200mm/20cm
1.5in	=	37mm/3.7cm	5.25in	=	134mm/13.4cm	8in	=	203mm/20.3cm
2pdr/1.575in	=	40mm/4cm	5.46in	=	138.6mm/13.86cm	8.27in	=	210mm/21cm
1.97in	=	50mm/5cm	5.5in	=	140mm/14cm	9.2in	=	234mm/23.4cm
6pdr/2.244in	=	57mm/5.7cm	5.9in	=	150mm/15cm	9.45in	=	240mm/24cm
2.9in	=	75mm/7.5cm	6in	=	152mm/15.2cm	10in	=	254mm/25.4cm
12pdr/3in	=	76.2mm/7.62cm	64pdr/6.3in	=	160mm/16cm	11in	=	280mm/28cm
3.46in	=	88mm/8.8cm	6.4in	=	164mm/16.4cm	12in	=	305mm/30.5cm
4in	=	102mm/10.2cm	6.5in	=	165mm/16.5cm	12.2in	=	310mm/31cm
4.1in	=	105mm/10.5cm	6.6in	=	170mm/17cm	12.6in	=	320mm/32cm
4.5in	=	114mm/11.4cm	7.1in	=	180mm/18cm	13in	=	330mm/33cm

List of Abbreviations/Acronyms

AA Anti-Aircraft
AAC Anti-Aircraft Common (US Navy term for the AA form of HE projectiles)
ACNS Assistant Chief of the Naval Staff (Royal Navy officer in charge of tactical policy and planning)
AFCT Admiralty Fire Control Table
AMC Armed Merchant Cruiser
AP Armour-Piercing
APC Armour-Piercing Capped
AR Action Report
ARA *Armada de la República Argentina* (Argentine Navy – also used as a warship designator for naval ships in Argentine service)
ASW Anti-Submarine Warfare
bhp brake horsepower (the measured horsepower of the rotating shaft of a steam turbine or internal combustion engine before any reduction gearing, cf., shp, ihp)
BLR Breech-loading rifle (a rifled naval artillery piece loaded from the breech – cf., MLR)
BuC&R Bureau of Construction and Repair (the US Navy department responsible for the named activities)
BuEng Bureau of Engineering (the US Navy department responsible for power systems)
BuOrd Bureau of Ordnance (the US Navy department responsible for guns and gunnery)
BuShips Bureau of Ships (formed in June 1940 by the merger of BuC&R and BuEng)
CID Committee of Imperial Defence (a standing committee of members of the British Cabinet, heads of the military services and Dominion Prime Ministers, intended to advise the Prime Minister on military strategy, in existence from 1902 until 1939)
CinC Commander-in-Chief (primarily a US Navy usage; pronounced 'sink'; in British usage it is often hyphenated, as 'C-in-C')
CO Commanding Officer
CNO US Navy Chief of Naval Operations
CPC/CPBC Common Pointed Capped/ Common Pointed Ballistic Capped (Typical QF shell used against armoured targets, a common shell given an armoured cap and, optionally, a ballistic cap, cf., SAPC/SAPBC)
CPO Chief Petty Officer
crh calibre radius head (a number – properly two numbers but almost always shown as a single digit – indicating the curvature of the nose of an artillery shell; the higher the number, the longer, more streamlined the nose – numbers normally range between 4 and 8)
DCT Director Control Tower
DNC Director of Naval Construction (the Royal Navy's head of the ship design bureau, generally a civilian marine architect)
DNO Director of Naval Ordnance (the RN's lead gunnery officer on Admiralty staff)
DP Dual Purpose (referring to guns that could be fired at aircraft and surface targets and the directors that controlled them)
EOC Elswick Ordnance Co
FY Fiscal Year (in US terminology, the budgetary year in which money was allocated for a ship; often does not coincide with the calendar year; expressed in the form 'FYyyyy', as in 'FY1928')
GM Metacentric Height (a measure, in feet, of the height of a ship's metacentre – the point where a vertical line from the ship's centre of buoyancy intersects the ship's inclined centreline)
GMT Greenwich Mean Time
GRT Gross Register Tons (a measure of a cargo ship's carrying capacity, only indirectly related to displacement)
HA High-Angle (generic descriptor for anti-aircraft-related equipment)
HACS High-Angle Control System (Royal Navy anti-aircraft fire-control direction system)
HADT High-Angle Director Tower (Royal Navy anti-aircraft fire-control position)
HC High-Capacity (synonymous with HE)
HE High-Explosive (synonymous with HC)
HMAS His Majesty's Australian Ship (Royal Australian Navy warship designator)
HMCS His Majesty's Canadian Ship (Royal Canadian Navy warship designator)
HMNZS His Majesty's New Zealand Ship (Royal New Zealand Navy warship designator)
HMS His Majesty's Ship (Royal Navy warship designator)
HTS High-Tensile Steel (homogenous armour-grade steel highly resistant to deformation under stress, widely used as a construction steel for warships after the First World War)
IFF Identification Friend or Foe (an electronic interrogation system that allowed a radar scope to display whether a contact was friendly or not)
ihp indicated horsepower (the theoretical energy output of reciprocating steam engines, as opposed to the measured energy output of rotating shafts, cf., bhp, shp)
IJN Imperial Japanese Navy
KC Krupp Cemented armour

KM *Kriegsmarine* (the German navy after 1935)[1]
KNC Krupp Non-Cemented armour (a homogeneous high nickel content armour steel used by the Royal Navy (and many others) between 1900 and 1925)
KNS Krupp Nickel Steel (a homogeneous high-percentage nickel alloy armour steel used by Germany during and immediately after the First World War, until replaced by the *Wotan*-series steels)
LA Low-Angle
LD laid down
MLR Muzzle-loading rifle (a rifled naval artillery piece loaded from the muzzle – cf., BLR)
MN *Marine Nationale* (the French navy)
NC Non-Cemented steel (the generic term for homogeneous armour plate used in the place of KNC after the First World War, frequently a high-Molybdenum content alloy)
NCM Naval Conference (Ministerial) Committee (a British Cabinet-level committee established in April 1934 to monitor naval matters)
NIACC Naval Inter-Allied Control Commission (board established by the Treaty of Versailles to oversee the post-First World War German Navy)
NIRA National Industrial Recovery Act (a law enact by the US Congress on 16 June 1933 that enabled FDR to restart naval construction in the United States)
NVNC New Vickers Non-Cemented armour (a homogeneous carbon steel armour used by the Japanese in the place of KC)
OpNav US Navy Office of the CNO
PM The British Prime Minister
PO Petty Officer
PPI Plan Position Indicator ('God's Eye View' 360° radar display)
QF Quick-firing
RAF Royal Air Force
RAN Royal Australian Navy
RCN Royal Canadian Navy
RDF Radio Direction-Finder (originally simply a passive system for identifying the direction from which a radio signal originated; sometimes used by the British as a synonym for radar)
RM *Regia Marina* (Royal Italian Navy – from 1861–1946)
RMA *Reichsmarineamt* (Imperial Naval Office – the pre-1918 German Admiralty)
RN *Regia Nave* (Royal Ship – warship prefix designator used by the *Regia Marina*)
RN Royal Navy
RPC Remote Power Control (a system of automatic gun-pointing controlled by a fire-control system)
rpm rounds-per-minute (rate-of-fire for a gun, meaningful only as a sustained rate, so care must be taken to assure that the given rate is not a burst rate artificially-supported by ready-service ammunition storage)
SAM Surface-to-Air Missile
SAP Semi-Armour-Piercing
SAPC/SAPBC Semi-Armour-Piercing Capped/ Semi-Armour-Piercing Ballistic Capped (later name for CPC/CPBC)
SecNav Secretary of the Navy (US Cabinet-level civilian in charge of the Navy, equivalent of British First Lord of the Admiralty)
shp shaft horsepower (the measured horsepower of the rotating shaft of a steam turbine or internal combustion engine after any reduction gearing, cf., bhp, ihp)
SMS *Seiner Majestät Schiff* (His Majesty's Ship – *Kaiserliche Marine* warship designator)
STCN *Service Techniques des Constructions Navales* (design bureau of the *Marine Nationale*)
STS Special Treatment Steel (a high nickel content armour-grade high-tensile-strength weldable steel used by the US Navy for vertical bulkheads and protective decks)
TBD Torpedo Boat Destroyer
TF Task Force (USN designation for a large ad hoc force given a specific task)
TG Task Group (USN designation for a subdivision of a TF)
TNT Trinitrotoluene (an explosive widely used in bomb and torpedo warheads and artillery shells, replacing Lyddite (trinitrophenol) as the preferred explosive at the beginning of the twentieth century due to its chemical stability and its ability to withstand shock)
TS Transmitting Station (RN term for the gunnery control station below decks; Plotting Room in USN parlance)
UK United Kingdom
USAAF United States Army Air Force
USN United States Navy
USS United States Ship (USN warship designator)
VLS Vertical Launch System
VTE Vertical Triple-Expansion (an advanced form of compound steam engine)
Wh *Wotan hart* (Krupp-made homogeneous nickel steel used for armour plate)
W/T Wireless Telegraphy (Royal Navy term for radio, particularly Morse as opposed to voice radio)
Ww *Wotan weich* (Krupp-made homogeneous nickel steel, somewhat more ductile than Wh, used primarily for holding bulkheads)
XO Executive Officer

Introduction

This book came about, in part, because in the course of writing *The Battleship Holiday*, I found it necessary to apologise to the reader for spending an inordinate amount of time and space discussing cruisers.[1] Simply put, the story of warship development in the critical period between the world wars, as often as not, centred on issues related to the size and numbers of cruisers the major naval powers wanted to build and would be allowed to build by the treaties negotiated in those years (and by the parlous state of most national economies during the 1930s). This book, starting with a necessarily brief look back at the emergence of the steam-powered, iron-hulled cruising ship in the 1860s, then following the multiple threads of development that led to the big armoured cruisers and the light cruisers of various sizes that fought in the First World War, will concentrate on the period of intensive development between the wars. It will then look at how the ships that emerged from that period stood up to the test of combat in the Second World War and, finally, glance, again very briefly, at the evolution of the cruiser type in post-war navies, at some ships that were (and are) called cruisers that perhaps should not be and at a few that are not and perhaps should be.

Author's Very Brief Note

The reader should be aware that the author intends in this introduction, and indeed in all the coverage of cruiser development up to the end of the First World War, to be very selective in the coverage of ships and lines of development. The evolution of the modern cruiser from the cruising ship of the age of wood and sail was fiendishly complex.[2] It has been the subject of multiple full volumes. Only those ships, ship types and events that had an impact on the cruisers that were designed and built during the primary time period under discussion will be covered in the introductory chapters.

Frigates, Corvettes, Sloops, etc

In the age of wood and sail, warships were either 'line-of-battle ships' or they were one of multiple categories of smaller cruising ships used for the remaining tasks required of a fleet. These tasks included scouting (and preventing enemy scouts from doing their job), protecting trade from raiding cruisers (or conversely raiding enemy trade routes), message delivery (in the days before wireless telegraphy, introduced to ships in the 1890s, made beyond-visual-range communication possible) and maintaining a military presence on distant colonial stations. After the 'locomotive torpedo' became a credible weapon in the mid-1870s, cruising ships also took on the task of defending the fleet against enemy torpedo attacks and leading the fleet's torpedo boat flotillas against the enemy.[3]

The transition from wood and sail to iron and steam was far from simple for any ship type, but it was far easier at the capital ship end of the scale. Battleships simply had to be the biggest, strongest ships in the fleet. When it came to cruising ships, it was clear that there could be no 'one size fits all' ship design that could perform all the tasks listed above equally well; they all called for more speed and endurance than a battleship, while requiring less firepower and protection, but needed these qualities in varying amounts depending on the task. Even before the transition, cruising ships came in a variety of types, with no hard and fast dividing line between them, but generally, from larger to smaller, cruising ships were classed as frigates, corvettes, sloops and scouts or avisos (dispatch boats). In general, frigates were intended for the longest-duration missions, so would be sent to colonial destinations or on trade protection or interdiction missions; corvettes and sloops would be used for scouting and protection of the fleet against enemy scouts. A navy might not have purpose-built small scouts or avisos for communications work; sloops were often used for that.

When the first ships were made of iron, it was natural that they would be designed as types that would replace their wooden predecessors. Nor was it in any way surprising, considering the comparative characteristics of iron vs wood and steam vs sail, that it proved far easier to create an iron/steam equivalent of a 'line-of-battle ship' than of any of the smaller cruising types. There were several reasons for this. Mainly it was because early steam engines were large, with low power-to-weight ratios, fitting more easily into larger hulls; it took years of technological advances to develop engines small enough and powerful enough to meet the requirements of cruising ships. Just as importantly, battleships in the second half of the nineteenth century had more limited range and speed requirements than any of the cruising types. This did not prevent the inevitable replacement of wood by iron and then by steel and the adoption of steam power in cruising ships of all types, but it does explain why sails were being removed from steam-powered battleships fifteen years earlier than from similarly-powered cruisers.[4]

When the first iron-hulled cruising ships were built in the second half of the 1860s, navies still used the traditional names to categorise the different sizes of cruising ships, calling them frigates, sloops and so on, but it soon became obvious that the names had little relevance in a world where the relationship of ship size and function was not nearly as easy to define as it had once been. While the term 'sloop' would remain in use in the Royal Navy to describe a small, handy, multi-purpose vessel, the term 'frigate' fell out of use in the 1870s and 'corvette' in the early 1880s. In their place, by the mid-1880s, a categorisation scheme came to be used that could only have been loved by legislators and accountants. Cruisers, at least in the Royal Navy, were defined as belonging to one of three classes, prosaically labelled 'first', 'second' and 'third', from large to small. These classes generally took on the roles of frigates, corvettes and sloops respectively from sailing-ship days, with first class cruisers used mostly for colonial and trade-protection duties, second class cruisers intended as fleet scouts and third class cruisers serving as flotilla leaders and liaison vessels.

Reactions, and Reactions to Reactions . . .

The first iron cruising ship was HMS *Inconstant*, laid down in November 1866 and completed in 1869. Despite her rather inauspicious name, she was so advanced that two sister-ships were completed to nearly-identical designs five and seven years later. She was classed as an unarmoured iron frigate, displacing 5780 tons, powered by a horizontal single-expansion engine driving a single raisable propeller shaft that allowed her to maintain 15.5 knots for a full 24 hours, at that time an unheard-of achievement. She mounted ten 9in muzzle-loading rifles (MLRs) and six 7in MLRs, all in single broadside mounts except for two of the smaller guns which fired through forward-facing insets in the bow. The guns were mounted this way, as they would have been in any ship built for the preceding hundred years, because the *Inconstant*s carried a full three-masted ship rig and a fixed bowsprit and that was seen as the most practical way to mount guns in a fully-rigged ship; they were considered fine sailers that could reach 13.5 knots under full top-gallants and royals before a fair wind. They were, at the time of *Inconstant*'s commissioning, the most advanced cruising ships in the world.

It is interesting to note that HMS *Shah*, the third and largest of the *Inconstant* class and not completed until 1876, found herself engaged in what was perhaps the earliest battle between iron warships, the Battle of Pacocha in May 1877. *Shah*, involved in the kind of colonial duty appropriate for a cruiser, was on the west coast of South America, when her captain was ordered to intervene to protect some British merchantmen captured by the Peruvian monitor *Huáscar* and being held at the port of El Callao. When the Peruvians heard of the approach of *Shah* and the smaller wooden screw corvette HMS

Third of the three-ship *Inconstant* class of unarmoured iron frigates, HMS *Shah* was not completed until 1876, ten years after the laying down of the lead ship of the class. By this time, an unarmoured cruiser mounting guns in broadside ranks like a Nelsonian ship-of-the-line was already obsolescent, if not totally obsolete. Nonetheless, the Royal Navy was not about to waste a brand-new, large iron and steam cruising ship and sent *Shah*, looking as she appeared in this image, off to the South American station to protect British interests, a typical assignment for a cruising ship. There, on the coast of Peru, in May 1877, she fought the Battle of Pacocha, an inconclusive engagement with the Peruvian monitor *Huáscar*, perhaps the earliest battle between iron warships. (NHHC)

Amethyst, *Huáscar* fled, finally being caught in Pacocha Bay.[5] In the ensuing battle, fought in the late afternoon of 29 May, the two British ships fired over 400 rounds of common shot – they carried only a few armour-piercing (AP) rounds – obtaining approximately sixty hits, not one of which did any serious damage to *Huáscar*, although her top-hamper was pretty well shot up and she suffered one man killed and several others wounded. *Huáscar*, which was undermanned, managed to get off only forty shots during the battle and could claim only some damage to one of *Shah*'s masts for the effort. *Shah* was clearly an anachronism, as much as *Amethyst*. Neither had any business in a gun battle with a well-armed and armoured turret ship. In just the eight years since *Inconstant*'s completion, *Shah* had become hopelessly outdated. Within two years, she would be paid off.

The critical descriptor used in reference to the *Inconstant*s was 'unarmoured'. Before *Shah* was completed in 1876, much less could be dispatched to South America, she was already being rendered obsolescent by newer designs that addressed her lack of protection in several different ways. When *Inconstant* was designed, there was simply no room for any protective armour in the plans for iron ships smaller and faster than capital ships. Nevertheless, it soon became obvious that the mission requirements of ships such as *Inconstant* would bring them into potential conflict with ships as strong or stronger and that the total lack of any protection to their vitals – magazines and engineering spaces – had to be considered a critical liability. As the naval architects of the day turned their talents at the beginning of the 1870s to the problem of how to protect a cruising ship, they, perhaps inadvertently, gave rise to the most important distinctions that would be used to categorise cruisers in the last decades of the nineteenth century.

The first to make the most obvious move in this direction were the Russians. In 1870, the 'belted cruiser' *General-Admiral* was laid down at the Nevskiy Yard, St Petersburg.[6] The term 'belted cruiser' was invented to describe a cruiser with a waterline armour belt; the term would almost immediately be replaced by 'armoured cruiser'. In the case of *General-Admiral*, the waterline belt, which ran the full length of the hull, was wrought iron 5in–6in thick, extending from 2ft above to 5ft below the load waterline. Six 8in/22 breech-loading rifles (BLRs) were grouped in a similarly-armoured central battery which extended out over the sides of the hull, allowing fire directly fore and aft from the corners of the battery. Although in most respects *General-Admiral* was an admirably advanced design, she suffered from two serious problems which limited her utility. One was her speed; her power plant generated approximately 4700ihp to drive a ship that displaced just over 5000 tons. It is small wonder that *General-Admiral* could barely reach 12 knots under steam on a good day. The other problem was that the completion of the ship proceeded very slowly; while she raised a great deal of interest at the time of her laying down in November 1870, by the time she was completed and entered service in 1875, she had been superseded by ships built to better designs, inspired, at least in part, by knowledge (or rumour) of her capabilities. *General-Admiral* did serve her country's several successive governments a long time, not being stricken until 1938, but almost all of that time was spent in second-line duties.

The ship the Royal Navy built in response to rumours of *General-Admiral* was HMS *Shannon*, begun on 29 August 1873 and completed in 1877 to a design in many ways similar to her Russian counterpart's. She too carried her largest guns in a central battery designed to fire forward as well as to the side; she also had a waterline armour belt, although hers did not run the full length of the ship; and she was also significantly underpowered, her Laird horizontal-return connecting-rod engines producing only 3370ihp, driving her 5670 tons at a maximum of 12.25 knots. On top of this slow speed, she proved to have inadequate range under steam and to be a poor sailer. All this limited *Shannon*'s utility. She saw only four years of seagoing service, only two of those on distant stations, before being brought back home and being reduced to coastguard duties.

Another class of armoured cruisers was designed and laid down by the Royal Navy before *Shannon* was launched, as if they sensed that she would leave much to be desired. The two ships of the *Nelson* class were enlarged *Shannon*s, almost all of

Perhaps the earliest armoured cruising ship to be laid down was the Russian *General-Admiral*, started at the Nevskiy Yard, St Petersburg, in 1870 and commissioned a year before *Shah*. She is seen here at the Columbian Exposition, held at New York City, in April 1893, after she had been re-engined, adding a second funnel. In order to allow better arcs-of-fire for her main battery of six 8in/22 guns, while retaining her full sailing rig, her designers gave her an armoured central battery extending out over the sides of the hull between her foremast and mainmast. Gun ports at the corners allowed limited fore-and-aft fire from the main battery. (NHHC)

As designers sought to marry armour, armament and steam with sail, they sometimes came up with extremely creative compromises, such as the French barbette ship *Bayard*, seen here about the time of her completion in 1882. She was wooden-hulled with steel upperworks and ram bow, and had a complete waterline belt of wrought iron as much as 10in thick and four 9.4in/19 guns in her main battery. The guns were sited in armoured barbettes, two next to each other forward under the bridge, one on the centreline immediately abaft the funnels and one more, also on the centreline, between the main and mizzenmasts. The hull, in characteristic French fashion, had considerable tumblehome, which caused the forward pair of barbettes to extend out from the hull in sponsons. Unarmoured hoods covered the barbettes, with cross-shaped slits that allowed the guns a limited range of elevation and train. (NHHC)

the added 2000 tons being given over to a larger power plant that almost doubled the power output; that bought only two additional knots of speed, which was a significant disappointment. However, their larger size gave them sufficient coal storage to add enough range to be of greater utility to the fleet.

And Now for Something Completely Different . . .

At the same time that the Royal Navy was stumbling through its first halting steps towards building a practical armoured cruiser, it laid down a pair of ships classed as 'despatch vessels' that would serve as an important step towards developing an alternative cruiser model. Critical in this development was the availability of affordable steel, made possible by the invention of the Bessemer and Siemens-Martin processes in the 1850s and 1860s.[7] Steel had significant advantages over iron, being stronger per unit weight, allowing the construction of ships that were lighter or stronger (or both). Navies began experimenting with steel in the place of iron as soon as the steel plates and structural members became available in sufficient quantities. The French were the first to use steel in large quantities in a warship, the *Marine Nationale* laying down the central-battery ship *Redoutable* in August 1873. Most of her structure was steel, but her armour was wrought iron. The Royal Navy would, in November 1875, lead the way in laying down an all-steel warship.[8] HMS *Iris* was born out of a desire to build a ship that was fast and inexpensive enough that it could be built in large numbers. She was small (3730 tons), had a large power plant (a horizontal direct-acting compound engine designed to produce 6000ihp), a very light barkentine rig and a relatively light weapons fit (ten 64pdr [6.3in] MLRs in the main battery).[9] The requirements placed on *Iris*' designer, Nathaniel Barnaby, were pushed by foreign developments.[10] Several potential rivals had produced cruisers made of wood or iron over the preceding few years that were significantly faster than anything the Royal Navy was building. Barnaby felt compelled to develop a ship that not only met the requirements of affordability, but could also exceed the speed of any of these competing designs. The only way to achieve these fundamentally incompatible goals was to forego all armour protection. *Iris* was completed with wide coal bunkers lining her sides from her double-bottom all the way up to her Main Deck. These served two purposes – providing some limited protection against at least torpedo boat-sized weaponry and giving what was, for the time, the impressive endurance under steam (for a ship of such small displacement) of over six days at half-power.

The next logical step came from the brilliant mind of the Italian designer Benedetto Brin. Like Barnaby, he was presented a set of goals that seemed impossible to achieve in one ship. The *Regia Marina* wanted a ship that had size, protection and armament equal or better than the best of contemporary battleships, but at the same time had all the qualities of a colonial cruiser, meaning it had to be significantly faster and have greater endurance than any battleship and be able to carry an infantry division (approximately 10,000 men) in addition to her crew.[11] To his credit, Brin produced a design of considerable ingenuity that met most, if not all, of the stated requirements. The ship he designed was laid down on 3 January 1876 at Castellammare and given the name RN *Stella d'Italia*, later shortened to just *Italia*. She had the size (13,678 tons normal displacement), the speed (17.8 knots), the armament (four 17in main-battery guns in a

The increased availability of steel, being relatively light and strong compared to iron, made the development of an all-steel warship simply a matter of time. The first such was HMS *Iris*, completed in April 1879, seen here as she appeared after being rearmed in 1886–7. She was intended to be the prototype of a new kind of inexpensive, high-speed cruising ship, protected by her speed rather than armour. What little protection she had was provided by an extensive belt of coal bunkers lining her sides, which also served to give her impressive range under steam power. Her light main battery of thirteen 5in guns was arrayed mainly in a broadside battery, with three in shielded Main Deck single mounts. (NHHC)

The true revolution in the design of cruisers came with the abandonment of sailing rigs. The designer of RN *Stella d'Italia* was able to make that move in part because, although this ship had all the characteristics of a cruiser, she was officially classified as a battleship, which type was already being built without sails when *Italia* was laid down in 1876. Her main battery of four 17in guns was truly battleship-sized, but her planned top speed of over 18 knots was befitting a cruiser (compared to the speed of contemporary battleships). She lacked an armour belt, introducing a domed armoured deck topped by a 'cellular layer' as waterline protection, plus an oval barbette of 17in sloped compound armour under the guns. Unfortunately, she took nine years to build, not completing until 1885, by which time she was no longer revolutionary. (NHHC)

diagonally-disposed central barbette), accommodation for troops (three complete decks above the engineering spaces and below the main battery running the length of the ship) and good range (approximately 5000nm). Where Brin's ingenuity was most on display was in her protective scheme. He knew, as Barnaby had with *Iris*, that he did not have the displacement available to give this ship an armour belt and still retain the other desired qualities. His solution was to give *Italia* a domed armoured deck just below the waterline, 4in thick over the ship's centreline, that extended the full length of the ship; above this was a 'cellular layer' – a layer of watertight compartments filled with coal or completely sealed to act as cofferdams – topped by an unarmoured horizontal deck. Brin's reasoning was that no vertical armour of any thickness that could be carried by a ship of *Italia*'s size would be effective against the main-battery guns then being mounted. It would be better, according to his reasoning, not even to try to defeat enemy shells, but rather to limit the damage they did by subdividing the waterline area into many small individually-buoyant compartments on top of a reasonably thick armoured deck protecting the ship's vitals. (Remember this was at a time when battles were expected to be fought at ranges well under 10,000yds, and plunging fire was not yet the threat it would become in the not-too-distant future.)

Although officially classed as a battleship, *Italia* was understood by all potential rivals for what she really was, an over-sized cruiser. More importantly, whether she is seen as a cruiser or not, the armour scheme Brin developed for *Italia* proved highly influential. None of the individual elements – the armoured deck or the cellular layer – was new, but the combination as the primary protection scheme for a warship intended to be fast and far-ranging, became a pattern that was picked up almost immediately by designers in other nations. (They did not wait for *Italia* to be completed, much less launched; the Italians were notoriously slow in the construction of many of their most revolutionary designs.[12] *Italia* was laid down in 1876, but not launched until 1880 and not completed until 1885.)

In mid-1880, follow-ons to the *Iris* class designed by Barnaby were laid down; three ships of the *Leander* class were laid down on 14 June 1880, though the first was not completed until May 1885. Well before HMS *Leander* was launched on 28 October 1882, however, an 'Elswick cruiser' being built for Chile was laid down. This ship, named

Esmerelda, was designed by George Rendel at the Armstrong & Co, Ltd, Elswick yard, Newcastle upon Tyne. She would set a new standard for small cruisers. ('Elswick cruiser' was a specific and also a generic term used to describe the large number of warships, mostly cruisers, built by British shipyards, mostly Armstrong's Elswick yard, for export to foreign navies between 1867 and the start of the First World War. Armstrong alone built 159 ships for eighteen navies during this period. Among these were even two originally ordered by Brazil that ended up being purchased by the US Navy for use in the Spanish-American War – USS *New Orleans* and *Albany*. 'Elswick cruisers' have been described as being 'designed to emphasize speed and gun battery rather than survivability, endurance, or ammunition supply; in modern terms, they showed concentration on visible rather than invisible qualities'.[13])

This description quite accurately fits *Esmerelda*, which, long before she was completed in July 1884, created a sensation because she seemed to embody all the qualities of Brin's *Italia* in a cruiser displacing only 2950 tons. What made this feat all the more remarkable was that *Esmerelda* had a full-length armoured deck (½in amidships, sloping down at the sides 1in thick), a well-subdivided cellular layer with a cork-filled cofferdam outboard, a powerful armament of two 10in and six 6in BLRs and a two-shaft horizontal compound (double-expansion) power plant capable of driving her at 18 knots.[14] She was the first cruiser to be completed without a working sailing rig, having instead two 'military' masts with fighting tops, She created this sensation despite the fact that she had very low freeboard fore-and-aft – only 11ft – which led to her being very wet in any sea and a rather unstable gun platform. This was not so much a problem in her first life in the relatively calm coastal waters off Chile, but, in November 1894 she was sold to Japan (via Ecuador); the Japanese were embroiled in the First Sino-Japanese War and faced the urgent need to strengthen their navy. The Japanese found the *Esmerelda*, which they renamed *Idzumi*, handled poorly in the rough waters in the Sea of Japan and she was taken in hand for major reconstruction, with new, lighter-weight armament replacing her main and secondary batteries.[15] Nonetheless, the set of characteristics brought together in *Esmerelda*/*Idzumi* clearly defined a type of cruiser not seen before, one that

One of the original 'Elswick cruisers', RN *Giovanni Bausan* was built for the *Regia Marina* at the Armstrong yard to a design by George Rendel, being laid down in 1882 and delivered in 1885. She is seen here at the Columbian Exposition, New York City, in April 1893. What made an 'Elswick cruiser' different from all those that came before was emphasis on speed and offensive power to the exclusion of all other ship characteristics. *Bausan* had a main battery of two 10in/30 EOC Pattern G breech-loading guns in single barbettes fore-and-aft with six 5.9in/26 guns in sponsons along the sides. Protection was limited to a 1½in armoured deck topped by a cellular layer bounded by cork-filled cofferdams. (NHHC)

Another Rendel-designed 'Elswick cruiser' was the Japanese *Naniwa*, laid down at the Armstrong yard in 1884. This image, dated 1885, shows Japanese officers, obviously from the contingent sent to take possession of their new cruiser, posing on or over one of the Krupp 20.6cm/35 main-battery guns in its barbette. (NHHC)

sparked a frenzy of emulation in other navies. This required a new type-descriptor; almost immediately, these small, fast cruisers, protected primarily by an armoured deck and watertight compartmentation, became known as 'protected cruisers'.

The protected cruiser appeared to provide the solution that all major navies were searching for in a cruising ship that had a good balance of size, speed, range, armament and protection. It is safe to say that every major navy reacted in some way to the idea – if not to the idea itself, then to the fact that everyone else was reacting to it. Before *Esmerelda* was completed in July 1884, four other nations had laid down ships that would come to be called protected cruisers (although they often had different type descriptors at the time); these were (in chronological order of laying down): the French *Sfax* (March 1882); the Italian RN *Giovanni Bausan* (21 August 1882), the Royal Navy's HMS *Mersey* (9 July 1883) and the Japanese *Naniwa* (27 April 1884). The laying down of five fairly similar designs for five countries in a period of three years was hardly coincidental. Three of those ships – *Esmerelda*, *Bausan* and *Naniwa* – were designed by George Rendel or his successor at Armstrong, William White, and were built at the Elswick yard.[16] *Mersey* was designed by White before he joined Armstrong, but he was well aware of *Bausan*'s design, to the extent that when he submitted his first design draft in May 1882, he made a pointed comparison between his design, drawn up to Admiralty requirements, and *Bausan*'s, noting the clear superiority of the Rendel design.[17] The Admiralty Board agreed with him and asked for an upgraded design. The one ship on that list not designed by Rendel or White, the French *Sfax*, was similar only in having an armoured deck and cellular layer for protection; otherwise, *Sfax* looked like she came from an earlier era, with a full barque sailing rig and her six 6.4in/28 main-battery guns mounted in forward-facing embrasures and side sponsons.

Nor was this the end of the close relationship in the designs of protected cruisers of the world's navies. The Chinese ordered a pair of Elswick cruisers laid down in October 1885 – *Chih-Yuen* and *Ching-Yuen* in old-style Wade-Giles transliteration.[18] The Russians ordered a large (5863-ton) protected cruiser from the French in 1886 – *Admiral Kornilov*. A trend towards larger protected cruisers had already begun, led by the French; soon after launching *Sfax* in 1885, the *Marine Nationale* laid down a second protected cruiser nearly half again as large. *Tage* had the same set of anachronistic features as *Sfax*, just writ much larger to the tune of 7469 tons normal

Above: Essentially a copy of *Naniwa*, USS *Charleston* (C2) was built at Union Iron Works, San Francisco, starting in 1887, from plans developed by William White at Armstrong. She was to have been armed with single 8in/35 guns in her main-battery barbettes, but when she was completed, these guns were not available, so a pair of shielded 6in/30 mounts, the same model gun sited in her broadside sponsons, were substituted in each barbette, as seen here. The larger guns were mounted in an 1891 refit. (NHHC)

Right: Seen as she looked shortly after her completion in June 1887, the French protected cruiser *Sfax* clearly appears to be from an earlier period of naval design than the Rendel or White-designed 'Elswick cruisers'. Her three-masted barque rig and main battery in embrasures and sponsons harkened backwards rather than forwards. (NHHC)

Below: The Germans also designed their own first protected cruisers at this time, such as SMS *Prinzess Wilhelm* (seen here) and her sister *Irene*. This image shows *Prinzess Wilhelm* after an 1893 refit during which all but the four 15cm main-battery guns in the two sponsons per side were replaced by 10.5cm guns, three of which can be seen here in shielded single mounts just forward of the after sponson. (NHHC)

displacement. The Germans developed their own design for a protected cruiser, laying down SMS *Irene* and *Prinzess Wilhelm* in 1886. The Americans were the last naval power to lay down a protected cruiser. In part this was due to the parsimony of Congress, which disliked spending any money on defence, particularly on warships, when there appeared to be no threat of war in sight, and, in part, it was due to inexperience on the part of American shipbuilders. The US Navy finally turned to the ultimate source of knowledge on the subject, acquiring a design from Armstrong that closely resembled *Naniwa*'s. USS *Charleston* (C2) was laid down at the Union Iron Works, San Francisco, CA, on 20 February 1887, the last of the first-generation protected cruisers.

Protected Cruisers in Battle

Elswick-built protected cruisers met in battle most famously halfway around the world in the Battle of the Yalu, on 17 September 1894, which was the major naval confrontation of the First Sino-Japanese War. The Chinese squadron was built around two large German-built battleships, and also comprised eight cruisers of very mixed quality, the best of which were the two Elswick-built *Chih-Yuen* and *Ching-Yuen*. The Japanese force was much more uniform in composition, being made up of eight cruisers, all of relatively recent construction, as well as three older ships. The four fastest of the cruisers, including *Naniwa* and her sister *Takachiho* (and an even newer Elswick-built protected cruiser, *Yoshino*), were grouped into a 'flying squadron', which manoeuvred independently from the main body.[19] The Japanese had nearly all the advantages; their ships were faster, their armament newer and better-served and their training and unit cohesion was far

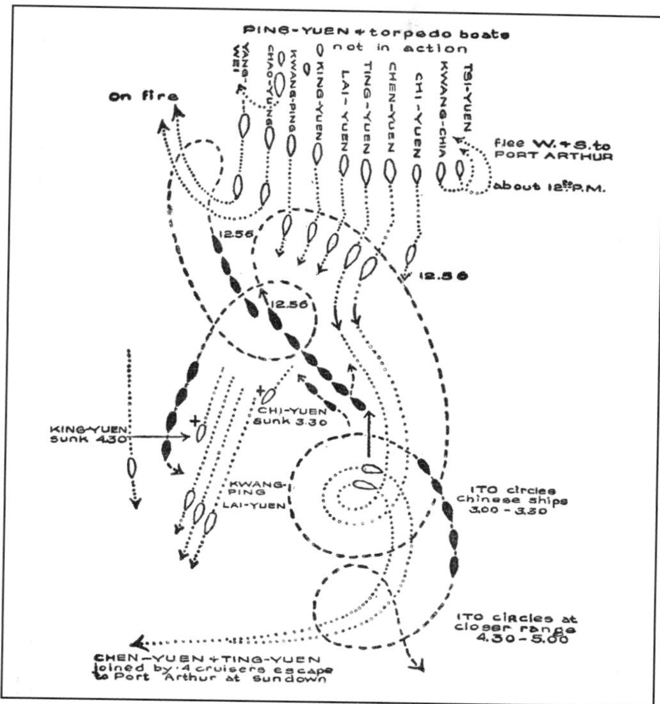

The Battle of the Yalu was fought on 17 September 1894 between a Japanese fleet, drawn up in two squadrons in line-ahead formation, shown in black in this chart, and a Chinese formation in line abreast centred on the two battleships *Ting-Yuen* (*Dingyuan*) and *Chen-Yuen* (*Zhenyuan*). The four newest and fastest of the nine protected cruisers (and three smaller ships) that comprised the Japanese force were positioned ahead of and to the port side of the main formation; this 'flying squadron', commanded by Rear Admiral Tsuboi Kozo, operated independently from the main body. It was mainly responsible for engaging the newer Chinese cruisers – the two Elswick-built protected cruisers *Chih-Yuen* (*Zhiyuen*) and *Ching-Yuen* (*Jingyuen*) and a pair of German-built belted cruisers *King-Yuan* (*Jingyuan*) and *Lai-Yuan* (*Laiyuan*). The Chinese formation shown in this chart, copied from Stevens and Westcott, *A History of Sea Power*, first published in 1920, is basically correct, except it uses unorthodox versions of the Chinese ship names and seems to have left *Ching-Yuen* entirely off the chart. *Chih-Yuen* (spelled *Chi-Yuen* in the chart) was set afire and attempted to ram *Naniwa*, the last ship in line in the 'flying squadron', but missed and sank soon thereafter. Tsuboi's squadron then concentrated on *King-Yuan* (spelled *King-Yuen* here), leaving her sinking. No Japanese ships were sunk, but Tsuboi's flagship *Yoshino* and the flagship of overall commander Vice Admiral Ito Sukeyuki *Matsushima* were both significantly damaged.

Rear Admiral Tsuboi's flagship and first ship in the line of the 'flying squadron' at the Battle of the Yalu was *Yoshino*. She was built at Armstrong's Elswick yard to a design by Philip Watts, completing in September 1893. Her main battery was four 6in/40 EOC QF guns, two in single shielded centreline mounts on the forecastle and quarterdeck and one each in sponsons abaft the foremast that allowed forward fire. At the time of her delivery, she was claimed to be the fastest cruiser yet built, with a top speed of 23 knots. (NHHC)

superior. The only advantage the Chinese had was their two battleships, which were larger and carried bigger guns and thicker armour than any Japanese ship. The battle can be described very quickly. The Japanese literally, as well as figuratively, steamed circles around the Chinese formation. Some of the Chinese ships fled at the beginning of the battle; two with wooden upperworks caught fire and burned to the waterline. For the most part the Chinese fought well but in a losing effort; the Japanese were unable to do serious damage to the two battleships, which broke off the action when they started to run low on ammunition for their main-battery guns. Two of the Chinese cruisers were sunk as well, including *Chih Yuen*; she apparently was hit by a shell that detonated one of her torpedo warheads, causing damage sufficient to sink her 'with screws racing in the air'.[20] The Japanese squadron took significant damage; four ships received damage described as severe, but none were sunk.

An interesting side note regarding this battle relates to the Elswick-cruiser *Naniwa* and the identity of her commanding officer, Captain Togo Heihachiro. He was a young officer on a rising career arc. He would command the Japanese fleet at the Battle of Tsushima in 1905.

Vice Admiral Ito's flagship *Matsushima* was surely one of the more bizarre-looking and, unfortunately, least-successful protected cruisers of the era. Built to a design 'suggested' by French naval architect Louis-Émile Bertin, she was one of three semi-sisters that shared a common size and shape and philosophical approach to naval warfare. Bertin was a leading proponent of the *Jeune École* (Young School) that promoted the idea that smaller navies (e.g., France or Japan) could take on large maritime powers (e.g., Great Britain or China) with small, fast, well-armed ships. In this scheme, protection took a backseat, because battles with well-armed enemy warships were to be avoided (by use of the aforementioned high speed). At Bertin's suggestion, the three *Matsushima*s carried a single very large main-battery gun, the 12.6in/38 Canet in a thick barbette with a 4in armoured hood over the top; unlike her two sisters, *Matsushima* carried hers aft, seen here under the awning. This gun was exceptionally powerful, firing a 990lb AP round or a 772lb HE round; unfortunately, it was extremely slow-firing. Its advertised rate of fire was one round every five minutes; its actual rate of fire in combat proved to be closer to one round every hour. During the Battle of the Yalu, *Matsushima* managed to fire four shots with her main battery, achieving one hit. In return, she was hit twice by 305mm shells from one of the Chinese battleships; she suffered more than half of the approximately 200 Japanese casualties that day. (NHHC)

The Decade of the Protected Cruiser

Among the lessons from the Battle of the Yalu, besides the obvious ones relating to the superiority of the line-ahead formation adopted by the Japanese and the critical importance of squadron speed and gunnery training, was the clear indication that while the protection provided by the armoured decks of the Japanese protected cruisers was effective in keeping those ships afloat in a gunfire engagement, it in no way prevented major damage or significant casualties. Nonetheless, the decade that stretched from the middle of the 1880s through the mid-1890s was dominated by protected cruiser development. Except for small, lightly-armed and armoured scouts and torpedo cruisers, which continued to be

One of the new Chinese belted cruisers, *King-Yuan*, is seen as she looked soon after launch at Vulcan, Stettin (Szczecin). A barbette forward held two 8.2in/35 guns under a thin armoured hood. A narrow belt of 9.4in-thick compound armour was completely submerged at full load. *King-Yuan* was badly battered and set afire by the QF guns in Tsuboi's 'flying squadron', mainly those in *Yoshino*, and sank in a cloud of smoke and flame. (NHHC)

built at a steady rate, almost all medium- and large-sized cruisers were built to protected cruiser designs.[21]

In Great Britain, the Royal Navy authorised no armoured cruisers between 1886 and 1897.[22] The Admiralty calculated that cruisers would require vertical side armour greater than 4in thick to resist gunfire by equivalent ships at the anticipated battle ranges. Starting from that basis, they then concluded that an affordable ship could not be designed with sufficient fighting qualities of speed and offensive power and at the same time carry enough armour of the requisite thickness. It was, in their opinion, better to leave the sides of cruisers unarmoured than too lightly armoured. The naval projectiles available in the mid-1880s were such that the shells would be unable to damage the armoured deck over the ship's vitals, and AP rounds, striking with flat trajectories, would likely pass through without detonating or causing much damage.[23]

The problem, as frequently happens, was that this reasonable conclusion began to look less reasonable as the decade passed, because the underlying assumptions on which it was based became increasingly invalid. The most obvious was the need to build small, affordable cruisers. As much as the Royal Navy may have wanted to build only modest-sized cruisers that could be turned out in large numbers – and they did build a truly large class of protected cruisers, the twenty-two ships of the *Apollo* class, starting in 1899 – the world seemed to conspire to create threats that small cruisers were insufficient to address. By the early 1880s, large, fast ocean liners were being built by several nations to ply the Atlantic and Indian Ocean routes, reaching sustained speeds in excess of 18 knots, and the financial incentives to claim the fastest and biggest liner was driving the competition to build ever larger and faster examples. Many of those liners were British, but some were not – in 1884, the fastest was the American-built SS *Oregon* – and other nations, particularly Germany, were joining the race.

The Royal Navy saw these ships as a potential threat; they were fast, long-ranging, and could be easily armed with a few small quick-firing guns and turned into armed merchant cruisers (AMCs) that could threaten Britain's long, vulnerable trade routes. What was needed was an equally fast, long-legged, but far better-armed cruiser that could make quick work of the potentially elusive but highly vulnerable AMCs. William White was asked to draw up a design for an big, fast cruiser. He was to take as his starting point, the design of the Royal Navy's last armoured cruisers, the seven ships of the *Orlando* class laid down in 1885–6. To White, they represented all that was wrong with the armoured cruiser type; they had a 10in-thick external armoured belt so short and narrow as to all but useless.[24] White was determined that not only would his 'AMC-catchers' be big and fast, but they would forego belt armour. His design was delivered to the Admiralty in June 1887, and was approved with few changes the following January; they would be the biggest, fastest cruisers any nation had yet built and they would be protected cruisers. HMS *Blake* would displace 9150 tons, measure 399ft 9in overall and be driven by a power plant based on new technology; vertical triple-expansion (VTE) reciprocating engines driving two shafts would deliver 20,000ihp at forced draft for a speed of 22 knots.[25]

As wonderful as the *Blake*s sounded on paper, in the water, the two ships in the class did not quite live up to expectations. Neither HMS *Blake* nor her sister *Blenheim* ever reached their contract speed. But White was not deterred. The *Blake*s were followed by nine ships of the *Edgar* class, 1800 tons smaller and designed for two knots less speed, but these ships, laid down in 1889–90, all exceeded their designed speed; they proved to be every bit the equals of the *Blake*s and served in the fleet to general approval.

The protected cruiser had one last great gasp before fading from the scene. In 1892, the Russians had launched a large armoured cruiser named *Rurik* which was causing alarm in Whitehall; as will be discussed in the next chapter, in some navies the type had never quite died out.[26] *Rurik* and two planned sisters, it was reported, were to be huge (almost 11,000 tons), with exceptional range – *Rurik* was reported to have been designed to be able to steam from Kronstadt in the Baltic to Vladivostok without coaling – which would suit them for the role of commerce raiders, the very thing that would most rapidly grab the attention of the Royal Navy.[27] The British felt compelled to reply; it mattered not that *Rurik*'s was in fact a poorly-executed, anachronistic design. Regardless, White responded with designs for what were again the largest cruisers (and the longest warships) yet contemplated by any navy when laid down in 1894. HMS *Powerful* and *Terrible* pushed the envelope in a number of dimensions. They displaced 14,200 tons, were 538ft long overall and had engines that produced 25,000ihp which drove them at 22 knots. The *Powerful*s retained essentially the same battery as the *Blake* class and had a similar armoured deck. (This whole series of large protected cruisers designed by William White had a designed-in provision for the later addition of side armour should that be decided upon, but White remained adamantly opposed to the idea and it was never done.[28])

The *Powerful* class did not mark an end to the production of protected cruisers by any means, but it certainly was the 'high-water mark' of the type, whose popularity dropped off rather rapidly soon after these ships were launched in 1897–8. Through no fault of their own, these two were considered 'white elephants', ships in search of a role to fulfil in the Royal Navy. In part this was because they pioneered some new technologies that were perhaps a bit too pioneering. They were the first large warships equipped with water-tube boilers, which had been successful in increasing endurance in commercial use, but in these ships, the forty-eight Belleville large-tube boilers proved troublesome from the start, leaking badly and, uncharacteristically, were surprisingly inefficient.[29] But the biggest problem facing these ships was that the Russian cruisers they were built specifically to counter proved to be fatally flawed; the *Powerful*s turned out to be a weapon without a target. For all intents, the era of the protected cruiser had come to an end.

The 'high-water mark' for the protected cruiser is best portrayed by the Royal Navy's HMS *Powerful*, seen here at Melbourne, Victoria, Australia. After a refit, she went into reserve until 1905, when she was made flagship of the Australia Station, which position she held until 1912. She had a main battery of two 9.2in/40 Mk VIII guns in single turrets and a secondary battery of 6in/40 QF guns arrayed in casemates along the sides. Despite the appearance of being at speed due to the thick plume of black smoke trailing from her two forward funnels, she is firmly anchored midstream. (SLV/AGC)

Chapter 1

Cruisers in all Sizes and Shapes – A First Glimpse of the Future: 1897–1914

1897 is an arbitrary year to choose as the dividing line between the first generation of steam and metal cruisers and the generation that would carry the type into and through the First World War, as there was no blinding flash of technical insight, no 'Trinity test' that jumpstarted the new era, so picking a point to mark the dividing line seems necessary. Still, a number of events occurred in that year, each in itself not important enough to have grabbed undo attention at the time, but together, in hindsight, sufficient to look like noticeable momentum in a new direction.

One reason for choosing that year is because it was the year in which construction was authorised for two classes of ships that were each, in markedly different ways, to have great influence on the further development of cruisers; one would stimulate the regeneration of a type that had been around from the beginning – the belted or armoured cruiser – while the other marked the genesis of a new type that would come to dominate the development of smaller cruisers – the light cruiser. One of these would grow to sometimes outsized proportions and – as will be seen – reach a dead end when put to the test in combat; the other would prove to be an adaptable, versatile platform that would serve as the basis for wartime development and beyond.

Driving this change were rapid advances in two interrelated fields of technology critical to naval development: explosives and metallurgy. Not that there had been sudden breakthroughs in either field in 1897, but in (or about) that year, the accumulating progress of the previous decade combined to bring about critical advances that pushed both fields forward rapidly. The development of the Bessemer and Siemens-Martin processes had made steel abundant and cheap beginning in the 1870s, but there things temporarily stalled, at least in terms of the use of steel for armour plate. Homogeneous 'mild' steel could be cast and rolled into plates of any thickness desired, and the protection provided was in direct proportion to the thickness of the plate, but so was the weight, and that was the problem for naval architects. (As noted above, the Royal Navy concluded in the mid-1880s that they could not provide armour thicker than 4in over a sufficient area of the side of a cruiser and still produce an affordable design.) Plates as thick as 22in were manufactured as early as 1876 by Schneider & Cie in France.[1] The problem was that homogeneous steel armour had some unfortunate characteristics, especially when compared to the iron armour it was replacing. Steel armour of any given thickness would resist penetration better than the same thickness of iron, but when the point of failure is reached, homogeneous steel loses its advantage. While steel did a good job preventing the penetration of the contemporary chilled cast-iron projectiles of the Gruson or Palliser types, once holed the armour would tend to break into pieces, becoming useless against further hits, whereas iron armour, if penetrated, would otherwise remain intact.[2]

In response to Schneider's functional monopoly on thick steel plate, the British firm of Charles Cammell & Co. began offering compound armour in 1877.[3] Compound armour was an attempt to combine the best qualities of wrought iron and mild steel by 'sandwiching' a plate of one to the other – the first compound armour was made by soldering the iron plate to the steel plate by heating them next to each other and then flowing molten steel between them. The compound plate was then further heated and rolled to assure adhesion, and finally quenched on the steel side to further harden that surface.[4] This process was later simplified by embedding the heated iron plate in the bottom of a clay mould and simply pouring molten steel over it to the required thickness. Compound armour was a successful idea; it did a better job resisting artillery projectiles than any existing plate. (An average Brinell Number for compound armour would have been 400/105, with the first number representing the hardness of the steel face and the second the hardness of the wrought-iron backing.[5]) However, this success was rapidly overshadowed by technological advances.

One of those advances was the introduction of nickel-steel by Schneider in 1889.[6] It was found that by adding between 3 per cent–7 per cent nickel into the steel, toughness could be increased substantially; the Brinell Number of a homogeneous plate went from 120–140 (for mild steel) to 180 (for nickel-steel). Since the manufacturing of a homogeneous plate was much simpler than the complex process required to make compound armour, it allowed nickel-steel plate to be offered at significantly lower prices. Add to that all the other advantages of steel over iron, in particular its lighter weight and greater structural strength, and it is easy to understand why the appeal of compound armour rapidly declined.

In 1890, the American inventor and metallurgist Hayward A Harvey set out to make a steel armour plate as successful at defeating armour piercing (AP) rounds as Gruson chilled cast-iron armour. (This latter was a specialised armour developed for land fortifications.) After heating a plate of nickel-steel to above its 'critical hardening temperature' – the temperature at which iron is able to accept significant amounts of carbon into its crystalline structure, generally above 723°C – one face was packed tight against a bed of bone charcoal for a period of two to three weeks, which allowed carbon to soak into the steel to an average depth of 1.25in. The plate was then heat-treated on the carburized (case-hardened) side to augment the hardening and finally quenched. This process, immediately called 'Harveyizing', produced a single plate with the characteristics of a compound plate; a Harveyized nickel-steel plate would typically have a Brinell Number of 680/190.[7] (The generic term for the process of carbon enrichment was 'cementing'. Armour types made this way were therefore called 'cemented' armours, and became so common that homogenous plates were often termed 'non-cemented'.) Harvey soon discovered that his process could be applied equally as well to mild steel plates, and a less expensive form of his armour was then offered with Brinell Numbers 680/140. It is small wonder that Harvey plate, almost overnight, became the preferred armour steel of the world's shipbuilders.

In 1893, in an attempt to break Schneider's monopoly in Europe, Friedrich Krupp acquired Gruson AG, in order to acquire that company's proprietary chilled casting technology. When they added that process to a cementing technique similar to Harveyizing and a new chemical recipe for steel that added chromium as well as nickel to the iron (which added another incremental upgrade in the toughness of steel plate), the resulting product, billed as Krupp Cemented (KC) armour and put on the market in 1894, proved to be immediately attractive to naval architects.[8] This was because, even though KC armour was considerably more expensive than Harvey plate, it was more effective per unit thickness.[9] The cemented layer was still just approximately 1.25in deep, but the Gruson process, generically called 'decremental hardening', resulted in a layer of gradually decreasing hardness that extended between 30 per cent–40 per cent of the thickness of the plate. This gave a Brinell Number of 680/225.

The one downside to these early cemented armours was that the manufacturing processes put limits on the thickness (or perhaps better to say, thinness) of armour plates. Because the face-hardened part had a normal depth of approximately 1.25in for Harvey plate and one-third of the plate's thickness in the case of KC, there was a practical minimum to the thickness of a plate of cemented armour. In the case of Harvey plate, the recommendation was that the 'soft' backing should be a minimum of three times the thickness of the cemented layer, which led to a recommended minimum of 6in armour plate. (Some instances are on record of 4in Harvey armour belts, but this was less than optimal usage.) Because the thickness of the cemented layer of Harvey armour was fixed regardless of the thickness of the plate, there tended to be little actual benefit in terms of increased protection against AP shot in increasing the thickness of a plate beyond 6in.[10] In this regard, KC had a distinct advantage, in that, because the backing steel was tougher than either the mild steel or nickel-steel used for Harvey plate and because the decremental hardening obtained from the Gruson chilling process was designed to work to a percentage depth of a plate (approximately one-third) regardless of its thickness, KC plates could be made to almost any thickness greater than 8cm (3.2in) and the amount of protection against penetration afforded by KC plate was a relatively direct function of plate thickness. The greater flexibility that KC afforded designers and the better protection for unit weight combined to explain why KC replaced Harvey as the preferred armour in cruiser design very rapidly. By 1897, that replacement was essentially complete.

For the sake of completeness, a very brief description of the development of the materials used in projectiles is necessary. As mentioned above, chilled cast-iron shell bodies became common for AP shells, beginning in 1866.[11] The compound plate introduced in 1876 proved itself relatively effective against the Palliser or Gruson shot then still in common use, although new materials were about to be introduced. (In 1878, the Royal Navy approved the adoption of the Whitworth shell, which comprised a mild steel body with a carburized (case-hardened) nose, that proved superior in tests to Palliser shell.) However, in separate tests run in the same year, it was discovered, quite unexpectedly, that the protective quality of compound plate was asymmetrical; it mattered which side the shell hit first. More so, it mattered not a little, but a lot. In the first tests, shots were fired at the front and back of a compound plate; shots that shattered on the hard face of the plate passed easily through the plate when they struck the softer back first. It was immediately apparent from examination of the plates that the accumulation of 'soft' iron around the point of the shell body protected the shell enough to facilitate its penetration. To verify this, the test was then repeated with a thin 'soft' wrought-iron plate clamped to the hardened outer face of the compound armour plate. The result again was increased penetration of the armour. The test was repeated once more with a mild steel 'jacket' fitted around the point of the AP shot. The result was the same. Thus Armour-Piercing Capped (APC) shells were invented; nonetheless, it was not until 1883 that the British fielded their first APC shells, and 1896 before the Royal Navy, followed quickly by other navies, began to adopt their first service rounds. Within several years, APC shells had become ubiquitous; by then mild steel caps had been supplanted by a decrementally hardened cap even harder than the Holtzer chromium steel that was adopted for AP shell bodies by many navies, including the US Navy, in the late 1880s.[12]

Something Old is New Again: The Re-emergence of the Armoured Cruiser

The preceding digression has been a chance to set the stage for a major shift in the direction of cruiser design driven (perhaps even necessitated) by another technical advance, in the field of explosives; the French adopted a new compound to fill their high-explosive (HE) shells in 1887, which they called Melinite. It combined a known explosive, guncotton (nitrocellulose), which was far more powerful than the gunpowder filler then in common use, with a newly-developed explosive, picric acid (trinitrophenol). Guncotton was notoriously shock-sensitive; it could not be used as a shell filler because it had a bad habit of premature detonation, sometimes in the barrel of the gun, but when mixed with picric acid, it became sufficiently stable to survive until striking the target. The British started manufacturing a similar explosive at a facility at Lydd in Kent, which they called Lyddite.[13] High-explosive shells filled with Melinite/Lyddite had much greater destructive power than shells filled with similar amounts of gunpowder.[14] When William White was made aware of these development in 1888, he downplayed their immediate impact on existing protected cruisers and his current and future designs, and the Royal Navy continued laying down large protected cruisers for another decade; other navies, the French in particular, saw the adoption of the more powerful explosive for what it was, the inevitable invalidation of the idea of the protected cruiser.[15] They saw that the new, more powerful HE shells had the potential to damage a protected cruiser's cellular/cofferdam layer above the armoured deck to the point where it would become more of a liability than an asset.

What was required was a cruiser that carried an armoured outer shell, not necessarily thick enough to keep out AP rounds, but sufficient to detonate HE rounds before they could penetrate. In 1888, the French laid down just such a ship. Precisely contemporaneous with White's *Blake*s, *Dupuy de Lôme* was a complete departure from previous French design practice and, really, from any cruiser yet built.

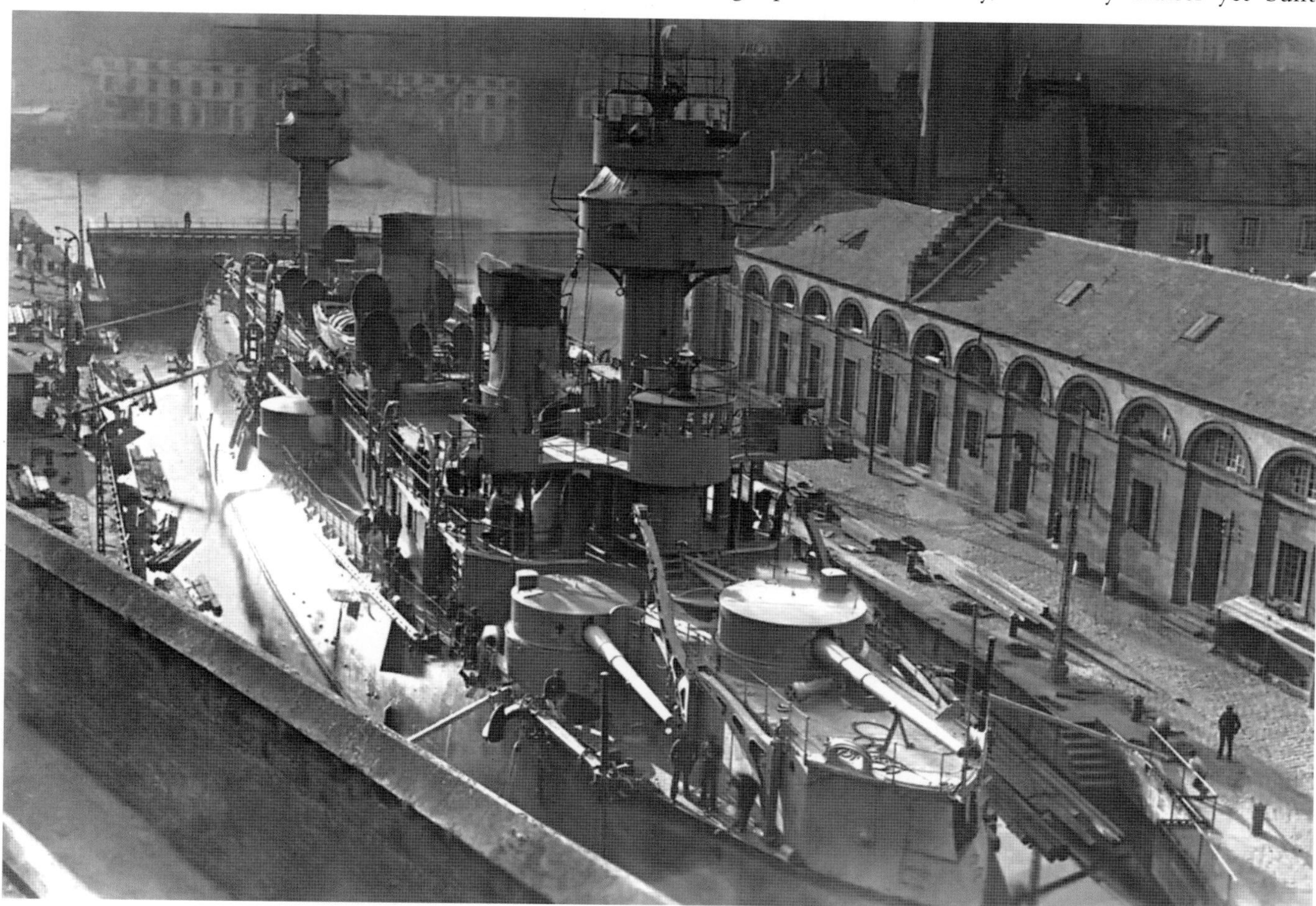

The French led the resurgence of the armoured cruiser as a type with ships such as *Dupuy de Lôme*, seen here at the celebrations for the re-opening of the widened Kiel Canal in June 1895. This was only a month after her delayed acceptance by the *Marine Nationale* due to persistent problems with her innovative *Amirauté* fire-tube boilers. She never met her designed speed of 20 knots. The exaggerated plough bow, tumblehome and cruiser stern were all designed to reduce the area needing armour protection, but at the same time, they made her a poor sea boat. The weight of the turrets in which all of her main- and secondary-battery guns were carried and the heavy military masts fore-and-aft did not help her stability.

Even though *Dupuy de Lôme* was extensively reconstructed starting in 1902 in an attempt to improve stability, she spent most of the rest of her short career in reserve. In this post-reconstruction image, dated c1918, it can be seen that she has been re-boilered – she now has three funnels rather than two – and the heavy military masts have been replaced by much lighter structures. (NHHC)

Designed by innovative naval constructor Louis de Bussy for fast, long-ranging, independent action, *Dupuy de Lôme* was given extensive offensive and defensive capabilities intended to allow her to deal with any enemy cruisers she might encounter. All her main- and secondary-battery guns were carried in single turrets, two 194mm/45s, mounted one on each broadside, and six 164mm/45s, laid out such that all could fire fore and aft, at least theoretically. (In practice, there was a great deal of interference between turrets and significant potential for damage to ship structures as arcs of fire approached the centreline.) But the ship's most noteworthy feature was her armour scheme, intended to allow her to survive any brush with enemy warships she could not outrun. For this purpose, she was given an impressively dense and redundant defensive system, starting with a 'shell' of 3.9in-thick homogeneous steel stretching from bow to stern and from 4.5ft below the waterline to the Upper Deck.[16] Curving up from the lower edge of the outer shell was a protective deck 1.2in thick, and below that was a splinter deck 0.8in thick; the 'tween-decks space was filled with coal. Above the protective deck, which was entirely below the waterline, was a tightly sub-divided cofferdam layer filled with cellulose, intended as a water-excluding material, to a height of 3.28ft above the waterline. (The cellulose used as a water-excluding material in cofferdams was most frequently sawmill waste, what the British term 'wood offal', a combination of sawdust and wood chips. It is a material that has the unfortunate tendency to rot if it gets wet.) De Bussy managed to pack all of these qualities, along with a power plant designed to move her at 20 knots, into a hull displacing only 6676 tons, 2500 tons less than the *Blake*s, a truly remarkable achievement. As if to call attention to the small displacement of this ship, and in what was a very real attempt to reduce the area of the ship under armour, *Dupuy de Lôme* had a remarkably long plough bow and exaggerated cruiser stern, all of which gave her an unusually squat appearance (and made her very wet at speed or in any sea).

These offensive and defensive aspects of the ship proved generally successful, but not without some serious teething problems. The complex curved steel armour plates proved to be of uneven quality and a number had to be remade when they were found to be visibly flawed. This delayed her commissioning for sea trials until April 1892, nor was this to be the last or worst of her difficulties. She had been built with an ingenious three-shaft engineering plant, with horizontal triple-expansion engines on the outer shafts and a vertical triple-expansion engine on the centre shaft. These were to be driven by steam generated by eleven *Amirauté* fire-tube boilers. (In an effort to increase the efficiency of early 'locomotive'-type single water-vessel boilers, various expedients were tried, including the water-tube boilers already mentioned and fire-tube boilers, which instead of a single fire-bed below the water vessel, substituted multiple fire-beds in tubes surrounded by the water vessel.) Much like the water-tube boilers tried out in the Royal Navy's *Powerful* class, these had problems when first introduced. Problems with these boilers, all of which had to be replaced at least once, delayed her final sea trials, acceptance and commissioning until May 1895. *Dupuy de Lôme* would never reach her designed speed of 20 knots, nor pose the threat to world (and particularly British) trade routes that she was designed to do, but she marked an important step in the re-emergence of the armoured cruiser as the dominant type of large cruiser.

Dupuy de Lôme generated immediate interest and reaction at home and abroad. The Russians picked up on the idea very quickly – they were very close followers of French practice at this time – producing the much-touted *Rurik* (described above) and following her with the even larger, and equally unsuccessful, *Rossia* and *Gromoboi*. The Russians were not shy when it came to technical innovation – *Rossia* had a very early Harvey nickel-steel belt as much as 8in

The US Navy in this period was ultra-conservative, as witnessed by ships such as USS *Brooklyn* (ACR3), seen here in the old-fashioned livery adopted after the Spanish-American War. *Brooklyn* displayed that anachronism by combining features of both the protected cruisers that had been the dominant type of the preceding decade and the armoured cruisers coming into vogue because new materials allowed and new munitions required better protection. This was hardly obvious in this view showing her not too long after the conclusion of the war, but another mix of features is. *Brooklyn*'s main battery of eight 8in/35 guns was mounted in well-armoured cylindrical twin turrets, a distinctly modern feature at the time of her laying down in 1893, but the turrets were nested inside raised barbettes of even thicker armour, a rather conservative touch. The military masts, the main-battery turrets carried in broadside sponsons, the pronounced tumblehome and the three tall, thin funnels, all contribute to *Brooklyn*'s old-fashioned appearance. (NARA)

thick, *Gromoboi* used KC armour 6in thick, among the first warships to do so – but the arrangement of armament remained anachronistic. The US Navy, despite, or perhaps because of, its strongly conservative bent, took to the armoured cruiser idea quickly. After a long period of parsimonious naval budgets, Congress authorised some serious shipbuilding in 1888. (Actually, it had started two years earlier, and a ship had been laid down classified as 'ACR1' – armoured cruiser number one – but this ship, USS *Maine*, was in reality a second-class battleship and, despite being famous for blowing up in Havana harbour in 1898, is of no interest to this story.) Renewed American cruiser building really started with USS *New York* (ACR2), laid down on 30 September 1890. Consistent with their conservative approach to design, *New York* had a full-length armoured deck, 6in thick in the sloping sections, with a well-subdivided cellular layer above that, plus a 4in-thick narrow waterline belt running the length of the engineering spaces, all armour being Harvey plate.[17] Of the main battery of six 8in/35 guns, four were in well-armoured twin turrets fore-and-aft, an advanced feature for cruisers at the time. The Italians produced only three relatively small, lightly-armed

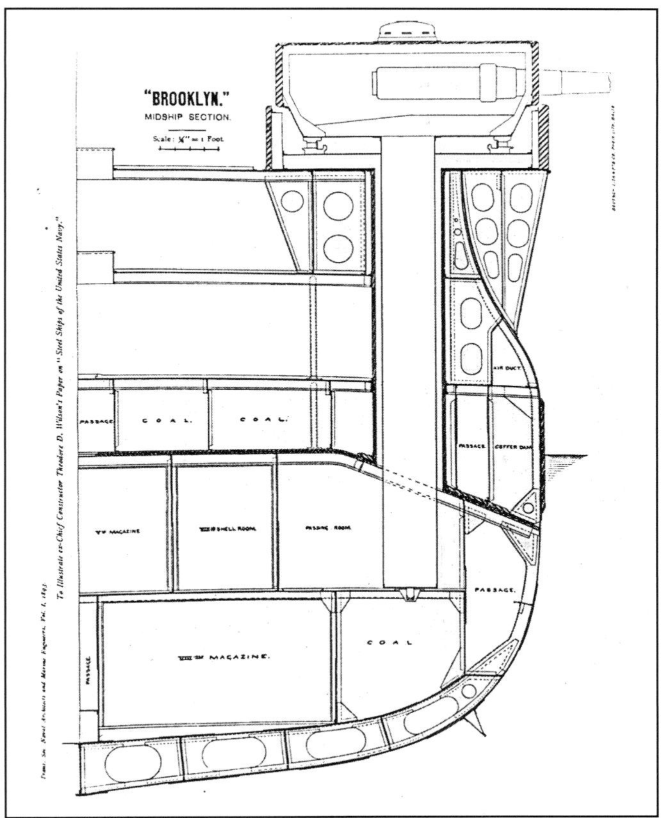

A cross-section plan of *Brooklyn* in way of her midships main-battery turret shows details of her armour scheme and the combination of conservative and advanced features that it included. Note that her armour scheme included both a domed armoured deck at the waterline, surmounted by a cellular layer of coal bunkers bounded by a cofferdam, all typical features of a protected cruiser, plus she had an external armour belt of 3in Harvey plate at the waterline, characteristic of an armoured cruiser. This cross section also shows one of the main-battery midships sponsons, built out over the tumblehome of the hull's shell plating, above which sits the barbette, 8in outboard and 3in inboard, inside of which sits the turret with 5.5in vertical sides. (TSNA&ME)

Seen in her later life, when she was employed as a training cruiser – the first of this name employed by the *Marine Nationale* in this role – *Jeanne d'Arc* is seen tied up alongside a pier in San Francisco, approximately 1920. Not much had changed in her appearance in the eighteen or so years since her completion at Toulon, at which time she was a leading example of a new type of super-large armoured cruisers noted for their great speed and range. However, she was criticised for being too lightly armed for her size; she carried a main battery of two 194mm/40 Mle 1893 in single turrets and a secondary battery of fourteen 138.6mm/45 Mle 1888 single mounts in Main Deck sponsons and unshielded forecastle-deck mounts. (NHHC)

armoured cruisers during this period. The Japanese, at this time, were building only small cruisers at home and were not yet convinced of the need to order another large cruiser from abroad.

If Big is Good, then . . .

In taking their time reacting to the French revival of interest in large armoured cruisers, the Japanese were only following the lead of their mentors, the British, who, following White's lead, were sceptical of about the value of a thin armour skin on a cruiser. Even the scare thrown into the British by rumours of the Russian giant *Rurik* and her follow-ons was not enough to shake White's belief in the protected cruiser with its 'soft' sides. It took the availability of KC armour to finally convince White that the time had come to reconsider the armoured cruiser type. Specifically, by White's reasoning, a belt of 6in KC plate could defeat the 100lb CPC/CPBC (4crh) 6in/45 QF rounds, hard-capped common shells then coming into regular use against armoured targets, the type he considered to be the greatest danger facing a cruiser. His logic was that the larger guns carried by cruisers at that time, ranging from 7.5in up to 10in, rarely exceeded a rate of fire of two rounds-per-minute (rpm) in practice, and, thus, presented a manageable threat. The 6in QF, on the other hand, which was liberally arrayed on contemporary cruisers as the main battery in smaller ones and the secondary battery in larger ones were capable of 4–5 rpm and could overwhelm any target within range that was not adequately protected.[18]

White, who had been taken ill in 1895, visited France and Italy during his recovery, a 'busman's holiday' during which he visited shipyards and naval ministries in both countries, coming away with information on their cruiser construction programmes, both of which appear to have influenced his thinking.[19] The French laid down *Jeanne d'Arc* in October 1896, which represented another jump ahead in cruiser design. She was the brainchild of Admiral Ernest François Fournier, who believed that fast, well-armed and well-armoured cruisers should be able to defeat large, slow battleships, and armoured cruisers should therefore be built in preference to battleships, particularly by nations like France with limited naval budgets. This led him to favour cruisers that were larger, faster, better-armed and better-armoured than any built before. *Jeanne d'Arc* did her best to meet that challenge. She was 11,100 tons, armed with two 194mm/40 main-battery guns in single turrets fore-and-aft and fourteen 138.6mm/45s in sponsons or single shielded mounts.[20] Her armour was Harvey nickel-steel 6in thick along the main belt at the waterline in way of the engineering spaces. This belt formed the outer edge of an 'armoured box' bounded by cofferdams and sub-divided into eighty coal bunkers. She had thirty-six du Temple-Guyot small-tube boilers situated in two widely-spaced fire rooms with her engine rooms in between; this gave her a distinctive silhouette with six funnels in two widely-spaced groups of three. Despite generating 33,000ihp, her three VTE engines drove her no faster than 21.8 knots, which was truly disappointing. Regardless of whether her speed or manoeuvrability was up to expectations, *Jeanne d'Arc* began a series of large armoured cruisers that would be the pride of the *Marine Nationale*; in the eyes of Fournier and the *Jeune École*, they were the true capital ships of the French navy for at least the next ten years. *Jeanne d'Arc* was criticised in some foreign navies for being under-gunned for her size; the ships that followed in the design series immediately after her – seven classes of eighteen ships laid down between 1898 and 1906 – were given a significantly stronger battery, but none of them carried armament equivalent to a contemporary battleship. It took an Englishman to take that step over the edge.

White also would likely have visited the Ansaldo yard at Genoa (Genova) where he would have seen the Italian armoured cruiser RN *Giuseppe Garibaldi* under construction. Designed by Edoardo Masdea, *Garibaldi* (6773–7628 tons) was a vast improvement over all preceding Italian cruisers and set a new standard for medium-sized cruisers, proving that the armoured cruiser concept was not restricted to only the largest ships. This design proved so popular that eleven more were ordered by three countries (including Italy), and ten were actually built over a period of ten years, serving in four different navies. Early ships in the class mounted two 10in/40 Elswick main-battery guns in single turrets fore-and-aft; later ships carried two 8in/45s in a twin turret aft in the place of the single 10in gun; at least two had the twin 8in guns fore-and-aft. A secondary battery of between ten and fourteen 6in/40 QFs were mounted in casemates and shielded mounts along the sides. Regardless, this meant that they were abnormally well armed for a ship that size. The armour type and thickness depended on the customer and when the hull was laid down. The first four built were bought by Argentina; they were completed with a waterline belt of 5.9in-thick Harvey steel (except for the fourth, which received KC); the

Setting a new standard for medium-sized armoured cruisers, the Italians laid down RN *Giuseppe Garibaldi* in 1895 at the Ansaldo yard, Genova-Sestri Ponente. So appealing was this design by Edoardo Masdea that the first five of the class were sold to foreign navies, including *Garibaldi*, seen here at completion at Genoa in 1897, after being turned over to the Argentines, who shared an equal admiration for her namesake and simply changed her name to ARA *General Garibaldi*. The angle of the sun makes the belt of Harvey plate, 5.9in thick up to the Main Deck in way of the magazines and engineering spaces, plainly visible. The large main-battery turrets fore-and-aft each held a single 10in/40 EOC Pattern R gun. The five casemates along the side each held a single 6in/40 QF EOC Pattern Z gun. (NHHC)

belt thinned to 3.1in at the bow and stern, but amidships was carried at full thickness up to the Main Deck. A thin (1.5in) curved armoured deck covered the full length of the ship at the waterline. They were good steamers, most making their designed speed of 20 knots. The Spanish navy, seeing how well-received the first ships were by the Argentines, bought the next ship to be laid down, naming her *Cristóbal Colón*. The Spanish were not happy with the cost of the Elswick 10in guns; *Colón* was delivered in 1897 with her main-battery turrets empty and was scuttled by her crew a year later at the Battle of Santiago in that condition.[21] The next three ships in the class were built for the *Regia Marina*, after which two more were built to a follow-on order by the Argentines, but, before they could be delivered, they were purchased by the Imperial Japanese Navy in 1904 as the last, extemporised, part of a programme of acquiring a squadron of world-class armoured cruisers in anticipation of war with Russia (see below). One more was ordered by the Spanish, a follow-on to *Colón*, but after the disastrous outcome of the Spanish-American War, the order was cancelled.

Regardless of the reasons, William White proposed following the long line of Royal Navy protected cruisers with an even-larger armoured cruiser version, the *Cressy* class (12,000 tons). Not only were the *Cressys*, authorised in 1897, to be larger than any previous Royal Navy cruiser, with the sole exception of the *Powerful* class, but they would match that class in armament and very nearly in speed, making them, finally, the ships White had wanted but had failed to achieve when he designed the *Powerfuls* four years earlier. The *Cressys* had, on top of their impressive size, armament and speed, a belt of KC plate 6in thick in way of their engineering spaces, which gave them the effective option of fighting any ship of equal or lesser size with a good chance of success and fleeing from anything bigger.

These were followed by the somewhat-larger *Drakes* and

Compare *Jeanne d'Arc*, seen above, to the contemporary HMS *Euryalus* of the *Cressy* class, seen here, the Royal Navy's answer to *Marine Nationale*'s large armoured cruisers. Designed by William White after his extended tour of French and Italian shipyards in 1895–6, the *Cressys* were bigger than *Jeanne d'Arc* by 1000 tons, but were shorter and beamier and, consequently, marginally slower. Their main-battery guns were bigger – a pair of 9.2in/47 Mk Xs in single turrets – and they carried fewer, but bigger, guns in their secondary battery. They accomplished this with stacked casemates fore-and-aft on each side, a feature that had limited utility in any sea, when the lower casemates would tend to be unserviceable. *Euryalus* is seen in this image sometime between 1908 and 1914, after the date when she had fire-control positions added to her masts and before the First World War started and her funnel bands were painted out. (LOC/BNS)

The Imperial German Navy's *Gazelle* class, represented here by SMS *Nymphe*, laid down in 1898 and completed in 1900, set a new standard for smaller cruisers. This image, taken by Arthur Renard of Kiel in 1901, shows *Nymphe* in her original configuration with an exaggerated plough bow; she would be one of the ships Germany would be allowed to retain after the First World War and had an extensive reconstruction then that included replacement of that bow form with a raked bow. Her armament of ten 10.5cm/40 guns was carried in shielded single mounts. Two were sited side-by-side forward and aft in thin breakwaters; the remainder were along her side in casemates and an amidships sponson. They are considered to be the prototypes of the light cruiser type. (NHHC)

the somewhat-smaller *Monmouths* and *Devonshires*. For the time being, the Royal Navy seemed content building armoured cruisers of approximately 10,000 tons, a policy that made good economic and political sense. It would not last.

The Need to Simplify: The Genesis of the Light Cruiser

Where the Royal Navy had defined the 'universe' of cruiser types as falling into three 'classes', each with a more-or-less discrete range of tonnage, armament and intended functions, other nations with lesser naval ambitions (or perhaps just smaller annual budgets) had to find a way to address the various roles of cruisers with fewer ships. One nation in particular, Imperial Germany, showed considerable ingenuity in designing ships that combined the characteristics of more than one 'class' of cruiser. They were particularly successful in doing this in the *Gazelle* class, which was laid down beginning in 1897, which combined the characteristics of the Royal Navy's second- and third-class cruisers, namely high-speed and armament sufficient to either scout for the fleet or work with destroyer flotillas in attack or defence, while still having sufficient protection and range to fulfil the role of colonial cruiser. The ten ships of this class, which were laid down over a period of four years, were classified as *Kleiner geschützter Kreuzers* (small protected cruisers) because their only armour was a curved protective deck of 1in–2in KC. They became known in Britain and America, almost immediately, simply as 'light cruisers'.

What made the *Gazelle* class so special that they deserved to be called the progenitors of a whole new type of cruiser? It was not any one single feature, but rather the accumulation of a number of incremental developments that together allowed for a type upgrade. These included:

- KC armour – which, being lighter and stronger, allowed useful armour protection to be achieved in ships that averaged 3033 tons normal displacement.[22]
- QF guns – the entire class mounted ten 10.5cm/40 BLRs with horizontal sliding-block breech closure that could sustain 15rpm per gun firing a 35.3lb AP shell or a 38.4lb HE shell.[23] The guns were located in single mounts arrayed two each side-by-side fore-and-aft, plus three on each broadside.
- VTE engines – the ultimate expression of the reciprocating steam engine, the vertical triple-expansion engine used three successively larger and lower-pressure cylinders to attempt to wring all the energy possible out of the steam generated by the more efficient water-tube boilers that were now becoming common.[24] These allowed good speed (20.75–21.5 knots) to be achieved from a relatively small (8500–9000ihp) and economical power plant. They had sufficient range to serve successfully in the colonial cruiser role.
- Radio – the first Marconi sets installed in warships preceded the laying down of SMS *Gazelle* by just two years, but the

Uncharacteristically, the normally conservative Americans picked up on the idea of the light cruiser fairly quickly. Perhaps it was because during this period the US Navy built so few cruisers that no opportunity to explore current design trends could be wasted. The three 'scout cruisers' of the *Chester* class shared a basic design, but little else; the navy took advantage of this opportunity to compare three different power plant systems. USS *Salem* (CS3), seen on the occasion of the Hudson and Fulton Celebration held at New York City in September–October 1909, a year after her completion, was one of the first American warships powered by turbines. The *Chester*s were very lightly armed, with a main battery of only two unshielded 5in/50 single mounts on the centreline. (LOC/BNS)

potential of this new communication technology, particularly in its ability to allow long-range scouting, was obvious. Now, fast ships could be sent out far ahead of a fleet to sweep wide arcs, their radius of reconnaissance limited only by their speed, numbers and the range of their radios.

It was this combination of features, previously only found in much larger ships, that had the greatest impact on foreign observers and caused their emulation in many navies.

The only serious criticism levelled at the *Gazelle*s – and this was equally true for the successor classes of light cruisers built by the Germans up until the *Wiesbaden* class of 1913 – was that they were considered too lightly armed. Most other navies considered the 10.5cm (4.1in) gun too small to be the main battery of a ship that was supposed to fill the roles of fleet scout or anti-torpedo-boat defence. As each of the other major navies laid down their own light cruisers, they tended to carry larger main batteries.

The Japanese were the next to produce a light cruiser, authorising the construction of *Tone* in 1903, although she was not laid down until 17 November 1905. She displaced 4100 tons, had a protective deck of 1.5in–3in-thick KC, was armed with two 6in/45 QF single-mount main-battery guns and ten 4.7in/50 single-mount secondary-battery guns.[25] The Americans, normally quite slow and conservative, actually started construction of their first light cruisers just a bit before the Japanese, laying down all three cruisers of the *Chester* class in August and September 1905.[26] There was no specific mention of the German *Gazelle*s in the design discussions leading up to the issuing of bids for proposals. The bid 'package' set certain parameters of speed and endurance that could be met by a 16,000ihp VTE propulsion system, but the bidders were invited to offer other options. The result was that the three cruisers in the class each had a different power plant. The three ships were all small with a normal displacement of 3750 tons, a main battery of two 5in/50s and a secondary battery of six 3in/50s and protection limited to short strakes of vertical 2in-thick KC plate in way of the engineering spaces and a protective deck 1in thick over the steering gear. Each had a different power plant; USS *Chester* (CS1) and *Salem* (CS3) were the first American warships to be turbine-powered.

The Americans found, as did all navies upon first adopting turbine propulsion, that these systems provide reliable power at high speed, but poor economy at slower speeds. (This problem was not completely solved until the introduction of reduction gearing in another ten years or so. In the meantime, nations employed various strategies to get more economy out of their power plants without giving up the great reliability of turbines. The most common of these was a 'staged' turbine system, venting steam from a high-pressure turbine into a lower-pressure turbine driving a separate shaft. Sometimes as many as four different turbines working at different pressures could be operated on the same steam line with the appropriate turbine being 'clutched' in-line as needed. Needless to say, this was an complex and expensive solution to a simple problem and, once the problem of manufacturing the reduction gearing necessary for geared turbines was mastered starting in approximately 1915, these rapidly replaced direct-drive turbines.)

The Italians and Austrians had their own private 'Adriatic Arms Race', building competing small, fast scout cruisers; the race began with the laying down of SMS *Admiral Spaun* in May 1908 at Pola. While only marginally smaller than *Salem*, seen in the preceding image, *Spaun* was longer, narrower, more lightly armed – her main battery was seven 10cm/50 guns in shielded single mounts – and, at a top speed of greater than 27 knots, more than 3 knots faster. This combination of light armament and high-speed set the pattern for the 'Adriatic scouts' built by both sides. (NHHC)

The Royal Navy resisted the lure of the light cruiser until 1908. The British had continued building small, very lightly-armed scout cruisers and larger, second-class cruisers, each designed to fit their own niche at the 'high' and 'low' end of a light cruiser's tasking.

The Italians and the Austrians had their own 'Adriatic Arms Race', entirely separate from any other naval rivalry going on at the time, largely expressed in the construction of surprisingly well-designed small scout cruisers. The first ship in the series, the first Austrian cruiser laid down in eight years, was SMS *Admiral Spaun* of 1908; she was small (3500 tons) and very lightly armed (seven 10cm/50 single mounts for the main battery), as befitted a fast scout. The first Austrian naval vessel equipped with turbines, she was given a complex power plant with six separate turbines driving four shafts, which never proved entirely problem-free. However, she was followed by a class of three more scouts, laid down in 1911–12, identical to *Spaun*, except they mounted two more main-battery guns and had a much simpler (and more successful) two-shaft turbine power plant.

The Italians, in response, built two somewhat similar classes of small scout cruisers, three ships in total, during this same time period – RN *Quarto* laid down in 1909 and the two-ship *Bixio* class of 1911. *Quarto*, in particular, was innovative in a number of ways, with a novel arrangement of main-battery guns clustered aft and shallow draft that, curiously, aided in their survival in the dangerous waters of the Adriatic.

Dressed to honour the Fourth of July in 1919 at Spalato (Split), Croatia, which was then in Italian hands, the Italian scout cruiser RN *Nino Bixio* shows off her own sleek lines. Like *Spaun*, she was long and narrow and, additionally, had a shallow draft – only 13ft 5in – which permitted her to operate in the often shoal waters of the northern Adriatic and gave her an unusual wave pattern along her side that often deceived adversaries as to her speed. Her main battery of six single 120mm/50 EOC Pattern EE guns were all mounted on the centreline except for two mounts side-by-side on the forecastle. (NHHC)

Their unusually shallow hull form caused them to have a peculiar wave pattern along their side when steaming at moderate speed; enemy torpedo boats and submarines tended to misjudge their speed, leading to narrow escapes on a number of occasions.

Some consider the *Boadicea*s, scout cruisers laid down in 1907–8, to be the Royal Navy's first light cruisers, but most think they were still too poorly protected and lightly armed to be considered true responses to *Gazelle* and her successors.[27] It is generally conceded that the first fully-realised British light cruisers were the five ships of the *Bristol* class laid down in 1909. (The fact that all the ships in this class and all their direct follow-ons were named for municipalities in the United Kingdom led to them being called the 'Towns'.) The *Bristol*s displaced 4800 tons, were armed with two 6in/50 Mk XI BLRs and ten 4in/50 Mk VII BLRs, had a speed of 25 knots and a range of over 5000nm powered by 4-shaft Parsons or 2-shaft Brown-Curtiss turbines and protection limited to an armoured deck with a maximum thickness of 2in. The only complaint against the *Bristol*s was that, if anything, they were not big enough. They were narrow for their length making them internally cramped and had a high metacentre, which made them exceptionally 'lively' gun platforms and definitely not the most comfortable ships in weather.[28]

The *Bristol*s were the largest and most heavily-armed small cruisers to date, although that distinction did not last long. It seems to be an inevitable rule of ship design that follow-on classes are expected to grow in capability – if fast is good, then faster is better, if well-armed is good, then better-armed is better, etc – and the Japanese followed that pattern with the *Chikuma* class that followed *Tone*, starting in April 1909. Displacing 5000 tons and armed with eight 6in/45 BLRs, they were bigger and more powerful than any previous light cruiser;

The Royal Navy did not finally start building true light cruisers until 1909 with the *Bristol* class, of which HMS *Liverpool*, seen here probably in late 1911 or early 1912, was the first to be laid down. The image can be dated relatively accurately because the short funnels with she was completed in October 1910 have been lengthened, which was done in 1911, but the searchlight platform that was added between her second and third funnels in 1912 is not yet present, nor does she have the funnel bands that were painted on that year. The *Bristol*s were bigger, at 4800 tons, and more heavily armed, with a pair of single 6in/50 Mk XI* guns fore-and-aft, than any light cruiser to date and, with a class of five laid down over a period of two months, were also more numerous than any other nation's. (NHHC)

they also had a speed advantage, getting 26 knots from 22,500shp and a range of 10,000nm at 10 knots.[29]

Of more direct interest to the British, the Germans continued to build light cruisers, follow-ons to the *Gazelle*s, which also grew in size, but remained smaller than the *Bristol*s or *Chikuma*s. The seven-ship *Bremen* class, laid down between 1902 and 1904, displacing 3750 tons and with a designed speed of 23 knots, were otherwise quite similar to the *Gazelle*s. One of this class (SMS *Lübeck*) was the first turbine-powered warship in the High Seas Fleet. The Germans continued laying down light cruisers at a steady pace of two or three a year; clearly they found the type useful and were committed

to building up the numbers in their fleet. Alone among the major navies, they resisted the temptation to continue increasing the size of each successive class. It was not until the laying down of the *Kolberg*s starting in 1907 that the Germans increased the size of their light cruisers to greater than 4000 tons. The four-ship *Kolberg* class (4362 tons) was the first that was entirely turbine-powered, giving a speed of between 25.5 knots and 26.7 knots – each was given a different manufacturer's turbine system in order to compare reliability and efficiency – and was the first to increase armament – increasing both the number and barrel length of the main battery, but not the calibre – to twelve 10.5cm/45.

At this time both the Royal Navy and High Seas Fleet took a significant and more-or-less parallel step forward in light cruiser design. Both nations decided, at much the same time, that their light cruisers needed to be better protected. The Germans actually started work on their new class first. The four ships of the *Magdeburg* class were all authorised in 1908, but they took abnormally long to complete. Having decided that a waterline belt of armour of between 2.36in and 0.71in thickness running 80 per cent of the length of the hull was necessary to improve the survivability of their next class of light cruisers, the German designers were left with the problem of determining how to work the weight of this armour into a hull that, with only a marginal increase in displacement, was to carry the same armament as the *Kolberg*s with greater speed and endurance. The solutions reached by

The Japanese, at this time closely allied to the British, were apprised of the 'Town' class light cruisers' development and responded with a similar design, somewhat larger in every dimension except width and also faster by one knot. *Yahagi*, seen here, was completed with six 6in/45 41st Year Type guns and four 3in/40 41st Year Type guns, all in single-mounts, but shortly after completion the smaller guns were replaced by an additional pair of 6in guns at the waist, giving *Yahagi* eight compared to two similar guns in *Liverpool*, and making the *Chikuma* class unusual in mounting a single-calibre battery. (NHHC)

the German designers were clever and innovative, but they took time to implement. Instead of bolting the armour belt through a layer of wood to the outside of an otherwise complete hull structure, as was common practice in capital ships and large armoured cruisers, the Germans designed the armour to be the outer shell of the ship, part of its integral structure. In a further effort to save weight, the designers borrowed a technique that had been pioneered by builders of large commercial vessels – longitudinal framing. Instead of building up a ship as a series of light, closely-spaced lateral frames attached to the keel, a system carried over from the days of wooden ships, a longitudinally-framed ship gets its strength from a series of heavier, more widely-spaced frames connected by multiple longitudinal girders paralleling the keel.[30] By replacing between four and six lighter frames with one heavier frame (plus the longitudinal girders), significant weight was saved with no loss in structural strength. Thus, the

Magdeburgs were able to carry the side armour, which joined a conventional 1.57in–2.36in-thick armoured deck at the bottom, and armament similar to the preceding *Kolbergs*, at a top speed of between 27.5 knots and 28.2 knots, all with only 200 tons of increased displacement (raising the normal displacement to 4570 tons). The only downside to this new design was that it included so many new technologies and design features, including a new hull shape with a forward-slanting bow that improved seakeeping and an overhanging stern, that the design process took a year longer than usual and the ships were not laid down until 1910 and not completed until 1912. Only three more light cruisers, the two ships of the *Karlsruhe* class and the first of two in the *Graudenz* class, were completed by the Germans before the First World War began. They were essentially repeat *Magdeburgs*, somewhat larger and faster, but otherwise the same.

At the same time that the *Reichsmarineamt* (RMA), the German Admiralty, was determining the design parameters of the *Magdeburg* class, the Royal Navy's Admiralty asked for bids for the 1911 light cruisers. In a series of design requirements that paralleled the changes made in Germany to a remarkable extent, the Admiralty asked for the inclusion of a full-length armour belt with a maximum thickness of 3in.[31] (It must be noted that Watts, who succeeded White as DNC in 1902, did not make all of the design 'leaps' the Germans did with the *Magdeburgs* in the *Chathams*. He did not, for example, make the armour belt of the *Chathams* part of the ships' structure, instead bolting it over the existing shell plating; the 3in total thickness was achieved by adding 2in of armour to 1in of structural plate.) The *Chatham* class also introduced an improved hull form with a flared 'plough' bow and overhanging stern, and an extended forecastle deck, all of which aided performance in bad weather, in a manner quite similar to the *Magdeburgs*. All this was achieved at an increase of only 150 tons over the *Weymouth* class, to a normal displacement of 5400 tons.

However, after laying down one more four-ship class of 'Towns', the British realised that these ships were still not the general-purpose light cruisers the Germans were building. They were too big and slow to act as flotilla leaders; however, the classes of smaller scout cruisers the Royal Navy had continued building were also not adequate for that task, being too short-legged and

SMS *Strassburg* was one of the *Magdeburg* class of light cruisers in which the Germans introduced a number of novel features including longitudinal framing and structural use of the external armour belt of nickel steel. Visible changes included the raked bow and raised forecastle deck which made the ships good sea boats. One criticism was the retention of the small 10.5cm/45 gun for the main battery. In 1916, sometime after this image was taken, the twelve 10.5cm guns were replaced by seven 15cm/45 single-mount guns, a more appropriate main battery. *Strassburg* survived the First World War and was turned over to the Italians, with whom she served on into the Second World War. (NHHC)

As appealing as the large 'Town' class light cruisers were to the Lords of the Admiralty, many in the fleet (and in Parliament) saw the value in building somewhat smaller (and less expensive) light cruisers, as the Germans had been doing. The Royal Navy responded to this pressure with the *Arethusa* class, as represented by HMCS *Aurora*, seen here at San Diego on 3 April 1921 on her sole cruise in Canadian service, which took her from Halifax to Esquimalt and back. Commissioned into the Royal Navy at the outbreak of the First World War, she fought at Dogger Bank and served in the North Sea for the remainder of the war before transferring to the Royal Canadian Navy. The *Arethusa*s were more than 30 per cent smaller than the last subclass of 'Towns', carried a mixed armament of two 6in/45 Mk XII and six 4in/45 Mk V QFs, and were seen as less useful as general-purpose cruisers, leading to their rapid retirement after the war. This image shows *Aurora* with all of the wartime changes made to the class, which included the replacement of the light pole foremast with a more substantial tripod supporting a fire-control top, the building up of the after control position to incorporate a pair of 3in/40 HA guns, the addition of a second pair of twin torpedo tubes and the partial remnants of a flying-off platform forward of her bridge that had extended over the forward 6in gun mount. (USAF)

299

slow to lead the newest generation of destroyers. The Royal Navy reacted by calling for the design of a new class of moderately-sized light cruisers, smaller than the 'Towns', but bigger than the scouts, and faster than either – the eight-ship *Arethusa* class, the last pre-war class and the prototype for most of the wartime light cruiser classes; they displaced 3750 tons, carried a main battery of two 6in/45 Mk XII BLRs with six 4in/45 Mk V QFs at a speed of 28.5 knots. With this class, the Royal Navy introduced the use of armour as a structural element; the *Arethusas* were protected by a 3in-thick armour belt and a protective deck 1in thick. Another new feature introduced with this class was a switch to oil fuel, which helped make the reduction in size practical.[32] Although the *Arethusas* were barely 80 per cent the size of the contemporary *Magdeburgs*, the follow-on classes of Royal Navy light cruisers increased in size very rapidly to more closely approximate their German counterparts; in keeping with its long-established policy of maintaining a substantial advantage over any rival navy, and as befitted the nation with the world's most highly-developed shipbuilding industry (in 1914), the Royal Navy would outbuild the High Seas Fleet in light cruisers, as in all other major warship types, before and during the upcoming war.

. . . Is Bigger Necessarily Better?

The Royal Navy's programme of moderately-sized armoured cruisers as established at the end of the century seemed adequate for their needs as long as the rest of the world followed suit. As would happen again, British hopes would be disappointed; the Russians and French, in particular, continued building large armoured cruisers, prompting the Royal Navy to respond.

The Royal Navy's 1903 building programme included a pair of armoured cruisers nearly the size of the *Drakes*, but

An important step in the growth of Royal Navy armoured cruisers came with the *Drakes* and the follow-on *Duke of Edinburgh* class, the lead ship of which is seen here at the Hudson and Fulton Celebration, New York City, September–October 1909 (which accounts for the American flag flying from her mainmast). This class introduced a greatly increased main battery; where the *Drakes* had two 9.2in/47 Mk X BLRs in single-turrets, HMS *Duke of Edinburgh* had six in single turrets, forcing her secondary battery of ten 6in/50 Mk XIs into Upper Deck casemates, where they could be served only in calm weather and at slow speeds. (LOC/BNS)

more heavily armed. Where the latter had carried a pair of 9.2in/47 Mk X BLRs as their main battery, the two ships of the *Duke of Edinburgh* class carried six in single turrets, compensating for the weight and space they took up by sacrificing six 6in/45 QFs from the secondary battery (leaving a total of ten in broadside casemates on the Upper Deck).[33] There were to have been four more identical follow-ons the next year, but even while the *Duke of Edinburgh*s were building, concerns were raised about their secondary battery, both its siting and its hitting power. Opinion from the fleet strongly urged adopting a heavier secondary battery, even if it meant carrying fewer guns, and carrying them higher, as guns at the Upper Deck level were often unserviceable in a seaway. The decision was made, therefore, to replace the ten 6in/50 Mk XIs with four 7.5in/50 Mk II in single turrets at the Main Deck level. It proved to be too late to make the change economically in the first two ships, and they were completed as designed. They displaced 13,550 tons, carried a belt of armour 6in thick at its thickest and could steam at 23 knots on 23,000shp. The four later ships, the *Warrior* class of 1903–4, are considered a separate class even though they differed only in the secondary battery.[34] A final design, the three-ship *Minotaur* class of the 1904 building programme, completed the series of large armoured cruisers for the Royal Navy. They were enlarged *Warrior*s, with twin 9.2in/47 turrets fore-and-aft and five single turrets for 7.5in/50s on each broadside. The displacement rose to 14,600 tons – exceeding even that of the *Drake*s – while armour and speed remained similar to the preceding classes.

Other nations were building similarly large armoured cruisers at this same time. These included the German *Scharnhorst* class in 1904–5; the Italian *Pisa* class starting in 1905; the American *Tennessee* class of 1903–5; the new Russian *Rurik* in August 1905 and the French *Edgar Quinet* class starting in 1905. The most telling statement that can be made about the *Warrior* class is that, unlike the lineage of light cruiser development, which was still just getting started in 1904, this was the last class of 'conventional' large cruisers laid down by the Royal Navy. (In all but one case, the classes listed above were the last of the type for each of the listed navies.[35])

The Apogee of the Armoured Cruiser: Ulsan – August 1904

Impressive as the *Minotaur*s were, they were about to be overtaken by events, and ultimately rendered irrelevant, by events at home and abroad. When Japan went to war with the Russians in 1904 over rival ambitions in Manchuria and Korea, the Japanese had been preparing for hostilities for a number of years. Aware that they could not build up their navy fast enough with local industrial capability, the Japanese looked abroad.[36] Already, in 1897, approval was given to alter an already-approved ten-year naval building plan, substituting six armoured cruisers for four planned protected cruisers. The six cruisers were ordered from European yards with expertise in cruiser construction – four from Armstrong Elswick

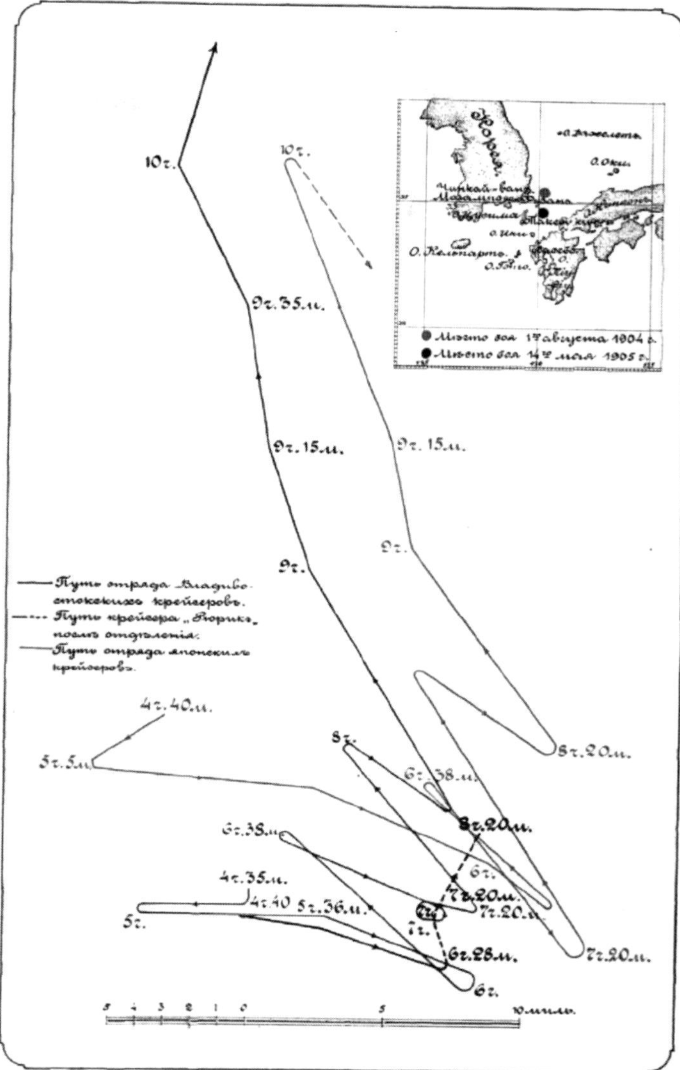

A Russian chart of the Battle of Ulsan, 14 August 1904, shows the tracks of the Russian squadron starting at the bottom at 04.35, just before Rear Admiral Jessen ordered the turn to the west, forming his line of battle, led by *Rossia*. Vice Admiral Kamimura's squadron is first noted at 04.40 towards the north-west, heading south-west. At 05.00, Jessen led around to the east, followed five minutes later by Kamimura. The point at which *Rurik* lost steering control and manoeuvred separately from her two squadron mates occurred shortly after 05.20, about halfway along the easterly track before Jessen turned to the east-south-east at 05.36. From that point onward the tracks get confusing as Jessen's two less-damaged ships manoeuvred back-and-forth. At one point, at around 07.00, *Rossia* and *Gromoboi* circled *Rurik*, whose path is now indicated by a dashed line; unable to provide more than temporary succour to the battered *Rurik*, Jessen resumed his zigzag path, not turning towards the north-north-west and Vladivostok until 08.20.

(*Asama*, *Tokiwa*, *Idzumo* and *Iwate*), one from Vulcan Stettin (*Yakumo*) and one from AC la Loire St-Nazaire (*Adzuma*). All six of these cruisers, with very similar characteristics, designed to form a homogeneous squadron, were completed within a period of two years between March 1899 and March 1901. They all displaced between 9300 tons and 9750 tons, were protected by waterline belt armour of 7in maximum thickness of Harvey nickel-steel in the earlier units and KC plate in the later ones, mounted a main battery of four 8in/45 Elswick Ordnance Co (EOC) guns in twin turrets and between twelve and fourteen 6in/40 QFs in the secondary battery and could make a top speed of 20–21.5 knots. These six new armoured cruisers, along with six battleships, made up the Japanese fleet that would be tasked with containing the Russian Pacific Fleet, based at Port Arthur (Lushun) and Vladivostok, and then meeting any reinforcing units sent east.

Rear Admiral Jessen's flagship *Rossia* is seen much as she would have appeared at Ulsan; the only significant change would have been the painting out of all the upper works, masts, funnels, boats and bow crest that stand out against her black-painted hull. Her main battery of four single 8in/45 guns was carried in sponsons abreast her bridge and mizzenmast. Most of her massive secondary battery of sixteen 6in/45 guns were in a broadside battery reminiscent of a Nelsonian man-of-war; she even had one protruding from her bow. She was hit thirty-one times at Ulsan, causing eleven hull leaks, and had a persistent fire forward, but survived because the Japanese squadron turned away rather than pressing their advantage. (NHHC)

The Japanese had been able to bottle up the Russian Port Arthur squadron, which comprised the bulk of Russian naval strength in the region, from the beginning of the conflict in February 1904. The only Russian force in the Far East able to move with freedom was a small squadron of cruisers that was operating from Vladivostok, comprising the armoured cruisers *Rossia* (flagship of Rear Admiral Karl Petrovich Jessen), *Gromoboi* and *Rurik*, and the new protected cruiser *Bogatyr*; however early in the conflict, on 14 May, *Bogatyr* was damaged by grounding, and played no part in the tale told here.[37]

The Russian Cruiser Division was active, sortieing regularly to prey on merchant traffic around Japan. The squadron went out twice in February, then not again until April. The unit carried out raids into the Korea Strait (Tsushima Strait) and east to Shimonoseki in mid-June and towards the central Korean coast at Wonsan at the end of the month. In mid-July, Jessen's squadron undertook its most ambitious raid, passing through the Tsugaru Strait between Honshu and Hokkaido out into the open Pacific and as far south along the east coast of Japan as the entrance to Ise-Wan. The importance of this long raid, which lasted until the beginning of August, was that it put significant wear on the three active Russian armoured cruisers. Jessen had hoped for some time to refit his ships, but within days of arriving back at Vladivostok, Admiral Vitgeft, commanding the Russian Pacific Fleet, alerted the Cruiser Division to be ready to support an impending breakout attempt from Port Arthur. Contradictory messages from Vitgeft left Jessen guessing as to how to proceed; eventually the three Russian cruisers sortied on 12 August, having performed little, if any, of the needed maintenance. *Rossia*, for example, left Vladivostok with four of her thirty-two boilers not fully functional. It was not surprising, therefore, that the best speed that the Cruiser Division could muster when operating together, was 13 knots, *Rurik*'s top speed.

The six Russian raids to date had netted a total of fifteen steamers carrying goods (or troops) between Japan and the war zone in Korea and were proving to be an embarrassment, if not worse, for the Japanese. They responded by leaving their II Division of armoured cruisers, commanded by Vice Admiral Kamimura Hikonojo, permanently assigned to guard the Korea Strait from a base at Pusan (Busan). Thus, when Jessen's force of three armoured cruisers approached on the night of 13/14 August 1904, arrayed in a sweep line – line-abreast formation with 2nm separation – it very nearly collided with Kamimura's line of four – the flagship *Idzumo* followed by *Adzuma*, *Tokiwa* and *Iwate*. Stationed further south, widely separated, were the old protected cruisers *Naniwa* and *Takachiho*, veterans of the Yalu.

The two forces passed close in the dark without sighting each other, the Russians steaming south looking for ships from the Port Arthur squadron which were to have attempted their breakout, and the Japanese steaming eastward to block the strait. Both forces turned back towards dawn; Jessen decided that he had reached the limit of his search range and, at 04.40 signalled his squadron to turn west into a patrol line; they were on the same parallel as the Korean fishing port of Ulsan. Somewhat earlier, Kamimura had reached the north-eastern end of his patrol line and had turned back. At first light, approximately 04.40, the two squadrons sighted each other, 30nm north-east of Tsushima Island; Kamimura was 8nm to the north of the Russians, heading south-westward, converging towards their line of advance. This was clearly not to Jessen's advantage, and he led his line around in a 180° turn to the east at 05.00. Kamimura saw this manoeuvre and, five minutes later, turned his line to a heading just south of east, so that he would continue closing the Russian line.

The two forces steamed eastward on these slowly converging courses until 05.10, when the range had dropped to 10,000yd, at which point the Japanese opened fire.[38] The Russians responded immediately, but the Japanese fire was faster, heavier and more damaging. The Japanese fired mainly HE shells with Shimose (a form of Melinite) filling, which were not intended to penetrate the Russians' armour; they were supposed to explode on contact and devastate any unprotected parts of their targets. American observer Lieutenant Commander Newton A McCully, who was attached to the Russian forces, reported:

> The Russians found ranges by taking masthead angles with an instrument called 'scholl' in form of a telescope with cross wires.[39] Range-finding officers were stationed in foretops, and ranges communicated by telegraphic connection, until these were carried away early in the action, then by means of messengers. One range-finding party in foretop of *Gromoboi* was entirely carried away by a shell which struck the top, only a portion of one man's body falling on the deck. The hits from which the Russian ships suffered most were the plunging fire on the upper deck which caused most of the casualties, and the funnel hits which damaged the boilers.[40]

The Japanese shot faster and more accurately from the beginning of the engagement. They hit *Rurik* forward and started a fire in her forecastle within minutes of opening fire. Then, at 05.23, they landed the first serious blows; exactly the kind of funnel hit described by McCully forced three boilers temporarily off-line in the Russian flagship *Rossia*. On top of the four boilers already operating at reduced capacity, the sudden loss of steam pressure from three more boilers caused a rapid drop in *Rossia*'s speed, forcing the following cruisers to swerve out of line to avoid collision, *Gromoboi* to port, *Rurik* to starboard. While executing this abrupt manoeuvre, *Rurik* was hit right aft by an 8in shell that penetrated her steering compartment and exploded there, jamming her rudder. From that point onward, *Rurik* no longer manoeuvred with the other two Russian cruisers; she steered only with great difficulty using her two screws, which further reduced her speed, causing *Rossia* and *Gromoboi* gradually to pull away.

The Japanese squadron, which had a three-knot speed advantage even before these events, began pulling ahead, while continuing to converge on the Russian line. Concerned about the shortening range, Jessen ordered a turn to the east-south-east at 05.36, a turn the Japanese followed almost immediately. The two forces continued on this course for another twenty-four minutes, every minute taking Jessen further away from his base. Fortunately for the Russians, Kamimura's cruisers did not slacken speed, so they gradually drew ahead of the Russians, giving Jessen the opening he needed. At 06.00, Jessen ordered a 18-point (202.5°) turn to starboard, a turn that would cause his two cruisers to loop around to the right across their track before settling on a course to the north-west that would take them around the rear of the Japanese formation heading towards Vladivostok and keep them between the Japanese and the lagging *Rurik*.[41] Kamimura saw the Russian turn, but initially misinterpreted what Jessen was doing; the Japanese force only turned 2 points (22.5°) further to the south-east, which allowed the Russians to make their turn in relative peace, but resulted in the Japanese concentrating their fire on *Rurik*, which had become exposed as the other Russian cruisers turned. Those were now moving off to the north-west at increasing speed as *Rossia*'s damaged boilers were brought back on-line. It was only after 06.05 that Kamimura turned to follow.

At 06.28, as the main forces were heading north-west on parallel courses, a drama was being played out behind them. *Rurik* had continued on to the east-south-east at slow speed, struggling to bring the flooding aft under control and regain control of her steering. Then, out of the rising sun (fittingly perhaps), appeared *Naniwa* approaching from the east.

Gromoboi, the second in Jessen's line, was three years newer than *Rossia*, but shared most design features. As can be seen here in this view taken at Melbourne, where she was making a formal visit to Australia in 1901 while on her way to her assigned station at Vladivostok, she carried her secondary battery in casemates at the Upper Deck level, which gave them somewhat better arcs of fire. The crisp white paintwork and gilded bow crest would be painted black before she went to war three years later. (SLV/AGC)

Steering with her engines, *Rurik* was able to turn slowly to the north-north-west, all the while being pounded at rapidly decreasing range. Ten minutes later, realising *Rurik* was in desperate straits, Jessen turned his two ships back through another 22-point turn, this time to port, in order to drive off *Naniwa*. At 07.00, *Rossia* and *Gromoboi* approached *Rurik* and circled the struggling cruiser, already battered almost beyond recognition, but largely intact below the waterline and not yet in any danger of sinking. While they succeeded in providing temporary respite for *Rurik*, the main body of Kamimura's squadron, which had turned back at the same time as Jessen, continued pounding away, and Jessen could not linger to protect his wounded compatriot. After one loop around *Rurik*, Jessen turned again to the north-westat at 07.20, followed again by Kamimura.

The rest of the battle can be described succinctly. At 08.00, Jessen turned back one more time in an attempt to intervene to protect *Rurik*, which was once again being hit hard by *Naniwa* and, since 07.50, also by *Takachiho*, which was coming up from the south-west. But, this time, after steaming towards the south-east for twenty minutes, it became obvious to Jessen that there was nothing more he could do to aid *Rurik*, which had been reduced to a state of near-immobility, with only a few gun mounts still serviceable. With reluctance, at approximately 08.20, *Rossia* and *Gromoboi* turned to the north-north-west and bent on their best speed, hoping to escape to Vladivostok. Kamimura turned once more to follow.

The accounts of what happened next are not totally clear, except that all agree that for the next hour-and-a-half the two squadrons continued steaming on parallel courses and maintaining a steady fire at each other, which was generally to the advantage of the Japanese, who had more guns and fired them with greater rapidity. However, at 10.00 or shortly thereafter, Kamimura turned back, ending the pursuit of Jessen's survivors, allowing them to escape. The reasons given for the abandonment of the chase are various; for example, it is stated that *Iwate* had received significant damage and *Adzuma*'s power plant was balky and could not have continued much longer at high speed.[42] One source states that Kamimura was incorrectly informed that his ammunition stocks were depleted, that only one-quarter remained when in fact the true number was closer to one-half, causing him to cease firing to retain a reserve sufficient to finish off *Rurik*.[43] Other possibilities put forward include that Kamimura was under orders not to leave the Korea Straits uncovered, but, regardless, his decision was fortuitous for Jessen.[44] *Rossia* was herself in terrible shape; she had twenty-six hits in the hull, which had led to eleven hull leaks of varying degrees of seriousness. Three of her four funnels were damaged, reducing the steam pressure she could generate.[45] Hits under her forward superstructure had started a persistent fire that forced the abandonment of her bridge area. *Gromoboi* had not been hit as hard, in terms of damage to her hull, but had a great many more casualties among her crew.[46] Regardless of the reason for Kamimura's turn away, it probably saved Jessen's remaining cruisers from destruction. As it was, at nightfall, feeling he had reached a safe distance from any pursuit, Jessen ordered both cruisers stopped, so that their crews could concentrate on assuring their ships' seaworthiness, particularly that of *Rossia*.[47]

As it turned out, the only ship lost this day was *Rurik* and she did not sink easily. The Japanese fired over 5000 8in and 6in rounds during the battle, achieving approximately 200 hits, three-quarters of them 6in hits on *Rurik* at relatively short range.[48] Obviously, no post-battle examination of *Rurik* was possible, but examination of *Rossia* and *Gromoboi* showed that '[t]here was no perforation of armour in either ship, and [the] protective deck also remained intact, but there were leaks, due

One of the Japanese armoured cruisers that fought at Ulsan was *Iwate*, seen here also at Melbourne, but many years after the preceding image of *Gromoboi*. In this image, most likely taken in 1928, after *Iwate* has been reduced to the role of a training ship, the lower rank of casemates have been plated over along the sides. *Iwate* shared many features with *Gromoboi*, having been launched only one year later, but had one clearly more 'advanced' element, the main-battery twin turrets fore-and-aft. (SLV/AGC)

to blows on the armour, opening up seams. The destruction caused by the plunging hits was exceedingly great, little escaping the large number of fragments.'[49]

Rossia was hit a total of thirty-one times, suffering 200 casualties, including forty-seven dead. As mentioned, *Gromoboi* was hit fewer times – twenty-seven hits altogether – but suffered 259 casualties, including ninety-three killed. Long after Jessen turned away to the north, *Rurik* continued to fight. Whatever else might be said about the Russian navy or its individual sailors, they proved themselves brave beyond any doubt this day. Facing two protected cruisers, with little means of defending herself, *Rurik* was pounded at shorter and shorter ranges far beyond the point at which she could have struck her colours without shame. Her three ranking officers were all dead by the end, command having been assumed by the fourth officer in line, a Lieutenant Ivanov. At approximately 10.20:

> The intention was to blow up the cruiser but [this] could not be executed for lack of fuze, which was destroyed in [the] conning tower, the remainder being in [a] filled compartment. Instead the bottom valves were opened and [the] cruiser gradually sank. When [the] Russians ceased firing, [the] Japanese also ceased, and when [the] cruiser sank they used utmost endeavor to rescue the crew who were floating about on mattresses, wooden articles, and swimming, all boats having been destroyed.[50]

Not surprisingly, the bulk of the Russian casualties occurred in *Rurik*, which suffered 408 casualties, including 192 dead. The Japanese rescued 625 survivors.

On the Japanese side, it appears that only *Iwate* was hit hard and took a significant number of casualties – seventy-seven, including forty dead.[51] On the remaining Japanese ships, total casualties were five killed and forty-four wounded. Three of the Japanese cruisers were briefly docked after the battle – *Idzumo*, *Adzuma* and *Iwate* – all reporting back for duty within weeks. Both surviving Russian cruisers were docked at Vladivostok for more than three months. They participated in only one more, abortive, raid, in August.

Spiralling Out of Control

The lessons drawn from Ulsan and from the action in the Yellow Sea just a few days earlier, when the Port Arthur squadron had attempted unsuccessfully to break the Japanese blockade, were several and mostly incorrect. At the Yellow Sea battle, which was primarily between battleships – and at which Japanese cruisers had proved to be largely ineffective, both offensively and defensively – the most remarkable – and memorable – fact was that, despite both sides mounting rangefinders with a maximum effective range of 6000yd, fire had been opened at about 16,000yd with their 12in main-battery guns, with hits being obtained at that range.[52] At that range, the 8in main battery of the armoured cruisers of either side could not penetrate the thick armour of enemy battleships. But the equally clear lesson drawn from the two battles was that speed was a clear advantage. One further point was made clear at Ulsan. The main batteries of armoured cruisers, as then conceived, were not capable of decisively defeating their own type, much less better-protected capital ships.

Looking at these engagements, a number of observers drew similar conclusions. The armoured cruiser was seen by many to be the warship of the future, as long as it carried significantly greater armament, but without sacrificing any of the speed that gave the type its tactical advantages. While by no means the first to think of the idea, the Japanese were the first to start construction of an armoured cruiser with capital-ship armament. The Imperial Japanese Navy had lost two of its six battleships right at the outbreak of the Russo-Japanese War when they ran upon a Russian minefield off Port Arthur in May 1904. Two new and particularly powerful battleships were under construction for Japan in England, but they had just been laid down and were two years away from completion. The Japanese had purchased two large and powerful new armoured cruisers from Argentina, which would have to stand in place of the missing battleships in Admiral Togo's I Division.[53] But what they really wanted, and intended to build as the first large warships built in Japan, were a pair of outsized armoured cruisers, almost as big, at 13,750 tons normal displacement, as a contemporary battleship, armed with four 12in/45 Armstrong BLRs in twin turrets fore-and-aft and twelve 6in/45 QFs in hull casemates on the Upper and Main Decks – identical armament, except for the number of 6in guns, to that carried by Japan's four battleships – at a speed

The Russians replaced the armoured cruiser *Rurik* lost at Ulsan with another armoured cruiser of the same name. This one, laid down in 1905 at the Vickers yard at Barrow-in-Furness and completed in 1908, was well in advance of any contemporary armoured cruiser in size, armament and protection, with a main battery of four 10in/50 in twin turrets and a secondary battery of eight 8in/50 also in twin turrets; she had the misfortune to be exactly contemporaneous with the Dreadnought revolution in capital ship/large cruiser design, which rendered her obsolescent from the day she entered service. (NHHC)

of 20.5 knots – 2 knots faster than those battleships – with armour 7in thick at its thickest – only 2in thinner than that of typical battleships. This was a true hybrid cruiser-battleship of a type that had been discussed, but never laid down before. Two ships of this design were laid down at Kure Navy Yard: *Tsukuba* on 14 January 1905 and *Ikoma* on 15 March. An enlarged *Tsukuba*, longer by 35ft, heavier by 850 tons, faster by 1 knot and carrying eight 8in guns in her secondary battery in the place of twelve 6in guns, was laid down in August 1905, with the name *Kurama*.

The idea of such a ship went back some years before the laying down of *Tsukuba*. A number of younger officers in several navies, particularly the Royal Navy, saw the emergence of large armoured cruisers as the solution of the problem of constantly rising costs of naval construction. One of those officers was John A 'Jacky' Fisher, who, when he was C-in-C Mediterranean Fleet (from 1899 to 1902), did his best to instil in his officers an aggressive spirit through a series of lectures in which he returned regularly to the themes of fleet speed and hitting power at the expense of all other features of ship design, to the extent that cruisers would replace battleships as the fleet's flagships and cruiser squadrons would form the fleet's primary battle force. Towards the end of his tenure there, in February 1902, he offered a very tangible expression of this idea, proposing the setting up of an Atlantic Fleet based at Gibraltar comprised of a dozen armoured cruisers, able to respond to crises in either home water or the Mediterranean as needed.[54]

At the same time that Fisher, as soon as he was installed as First Sea Lord in October 1904, actively pushed the development of the revolutionary 'all-big-gun' battleship *Dreadnought*, he pursued the idea of an 'all-big-gun' armoured cruiser with equal (if not greater) vigour. In a famous paper written in July 1904, outlining the plans he had in mind for his tenure at the Admiralty, Fisher called for the development of both new types, but added cryptically 'no one can draw the line where the armoured cruiser becomes the battleship'.[55] At this time, Fisher was still thinking of distinct armament for the two types, preferring sixteen 10in guns for the 'all-big-gun' battleship – preferring this main battery over the then-standard 12in gun because of its higher rate of fire – and sixteen 9.2in guns for the 'all-big-gun' armoured cruiser – again liking the smaller gun because of its yet higher rate of fire.

Whatever else may be said about 'Jacky' Fisher, positive or negative, he was willing to listen to people who knew more than himself. From the earliest days of his rise to command, he had surrounded himself with younger officers, chosen for their technical expertise (and loyalty), a group that became known as the 'Fishpond'. Among the members of the 'Fishpond' to gain fame on their own were Admirals John R Jellicoe, Percy M Scott and Reginald H S Bacon, all gunnery experts. When Fisher took over as First Sea Lord, both Jellicoe and Bacon were also posted to Whitehall and were immediately 'drafted' into an informal 'Committee of Seven' to advise Fisher on technical matters as he rushed to jumpstart his ambitious programme of shipbuilding and organisational reform.[56] (This group was the precursor of the formal Committee on Designs, set up in late 1904, tasked with defining the specifications of the 'all-big-gun' battleship and the 'all-big-gun' armoured cruiser among other items.) It was Bacon in particular who argued forcefully in favour of the

12in gun both for the battleship design and, even more significantly, for the armoured cruiser.

> For weeks, however, discussion continued about the armament . . . 9.2-inch versus 12-inch; but in the end the 12-inch gun won on the unanswerable plea that ships, of the size and tonnage necessary . . . should have an additional use in being able to form a fast light squadron to supplement the battleships in action, and worry the ships in the van or rear of the enemy's line.[57]

While Bacon's account, written many years after the event and informed by hindsight, goes on to add that these 'all-big-gun' armoured cruisers were 'never intended to *engage battleships singlehanded* [his italics]', that was far from the view at the time. In the Report of the Committee on Designs, Fisher referred several times to what the Japanese were doing with the *Tsukuba* design, making the point that this offered a model for saving money in the naval budget, very much an issue at that time.[58] Fisher stated that the Japanese had effectively replaced a battleship with a 'glorified armoured cruiser' because they could not afford to build both; he argued that 'these armoured cruisers are battleships in disguise'. He was not successful then in persuading the Committee to drop the 'all-big-gun' battleship in favour of the 'all-big-gun' armoured cruiser, nor did he emerge victorious later, in March, when he took his arguments to the full Admiralty Board, but he could claim some success. The 1905 building programme that emerged from those discussions included money for one 'all-big-gun' battleship (HMS *Dreadnought*) and three 'all-big-gun' armoured cruisers (the *Invincible* class battlecruisers).[59]

The story of the catastrophic career of the Royal Navy's battlecruisers need not be recounted here.[60] Suffice it to say that the emergence of the 17,373-ton, 25.5-knot *Invincibles* armed with eight 12in main-battery guns effectively rendered every armoured cruiser obsolete, although, regrettably, they were allowed to linger in the world's fleets. The Germans, because they initially only heard rumours of the capabilities of the *Invincibles*, reacted in an understandable but totally misguided manner. They laid down SMS *Blücher* in 1907 as an answer to Fisher's initial concept of an 'all-big-gun' armoured cruiser armed with 9.2in guns. *Blücher* was the last and 'best' armoured cruiser, 15,590 tons, armed with twelve 21cm/45 in six twin turrets. She was, nonetheless, a dead-end design, neither fish nor fowl, with no natural role to play in a modern fleet. Too late to change *Blücher*, the Germans began to get more accurate information on the actual characteristics of the *Invincibles* (and *Tsukuba*), and followed up with a design with significantly greater armour and armament.[61] Because the information coming to them from their attaché in London did not mention that the *Invincibles* had armoured cruiser-type armour – an armour belt 6in–4in thick – the Germans gave their first battlecruiser SMS *von der Tann* an armour belt 9.84in–3.15in thick, as well as eight 28cm/45 main-battery guns and four-shaft Parsons turbines driving her at 24.75 knots on 43,000shp. In *von der Tann*, the Germans had produced the 'hybrid' cruiser-battleship Fisher wanted, or something quite close to it. The development of armoured cruisers had truly reached a dead end.

Anticipating the Dreadnought revolution, which saw a move away from similarly-sized main and secondary batteries – such as *Rurik*'s 10in and 8in batteries – and equally anticipating 'Jacky' Fisher's drive towards an 'all-big-gun' armoured cruiser (which became HMS *Invincible*), the Japanese responded to the loss of two battleships at the beginning of the Russo-Japanese War in 1904 by ordering a pair of 'hybrid battleship-cruisers', with the main battery of a pre-Dreadnought battleship – four 12in/45 guns in twin turrets – but with armour and speed more appropriate to an armoured cruiser. The result was *Tsukuba*, seen here at the Jamestown Exposition Naval Review on 2 May 1907, barely four months after her completion. She created quite a sensation for a year, until *Invincible* was commissioned and the 'true' battlecruiser, with eight 12/45 guns burst on the scene and effectively obsoleted all large, mixed-battery armoured cruisers. (NARA)

Chapter 2

The Test of Battle, Part 1: 1914–1916

When war broke out in Europe in July 1914, the navies of the major combatants (and those still just looking on) had been stocked with cruisers in a myriad of sizes, shapes and capabilities. The demands of war, whether it was the tedious steaming of long-ranging missions searching for enemy commerce raiders or the sharp action of combat, soon tested the mettle of designs long assayed only theoretically. This chapter will cover engagements in the First World War that exclusively or primarily involved cruisers (or parts of larger battles involving cruisers) and that allow conclusions to be drawn about the qualities of the types of cruisers that evolved up to 1914.

Pacific Sunset: Coronel – 1 November 1914

The start of the war found German cruisers literally scattered around the world. Two were trapped in the Mediterranean by the sudden rush of events after the assassination of the Austrian archduke in Sarajevo; the *Magdeburg* class light cruiser SMS *Breslau*, along with the equally new battlecruiser

One of Germany's newest and best light cruisers, SMS *Karlsruhe*, had just been in commission a few months when she was sent to the Caribbean to relieve the station cruiser there, SMS *Dresden*. *Karlsruhe* is seen here provisioning at San Juan, PR, on 9 or 10 August 1914; she arrived there with nearly-empty bunkers, having been chased by British cruisers. She was longer and faster than *Strassburg* seen in the preceding chapter, but otherwise similar. Perhaps the newness of the ship and her crew played a role in the briefness of her career. At the outbreak of war, she set off on a highly successful commerce-raiding voyage south along the South American coast, but was back near Barbados when she was destroyed by a cataclysmic internal explosion, probably caused by the mishandling of munitions in the forward magazines. (LOC/BNS)

SMS *Goeben*, fled east from the coast of Algeria, followed by rather inept Royal Navy pursuit, reaching Constantinople (Istanbul) on 10 August 1914 and transferring to Turkish control a week later. The brand-new light cruiser SMS *Karlsruhe* was just taking up station in the West Indies as replacement for SMS *Dresden* when war broke out. *Karlsruhe* was surprised by a Royal Navy patrol in the Caribbean while attempting to transfer weapons to a German liner, but was able to escape using her 27-knot speed. She then went on an extended raid down the Atlantic coast of South America, as far south as Recife (Pernambuco), Brazil, sinking or capturing sixteen ships before turning back north again towards the end of October. She was approaching Barbados on 4 November when she suffered a catastrophic internal explosion that tore off her bow aft of the bridge. The forward part sank quickly, taking most of her crew and her captain with it; the after part remained afloat long enough for 129 of her crew to transfer to an accompanying supply ship. Another light cruiser, SMS *Königsberg*, briefly ran free among the sparse merchant traffic off the east coast of Africa before being bottled up in the Rufiji River delta.

SMS *Scharnhorst* was the flagship of Vice Admiral Maximillian von Spee's German East Asia Squadron. She is seen here in a famous pre-war image made by Arthur Renard. Excluding the ill-conceived SMS *Blücher*, she and her sister SMS *Gneisenau* were the last and best of Germany's armoured cruisers. They fought well at Coronel, their main battery of eight 21cm/40 guns, disposed in twin turrets and Upper Deck casemates, scored early and effectively against Cradock's armoured cruisers. When put up against the two *Invincible*s sent south from the Grand Fleet, they proved hard to sink, but utterly unable to damage seriously the British battlecruisers. (NHHC)

The outbreak of war had prevented *Dresden* from returning home after being relieved in the Caribbean. Instead, she too headed south, operated briefly off the east coast of Brazil, stopping at Trinidade Island and then Isla Hoste at the southern tip of the continent to spend a week-and-a-half at Orange Bay on engine maintenance, it having been almost a year since *Dresden* had last seen yard time. Informed that there were good targets along the western side of South America, *Dresden* started up the Chilean coast. Near the Juan Fernández Islands, radio contact was established with Vice Admiral Maximillian von Spee, commanding the German East Asia Squadron, with which *Dresden* rendezvoused at Easter Island (Rapa Nui) – famous for its megalithic standing heads, 1900nm from the Chilean coast – on 12 October 1914.

Spee's squadron, which had been at Ponape (Pohnpei) in the Carolines (Federated States of Micronesia) when war broke out, consisted of the large armoured cruisers *Scharnhorst* and *Gneisenau*. It was joined there on 6 August by the light cruiser SMS *Nürnberg* which had been on the west coast of the United States, after which the three ships left together for Pagan in the Marianas. Spee was following instructions from Berlin, which gave him a few general guidelines and considerable latitude to direct his movements as he thought best.

Spee was joined at Pagan by the light cruiser SMS *Emden*, which had been at Tsingtao (Qingdao) when the war began. He wanted then to head east towards Eniwetok (Enewetak) in the Marshalls, but *Emden*'s captain persuaded Spee to allow him to detach and take his chances as a commerce raider. (*Emden*'s brief, but spectacular, career as a solo raider mainly in the Indian Ocean lasted until she was caught and sunk by the *Chatham* class light cruiser HMAS *Sydney* at the Cocos Islands on 9 November 1914.) From Pagan also, *Nürnberg* was detached to carry mail and dispatches to Honolulu for forwarding to Berlin. The squadron continued meandering generally eastward, stopping at uninhabited Christmas Island (Kiritimati) in the Line Islands (Kiribati) – where *Nürnberg* rejoined – then Samoa and Tahiti – where a French gunboat was sunk – and finally Easter Island. There the squadron was joined by *Dresden* and also by the light cruiser SMS *Leipzig*, which had replaced *Nürnberg* on the west coast of North America, and had arrived at Easter Island via San Francisco, Mazatlán and the Galapagos Islands.

From there, Spee took his squadron, now five ships strong, towards South America. Approaching the coast of Chile, he learned from a German trade representative that the Royal Navy *Bristol* class light cruiser HMS *Glasgow* was in the harbour at Coronel, a seaport on that country's south-central coast, and determined to destroy her. *Glasgow* was actually part of a larger British squadron, the remnants of Rear Admiral Christopher G F M Cradock's North American and West Indies Station command. Unlike Spee, Cradock was receiving regular, detailed and often conflicting orders from his superiors in Whitehall. By stages, these orders moved him south from his original station. After receiving reports on 13 August that *Dresden* had been sighted off the mouth of the Amazon and *Karlsruhe* was near Curaçao, he transferred his flag at Halifax, Nova Scotia, to the *Drake* class armoured cruiser HMS *Good Hope* and set off south to take personal command of the pursuit of the two German light cruisers.[1] By the beginning of September, the pursuit had taken him as far south as St Peter and St Paul Rocks and Fernando de Noronha before he put in at Recife on 5 September. There he was met with orders putting him in charge of a South-eastern Coast of South America Station, with a scattered squadron under his command comprising, besides his flagship, the armoured cruisers HMS *Berwick* and *Monmouth*, the light cruisers HMS

One year older than *Dresden*, which had been stationed in the Caribbean, SMS *Nürnberg* had a similar posting on the west coast of the Americas. She is seen here on 18 May 1914 at Mazatlán, Mexico, where she was making a port call. *Nürnberg* missed most of the action at Coronel, catching up with Spee's squadron only after dark, in time to finish off HMS *Monmouth*. She did not survive the Falklands battle. (NHHC)

Above: By the time the Royal Navy was building the *Chatham* class, of which HMAS *Sydney* was an example, seen as completed in 1913, the issues with the *Bristol*s had been resolved by adding two feet to the beam and employing a single-calibre main battery of six 6in/45 Mk XIIs in single mounts. After SMS *Emden* separated from Spee's squadron at Pagan in the Pacific and began a commerce raid into the Indian Ocean that briefly panicked the Royal Navy, *Sydney* was one of the ships earmarked to attempt to track down the elusive German raider. (SLV/AGC)

Right: *Emden* was found and overwhelmed in a short, sharp firefight with *Sydney* at the Cocos Islands on 9 November 1914. *Emden* fought gamely, but was hopelessly outgunned by the bigger and better-armed *Sydney*, and was soon reduced to a sinking wreck. Her captain decided to beach her on the reef off North Keeling Island to save what remained of her crew. As it was, she lost more than a third of her complement of 376. She is seen here sometime after that battle, wedged well up on the reef. There had been talk of a salvage operation in 1915, but constant wave action broke apart the wreck fairly rapidly; by 1919, reports indicated little of the ship remained visible above water. (SLV/AGC)

Bristol and *Glasgow*, and a number of AMCs. Cradock kept most of his squadron with him, patrolling between the Abrolhos Rocks (off the Brazilian coast midway between Bahia and Rio de Janeiro) and the mouth of the River Plate (Rio de la Plata), but he detached three ships – *Glasgow*, *Monmouth* and one of the AMCs, HMS *Otranto* – to cover the Strait of Magellan to prevent *Dresden* slipping away to the west.

After sinking a freighter off the Plate on 26 August, *Dresden* had continued on south. Cradock did not receive this news until a week later along with the incorrect information that *Dresden* had then moved to the north. Cradock met up with the *Glasgow* detachment on 14 September; on that same day, he was ordered to shift his base of operations south to the Falklands Islands in the South Atlantic, with the intention of blocking any move by Spee around Cape Horn.[2] Two days later, the pressure seemed to have eased, as news arrived from London that Spee had made landfall at Samoa on the 14th and had departed in a north-westerly direction, indicating the Germans were heading away from South America.[3] Cradock was therefore instructed that his squadron 'need not be concentrated', that he should send two cruisers and *Otranto* to and through the Strait of Magellan to the west coast of South America to disrupt 'German trade' and search for *Dresden*. What is curious about this order is that the Admiralty knew full well that there no longer was any 'German trade' worth interdicting; by this point of the war any German merchant shipping had run for home, been sunk, captured or was hiding out in neutral harbours.

Cradock departed the Plate estuary on 22 September, heading south, searching for the elusive *Dresden* at every bay and inlet along the way. Three days later, by pure chance, he happened on the British liner *Ortega*, which passed on the news that a week earlier, on the Pacific side of the Magellan Strait, *Dresden* had chased her into Chilean waters. With this first definite word of *Dresden*'s location in weeks, Cradock set off for Punta Arenas, the major port on the Strait of Magellan. There, he learned that *Dresden* had last been seen holed up at Orange Bay, perhaps 175nm further south. Wasting no time, he took his squadron to the west of Tierra del Fuego and east around False Cape Horn at the southern tip of Hoste Island, only to find Orange Bay empty. Now short on coal, he sent *Otranto* back to Punta Arenas while he took his three cruisers to provision at Port Stanley in the Falklands.[4] From there, *Glasgow* and *Monmouth* departed on 3 October to pick up *Otranto* and carry out the prior orders to patrol off the west coast of South America.

Once again this plan was overtaken by events. *Otranto* intercepted radio signals that seemed to indicate activity at Orange Bay, and *Good Hope* followed after the others two days later, but a second foray into that desolate bay proved equally fruitless, and *Good Hope* returned to the Falklands while the rest of the squadron headed into the Pacific with orders to go no further north than Valparaiso. Back at Port Stanley, Cradock ordered the old battleship HMS *Canopus*, which had been transferred to his command, to join him in the Falklands.

Back in London, there was turmoil at Whitehall. The First Sea Lord, Prince Louis of Battenberg, was under increasing fire for the fact that he was of German origin; this kerfuffle distracted the leadership of the Admiralty at the very time when it should have been giving Cradock firm guidance (or leaving him alone). On 13 October, Battenberg and the First Lord of the Admiralty Winston S Churchill generated a memorandum in which they expressed the belief that Cradock knew Spee was headed in his direction and that he should, if faced with a superior enemy force, shadow that force until he

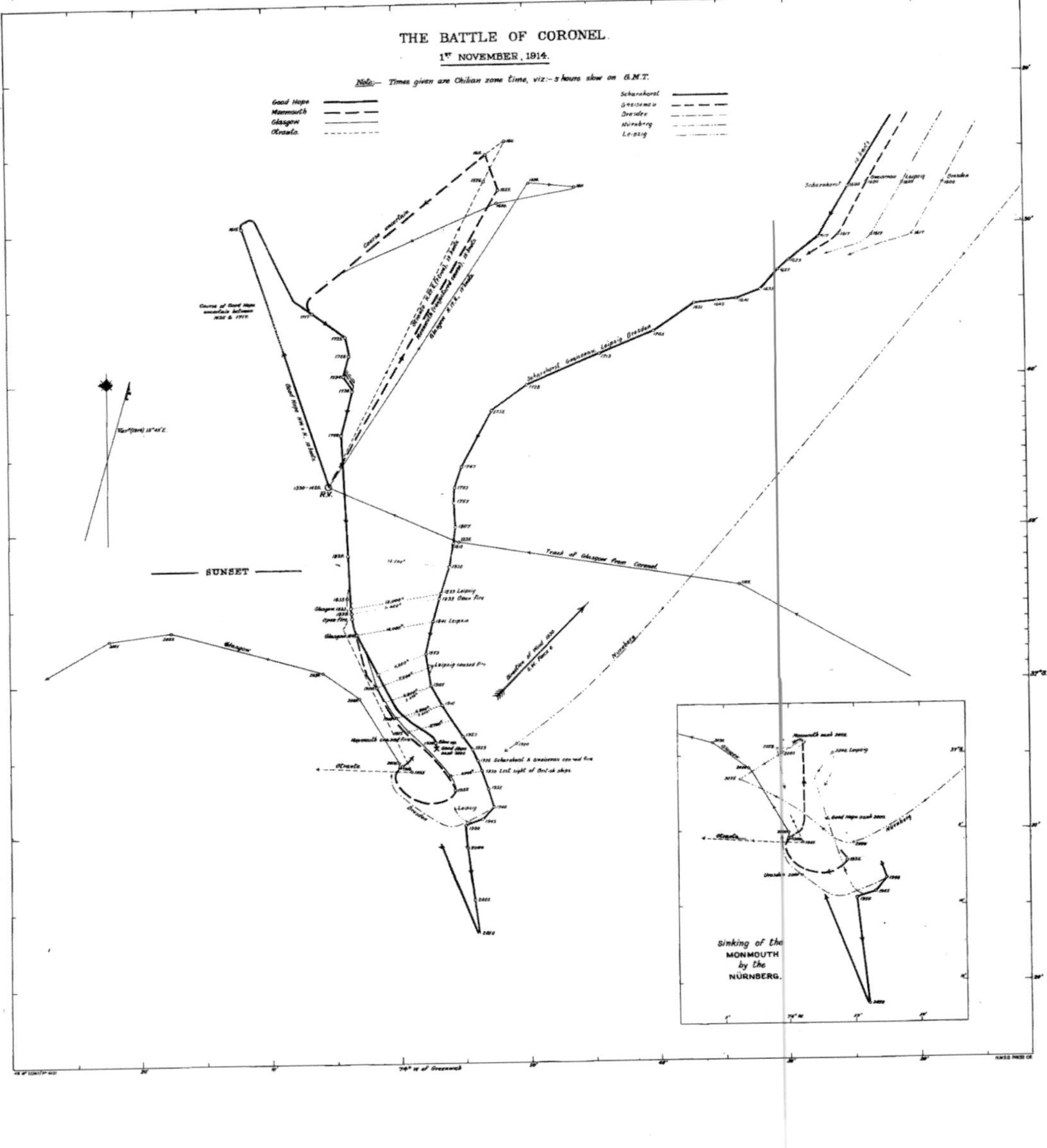

This excellent track chart of the Battle of Coronel is from the Royal Navy's Staff Monographs Vol IX. The thin line coming from the south-east is HMS *Glasgow* returning from Coronel to the rendezvous with Cradock's squadron, marked 'R.V.' on the chart. From there the squadron dispersed into scouting formation until HMS *Otranto* sighted smoke to the east at 15.56 and *Glasgow* turned to investigate at 16.00. At that point, Cradock could still have avoided combat, but once he assembled his battle line on a converging course with Spee's squadron, he was committed to an unequal and unfortunate fight which he ultimately lost. (RNSM)

Rear Admiral Christopher Cradock's flagship was HMS *Good Hope*, a *Drake* class armoured cruiser, seen here on 2 May 1907. Besides the two large single turrets with 9.2in/47 Mk X guns, she had eight 6in/45 Mk VIIs on each side in two-level casemates; the lower rank of these guns proved serviceable at Coronel only because of director control. It appears that some elaborate event is going on in this image – she was flagship of 1st Cruiser Sqdn, Atlantic Fleet at this time – given the extensive awning over the quarterdeck and the two accommodation ladders, one in use, visible aft. (NHHC)

could be reinforced.[5] However, the message they sent him that day not only did not express those sentiments, it stated explicitly that he was to take his entire force, including *Canopus*, to seek out Spee, and that there would be no further direct reinforcements. Cradock waited at Port Stanley for five more days for *Canopus* to arrive, only to be informed the old ship would require a minimum of five days in port to clean boilers and refurbish her engines. Equally as distressing was the news that, even then, her maximum sustained speed would be 12 knots.[6] Therefore Cradock left *Canopus* behind with orders to follow as best she could, escorting a pair of colliers; he set out from Port Stanley, heading for a rendezvous with the other three ships of his squadron at Vallenar Roads (Rada Vallenar) on the southern Chilean coast on 27 October.

Cradock's squadron finished coaling at Vallenar and departed two days later, at the same time that *Canopus* was arriving. *Glasgow* was detached to run ahead to Coronel to deliver dispatches and pick up mail. However, almost as soon as the squadron departed Vallenar, *Glasgow* started picking radio transmissions from *Leipzig* and, acting on prior instructions from Cradock to the effect that finding Spee was more important than his communications mission, spent the 30th and most of the next day cruising slowly off the coast near Coronel, listening for further signs of German activity. *Glasgow* delayed entering Coronel until 19.00 on 31 October, so as to avoid being trapped by Spee's squadron.[7]

Both sides had a very distorted picture of each other as they neared on 1 November 1914. Cradock's squadron, which had been tracking *Leipzig* through her radio activity, knew she was close, and swept up the coast of Chile expecting to meet only one light cruiser. Spee knew only of *Glasgow*, which had been reported at Coronel the night before, and approached the coast, disposed to trap a single light cruiser that would be required by neutrality rules to leave port within 24 hours. By late afternoon, the Germans were sweeping down the coast from the north, close inshore, in very loose formation, with *Scharnhorst* leading, *Gneisenau* trailing by perhaps two miles, followed at increasing intervals by *Leipzig*, *Dresden* and *Nürnberg*.[8] The orders were for the light cruisers to close on *Scharnhorst*, which would take position off the main, northern exit from Arauco Bay, on which Coronel was located, while *Gneisenau* covered the smaller, southern exit. If *Glasgow* had not appeared by 18.00, one of the light cruisers would enter the port to 'remind' the port authorities that international law required the departure of the British cruiser.

What Spee did not know was that *Glasgow* was long gone. She had been tracking *Leipzig*'s radio traffic and knew the German light cruiser was close, so Cradock ordered *Glasgow* to leave Coronel in the morning, which she did at 09.15, heading for a rendezvous with the rest of Cradock's squadron 50nm west of Coronel. This took place at approximately 13.15, after which Craddock organised his four ships into a sweep line heading north-north-east, with 15nm separation, in order (from west-to-east) *Good Hope*, *Monmouth*, *Otranto* and *Glasgow*, speed 15 knots. They started to spread out into this search formation at about 13.45 and still had not reached full separation when, at 15.56, *Otranto* sighted smoke on her starboard bow and signalled *Glasgow* to that effect; the light cruiser turned to investigate at 16.00.[9] Eleven minutes later, *Glasgow* had the two German armoured cruisers in sight and turned back to west-by-south to spread the alarm, her turn mirrored by *Otranto* and *Monmouth*. The Germans did not sight *Glasgow* until 16.17.

(A quick note about the weather is necessary for an understanding of events. The sky was almost entirely cloudless, an early mist having cleared, but a strong steady breeze just east of south kicked up at noon, increasing in strength considerably by sunset and gradually swinging around to the south-west, driving steep seas in front of it. The sun would set shortly before 18.30. The moon, one day short of full, was going to rise right before sunset, but would have to clear some cloud build-up over the Andes before it would provide any light.)

The first news of contact spurred both commanders to make the obvious calls. Spee simply ordered a 1-point (11.25°) turn towards the south-west and instructed his squadron to close on the flagship. Craddock had a more complicated problem to solve for a number of reasons. He had to concentrate his squadron which was stretched over almost 40nm of ocean and bring it to bear on a target at least as fast as all but one of his ships, and a full 5 knots faster than his slowest ship, if he kept *Otranto* with his squadron. He turned *Good Hope* to the south-south-east at approximately 16.15. The critical decision point for Cradock came five minutes later, when he received *Glasgow*'s report that Spee's two armoured cruisers were in sight. He now knew he was up against a superior force that was in a tactically advantageous

position. He never hesitated; at 16.40, he ordered all ships in the squadron to concentrate on *Glasgow*.[10] With this one decision he committed his squadron to battle against an opponent which had superior armament and speed, and advantages of weather and light that would only increase as time passed.

Spee gradually turned *Scharnhorst* onto a course that paralleled *Glasgow*'s to the west-south-west and increased speed to match, which actually delayed the rate at which *Gneisenau* and the light cruisers could join up with the flag. Cradock's line reformed at 17.17 heading south-east-by-east and gradually bore around to the south-south-west; Spee was headed south-west-by-west, a converging course, albeit a slow convergence. At 17.34, the two lines now separated by 18,000yd, Cradock realised he had less than an hour before sunset and, with the sun behind him and therefore shining directly in the eyes of the German gunners, he would never have a better tactical position. Therefore, he ordered a 4-point (45°) turn together to port, towards the enemy, that would close the range and initiate the engagement much more rapidly. Spee understood Cradock's intent and ordered a 2-point (22.5°) turn away. At the same time, he slowed *Scharnhorst* so that the rest of his squadron could catch up. Four minutes later, realising Spee would simply match any turn of his, Craddock reformed his line by a 4-point turn together to starboard and the two sides resumed a gradually converging run to the south. At 17.50, Cradock made another 1½-point (16.875°) turn towards Spee, to which the Germans did not react; quite possibly it was not noticed.

Shortly after 18.00, with the sun hanging at the western horizon, it was finally Spee's turn to take the initiative. The range had now down to approximately 14,000yd, still too long for Spee's liking. (Cradock had the biggest guns at Coronel, *Good Hope*'s two 9.2in/47s, but there were only two of them.[11] They had a theoretical range of 22,000yd, but in the conditions at Coronel, the practical range would be far shorter. Spee's two armoured cruisers could each bring six 21cm/40s to bear on a broadside; these had a theoretical range of over 17,000yd, but, because of the limitations of the twin turrets in the *Scharnhorst* class, the practical maximum range was 13,560yd.[12]) At 18.07, Spee turned 1 point towards the British to begin shortening the range more rapidly.

Just before 18.30, the sun disappeared below the western horizon and the range had dropped to just under 11,500yd;

The other armoured cruiser lost at Coronel was HMS *Monmouth*. She was a third smaller than *Good Hope* in displacement and carried a uniform battery of fourteen 6in/45 Mk VIIs in turrets and casemates. Like her squadron-mate, she was hit early and hard in the action at Coronel and she dropped out of line, as indicated in the chart reproduced above; *Glasgow* followed her until around 20.00. After that, burning from numerous fires, listing and down by the bow, she struggled on to the north for most of an hour before *Nürnberg* arrived to deliver the *coup de grâce*.

Spee finally had the conditions he wanted. *Scharnhorst* led the German line, *Gneisenau* trailed by 600yd, *Leipzig* was 1000yd further back and *Dresden* was closing rapidly. Silhouetted against the bright western sky, Cradock's line – *Good Hope* followed by *Monmouth*, *Glasgow* and *Otranto* in that order – was a clear target; Spee ordered fire to be opened at approximately 18.30. *Scharnhorst*'s ranging salvos were with 21cm HE rounds. The first two fell short, but on her third salvo she found the range and was rewarded with a burst of flame visible between *Good Hope*'s forward turret and conning tower; at virtually the same time, *Gneisenau* hit *Monmouth*'s forward 6in turret, igniting powder charges waiting to be loaded, blowing the turret overboard. *Good Hope*'s crew made some progress controlling the fire forward but, only minutes later, a second hit in almost exactly the same spot ignited powder charges in the secondary battery, after which the fire forward was never fully contained. It appears *Good Hope*'s forward main-battery turret ceased functioning at this point. Once they found the range, the German armoured cruisers switched over to firing AP rounds from their 21cm batteries, while continuing to fire HE from their secondary batteries. Within minutes, the battle was all but over.

As *Scharnhorst* and *Gneisenau* battered their opposite numbers, *Leipzig* and *Dresden*, with much smaller and shorter-ranging 10.5cm guns and suffering more from the rough seas than the bigger armoured cruisers, were causing much less damage to their British opponents. This was particularly true in the case of *Otranto*, whose captain, even before the shooting started, had asked permission to withdraw out of range, a fitting request given that his ship was never intended to fight other warships. The reply he got from Cradock was a garbled non-answer, which he took to be permission to haul out of line and find shelter on *Glasgow*'s unengaged side. That ship, whether from luck or poor shooting on *Leipzig*'s and *Dresden*'s part, got through the engagement receiving only five hits, only one of which caused serious damage, a 6ft-square hole at her waterline above her port outer screw.

The fates of *Good Hope* and *Monmouth* were as horrific as one might expect. As the range closed Cradock made small turns towards Spee at about 18.40 and again around 19.07, in what appears to have been an attempt to increase the effectiveness of his squadron's gunfire. Already by about 18.50, *Monmouth* was no longer able to maintain her position in line and, ablaze between decks along much of her length, slowly losing way and down by the head, she fell away to starboard. *Glasgow* had to slow abruptly to avoid her.[13] *Glasgow* then followed after *Monmouth*, which continued on to the south-east. At approximately 19.00, *Leipzig* ceased firing and turned away from the battle, it being reported that Spee had ordered an 8-point (90°) turn to port. While this was quickly shown to be in error and the ship was brought back into line, she did not resume firing, as she could no longer find a target.

At 19.20, *Good Hope* suffered a major internal explosion; the fires had reached a midships magazine. This brought her to a halt and, after firing a few more rounds from her after guns, silenced her battery. To observers in *Glasgow*, it seemed . . .

> . . . that the ship could not recover from the shock. Flames shot up and debris was thrown up to a great height; then the fires died down, and the *Scharnhorst* ceased firing on her; and as the British and German lines drew past her to starboard and port the blackened hull was lost to sight in the darkness.[14]

According to eyewitnesses, presumably also in *Glasgow*, the explosion broke the ship in two parts and only the after half continued floating.[15]

The rest of the story got more complex as it split into multiple sub-actions. Spee continued on to the south-south-east; his armoured cruisers ceased firing at 19.26 and lost sight of any British ships four minutes later, even though the range had now come down to 4000yd. After slowly bearing towards the west in hopes of regaining contact, Spee finally decided that no good could come from keeping his two armoured cruisers so close to enemy ships carrying torpedoes, and, at approximately 19.35, he ordered his light cruisers to search for and attack any surviving British ships. Ten minutes later, he turned away, just east of south, intending to turn back again once the moon had risen high enough to give him better visibility.

The attack Spee had ordered would not be an easy task to accomplish, as the three light cruisers were now each operating alone. At about 19.35, the captain of *Otranto* decided that, in his case, discretion was the better part of valour, and he turned away to the west, departing the scene. At the same time, realising he was losing the battle against the head seas, the captain of *Monmouth* turned his ship through approximately 220° so that she was now heading north-north-east with her stern to the breaking waves. *Glasgow*, which had faithfully followed *Monmouth* to this point, made the hard, but necessary, choice to abandon the stricken cruiser, which could clearly neither fight nor flee and, given the weather and presence of nearby enemy ships, could not be towed or otherwise succoured. At about 20.00, *Glasgow* departed to the north-west. Impetus in making this decision was supplied by *Dresden*, which appeared out of the gloom from the south. As *Glasgow* quickly accelerated to high speed, *Dresden* gave chase.

Right: HMS *Glasgow* was a *Bristol* class light cruiser, from the first of the Royal Navy's 'Town' classes, seen here in a pre-war image. She was the newest and fastest of Cradock's cruisers, so she got used for tasks such as running in and out of ports such as Coronel to drop off messages. Their mixed armament of two 6in/50 Mk XIs and ten 4in/50 Mk VIIIs proved unfortunate, as did their narrow beam, which caused a cramped interior and made these ships poor gun platforms. *Glasgow*'s speed allowed her to escape the carnage at Coronel and exact a measure of revenge at the Falklands where she helped bring SMS *Leipzig* to heel. (NHHC)

These were the fastest ships in their respective squadrons, with trials speeds of excess of 24 knots. Neither could be expected to reach those speeds in this weather and after months at sea, but *Glasgow* had all the advantages in this race, being one-third bigger and having been docked much more recently. She drew steadily away from *Dresden* and by 20.20 was lost to sight.

Leipzig turned north at 19.48, having sighted what was described as a 'dimly visible glare' in that direction, but, as she approached, the light vanished.[16] Ten minutes later, as she passed through the waters where the 'glare' had been seen, crewmen on deck tossing powder cases overboard noted a large field of debris and floating bodies. Officers on *Leipzig*'s bridge saw nothing and the ship continued on without stopping. The glare originally seen from *Leipzig* could only have been the last fires burning in what remained of Cradock's flagship, meaning that it sank between 19.48 and 19.58. As curious as the fact that the officers on *Leipzig*'s bridge did not see the gruesome flotsam through which the ship steamed is the fact that no-one on the bridge or deck reported hearing any survivors calling for rescue.[17]

That left only *Monmouth* to be 'cleaned up'. At 21.25, *Glasgow* noted in her log 'a searchlight flicker below the horizon', followed by 'seventy-five flashes' of gunfire.[18] This could only have been *Nürnberg*'s belated arrival on the scene. After bending on all speed to make up the distance she was lagging behind the squadron, *Nürnberg* had sighted *Scharnhorst* only at 17.30; after that she followed the battle in the increasing dusk as best she could. At 20.05, she caught a brief glimpse of *Glasgow* in the distance, but then lost her in the darkness. She then came upon *Monmouth*, obviously in distress, down by the bow and listing to port, but still under way and with her colours still flying. As was customary under the circumstances, *Nürnberg* opened fire at 20.50 after briefly illuminating her with searchlights. The latter gesture was done both as a double-check on the identity of the target and a warning to *Monmouth* of what was to come. *Nürnberg* made

a slow firing pass along *Monmouth*'s starboard side. As the colours remained flying defiantly, *Nürnberg* then looped around and commenced a second firing run, during the course of which *Monmouth* rolled over on her port side and slid bow-first under the waves. The time was recorded as 20.58. No attempt was made to pick up survivors. The reasons given by *Nürnberg*'s survivors were the sea state, which made the launching of boats impossible, and the sighting of smoke columns on the south-western horizon which *Nürnberg* turned to investigate. (These turned out to be Spee's two armoured cruisers.)

Except for four men wounded in *Glasgow*, all of the British casualties were from the sinking of *Good Hope* and *Monmouth*, which took 1570 men to their graves. *Scharnhorst* was hit twice by *Glasgow* for no significant damage. *Gneisenau* was hit by four shells fired by *Monmouth*, one of which temporarily jammed her after main-battery turret; this wounded three of her crew, the only casualties suffered by the Germans that day.

The rest of the story of Spee's squadron is well-known and need not be covered in detail. Suffice it to say that he took his squadron around Cape Horn only to be met by a vastly superior Royal Navy force at the Falklands where he was defeated as utterly as he had Cradock. Of his five ships, only *Dresden* escaped, and that only for a short time.

The question, then, must be asked, why Cradock accepted battle against a superior foe in a tactically disadvantageous position. (Of course, it is reasonable to ask whether he had the option to avoid the battle; it certainly appears, given the lateness of the hour at which contact was made, that it is quite reasonable to presume that he had the option to keep out of range of Spee's guns until night fell.) It is easy to write off Cradock's actions as a very late example of Victorian-era-style derring-do – a 'Charge of the Light Brigade' moment inspired more by schoolboy tales of bravado than real-world calculation – but if one tries to imagine oneself in his place, with very incomplete tactical and strategic situational awareness, with limited and generally unsatisfactory communication with his superiors in London, unsure of what, if any, support would be forthcoming if he deferred action and keenly aware of what had happened to his friend Rear Admiral Ernest C T

After Coronel, part of Spee's squadron put in at Valparaiso – neutrality law permitted only three belligerent ships to enter at a time – which allowed Spee to come ashore on 3 November and exchange messages with Berlin. (It was from intercepts of this message traffic that the British first learned of Cradock's defeat.) This image shows Spee (centre, foreground) seated in his pinnace, coming alongside the pier at the Chilean capital. (NHHC)

Probably the sweeter revenge for *Glasgow* was the final entrapment of *Dresden* at Más a Tierra, one of the Juan Fernández Islands off the coast of Chile. *Dresden*, which had not seen a dockyard in several years and had now steamed hard for several months since leaving the Caribbean, was ordered home after escaping the destruction of Spee's squadron at the Falklands, but her captain judged her incapable of making the journey. Instead, he took her around the Horn and finally interned her at Más a Tierra, turning the ship over to the Chilean authorities there on 9 March 1915. She was in Cumberland Bay there on 14 March when *Glasgow* and HMS *Kent* arrived. *Dresden* signalled that she was unmanoeuvrable and no longer a combatant, but these messages were ignored and the British opened fire. After *Dresden* ran up a white flag, the British stopped firing, but when negotiations reached an impasse – the captain of *Glasgow* refusing to accept that *Dresden* was now a Chilean vessel and demanding that she surrender to the British – the German crew set off scuttling charges causing *Dresden* to sink slowly by the bow, as seen here. (NHHC)

Troubridge, who was facing a court martial for the 'crime' of allowing the German Mediterranean Squadron slip past him, his actions become more understandable.[19] Perhaps he thought he could damage some of Spee's ships or, at a minimum, cause him to fire off much of his irreplaceable stock of ammunition. (He was successful in this latter goal, if not much else, not that it had any marked impact on the outcome of the subsequent Falklands engagement.[20])

On the other hand, a more imaginative commander might have thought of a use for his resources that would have allowed him to report Spee's presence to London and to shadow the German squadron, so as to buy time for the Admiralty, with its vast resources, to bring in the forces necessary to contain the threat (which is, in fact, exactly what they did after they learned of the disastrous defeat at Coronel). That would have been a complex manoeuvre to orchestrate ad hoc, without prior arrangement with his squadron's commanders, but by no means impossible. He had a fast light cruiser in *Glasgow*, faster than any of Spee's ships, that could perform the shadowing; his two armoured cruisers could carry out sweeps behind and to sea, to make sure Spee did not make a radical loop around or try dividing his command; and *Otranto*, not fit for much else, could run in and out of ports delivering messages, until *Canopus* joined up and the British squadron had enough firepower to take on the Germans with a better chance of success. It could have been arranged.

Tragically (and more than a little ironically) the Admiralty, now with 'Jacky' Fisher once again in the post of First Sea Lord, sent out an order to Cradock on 3 November – they would not learn of the disaster at Coronel, from listening in to German reports, until the next day – clarifying his instructions and assuring him of reinforcement.[21] He was told that *Defence*, a newer and larger armoured cruiser, then at Montevideo, would be sent forward as rapidly as possible, and emphasised the importance of concentrating his squadron, including *Canopus*. In the meanwhile, he was to use *Glasgow* to shadow Spee's movements. The clear implication was he should not seek battle until such a concentration took place.

Finally, one must ask, how well did the ships engaged in this battle perform? Neither side shot well, but at this stage of the war, good shooting was not an expected goal of any navy, particularly in ships smaller than capital ships and particularly in such sub-optimal weather conditions as prevailed at Coronel. The only fire-control equipment carried on most cruiser-sized warships in 1914 were rangefinders, and, while these had improved incrementally since Ulsan, they still had limited range and their utility decreased as a direct function of reduced visibility. In *Good Hope* and *Monmouth*, Cradock had the advantage of a centralised fire-control director sited in the foremast spotting top. This certainly helped, but technology could only partially offset the advantages of light and weather held by Spee; while both lines were heading into a stiff breeze and taking water over their bows, the British cruisers had more guns in Upper Deck casemates that proved to be unserviceable due to the high seas, and the visibility was entirely favouring the Germans, silhouetting Cradock's line while hiding Spee's in gathering gloom. In commenting on the effectiveness of each side's secondary batteries, the Royal Navy staff assessment, written a decade after the battle, stated:

> The German ships pitching and rolling heavily, but the *Scharnhorst* and *Gneisenau* were able to fire their lower 5.9in. guns, though the guns' crews had at times to work in water up to their knees. The main deck 6in. guns of the *Good Hope* and *Monmouth* were mounted lower than those of the enemy, and it is doubtful whether, in the absence of the director, they could be fired at all.[22]

The difference in the visibility offered to the sightsetters on the opposing sides at Coronel accounted for a great deal of the disparity in the success of the gunfire of the Germans and the British that evening, that and training, seeing as how the German ships had been in commission with largely the same crews for several years, while most of Cradock's ships were newly-recommissioned from reserve status with relatively 'green' crews who were new to their ships and each other.[23] Nor were the British helped by the rather poorer quality of their ammunition; for example, the two 4in shells fired by *Glasgow* that hit *Scharnhorst* failed to explode.[24]

Nonetheless, the question of how well the ships that fought at Coronel performed offensively and defensively needs to be explored. On this day, *Scharnhorst* fired off 422 21cm (188 HE; 234 AP) and 215 15cm (148 HE; 67 AP) rounds, all but a few at *Good Hope*, and achieved an estimated thirty-five hits.[25] This would give a hit rate of 5–6 per cent, as good or better than the best sustained rate achieved by any capital ships at Jutland.[26] Of course, *Scharnhorst* faced far different battle conditions, including ranges that, towards the end of the engagement, had come down to less than 5000yd, but this was with a rising sea and failing light, so it was hardly target practice. British shooting was significantly worse, achieving six hits for all the shots taken by three ships, but must be understood within the context of poor visibility and weather conditions.

Good Hope and *Monmouth* proved to be difficult to sink. *Good Hope*, as noted, took over thirty-five hits from shells 15cm or larger before succumbing; it is not clear how many large-calibre hits *Monmouth* took, but it is known that she was hit by 135 10.5cm HE rounds from *Nürnberg* during the final attack.[27] When it became the turn of *Scharnhorst* and *Gneisenau* to meet a superior foe at the Falklands a month later, they proved every bit as tough. It is known that *Gneisenau* absorbed some fifty 12in/45 rounds fired by a pair of Royal Navy battlecruisers and ended up hastening her own demise by opening her seacocks.[28]

Showdown at 'Windy Corner': Jutland – 31 May 1916

The Battle of Jutland at the end of May 1916 is justifiably famous as the most massive confrontation of capital ships in the age of steel and steam, though it is certainly more famous for what did not happen than for what did. Most importantly, it did not prove decisive to the war in any manner. What it did change was the perception of certain ship types, in some cases dramatically. The cataclysmic destruction of three of 'Jacky' Fisher's prized battlecruisers exposed a serious flaw in his concept of a ship pairing capital ship armament with armoured cruiser speed and protection. Despite the fact that the German battlecruisers present that day, which were designed to a different paradigm, showed themselves to be fast, hard-hitting and much more resistant to damage, the general perception of the battlecruiser type by professional as well as popular observers changed abruptly from strongly positive to sharply negative.

Two other cruiser types were present at Jutland and had the opportunity to demonstrate their capabilities in the most extreme battle conditions. That the light cruiser type and the armoured cruiser type performed very differently in the test of combat probably surprised no-one. The armoured cruiser as a type had been effectively superseded by the battlecruiser, but the Royal Navy, at least, had built so many armoured cruisers that even in the spring of 1916, eight were still assigned scouting duties with the Grand Fleet. (The Germans had lost *Blücher*, *Scharnhorst* and *Gneisenau*, their newest armoured cruisers, by this point in the war, and the rest had been reduced to second-line duties. The High Seas Fleet steamed to Jutland with no armoured cruisers.) The eight British armoured cruisers were organised into two four-ship squadrons – 1st Cruiser Sqdn (1CS): HMS *Defence* (Rear Admiral Arbuthnot), *Warrior*, *Duke of Edinburgh* and *Black Prince*; 2nd Cruiser Sqdn (2CS): HMS *Minotaur* (Rear Admiral Heath), *Cochrane*, *Shannon* and *Hampshire* – arrayed in a broad sweep line 13nm ahead of the main body of the fleet on a front 30nm wide. The cruiser screen maintained this formation as the British and German battlecruiser forces ran to the south, encountered the main body of the High Seas Fleet, turned and ran back to the north.[29]

Much further ahead of the Grand Fleet were the three battlecruisers of Rear Admiral Hood's 3rd Battlecruiser Sqdn (3BCS) – HMS *Invincible*, *Inflexible* and *Indomitable* – led on his port and starboard bows by the new light cruisers HMS *Canterbury* and *Chester* respectively. At the very first contact between the enemy scouting forces, Hood had taken it upon himself to increase speed and turn to the east in order to block a possible German retreat through the Skagerrak.[30] When he learned that the battlecruiser forces had turned south, he led his force around to the south-east. By the time contact was made between the Grand Fleet and the approaching German force, Hood was at risk of being cut off from the main body of his fleet by enemy battlecruisers if he did not double back immediately.[31]

On the German side, the lead scouting group was a line of four of Germany's newest and best-armed light cruisers, the IIAG (*II Aufklärungsgruppe* – 2nd Scouting Group) comprising SMS *Frankfurt* (Rear Admiral Bödicker), *Pillau*, *Elbing* and *Wiesbaden*, leading Vice Admiral Franz Hipper's five battlecruisers by approximately 5nm.

Sister-ship to SMS *Wiesbaden*, which fought so gallantly at Jutland, SMS *Frankfurt* is seen here after the German surrender, flying American colours; she had been turned over to the US Navy as reparations at the end of the war. (Her crew tried unsuccessfully to scuttle her with the rest of the fleet at Scapa Flow.) The *Wiesbadens* differed from earlier German light cruisers pictured here, even ones as new as *Karlsrühe*, in that their main battery was eight 15cm/45 in shielded single mounts, which gave them a far more respectable offensive punch than their predecessors. (NHHC)

HMS *Chester* was one of a pair of light cruisers ordered by the Greek Navy in 1913 and laid down the following year, based on the design of the *Chatham* class. Taken over by the Royal Navy when the war began, *Chester* had begun fleet service only the month before she found herself fighting four of Germany's newest and best light cruisers at 'Windy Corner'; attached to Rear Admiral Hood's 3rd Battlecruiser Sqdn, which was only temporarily assigned to Jellicoe's Grand Fleet, *Chester* and the equally new *Cambrian* class light cruiser HMS *Canterbury* found themselves engaged with the German IIAG, which included *Frankfurt* and *Wiesbaden*. *Chester* carried an unusual (for the Royal Navy) main battery of ten 5.5in/50 Mk I, the weapon chosen by the Greeks because the rounds were almost 20 per cent lighter than the standard British 6in guns, but offered similar range and penetration characteristics. (NHHC)

As the two battlecruiser forces, now followed closely by the entire German fleet, neared the Grand Fleet, approaching from the north-west, the 'crisis' of the battle was also approaching, the point at which Admiral Sir John Jellicoe would need to deploy his fleet into a single battle line. The problem was, in order to make the correct decision, Jellicoe needed information and of this he was receiving precious little, and what little he was receiving was contradictory.

Then, suddenly, things began happening in a rush. The light cruiser *Chester*, which had reached a position 6nm to the west-north-west of 3BCS, heard gunfire to the south-west at 17.27 and turned in that direction to investigate.[32] Advancing through smoke and haze that sometimes reduced visibility to 2000yd, *Chester* sighted a three-funnelled cruiser heading north-north-eastward at 17.36, which flashed the correct British recognition signal. Assuming this was the leading cruiser of one of Beatty's scouting squadrons, *Chester* reversed course and set a course towards the north-east, as three more cruisers came into view behind the first. *Chester*'s captain presumed he was leading Beatty to join up with Hood's squadron; he was mistaken in that presumption and would pay dearly for it, because he had, in fact, happened upon Bödicker's IIAG. (Beatty had been consistently misreporting his position to Jellicoe, and was at least 20nm north-west of where Jellicoe expected him to be.[33]) The Germans had the British recognition signal because it had been broadcast by radio earlier in the day.[34]

With the range down to 6000yd, *Frankfurt* opened fire on *Chester* at 17.38, followed rapidly by the other three light cruisers in IIAG. So dense was the gunfire that it was impossible to track fall of shot, causing Bödicker immediately to order *Elbing* and *Wiesbaden* to cease firing; so accurate was the gunfire that *Chester* got off only one full salvo in reply. On *Frankfurt*'s third or fourth salvo, *Chester* was hit hard. A direct hit knocked out her forward portside gun, killing the crew of that gun and many in the crew of two of three other guns on that side; after her first salvo, another hit penetrated just above her armour belt, severing the voice-pipe from the transmitting station, so directed gunfire would have been impossible even if many of her guns had not been rendered inoperable.[35]

A Brief Digression – Fire Control in Cruisers in 1916

The introduction of a below-decks compartment dedicated to the accumulation and processing of fire-control information in a cruiser – called a transmitting station (TS) in the Royal Navy or a plotting room in the US Navy – was independent of the introduction of any individual element of fire-control equipment. The first experimental TS in the Royal Navy was set up in the armoured cruiser HMS *Duke of Edinburgh* in 1906 in an attempt to move the gunnery control officers and their communications equipment away from the noise and smoke of the spotting tops. While there was concern that being isolated in the ship's interior would detract from the ability of fire-control operators to communicate timely and accurate information to the guns, this proved not to be the case, especially after battle experience showed the vulnerability of men and equipment in spotting tops to injury or damage. The equipment typically found in the spotting top at this time might have included a spotting telescope to designate the target and possibly also a Dumaresq to determine range and deflection rates of change, with a 9ft-basis Barr & Stroud rangefinder generally mounted lower down, on the bridge roof.[36] Information from these devices was sent to the TS via both automatic and voice links; the TS would have minimal equipment in a cruiser at this point, generally nothing more than a range clock, if that, because the job of the TS was primarily the control of salvo fire. (The cruisers of IIAG, the newest in the High Seas Fleet, were equipped with an *E-Uhr*, the German equivalent of the Vickers Range Clock, a spring-motor-driven device, that, when set with a range-change-rate and a known target range, would show future ranges, assuming the range-rate remained constant.[37]) Range and bearing data sent from the rangefinder and Dumaresq would be integrated and transmitted to each bearing gun mount and, when all guns reported ready, the firing key pressed to initiate salvo fire. When voice-pipes to *Chester*'s TS were severed at the beginning of her engagement with the IIAG, she lost what ability she had for directed salvo fire.

As practised in the Royal Navy, one of the most important functions of the fire-control system, particularly for cruisers with their proliferation of similarly-sized guns, which would make correction by observation of shell splashes impossible if the guns fired independently, was to organise a ship's guns into groups and manage the information sent to each group so that they acted, as much as possible, as a coherent unit.

> The system adopted in H.M. Ships for the control of fire by means of electrical instruments, consists of dividing the guns into various groups, and supplying each with information separately.
>
> The control officer is in general not in electrical communication with the guns, but is only in communication with them through the 'Transmitting Stations,' which is situated low down in the ship behind armour. . .
>
> All ships have several control positions, so that if one is knocked out, the transmitting stations may receive information from another. Nearly all ships . . . have two transmitting stations, . . .[38]

The equipment used in the Royal Navy to transmit range and deflection from the transmitting station to the guns varied considerably from ship to ship. For example, *Glasgow*, which fought at Coronel, had Vickers 'Follow-the-Pointer' Instruments, Mk II.[39] *Warrior* had Vickers, Son, and Maxim, with Barr and Stroud rate instruments, while *Defence* had a complete Barr and Stroud Mk II system.[40]

The use of these systems was described as being comparable to the use of a machine gun on a land battlefield.

Citing a battle practice from 1 December 1912, the handbook notes that this applied particularly in the case of light cruisers:

> In organizing the fire discipline of a [ship], it is useful to consider her as a 'Maxim Gun' and to employ the same method of firing, viz., to open fire with salvoes (corresponding to single shot firing) with all sights with the same adjustment; and then, when the range is found, to develop rapid bursts of independent firing (representing the firing key being pressed) while the target is passing through the zone of the pattern. The control officer meanwhile predicts the next alteration of the position of the pattern, and when the target has passed through the zone, 'Check Fire' is ordered, or to use the Maxim gun simile, the firing lever is eased; and, during this time, transmission of the new sight adjustment is proceeded with. When the sights are readjusted each gunlayer is at liberty to fire again as his sightsetter reports 'On.'[41]

Showdown at 'Windy Corner': Jutland – 31 May 1916 – Continued

Within minutes, *Chester* had only one functioning gun facing the enemy operating under local control. The light cruiser survived this ordeal by dint of good luck, excellent seamanship and the cool head of her CO who rang up emergency flank speed and then turned her away, chasing shell splashes until she drew out of range without accumulating any further damage. (*Chester* was hit seventeen times, had three holes in her side armour and had four guns disabled, but her power plant remained intact, enabling her escape; she suffered thirty-five dead and forty-two wounded.[42])

In the process, her CO accomplished at least part of what he had originally set out to do, drawing enemy forces towards the big guns of Hood's battlecruisers. As Bödicker chased *Chester* to the north-east, the three *Invincible*s of 3BCS emerged from a patch of fog to the east at a range of 9000yd.[43] Hood had been slow to react the action to his westward, not turning until 17.38. Twelve minutes later, *Invincible* opened fire on *Frankfurt*, taking IIAG completely by surprise; the Germans were unable to see more than the flashes of 3BCS's guns until late in this brief engagement. Reacting quickly, Bödicker ordered a 180° turn together to starboard, a manoeuvre that caused the range to drop to 8000yd or less.

Not for the last time this day, 3BCS shot exceptionally well.[44] *Pillau* was hit by a 12in shell, probably fired by *Inflexible* at 17.58. The shell detonated below *Pillau*'s chart house in the officers' head, most of the explosive energy venting outboard on her starboard side, but some damaged the uptakes to her forward funnel and forced the temporary shutting down of all the coal-fired boilers in her forward fire rooms. Fortunately, the remaining four oil-fired boilers supplied enough steam to allow her to maintain 24 knots and keep up with the squadron as it disappeared in the smoke. Four men were killed in *Pillau*.

While this was going on, the roiled waters where Hood's

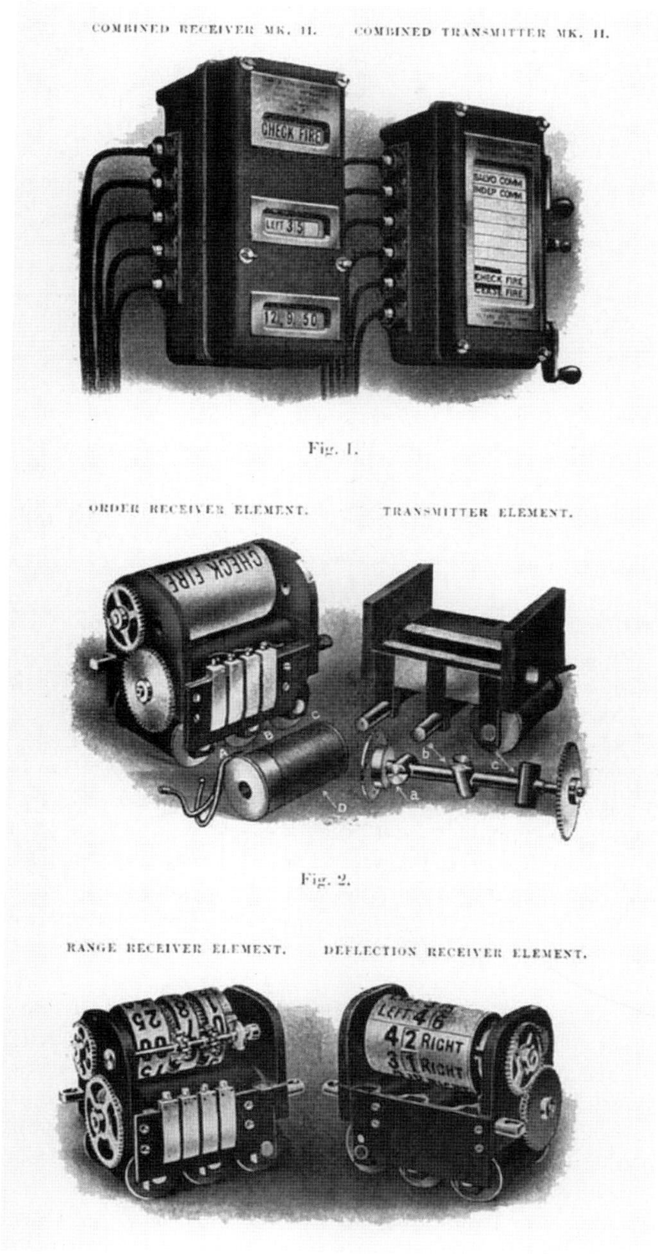

Elements of the Barr and Stroud Mk II fire-control system, as fitted in HMS *Defence*, are seen in this illustration from the Royal Navy's *Handbook for Fire Control Instruments, 1914*. The transmitting instruments illustrated here would be situated in the TS, where the control officer used the Combined Transmitter Mk II to send the gun order, deflection and range to each gun in the group he was controlling. When controlling salvo fire, each gun would signal when the indicated range and deflection had been set and, when all guns in the group indicated they were set, the control officer fired the salvo. (NA)

HMS *Chester*'s brush with IIAG was brief and violent, as can be seen in this view of her port side taken after the Battle of Jutland, June 1916. At least five shell holes can be seen here, three of which appear to have penetrated her 2in belt armour. All but one of the guns bearing on this side were knocked out of action. Critically, she was able to steam and steer, which enabled her to 'chase salvos' long enough to make her escape. (NHHC)

and Bödicker's squadrons met – dubbed 'Windy Corner' by the British – were about to get much more crowded. HMS *Warrior*, which was still following Arbuthnot's flagship *Defence* on the starboard bow of the oncoming Grand Fleet, had begun edging over eastward in anticipation of meeting Beatty's battlecruisers, expected to be approaching from the south-east. Passing across the front of the Grand Fleet, *Warrior*'s Captain Vincent B Molteno stated:

> At 5.40 p.m., while still 10 miles ahead of our battle fleet, and with speed now increased to 20 knots, gunfire was heard and gun flashes seen about 30 degrees before our starboard beam, but on a bearing west of south, instead of the bearing east of south on which, by plotting the reports of the enemy from our battle cruisers, we had calculated that we should join the action. The time was also about half an hour earlier than we had expected.[45]

Assuming *Warrior*'s clocks were accurate, the gunfire observed at 17.40 was between *Chester* and IIAG; 3BCS would not enter the fray for ten more minutes. This would be the first contact between the main body of the Grand Fleet and the leading elements of the High Seas Fleet.

> A few minutes later, on almost the same bearing as the gun flashes, light cruisers belonging to our battle cruiser fleet were sighted,[46] . . . At about 5.47 I sighted three, or, possibly, four enemy light cruisers about 20 degrees on my starboard bow, and I now increased speed to 21 knots to close from ½ a mile to ¼ of a mile astern of *Defence*. *Defence* then altered course about 20 degrees to port, bringing the nearest enemy cruiser–the *Wiesbaden*–on to a bearing of Green 80 and signalled 'Open fire, ship interval 12 seconds'.[47]

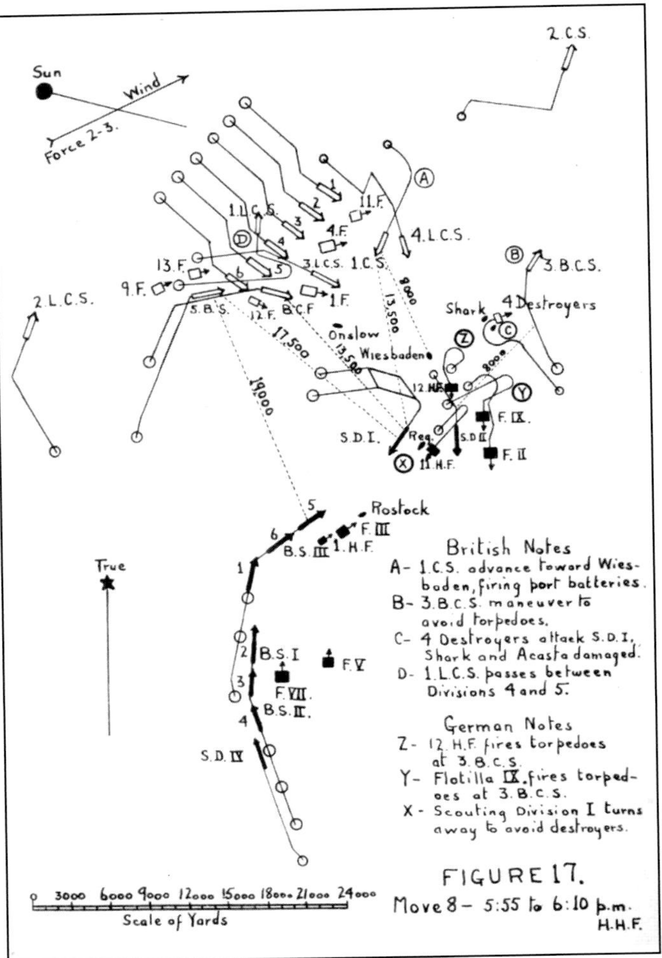

American Lieutenant Commander H H Frost made an excellent analytical study of the Battle of Jutland for the US Navy in 1921 that included a clear set of charts breaking down the action into short stages. His Fig 17, reproduced here, shows the first part of the critical action at 'Windy Corner', between 17.55 and 18.10. All the major 'players' can be seen here: *Wiesbaden* is already isolated between the fleets to the right of centre; above and a bit to the left is 1CS, which comprised *Defence* and *Warrior*; steaming away to the south is the rest of SDII, which is Frost's name for IIAG, as marked on his chart; the destroyer HMS *Onslow*, which delivered the fatal torpedo attack on *Wiesbaden*, is to her left and off to the right is 3BCS, which is the three *Invincibles*. (USN)

It is curious that Captain Molteno, whose narrative is being quoted here, claimed *Wiesbaden*, the last in Bödicker's line, was the closest enemy cruiser. This is certainly the wisdom (or some other quality) of hindsight, as, in an earlier report, Molteno described the cruiser at which he was firing as one of the *Pillau* class.[48]

> . . . Three salvos were fired by each of us at extreme range

under the concentrated pair ship fire organization which the squadron had worked up, but all the shot falling short, we checked fire, and *Defence* altered course directly towards *Wiesbaden*.[49]

'Concentrated pair ship fire organization' was an arrangement whereby two ships fired their main-battery weapons under the control of one of the ships, generally the leading ship, with an agreed-upon time interval between the salvos fired by the two ships, in this case 12 seconds. The lead ship took the responsibility for determining range and deflection to the target and making any necessary corrections, transmitting the information to the trailer by flag or signal lamp.[50]

. . . At 6.1 p.m. the *Defence* again altered course and brought *Wiesbaden* on to a bearing 40 degrees on the port bow. Just after this the light cruisers of our battle cruiser fleet passed astern, and we came under fire from the enemy light cruisers.

Defence and *Warrior* then opened fire, and the second salvo of both ships hit the *Wiesbaden*, setting her on fire, and causing a great escape of steam on board her. In a few minutes she was seen to be stopped.[51]

Here Molteno, perhaps understandably, misinterpreted what he was witnessing, because, when *Defence* and *Warrior* opened fire on *Wiesbaden* over their port bows at 18.05, the German light cruiser had already received the damage that disabled her power plant. At 18.00, as IIAG was completing its turn together to the south-south-west, *Wiesbaden* took a 12in shell in her engine room, most likely from *Invincible*, which disable both her turbines and left her without power. (It is believed that a second 12in shell hit her at this time, but this cannot be stated with certainty. She was most likely hit by six 9.2in or 7.5in shells fired by *Defence* and *Warrior* between 18.05 and 18.19, but she had already been disabled.[52]) She had been steaming at full speed when she was hit, so it would take some time before she drifted to a stop; when Arbuthnot re-opened fire at 18.05, at a range of 8000yd, she must have still had way on, making it seem to the eager observers in *Warrior*, that it was their gunfire that caused the venting of steam and the loss of speed that they witnessed. Indeed, so intent were Arbuthnot and his men on crippling this enemy cruiser, which appeared to threaten their approaching fleets, that they seemed oblivious to their own looming danger.

. . . but as she was still in a position favourable for firing torpedoes at our battle cruisers, we, *Defence* and *Warrior*, continued hitting her again and again with our port guns, closing her to within 6,000 yards before turning away. . . When both *Defence's* and *Warrior's* second salvoes hit the enemy, I remember remarking to the Navigator : 'We have never had a practice concentration of fire go off so smoothly and successfully'. . .

As we closed the *Wiesbaden*, we passed about a mile ahead of our battle cruiser squadron, and came under heavy fire from the enemy battle cruisers[53] . . .

During this fighting *Warrior* was a quarter of a mile astern of *Defence*, and I twice thought *Defence* had been hit by the enemy battle cruisers because of sudden puffs of black smoke which came from her. At 6.19 she commenced to turn away to starboard, and was then hit by two salvoes in quick succession. Then she blew up and completely disappeared.[54]

In these few brief sentences, Captain Molteno wrote *finis* to the armoured cruiser type in the Royal Navy. As long as battles for sea control were between capital ships carrying big guns, the captains of large, well-armed cruisers, be they battlecruisers or armoured cruisers, seemed unable to resist the temptation to engage with the 'big boys' with, as Jutland would so emphatically demonstrate, disastrous results. In the case of *Defence*, it took the Germans barely four minutes to deliver the verdict. She was sighted at about 18.15, immediately after clearing *Lion*, from the leading ships of Hipper's IAG.[55] The gunners in SMS *Derfflinger* hesitated to open fire – *Defence*'s four-funnelled silhouette somewhat resembled that of a German light cruiser – but those in SMS *Lützow* did not and opened fire at 18.16. No more than a minute later, as many as four of the leading battleships of the High Seas Fleet joined in. It is impossible to identify which of these ships fired the

This image shows HMS *Minotaur*, sister-ship of HMS *Defence*, soon after her completion in 1909. These were the last armoured cruisers built by the Royal Navy, which, like the last pre-Dreadnought battleships, showed how far the paradigm had been pushed beyond its practical limits. This ship had four 9.2in/50 Mk XI guns in twin turrets in their main battery and ten 7.5in/50 Mk V in single turrets along the sides as their secondary battery; as a practical matter, it would be impossible to distinguish the fall of shot of the main and secondary batteries. Perhaps the biggest problem, however, was that these ships looked so much like their battleship counterparts that the temptation to lead them into battle against capital ships was too much for some captains to resist. That, as much as anything, led to the catastrophic loss of *Defence* at Jutland. (NHHC)

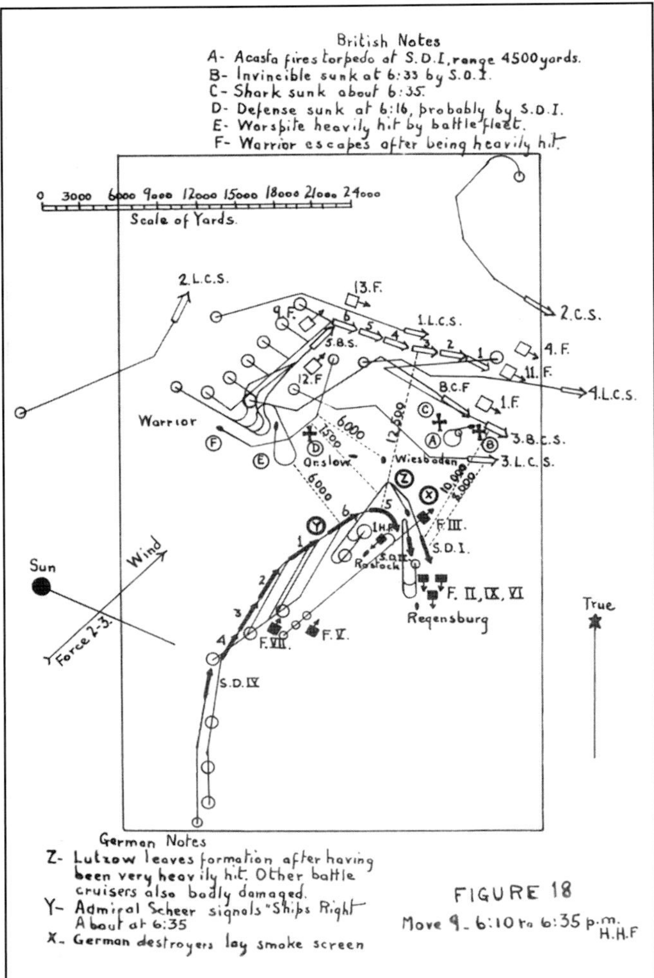

The next chart in Lieutenant Commander Frost's series shows the action at 'Windy Corner' from 18.10 to 18.35. *Wiesbaden* is still stranded between the battle lines, which are now bending away to the east and south. *Onslow*, which was disabled in making her attack on *Wiesbaden* is also still there; she survived. The point where *Defence* exploded is marked with a cross and the letter 'D'. The route followed by *Warrior* as she escaped is marked with the letter 'F'. (USN)

fatal salvos. The terrible drama was witnessed by much of the Grand Fleet, which was itself beginning to engage the German fleet. Some, at least, questioned the wisdom of Arbuthnot's decision to charge in between the approaching fleets:

> ... the 1st Cruiser Squadron ('*Defence*', etc.) broke through the centre of our Squadron [3rd LCS] as we made to the eastward. Admiral Arbuthnot's Squadron then wheeled round to starboard on to a westerly course and opened fire on a German light cruiser which hove in sight on our starboard bow. Apparently Admiral Arbuthnot was anxious to engage any enemy that might turn up, and pressed forward with great impatience ... almost immediately they found themselves within close range of the German battle cruisers and battleships, and before they could turn away–there was practically no direction clear to which they could turn–they were being concentrated upon by overwhelming gunfire from the enemy ships ...[56]
>
> A few minutes after we opened fire, the '*Defence*' and '*Warrior*' appeared on our engaged side, steaming on an opposite course.[57] The ships were practically continuously hidden by splashes, they were being repeatedly hit by heavy shell, and must have been going through hell on earth. . .[58]
>
> At first, the '*Defence*' did not seem to be damaged, but she was being heavily engaged, and salvos were dropping all around her. When she was on our bow three quick salvoes reached her, the first one 'over', the next one 'short', and the third all hit.[59] The shells of the last salvo could clearly be seen to hit her just abaft the after turret, and after a second a big red flame flashed up, but died away again at once. The ship heeled to the blow, but quickly righted herself and steamed on again. Then almost immediately followed three more salvoes. . . . again the shell of the hitting salvo could be clearly seen to strike, this time between the forecastle turret and the foremast funnel. At once the ship was lost to sight in an enormous black cloud, which rose to a height some hundred feet, . . .[60]
>
> At about 6.15 p.m. we witnessed the action of the 1st Cruiser Squadron and the blowing up of '*Defence*'. We thought she had been gone about a minute before she finally blew up, as she completely disappeared in a mass of spray, smoke, and flame. But she came through it apparently still intact, only to disappear a few seconds later in a tremendous belch of vivid flame and dense black smoke, from which some dark object, possibly a boat or a funnel, was hurled through space, twirling like a gigantic Catherine-wheel.[61]
>
> The foretop fell with a sickening splash into the water, and then the '*Warrior*', herself damaged, listing to starboard, and in places on fire, raced over the spot where the '*Defence*' had been, through the smoke-cloud of her flagship's explosion.[62]

Molteno managed to extricate *Warrior* from her immediate peril, chasing salvos as *Chester* had done, heading westward, covered in part by smoke from a hit that wrecked her bridge and started a fire at 18.17. At first, he had intended to fall in astern of the 5th Battle Squadron, which was now steaming to the north-east attempting to attach itself to the end of Jellicoe's battle line, but he found that the damage *Warrior* had received, which included at least fifteen hits by large-calibre shells, made that impossible. One shell, in particular, had done tremendous damage, hitting *Warrior* amidships on the port side near the waterline, passing through a coal bunker and across the port engine room, exploding upon striking the centreline bulkhead; the detonation damaged the port engine, while major shell fragments tore through the starboard engine room, ripping holes in the double bottom. Steam lines were severed on both sides and uncontrollable flooding began to starboard, spreading rapidly to the port side. Losing power rapidly, Molteno was barely able to steer *Warrior* clear of *Warspite*, which was circling aft of the Grand Fleet due to a jammed rudder. Fortunately, the seaplane carrier HMS *Engadine* was nearby, and Molteno was able to signal her to stand by and prepare to take *Warrior* under tow.

By 21.00, the tow had been rigged and the two ships were proceeding towards the dockyard at Cromarty at 8 knots. The amount of damage *Warrior* had sustained, however, and the falling barometer, combined to make it impossible to save the ship. As late as 04.00 the next morning, it appeared that damage control crews might be able to stem the flooding, but by 06.00 the ship was noticeably settling, the Main Deck was submerged to the depth of 2ft aft, the ship had a 6°starboard list and rising seas were beginning to enter through holes punched in the Upper Deck. Most seriously, she had only progressed approximately 100nm towards safety; she was still 160nm east of Aberdeen. At 07.15, Molteno ordered *Engadine* to cast off her tow and come alongside to begin evacuating the wounded, followed not long after by the remainder of the crew. *Warrior* was actually still afloat when *Engadine* steamed away at 08.25; when 2CS crossed the site where she was abandoned later that day, nothing was seen. In all seventy-one officers and men died in *Warrior* and thirty-six were wounded; 903, the entire complement, were lost in the destruction of *Defence*.

Left: HMS *Cochrane* was a sister of HMS *Warrior*, which followed *Defence* into battle at 'Windy Corner' at Jutland, 31 May 1916. One class older than *Defence*, the *Warrior* class carried the same combination of similarly-sized main- and secondary-battery guns, but rather differently arranged. Where *Defence* had her main battery in two twin turrets, *Warrior*'s was in six single turrets on the centreline and in wing positions. The secondary battery was in four single turrets between the wing main-battery turrets. Nothing in *Warrior*'s design or construction inclined her to survive the onslaught at 'Windy Corner' any better than *Defence*, but through a combination of luck and skill, her captain managed to escape from the immediate danger, although she sank early the next day. (NHHC)

Nor would that be the end of the devastation to be visited upon Royal Navy armoured cruisers this day. A third member of 1CS, HMS *Black Prince*, would stumble upon the head of the German battle line as it felt its way across the rear of the Grand Fleet's formation in the dark. She was behind the main body of the fleet, amongst the destroyer flotillas, when, right after midnight the German dreadnoughts SMS *Nassau* and *Thüringen* simultaneously sighted and illuminated a four-funnelled cruiser. It appears *Black Prince* momentarily thought she had happened upon friendly forces, until, being challenged with an unrecognised code, she turned away, too late to save herself. *Thüringen* opened fire with her secondary battery, claiming fifty-one hits, leaving the cruiser afire along her entire length before she drifted aft to be engaged by three other German battleships. *Black Prince* exploded in a massive cataclysm at 00.15, approximately eight minutes after first being illuminated; 857 officers and men, her entire complement, perished in her.

That leaves only *Wiesbaden* to account for. She was last seen at 18.05, already disabled and drifting to a stop between the battle lines, under fire from *Defence* and *Warrior*. She could have hardly been in a less auspicious location, because as each successive British dreadnought turned to port as the Grand Fleet deployed, often the only enemy in sight was this solitary derelict adrift between the fleets. As such she became a target of opportunity for a long list of British warships (listed in approximate chronological order):

18.05–15 Simultaneous with Arbuthnot's charge, the destroyer HMS *Onslow*, which had been assigned to escort *Engadine*, noticed *Wiesbaden* in a position to launch torpedoes at the British battle line and turned to attack. She fired fifty-eight rounds of 4in shells at ranges between 2000–4000yd, so most of them undoubtedly hit, and fired off two torpedoes, one of which hit *Wiesbaden* well aft, causing tremendous damage. (This torpedo hit was the largest contributing factor to *Wiesbaden*'s eventual sinking.)[63]

18.07–12 HMS *Tiger*, one of Beatty's battlecruisers, fired her 6in secondary battery at *Wiesbaden* for lack of any other visible target.

18.07 HMS *Falmouth* and *Yarmouth*, light cruisers of

the 3LCS, opened fire on *Wiesbaden* at a range of approximately 5000yd with their 6in/50 main batteries and fired one torpedo at her. An unknown number of hits were obtained; the torpedo missed.

18.20–39 Sixteen of the twenty-eight battleships that comprised the Grand Fleet fired one or more salvoes of main-battery fire at *Wiesbaden* during this period.[64]

18.54 HMS *Marlborough* was hit by a torpedo in her starboard side under her bridge. While it is not possible to be certain, the most likely source of this torpedo was *Wiesbaden*.

18.54–19.05 Six battleships fired at *Wiesbaden* in a second period of visibility, including two (HMS *Collingwood* and *St Vincent*) which had not participated in the first period of capital ship bombardment. In total, it appears most likely that thirteen shells of 12in calibre or larger, plus a large, but unknowable, number of smaller-calibre shells had hit *Wiesbaden*, leaving her a shambles, but still defiantly afloat.

After this, the battle moved off to the south, leaving *Wiesbaden* behind. Her demise was inevitable given the extent of the damage she had suffered, but her survival until at least 01.45 the next morning was a testament to the solidity of her design and construction. Of the sixteen watertight compartments into which her hull was divided, seven of the eight middle compartments were ruptured by shellfire. Still, she might have survived had it not been for the torpedo damage aft. Five hundred and eighty-nine officers and men died in her, the second-highest casualty total in any German ship at Jutland (exceeded only by that of the pre-dreadnought SMS *Pommern*, which exploded). It is not certain how many of her crew made it into the water on extemporised rafts, but all but one fell victim to exposure as they drifted in the cold rough seas for more than a day. Eventually, only one man, Leading Stoker Hugo Zenne, was rescued, by the passing Norwegian steamer *Willi* more than thirty-eight hours after *Wiesbaden* sank.

As poorly as the armoured cruiser (and battlecruiser) type performed at Jutland, at least as conceived and built by the Royal Navy, the light cruiser as a type put a stamp on its success as an 'all-purpose' cruiser type. The British lost no light cruisers at the battle, even though five of them – *Calliope*, *Castor*, *Chester*, *Dublin* and *Southampton* – sustained multiple hits by guns of varying calibres, their power plants remained intact and all returned to port under their own power. The Germans lost four light cruisers at Jutland; besides *Wiesbaden*, these were: *Frauenlob*, of the old *Gazelle* class, and the much newer *Elbing* and *Rostock*. Of these, only *Frauenlob* sank quickly, and that only after being torpedoed in her after engine room. The other two were disabled, one by torpedo and the other by ramming; both were under tow towards home and were in no danger of sinking when they were overtaken by Royal Navy patrols and were scuttled to prevent capture.

Why did light cruisers so dramatically out-perform armoured cruisers at Jutland in terms of their ability to absorb punishment and survive? There is no single, simple answer to that question. For the most part, the Royal Navy light cruisers damaged at Jutland were newer, smaller and faster than the armoured cruisers, which enabled them to escape from danger more readily, but that alone is insufficient to explain the difference. Two of the three armoured cruisers lost at Jutland (and also *Good Hope* at Coronel) were lost to cataclysmic magazine explosions; none of the light cruisers on either side suffered a similar fate. This cannot be explained by simple examination of armour schemes; the light cruisers involved had, in general, not much better armour protection than the older armoured cruisers. Nonetheless, they survived punishment better than the older armoured cruisers. *Chester* was hit seventeen times, but steamed away; admittedly none of those hits impacted her ability to steam, which was critical to her survival. *Pillau*, which had no external armour, was hit by a 12in shell which detonated under her charthouse and did temporarily impact her engineering plant, but she survived; that hit with a large-calibre shell was in the general vicinity of her forward magazines, but she did not explode. *Wiesbaden* endured a legendary pounding and, incredibly, might have survived had she not received one torpedo hit aft. There is no question that, being generally newer, the light cruisers at Jutland were unquestionably better subdivided and structurally stronger than the older armoured cruisers.

Still, it is unclear if any of that is sufficient to explain the difference in the survival rates of the two ship types at Jutland. Absent any other explanation, one of the few remaining factors that could explain the different outcomes is the quality (or 'style') of command of the individual ships. This author has the distinct impression that the captains of the armoured cruisers at Jutland fought their ships differently, more recklessly, than did the commanders of light cruisers, and paid a steep price for their incaution. Had any of the light cruisers in the Royal Navy suffered the damage inflicted on *Defence* or *Black Prince*, would she have survived? The answer can only be speculative, but, in this author's opinion, probably not. The one light cruiser that day that did receive commensurate damage was *Wiesbaden* and she did not survive; critically, however, she failed, but she did not fail cataclysmically. It is this author's opinion that light cruisers emerged from Jutland with an untarnished reputation in great part because they were a fundamentally superior design paradigm, but also because in this battle they were better led and far luckier. Regardless of the reason, the idea that the light cruiser 'line' had great potential for further development was only reinforced at Jutland.

Chapter 3

War Production and the Gold Standard – The *Hawkins* Class and their Contemporaries: 1914–1922

It is unquestionable that the only cruiser type to emerge from the early war years with an untarnished reputation was the light cruiser, which proved it could perform the scouting, trade protection and other related duties expected of a cruiser and survive tremendous punishment. Clearly this was a type capable of further development. This became all the more apparent as war experience accumulated, showing that light cruisers could serve as a capable, high-speed gun platform for main batteries of 6in and even larger size.

Incremental Improvements for the Royal Navy . . .

Starting from the *Arethusa* class of 1912 as a base, the Royal Navy followed a relatively straight line of development with its war-production cruisers, as each succeeding class grew in size and capability. The first wartime class – all eight were laid down before the war began, but were launched and completed after the outbreak of hostilities – was the *Caroline* class, the first of a series of wartime classes all given names starting with the letter 'C'. They displaced 450 tons more than the *Arethusas*, using that extra tonnage to add 10ft in length and, more importantly, 2.5ft in beam, which greatly improved stability. They carried two extra 4in/45 guns, and re-arranged their main battery, so that both 6in/45s were mounted aft; the extra 4in guns were carried side-by-side on the forecastle in a rather unfortunate arrangement that was replaced in most ships during the war by a single 6in mount.[1] The last two ships in this class are often considered a separate class because they were used to experiment with geared turbines, one with four shafts and one – HMS *Champion* – with two shafts, which proved very successful. A follow-on class of four virtually identical ships, the *Cambrian* class, were started before all the lessons had been learned from experience with the *Carolines*.

Typical of the Royal Navy's war-production 'C' class light cruisers was HMS *Caradoc* (D60) – note that she has a pennant number given here because she and her two sisters which survived the First World War served on into the Second World War, the oldest class of Royal Navy cruisers to do so. *Caradoc* is seen as she appeared in 1918, a year after her completion, as can be ascertained by the searchlight platform aft and the range clock hanging on her mainmast, both of which were fitted that year. Her main battery of five 6in/45 Mk XII single mounts were all carried on the centreline. Three of them can be seen in this image; two are under the awnings spread abaft the forward superstructure and on the quarterdeck. Note the large fire-control top forward, which necessitated a tripod foremast to support it. (NHHC)

It was not until the laying down of the two-ship *Centaur* class in early 1915 that the Royal Navy first put the benefits of war lessons learned into cruiser design. By then, the early battles fought at Coronel, the Falklands and Heligoland Bight had shown dramatically that the 4in gun was essentially useless as a weapon against other cruisers, that mixed-calibre main batteries simply confused the fire-control problem and that director control would solve any lingering problems associated with carrying a heavy (6in) main battery in a relatively small (4165-ton) ship.[2] The decision to adopt five 6in/45s arrayed on the centreline for the main battery of the *Centaurs* was not without opposition, especially in combination with the adoption of director control, in part because many in the fleet considered *Arethusa* and her descendants to be primarily intended to fight destroyers, often many at a time, for which more, smaller guns would be an advantage and a fire-control director would be useless topweight. Nevertheless, that decision was made, no doubt because the driving force behind the decision was the newly re-appointed First Sea Lord 'Jacky' Fisher. It was not until the five-ship *Ceres* class of later in 1916 that the Royal Navy settled on a 'standard' war production light cruiser design, with five 6in/45s – still all in single mounts, but now superfiring fore-and-aft, plus all the other features accumulated along the way, enabled by adding 8in to the ships' beam. This added 70 tons and further increased stability.

The *Ceres* class were the last 'main-sequence' light cruisers to be completed during the war. A further follow-on class of five nearly-identical ships, the *Capetown* class, was started in 1917–18 and not completed until after the end of the war. The main difference from the preceding class was an attempt to improve seakeeping by raising the height of the bow. Where the *Ceres* class had a freeboard at the bow of 23.5ft, the *Capetowns* were given a raised 'trawler' bow with a freeboard of 28.5ft. However, the designers had one serious concern about this increased bow height; the fear was that if the existing flare of the bow was simply continued upward and outward, it would offer too much 'slamming surface' to the waves in rough weather, threatening the structural integrity of the forecastle. Rather than redesign the bow with a reduced flare, they opted to carry the shell plating up from the old sheer line at a much reduced flare, introducing the 'knuckle' in the bow characteristic of nearly all Royal Navy cruisers between the wars.[3]

With the class following the *Caradocs*, the Royal Navy addressed some of the remaining problems with their small light cruisers, namely stability and forward firepower, by marginally increasing the beam and by moving the bridge aft enough to allow 'B' mount to be moved into a superfiring position forward. Both moves were considered highly successful. This view shows HMS *Curacoa* (I41), apparently in the mid-1930s, when she was serving as the Gunnery School ship, because it appears that her torpedo tubes, two banks each side, have been removed. The image can definitely be dated to after 1927, because the aft end of one of the *Nelson* class battleships can be seen in the right background. (NHHC)

Simultaneous with the development of the *Capetowns*, the Royal Navy ordered the first three of an eventual nine enlarged *Ceres* type in response to intelligence reports that the Germans were building light cruisers armed with eleven or twelve 15cm guns.[4] (In fact, these reports proved to be unfounded – see below.) The British already had a significantly larger and better-armed cruiser design in the works (the *Hawkins* class 'colonial' cruisers described below), but wartime shipbuilding priorities being what they were, they understood that a more rapidly-constructed alternative, smaller than a *Hawkins* but larger than a *Ceres*, would meet their immediate needs. The result was the *Danae* class, the first of which was laid down before the end of 1916, and two of which were actually completed before the end of the war. They really were just an

Top: Twenty-one more feet of length and two more feet of beam bought the *Danae* class enough room to mount one more main-battery gun and a considerable improvement in habitability. In this image, the lead ship is seen at Melbourne on 7 January 1937. HMS *Danae* (D44) was active in the Far East during this period, often stationed at Hong Kong or Shanghai, so that visits to Australia were not uncommon. Another increase in weaponry was a change from double to triple torpedo tube mounts. To save room, the third tube was carried above the first two. (SLV/AGC)

Middle: A good close-up of the forward superstructure of HMS *Delhi* (D74), seen at Long Beach, CA, probably in July 1924, during the Special Service Cruise, which took HMS *Hood* (51) and a squadron of 'D' class cruisers around the world on a goodwill mission. *Delhi* was the lead ship of the second group of 'D' class cruisers which differed mainly in having the higher 'trawler' bow, introduced for better seakeeping with the *Capetown* class. The fire-control position on the foremast can be seen in some detail; the large control top, where the gunnery officer would be located with his spotting glasses, is located above the cylindrical director position, not yet fitted with its own rangefinder. Note the multitude of voice pipes leading down from the control top to the open bridge and then on down to the next level, which was serving as a flag bridge. At this time *Delhi* was flagship of the Royal Navy's 1st Light Cruiser Squadron; the boat at the davits to the right carries the painted flag of a rear admiral. (NHHC)

Below: HMS *Diomede* (D92) was one of the second group of the Royal Navy's 'D' class light cruisers, seen here on 10 July 1929. Of particular note, besides the 'knuckle' in the 'trawler' bow, was the experimental enclosed mounting for the 6in/45 Mk XII gun in 'A' position. This mount was quite successful, providing all-weather coverage and blast protection when the gun in 'B' position was fired; test evaluators recommended that all future ships with similar weapons be provided with this mount, but no ships with 6in single mounts were developed for the Royal Navy after this time. (SLV/AGC)

enlarged *Ceres* type. Adding 21ft of length, 2ft of beam and 700 tons of displacement enabled one more main-battery gun to be mounted between the foremast and fore funnel, and triple torpedo tubes to be substituted for doubles.

Upon hearing the first intelligence reports of the pair of fast cruiser-minelayers included in the German 1916 building programme, the Royal Navy reacted by pushing through the design and development of the *Emerald* (or 'E') class, the final wartime class of light cruisers developed by the British; laid down in 1918, only two of the three were eventually completed and those not until 1926.[5] They were almost 100ft longer and displaced over 2620 tons more than the *Danae*s, reaching 7550 tons normal displacement, which bought only one more 6in/45 mount; almost all the added tonnage went into a doubling of power output that increased top speed from 29 knots to 33 knots.

. . . and Across the North Sea

While the British were building successively improved iterations on the pattern established by the *Arethusa* class, the Germans were doing much the same based on the *Graudenz* class, which was itself essentially a repeat of the earlier *Magdeburg* class. The most important change introduced into this orderly succession was actually done with impetus provided by the Russians. In 1912, the Russian Navy had contracted with the Schichau yard at Danzig (Gdansk) to build a pair of light cruisers; they were different in many ways from contemporary German designs, for example, lacking belt armour and being designed to carry a main battery of eight Russian-supplied 13cm/55 guns. They were approaching completion when war broke out and, with Russia now an enemy, the two cruisers were taken over by the Germans and completed for the High Seas Fleet. Nothing could be done to

The last class of wartime light cruisers built by the Royal Navy was the 'E' class, intended to counter the German's rumoured high-speed minelaying cruisers. Three were ordered in 1918, but only two actually started and they were not completed until 1926. For being more than 2000 tons heavier than the 'D' class, they carried only one more 6in/45 gun mount. HMS *Emerald* (D66) seen here is as-built condition, carried seven single mounts as her main battery. She had an aircraft platform just forward of her mainmast. Her sister, HMS *Enterprise* (D52), was completed with a twin turret forward in the place of *Emerald*'s two single mounts. (NHHC)

The last generation of German light cruisers were bigger than the *Wiesbadens*, but otherwise similar. SMS *Karlsrühe* (ii) is seen here at the surrender of the High Seas Fleet, 21 November 1918. She was the flagship of the surrendering light cruisers, flying the flag of Commodore Viktor Harder. Between her after funnel and mainmast, she carried a pair of 8.8cm/45 Flak (*Flugabwehrkanone* – AA gun) single-mount guns. The old French armoured cruiser *Amiral Aube* can be seen in the left background. (NARA)

remedy the problem of the missing belt armour, but the ships' guns, which had not been delivered from Russia, could be readily replaced by a German equivalent. Up to this point, all German light cruisers had been equipped with the 10.5cm/45 as their main battery, a reliable and handy weapon firing a 56.2lb all-up round, but which was frequently criticised for being too small, particularly after the Royal Navy began mounting 6in guns in their light cruisers starting in 1909. Regardless of the reason, the decision was made to arm these two, named SMS *Pillau* and *Elbing*, with eight 15cm/45, the first German light cruisers to mount this larger gun. Thereafter, all Imperial German light cruiser classes would carry this gun as their main battery.

In 1913 and 1914, the Germans continued their steady, two-a-year construction of cruisers, laying down the extremely successful *Wiesbadens* in 1913, which were enlarged *Graudenz* types with the strengthened main battery introduced in the *Pillaus*, and the first two of four of the even-larger *Königsberg* (ii) class in 1914. Finally, in 1915, the pace of construction increased dramatically, as the Germans saw how heavy a price they had paid for having dispersed their cruiser assets around the globe at the beginning of the war. It was too late, however, to impact the course of the war; no fewer than nine light cruisers and two cruiser-minelayers were laid down that year, but only four of the light cruisers, as well as the cruiser-minelayers, were completed before the end of the war and many of those were completed too late to be of much use. (However, a number of the later German light cruisers that survived the war were turned over to the Allies after the war as reparations; while the British, Americans and Japanese scrapped their reparation cruisers or, in more than one case, used them as bombing or explosives trials targets, the French and Italians incorporated some of theirs into their navies and two lasted into the Second World War.[6])

In general, the German cruiser designs after the *Magdeburgs* were highly successful, especially after the 15cm gun was adopted as the main battery. They demonstrated, particularly in the extreme case of *Wiesbaden*, an ability to survive extraordinary punishment. Yet, due to the fact that the Germans lost the First World War, it seemed that their design lineage was doomed to die out, all of the best ships of the type destined to be scrapped, sunk as targets or, at best, to serve as second-line units in one of the victor's navies. Except that, curiously, a provision of the Versailles Treaty, which regulated the post-war German navy (*Reichsmarine*), allowed for a resurrection of sorts, as will be recounted below.

A Great Leap Forward

Not long after the war broke out, the Royal Navy realised that, even with the defeat of Spee's cruiser force at the Falklands, they lacked a ship fully capable of protecting their trade routes against the possible predations of German AMCs. The ideal ship was probably a battlecruiser, but their availability to fight at the Falklands had been an exceptional response to an emergency situation, not something that could be relied upon. The cruisers next best suited to the job, the 'Towns', were needed for fleet support as much as the battlecruisers and were

thought to be under-gunned for the task. What was called for was a purpose-built 'colonial cruiser' designed for long-distance missions, with high top-end speed to chase down speedy AMCs and a heavy-enough armament to overcome quickly any enemy vessel that might possibly be encountered beyond home waters.

As early as October 1914, a proposal for a ship of this type was placed before the Admiralty Board.[7] Various armament combinations were proposed, ranging all the way from a new 5.5in/50 gun – ordered by the Greek navy for the light cruisers taken over as HMS *Birkenhead* and *Chester* – to the 9.2in/47 gun – as carried in the *Warrior* class. Finally, in mid-1915, the decision was made to opt for a single-calibre main battery of seven 7.5in/45s in single mounts. This was the same calibre as the secondary-battery gun carried in the *Minotaur*s and *Warrior*s, but with a shorter barrel, which facilitated more rapid, power-assisted training and elevation. Also, this gun was approximately halfway between the smaller and larger alternatives in terms of weight per mount, which no doubt influenced the decision. To obtain the best possible range, these ships reintroduced mixed coal-oil fired boilers, the idea being that on colonial stations, oil fuel might not always be available, but coal was ubiquitous; as an added bonus, the coal bunkers along the ships' sides in way of the engineering spaces would enhance their survivability. To carry the number and size of guns planned for these ships would require a platform significantly larger than that of the *Emerald*s, even without any increase in protection.[8] The resulting hull was 35ft longer and displaced 2200 tons more, for a normal displacement of 9750 tons. (This was approximately the same size as the *Monmouth* class armoured cruisers, though a good deal smaller than *Warrior* or *Defence*.) To further protect them underwater, the hulls were given 5ft bulges amidships. Another 'anachronistic' feature was the almost total lack of sheer forward. These ships were remarkable for having a very low quarterdeck, on which two of the main-battery guns were located, and were notorious for the wetness of these positions in any weather, but one CO commented that those guns did not suffer as much in rough conditions as did 'A' turret at the bow due to the lack of sheer.[9]

One of the *Hawkins* class cruisers, HMS *Cavendish*, was converted to an aircraft carrier before completion by the addition of a large hangar forward of her bridge topped by a flying-off deck and a separate landing-on deck aft. Re-christened HMS *Vindictive* (D36), she served only briefly in that role before being reconverted back into a cruiser, with most of her guns re-emplaced and the flight decks removed, although the large hangar structure remained forward of her bridge. The oddly-shaped structure at the forward edge of her hangar, seen in this image taken in July 1927, is an athwartships catapult (wrapped in tarpaulin here); aircraft would be lifted out of the hangar through a large hatchway in the overhead and positioned on the catapult for launching. (USAF)

One of the *Hawkins* class cruisers was extensively reconstructed in the late 1930s. HMS *Effingham* (I98) was taken in hand in 1937; she was reboilered, which allowed her after funnel to be deleted, and her main battery of 7.5in guns was replaced by nine 6in/45 Mk XIIs in shielded single mounts, all but two on the centreline. This was supposed to be the model for the reconstruction of the remaining members of the class, but neither the time nor the money were available before the next war broke out. (NHHC)

The first of these new ships, by far the largest cruisers the Royal Navy had laid down since the *Minotaur* class of 1905, were ordered in December 1915 and laid down in June 1916. They were named the *Hawkins* class; all were to be named after Elizabethan-era sea captains. In all, five were laid down and four completed as cruisers; one, HMS *Cavendish*, was converted into an aircraft carrier, with a large box hangar for seaplanes in the place of 'B' turret forward of the bridge, a 'flying-off' deck on top of that hangar for launching aircraft and a long (193ft) 'flying-on' deck aft of the funnels in the place of 'X' and 'Y' turrets. In this form, she was renamed HMS *Vindictive* (D36). Only one attempt was made to fly aircraft aboard *Vindictive*, soon after her completion in October 1918; that attempt was successful and she was commissioned into the Flying Squadron, Grand Fleet, and sent to the Baltic to support operations against the Bolsheviks, but there she ran aground and sustained serious damage. By the time she emerged from Portsmouth after repairs in March 1920, she had been reconverted back into a cruiser, losing her flight decks and regaining 'X' and 'Y' turrets, but retaining the box hangar forward and the name *Vindictive*.

. . . and Even Farther Afield

Other nations besides Great Britain and Germany were developing cruisers, or at least considering it, during this period, although the war impacted the development of these designs in one fashion or another. For example, the French *Marine Nationale* defined a long-range building programme in March 1912 that included a class of ten 'fleet scout cruisers'; they would be the first cruisers laid down by the French since 1906. Initial designs were for a 6000-ton ship, but these were rejected in favour of a smaller ship of 4500 tons, quite similar in many respects to the German *Magdeburg*s. They were to have mounted eight 138.6mm/55 guns in single mounts superfiring fore-and-aft and in broadside mounts, have minimal armour (1.1in) in way of the magazines and engineering spaces, and a four-shaft power plant capable of 29 knots.[10] The first *tranche* of this class was to have been laid down at Toulon in November 1914, but the beginning of the war brought new warship construction to a halt in France; the first of them was to have been named *Lamotte-Piquet*. In July 1915, the *Service Techniques des Constructions Navales* (STCN), the design bureau of the *Marine Nationale*, met to consider possible modifications to the *Lamotte-Piquet* design in light of war experience. The design was re-endorsed with relatively minor modifications, but there was no chance that any of the class would actually get built with the war going on. But, in a manner somewhat similar to that which took

The Soviet light cruiser *Chervona Ukraina* (ex-Imperial Russian *Admiral Nakhimov*) was laid down in 1913 and launched a year later, but not completed until 1927. Completed to essentially the original design, she could hardly have been more anachronistic from the day she entered service. Her main battery was fifteen 130mm/55 Pattern 1913 guns, six of which were in casemates, the rest in single mounts. She served in the Black Sea, where she was sunk by dive bombers in 1941. Raised after the war, she served briefly as a training hulk before being sunk again as a target in 1950. (NHHC)

place in Germany, this design did not fade away; it sprang to life again after the war, as recounted in the next chapter.

The Russians became interested in the light cruiser type rather later than most other navies; the first pair they ordered, in 1912, to be built in Germany by the Schichau yard, were taken over, nearly complete, by the Germans when the war began, becoming SMS *Elbing* and *Pillau*. Under the same 1912 building programme, six larger cruisers were authorised for domestic production, to be armed with fifteen 130mm/55 guns in single mounts and casemates. Four, to be built at Baltic yards, and two more at Black Sea yards, were laid down in 1913 and launched in 1915–16, but the upheaval of the Russian Revolutions brought all work to a stop. The fates of those that were launched varied considerably. One of the four Baltic ships, *Svetlana*, renamed *Profintern* after the Communist Revolution, was completed to more-or-less the original design in July 1928. She transferred to the Black Sea, was renamed *Krazniy Krim* and served throughout the Second World War. Two more of the Baltic hulls were completed as merchant tankers in 1926. The last remained incomplete until broken up on the ways at the Putilov Yard, St Petersburg in 1956–7! In the Black Sea, *Admiral Nakhimov*, renamed *Chervona Ukraina*, was completed in 1927 to much the original design, served the Soviet navy into the Second World War, was sunk by a German air raid at Sevastopol in November 1941, raised in 1947 and served three more years as a training hulk, before being sunk in 1950. The other Black Sea cruiser, *Admiral Lazarev*, renamed *Krazniy Kavkaz*, was completed to a substantially modified design. The Russians had wanted to fit her with a more powerful armament, but, determining that her lightly-constructed hull could not take too much added topweight, ended up giving her four 180mm/60 in massive single turrets and a large catapult and aircraft-handling crane abaft her second funnel. Soon after her

completion in 1932, she collided with another ship, requiring major reconstruction forward; she emerged with an extended, flared bow, quite different in shape than that of any of her sisters. She was active through much of the Second World War, before being designated a training ship in 1947 and sunk as a target in November 1952.

The Japanese were the only other nation, besides the British and Germans, to lay down cruisers during the First World War. They were able to do this because they were in the unique position of being a belligerent on the Allied side almost from the beginning of the war, but this never required them to commit troops or a significant portion of their national economy to the war effort. Nevertheless, the Imperial Japanese Navy kept a wary eye on technical developments in the Royal Navy and in 1916, having been impressed by the role played by British light cruisers at Jutland, two small light cruisers loosely modelled on the Royal Navy's 'C' class cruisers were included in the next building programme.[11] This first pair of new cruisers in seven years were classed as '3500-ton small-model cruisers'; intended primarily as flotilla leaders, the *Tenryu* class was given high speed (33 knots) with a three-

The *Tenryu* class was Japan's response to the Royal Navy's 'C' class light cruisers. Seen here from USS *Houston* (CA30) at Shanghai, probably in May 1932, *Tatsuta* shows her sleek lines, which allowed her high speed, but at the cost of limited armament – four 14cm/50 3rd Year Type in shielded single mounts – a cramped interior and marginal stability. *Tatsuta*, normally home-ported at Sasebo, had been sent to Shanghai to return the remains of a Japanese general who had been assassinated there by a Korean dissident. (NHHC)

Kraznyl Kavkaz (ex-*Admiral Lazarev*), sister to *Chervona Ukraina*, was completed to a much-modified design, as seen in this image from sometime after the 1932 collision in which her bow was damaged and rebuilt as seen here, with two funnels instead of three. The Soviets had wanted to give her significantly stronger armament, but concluded that her lightly-built hull could not take the weight or stress of a much bigger weapon than that for which she had been designed and ended up fitting her with four 180mm/60 B-1-K Pattern 1931 guns in massive single turrets, with none of the casemates and only four 76.2mm/30 8-K Pattern 1914/15 AA guns for a secondary battery. Note the substantial aircraft-handling crane looming over the catapult abaft her second funnel that was not mounted until 1935. This image probably dates to 1940, because the 76.2mm AA guns have been replaced by an equal number of Italian-made 100mm/50 'Minizini' twin-mounts. (NHHC)

shaft geared-turbine power plant developing 51,000shp[12] To achieve that speed on that displacement, especially considering they carried 2in–2.5in of side armour, steps had to be taken to save weight elsewhere. One step was the extensive use of high-tensile strength steel throughout, allowing for lighter structural members; another was the adoption of longitudinal framing. Weight was further saved by adopting a very narrow 'destroyer-like' hull form, with a short forecastle extending just past the bridge and no sheer to the hull. Armament was limited to four 14cm/50 3rd Year Type shielded single mounts, all on the centreline, and two triple 53cm torpedo tube mounts. Both ships easily exceeded their designed speed during trials and were considered highly successful designs, except for their relatively weak main-battery, and they served continuously until 1938, when they were placed in reserve. Refitted and minimally modernised in 1940–1, they served in the Second World War, during which both were sunk by US Navy submarines.

Barely had construction begun on the *Tenryus* when details began to arrive in Japan of the American 'Big Navy Act' of 1916, which called for dramatic expansion of the US Navy.[13] The Japanese reacted with their own '8-4 Fleet Completion Programme' of 1917 calling for, among many other ships, the construction of nine new cruisers.[14] These were to include six of an 'Improved 3500-ton type' and three 7200-ton scout cruisers. But, by mid-1917, details had begun to arrive in Tokyo of the light cruisers included in the American 1916 programme; these reports indicated they would displace approximately 7100 tons (normal), possess a 35-knot top speed

Despite their small size, the *Tenryus* were considered successful and served as the model for a large class of enlarged follow-ons, the *Kuma* class followed by the nearly-identical *Nagara* class. This image shows *Kinu*, one of the *Nagaras*, with the characteristic large forward superstructure incorporating a hangar for aircraft and the flying-off platform extending forward from it over No 2 main-battery turret. These ships were 1500 tons larger than the *Tenryus*, more than 60ft longer and 3 knots faster. The greater size enabled them to carry three more main-battery guns. (USAF)

and mount eight 6in guns, four torpedo tubes and two aircraft catapults with provision to carry up to four aircraft. In view of this information, which was correct in some respects and wildly inaccurate in others (see below), the planned 'Improved 3500-ton type' would be totally inadequate and even the projected scout cruisers needed to be rethought. In their place, it was now proposed to build eight light cruisers of 5500 tons, the first two of which would be laid down as rapidly as possible. Additionally, money was to found to build a ninth cruiser to a design that would intentionally 'push the envelope', incorporating as many novel features as possible.

In order to generate a design that could be ready for laying down in August 1918, it was extrapolated from the *Tenryus*'; the *Kuma* class, which eventually comprised five ships, was 64ft longer, had almost double the power and a four-shaft power plant giving a top speed of 36 knots, mounted seven 14cm/50 main-battery guns in single mounts, eight torpedo tubes (in four twin mounts) and provision to carry forty-eight mines. Three more *Kumas* were laid down the next year and two more in 1920 followed by four more funded by the '8-6 Fleet Completion Programme' of 1918. The last six differed in having a larger bridge that incorporated an aircraft hangar, complete with a 'flying-off' platform that extended out over the forward main-battery guns. Additionally, the six cruisers of this *Nagara* sub-class carried larger 61cm torpedoes. Seven more of the class were authorised by the '8-8 Fleet Completion Programme' of 1920. These had a re-arranged power plant, with greater subdivision of fire rooms, that required a fourth funnel to be added, and caused the hull to be lengthened by 2ft 9in. The first four of the *Sendai* sub-class were not laid down until 1922. Only three of them were completed; the fourth was broken up on the slipway and the last three never started under the provisions of the Washington Treaty (see the next chapter).

Rendering passing honours as she exited Shanghai, probably between September and November 1936, the crew of *Nagara* stands stiffly at attention. Given the gathering of warships of all major powers that assembled at Shanghai in those years, it was customary for any item of equipment considered at all secret or sensitive to be covered in canvas, or otherwise hidden, as are the catapult, aircraft cockpits and torpedo tubes on *Nagara* in this view. A number of modifications have been made since her completion, including the removal of the flying-off platform forward, its replacement by the catapult abaft the third funnel and the replacement of the pole mainmast by a more substantial tripod mast with an aircraft-handling crane. (NHHC)

The aforementioned 'Big Navy Act' of 1916 authorised the construction of ten scout cruisers, which would be the first cruisers built by the US Navy since 1905. The General Board, made up of senior admirals for the purpose of advising the Navy on, among of things, the design of new ships, was asked in 1915 to define the design of a scout cruiser for the fleet.[15] Recent history, including exercises in the North Atlantic, had underlined the US Navy's glaring lack of modern cruisers; doctrine called for destroyers to perform general scouting duties, but the foul weather common in the North Atlantic much of the year often left the fleet without adequate scouting capability. Specifically, Rear Admiral Frank F Fletcher, commanding the Atlantic Fleet, submitted a proposal to the

An indication of just how conservative the US Navy was in 1918 can be seen in this image of USS *Milwaukee* (CL5, ex-CS5), seen at Tacoma, WA, in 1923, when one realises that the twin gunhouse for the 6in/53 guns on the forecastle (and a similar one on the quarterdeck) was an afterthought, added at the last minute, after *Milwaukee* was almost ready to launch, when it was realised how under-gunned these ships would be compared to foreign contemporaries. The stacked casemates at the corners of the forward and after superstructures, where the majority of the twelve main-battery guns were sited, were a feature last seen in ships designed almost two decades earlier. (NHHC)

Navy Secretary for a scout capable of maintaining a 5-knot speed advantage over battleships in any weather – then generally capable of 21 knots in most conditions – and armed well enough to penetrate an enemy cruiser screen.[16] Asked to explore the feasibility of such a vessel, the General Board turned to the Preliminary Design Section of the Bureau of Construction and Repair (BuC&R), requesting sketch designs that would meet these rather loose parameters. BuC&R responded in April 1915 with a series of more than twenty sketch designs that started at 10,500 tons normal displacement ranging all the way up to 26,800 tons, armed with from ten 6in up to four 16in guns in the main battery. This design series eventually evolved into the *Lexington* class battlecruisers laid down in 1920–1.

The General Board well understood that even the smallest of the April 1915 scouts was much bigger than needed for the fleet scouting role envisaged by Fletcher. With that in mind, the board came back to Preliminary Design in late 1915 with a much more narrow set of characteristics for the scout cruisers; the new scouts were to displace approximately 8000 tons, have a speed in excess of 30 knots, a range of at least 10,000nm, mount six or more 6in guns in the main battery and carry a 3in armour belt. The Chief Constructor – the American DNC – Rear Admiral David W Taylor, wanted to build a larger ship, in the 11,000–12,000-ton range, with a speed of 35 knots, but the General Board pushed back; on 22 December 1915, an agreement was reached on a sketch design for a 35-knot ship of 6750 tons, with a hull 550ft in length, cut down fore-and-aft to save weight, billboards instead of hawsepipes forward for handling the anchors, no provision for aircraft stowage or handling, no ammunition hoists, not even wooden planking on the weather decks or tiling in the crews' showers, so stringent were the weight-saving measures taken in the design process. (When concerns were raised about the

This view of the starboard quarter of USS *Memphis* (CL13, ex-CS13) shows the clear downside of the stacked casemates combined with the rising sheer line of forecastle deck. While the lower casemate forward was well clear of the water in all but the most violent of weather, the same cannot be said for the lower casemate aft, nor the after twin gunhouse on the tiny quarterdeck for that matter. *Memphis* is riding quite high in this view taken on 10 June 1927; were she at normal load, the lower casemate guns aft would be unserviceable in any serious weather. Note the catapult with a Vought UO-1 floatplane just abaft the aftermost funnel. Just visible under the flare of her forecastle, it can be seen that *Memphis*, like all but the first two *Omaha*s, had hawsepipes rather than billboards for handling their forward anchors. (NPL/VPC)

seaworthiness of the design, the cut-down deck forward was eliminated and a conventional forecastle deck added in.) The main-battery arrangement was unusual and more than a bit anachronistic. Ten 6in/53 guns were to be arrayed in single mounts; two were to be positioned in stacked casemates at each corner of the forward and after superstructures and the other two in open mounts on each broadside amidships. In theory, this would allow four guns to fire directly fore-and-aft and five on each broadside, while leaving the low quarterdeck free for the later fitting of aircraft facilities, if that was decided upon.[17] In March 1916, at the suggestion of Taylor, the General Board approved the deletion of the amidships main-battery mounts in exchange for armour protection in way of the steering gear. On this basis, contract plans were signed off in July 1916.

There matters stood while higher priorities of war production of destroyers and merchant hulls kept American shipyards busy for the next several years. The first two of the new cruisers – USS *Omaha* (CS4) and *Milwaukee* (CS5) – were laid down in December 1918.[18] Eight more would be laid down in 1920. In October 1920, as the first pair were nearing time for launch, the General Board approved a significant upgrade to the ships' armament. Experience gained in the relatively brief American involvement in the naval war had impressed many in the US Navy with the utility of the Royal Navy's light cruisers; it was impossible for the Americans not to note that ships such as the Royal Navy's 'C' class cruisers, while 2500 tons smaller than the planned *Omaha*s, had a broadside with one more 6in gun, and that the somewhat larger *Danae*s had two more. While pleased that the 35-knot *Omaha*s would be the fastest cruisers in the world (when launched), the weak broadside was a matter that needed addressing. The launch of *Omaha* and *Milwaukee* was put on hold while a twin mount for the 6in/53 in an enclosed blast-proof gunhouse was designed and the requisite foundations, hoists and magazines retrofitted into the forecastle and quarterdeck. Consideration was given to suppressing the eight single-gun casemates in favour of a second pair of 6in twin-mount gunhouses, which would have left the ships with the same broadside, but this was rejected by the General Board on the grounds that as scouts, they might be expected to encounter multiple enemies at the same time and the ability to engage on both sides simultaneously would be advantageous. The added 175 tons cost perhaps a half-knot in speed; more serious was the addition to the cumulative increase in displacement, now up to 7050 tons normal, which raised the waterline; this caused the torpedo tubes and aft casemates and quarterdeck to be wet in any weather, a problem made only worse when a pair of catapults and other aircraft-handling equipment were added abaft the funnels soon after completion.

Germania Redux . . .

The Treaty of Versailles left Germany stripped of all but a token naval force. The once proud High Seas Fleet was reduced to handful of antiquated pre-dreadnought battleships and eight equally old light cruisers of the *Gazelle* and *Bremen*

Not many changes were made to the *Omaha*s before the Second World War broke out. As early as 1928, the removal of the lower after casemates was authorised, but, as can be seen in this image taken during a visit to Sydney, Australia, in February 1938, that has clearly not been done yet to USS *Trenton* (CL11, ex-CS11). What has been done is the movement of the large armoured rangefinder from the after superstructure to the roof of the pilot house, the replacement of the searchlight under the foremast fire-control top by an enclosed lookout position and the placement of an AA platform with four .50cal/90 Browning MGs atop the foremast fire-control top. (NHHC)

classes (six in active commission and two in reserve). The newest of the light cruisers had been launched in 1903, the oldest in 1899. One of the key provisions of the Versailles Treaty was Article 190, which established 20 years from launch date as the point at which Germany could replace any of their old cruisers and 6000 tons as the maximum allowable displacement.[19] The treaty was not explicit in any way about how displacement was to be measured nor about what was meant by the word 'ton'. As a result, the Germans set about designing their first new large warship in the post-First World War era with what turned out to be a number of misconceptions regarding the limits to which they could build.

This new ship, a light cruiser, was largely based on the design of the highly-successful *Königsberg* (ii) class of 1914–15. A set of plans for SMS *Karlsruhe* (ii) had survived the war, and was used as a starting point by the design staff of the *Reichsmarine* – the name adopted by the navy of the Weimar Republic as the successor to the Imperial German Navy (*Kaiserliche Marine*). The new ship, given the contract name Ersatz-*Niobe*, was remarkably similar to its 1915 prototype. The new ship was 12ft longer (508ft 10in overall) and displaced 160 tons more (5600 tons standard); she had a mix of coal-fired and oil-fired boilers like *Karlsruhe* (ii), which drove a similar two-shaft power plant, giving a top speed of 29.4 knots, just about two knots faster than her predecessor; her main battery was similar, also comprising eight 15cm/45 guns in single mounts, the only difference being that the forward pair in Ersatz-*Niobe* were superfiring rather than side-by-side; the armour belt of the new ship was 2in thick, an inch thinner than that in *Karlsruhe* (ii).[20]

In this form, the proposal to construct Ersatz-*Niobe* was included in the 1920 Naval Estimates and approved in March 1921. The contract was let with the former Imperial Dockyard at Wilhelmshaven, now known as the *Marinewerft*, on 7 April 1921, and her keel was laid on 8 December. This, however, was far from the end of the story of how the German light cruiser *Emden* acquired her eventual shape. At the conclusion of the Washington Conference in February 1922, the Germans received a number of rude shocks; to their chagrin, they discovered that they had been using both the wrong definition of 'ton' and the wrong measure of displacement in calculating the size of Ersatz-*Niobe.* The Germans had been using metric tonnes in all their calculations, but the Versailles Treaty and Washington Treaty had been written with the long ton in mind. This made a significant difference; a metric tonne was 98 per cent the size of a long ton, A ship that displaced 6000 tons in metric tonnes would displace only 5880 tons in long tons. Even more significant was the German use of 'design displacement' in their calculations; the Washington Treaty used a definition of 'standard displacement' that calculated displacement very differently, and which, because of its use in that treaty, became the predominant definition in use among the world's navies.

The Germans had been using what was known as 'design displacement', which calculated displacement with between one-third and two-fifths of maximum fuel and boiler feedwater aboard. (For what it is worth, Royal Navy practice up to the time of the Washington Treaty was to use 'normal displacement', which measured a ship with all equipment and two-thirds of consumables aboard.) At the Washington Conference, the Americans pushed successfully for the adoption of their definition of 'standard displacement' which was with full equipment, crew and consumables, but with no fuel or boiler feedwater. In general, a ship would displace about 5 per cent less when measured by 'standard displacement' than by 'normal displacement', with 'design displacement' giving a figure in-between the two.

The upshot of this confusion was that, in mid-1922, with construction of Ersatz-*Niobe* still just getting started, the Germans asked the Naval Inter-Allied Commission of Control (NIACC), which had to approve all new naval construction under terms of the Versailles Treaty, for permission to modify the design of the new cruiser. Specifically, the Germans asked for permission to replace the eight single 6in mounts with four twin mounts of the same calibre, but with a longer barrel, and to increase the number of torpedo tubes from four to eight in twin mounts, but these requests were denied and the construction continued as originally planned. Because of the slow delivery of materials, Ersatz-*Niobe* was not launched until 7 January 1925, at which time she was christened *Emden*.

Seen during a visit to Yokohama in 1931, this overhead view of *Emden* demonstrates just how much she resembled the late-war Imperial German light cruisers on which her design was based. Except for her forward gun mounts being superfiring rather than side-by-side, the presence of a tall cylindrical foremast and needing only two rather than three funnels, she could have passed for a sister-ship to any of the light cruisers laid down after 1914. (NARA)

Chapter 4

The Washington Treaty and its Immediate Consequences: 1920–1922

The Washington Conference on the Limitation of Armament was called primarily to forestall a renewed international competition in the building of capital ships, the kind of 'arms race' that many believed to be a primary cause of the First World War. It is more than a little ironic that the call for such a conference should come from the United States, because it was the Americans who, more than any other nation, were pressing ahead with the construction of more large warships despite the end of global hostilities. The 'Big Navy Act' of 1916 had authorised the construction of ten battleships and six battlecruisers at a time when only the British and Japanese were starting new capital ships and those in very small numbers.[1] But the real 'back-breaker' was the new building programme proposed by the Americans in 1918. In October of that year, with the war winding down, the General Board of the US Navy, with the full encouragement of Navy Secretary Josephus Daniels, proposed a new three-year programme of no less than twenty-eight more capital ships.[2] Aware that even he could not sell this programme to an increasingly isolationist Congress, President Woodrow Wilson had the request trimmed down to sixteen capital ships. In the end, the 1918 programme became a bargaining chip used by Wilson to good effect at the Paris peace negotiations, but the 1916 programme, though delayed, remained in effect and increasingly an irritant in Anglo-American relations.[3] All of this was a very good reason for reasonable folk to want, with the 'War to End All Wars' behind them, to attempt to avoid needlessly provoking another one. What, a reader might ask, has this issue of building battleships and battlecruisers to do in a narrative about the development of cruisers? Surprisingly, the answer is a great deal.

Irritants Here and There . . .

For two allies, bound together by a common language, a common belief in democratic institutions and, most recently, by the bonds forged by fighting a common enemy, the British and Americans still had very little trust in each other's motives with peace rapidly approaching. There were some valid reasons for this. The post-1918 world was bound to look very different from that before the war in ways that, for the most part, were not to Britain's advantage. Despite having defeated their most threatening enemy, Britain was not emerging from the war in a stronger geopolitical position. If anything, the United Kingdom had not been in a weaker position in over a hundred years. There were multiple reasons for this. For one, the British Empire was increasingly fractious. The major 'white' colonies – Canada, Australia, New Zealand and South Africa – were increasingly unwilling to follow Britain's lead blindly; even India was pushing for greater independence. The Empire could no longer be relied upon to supply ships and men automatically to defend the 'mother country', especially not in times of peace. At home, things were even worse. Britain had sustained devastating losses in the war, losing much of a generation in the bloodbath. Any return to a robust peacetime economy would be impeded by an ageing industrial infrastructure worked by a restive labour force that had been asked to postpone raises and other benefits for the duration and was eager to be paid what it believed was overdue compensation.[4] Rationing of fuel and food, which had been introduced in 1918, would take some time to go away, because the British merchant fleet had suffered terrible losses during the war.[5] Slowing any recovery was the massive national debt left by the war; the conversion to a peacetime economy would have to take place without any significant infusion of public money.

The Americans emerged from the war in a very different condition. Where the British were deeply in debt, the Americans were now the world's creditor nation, holding huge amounts of debt that had been used by Britain, France and, to a lesser extent, most of the other Allies, to pay for the weapons that defeated Germany. (Of course, things are rarely as simple as they seem on the surface. Of the over $10 billion in debt owed the United States by the Allies, almost all the borrowed money had been spent in the United States to purchase war materiel, so many in Europe felt that the Americans were effectively 'double-dipping'.[6] The Americans sympathised, but still insisted on repayment of the war debts. The British proposed repaying the Americans in finished goods rather than in cash, but the Americans would have none of it.) Where the British economy would struggle to shift gear from wartime production, the American economy would have no similar problem, because the civilian economy had never seriously contracted during the war.

Hoping, perhaps, to steal a march on their presumptive ally, a diplomatic mission led by Ambassador Maurice W E de Bunsen was dispatched from London to South America, ostensibly to show Britain's great appreciation to those states that had supported the Allied cause (or at least had abstained from supporting Germany). It was obvious to the Americans, and de Bunsen himself made no secret of his intent, that the mission, which left Devonport on 21 April 1918, was very much about bolstering Britain's diplomatic and economic ties with the major South American markets.[7]

Needless to say, the Americans were none too pleased with what they considered to be British 'poaching' in their backyard. Nor were American feelings improved by a revival of the idea of 'Imperial Preferences', a system of protectionist tariffs designed to promote trade among British colonies and reduce competition from outside the Empire. These actions on the part of the British ran up against two basic tenets of American foreign policy, positions that Americans, regardless of political party, would have been unwilling to compromise: free trade and the Monroe Doctrine.[8]

The American reaction was, at least at first, limited to an increase in the vocal anti-British sentiment harboured by some elements in American society.[9] The timing, however, was unfortunate, coming as it did at a time when the British were pushing hard for the Americans to increase their commitment to the war effort and, at the same time, to recognise, formally and informally, the many sacrifices the British had made while America sat on the sidelines. Where the British were concerned that the Americans were building a massive new navy which, from the British point of view, they did not need, the Americans saw the British profiting greatly by the end of the war – both because the Royal Navy would no longer have to concentrate at home and could gain greatly from taking over the German ships interned at Scapa Flow – and, by dint of the Anglo-Japanese Alliance, potentially threatening the United States with war on both coasts.

When the Americans finally did react, it was the turn of the British to be displeased. Where the British had sent de Bunsen on a commercial mission poorly-disguised as a diplomatic tour, the Americans sent out genuine humanitarian

Political will meets naval force. Given the strongly conservative mood of the American electorate that swept the Republicans and their standard-bearer, Warren G Harding, into office in 1920, it is not surprising that Harding should have been the one to call a disarmament conference to convene in Washington in 1921, nor was it a shock that the emphasis was on naval arms and on capital ships in particular, the most expensive of armaments. Nowhere could those forces be seen in more perfect juxtaposition than in this image of Harding, arms folded across his chest, addressing the sombre-looking officers of an American battleship under the looming barrels of that ship's aftermost main-battery turret. (LOC/HEC)

relief missions after the end of the war to a number of countries in Europe and the Middle East, the latter an area the British considered one of their proprietary 'spheres of influence'. What alarmed London was that, along with the bags of flour and other food aid, the Americans sent representatives of financial and commercial interests.[10]

These matters roiled Anglo-American relations at the Paris Peace Conference, but an agreement was finally reached that gave the Americans acknowledgement of the Monroe Doctrine and Wilson the League of Nations Covenant, while avoiding the 'freedom of the seas' issue. The major British 'want' with which they had come to Paris – an agreement with the Americans that would formalise British naval superiority – was put on hold, to be the subject of future negotiations. The British took this promise of negotiations seriously and in late September 1919, barely three months after the signing of the Versailles Treaty, the former Foreign Secretary Edward Grey was dispatched to America to meet with Wilson and begin negotiations that would acknowledge Britain's need for a larger navy because of her greater dependence on imports for survival.

Grey's mission never had a chance to succeed because President Wilson suffered a breakdown in health at exactly the same time that the British negotiator arrived in America. Regardless, whatever goodwill may have remained between the two nations evaporated completely a year later when, on 8 September 1920, the British Treasury filed a formal claim for reimbursement for expenses incurred by Great Britain in support of the American forces that had fought in Europe.[11] It can safely be stated that the period between the end of the Paris Peace Conference in 1919 and the beginning of Washington Conference on the Limitation of Armament in 1921 represented a low point in Anglo-American relations.

Cruising the Potomac

It is probably not possible and certainly not important to determine where the movement toward post-war arms limitation began. The Grey mission to the United States in 1919 had as its primary goal a reduction in American naval construction, so that Britain would not feel pressured to match American expenditures, but this was not part of a global arms-reduction initiative. The American Republican Party, which advocated fiscal conservatism and political isolationism, gained in voter appeal with the end of the First World War. Many Americans saw the war as a waste of American lives and money with little gain for the country to balance the expense; a common criticism of Wilsonian globalism was to ask what America had gained from the defeat of the Central Powers beyond a stack of uncollectable debts. To many Americans, the defeat of Germany and Austria was more the destruction of a market than the removal of a dire threat.

In December 1920, Idaho Senator William E Borah introduced a resolution calling for the United States, Great Britain and Japan to agree on 'promptly entering into an understanding or agreement by which the naval expenditures and building programs . . . shall be substantially reduced annually during the next five years'.[12] While Borah was not the first to suggest such a move, he was probably the most influential to do so. His resolution was approved unanimously in the US Senate and was attached to a naval appropriations bill that was vetoed by President Wilson. The following April, with a new Republican President, Warren G Harding, now in office, the Borah Resolution was re-introduced and passed both houses of the United States Congress in May and June by overwhelming votes. Arthur H Lee, the new First Lord of the Admiralty, had stated his nation's willingness to agree to naval disarmament in a speech he gave on 16 March 1921.[13] Speaking to the British Institute of Naval Architects, he stated:

> We see the United States Senate is laying down the principle that America shall maintain a navy at least equal to that of any other Power. That is a claim to equality which this country has never accepted in the past and never would accept save in connection with the great English-speaking nation that has sprung from its loins and must ever hold a great place in our regard and confidence.[14]

Despite the somewhat lurid style of Lee's oratory, his statement laid an essential building block for a naval conference because, for the first time, it formally stated Great Britain's abandonment of all previous 'power standards' and acceptance of parity with the US Navy. He went even further on that occasion, stating explicitly:

> . . . if an invitation comes from Washington, I am prepared personally to put aside all other business . . . in order to take part in a business than which there can be nothing more pressing in the affairs of the world.[15]

Again, on 22 April, when the publisher of *The New York Times*, Adolph S Ochs, who openly advocated naval disarmament, was in London, Lee requested a meeting and returned to the theme of British willingness to participate in arms reduction negotiations, signals which Ochs duly reported to his contacts at the American Navy Department.[16]

Two days later, on 24 April, the Japanese expressed very similar sentiments through very similar channels; the director of the East and West News Bureau in New York, Dr Iyenaga Toyokichi, considered to be a reliable Japanese Government spokesman, issued a press release:

> The Japanese Government would welcome a conference looking toward reduction of naval programs. It is utterly foolish to think that Japan could compete with the United States in a program of huge naval expansion . . . The expense for the United States would be heavy, and for Japan practically ruinous.

> . . . Japan was willing to consider a reduction in her naval program if the United States and Great Britain would agree to a conference, and succeed in devising a certain formula of naval equipment in accordance with the needs of the respective countries as dictated by geographical, political and other considerations.[17]

Whether Harding truly intended, on becoming president, to take the lead in a world-wide disarmament movement is ultimately irrelevant. He now had so much pressure on him at home and abroad that he had little choice but to issue invitations to the leading military powers – not just Britain and Japan, but also France and Italy – to meet in Washington in November to discuss disarmament in general and naval disarmament in particular. The invitations went out from US Secretary of State Charles Evans Hughes on 8 July 1921.

Of course, the enthusiasm all parties felt for the prospect of the economies and lessened international tensions that could potentially emerge from a successful naval disarmament conference all hinged on what Dr Iyenaga had quite accurately identified as the critical component – success in 'devising a certain formula' of reductions that would satisfy all parties. In order to concoct such a formula, it was necessary to know from what point the reductions were starting. What was the actual state of the world's navies in mid-1921? It is doubtful that the senior naval leaders of any two of the world's navies would have agreed on much in such an assessment at the time. For example, commenting on the relative strength of the American and British cruiser fleets of this period, Roskill stated:

> As regards cruisers . . . the USA possessed many fewer modern ships than Britain, but the ten *Omaha* class light cruisers (7,050 tons, armed with ten or twelve 6-inch guns) which had been authorized in 1916 . . . were the most powerful ships of their class so far designed.[18]

This was, in more ways than one, a very curious statement to make almost a half-century after the fact, no doubt reflective of the Royal Navy's sense of the state of the world's navies at the time. On a ship-for-ship basis, there was little to choose between the US Navy's *Omaha*s and the Royal Navy's *Emeralds*; they were virtually the same size, with essentially the same broadside – six 6in guns if the lower casemate guns of the *Omaha*s were discounted, as they were useless in any but the most ideal conditions – with almost the same speed and the same armour. The fact that the Americans built ten *Omaha*s to the two *Emerald*s was more than offset by the fact that the US Navy had laid down no cruisers before the *Omaha*s since 1905. It is probably needless to point out the incredible understatement in Roskill's use of the term 'many fewer' to describe the number of modern cruisers the Americans possessed in the period before the Washington Conference compared to the Royal Navy; it is only necessary to note that since 1905, a period during which the Americans had laid down only the ten *Omaha*s, the Royal Navy had laid down eighty cruisers, all classed as scout cruisers or light cruisers, with the possible exception of the five ships of the *Hawkins* class. Of these, seventy-two had been completed as cruisers by 1921 and fifty-five of those were still be in service at the commencement of the Washington Conference.[19]

The other navies of interest to this account all also had 'many fewer' modern cruisers than the Royal Navy. Of the states that would attend the Washington Conference, the following totals of cruisers were in service in November 1921:

France: The French had built primarily large armoured cruisers before and after the turn of the century. Their planned class of ten light cruisers, intended to be laid down starting in 1914, never materialised due to the demands of war production. Of necessity, therefore, the *Marine National* had to make do with their obsolescent armoured cruisers. In November 1921, they still had seventeen in service, some as old as 27 years; the newest was *Waldeck-Rousseau*, a mere ten years old.

Italy The Italians, unlike the French, completed some small cruisers just before and during the war, a total of six, of which five were still in service in November 1921. These, along with five older armoured cruisers, comprised the cruiser forces of the *Regia Marina* at the time of the Washington Conference.

Japan Like the Americans, the Japanese had an active shipbuilding programme largely unaffected by the war. Between 1905 and November 1921, they laid down sixteen light cruisers, of which eleven had been completed. Another *Nagara* class cruiser would be laid down a month after the conference began. The Imperial Japanese Navy also retained numerous old armoured and protected cruisers in coastal defence and training roles.

The other navies of interest to this account, Germany and Russia, were not invited to Washington for different reasons. Germany's navy, as recounted in the preceding chapter, was controlled at this point by the Treaty of Versailles and limited to six old light cruisers, although the first of their allowed replacements would be laid down soon. Soviet Russia had essentially cut all diplomatic ties with its former allies and had stopped work on the cruisers building at the Baltic and Black Sea shipyards, so its navy seemed of little interest or importance at this point. A few old armoured and protected cruisers remained, but they were in poor repair and were

The best way to test a design was to subject it to the real-world stress it would face in battle. Some of the victorious Allies, the ones that did not need the ships to fill out their war-depleted fleets, took advantage of the German ships distributed as reparations to use them as targets. This allowed them to test both the quality of the German designs and, in the case of the Americans, to try out the new-fangled art of aerial bombardment against real ships. Here, a pair of officers, one of whom, at least, seems quite relaxed, watch while a cameraman films the bombing of the former SMS *Frankfurt* off the Virginia Capes on 18 July 1921. The lighter-than-air ship visible to the right of the plume of water was there as an observer, not as a bomber. (NHHC)

After having been hit by twelve bombs, including a number of 600lb bombs, dropped by US Army bombers led by Brigadier General William L 'Billy' Mitchell, *Frankfurt* settled by the bow and sank on an even keel. Of course, as a test of air power versus ships, these were hardly realistic trials, as the ships were anchored and unmanned, so no damage control was possible to minimise flooding. Nonetheless, Mitchell touted the sinking of *Frankfurt* and other ships as proof that aircraft were sufficient to defend the coasts of the United States and that ships (other than aircraft carriers and escorts) were made obsolete by aircraft. (NHHC)

almost all destined to be scrapped in the next few years. Five of the incomplete light cruisers laid down in 1913 were completed after the war, to modified designs, between 1926 and 1932.

The Washington Conference on the Limitation of Armament started off with a 'bang' on 12 November 1921. Invitations had been sent to a long list of nations in Europe, the Americas and Asia, although the focus was on disarmament discussions between the United States, Great Britain and Japan. After the expected *pro forma* introductory remarks by the American President – a standard diplomatic address, welcoming the delegations and encouraging them to work diligently – the Secretary of State then took to the podium. His address was anything but boilerplate. Hughes, who had been appointed presiding officer of the conference, opted to forego generalities and platitudes, choosing instead to present a remarkably specific plan, complete with ship numbers and names, listed nation-by-nation, for how many ships should be scrapped and how many tons retained under his proposed disarmament regime. It was a stunning *tour de force*.

After a brief introduction explaining who was at the conference and why – and after describing some of the history of previous, failed attempts at such initiatives – Hughes dove straight into the subject. He was particularly critical of prior attempts at disarmament that had tried to slow the growth of armaments, but allowed their production to continue at a reduced rate. He had a much more radical approach in mind, an approach he had worked out within a small group of advisors, taking very nearly all of the delegates, including most of the Americans, completely by surprise.

> . . . the core of the difficulty is to be found in the competition in naval programs, and that, in order appropriately to limit naval armament, competition in its production must be abandoned. Competition will not be remedied by resolves with respect to the method of its continuance. One program inevitably leads to another, and if competition continues, its regulation is impracticable. There is only one adequate way out and that is to end it now.[20]

Not only did Hughes propose a clean and sharp ending to the competition in naval construction, he made it clear that he intended to turn a deaf ear to all 'special pleadings' by any nation that claimed unaddressed needs or specific requirements:

> . . . one nation is as free to compete as another, each may find grounds for its action. What one may do another may demand the opportunity to rival, and we remain in the thrall of competitive effort.[21]

He proposed starting from the position that a navy's relative strength could be accurately measured by adding up its current capital ship tonnage, and that figure should be the sole basis for establishing future strength ratios. Regarding cruisers (and other warship types), Hughes proposed:

> That 'auxiliary combatant craft' tonnage, meaning the numbers and aggregate tonnage of all other ship types, would be allocated in the same ratios as capital ship numbers and tonnage.[22]

An observer described Admiral Beatty, the leading naval delegate for Great Britain, as sitting up in his chair with a 'slightly staggered and deeply disturbed expression'.[23] That probably was understating the impact of Hughes' proposals on Beatty and most other delegates.

Hughes went on to propose that 'auxiliary combatant craft' would be sub-divided into three categories: submarines, aircraft carriers (and other aircraft-handling vessels) and 'auxiliary surface combatant craft', this latter group to include cruisers, flotilla leaders and destroyers displacing more than 3000 tons, with a top speed in excess of 15 knots and a main battery greater than four 5in guns. Under Hughes' proposal, the United States and Great Britain would be allowed 450,000 tons of this last category of ships and Japan 270,000 tons, in keeping with the 5:5:3 ratio he had proposed for capital ships, with the proviso that, if current tonnage exceeded those levels, no scrapping need take place until such time as they would normally be retired. At that time, the tonnage limits would be imposed. The replacement rule proposed by Hughes for cruisers stipulated that a ship could be replaced when it was 17 years old (measured from the date of its completion), with the laying of the keel of a replacement ship permitted two years prior to the replacement date. In a separate provision, the maximum calibre for guns in 'auxiliary surface combatant craft' was to be set at 8in.[24]

Clearly, this was a great deal for the delegations to absorb, and Hughes adjourned the conference for three days to allow for official reactions to be formulated. The British delegates were generally favourable to Hughes' overall approach, at least as applied to capital ships and especially in that it would put an end to the massive American and Japanese building programmes, to which Great Britain was poorly placed to respond. Beatty was less happy about the idea of a ten-year 'holiday' in capital ship construction, being concerned about the survival of Britain's shipbuilding industry; he proposed that the British counter Hughes' 'holiday' idea with a process of low-rate replacement of older ships that would keep a steady flow of work to the shipyards. Further, he was unhappy with any restriction on the number of cruisers the Royal Navy could deploy, citing what he saw as the British Empire's unique dependence on seaborne trade and the need for cruisers both for fleet duties and for trade protection. Beatty lobbied hard for these points despite them both being precisely the kind of 'continuance' and 'special pleadings' that Hughes had argued against in his opening address.[25]

When the conference convened again on 15 November, the head of the British Empire delegation, Arthur Balfour, a former Prime Minister and Foreign Secretary, rose first to give his delegation's formal response. Described as a white-haired man, weighed down by the burden of his responsibilities, Balfour spoke slowly, without notes.[26] He started by stating Great Britain's general agreement with the capital ship tonnage limits and fleet sizes proposed by Secretary Hughes, but then he began to list the points on which the British desired further discussion. He stated that the British also wanted to discuss the matters of replacement schedules and the numbers of cruisers allocated to the Royal Navy for trade protection as opposed to fleet duties. These, he said these would be submitted in to the newly-formed sub-committee of naval experts, under the chairmanship of American Colonel Theodore Roosevelt, Jr.[27]

Balfour was followed at the podium by the chief Japanese delegate Admiral Kato Tomosaburo. His remarks were brief and to the point, unlike Balfour's rambling address. After two brief paragraphs praising Hughes' high ideals, Kato went straight to the heart of the Japanese position. He concluded by explaining that, although the Japanese were asking for an adjustment in their allocation ratio, they were not asking for parity with the United States or Great Britain, which must surely make it obvious that Japan 'had never in view preparations for offensive war'.[28]

Speaking for the French, the veteran diplomat Aristide Briand was uncharacteristically blunt, stating basically that the war had done much of the job of naval arms limitation for the *Marine Nationale*. The French position, Briand made clear, was that they had no need to make further sacrifices. The late war had largely been fought on French soil at the cost of a generation of Frenchmen; the *Marine Nationale* had added no new major warships during the war except for a few that had been almost complete when war broke out.

Much more information came out when the delegations held impromptu press conferences before and after the main conference session. This gave Balfour a chance to elaborate on some of the other issues that had been on Beatty's mind. For example, he emphasised the point about Great Britain's greater need for cruisers because of her greater dependence on imported resources; he took direct aim at Hughes' contention that the current size of each nation's capital ship fleet should be taken as the basis for its requirements of all other ship types. He promised to deliver a detailed report in the coming days outlining the British Empire's needs for cruisers of all types.

The Japanese, in keeping with their accustomed caution in negotiating publicly, said little more than Admiral Kato had stated in the public session, but the news still leaked out about their desire for their ratio to be increased from the 60 per cent of that allowed the Anglo-Saxon Powers to a number closer to 70 per cent.[29]

What was obvious from the opening sessions of the Washington Conference was that Hughes' dramatic proposal had received general approbation, at least from the two largest navies. With the application of some additional pressure, the capital ship agreement would be extended to incorporate the next two largest navies – Italy and France. Reaching agreement on this part of the problem – the part that most observers would have thought beforehand was the hardest to solve – proved relatively easy. After much grumbling, a ratio of 5:5:3:1.75:1.75 for capital ship tonnage was accepted by the five Contracting Powers.[30] It was in the idea that the same limitation ratio assigned for capital ships could simply be carried over without further adjustments to establish tonnage limitations for 'auxiliary combatant craft' that Hughes' plan broke down.

When an explosive is detonated next to a caisson, its effects can be precisely measured, not only by photographing the explosion itself, as in in this image of a caisson test conducted at Norfolk, VA, on 20 June 1912, but also by examination of the caisson after the test. Even if the caisson sinks – especially if it sinks – its recovery is assured because it is tethered by multiple lines and it is sinking in known, shallow waters. (NARA)

The simple fact was that none of the other Contracting Powers looked on the issue of limiting smaller warships in the same way that the United States did. To the Americans, the fleet was a force for power projection. In 1921, the United States had no reason to fear attack by sea by any nation, so once the needs of the main battle fleet for 'auxiliary combatant craft' were defined, a definite limit on the requirements for such craft could be established.[31] No other navy was in quite so fortunate a position. Every other of the Contracting Powers had some issues of coastal defence against potential invasion or the protection of trade carrying resources vital to national survival which were in excess of the needs of the main battle fleet. At the opposite extreme to the Americans were the British, who, as Balfour took pains to point out on 16 November, never had more than seven weeks of food in reserve during the recent war.[32]

The problem with bombing or shelling test ships is that the evidence of the damage that caused them to sink, the details of which designers would greatly desire to examine, ends up on the seafloor. A much better approach, at least for testing underwater protection schemes, is a test caisson, such the one seen here in the Norfolk, VA, Navy Yard on 30 March 1920. A caisson like this can be submerged to the desired depth and a precisely measured explosive charge detonated at a known depth of water and a known distance from it. (NARA)

The Japanese made it clear that not only were they displeased with the 60 per cent ratio in regard to capital ships, but felt that this ratio was even more prejudicial to their interests when applied to 'auxiliary surface combatant craft'. Kato stated on 17 November:

> Because of her geographical position, Japan deems it only fair at the present time that the other interested countries should agree that she maintain a proportion in general tonnage slightly greater than 60 per cent., and in a type of vessel of strictly defensive character, she might desire even to approximate that of the greater navies.[33]

He would not specify what he meant by the term 'vessel of strictly defensive character'.

The French considered themselves as dependent on trade with their overseas colonies as the British were. Add to this the French contention that, since they had such a significantly less powerful fleet than their closest neighbours, they had to look towards submarines and other 'auxiliary combatant craft' to defend their shores. Pressured into accepting a ratio of capital ship tonnage only slightly more than half the Japanese 60 per cent allocation, the French responded by demanding a larger allocation of submarine tonnage.[34] When told that the British were reacting negatively to this demand, Briand replied sarcastically:

> When the British retain 500,000 tons of capital ships, I

> do not say it is against France, although England is a friend of America, an ally of Japan, and Germany and Russia have no fleets.
>
> Perhaps the English want their capital ships to fish for sardines. Well, we want submarines to study the flora at the bottom of the sea for the benefit of our botanical societies.[35]

The Italians maintained the simplest position throughout the conference discussions, stating they wished parity with the French, so if the *Marine Nationale* were granted permission to construct more 'auxiliary' craft, the *Regia Marina* would expect similar allocations.[36]

Balfour made clear from his very first address to the conference that the British had 'questions connected with cruisers which are not connected with or required for fleet action'.[37] The next day, the British delegation received direction from the Admiralty, instructing that light cruisers and destroyers should, if possible, be placed in separate categories in regard to tonnage limitation, and suggested that the British should propose to Hughes that the Royal Navy should be allocated 450,000 tons of cruisers, the United States Navy 300,000 tons and the Imperial Japanese Navy 250,000 tons, based on need and that, because so many of the Royal Navy's cruisers had seen hard service during the war, the 17-year replacement cycle should be shortened for cruisers.[38]

Hughes had no interest in this proposal by the British, and it was almost immediately forgotten in the 'noise' generated by the Japanese demand for an allocation of cruiser tonnage in excess of the 60 per cent ratio assigned by the Hughes plan. These matters came to a head at the ninth meeting of the Committee on Limitation of Armament, the primary sub-committee comprising the heads of the delegations of the five naval powers, meeting on 28 December. The French started out by stating that the entire matter of naval arms limitation had been referred back to their Cabinet and the Supreme Council of National Defence and that those august bodies had, with great reluctance, accepted the limitation on capital ship tonnage under the Hughes plan, but could not, without compromising the security of the nation, accept limits lower than 330,000 tons of 'auxiliary surface combatant craft'.[39]

Balfour responded with sarcasm as barbed as Briand's, but without the Frenchman's wit. After stating that he 'rejoiced' that the French were willing to accept their assigned ratio of capital ship tonnage, he immediately mocked the notion that this represented any real concession by their erstwhile ally:

> He did not feel himself that the sacrifice on the part of France was in itself of an overwhelming character, even in regard to capital ships, . . .
>
> But when he turned . . . to the matter of other craft he confessed that a very different picture met the eye. . . . It had further to be noted that their French colleagues . . . intended greatly to increase the tonnage of their auxiliary craft. It must be acknowledged that this constituted a somewhat singular contribution to the labors of a Conference called for the diminution of armament. . . .[40]

By itself, this was an extraordinary display of diplomatic hypocrisy, given that the British themselves were asking for their special needs to be taken into consideration by the conference and their navy be granted an exemption from Hughes' rigid ratios when it came to 'auxiliary surface combatant craft' tonnage, but this statement effectively doomed any hope that might have existed for a quantitative limit on 'auxiliary combatant craft' being included in any agreement reached at Washington. While it is not clear that this was an explicit goal of the British once they learned of Hughes' intent to establish tonnage limits for all warship types, it is evident from their reactions both during and after the negotiations that this was an outcome very much to their liking.[41]

Hughes decided that he had to make the best of a bad situation and act quickly to prevent what he feared would be the natural evolution of cruisers, if not restrained, into larger and larger quasi-capital ships in much the same manner that armoured cruisers had evolved into battlecruisers, effectively skirting the capital ship tonnage limits that seemed to be gaining general acceptance. The best alternative that presented itself was one he disliked – replacing quantitative limits with qualitative limits. Hughes' original proposal included the idea of limiting the guns of 'auxiliary surface combatant craft' to 8in calibre.[42] There is some disagreement among sources as to whether the British or the Americans originated the idea of a 10,000-ton upper limit on the displacement of individual cruisers.[43] Regardless, Hughes was ready to respond immediately to the obvious impasse that had been reached in negotiations over tonnage limits for 'auxiliary surface combatant craft'. The American Secretary of State proposed the following resolution be adopted by the conference:

> No ship of war other than a capital ship or aircraft carrier hereafter built shall exceed a total tonnage displacement of 10,000 tons and no guns shall be carried by any such ship with a caliber in excess of 8 inches.[44]

This wording was generally agreed to with little objection; only the French balked briefly at the idea that their cruisers should be limited in any way.[45] With only slightly changed wording, Hughes' proposed resolution of 28 December became Articles XI and XII of the final treaty signed 6 February 1922. To the relief of all parties, the acrimonious interchange between Balfour and the French was soon forgotten.

The Last 'Pre-Treaty Cruisers'

The Washington Treaty for the Limitation of Naval Armament would include no overall tonnage limitation on

One of the post-First World War cruisers whose construction was not impacted by the Washington Conference was the French light cruiser *Primauguet*, seen here not too long after her completion in 1926. This dating can be stated with some assurance because she is lacking the large bi-level DCT atop her tripod foremast that was installed in 1928–9. This ship had the serious misfortune of being sunk by American naval forces at the Battle of Casablanca in November 1942. (NHHC)

the cruisers, but bound the five Contracting Powers to build non-capital warships that were no larger than 10,000 tons standard displacement and carried main-battery guns no larger than 8in calibre. Inevitably, that meant that no sooner was the ink dry on the treaty in February 1922 than the naval commands of all five signatories were directed to begin the design of 'treaty maximum' cruisers. But two of the affected nations had cruiser-size ships in the process of being built, far enough along in the process that re-working them to become 'treaty maximum' cruisers was simply not practical.

France: Delayed Gratification

The much-delayed *Lamotte-Piquet* scout cruiser design, last reviewed in 1915, sat untouched through the rest of the First World War while France struggled to survive the German onslaught. It was not until September 1919 that the *Marine Nationale* had the luxury of revisiting their needs, asking the STCN to take another look at the scout cruiser design in light of wartime experience. On 13 February 1920, Navy Minister Georges Leygues announced a major building programme, *Projet 171*, that included the construction of six new small cruisers.[46] The *Projet 171* cruisers differed from the 1915 sketch designs in a number of important features; the new ships were to mount the same number of 138.6mm/55 main-battery guns, but in four power-operated twin mountings rather than eight single mounts, and the torpedo and anti-aircraft (AA) batteries were to be upgraded. However, not long after the announcement of these characteristics, the French learned details of the American *Omaha*s and British *Emerald*s, and realised that both the armament and speed of these projected small cruisers would need to be greatly improved. The STCN quickly recast the cruiser design with 155mm/50 guns in the main battery and speed raised from 30 knots to 34 knots, which required an increase from 54,000shp to 102,000shp and an increase in length of almost 100ft. Unfortunately, this also meant an increase in estimated cost per ship of almost 75 per cent; since the budget available to the *Marine Nationale* remained fixed, the programme as ultimately approved in March–April 1922 included three, rather than six, cruisers, with the following specifications:

1922 Programme 8000-ton Cruisers: Duguay-Trouin Class

Displacement (std):	8000 tons
Length (oa):	595ft 9in
Beam:	56ft 5in
Draft:	17ft
Power plant:	102,000shp; Parsons geared turbines driving four shafts; eight Guyot du Temple boilers
Speed:	34 knots (designed); 33 knots (actual)
Range (designed):	3600nm @ 15 knots; 1400 tons oil fuel
Range (actual):	c3500nm @ 15 knots; 1200 tons oil fuel[47]
Protection (side):	0.75in (shell plating in way of main-battery magazines)
Protection (horiz):	0.5in–0.87in (deck plating over main-battery magazines and engineering spaces)
Armament (main):	8 x 155mm/50 Mle 1920 (4 x 2 – two forward and two aft)
Armament (AA):	4 x 75mm/50 Mle 1922 (4 x 1)
Armament (torp):	12 x 550mm Mle 1923D (4 x 3)[48]

These ships were ordered after the signing of the Washington Treaty, which means the French had the option of cancelling this programme and waiting until 'treaty maximum' cruiser plans could be drawn up, but they opted not to take that route. There were several reasons for this. One had to do with

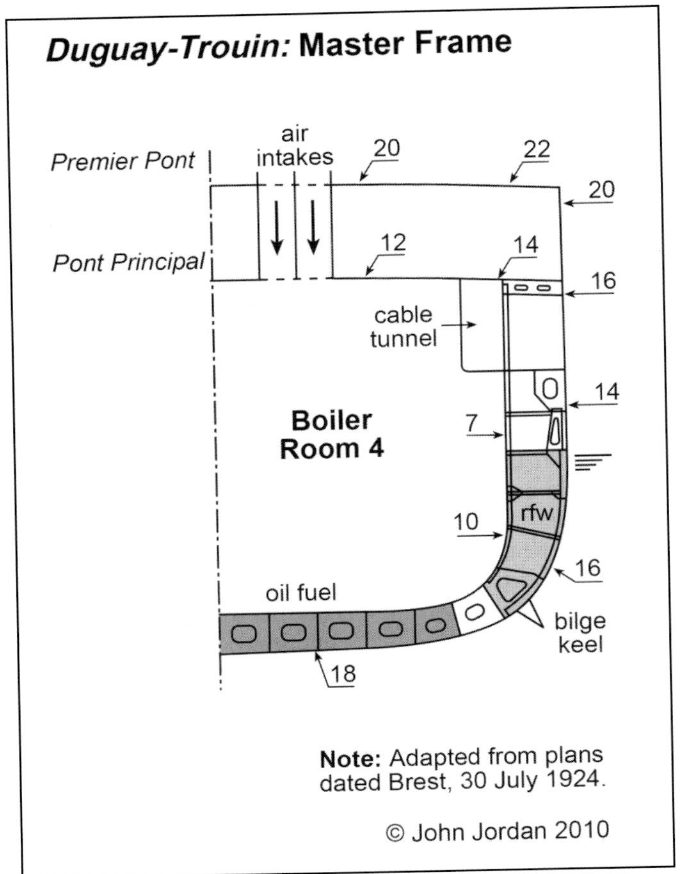

This cross-section drawing of the ships of the *Duguay-Trouin* class in way of the after fire room shows clearly that these ships were unarmoured. The thicknesses of structural steel plating are shown by the numbers in the drawing which denote millimetres of steel plate at the indicated point. Underwater protection was provided by the double bottom; given the tonnage restrictions on cruisers that the treaty regime would impose, no cruiser built over the next 20 years would have much greater protection against torpedoes or mines. (John Jordan)

the notorious instability of French governments after the end of the war; there had already been six changes of government since the Armistice, and there clearly was a mind-set in the *Marine Nationale* that it would be better to commit the nation to the construction of the three authorised cruisers while the money was available rather than assume it would still be there some months (or years) in the future when revised plans would be ready. (It would take over two-and-a-half years after the signing of the treaty for the first French 'treaty maximum' cruiser to be laid down.) The other undoubtedly had to do with the fact that the newest French cruisers at this point were the two *Quinet* class armoured cruisers laid down in 1905–6 and completed in 1911. The *Marine Nationale* was desperate to acquire any modern cruisers with acceptable characteristics. The first of three new cruisers, *Duguay-Trouin*, was laid down at Arsenal de Brest on 4 August 1922.

All three of the ships of this class were delivered in 1926–7 without their main-battery fire-control system. This was to have included a massive bi-level director control tower (DCT) incorporating two rangefinders – a 13ft 1in coincidence model for target ranging and a 9ft 10in stereoscopic model for scartometry, ranging on shell splashes to assist in correcting for shots falling short – at the top of the tripod foremast and a Mle 1923 fire-control computer in a plotting room below decks. In addition to this planned fire-control setup, a second 13ft 1in coincidence rangefinder was installed on top of the conning tower in a smaller bi-level housing. Two more similar rangefinder towers to support the 75mm battery were located one each port-and-starboard between the funnels.[49] They were also intended to mount a pair of high-angle (HA) fire-control directors, but these also were unavailable at the time of their completion. The large DCT sited on their foretop was ready for installation beginning around 1928–9. The open-topped HA directors were installed, one on each bridge wing, starting in 1933. These were served by a single HA fire-control table, so only one target could be engaged with controlled fire at a time.

Subsequent modernisations were piecemeal and relatively minor. In general, the bridge structure was enlarged in order to improve command efficiency and permit these ships to serve as flagships. In some cases, shields were fitted to the 75mm guns. An enlarged and improved, fully-enclosed HA director was substituted for the older model at the bridge wings. A number of 13.2mm/76 Hotchkiss Mle 1929 twin-mount machine guns were added to strengthen the AA fit.

Japan: Steady Improvement

As described above, the '8-8 Fleet Completion Programme' of 1920 included monies to start construction of four of the eight *Sendai* class light cruisers planned to fill out the Imperial Japanese Navy's scouting forces. None of them had yet been laid down by 6 February 1922 when the Washington Treaty was signed; however, nothing in that treaty impacted the plans for these ships. Indeed, when, on the day before the signing, the Naval General Staff ordered that all construction of capital ships at yards in Japan be stopped immediately, they ordered the acceleration of work on all non-capital ships.[50] So it is unsurprising that all four authorised and funded *Sendai* class light cruisers were laid down soon thereafter; three at private yards and one at the Sasebo Navy Yard.

The Japanese Navy Minister (and chief delegate at the Washington Conference), Admiral Kato, took advantage of the enforced leisure of the weeks-long ocean crossing returning home after the conference to rework the '8-8 Fleet Completion Programme' into a plan based on increased construction of larger cruisers. Within days of his arrival back in Japan on 10 March, the order went out to the Sasebo yard halting work on the one *Sendai* class cruiser being built at a

Another post-war, pre-treaty cruiser was the experimental *Yubari* built by the Japanese, completed in 1923. *Yubari* was an attempt to cram (very nearly all) the offensive power of the *Kuma* class cruisers into a ship intended to have just a bit more than half the displacement. The experiment was generally considered successful. This image, dated 15 November 1924, shows her after the height of her funnel was increased, but before protective hoods were fitted to her torpedo tubes. The fact that she turned out to be almost 500 tons overweight on completion is demonstrated by how close the lower row of scuttles is to the water; they would have to be closed whenever the ship was underway and in all but the calmest weather when in port. (NARA)

government-run facility; work on the three *Sendai* class hulls under construction at the privately-owned yards was allowed to continue to protect the fiscal health of those *zaibatsu*.[51]

The planned experimental cruiser, also funded in the 1920 programme, was almost immediately laid down at the Sasebo yard.[52] Lieutenant Commander Fujimoto Kikuo, the principal assistant to the IJN's Chief Constructor, Captain Hiraga Yuzuru, had been given the task of designing this ship. The idea was to fit the armament and speed of a standard 5500-ton light cruiser into as small a hull as possible. The ideas Fujimoto incorporated into this experimental design included: extensive use of high-tensile steel for structural framing; an internal, inclined 2.3in armour belt which, as had been pioneered by the Germans ten years earlier, was a strength member; superfiring twin turrets fore-and-aft which allowed the same broadside and better gunfire concentration ahead and astern than the conventional 5500-ton light cruisers; a recurved 'swan' bow and high, widely-flared forecastle designed to make for better weather performance; a larger bridge structure intended to concentrate more of the command activities in a centralised location; and a gracefully raked and trunked funnel intended to lead the smoke well clear of the bridge.[53] All of this was to be done in a hull 65ft shorter than the 500ft *Sendai*, with a designed displacement of 2890 tons standard. The resulting ship, named *Yubari*, was built in record time; she was completed just 13 months after being laid down in June 1922. The actual specifications to which she was completed were as follows:

Yubari

Displacement (std):	3387 tons
Length (oa):	457ft 6in
Beam (max):	39ft 6in
Draft:	11ft 9in
Power plant:	57,900shp; Mitsubishi-Parsons geared turbines driving three shafts; eight Kanpon three-drum water-tube boilers
Speed:	35.5 knots (designed); 34.8 knots (actual)
Range (designed):	5000nm @ 14 knots; 916 tons oil fuel
Range (actual):	3310nm @ 14 knots; 830 tons oil fuel
Protection (side):	2.33in NVNC internal 10° slope (engineering spaces only); intended to protect against USN 4in gunfire[54]
Protection (horiz):	1in NVNC (over engineering spaces)
Armament (main):	6 x 14cm/50 Type 3 (2 x 2 – one forward and one aft (superfiring); 2 x 1 – one forward and one aft)
Armament (AA):	1 x 8cm/40 Type 3 (1 x 1); 2 x 7.7mm/87 Lewis gun (2 x 1)
Armament (torp):	4 x 61cm (2 x 2)
Armament (mines):	48 Type 1 mines[55]

The fact that *Yubari* as completed was almost 500 tons heavier than designed proved to be of very little practical consequence. At normal load, she sat 11in deeper than planned, which brought the lowest row of scuttles forward seriously close to the waterline, but her stability proved to be more than adequate. After the *Tomozuru* incident in March 1934, when a torpedo boat capsized in a typhoon, the Japanese reexamined all their warships with an eye towards increasing stability, and *Yubari* had 124 tons of ballast added as a precaution. In general, *Yubari* was considered to have been a successful experiment; the 'A' class cruisers that followed soon after benefitted directly from the experience gained with her. She remained in service, very little modified, up to and into the Second World War, although she was not a popular ship to serve in; her crew accommodation was often poorly-ventilated due to the need to close her lowest row of forward scuttles when she was underway.[56]

Such was the confidence in the quality of the design work of Hiraga and Fujimoto, that even before *Yubari* was launched, the Japanese had proceeded with the laying-down of a pair of cruisers based heavily on the experimental cruiser's design. At the same time that Admiral Kato was proposing the cancellation of the remaining 5500-ton light cruisers and urging the expedited construction of the experimental *Yubari*, he also proposed the immediate substitution of two large scout cruisers of 7500 tons normal displacement (7100 tons standard displacement) in the place of the cancelled light cruisers. This 'emergency' proposal, coming immediately upon his return to Japan on 10 March 1922, was followed on 3 July by a more comprehensive programme, replacing the '8-6 Fleet Completion Programme' of 1918 and the '8-8 Fleet Completion Programme' of 1920 (both based largely on the construction of capital ships) with the 'Naval Armaments Limitation Programme', which, in the place of the cancelled 5500-ton light cruisers (and four 8000-ton scout cruisers which had been authorised but had never advanced beyond the sketch design phase), substituted, in addition to the two 7500-ton scout cruisers already authorised, two more scout cruisers of similar size and then four 'treaty maximum' cruisers.

For the large scout cruisers, Captain Hiraga offered a completely new design derived from the work he and Fujimoto had done on *Yubari*. For example, this new design took the long widely-flared forecastle of *Yubari* and extended it the full length of the ship, but allowed the sheer line of the main deck to undulate, specifically to slope downward aft alongside the bridge and then again further aft in way of the after superstructure. This led to a sinuous Main-Deck line that characterised most Japanese warships through the end of the Second World War. It provided a continuous longitudinal structure to the upper hull that added strength and allowed freeboard to be tailored to the wave pattern thrown up by a ship at speed. The main battery in Hiraga's new design would be six of the new 20cm/50 guns in single mounts then under development, three forward and three aft. The armour, which would be thicker than *Yubari*'s, would remain a structural element, but would be moved to the outer shell of the hull, where it would slope inward in a more conventional manner.

The one point on which Hiraga found himself overruled by the Naval General Staff was in regard to torpedo armament. The staff insisted that these scout cruisers be able to act in the role of large torpedo boats – Japanese naval doctrine had evolved to include heavy emphasis on night torpedo attacks as a major force equaliser – carrying twelve torpedo tubes with a full set of reloads. Hiraga fought hard to have this major source of topweight reduced but was repeatedly overruled. He finally was able to convince the staff to allow the torpedoes to be carried in fixed tubes within the hull at the Middle Deck level, which partially solved the stability issues caused by the excessive topweight, but added significant danger due to the hazard of storing the torpedo warheads in unprotected spaces above the ships' armour. The Naval Staff declared itself ready to accept this risk (and the tactical issues that accompanied fixed torpedo tubes) in order to gain the added offensive capability.[57]

The basic design of the 7500-ton scout cruiser was approved by the Naval General Staff in August 1921, with the following specifications:

'A' class Scout Cruisers: Furutaka Sub-class

Displacement (std):	7100 tons (designed); 7950 tons (actual)
Length (oa):	607ft 6in
Beam (max):	54ft 2in
Draft (mean):	14ft 9in
Power plant:	102,000shp; Mitsubishi-Parsons (*Furutaka*)/Kawasaki-Brown-Curtis (*Kako*) geared turbines driving four shafts; twelve Kanpon three-drum water-tube boilers
Speed:	34.5 knots (designed); 34.8 knots (actual)
Range (designed):	7000nm @ 14 knots; 1400 tons oil fuel
Range (actual):	6000nm @ 14 knots; 1010 tons oil fuel
Protection (side):	3in NVNC external 9° slope (engineering spaces only); intended immune zone against USN 6in/53 between 12,000m–15,000m[58]
Protection (horiz):	1.33in NVNC (over engineering spaces)
Protection (torp):	Shallow, unarmoured bulge below belt armour; 0.4in HTS torpedo bulkhead inboard
Armament (main):	6 x 20cm/50 3rd Year Type 1 (6 x 1 – three forward and three aft (middle gun superfiring))
Armament (AA):	4 x 8cm/40 Type 10 (4 x 1); 2 x 7.7mm/87 Lewis gun (2 x 1)
Armament (torp):	12 x 61cm (6 x 2)
Aircraft:	1 (1 x Heinkel HD-25)[59]

While the first two 7500-ton scouts were under construction – both *Furutaka* and *Kako* were laid down before the end of

The Japanese built four 8in-gunned cruisers – what would come to be called 'heavy cruisers' after the First London Conference – designed before the Washington Conference. These were to carry six 20cm/50 3rd Year Type 1 guns in large single gunhouses constructed of high-tensile steel up to an inch thick. This image shows *Furutaka*, the first to be completed, in the foreground, at Shinagawa on 10 October 1935. Note the sinuous line of her Main Deck, a feature introduced by Constructor Captain Hiraga to save weight without sacrificing strength; it would remain a feature of Japanese warships throughout the following decades. The most notable alteration of this ships since her completion has been the heightening of her funnels, done in 1927. Behind *Furutaka*'s bow is *Aoba*, one of the second pair of 'A' class scout cruisers, which can be readily distinguished at this time by their twin turrets in the place of the single gunhouses. In 1936–7, the two ships of the *Furutaka* sub-class were taken in hand for reconstruction, which gave them, among other changes, three twin turrets for their six main-battery guns like the *Aoba*s. (NHHC)

1922 and were ready to be launched at the beginning of 1925 – design work proceeded on the two follow-on 7500-ton scouts and on the first of the 'treaty maximum' cruisers. One of the important features planned for the larger cruisers was the mounting of the 20cm main-battery guns in twin turrets. Design on this gun turret had proceeded in parallel with design work on the second pair of 7500-ton cruisers, so that when *Aoba* and *Kinugasa* were laid down in early 1924, the intent was to fit them with three of the new twin turrets in place of the six single mounts. The Naval General Staff now wanted to know if these turrets could be retrofitted into the first two 7500-ton scouts, but the work on *Furutaka* and *Kako* was too far along and the delivery of the first of the twin turrets, the early type 'C' Model turrets, would not happen until at least six months after the ships would be ready for launch, so the decision was made to complete the first two as designed. The staff also wanted the new-model AA gun then entering service, the 12cm/45 10th Year Type, to be substituted for the older, less-capable 8cm/40, but again, the substitution would have delayed the launch of the first two cruisers, and so was put on hold.

Because the development of catapults for the launching of aircraft from ships was still in the experimental stage, *Furutaka* and *Kako* were each to be completed with a complex semi-rotating flying-off ramp, partially mounted on the foremost of the after gunhouses and partially on a semicircular rail system forward of that. In fact, the flying-off ramp system was found to be difficult to operate, and most frequently, aircraft were launched by hoisting them overboard and letting them take off from the water.[60] Fire control was relatively sophisticated for ships of this size and time, roughly equivalent to the systems being fitted in Royal Navy cruisers immediately after the First World War. Building on experience designing the centralised bridge structure of *Yubari*, the *Furutaka*s had a relatively massive forward superstructure, seven levels in height, built up around a plated-over, tapering internal tubular structure, referred to as a *tojo kyoko* ('pagoda-like' tower structure).[61] At the highest level was a glassed-in main-battery control platform with a Type 14 director (*hoiban*). From this position, the ship's gunnery officer identified targets and controlled salvo fire. The next level below, also a glassed-in platform, was the main-battery spotting platform in which were located two sets of high-powered binoculars, one each port and starboard, for spotting the fall of shot. Next down was the open target-survey platform, at which level was sited, also one each port and starboard, a pair of Type 13 *sokutekiban*, an inclinometer used to determine target course and speed. Also on this platform was the Type 11 change-of-range calculator. These devices together enabled the director to control a follow-the-pointer system for providing range and deflection orders to the main-battery turrets.[62] Below these gunnery-control platforms were three command platform levels.[63]

As the second pair of 7500-ton scouts were getting ready to be laid down in early 1924, the decision was made to include a number a features that had not been ready in time to be included in the *Furutaka*s. Besides the main-battery twin turrets, these included the heavier 12cm AA battery and the newly-available catapult to replace the flying-off ramp tested in the first pair of large scouts.[64] The specifications of the second pair were as follows:

'A' class Scout Cruisers: Aoba Sub-class

Displacement (std):	7100 tons (designed); 8300 tons (actual)
Length (oa):	607ft 6in
Beam (max):	54ft 2in
Draft (mean):	14ft 9in
Power plant:	102,000shp; Mitsubishi-Parsons (*Aoba*)/Kawasaki-Brown-Curtis (*Kinugasa*) geared turbines driving four shafts; twelve Kanpon three-drum water-tube boilers
Speed:	34.5 knots (designed); 34.8 knots (actual)
Range (designed):	7000nm @ 14 knots; 1400 tons oil fuel
Range (actual):	6000nm @ 14 knots; 1010 tons oil fuel
Protection (side):	3in NVNC external 9° slope (engineering spaces only); intended immune zone against USN 6in/53 between 12,000m–15,000m
Protection (horiz):	1.33in NVNC (over engineering spaces)
Protection (torp):	Shallow, unarmoured bulge below belt armour; 0.4in HTS torpedo bulkhead inboard
Armament (main):	6 x 20cm/50 3rd Year Type 1 (3 x 2 – two forward and one aft)
Armament (AA):	4 x 12cm/45 Type 3 (4 x 1); 2 x 7.7mm/87 Lewis gun (2 x 1)
Armament (torp):	12 x 61cm (6 x 2)
Aircraft:	1 (1 x Nakajima E2N Type 15 reconnaissance seaplane)[65]

Between 1931 and 1933, *Furutaka* and *Kako* went through refits during which their 8cm AA guns were replaced by the newer 12cm model and they were fitted with catapults for their aircraft. Between 1936 and 1939, they underwent more substantial rebuilds that saw the replacement of their single gunhouses with twin turrets similar to their half-sisters.

Chapter 5

Treaty Cruisers – The First Generation: 1922–1926

No sooner had the ink dried on the Washington Treaty than the navies of every one of the signatories began pushing their respective design bureaux to come up with plans for the optimal 'treaty maximum' cruiser. It would not be an easy task. It was not that there was anything particularly extreme about the specific limits chosen at Washington – 8in maximum main-battery gun calibre and 10,000 tons standard displacement – it is just that, whatever numbers had been chosen, it would be a significant technical challenge to design a ship that combined hitting power, speed, endurance and survivability in a hull with a strict tonnage limit. (The designers of capital ships had a somewhat easier task because they could generally sacrifice speed in order to gain firepower and protection; a cruiser's designer did not have that luxury.)

A Five-Way Tie?

The British were the first to lay down and complete 'treaty-maximum' cruisers, but their advantage was in some cases only a few months, so there was little significance in this case to being first. What is of much greater interest is to examine the paths taken in each nation to define the characteristics of these first-generation 'treaty maximum' cruisers and the energy with which each nation set about building these still highly experimental vessels.

Probably the first to act formally on their need for a 'treaty maximum' cruiser were the Japanese, followed almost immediately by the French. As noted above, the Japanese Navy Minister, Admiral Kato Tomosaburo, who as of 12 June 1922 had become Prime Minister, outlined a new naval construction programme on 3 July 1922 that included four 10,000-ton 'treaty maximum' cruisers.[1] The task of designing these ships fell automatically to the Design Section (Fourth Section) of the Navy Technical Department, headed by Chief Constructor Hiraga.

The French followed the lead of the Japanese only three days later, producing a staff requirement for no fewer than twenty-one 'treaty maximum' cruisers on 6 July.[2] These ships were to be fast enough to escape from any stronger ship that might be encountered while carrying out their scouting or trade protection duties – the STCN was instructed to design a ship that could outrun any existing (or planned) battlecruiser in the navy of any potential enemy (meaning, in this case, Great Britain or Japan, because Italy had no battlecruisers), in particular HMS *Hood*'s announced 31-knot top speed, placing a clear emphasis on speed as the most important characteristic in the design criteria.[3]

In February of that year, when the Washington Treaty was signed, the Royal Navy's assessment of its immediate need for cruisers was sanguine, given that, in addition to the numerous war-production cruisers still in service, a significant number of late-war light and 'colonial' cruisers were either newly-delivered or still under construction.[4] However, this feeling of self-satisfaction lasted only a short while as, in June 1922, the Assistant Chief of the Naval Staff (ACNS) delivered a report noting that, due to the strain of war duty, in approximately ten years a large proportion of the Royal Navy's cruiser force would approach obsolescence *en bloc*. He went on to note how difficult replacing so many cruisers at the same time would be in terms of both physical infrastructure (shipyards and skilled workforce) and financial feasibility (budgetary constraints). Therefore, the ACNS strongly recommended a planned programme of cruiser replacement starting sooner rather than later.[5] Acting on this recommendation, and taking impetus from the unfortunate loss of the brand-new 'colonial' cruiser HMS *Raleigh*, which ran aground in fog at Point Amour, Labrador on 8 August 1922 and was irrecoverable, the Royal Navy Controller in October asked DNC to produce a design for a 'treaty maximum' cruiser, with endurance sufficient to allow operations on patrol for a distance of between 1920nm and 2300nm from Singapore (to points near Hong Kong and Japan) at 16 knots, with five days on patrol before returning, all without refuelling (a total endurance therefore of approximately 6500nm at 16 knots) and a top speed of 33 knots.[6] In mid-1923, the Royal Navy's Director of Plans, looking to have a seventy-cruiser fleet in place by 1929, of which ten could be overage ships held in reserve, proposed a building programme that would see the laying down of eight new 'treaty maximum' cruisers in each of the next three years and four per year on a steady basis thereafter.[7]

The United States Navy had no such difficulties about resolving its need for additional cruisers. The construction of some of the ten authorised *Omaha* class light cruisers had been suspended for the duration of the Washington Conference – but that work resumed as soon as the conference concluded. The US Navy's General Board had been looking at larger cruisers to follow after the *Omaha*s, specifically thinking in terms of countering the Royal Navy's *Hawkins* class 'colonial' cruisers. In May 1922, the General Board called for sixteen new 'treaty maximum' cruisers, with eight of them to be authorised and funded in FY1924, which would have required Congressional action well before the start of 1923.[8]

The Japanese heavy cruiser *Haguro* of the *Myoko* class is seen fitting out at the Mitsubishi yard in Nagasaki on 6 April 1929. The *Myoko*s were essentially enlarged *Aoba*s, bigger by almost 3000 tons, lengthened by 50ft and mounting two more main-battery turrets. In this view, *Haguro* is very nearly complete; she would be commissioned before the month was out. This photograph was taken by an American naval officer on a destroyer tender making a port visit. Such visits, by all navies, were always an opportunity for an officer with a camera to help out his naval intelligence department. (NHHC)

That left only the Italians unaccounted for. Their traditional enemies were the Austrians and the French; the former had been reduced by their recent defeat to a non-threat, while the French were, in theory at least, an ally. The British were a potential adversary, with a strong interest in maintaining a naval presence in the Mediterranean. (In late 1922, Mussolini had just begun to consolidate power in Italy and Italian foreign relations were not yet as openly – and cynically – anti-democratic as they would soon become. The interest of the *Regia Marina* at this point, particularly after the conclusion of the Washington Conference, was to maintain parity with the French.) The Italians hesitated only long enough to ascertain that the French were indeed proceeding with their 'treaty-maximum' cruiser programme and they too followed along the same lines. Without the need to support colonial outposts stretching around the world, the Italian designers were given design criteria that put more emphasis on firepower and protection than on range.[9]

Building on a Solid Foundation: The *Myoko* Class

In June 1922, Chief Constructor Hiraga was promoted to the rank of Rear Admiral; there was a strong suspicion that, at least in part, this was done in an attempt to remove him from direct involvement in the design process of the new 'treaty-

maximum' cruisers. This was only partially successful. The original planning for the design and development of these ships had followed a normal process that began towards the end of 1922. It saw the Naval General Staff providing the Design Section with a list of requirements that included: 1) a main battery of eight 20cm guns in twin turrets to be arranged three forward and one aft; 2) an AA battery of four 12cm single mounts; 3) eight fixed torpedo tubes at the Upper Deck level; 4) armour protection against 'direct' hits by 6in shells and 'indirect' hits by 8in shells; 5) anti-torpedo protection in the form of a wide bulge below the waterline armour belt in way of the engineering spaces; 6) a top speed of 35.5 knots; 6) endurance of 10,000nm at 13.5 knots; and 7) equipment to stow, launch and recover two reconnaissance aircraft.[10]

Rear Admiral Hiraga studied these requirements and offered a counter-proposal that he believed addressed the most significant issues raised by the staff requirements. He proposed: 1) adding a fifth 8in main-battery turret aft for a more balanced weight distribution; 2) adding an armoured bulkhead inboard of the anti-torpedo bulge for greater protection; 3) reducing the endurance to 8000nm at 13.5 knots, because IJN strategic doctrine at this time called for the interception of the American fleet approaching Japan within the arc of the Bonin and Marianas Islands; and 4) the elimination of the torpedo tubes because the torpedo warheads represented a serious danger stored in a lightly-protected part of the ship and because the latest model 24in torpedo (Type 8 No 2) was so nose-heavy as to be impossible to launch from the height above the water proposed in the staff requirements.[11] The Naval General Staff reacted positively to the first two of Hiraga's proposed changes, but was less than pleased with his resistance on the other points. (The problem with Hiraga's resistance on any point of a design was his stubborn refusal to compromise; if he believed he was correct on an issue within his realm of competence, he would simply refuse to be budged. He had become so notorious among the naval leadership for his stubbornness that he had acquired the nickname 'Fuyuzuru', a play on his first name – Yuzuru – and on the Japanese word 'Fukutsu', meaning 'persistence'.[12])

The Japanese system of governance tended to avoid confrontation, preferring to reach decisions by consensus, so that a stubborn individual in a relatively minor position in the power structure could wield outsized influence, which was true in this case. Where someone in Hiraga's position in any other navy would have simply been overruled, ignored or even dismissed, in Japan he was often able to have his way; although the design work was done by Fujimoto, it was under Hiraga's close supervision. A design with the following specifications was presented to the Naval General Staff on 18 May 1923:

10,000-ton 'A' Class Cruiser

Displacement (std):	10,000 tons
Power plant:	130,000shp
Speed:	35.5 knots (designed)
Range (designed):	8000nm @ 13.5 knots
Armament (main):	10 x 20cm/50 3rd Year Type 1 (5 x 2 – three forward (middle turret superfiring) and two aft)
Armament (AA):	4 x 12cm/45 (4 x 1)
Aircraft:	2[13]

The debate over this submission was sometimes contentious, but Hiraga was true to his reputation for stubbornness, and the design that was approved for construction on 25 August was essentially unchanged. However, entrenched power structures are difficult for a solitary crusader to defeat in the end. Finally, in October 1923, the Naval General Staff got its way; Hiraga was sent on an extended trip to the United States and Europe, ostensibly to learn first-hand the latest construction methods in use overseas, but in reality to facilitate his replacement as head of the Design Section of the Navy Technical Department by the much more compliant Commander Fujimoto.[14] Because of the devastation caused by the Great Kanto Earthquake of September 1923, the laying down of the first of the class of 'treaty maximum' cruisers was delayed; Hiraga was unable to witness the laying down of *Myoko* at Yokosuka Navy Yard on 25 October 1923.

Ashigara, another of the *Myoko* class 'treaty maximum' cruisers, is seen at anchor off Tsingtao in 1938. Significant changes have been made during the course of a reconstruction that had been ongoing in four discrete stages since November 1934. The most noticeable of these was the addition of a large shelter deck, wider than the original Main Deck, added between her after funnel and turret No 4 on which were mounted two catapults (where she previously had one) and two of the four new twin 12.7cm/40 Type 89 HA guns that replaced the previous heavy AA battery. The mounts on each side were supported by a Type 91 HA fire-control director located either side of the rebuilt, enlarged bridge structure and a separate 14ft 9in Type 89 or Type 91 HA rangefinder visible just forward of her after funnel. She has a Type 94 main-battery DCT atop her forward superstructure. (NHHC)

No sooner was Hiraga overseas – he did not return for almost three years – than pressure was put on Fujimoto by the individual interest sections of the naval establishment, each promoting its own agenda. The Torpedo Branch managed to persuade Fujimoto to re-introduce the eight 24in fixed torpedo tubes, exactly the mounts that Hiraga had successfully suppressed, and the General Staff ordered the increase of the AA battery from four to six 12cm single mounts, which Fujimoto also approved. When it was discovered that fitting the torpedo tubes into the Middle Deck area above the engineering spaces significantly reduced berthing space for the crew, a broad deckhouse was added in way of the bridge and fore funnel to accommodate the displaced men. The foremost pair of AA guns was sited one deck higher than the others, on top of this deckhouse. The pressure to increase the weaponry carried by these ships continued; in 1925, Fujimoto agreed to the increase in the torpedo battery from eight tubes to twelve by substituting triple fixed tubes for the planned twin mounts.[15] A second pair of cruisers to this design, funded the following year, was laid down early in 1924.

With all the added armament, it is not surprising that these ships ended up overweight. What is surprising is how much overweight they ended up. The best analysis seems to indicate that the added armament and shelter deck accounted for at least one-third of the 980 tons by which they exceeded the target of 10,000 tons standard displacement.[16] The rest is harder to account for; what seems certain is that it was not intentional on the part of Hiraga and Fujimoto, because these ships rode deeper in the water than designed, and suffered lower endurance and less stability than planned because of their chronic overweight condition. Their 'as-built' specifications are as follows:

'A' Class Cruisers: Myoko Class

Displacement (std):	10,000 tons (designed); 10,980 tons (actual)
Length (oa):	668ft 6in
Beam (max):	62ft 4in
Draft (mean):	16ft 6in (designed); 20ft 5in (actual)
Power plant:	130,000shp; Kanpon geared turbines driving four shafts; twelve Kanpon three-drum water-tube boilers
Speed:	35.5 knots (designed); 35.2 knots (actual)
Range (designed):	8000nm @ 14 knots; 2470 tons oil fuel
Range (actual):	6600nm @ 14 knots; 1650 tons oil fuel
Protection (side):	4in NVNC external 12° slope (from Middle Deck in way of engineering spaces only; from Lower Deck in way of main-battery magazines)
Protection (horiz):	1.33in NVNC (over engineering spaces at Middle Deck level); 1.33in NVNC (over magazines at Lower Deck level)
Protection (torp):	Unarmoured bulge below belt armour with max width of 8ft 2.5in; curved anti-torpedo bulkhead 2.28in HTS inboard of bulge; vertical anti-torpedo bulkhead of 1in–0.33in HTS above bulge extending to armoured deck; inner splinter bulkhead of thin HTS from armoured deck to double bottom
Armament (main):	10 x 20cm/50 3rd Year Type 1 (5 x 2 – three forward (middle turret superfiring) and two aft)
Armament (AA):	6 x 12cm/45 Type 3 (6 x 1); 2 x 7.7mm/87 Lewis gun (2 x 1)
Armament (torp):	12 x 61cm (4 x 3); 12 reloads
Aircraft:	2 (2 x Nakajima E2N Type 15 reconnaissance seaplane), one catapult[17]

In many ways, the derivation of the *Myoko*s from the preceding *Furutaka*s was obvious. The large, centralised bridge structure of the earlier class became even larger in the *Myoko*s, because this class was specifically designed to serve as squadron flagships, and two of them – *Myoko* and *Ashigara* – were additionally fitted out to serve as fleet flagships, with the commensurate bridge space that these duties would require. The fire-control outfit was intended to be identical to the *Furutakas*, but as they were being completed, separate AA director equipment was coming into service and provision was made to mount a Type 89 14.76ft HA rangefinder with its associated computer on either side of the after funnel.

Each of the ships of this class was taken in hand for reconstruction between November 1934 and February 1935. (This first reconstruction of the *Myoko*s was actually done in four discrete stages with short intervals in between, but for all intents, it was as if they were under refit through June 1936.[18]) The changes carried out during these extensive reconstructions included the replacement of the main-battery guns with 20cm/50 3rd Year Type 2 guns which had an actual bore diameter of 203mm, which is exactly 8in. These guns fired a heavier shell (277.4lb v 242.5lb AP shell), but required a completely redesigned magazine and shell and powder hoist arrangement. The existing AA battery was removed, as were the fixed torpedo tubes. The six 12cm/45 single-mount AA guns were replaced by four 12.7cm/40 Type 89 twin mounts, with their associated Type 91 directors, which were mounted one each port-and-starboard abreast the after funnel and at the Upper Bridge Deck level of the forward superstructure. The main-battery fire-control suite was upgraded piece-by-piece; it now comprised a Type 94 director (*hoiban*), a Type 92 *sokutekiban* and, in a newly-created below-decks Main Commanding Room, a Type 92 low-angle (LA) fire-control computer (*shagekiban*), all now linked to a newly-fitted 19.7ft Type 14 rangefinder mounted above the director top.[19] The torpedo tubes were replaced by a single trainable quadruple mount port-and-starboard at the main deck level with a full set of reloads (sixteen Type 90 torpedoes in total). A small hull blister was added above the existing anti-torpedo bulge.

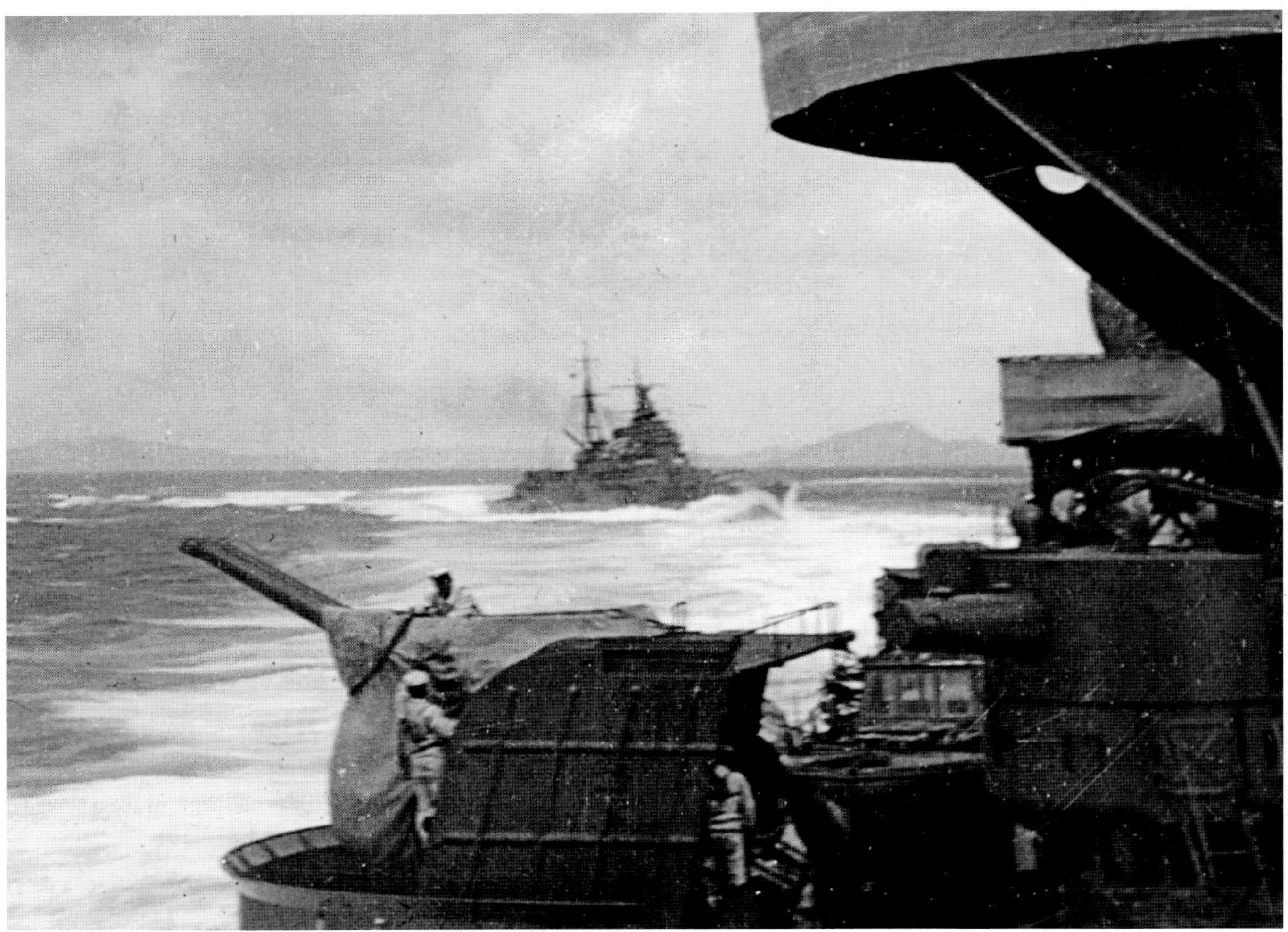

This image shows *Haguro* in the background, as seen from one of her sister-ships, manoeuvring at high speed, sometime during 1937. What makes this image interesting is the detail it shows of the starboard after 12.7cm/40 Type 89 HA mount abreast the after funnel and the associated 14ft 9in HA rangefinder in its cylindrical housing with the electrical cables coming out of the top that carry range data to the director at middle-bridge-deck level of the forward superstructure. (NHHC)

Looking Off into the Distance: The *Duquesne* Class

When the STCN was given the task of designing a 'treaty maximum' cruiser to follow after the *Duguay-Trouin* class, they had one advantage that perhaps other nations' designers did not. They knew that at least one task often on the list of a cruiser's duties, leading destroyer attacks and protecting the fleet from enemy destroyer attacks, would not need to be handled by this new ship. The flotilla leader role would be filled by a newly-conceived class of large destroyers – some considered them to be almost small cruisers – called *contre-torpilleurs*. Off-loading this role freed the designers of the new ships to concentrate on those duties of a cruiser that required speed and great endurance, such as fleet scouting, trade protection and colonial station-keeping. They had another advantage in that they had just completed the *Duguay-Trouin* class design, with which they were generally pleased, so they had an agreed-upon starting point from which to work.

The Naval General Staff (*État-major général de la Marine*) determined that, even with the addition of the three *Duguay-Trouins*, the *Marine Nationale* need twenty-one additional 'treaty maximum' cruisers.[20] In its proposal to construct these new cruisers, the staff assessment stated that the general requirements and characteristics of the new cruisers would not differ radically from those already defined for the *Duguay-Trouins*. The additional 2000 tons would be taken up providing the larger guns (203mm v 155mm) and associated turrets, barbettes and the larger hull and other support structures the new cruisers would require.

The staff requirement delivered to the STCN on 6 July 1922 was as follows:

French naval might, new and old, seen at Villefranche along the Mediterranean coast, probably in 1938. To the left is the old battleship *Courbet*, launched in 1912, reconstructed in the 1930s, but still an exemplar of obsolescent warship technology. In the foreground is the *contre-torpilleur Vauban*, one of the *Guépard* class 'super-destroyers'; these were the ships, particularly the *Guépard* class and their follow-ons armed with 138.6mm/40 Mle 1923 guns, making them for all intents small cruisers, that inspired the Italian *'Condottieri'*. In the right background is one of the *Duguay-Trouin* class light cruisers, now fitted with the large DCT atop her foremast. (NHHC)

10,000-ton Croiseur Léger (July 1922)[21]

Displacement (std):	10,000 tons
Range (designed):	5000nm @ 15 knots
Armament (main):	8 x 203mm (in three or four lightly-armoured turrets)
Armament (AA):	4 x 100mm (4 x 1)
Armament (torp):	8 x 550mm (2 x 4)
Armament (ASW):	4 x 24cm Thornycroft AS mortars (4 x 1)[22]

These instructions neglected to mention the inclusion of aircraft and left the issue of ship speed up in the air; the instructions to the STCN on that matter were that the staff wanted to see two sketch designs – one for ship with no protection beyond extensive watertight compartmentation and a second with 2 knots less speed and whatever weight was saved by reducing the speed put into vertical and horizontal protection. The more the naval staff thought about this set of requirements, the less they liked them, thinking them inadequate in AA weaponry and concerned about the lack of aircraft for scouting. To remedy these problems, a new set of staff requirements was generated in November 1922; to compensate for the added weight of the new equipment, the STCN was instructed to substitute triple torpedo tubes for the quadruple tubes previously specified:

10,000-ton Croiseur Léger (November 1922)

Displacement (std):	10,000 tons
Range (designed):	5000nm @ 15 knots
Armament (main):	8 x 203mm (in three or four lightly-armoured turrets)
Armament (AA):	8 x 100mm (8 x 1); 8 x 40mm (8 x 1); 12 x 8mm machine guns (12 x 1)
Armament (torp):	6 x 550mm (2 x 3)
Armament (ASW):	4 x 24cm Thornycroft AS mortars (4 x 1)
Aircraft:	1 (with trainable compressed-air catapult)[23]

The first French 'treaty maximum' cruisers were the two ships of the *Duquesne* class; this image shows *Tourville* at Melbourne in 1929 on her first 'round-the-world' trip. The rangefinder on her bridge was a 16ft 5in SOM coincidence rangefinder in a weatherproof housing. She has not yet had the large DCT fitted to her foremast. The HA directors intended for placement on her bridge wings were also not yet ready, leaving these ships with a somewhat bare appearance. The three 'cross-shaped' projections above the CAMS 37A aircraft on her catapult are from a three-masted sailing ship in the distance behind her. (SLV/AGC)

Quick calculations by the STCN showed that this ship could not be built without exceeding the 10,000-ton limit by at least 200 tons. (The 'sacrifice' of two torpedo tubes proved to have marginal impact.) Only by significant reduction in power – and consequently in speed – or by reducing the armament could the Washington displacement limit be met. The staff agreed to allow the replacement of the 100mm AA guns with the 75mm/50 Mle 1924 and the newly-developed 37mm/50 Mle 1925 in the place of the 40mm, but these also produced only minimal weight savings. The anti-submarine mortars were deleted (for the time being), which again produced only minor savings. Protection was only slightly greater than that in the *Duguay-Trouin*s, an internal 'box' of approximately 1.2in armour around each of the main-battery magazines and a similar 0.7in 'box' around the steering compartment. The STCN recommended that 2 knots of speed be sacrificed – from 34 knots to 32 knots – to gain some protection for the engineering spaces, but this was rejected by the naval staff. The final specifications were as follows:

Duquesne Class Croiseurs Légers

Displacement (std):	10,000 tons
Length (oa):	626ft 8in
Beam:	62ft 4in
Draft:	20ft 9in
Power plant:	120,000shp; Rateau-Bretagne geared turbines driving four shafts; eight Guyot du Temple boilers
Speed:	34 knots (designed); 33.25 knots (actual)
Range (designed):	5000nm @ 15 knots; 1842 tons oil fuel
Protection (side):	1.2in (main-battery magazines); 0.7in (steering compartment)
Protection (horiz):	0.75in (deck plating over main-battery magazines and steering compartment)
Armament (main):	8 x 203mm/50 Mle 1924 (4 x 2 – two forward and two aft)
Armament (AA):	8 x 75mm/50 Mle 1924 (8 x 1); 8 x 37mm Mle 1925 (8 x 1)
Armament (torp):	6 x 550mm Mle 1923D (2 x 3); 3 reloads
Aircraft:	2 (2 x CAMS 37A); one trainable compressed-air catapult[24]

Funding for two ships to this design was approved towards the end of 1924. The order for the lead ship, to be named *Duquesne*, went to Arsenal de Brest, where she was laid down on 30 October 1924. Both were completed in early 1929.

They were to have a fire-control suite similar to the preceding *Duguay-Trouin*s. In similar fashion, the large foretop DCT was not ready when the ships were completed and had to be fitted later. One difference from the earlier model was that the main DCT had a 16ft 5in coincidence rangefinder for primary rangetaking. They were to have a similarly-sized rangefinder on the conning tower in a weatherproof trainable

On the same cruise that took her to Melbourne, *Tourville* transited the Panama Canal on 1 May 1929. While in the Gatun Locks, at the Atlantic entrance to the canal, US Navy intelligence took advantage of the opportunity to take a series of detailed images of the new ship as she passed through. In this view, details of the forward main-battery turrets, each with two 203mm/50 Mle 1924 guns can be seen, as well as the weatherproof rangefinder atop her conning tower. The weatherproofing was a prudent precaution; as can be seen in this and the next images, it has apparently just finished raining. The officers all came prepared for the tropical weather, decked out in their white uniforms and pith helmets. (NHHC)

housing, but these were also not ready upon completion; they were temporarily given earlier models. Turrets II and III had trainable armoured hoods on top enclosing 16ft 5in rangefinders; these could rotate through 15° either side of the turret axis, allowing them to track a target while the turret was offset for deflection. These ships had a Mle 1924 fire-control computer in their plotting room. High-angle fire-control directors were to be fitted at completion but were not ready for placement on the bridge wings until the mid-1930s.[25]

Another view of *Tourville*'s forward main battery and bridge, taken from higher up, shows good detail of 16ft 5in rangefinder inside its armoured hood on the roof of Turret II. This was the early, fixed version of the turret rangefinder; a later refit gave them a larger hood which allowed the rangefinder to deflect up to 15° either side of the turret axis. Note the aerial recognition marking, the letter 'T', painted in black on the turret and on the rangefinder hood. Note also the textured pattern of the decking, clearly intended to provide some skid-resistance when the deck gets wet, as it is here. (NHHC)

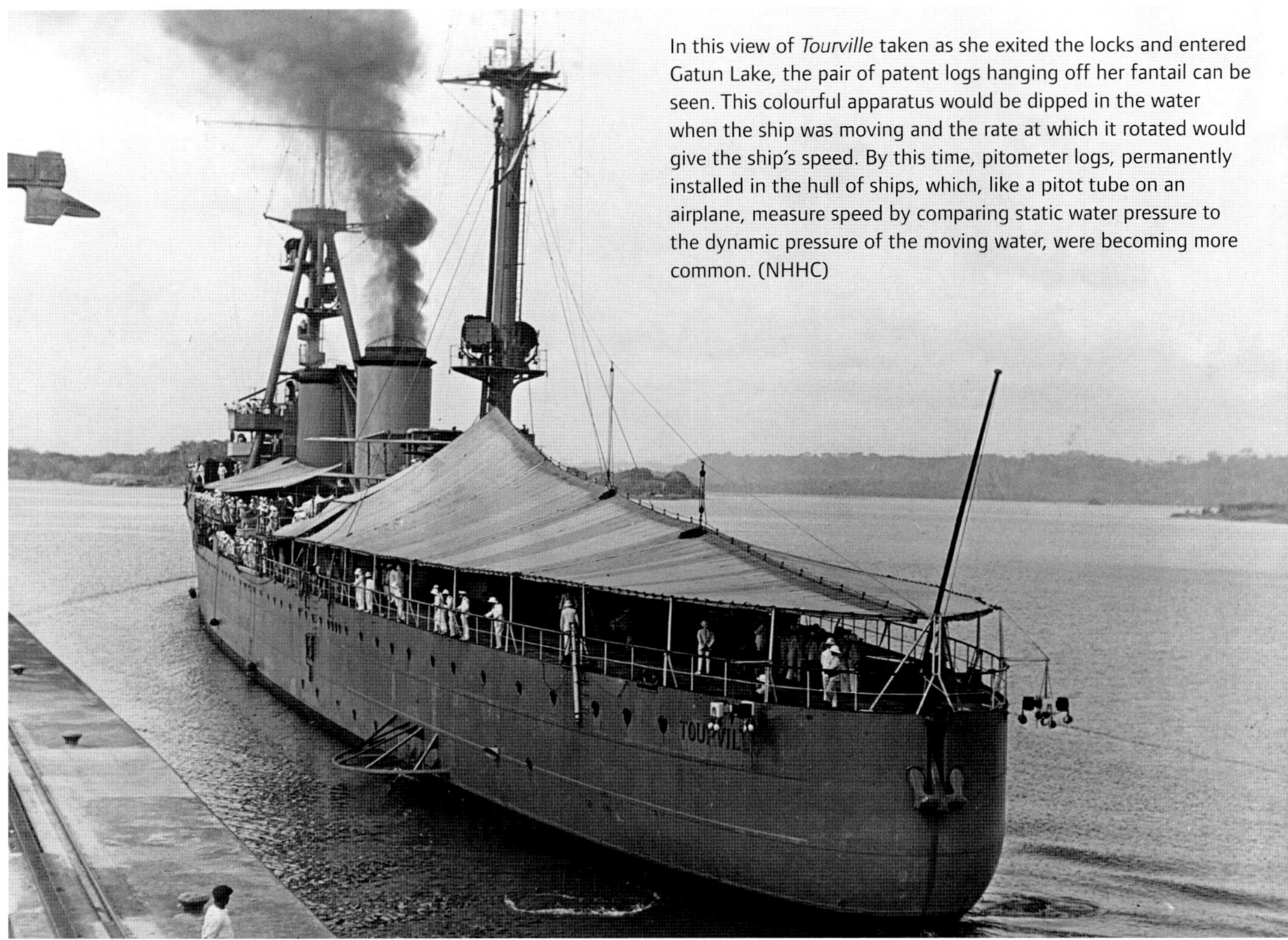

In this view of *Tourville* taken as she exited the locks and entered Gatun Lake, the pair of patent logs hanging off her fantail can be seen. This colourful apparatus would be dipped in the water when the ship was moving and the rate at which it rotated would give the ship's speed. By this time, pitometer logs, permanently installed in the hull of ships, which, like a pitot tube on an airplane, measure speed by comparing static water pressure to the dynamic pressure of the moving water, were becoming more common. (NHHC)

Both were modified somewhat in the mid-1930s. Splinter shields were added to the 75mm mounts, and four of the 37mm mounts were relocated to make room for an equal number of 37mm Hotchkiss twin mounts.

Something Completely Different: The *Kent* Class

Eustace Tennyson d'Eyncourt, who had succeeded Phillip Watts as DNC in 1912, was busy on the *Nelson* class design, so he turned the 'treaty maximum' cruiser project over to one of his assistants, Charles S Lillicrap. DNC made it quite clear to Lillicrap that he was not to base his design on that of the *Hawkins* class. Indeed, none of the designs for the cruisers the Royal Navy was then still building were considered adequate to serve as a model for the next cruiser that Great Britain needed.

The path by which the Royal Navy had reached this point was a remarkably straight line. It appears that, at no point in the immediate aftermath of the Washington Conference, did the British seriously consider building anything other than a 'treaty maximum' cruiser as a follow-on to those ships currently completing.[26] In Admiralty Board discussions, the examples of American and Japanese plans for 'treaty maximum' cruisers were regularly raised as sufficient grounds to explain the British need for ships of similar capability. An early 1923 staff estimate pointed to the possibility of Japanese cruisers raiding British trade routes as justification for a recommendation that the Royal Navy should build seventeen '10,000 ton light cruisers as soon as possible'.[27] This estimate was revisited later in 1923; at that time, the Director of Plans calculated the need for seventy cruisers and set forth the highly optimistic plan to lay down eight 'treaty maximum' cruisers per year for three years starting in 1924. Following this plan, he calculated, the Royal Navy would possess fifty-nine cruisers by 1929. From that total, thirty-one would be required for fleet work, leaving only twenty-eight for trade defence, eleven fewer than he thought necessary.[28]

The directions Tennyson d'Eyncourt gave to Charles Lillicrap on 2 November 1922 were a combination of extremely specific and quite general.[29] Lillicrap was told to make maximum structural use of high-tensile-strength steel in

Part of the pressure on the Royal Navy to start building new 'treaty maximum' cruisers, despite still having many relatively new war-built light cruisers, came from the loss of one of their newest and best cruisers when HMS *Raleigh* grounded off Point Amour, Labrador, on 8 August 1922. She was moving at high speed through the Belle Isle Strait when she ran hard aground, so well wedged-up on the rocky shore that no amount of pulling could drag her off. She remained there, relatively intact, for four years, an acute embarrassment to the Royal Navy, before the hulk was stripped and blown up. (NHHC)

order to lighten the hull structure. Armament was to be 8in guns, preferably in four twin turrets, although Lillicrap was encouraged to explore alternatives such as triple turrets and an all-forward main-battery turret grouping as had been adopted for the 'G3'/*Nelson* design. Space for two aircraft with hangar protection was desirable. Speed was to be 33–34 knots. The only specific mention of protection in Lillicrap's instructions was to provide the new cruiser with an anti-torpedo bulge and, if there was displacement to spare, deck armour over the steering gear and magazines.

As work on the design proceeded, it became clear that not everything on DNC's wishlist could be accommodated in 10,000 tons. In January 1923, Lillicrap was given an additional list of instructions that further narrowed his design options. The power plant of the new cruiser was to be limited to 100,000shp, which would drive a ship of 10,000 tons standard displacement at an optimal maximum speed of 32 knots. The engineering spaces were to be given protection against splinters and small-calibre fire by a thin, shallow armour belt, while the magazines were to get a more substantial protective box capable of defeating cruiser-grade gunfire.[30] After working out the weights of the hull structure, power plant, armament and other equipment, Lillicrap calculated that he had 830 tons to devote to protection. By July, therefore, he had a sketch design on the table that had 2in of belt armour in way of the magazines and engineering spaces, with a deck that varied between 1in and 2in over these spaces and the steering gear. Lillicrap argued strongly against this scheme, stating that it spread the protection too thinly over too large an area, and that it would fail to protect against destroyer gunfire at any range or bombs from any altitude. He wanted instead to concentrate thicker armour around the magazines and leave the engineering spaces to all intents unprotected. He must have been persuasive, because this is essentially the scheme that was adopted.

In October, the Admiralty Board was offered alternatives that would have provided a 33-knot ship with six or eight guns in the main battery or an eight-gun ship with more endurance and more rounds per gun but a top speed of only 31 knots. The Board chose the slower alternative, with the proviso that some of the weight saved in reducing the size of the power plant (from 100,000shp to 75,000shp) be put back into providing marginal side armour in way of the engineering spaces. With this final touch, the sketch design was approved by the First Sea Lord at the beginning of November and complete specifications were approved by the Admiralty Board on 13 December 1923.[31]

That left the issue of finding the money to pay for them.

HMAS *Canberra* (D33), one of the *Kent* class 'treaty-maximum' cruisers, is seen quite early in her career, before 1932 when a crane for handling her aircraft and boats was added alongside her after funnel and a protective hood was added to the rangefinder on her after superstructure. This image shows her riding high in the water, which allows the top of the anti-torpedo bulge under her narrow waterline armour belt to be seen. Note the large, two-level spotting and fire-control position, topped by a shielded rangefinder, located atop her bridge. Note also the aircraft platform, not yet fitted with a catapult, abaft her after funnel. (SLV/AGC)

On the occasion of the conclusion of the 1923 Imperial Conference, at which only the Australians showed any strong inclination to contribute in any meaningful way to the post-war sustainment of the Royal Navy, the Admiralty Board submitted its 1924 Naval Estimates to the Cabinet.[32] As proposed by the Director of Plans, the original submission called for eight new cruisers, along with other ships, but this was more than the newly-elected Labour-led government would tolerate. The Admiralty Board approved the proposal for eight cruisers on 21 November 1923, but it never had a chance of winning Cabinet approval. Beatty countered with a proposal for four cruisers in 1924 and five the following year, if the shortfall was made up later; Ramsay MacDonald, the new Prime Minister, concerned about unemployment in Scotland and the North Country, where most of Great Britain's private shipyards were located, eventually submitted a bill for five cruisers to Parliament in February 1924.[33] The Australians, true to their word, agreed to build two more, which were ordered from the John Brown yard, Clydebank, the following year. The as-built specifications of the *Kent* class cruisers were:

Kent Class

Displacement (std):	10,000 tons; 13,810 tons (deep)
Length (oa):	630ft
Beam (max):	68ft 4in
Draft (mean):	20ft 6in (actual)
Power plant:	80,000shp; Parsons or Brown-Curtis geared turbines driving four shafts; eight Admiralty three-drum water-tube boilers
Speed:	31.5 knots (std); 30.5 knots (deep)
Range (designed):	8000nm @ 12 knots; 3424 tons oil fuel
Protection (side):	1in Ducol external shell plating (in way of engineering spaces only); 4in KNC (side plating in armoured box citadel around main-battery magazines)[34]
Protection (horiz):	1.25in Ducol (over engineering spaces at Middle Deck level); 2.5in KNC (crown of armoured box citadel around main-battery magazines)
Protection (torp):	Shallow unarmoured bulge below belt armour
Armament (main):	8 x 8in/50 Mk VIII (4 x 2 – two forward and two aft)
Armament (AA):	4 x 4in/45 QF Mk V (4 x 1); 4 x 2pdr Mk II pompom (4 x 1)
Armament (torp):	8 x 21in (2 x 4)
Aircraft:	1, one catapult (space provided aft of funnels, but aircraft & catapult not fitted at commissioning)[35]

These ships were laid down within a very narrow window of time; the five Royal Navy hulls were all begun between 15 September 1924, when HMS *Berwick* (65) was laid down at the Fairfield yard, Glasgow, and 15 November 1924, when HMS *Kent* (54) was started at the Chatham Dockyard. The two Australian hulls – HMAS *Australia* (D84) and *Canberra* (D33) – were laid down at the John Brown yard in August and September 1925 respectively. All seven were completed in 1928.

The ships that emerged from this arduous design process were considered highly successful on nearly all counts by the Royal Navy. Their hull, with its high freeboard and continuous Main Deck made them excellent sea boats; their relatively broad beam made them stable, so they were good gun platforms and provided comfortable accommodations for officers and crew, which made them popular in the fleet. The bridge was topped with a compact two-level tower block modelled on that fitted in HMS *Frobisher* (D81), one of the final pair of *Hawkins* class 'colonial' cruisers, nearing completion at Devonport. For the same reasons that the Japanese had tried out a large bridge structure in their experimental cruiser *Yubari*, the idea was to concentrate more of the command personnel in a central location in order to facilitate decision-making and the communication of orders. The *Kent*s were fitted with the new Admiralty Fire Control Table (AFCT) Mk II, the successor to the competing Dreyer and Pollen fire-control systems, with some features of the American Ford Rangekeeper added in.[36] The AFCT was supposed to have been driven by data from a newly-designed DCT sited on top of the tower bridge. The DCT integrated the functions of a fire-control director with a main-battery rangefinder and added in the ability to cross-level – detect and compensate for roll along the ship's long axis – and included positions for spotters and for the ship's gunnery officer so that, unlike as happened in some Royal Navy ships at Jutland, rangefinding and shell spotting would all be on the same target. Unfortunately, the first prototype DCTs were still under test, having been installed in the *Nelson*s and in the light cruiser *Enterprise* in 1926 and 1927, and production versions were not available when the *Kent*s were completing in 1928. In the place of the DCT, the *Kent*s had a two-level, box-like spotting and fire-control position atop their bridge with a combined rangefinder/director above, similar to that mounted on the conning towers of Royal Navy dreadnoughts during the war.

The main-battery mounts proved troublesome, primarily because of requirements laid down by the Admiralty Board in the wake of the Washington Conference mandating that all ship's guns, even main-battery guns, have AA capability. In the case of the new 8in/50 Mk VIII gun adopted for the *Kent* class, the Board required that these guns be able to elevate to 70° and be able to fire at a rate of 12rpm. These were extraordinary specifications for a gun of this size at this time; to give some idea of what was a more 'normal' main-battery gun specification for this time period, the 7.5in/45 Mk VI main battery in the *Hawkins* class had a maximum elevation of 30° and a rate of fire of 5–6rpm.[37] Attention must also be paid to the loading angles of the gun. Larger-calibre guns had multi-part shell and powder charges brought into the turret on separate hoists and then positioned in a loading tray in the correct order behind the gun's breech – each individual element too heavy to be manhandled – before being mechanically rammed into the firing chamber. They could only be loaded at certain angles of elevation; the 7.5in gun of the *Hawkins* class could be loaded only between -5° and +10°. If firing at a higher elevation, the gun would have to be lowered, loaded and raised again between each shot.[38]

From the first tests of the guns and their mountings, it was obvious that they would not be able to meet the board's expectations in either rate of fire or ability to track even slow-moving aircraft. Even before the *Kents* entered service, the rate-of-fire requirement had been reduced to 6rpm, but even this proved unsustainable. One time, during trials, *Kent* was able to reach 5rpm, but in practice 3–4rpm was the maximum sustainable rate. Add to that the fact that, even though the turrets were designed to elevate the guns at 10°/second and train them at 8°/second, neither of those rates were ever achieved in reality. The actual rates were slightly more than half the designed rates.[39] On 26 July 1929, HMS *Devonshire* (39), of the follow-on *London* class, suffered a catastrophic breech failure in one gun in 'X' turret during a practice shoot, igniting a shell and several powder charges in the turret, blowing the roof off the turret and killing eighteen officers and men. As late as June 1938, a report from HMS *London* (69) noted the inability to conduct a practice shoot of twenty rounds without a material failure. It is therefore not very surprising that in this gun, the Royal Navy, in Roskill's words, 'produced the least successful armaments ever fitted to British warships in modern times'.[40]

Most of the *Kent*s were modernised to some extent during the 1930s, but in nothing like the systematic fashion that the Japanese updated the *Myoko*s. All five Royal Navy *Kent*s and *Australia* had an external armour belt of 4.5in thick cemented armour (CA) added in way of the engineering spaces and transmitting station, starting above the anti-torpedo bulge and continuing down behind it. The belt was rather shallow, being just 6ft in height. The same six ships – all the *Kent*s except *Canberra* – had their bridge structures modernised. The original bridge, with its boxy fire-control tower, had proved to create a wind shadow when the ship was steaming at any speed, trapping funnel smoke. The short-term solution was to increase the height of the funnels, initially by 15ft; in the two Australian ships, the funnels were raised a further 3ft. Part of the process of modernising the bridge structure of most the *Kent*s was the removal of the fire-control tower and its rangefinder/director, replacing them with a DCT. (This appears to have been done on all the *Kent*s except HMS *Suffolk* (55) and *Canberra*.) On several of the *Kent*s, the after superstructure and rotating catapult were removed, being replaced by a fixed athwartships catapult and large hangar, so that three aircraft could be carried. All of the *Kent*s had their single

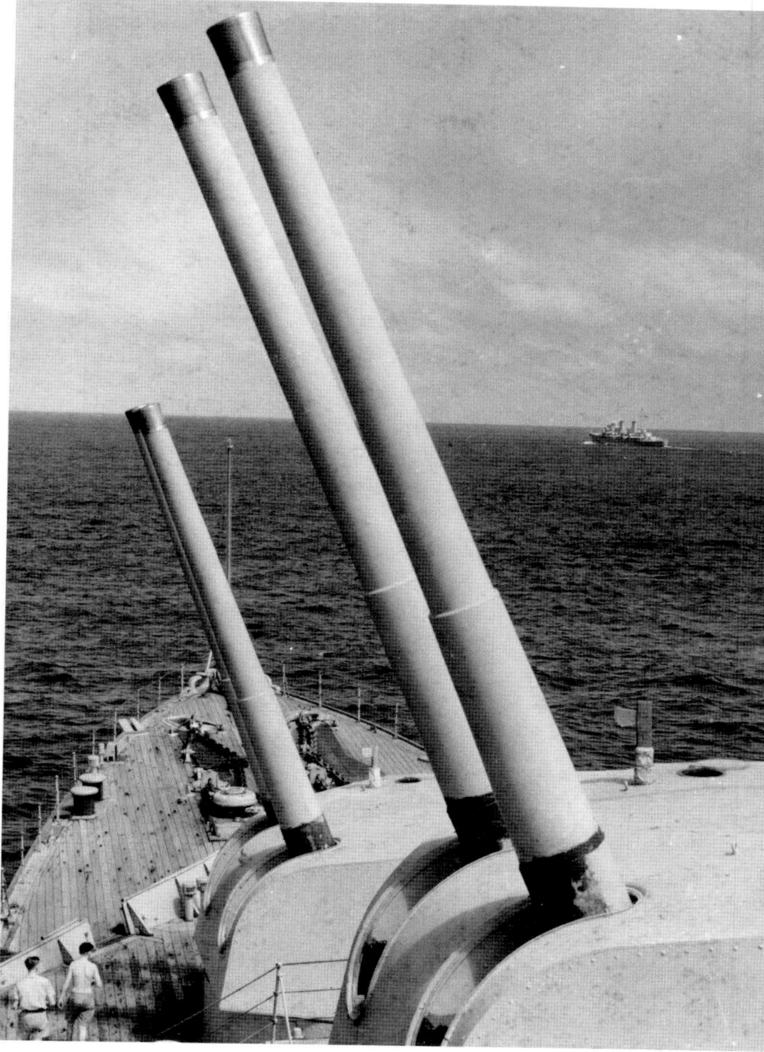

The 8in/50 Mk VIII gun, used in the *Kent* class and all of the succeeding classes of Royal Navy heavy cruisers built between the wars, was a weapon that proved troublesome from the beginning. Part of the problem was the gun itself; a breech failure caused a fatal turret explosion in HMS *Devonshire* (39) during her initial trials in 1929. Even more of the problem was with the mount, which, as can be seen here in this image of HMAS *Shropshire* (73) – she transferred to the RAN in late 1942 to make up for the loss of *Canberra* – allowed the main-battery guns to elevate to 70° and be used, theoretically, as AA guns. HMAS *Hobart* (D63) can be seen in the background. (SLV/AGC)

4in/45 Mk V AA mounts replaced by twin Mk XVI mounts and the single 2pdr pompoms replaced by quadruple or, in some cases, octuple mounts.

To find the weight for all these additions, two of the ships, *Suffolk* and HMS *Cumberland* (57), had their fantails cut down one deck aft of 'Y' turret. All ships of the class landed their

torpedo tubes. Nevertheless, most of the *Kent*s gained significant displacement during the modernisation process. When the belt armour was added to ships of this class, the intent had been that only 1ft of the belt was to extend below the waterline, but as more and more weight was added in the form of AA weapons, fire-control systems and sensors, the ships' displacement increased to the point that photographs of *Kents* taken during the Second World War rarely show more than a foot or two of the belt evident above the waterline.

Puttering Along on the Potomac: The *Pensacola* Class (CA24–CA25)

As much as the US Navy's General Board may have wanted more cruisers, the Republican-dominated, strongly isolationist Congress would not be rushed; they refused to authorise any new cruisers in the FY1924 budget.[41] On 7 April 1923, the General Board upped the ante, asking for twelve in FY1925. This time Congress moved, albeit not nearly as far or as fast as the General Board would have liked. The original eight requested cruisers were finally authorised on 18 December 1924, when Congress passed the Cruiser Act of 1924. However, money for only the first two was included in the FY1925 budget approved in early 1925.

At this point, the US Navy was far from having an agreed-upon design or even a set of characteristics for the cruiser it wanted to build with this new money. Some sketch design

Most of the *Kent*s were reconstructed in the late 1930s. One which had the most work done was HMS *Suffolk* (55), seen here emerging from a refit on the Tyne, 30 June 1942. Most of the notable changes from her original form were done in a major rebuild carried out in 1936; these included adding the large hangar topped by a HACS director in the place of her after superstructure abaft a fixed athwartships D-I-H catapult, adding AA guns, putting new armour behind the anti-torpedo bulge and cutting down the quarterdeck in partial compensation for all the added weight. The fairly short 1942 refit mainly saw the upgrading of her radars; a Type 273 microwave surface-search set in its 'lantern' was added atop the hangar and Type 281 antennas replaced the earlier Type 279s at the mastheads. (NARA)

work had begun as early as February 1919 with the intent to improve upon the design of the *Omaha*s, which were by then universally considered to be undergunned for their size.[42] The designs generated at this early stage took one of two general forms; they were either repeat *Omaha*s, only smaller and faster, or they were somewhat larger ships to be armed with a proposed 8in/50 gun. None of them, with one exception, would have been larger than approximately 8000 tons standard displacement; that exception was the sketch design labelled '*C-1*', which was for an American response to the Royal Navy's *Hawkins* class, which would have been 10,000 tons, armed with seven of the new 8in guns in a mix of twin and triple turrets and capable of 33.5 knots.

This last sketch design garnered the most interest from the General Board and served as the basis for a new series of design studies, presented in April 1921, which started with a baseline design of a cruiser with eight 8in guns in the main-battery (4 x 2), a 5in armour belt (which, together with the armoured deck, would provide an immune zone against 8in gunfire between 16,000–21,000yd), a 3in armoured deck with 4.5in sloped edges and a speed of 34 knots. This could all be packaged in a ship that displaced 12,000 tons standard.[43] Preliminary Design knew that the General Board would undoubtedly be displeased with the size of this proposed ship and offered four alternatives, each of which sacrificed one or more of the desirable features of the base design – speed, gunpower or protection. None of the proposals won the outright endorsement of the Board, but the one that got the most support was Proposal 1921-1b, which sacrificed armour while retaining most other characteristics at or near the full values in the baseline design. The design proposal was as follows:

US Navy Cruiser Proposal 1921-1b

Displacement (std):	10,000 tons
Power plant:	118,000shp
Speed:	34.5 knots
Range (designed):	10,000nm @ 10 knots
Protection (side):	1.5in (in way of engineering spaces only)
Protection (horiz):	1in horizontal; 1.5in slopes (in way of engineering spaces only)
Armament (main):	8 x 8in/50 new design (4 x 2 – two forward and two aft)
Armament (AA):	4 x 5in/25 (4 x 1)
Armament (torp)	6 x 21in (2 x 3)[44]

It was this design that the American delegation had in mind when they proposed limiting cruiser displacement and gun calibre at the Washington Conference in 1921. The end of the conference sent everyone, quite literally, back to the drawing board. The role of cruisers, in the minds of the 'greybeards' of the US Navy's General Board, suddenly got significantly more important. It may have been pure coincidence, but a number of extremely relevant events altered the US Navy's view of their needs at this time vis-à-vis a possible Pacific war. One was obviously the Washington Treaty, which, when it was signed in February 1922, had several major strategic implications for the United States. Not only would the Americans be required to abandon construction of eleven new capital ships, but they would also have to scrap seventeen older battleships. Some of those ships were obsolescent and ready for the breakers, but by no means were all of them too old to figure in the US Navy's plans for a possible war with Japan. This was particularly true because of another 'feature' of the Washington Treaty; Article XIX of the treaty specified that no new fortifications or upgrades to existing naval facilities could be made in the Pacific by any of the signatories, with the exception of the Hawai'ian Islands (and Singapore in the case of the British). This specifically prevented the Americans from upgrading the defences at Guam or the Philippines, both staging points on a trans-Pacific crossing by an American fleet. That plus the loss of critical support that the older battleships would have provided for convoy escort and shore bombardment – remember that the US Navy in 1922 possessed no cruisers other than the ten *Omahas* – forced the US Navy to conclude that neither Guam nor the Philippines was defensible in the event of war with Japan.[45]

A version of War Plan Orange, the strategic plan for the American reaction to a Japanese declaration of war (and the presumed attack on American assets in the western and central Pacific), was produced in September 1922 calling for a stepwise progression of American forces across an assumed-hostile Pacific.[46] This plan would not stand for long. Too many people in the United States military, particularly in the Army, had too much invested in the Philippines to simply let the American presence there be written off at the beginning of a war with Japan. When Harding's Navy Secretary Edwin C Denby met the Governor General of the Philippines, Major General Leonard Wood, later in 1922, the latter protested vehemently against the 'abandonment' of the Philippines, which he stated would be a 'national dishonor'.[47] Neither Denby, nor Harding, could afford to ignore his opinion. The September 1922 plan was almost immediately forgotten; by the middle of 1923, Wood was informed that a new War Plan Orange was being prepared that called for the dispatch of a large naval expedition escorting more than thirty troop transports on an uninterrupted voyage straight through from Honolulu to Manila Bay.[48] The Joint Army and Navy Board, which comprised the chiefs of staff of the US Army and Navy approved a broad outline of this new 'through ticket' plan in August 1924, with the details of this first Joint War Plan Orange being completed in January 1925.

The only problem with this plan was that the Navy did not have nearly the resources envisaged by the planners to carry out the aggressive trans-Pacific sweep it called for. The plan assumed that the fleet, amounting to over 500 ships of all kinds, would assemble in the Hawai'ian Islands within fourteen days of a declaration of war by the Japanese. On the assumption that the Philippines could hold out for 60 days until relieved, the fleet would then have less than 50 days, steaming at 10.5 knots, to cover the 5000nm between Honolulu and Manila. On paper, that may have seemed an easy task, but there were huge obstacles to overcome. First, the US Navy did not possess and could not obtain the number of ships required without long planning and significant allocation of money. Second, underway replenishment would be required and was still a relatively unproven capability.[49] Finally, at least part of that passage would undoubtedly be contested. It was at the points where the US Asian Expeditionary Force (USAEF) would pass through the relatively narrow waters between the Volcano Islands and the northernmost of the

One of the first American 'treaty maximum' cruiser was USS *Salt Lake City* (CA25, ex-CL25), seen here on 20 May 1930, in essentially as-built condition, at the Fleet Manoeuvres held off Guantanamo Bay, Cuba, with President Hoover aboard. Like most of the first generation 'treaty maximum' cruisers, she was flush-decked, but stood out for the curvature of her sheer line, designed to save weight while still providing good weather handling forward. She and her sister were unusual also in having a mix of twin and triple turrets in their main battery. (NARA)

Marianas – a gap of some 270nm and then further through the Luzon Strait between Formosa and Luzon, the northernmost of the Philippine Islands, that were identified as being where the danger of Japanese attack would be the greatest. It was at these points that old battleships and cruisers would be most sorely missed.[50]

Armed with this demonstrable shortfall in the Navy's ability to carry out the mandated strategic policy of the President and his Administration, it was, for once, not difficult to push legislation with the necessary authorisation for eight 'treaty maximum' cruisers through Congress in December 1924, nor to get funding approved for the first two. That did not, however, bring any resolution to the question of what exactly the characteristics of those ships were to be.

There simply was no consensus among the navy bureaux regarding what was the proper set of priorities for divvying up the very limited tonnage allowed in a 'treaty maximum' cruiser. The starting point of most discussions was the performance of the new 8in/55 Mk 9 main-battery gun then under development, with a projected range well in excess of 30,000yds and armour penetration exceeding that of the preceding generation of similarly-sized guns.[51] It was an axiom of warship design that a ship's protection should be sufficient to defeat its own main-battery at expected combat ranges, but this was clearly not possible in a 10,000-ton ship without unacceptable sacrifices in other qualities such as firepower (battery size), speed and endurance. (It did not help that the new American 8in gun was unusually heavy.) One faction in the Preliminary Design section argued vehemently that better catapults and shipborne aircraft, along with more reliable radio communications, made the necessity of extremely high speed (34 knots or more) unnecessary; cruisers could fulfil their scouting role without getting dangerously close to superior enemy forces. Better protection could be bought by the sacrifice of extremely high speed (opting for 32 knots instead of 34 knots could save 15 per cent–20 per cent of the weight and size of the power plant).[52]

This debate continued throughout 1923 and most of

1924. Interestingly the General Board consistently came down in favour of more lightly-protected (or even totally unprotected) high-speed designs, rather than the somewhat slower, more balanced designs. At the end of 1924, when it was realised that money would finally become available to build the first of these new cruisers, the academic debate suddenly got serious. The General Board asked for a new design, starting from the design of the *Omaha* class as a baseline. Preliminary Design was ordered to present a full series of sketch designs running the gamut from unprotected schemes optimised for high speed to well-protected schemes – immune against 6in gunfire at short range and 8in gunfire at long range – and with main batteries of between eight and twelve 8in guns. In March, the General Board selected a scheme that was in the mid-range of armament, speed and protection, which was developed into the *Pensacola* class with the following specifications:

Pensacola Class

Displacement (std):	10,000 tons (design); 11,568 tons (full load)
Length (oa):	585ft 6in
Beam (wl):	65ft 3in
Draft (mean):	19ft 6in (full load)
Power plant:	107,000shp; Parsons geared turbines driving four shafts; eight White-Forster boilers
Speed:	32.5 knots (design)
Range (designed):	10,000nm @ 15 knots; 3952 tons oil fuel
Protection (side):	2.5in STS external belt (in way of engineering spaces); 4in STS external belt (in way of main-battery magazines)[53]
Protection (horiz):	1in STS (over engineering spaces); 1.75in STS (over main-battery magazines)
Armament (main):	10 x 8in/55 Mk 9 (2 x 2 – one forward and one aft; 2 x 3 – one forward (superfiring) and one aft (superfiring))
Armament (AA):	4 x 5in/25 Mk 10 (4 x 1)
Armament (torp):	6 x 21in (2 x 3)
Aircraft:	4, two catapults[54]

The most interesting design features of the two ships of this class derive from attempts to save weight; being the originators of the limitation formulas imposed by the Washington Treaty, it clearly behoved the Americans, of all people, to abide by the letter of the law. The most obvious weight-saving feature was the sacrifice of a forecastle deck and the adoption of a curved sheer line, for similar reasons that the Japanese adopted the sinuous sheer line for *Yubari* and later cruisers; this saved significant weight and the curved sheer line similarly allowed lower freeboard amidships where it was not needed. In an attempt to make up for the lower freeboard forward due to the lack of a forecastle deck, they were given more flare at the bow than previous American designs. Because the hulls of these ships were relatively short but still were expected to maintain high sustained speed, they were given extremely fine lines fore-and-aft, especially forward.[55] This led to another unusual feature of the design. In order to mount a main battery of ten 8in guns, the designers could have opted for five twin turrets, as the Japanese did in the *Myoko* class, but that would not have been possible in such a short hull form. Instead, Preliminary Design proposed mounting two twin mounts and two newly-designed triple mounts, in superfiring pairs fore-and-aft.[56] In a case like this, the normal practice would have been to position the heavier triple mounts low and the twin mounts above them, as this would benefit stability, but this was not possible in the *Pensacola*s because of the extremely fine lines fore-and-aft; the larger barbette of the triple mount would not have fit in the narrow hull forward, forcing the designers to put the smaller twin mount on the Main Deck forward and the triple mount in the superfiring position. This pattern was reproduced aft.

Main-battery fire control in the *Pensacola*s very closely resembled that in the *Myoko*s, as completed, only mounted higher at the top of a tripod foremast. The fire-control top on the *Pensacolas*' foremast comprised two levels, both enclosed by glassed-in panels that could be lowered to improved visibility. The smaller top platform had seven panels and twelve glass ports enclosing a Mk 18 director with basic plotting capability, making it a self-contained fire-control calculator and salvo fire-controller.[57] The much larger lower level had ten drop-down panels, each with two glass ports; this level housed the spotters and enemy course detectors, performing functions very much like those done on the second and third levels of the *Myoko*s' 'pagoda mast'.

As with all of the other nations' first-generation 'treaty maximum' cruisers, the *Pensacola*s were modernised during the 1930s (and even up to 1941), though not very extensively. The modernisation took place in several stages. In the first stage, undertaken in the mid-1930s, their torpedo tubes were landed and the Mk 18 director in the foretop updated with an integrated rangefinder on top, which allowed the removal of the lower platform of the spotting top; those changes and the widening of the bilge keels from 18in to 36in was done in an attempt to alleviate a problem with snap rolling in all but the calmest seas that made the *Pensacola*s poor gun platforms.[58] This was due to excessive topweight on a lightly-constructed hull which caused them to have a high metacentre, which in turn causes a ship to be overly sensitive to wave action, particularly in cross-seas. Exacerbating the problem was the fact that the *Pensacola*s suffered from the opposite problem that affected their Japanese counterparts; they were found on completion to be almost exactly 900 tons under the target of 10,000 tons standard displacement. (It is necessary to remember that in the days before computers, ships were designed by dozens of engineers and hundreds of draftsmen armed with slide-rules, triangles and No 2 pencils. It cannot be a surprise that upon completion the calculation of the tonnage of a ship in the design phase could be off by as much as 3–5 per cent, in either direction, from the intended displacement of the ship. Even in those days, 10 per cent represented a serious error in calculation.)

Unfortunately, the problem of excessive metacentric height would not go away because the tendency was to continue adding weight high up in these ships. Major refits between 1939 and 1941 saw the cutting down of the mainmast to a stump, but any weight saved by that was more than replaced by the addition of large, heavy Mk 33 dual-purpose (DP) directors on her pilot house and mainmast and the doubling of the AA battery from four to eight 5in/25 single mounts. As more and more sensors and AA weapons were added to these ships they rode lower and lower in the water, which only served to emphasise the long curved sheer line of their weather deck; *Salt Lake City*, the second in the class, became known in the fleet as 'Swayback Maru'.

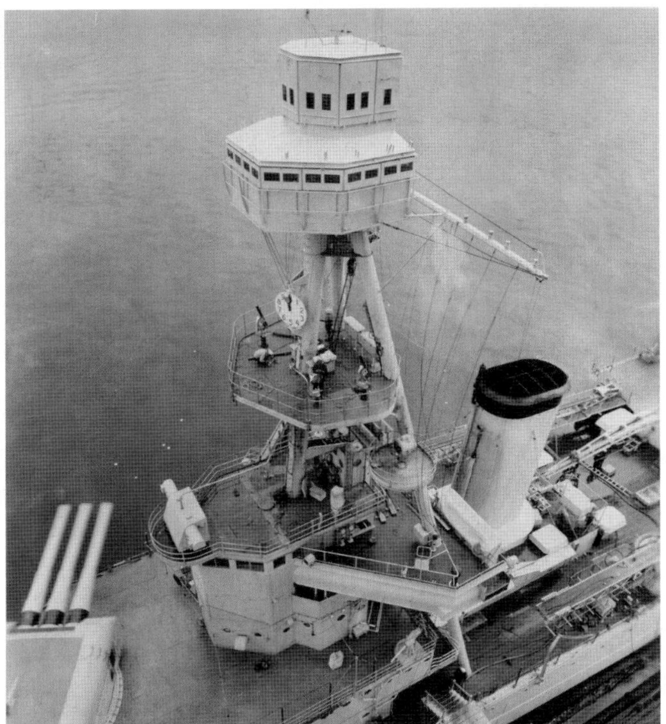

Salt Lake City is seen during a 1934 refit that saw, among other changes, the addition of an AA platform to each of her masts. The platform on her foremast, seen here, held four .50cal/90 Browning MGs. The bi-level fire-control top held a Mk 18 main-battery director at the top level; the larger, lower level held the battle lookouts with their spotting glasses and inclinometers for estimating enemy course. Note the range clock still carried on her foremast. (NHHC)

Classical Beauty: The *Trento* Class

The information the *Regia Marina*'s design staff had to work with was very limited. They knew that the French had gone ahead with the pre-treaty *Duguay-Trouin* class immediately after the Washington Treaty was signed and that more cruisers were in the works. They mainly could look back on their experience in the late war, during which they had been deeply impressed by the Austro-Hungarian Navy's scouts of the *Helgoland* class, which were fast, well-armed for their small size and served throughout the war with distinction, causing the Italians many problems with their hit-and-run raids, being able to outrun the Italian scouts and Royal Navy light cruisers based at Brindisi.[59] This helped the Italian naval staff (*Stato Maggiore della Marina*) establish their priorities for their post-Washington 'treaty maximum' cruisers, which they saw fulfilling the same role of extremely fast, hard-hitting raiders, for which speed would serve as the primary defensive characteristic. Great endurance was not a concern for this design; the expected theatre of operations was the western Mediterranean with the French as the expected enemy.

Early sketch designs, prepared by MARICOMINAV (*Comitato Progetti Navi* – Naval Projects Committee) in 1923 under the overall direction of General (GN) Giuseppe Rota,

This drawing reproduces the original sketch design generated by General (GN) Giuseppe Rota of MARICOMINAV, based on the *San Giorgio* class armoured cruisers of 1905, for the 'treaty maximum' cruiser design requested by the *Stato Maggiore* of the *Regia Marina*. It was to have been armed with eight 203mm main-battery guns in twin turrets and twelve 102mm/45 DP guns in the secondary battery. (Gino Chesi via Enrico Cernuschi)

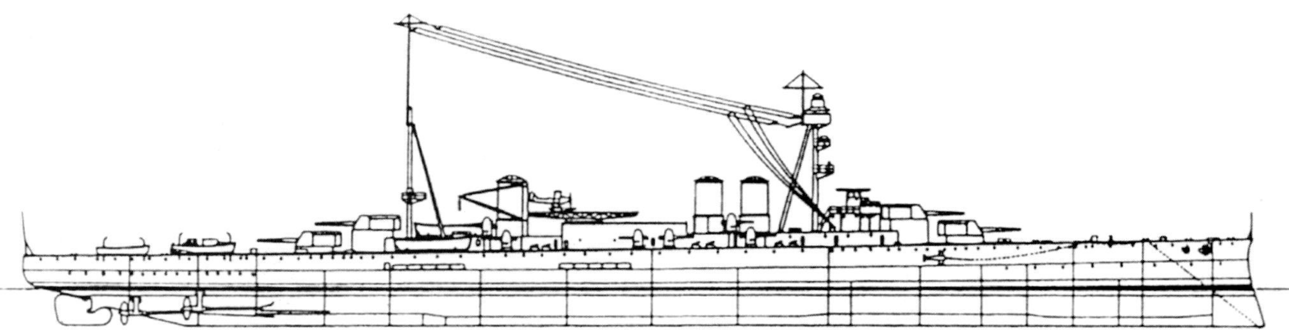

The final design to which RN *Trento* was built bore some resemblance to Rota's original sketch, but differed in having the two forward funnels trunked together into one, in replacing the twelve single mounts in the secondary battery with four 100mm/47 Mod 1924 twin mounts and in building up the forward superstructure substantially. This view shows *Trento* soon after her completion in 1929; she has her main-battery DCT at the top of what is still a tripod foremast, but appears to have only one of the six other smaller directors that would populate her masts and superstructures – the backup main-battery director on her forward superstructure appears to be in place. (NHHC)

were based on the most successful of the *Regia Marina*'s earlier big cruiser designs, the armoured cruiser RN *San Giorgio*, but armed with eight 203mm guns of a new design in the main battery and a secondary battery of twelve 102mm/45 single mounts.[60] Like most of the first-generation 'treaty maximum' cruiser designs, the MARICOMINAV designers chose a flush-deck design for the double benefits it provided – greater hull strength and weight savings over the considerably longer hull the new cruiser would require. Some features of the *San Giorgio* design were retained, most notably the unit system of the engineering plant; this placed the forward engine room between the two sets of fire rooms, in the hope that a single torpedo could not completely disable the ship. This arrangement explains the wide gap between the two forward funnels and single after funnel in the MARICOMINAV sketch design. That the *San Giorgio*s needed four funnels to serve fourteen boilers in a power plant that produced 23,000shp, while the new cruiser would need only three funnels to serve the twelve boilers that would produce an estimated 150,000shp gives some indication of the progress made in steam engineering in 20 years.[61]

In late 1924, with money from the 1923/1924 building programme for the first two 'treaty maximums' available (and needing to be spent) – the orders for the two cruisers had actually gone out in April 1924 – General Rota knew that it would be necessary to accelerate the completion of the design process. To that end, he assigned the project to one of his most talented designers, Colonel (GN) Filippo Bonfiglietti, who was given extensive license to refine the design as necessary. Bonfiglietti made a number of alterations large and small to the original MARICOMINAV design, some of which were made after they were laid down, which caused the construction to stretch out over more than four years in the case of the lead ship, RN *Trento*. He changed the bow form to one with more flare and forward rake to provide better seakeeping. He trunked the two forward funnels together to help clear smoke away from the bridge structure which he enlarged in order to concentrate command functions in one location. He strengthened and increased the number of weapons in the secondary battery to improve AA defence. The first of the pair, RN *Trento*, was laid down at OTO, Livorno, on 8 February 1925.[62] As built, the *Trento*s had the following specifications:

Trento Class

Displacement (std):	10,000 tons (design); 10,500 tons (actual)[63]
Length (oa):	646ft 2in
Beam (wl):	67ft 7in
Draft (mean):	22ft 4in (deep)
Power plant:	120,000shp (design); 150,000shp (actual); Parsons geared turbines driving four shafts; twelve Yarrow boilers
Speed:	34 knots (design); 35.6 knots (actual)[64]
Range (designed):	4160nm @ 16 knots; 2214 tons oil fuel
Protection (side):	2.76in KNC external belt (in way of main-battery magazines and engineering spaces)
Protection (horiz):	2in KNC (main deck over main-battery magazines and engineering spaces)
Armament (main):	8 x 203mm/50 Mod 1924 (4 x 2 – two forward and two aft)
Armament (AA):	16 x 100mm/47 Mod 1924 (8 x 2); 4 x 40mm/39 Vickers-Terni (4 x 1); 8 x 12.7mm machine guns (4 x 2)
Armament (torp):	8 x 533mm (fixed, main deck)
Aircraft:	3 (3 x Piaggio P6 bis); one catapult (fixed in forecastle)[65]

One important change Bonfiglietti made late in the construction process was to add in state-of-the-art fire control for the main and AA batteries. This involved the siting of seven director positions high up in the superstructure and masts of the *Trento*s, starting with the primary main-battery DCT at the top of the tripod foremast. This was a multi-level fire-control director which, in its original configuration, had a single 9.84ft stereoscopic rangefinder (*Tipo ST*) on its upper-level. (During initial service, it was found that these foremast positions suffered from excessive vibration and, during refits in 1931, two addition support legs were added to their foremasts, running upwards from the bridge, making their foremasts into pentapods.) Two other rangefinders were in place at the time of the *Trento*s' entry into service – the backup main-battery director on top of the forward superstructure with a 16.4ft coincidence rangefinder (*Tipo OG25* – manufactured by Officine Galileo) and a similarly-equipped, but smaller, auxiliary director on a small lattice tower abaft the after funnel. Each of these director positions had a port or periscope for a gyroscopically yaw-stabilised inclinometer (*gimetro*), used to measure target angle. Target bearing, range, angle and estimated speed, along with environmental data such as wind speed and direction (supplied by a mast-mounted anemometer) and own-ship course and speed (supplied by gyro-compass and pitometer log), were fed to a Barr & Stroud analogue computer, as further developed by Galileo, located in a below-decks Central Control Station (*Centrale di tiro*), which developed fire-control solutions and transmitted gun orders to the main-battery turrets.[66] As a further backup, in case centralised fire control proved impossible, each of the four main-battery turrets incorporated a 16.4ft coincidence rangefinder.

No later than the time of the 1931 refits, a longer base-line 16.4ft coincidence rangefinder was added to the lower level of the main foretop DCT, which allowed the shorter stereoscopic rangefinder at the upper level to be used for scartometry, as originally planned. In the same time frame, four secondary-battery directors with DP capabilities (and 9.84ft coincidence rangefinders) were added to positions on the foremast and mainmast port-and-starboard.

All the fire-control capability for the main battery initially proved to be of little benefit because the Ansaldo-built 203mm/50 guns were mounted in a common sleeve in very close proximity to each other – they were separated by only 39.4in centre-to-centre.[67] This contributed to dispersion problems when the guns were fired. A more serious component of the dispersion problem was the extremely high muzzle velocity of these guns. A lighter shell was produced and a smaller powder charge utilised that lowered the muzzle velocity from 2969fps to 2756fps, which went a long way towards resolving the problem. Italian fire-control doctrine, in a manner similar to that employed by the Germans during the First World War, called for the firing of half-salvos – one gun from each of the four turrets – in 875yd 'ladders' during the ranging phase at the beginning of an engagement. To prevent interference after that, when full salvos were fired, a millisecond delay through the use of a solenoid was introduced into the firing circuit for one of the barrels of each turret – a technology introduced by most other navies to solve similar problems – which appears to have effectively resolved the issue.[68]

The fixed catapult, set into the forecastle of the *Trento*s, was a unique feature. All the nations followed in this account agreed in the belief that carrying aircraft was essential to the scouting role that these cruisers were intended to carry out, and all had a difficult time finding the space and the displacement to fit the catapults and the aircraft necessary to this role. Each nation came up with its own unique solution to this problem; in the case of the first-generation 'treaty maximum' cruisers, most, if not all, would agree that the solution tried out were far from ideal and could stand considerable improvement. It is safe to say, however, that no nation's attempted solution was as radical, or as unsatisfactory, as the placement of a fixed catapult forward of the main-battery turrets and a hangar set into the forecastle deck in the *Trento*s. This arrangement of both hangar and catapult proved to be unfortunate for a number of reasons. Any aircraft carried in the 'ready' position on the catapult would, of necessity, interfere with the arc of fire of the forward main-battery turrets. Even if, it might be argued, such an aircraft would be launched before the ship went into action, and therefore resolve any interference issues, any subsequent need to launch one of the aircraft stowed in the hangar would, if anything,

Like many of the early 'treaty maximum' cruisers, *Trento* would be sent to Shanghai to protect Italian interests in that perpetually-embattled city. In this image taken in January 1932 from USS *Houston*, *Trento* is alongside the destroyer RN *Espero*. Obvious changes from the preceding image are the added legs to the foremast to stabilise her large main-battery DCT, and she appears to have all the remaining directors, including the four HA directors – two each on her foremast and mainmast – to complete her fire-control suite. Note the Piaggio P-6ter floatplane on its awkwardly-sited catapult on her forecastle. Just to her left in the background is a British cruiser, probably HMS *Berwick* (65), tied up alongside a godown. (NARA)

make the problem worse. Raising or lowering an aircraft out of or into the hangar required the erection of a collapsible derrick that would interfere with the forward turrets every bit as much as an aircraft. Also, since aircraft could only be stored in the narrow hangar space in disassembled form, the process of launching or stowing an aircraft would necessarily be slow. Finally, any aircraft carried in the 'ready' position on the catapult was exposed to any seas that might break over the forecastle, a far more vulnerable position than the sites further aft between or abaft the funnels chosen by other navies.

These ships were refitted in the mid-1930s, but not extensively altered, the main changes being incremental upgrades to their AA suites. The aftermost pair of twin 100mm mounts were removed and eight 37mm/54 Breda Mod 1932 in four twin mounts added in. Before the start of the Second World War, the 40mm mounts had been removed and the 12.7mm twin mounts replaced by twin 13.2mm/75.7 Mod 1931 mounts. Both ships also had prominent funnel caps added in 1939 in an attempt to prevent smoke interference with operations on the bridge.

Performing one of the difficult, but necessary, tasks that keep a warship in operation, sailors from RN *Trieste*, sister to *Trento*, load a 533mm torpedo – minus its warhead – through the starboard loading door, where it would positioned across from the after port side pair of fixed torpedo tubes. The openings for the starboard forward pair can be seen to the right. (NHHC)

Berlin Tries Again: The 'K' Class and Beyond

Having learned the hard way in designing *Emden* that assumptions should never be made and that basing the design of their new cruiser on an old design was a false economy, the Germans were determined that they would not make those same mistakes again; inevitably, they would find that there were new mistakes to be made. The Germans were still bound by the terms of the Versailles Treaty, which restricted them to warships no larger than 6000 tons displacement and allowed them to replace their old pre-war light cruisers only when they were more than 20 years old. The age restriction would no longer be a problem by 1924; every one of the cruisers left to the *Reichsmarine* had been launched in or before 1903.

In mid-1924, the *Reichsmarine* began designing a new class of light cruisers to follow after *Emden*. The instructions given the designers were loosely-framed, but the past actions of the NIACC had made it clear that guns larger than 6in calibre would not be approved for replacement light cruisers.[69] If the designers of other nations had difficulties defining ships with a balanced set of characteristics within the 10,000 tons allowed by the Washington Treaty, imagine what the Germans faced with a displacement limit of 6000 tons.

Weight had to be saved by any and all means possible. Even in the few years that had passed since the designing of *Emden*, new materials and technologies had become available to the naval architect that made weight savings somewhat easier, but there was a limit to how much those would help. Making their job harder, at the same time the designers were being asked to develop a design that carried a more powerful main battery, was better protected and developed almost half-again as much power. Based on the belief that the strictness with which the

Inter-Allied Control Commissions were enforcing the 'spirit' of the Versailles Treaty had eased considerably in the years since 1921, the decision was made early-on in the design process to adopt the new, longer 15cm/60 SK C/25 in an equally-new triple turret. It was a gamble, given that the NIACC had rejected the longer gun and twin turrets for *Emden*, but this time, the main battery was approved without objection.

Even though it would take four fewer boilers to generate the requisite steam to provide 65,000shp than it took to generate *Emden*'s 45,900shp, not much weight or space was saved because the *Reichsmarine* wanted diesel cruising motors on both shafts to provide greater endurance. While the two MAN 10-cylinder four-stroke diesels were extremely lightweight, they drove the two propeller shafts through a hydraulic clutch system that did not permit the steam turbines and the diesels to be connected at the same time, so they were dead weight when the turbines were in use. The captain could chose the economy of the diesel drive, which provided 1800bhp that could drive the ships at a maximum speed of 10.5 knots and gave them a range of 8000nm, or the speed of the turbine drive, which could push the ships to a maximum of over 32 knots and still provide decent endurance (7300nm) at 17 knots.[70]

Digging deep into their toolbox, the designers opted to employ welding for 85 per cent of hull seams, saving significant weight over traditional riveted construction. Light metal, such as duralumin, was used for most non-structural applications. The adoption of triple turrets for the main battery allowed nine guns to carried, all of which could bear on the broadside, where *Emden* had eight smaller guns of which only six could bear on either side. The design, which the *Reichsmarine* staff approved early in 1925, included a unique arrangement of the main battery. No doubt influenced by the disadvantageous strategic and tactical situation in which these ships would find themselves if faced by foreign contemporaries, it was decided to mount two of the three main-battery turrets aft, where they could more easily bear in situations when these ships were fleeing from an enemy. However, to give these after turrets a better arc of fire forward of the beam, they were offset from the centreline, 'B' turret (*Bruno*) to port and 'C' turret (*Cäsar*) to starboard, though any gain in arc was negligible. More important was the lack of any after superstructure near these turrets, which meant they could theoretically be fired as much as 45° forward of the beam, although that could only be done if the personnel immediately forward of these turrets had taken shelter.

The Reichstag authorised funding for the first of the new cruisers in 1925, which was ordered as *Kreuzer 'B'* (Ersatz-

The *Reichsmarine* built three similar light cruisers to a design that would (more-or-less) follow the spirit, if not quite the letter, of the restrictions in the Versailles Treaty. Unlike *Emden*, these were a 'clean sheet' design, mounting their main battery of nine 15cm/60 SK C/25 guns in triple turrets arrayed in a unique arrangement, with two of the turrets aft, offset from each other to improve their arcs of fire. In order to keep the displacement close to the treaty-mandated limit of 6000 tons, they were very lightly constructed, which would cause each of them, such as *Köln* seen here visiting Melbourne in April 1933, problems throughout their careers. (SLV/AGC)

Thetis) from the *Marinewerft*, Wilhelmshaven, on 28 March 1925. For a time, it was hoped that the second and third ships of the class might be given a heavier main battery, a new 19cm gun then being discussed, to be mounted in twin turrets, but when it was realised that the gun and its mountings could not be ready before 1929 (and that NIACC approval was unlikely under any circumstances), the decision was made to proceed with *Kreuzer 'C'* (Ersatz-*Medusa*) and *Kreuzer 'D'* (Ersatz-*Arcona*) to the same design as *Kreuzer 'B'*, both funded in 1926.[71] The 'as-built' specifications of these ships were as follows:

'K' Class

Displacement (std):	6000 tons (design); 6650 tons (actual)
Length (oa):	570ft 10in
Beam (wl):	50ft 2in
Draft (mean):	18ft 3in (design); 20ft 7in (deep)
Power plant (steam):	68,200shp; Marine geared turbines driving two shafts; six Schulz-Thornycroft double-ended water-tube boilers
Power plant (diesel):	1800bhp; two MAN W10 V 26/33, 10-cyl, 4-stroke inline engines
Speed (steam):	32 knots (design); 32.1 knots (actual)
Speed (diesel):	10 knots (design); 10.5 knots (actual)
Range (steam):	7300nm @ 17 knots; 1083 tons oil fuel
Range (diesel):	8000nm @ 10 knots; 137 tons diesel oil
Protection (side):	1.97in KNS external belt (in way of main-battery magazines and engineering spaces)[72]
Protection (torp):	0.59in KNS vertical bulkhead (6ft 2in inboard of external belt); 0.39in KNS sloping bulkhead (between bottom of vertical torpedo bulkhead and bottom of external belt)
Protection (horiz):	0.79in KNC (flat upper deck over main-battery magazines and engineering spaces)
Armament (main):	9 x 15cm/60 SK C/25 (3 x 3 – one forward and two aft)
Armament (AA):	2 x 8.8cm/45 Flak L/45 (2 x 1 – *Köln* completed w/4 x 8.8cm/75 SK C/25 (2 x 2)); 8 x 3.7cm/83 SK C/30 (4 x 2); 8 x 2cm/65 C/30 (8 x 1)
Armament (torp):	8 x 50cm (4 x 3)[73]

Kreuzer 'B' was laid down on 12 April 1926, launched on 26 March 1927 and named *Königsberg*; her two sisters were given names that began with the same letter.

From their entry into service, the 'K' class cruisers were used primarily as training ships for successive classes of midshipmen and other recruits joining the *Reichsmarine*, which meant they often were sent on lengthy ocean cruises which exposed their light construction to dangerous stresses. This became painfully obvious in 1936, when, on her fifth extended training cruise – it would be her third circumnavigation of the globe – *Karlsruhe* encountered a typhoon with Force 12 winds after departing Japan heading east.[74] The winds and accompanying seas were strong enough to buckle frames and cause tears in her outer shell plating, forcing her to heave-to in an attempt to ride out the storm. After the storm blew itself out on 21 March, she limped into Dutch Harbor in the Aleutians on the 23rd, where her crew attempted emergency repairs. Five days later, satisfied she could proceed in relative safety, she headed for San Diego, California, where she was dry-docked, and her buckled frames were braced and external patches were welded over the tears in her hull. This seems to have resolved the immediate concerns well enough for her to continue her route back to Germany. Once home she received a minor refit only, similar to those given her sisters, involving added deckhouses and upgraded AA armament. Finally, in 1938, she was taken in hand for a major rebuild, involving the widening of the hull by 5ft 3in amidships, adding a new external armour belt above the existing one, of 0.55in of *Wotan Härte*, a new formula homogeneous armour from Krupp, and a Main Deck of 0.63in of the same material. The widened hull formed a blister outside the existing shell plating from the turn of the bilge all the way up to the main deck, improving buoyancy and stability, but at a cost in speed. It was intended to make the same alteration to the other two 'K' class cruisers, but the start of the Second World War prevented that from happening.

Two more light cruisers would complete this series for the *Reichsmarine*. *Kreuzer 'E'* (Ersatz-*Amazone*) was authorised in 1928, laid down on 18 April of that year at the *Marinewerft* and was launched on 18 October 1929 with the name *Leipzig*. *Kreuzer 'F'* (Ersatz-*Nymphe*) was not authorised until 1933, was laid down on 4 November of that year at Deutsche Werke and was launched on 8 December 1934 with the name *Nürnberg*. In the five years that elapsed between the ordering of the fourth and fifth of this series, thoughts had once again turned to mounting a heavier main battery, but the decision was made to proceed with *Nürnberg* as an only slightly-modified *Leipzig* because design work was already underway on a true heavy cruiser, and it was correctly perceived that an up-gunned *Leipzig* would be a ship without an obvious role to play in a modern navy.

These ships were direct follow-ons to the 'K' class which they resembled in size, armament layout and general form. The most obvious differences from the earlier ships was the single large funnel replacing the two smaller ones and the placement of the after main-battery turrets on the centreline. The biggest difference was not visible; these two ships were given a third central propeller shaft to which their four cruising diesels were permanently clutched via a Vulcan hydraulic gearbox. This was a far superior arrangement to that of the preceding 'Ks', in that the diesels and turbines could be run

Left: This image, taken from *Köln*'s quarterdeck, demonstrates the degree of offset of the after main-battery turrets of the 'K' class light cruisers, Turret *'Bruno'* to port and Turret *'Cäsar'* to starboard. (via Ken Macpherson)

simultaneously, theoretically boosting the top speed achievable by turbines alone. When the ships were running on diesels alone, the outer shafts were turned at slow revolutions by small electric motors to prevent drag. The central shaft had a recently-developed adjustable-pitch propeller to allow the speed to be adjusted while running the diesels at optimal speed; this turned out to be a flawed system and, on *Leipzig* at least, it was replaced by a fixed-pitch screw. The diesel sets in these ships produced 12,400bhp for a speed of 18 knots. The diesels in both, particularly in *Leipzig*, were troublesome, but by the time the Second World War broke out, their problems had been largely resolved.

These ships were similar, but not identical. Both were somewhat longer and beamier than the 'Ks', *Nürnberg* somewhat more so than *Leipzig*, but they were just as lightly-built and poorly-protected, making them inferior sea boats and questionable assets in wartime. They could be distinguished visually by the prominent searchlight platform around *Nürnberg*'s funnel and the latter's larger bridge structure.

Below: The Germans built two more light cruisers after the three 'Ks'. They suffered many of the same problems of light construction and poor protection as the preceding cruisers and they fared poorly once war broke out. This image shows *Leipzig* during a towing exercise in August 1937. The external differences from the three 'Ks' can be seen. Their uptakes were trunked into a single funnel, which allowed room for a catapult and aircraft to be fitted between the bridge and the funnel, and the two after main-battery turrets are now mounted on the centreline. (NARA)

Chapter 6

Treaty Cruisers – Trying to Stem the Tide: 1926–1930

No sooner were the first 'treaty-maximum' cruisers on the ways – or in some cases even before they were laid down – than each of the naval powers was deep into planning follow-on designs that would address anticipated inadequacies in their initial attempts at the type. In every case, the most glaring of the perceived shortfalls was in the amount of protection provided; every one of these nations wanted to give their second-generation 'treaty-maximum' cruisers better, more extensive protection. The main difference between those nations was what, if anything, their designers (and the military and political leaders giving direction to the designers) were willing to sacrifice to compensate for the added weight of armour.

The coverage of ship development during this period is broken down into two phases, interrupted by an initial, abortive attempt to slow down cruiser construction at a hastily-called conference in mid-1927. When that failed utterly to achieve its goal, a second, somewhat better-planned, conference would be convened in 1930, as described in the next chapter.

More of the Same – More or Less: The *London*, *Norfolk* and *York* classes

Despite the obvious success of the Washington Conference in imposing the 'Battleship Holiday' that effectively curtailed capital ship construction for ten years starting in 1922, many felt that its success was, at best, incomplete, because the much-feared naval arms race in battleship construction appeared simply to have been replaced by one in cruiser construction. The Royal Navy remained firm in its commitment to the need for seventy cruisers in a time of changing political leadership in Great Britain. The governments of Asquith and Lloyd George had not always been the strongest supporters of military spending, but once committed to war, they had made the funds available to build up the Royal Navy to wartime strength. But, since 1922, the political climate had become less settled; seven years of Conservative leadership, interrupted only by nine months of Labour government in 1924, were far less forthcoming with support for warship construction.

In January 1924, when Ramsay MacDonald's Labour Party was beginning its first brief stint in power, the Admiralty submitted a ten-year building programme – which, admittedly, had been prepared before the defeat of Stanley Baldwin's Conservative government – that called for the Royal Navy to have its seventy cruisers by 1929, thirty-one for fleet service and thirty-nine for trade protection, of which only ten would be more than 15 years old.[1] Curiously, the 'point man' in the Conservative government's drive to trim naval expenditures in November 1924 was Winston S Churchill. The former First Lord of the Admiralty, now the Chancellor of the Exchequer, found himself using many of the same arguments that Lloyd George had used against him. The first Naval Estimates over which Churchill had oversight covered the 1925 building programme. Perhaps believing that, because of his experience in Whitehall, he would be sympathetic to the Royal Navy's proposals, the Admiralty approached Churchill in advance of their formal presentation of the Estimates to Parliament in March 1925, but, to their dismay, Churchill attacked them point-by-point and proposed his own naval budget with no shipbuilding funds beyond funding for a few submarines.[2] The only sop he threw the Admiralty was to propose the establishment of a subcommittee of the Committee of Imperial Defence, the Naval Programme (or Birkenhead) Committee, to study the Royal Navy's need for cruisers.

Churchill (and Baldwin) were faced with an equally obdurate pair at Whitehall in First Lord of the Admiralty William C Bridgeman and First Sea Lord Beatty. Bridgeman, a former Home Secretary, had no naval experience, but was a competent administrator and served the Royal Navy well for five years. Beatty was among the best-known and most popular public figures in Great Britain; whatever his qualities may have been as a tactical commander of ships in battle, he proved to be a forceful advocate for the Royal Navy at a time when one was needed. In July, based on the Birkenhead Committee recommendations, Baldwin crafted a compromise position that gave the Admiralty some of what it wanted.[3] The Royal Navy would get four cruisers in the 1925 building programme and three more in the 1926 programme, but there were some caveats attached.[4] One was that the start dates of some of those ships were to be delayed until the later part of their respective fiscal years; the other was a strong injunction to find cost savings wherever possible in the design of those ships.

This latter, of course, came as no surprise to the Admiralty. As early as January 1924, the Royal Navy was looking at smaller cruiser designs as an alternative to the already-standard 'treaty maximum' cruiser.[5] They looked at a variety of options, ranging from switching from twin turrets to triple turrets, which would allow the construction of a somewhat shorter ship with one more main-battery gun than carried by the *Kent*s, to simply downsizing the *Kent* design with three or even two twin-mount main-battery turrets or even substituting a

6in main battery for the 8in gun allowed by the Washington Treaty and adopted by all the major navies. After much back-and-forth, in October 1924 the new DNC, William J Berry, asked Lillicrap for a pair of sketch designs. One would be a revised *Kent* without the torpedo bulge; the weight saved would be used to provide aircraft-handling facilities and somewhat better protection. The improved underwater lines promised to increase speed by close to a knot. The other design would be similar but with no protection at all, in order to obtain maximum speed. On 2 January 1925, the board opted for the first of the two designs and Lillicrap proceeded to detailed design. In the end, the four-ship *London* class was virtually identical to the preceding *Kent* class except for the lack of an anti-torpedo bulge and, therefore, vertical, rather than inward sloping sides to the hull. The hull was 2ft 4in narrower, which allowed the power plant to give them 0.8 knots more speed, for a top speed of 32.3 knots.

The funding for three more cruisers came through in the 1926 budget as promised and the Admiralty looked again at the option of building a smaller cruiser. The pressure to get the construction of these ships underway caused two of them to be ordered to an almost identical design as the *London* class. The two *Norfolk* class cruisers, laid down in mid-1927, differed only in having a new-model, improved twin main-battery turret that added some protection and simplified the ammunition supply train.[6] This design was approved on 28 October 1926.[7] The following spring, it was learned that the long-delayed DCT would finally be ready for installation in new-construction cruisers and the bridge design of the *Norfolk* class was modified to mount the more compact fire-control director in the place of the multi-level tower structure fitted in the *Kent*s and *London*s. (Most, but not all, of these earlier cruisers had DCTs installed during refits before the Second World War.)

The *London*s and *Norfolk*s were refitted to varying degrees late in the 1930s. In general, they all received an added external waterline armour belt of 3.5in-thick KNC plate, as well as twin 4in/45 QF Mk XVIs replacing the single mounts and octuple 2pdr pompoms replacing the earlier marks. *London* herself was taken in hand for a major rebuild in December 1938, which lasted until March 1941, and saw her emerge from Chatham Dockyard with a completely revised silhouette, including a massive bridge structure resembling that of the 1938–9 *Fiji* class and two funnels.[8] There were discussions about modernising the remaining *London*s and *Norfolk*s in the same fashion, but limited funds and the coming of war prevented that from happening.

A detail view of the midships section of HMS *Sussex* (96), one of the preceding *London* class, seen in the mid-1930s, showing the extensible catapult on its rotating platform. This was a clever, if complex, way to resolve the problem of fitting a long catapult in the small space available. A Hawker Osprey sits ready for launching. Below and to the right is a 4in/45 Mk V HA single-mount gun. The ship's band in full regalia is assembling on the Main Deck, ready to play someone aboard. (NHHC)

HMS *Norfolk* (78), the lead ship of a two-ship class, the last 'treaty maximum' cruisers built by the Royal Navy, is seen visiting her 'sister city', the main American East Coast naval base, Norfolk, VA, on 29 September 1933. She shows all of the features the *Kent*s were intended to carry, but which were not ready for installation when they were completed; they include the DCT on her forward super-structure, a rotating, extensible catapult abaft her third funnel and the HACS tower, with its 'domed' canvas cover, immediately aft of that. Not in any way obvious, but just as important, was the change in the turrets to the Mk II gun mounts, which only allowed elevation to 50°, but proved to be far more robust. (NPL/VPC)

In February 1925, Lillicrap was again asked to look at the possibility of a smaller cruiser, starting with a scaled-down *Kent*-like design, but with eight 6in guns in the main battery.[9] Almost as an afterthought, he added an option for a version of this design with three twin 8in main-battery turrets, which would add 175 tons. At first DNC was far more interested in the 6in-gunned variant, but feedback from the fleet favoured the 8in-gunned version, especially if a way could be found to work in better protection. By August 1925, sentiment had hardened in favour of this variant, with 3in belt armour and a 1.5in armoured deck protecting the engineering spaces. Lillicrap was asked to produce a detailed design of this ship, which was approved by the Admiralty Board on 25 February 1926. (In Royal Navy parlance, this smaller type became known as a 'B' cruiser, with the 'treaty maximum' classes, by default, called 'A' cruisers.) The specifications of this ship, which became HMS *York* (90), were as follows:

'B' Cruiser: HMS *York*

Displacement (std):	8250 tons
Length (oa):	575ft
Beam (max):	57ft
Draft (mean):	20ft 6in (deep)
Power plant:	80,000shp; Parsons geared turbines driving four shafts; eight Admiralty three-drum water-tube boilers
Speed:	32.25 knots (std); 31.25 knots (deep)
Range (designed):	10,000nm @ 14 knots; 1900 tons oil fuel
Protection (side):	3in KNC external belt armour (in way of engineering spaces only); 4.375in KNC (side plating in armoured box citadel around main-battery magazines)
Protection (horiz):	1.5in Ducol (over engineering spaces at Middle Deck level); 3in KNC (crown of armoured box citadel over main-battery magazines)
Armament (main):	6 x 8in/50 Mk VIII (3 x 2 – two forward and one aft)
Armament (AA):	4 x 4in/45 QF Mk V (4 x 1); 2 x 2pdr Mk II pompom (2 x 1)
Armament (torp):	6 x 21in (2 x 3)
Aircraft:	1, one catapult (originally planned for two catapults, but light catapult on 'B' turret deleted during construction)[10]

York was laid down on 16 May 1927, almost two months before *Norfolk*. There was considerable enthusiasm for this design within the Royal Navy, as it was estimated that it would cost 10 per cent less than a 'treaty maximum' cruiser to build, making the job of persuading an increasingly parsimonious Parliament to fund the construction of cruisers somewhat easier.[11]

Besides being smaller than the three preceding classes of 'treaty maximum' cruisers, several features immediately stand out looking at *York* compared to her immediate predecessors. For the first time, the Royal Navy subjected models of this design to wind tunnel tests in an attempt to anticipate problems with funnel smoke interference. *York* was designed with a compact but relatively tall bridge structure that, the tests proved, created serious eddies in its wake if the ship was steaming into the wind. Smoke would gather in the lee of the bridge and then be forced down onto the deck and would trail off aft, affecting any personnel manning the after control positions and the quarterdeck.[12] Alternative solutions, such as raising the funnels 15ft or more, rounding off the forward face of the bridge or cutting away much of the lower bridge structure seemed to offer no relief. What did help somewhat was to trunk the two forward funnels together and increase the height of the two remaining funnels by 10ft; nonetheless, she suffered from smoke interference throughout her career when steaming directly into the wind, particularly at moderate speeds. The three-turret, two-funnel silhouette, with a large gap between the tall, compact bridge and the first funnel, was one distinctive feature of *York*. Another was the adoption of a 'traditional' cruiser hull with a raised forecastle deck forward and reduced freeboard aft. (The *Norfolk* class were the last Royal Navy cruisers with flush-deck hulls.)

Beyond the installation of a catapult between the second funnel and the after superstructure and the landing of the two single pompoms, *York* was very little modified between her commissioning in May 1930 and the outbreak of the Second World War.

Reluctant Warriors: Late Starts in America

At the beginning of 1925, a committee set up by US Secretary of the Navy Curtis D Wilbur to determine the critical needs of the US Navy, chaired by the Chief of Naval Operations (CNO) Admiral Edward W Eberle, reported its findings, a list of seven priority items.[13] Construction of eight new 'treaty maximum' cruisers came in only fourth on this list. (The first three items on the list were modernisation or conversion projects.) Thus, even though the construction of new cruisers was not right at the top of the list, it was the highest-listed of new-construction projects, which tended to be seen in a different, more critical, manner by the American legislature. (Congress, at this time, was far more willing to spend money on maintaining the fighting efficiency of existing ships than on building new ones.) The listing of the eight cruisers at the top of the US Navy's 'wishlist' of new-construction projects gave them a reasonable chance of being approved. Wilbur passed along Eberle's report with its implicit funding recommendations to President Calvin Coolidge (who had succeeded Harding when the latter died in office in 1923 and then had been elected in his own right in 1924), who submitted to Congress a much smaller funding request than the US Navy had wanted. Congress did, in fact, authorise the construction of eight 'treaty maximum' cruisers – by passing the Cruiser Bill of 18 December 1924 – but in the United States, the process of Congressional approval of naval construction was a two-step process, of which authorisation was only the first step. Funding the construction of a new ship was a second, independent step, which might, or might not, come at the same time as authorisation. In this case, the funding for only the first two cruisers came in 1924 – these became the *Pensacola*s. The remaining six ships in that initial authorisation that would become the *Northampton* class were funded in appropriations bills passed in May 1926 and March 1927. Anticipating that funding, the General Board of the US Navy had, in fact, been working since February 1926 on a new cruiser design to follow-on after the *Pensacola*s.[14]

As with all other nations looking back at their first-generation 'treaty maximum' cruisers, the US Navy wanted better survivability for their next designs. The General Board asked Preliminary Design to look into improving the subdivision of the power plant, particularly the fire rooms,

The US Navy's General Board wanted improvements on the *Pensacola* class in both survivability – they wanted better subdivision in the engineering spaces – and habitability – they wanted a forecastle deck, which would make the ships drier forward and provide more accommodation space for officers and petty officers. They were willing to sacrifice one main-battery gun to get this, going to a nine-gun arrangement with three triple turrets. Thus was born the *Northampton* class, of which USS *Louisville* (CA28, ex-CL28) was one, seen here at Melbourne, 15 February 1938. She has the Mk 24 main-battery director on her foretop, but has yet to be fitted with her HA directors. The rangefinders in hoods on her pilot house and after superstructure are for navigational purposes. The tube running along her near side to the aft end of her well deck is the avgas line, carrying fuel for the aircraft in her hangars from the tanks in her bow. (SLV/AGC)

which in the *Pensacolas* had been two large, undivided compartments. There was considerable resistance to this idea, as inserting a pair of watertight bulkheads into the *Pensacola* design in the engineering spaces would add almost 20ft to the length of the hull and increase the displacement as much as 200 tons.[15] Another feature very much desired by the General Board was a forecastle deck, to improve freeboard forward and provide needed room for accommodation for officers and men, but which would add another significant weight penalty. To counteract these additions, the designers were instructed to consider reducing weight by sacrificing one or two main-battery guns; instead of the *Pensacolas*' ten-gun main battery, designs were requested for a nine-gun ship with three triple turrets and an eight-gun ship with four twin turrets. Not too surprisingly, the nine-gun design proved to make better use of space and displacement and was strongly favoured. By the beginning of 1927, the General Board had a design they approved and sent on to Secretary Wilbur. The specifications of this ship, which would become the first of six ships of the *Northampton* class, were as follows:

Northampton Class

Displacement (std):	10,000 tons (design); 11,574 tons (full load)
Length (oa):	600ft 3in
Beam (wl):	66ft 1in
Draft (mean):	19ft 5in (full load)
Power plant:	107,000shp; Parsons geared turbines driving four shafts; eight White-Forster boilers
Speed:	32.5 knots (design)
Range (designed):	10,000nm @ 15 knots; 3067 tons oil fuel
Protection (side):	3in STS external belt (in way of engineering spaces); 3.75in STS external belt(in way of main-battery magazines)
Protection (horiz):	1in STS (over engineering spaces); 2in STS (over main-battery magazines)
Armament (main):	9 x 8in/55 Mk 9 (3 x 3 – two forward and one aft)
Armament (AA):	4 x 5in/25 Mk 10 (4 x 1)
Armament (torp):	6 x 21in (2 x 3)
Aircraft:	4, two catapults[16]

All six ships in the class were laid down over a period of six months in 1928, starting with USS *Chester* (CL27) on 6 March. As with the *Pensacolas*, they were originally classed as light cruisers (CLs), because of the relative lightness of their armour – it had nothing to do with the fact that they were even more under their designed displacement than the *Pensacolas*, in some cases as much as 1000 tons – but were later reclassified as heavy

The well deck in the *Northampton* class cruisers, such as seen here on USS *Augusta* (CA31, ex-CL31), was a large empty space forward of the hangars and between the catapults specifically for the handling of aircraft. However, images of these ships, such as the previous view of *Louisville*, show that aircraft were rarely stowed in the hangars, except when they needed to be serviced. This left the well deck open for other activities, such as this Change of Command Ceremony for the US Asiatic Fleet, at this time (25 July 1939) the only geographically-assigned fleet in the US Navy. Admiral Harry E Yarnell was being relieved by Admiral Thomas C Hart; appropriately enough, the ceremony was held in the middle of the Whangpoo (Huangpu) River that bisects Shanghai. (NHHC)

cruisers (CAs) on 1 July 1931 to comply with the terms of the First London Treaty. Compared to the *Pensacola*s, the armour of the *Northampton*s was somewhat thicker, but not dramatically so. At the time of their completion, the *Northamptons*' fire-control set-up resembled that of the *Pensacola*s, except that the *Northampton*s had a below-decks plotting room. In the early 1930s, they were fitted with a pair of Mk 24 main-battery directors at their foretop and after control position and a pair of Mk 19 DP directors fore-and-aft served by separate surface and AA rangefinders. These rangefinders were later consolidated into a single large, boxy structure called the Director Mount Mk 1.[17]

Building Castles: The *Takao* Class

There was nothing steady or inexorable about the course of Japanese politics during the years of the Taisho Emperor – Yoshihito, the son of the Meiji Emperor, who ruled from 1912 to 1926.[18] Yoshihito was an extremely weak ruler, especially compared to his father; he suffered from poor health and declining mental capacity that effectively left Japan without an emperor for many years. This lack of leadership, particularly between approximately 1914 and 1921, led to a period of relatively unfettered parliamentary rule in Japan, that became known as the 'Taisho Democracy'. On 25 November 1921, his 20-year-old eldest son Hirohito was named Prince Regent, making him titular ruler of the state, although it would take a number of years before he fully consolidated his power.

This story is of interest to us because, when Navy Minister Admiral Takarabe Takechi presented the proposed 1925 naval programme to the Diet in September 1924, a programme that called for twelve new cruisers to be laid down over a span of six years, it was rejected by the recalcitrant Diet.[19] A scaled-back five-year programme was presented to the legislature in February 1925 calling for only four new cruisers, but this was rejected as well. Trying again in August 1926, Admiral Takarabe submitted a plan covering four years and yet fewer ships overall, though still calling for four new cruisers. This time it was not rejected outright; the parliamentary budget committee approved a budget that allowed the Imperial Navy to build eighteen new ships, including two new cruisers. Then, in December 1926, Hirohito became Emperor upon his father's death, and a new spirit of urgency suffused the government – and loosened the Diet's purse strings; within months, a new five-year naval programme was approved that restored most of what Takarabe had requested the previous August, including all four new cruisers.

The Design Section of the Naval General Staff, now directed by Captain Fujimoto Kikuo, produced a design based on that of the *Myoko* class, with which the staff was generally pleased, so not much was considered to be needed in terms of improvement. One major change was the adoption of D-steel (Ducol steel) as the main structural and thin armour plate material in the place of the high-tensile steel (HTS) used in the *Myoko*s. The protection scheme was similar to that in the preceding class, but incrementally improved; for example, the extended armour belt in way of the magazines was tapered and extended deeper than in the *Myoko*s, thicker at the top (5in of NVNC) and thinner at the bottom (1.5in of NVNC) where it reached the turn of the bilge. Other changes included the fitting of rotating torpedo tubes above the armoured deck, in what was considered to be a move to improve safety, and the fitting of two aircraft catapults instead of one. An upgraded main-battery gun turret was installed in this class, the 'E' Model turret replacing the 'D' Model; the primary difference was that the guns in the 'E' Model turret could elevate to 70°, compared to 40° in the earlier model, giving them, theoretically, some AA capability, but, like all other similar main-battery turrets of this era with high angle of elevation capability, they could not elevate or train fast enough to be used in any other than 'barrage' mode.[20] The 'E' Model turret was visually distinguishable from the earlier model in having a flat roof and 'facetted' sides, where the earlier model had a curved roof and sides.

However, the most noticeable change was the adoption of a significantly larger bridge structure in a continuing effort to centralise all command functions in one location, as well as make room for a fleet command staff as these ships were intended to serve as flagships. As originally designed, the bridge of this class would have been quite similar to that of the *Myoko*s, and it was this design that Fujimoto presented for approval to the Naval General Staff and which Hiraga Yuzuru signed off on when he returned from his extended travels in 1926 and resumed his former position. However, while these

The second class of Japanese 'treaty maximum' cruisers was the *Takao* class, marked by the huge 'castle-like' forward superstructure and broad shelter deck behind it with insets for two sets of twin torpedo tubes. This image shows the midships section of *Atago* in November 1934, two years after she was completed, so she is essentially in as-built condition. This means she still has the single 12cm/45 10th Year Type AA guns in her secondary battery, that would be replaced by twin 12.7cm/40s, and the shelter deck has not yet been extended to meet the after superstructure. (NHHC)

ships were under construction, advice was sought from various divisions within the Imperial Navy's Technical Department, including Gunnery, Torpedoes, Navigation and Communications, each of which demanded space for their equipment and its operators. As is almost always true in such cases, this bridge structure grew in size seemingly without restraint, especially since the moderating influence of Hiraga was increasingly ignored. Apparently, there was some concern about the size to which this structure had grown, because, after the first of the class was launched in May 1930, the decision was made to build a wooden mock-up of the bridge on the now-completed hull, to allow representatives of the various technical divisions to test its suitability. It apparently was considered satisfactory, because the bridge design as built was essentially the same as the wooden mock-up. Where the bridge of the *Myoko*s had weighed 114 tons at completion, the forward superstructure of this new class was wider and longer, enclosing almost three times the volume and weighing 160 tons. Where the *Myokos*' bridge had eight levels, these would have ten.

Several sources claim, probably correctly, that this was the most massive bridge structure ever fitted on a cruiser hull, describing it as 'castle-like'.[21] Indeed, it was so large that critics within the fleet predicted it would cause significant wind resistance, acting much like a large sail, when attempting to manoeuvre the ship at slow speeds and close quarters. However, advocates of the centralisation of command functions held sway and the ships were completed with this extraordinary bridge structure. The 'as-built' specifications for the four ships in this class are as follows:

'A' Class Cruisers: Takao Class

Displacement (std):	9850 tons (designed); 11,350 tons (actual)
Length (oa):	668ft 6in
Beam (max):	62ft 4in (below waterline); 67ft (upper deck)
Draft (mean):	20ft 1in (designed); 20ft 5in (actual)
Power plant:	130,000shp; Kanpon geared turbines driving four shafts; twelve Kanpon three-drum water-tube boilers
Speed:	35.5 knots (designed); 35.3 knots (actual)[22]
Range (designed):	8000nm @ 14 knots; 2645 tons oil fuel
Range (actual):	7000nm @ 14 knots; 2570 tons oil fuel
Protection (side):	4in NVNC external 12° slope (from Middle Deck in way of engineering spaces only); 5in–1.5in NVNC (from lower deck in way of main-battery magazines)
Protection (horiz):	1.33in–1.25in NVNC (over engineering spaces at Middle Deck level); 1.33in NVNC (over magazines at Lower Deck level)
Protection (torp):	Unarmoured bulge below belt armour with max width of 8ft 2.5in; curved anti-torpedo bulkhead 2.28in Ducol steel inboard of bulge; vertical anti-torpedo bulkhead of 1in Ducol steel above bulge extending to armoured deck; inner splinter bulkhead of thin HTS from armoured deck to double bottom
Armament (main):	10 x 20cm/50 3rd Year Type 2 (5 x 2 – three forward (middle turret superfiring) and two aft)
Armament (AA):	4 x 12cm/45 Type 10 (4 x 1); 2 x 40mm/62 HI Type 91 (2 x 1); 2 x 7.7mm/94 HI Type gun (2 x 1)
Armament (torp):	8 x 61cm (4 x 2); 8 reloads
Aircraft:	3 (3 x Nakajima E4N2 Type 90-2-2 reconnaissance seaplane), two catapults[23]

The first in the class, the name ship, was laid down at Yokosuka Navy Yard on 28 April 1927, launched with the name *Takao* on 12 May 1930 and commissioned on 31 May 1932. Upon completion, the *Takao*s were found to be significantly overweight, much like the *Myoko*s before them. The number generally given for their standard displacement at completion is 11,350 tons.[24] Contrary to popular opinion in the United States at the time (and, to a great extent, to this day), it is quite obvious that the overweight condition of these ships was not intentional. This can be seen from looking at the submergence of the armour belt. The main belt in way of the engineering spaces had an overall height of 11ft 6in, of which approximately half was intended to extend above the waterline at ⅔-trials displacement, but at completion only 4ft 3in was exposed.[25] That meant that the *Takao*s were sitting 1ft 6in deeper in the water at trials displacement than planned. Not only did the overweight condition reduce the effectiveness of the armour scheme, but it impacted multiple aspects of ship performance, causing them to have reduced freeboard and to be slower and have less endurance than planned. However, the most serious impact was on the stability of the ships. Because of the added weight, the metacentric height (GM) of the *Takao*s was approximately 3ft 11in in ⅔-trials loading and 4ft 5in at full load, both figures sub-optimal.[26] (As stated above, the ideal range for GM (in a large ship) is 6ft–9ft.) In light condition, such as might be the case for a ship at the end of a long mission, when a large percentage of fuel and other stores has been consumed, the GM dropped to 1ft 3in, which would have been dangerously low in bad weather. To make matters worse, because these ships carried a disproportionate amount of their weight high above the waterline, their righting moment (GZ) – the tendency of a ship to return to an upright position when heeled over by a wave or turn – was reduced. There were few options available to the Imperial Navy in the short term to remedy these problems and none of them were appealing. As a stopgap measure, it was decided to add 250 tons of liquid ballast (seawater) when the ship was in light

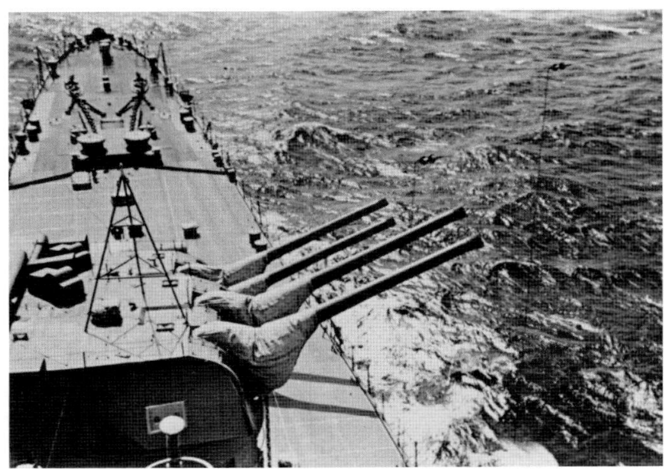

Maya, the fourth ship of the *Takao* class, was given somewhat different main-battery turrets than her sisters, the 'E$_1$' Model, which allowed less elevation, but otherwise was similar. The Japanese put a mast structure on top of No 2 turret to support radio antennas that ran up to the foremast. The two forward main-battery turrets both had 19ft 8in rangefinders partially enclosed within the rear of the turret structure; when these ships were reconstructed starting in 1939, the rangefinder in No 1 turret was moved to the top of the forward superstructure. (NHHC)

condition. After the *Tomozuru* Incident in March 1934, the amount of ballast was increased to 450 tons in an attempt to increase further the range of stability and GM.

Two ships in this class, *Takao* and *Atago*, underwent major modernisation in 1939–40, receiving an extensive bulge at the waterline and below to improve stability and underwater protection, increasing the maximum beam to 68ft. They traded their four 12cm single-mount DP guns for an equal number of twin-mount 12.7cm/40 Type 89s. Their lighter AA guns were replaced by four twin 25mm/60 Type 96 mounts and two twin 13mm/76 Type 93 mounts. The torpedo tubes were replaced by four quadruple tubes firing the new Type 93 Model 1 Mod 1 'Long Lance' oxygen torpedo. The other two ships received much less extensive refits, mainly focusing on AA and torpedo upgrades.

Incremental Improvements: *Suffren* and Her Half-Sister

With the *Duquesne* class finalised and laid down at the beginning of 1925, the French naval staff began consideration of the next cruiser design to follow. They were fully aware of how poorly protected the first two French 'treaty maximum' cruisers were, even in comparison to other nation's sparsely-armoured first-generation efforts. They were particularly concerned when they learned details of the Italian *Trento*s, which, as they discovered, had similar armament and speed but significantly better protection. As early as February 1924, the STCN was working on the next cruiser design, with the intent to retain the positive features of the *Duquesne* class, while finding a means to increase protection.[27] There really were not many options available to save weight, as the staff was insistent that nothing of consequence was to be reduced. New requirements aimed at survivability included side protection able to survive a hit by a 21in torpedo or a near-miss by a 220lb bomb and horizontal protection able to resist a 5.5in shell or 220lb bomb. The STCN's initial reaction was to report that this level of protection could only be achieved by sacrificing one-quarter of the power plant – from 120,000shp to 90,000shp and four shafts to three – which, given the laws of hydrodynamics, would only reduce the top speed by 2 knots, from 34 knots to 32 knots.

This sacrifice of two knots of top speed bought considerably upgraded protection compared to the *Duquesne* class. For the length of the engineering spaces, an external belt of 1.97in 60kg steel plate would run from 3ft 3in below the waterline to 5ft 3in above.[28] The main deck over the engineering spaces was to be 0.98in 50kg mild steel with a 0.47in splinter deck at Upper Deck level. The after fire rooms and engine room, because they would have only a single boiler and turbine in each, allowed enough hull width that a two-layer torpedo protection system could be fitted, with the outer layer serving as an oil fuel tank and the inner as a coal bunker, with the inner bulkhead varying in thickness between 0.79in and 1.57in.[29] The magazines had box protection similar to that in the *Duquesne*s, except that the sides of the boxes would be 1.97in 60kg plate and the main deck would be 0.79in mild steel.

This design was accepted by the naval staff with very little discussion. One ship was funded in the 1925 *tranche* by National Assembly, which would be named *Suffren*; she was laid down at Arsenal de Brest on 17 April 1926. She would be built to the following specifications:

The second generation of French 'treaty maximum' cruisers was represented by *Suffren*, seen here on 6 March 1934. The French designs always stood out for their general simplicity of line; even though, like the Royal Navy's 'treaty maximum' cruisers, they carried eight main-battery guns, the turrets and guns seemed relatively smaller in proportion to the overall size and shape of the ship. What makes *Suffren* particularly distinctive was the carrying of her two command bridge levels suspended above the forward superstructure on the heavy tripod foremast. (NHHC)

Suffren Type Croiseurs Légers

Displacement (std):	10,000 tons
Length (oa):	636ft 6in
Beam:	63ft 2in
Draft:	21ft 4in
Power plant:	90,000shp; Rateau-Bretagne geared turbines driving three shafts; six Guyot du Temple boilers; two small 'cruising' boilers
Speed:	32 knots (designed); 31.33 knots (actual)
Range (designed):	4600nm @ 15 knots; 1876 tons oil fuel; 500 tons coal; 2000nm @ 11 knots on 'cruising' boilers
Protection (side):	1.97in 60kg plate (in way of engineering spaces and main-battery magazines); 1in 60kg plate (steering compartment)
Protection (horiz):	0.98in–0.75in 50kg mild steel (over main-battery magazines and engineering spaces); 0.71in 50kg mild steel (over steering compartment)
Protection (torp):	Two-layer 'sandwich' with 1.57in–0.79in torpedo bulkhead (in way of after engineering spaces)
Armament (main):	8 x 203mm/50 Mle 1924 (4 x 2 – two forward and two aft)
Armament (AA):	*Suffren*: 8 x 75mm/50 Mle 1924 (8 x 1); 8 x 37mm/50 Mle 1925 (8 x 1) *Colbert*: 8 x 90mm/50 Mle 1926 (8 x 1); 6 x 37mm/50 Mle 1925 (6 x 1)
Armament (torp):	6 x 550mm Mle 1923D (2 x 3); 3 reloads
Aircraft:	3 (3 x GL 810 HY); two trainable compressed-air catapults[30]

A second, almost-identical ship, to be named *Colbert*, was funded the following year, and would be laid down at Brest on 12 June 1927, a month after *Suffren* was launched. The hull, protection and propulsion systems would be the same as in *Suffren*, but above the main deck, there would be a number of differences that distinguished *Colbert* from her near-sister. Where *Suffren* had two bridge levels mounted on her substantial tripod foremast above her conning tower, *Colbert* had a more conventional bridge structure, with her two upper bridge levels built behind and around her conning tower. *Colbert* had the new, larger 90mm/50 AA guns in place of the 75mm/50s in *Suffren*. To compensate for the greater weight and size of the 90mm AA guns, *Colbert* carried two fewer 37mm mounts. Probably the most noticeable change was the placement of the catapults in *Colbert* between the two funnels; this proved to be a more practical arrangement, better served by two smaller cranes alongside her after funnel in the place of a single, much larger crane amidships between the funnels.

Both ships underwent extended refits in the mid-1930s; the main result of these was the installation of a pair of HA directors with 9.84ft stereoscopic rangefinders that were intended to have been fitted at completion, but which were not ready until much later. On *Suffren*, these were mounted port-and-starboard abreast the forward funnel; on *Colbert*, they were placed on opposite bridge wings.

Atop her heavy foremast, *Suffren* had a large bi-level DCT, as seen in this image dated 15 October 1931, with a 16ft 5in SOM coincidence rangefinder at the back of the lower level for target ranging and a 9ft 10in Zeiss stereoscopic rangefinder in front for scartometry, the measurement of the distance between short shell splashes and the target. The upper level housed the Assistant Gunnery Officer and his team; the former had a periscope that protrudes from the roof of the 'step' at the front of the top level of the DCT. (NHHC)

Meandering on the Tiber

The Italians, having laid down the *Trento*s in 1925, looked across the Ligurian Sea with mixed feelings; while there was no doubting that the *Trento*s were more than a match for the *Duquesne*s, there was considerable concern about the other ships the French were building at the same time, the *contre-torpilleurs* – large destroyers, some would even describe them as small cruisers – starting with the six *Jaguar* class in late 1923. The *Stato Maggiore* reacted to the French decision to order six ships in the 2126-ton *Jaguar* class in their 1922 *tranche* with two different responses, both of which were pursued, at rather deliberate speed. One was to order their own new-design large destroyer types, starting with the '*Navigatori*' class, a class of twelve that were funded in the 1926 budget.[31] In the game of 'tit-for-tat' that the French and Italians were playing in the Mediterranean, each worried that the other might gain an advantage; when the French followed the order for three enlarged *Jaguar*s *(Guépards)* in 1925 with three more in 1926 – a ship type that was 25 per cent bigger and better-armed than the '*Navigatori*' – the Italians responded by looking towards a ship that would utterly dominate any 'super-destroyer'.

Unwilling to simply 'one-up' the French with a (hypothetical) 'super-*Navigatori*' that might displace a few hundred more tons and mount a few more guns, the Italians instead looked for their inspiration to the much-liked scout cruisers *Quarto* and *Bixio*, which had been designed before the First World War. What was wanted was a similar combination of destroyer-like speed and cruiser-like gunpower. As early as 1912, the *Regia Marina* had asked then-Captain (GN) Bonfiglietti to develop an improved *Quarto* of 5000 tons to be armed with eight 6in main-battery guns. Three ships to this design were ordered in 1914, but the cessation of shipments of steel from Great Britain at the beginning of the First World War, upon which Italian naval shipbuilding was then largely dependent, meant such large ships could no longer be contemplated. After the war, plans were made to update Bonfiglietti's 1912 design and reorder the scout cruisers starting with the 1921 programme, but a severe budget crisis in 1921–2 made that impossible. It would not be until 1925, when, now a Fascist state firmly under Mussolini's control, the Italian economy could again support the construction of larger warships and the idea of a larger complement to the '*Navigatori*' could again be considered.[32]

RN *Alberto di Giussano*, the first of the numerous '*Condottieri*', the Italian light cruisers intended to outclass the French *contre-torpilleurs*, were intended to be part of a fleet of light, heavily-armed and ultimately expendable warships designed for 'hit and run' tactics. To that end, they were very fast, with a top speed of over 36 knots, but had very light armour. When employed in more conventional warfare in the Second World war, they fared very poorly. One of the problems they had, which was overcome only with difficulty, was excessive salvo dispersion of the main battery of eight 152mm/53 Mod 1926 guns carried in four twin turrets, caused by this being a high-velocity weapon with the two barrels in each turret mounted too close to each other in a single cradle; the problem was resolved by firing a lighter projectile with a smaller charge at a lower velocity and introducing a delay between firing the two barrels. (NHHC)

The task of designing these new ships, designated 'large scouts' (*grandi esploratori*), fell to General (GN) Giuseppe Vian, under Rota's direction.[33] The directions given to Vian in 1926 by the *Stato Maggiore* called for a ship capable of carrying a main-battery gun bigger than the 130mm/40s of the *Jaguar*s and the 138.6mm/40s of the *Guépard*s, while being able to achieve a top speed of better than 36.5 knots. Of necessity, this would mean sacrificing protection; it was accepted that these ships would be armoured only against destroyer gunfire. The design that Vian presented to the staff in early 1927 was for a small, fast light cruiser with the following specifications:

'Condottieri' Type – 1st Group

Displacement (std):	5200 tons (design); 5110 tons–5170 tons (actual)
Length (oa):	555ft 5in
Beam (wl):	51ft 2in
Draft (mean):	19ft 4in (deep)
Power plant:	95,000shp (design); Belluzzo geared turbines driving two shafts; six Yarrow boilers
Speed:	36.5 knots (design)
Range (designed):	3800nm @ 18 knots; 1230 tons oil fuel
Protection (side):	0.94in AER shell plating with 0.71in AER splinter bulkhead inboard (in way of engineering spaces); 0.79in AER shell plating with 0.71in AER splinter bulkhead inboard (in way of main-battery magazines)[34]
Protection (horiz):	0.79in AER (Upper Deck over main-battery magazines and engineering spaces)
Armament (main):	8 x 152mm/53 Mod 1926 (4 x 2 – two forward and two aft)
Armament (AA):	6 x 100mm/47 Mod 1927 (3 x 2); 4 x 40mm/39 Vickers-Terni (4 x 1); 8 x 12.7mm machine guns (4 x 2)
Armament (torp):	4 x 533mm (2 x 2)
Aircraft:	2 (2 x Ro.43 reconnaissance floatplanes); one catapult (fixed in forecastle)[35]

Funds for four of these ships, which would carry the names of famous Italian mercenary captains (*condottieri*) of the Middle Ages and Renaissance periods, were included in the 1927 budget, though none would be laid down until the following year. (The first would be named *Alberto di Giussano*.) The intent, according to a plan developed at this

The *Regia Marina* did not scrimp in providing director towers and rangefinders on their cruisers, even intentionally small ones like the first group of *'Condottieri'*; besides the large main-battery DCT atop the tetrapod foremast, there was an identical DCT atop the conning tower forward (the aft part of it is just visible in the close-up of the forward superstructure of RN *Alberico da Barbiano*). Two HA directors can be seen here on the foremast wings. Also, there was an auxiliary DCT on the after superstructure, and two large rangefinders on Turrets No 2 and 3. (NHHC)

The Italian heavy AA gun, the 100mm/47 Mod 1927 twin mount, was designed so that it could be loaded at any angle, up to its maximum elevation of 85°, by the expedient of raising or lowering the height of the guns' trunnion as the angle of elevation changed, thus keeping the height of the loading trays constant. This was ingenious technology, but was complex engineering, and slowed the elevation rate of the guns, making them less effective against high-speed aircraft. This image shows a training session on RN *Giovanni delle Bande Nere*. It might have been staged specifically for the photographer; no-one in this image is taking the event too seriously, not the onlookers, who are in various relaxed poses, or even the gun crew itself. Note the life-preservers draped over railings and splinter mats; the fourth gunner from the left even has his helmet on backwards. Note also the racks for ready-service rounds inside the gun shield. (NHHC)

time by Chief of the *Stato Maggiore* Admiral Alfredo Acton and Rear Admiral Costanzo Ciano – the former ending a long, distinguished career, the latter a war hero who became an early supporter of Mussolini – was to base the future *Regia Marina* around a force of twelve '*Condottieri*' and twenty-four '*Navigatori*', 'stiffened' by the three *Trento*s and whatever capital ships might be in service.[36] The idea was that this would be a force of fast, powerful, but ultimately expendable, craft that would harass enemy forces with 'hit and run' tactics. But with the retirement of Acton in 1927 and Ciano's increasing involvement in politics, the direction of naval policy was taken over by others and shifted towards more conventional strategy and the initial '*Condottieri*' would increasingly find themselves ships without an obvious strategic or tactical role to play.

Swing and a Miss: Geneva 1927

No-one thought the Washington Conference had resolved all the issues of naval armaments, especially not with the nagging question of cruiser numbers and overall tonnage clearly left unresolved, but there was hope that future initiatives would carry the effort to a successful conclusion. The leading force in this effort, other than the governments themselves, was the League of Nations, which, even though the United States had not signed on, still embodied the hopes of many that reasonable men could lay the groundwork for global disarmament. (Despite not ratifying the Treaty of Versailles or formally joining the League, the Americans sent observers to attend all major League activities and, to all intents, acted like a member.) So, it transpired that while the naval powers were building their first generation of 'treaty maximum' cruisers as defined at Washington, diplomats in Geneva began the process of organising a conference to mandate global disarmament, not only of navies but of all arms, a massively complex undertaking. As with almost everything the League did, the General Disarmament Conference started with grand proclamations of intent and majestic rhetorical flourishes, and immediately bogged down in a seemingly-endless series of meetings by a preparatory commission starting in May 1926.

The 'way out' had been provided by Coolidge, the American President, who, under considerable pressure from his own party in Congress to rein in defence spending – the US Army had already been pared to the bone, so the only 'discretionary' military spending left was on new warships – proposed a new naval disarmament conference independent of the League process on 10 February 1927. Such was the urgency he felt to get the process moving that his Secretary of State Frank B Kellogg sent invitations out to the four other Contracting Powers from the Washington Conference on 14 March to gather in Geneva in mid-June. Even today, this would not give nations much time to prepare for a major international conference; in the days before jet airliners and instant connectivity, this was preposterously short notice for such an event.

Neither France nor Italy had left the Washington Conference happy with the result. Regardless of geopolitical realities, neither liked being categorised as only slightly more than half as 'major' as Japan and even less compared to Britain or the United States. Within days of receiving Kellogg's invitations, both France and Italy had respectfully declined to attend, although, in the end, both ended up sending representatives to observe the proceedings.

The Admiralty was under its own pressure to cut costs. Having approved the smaller and marginally cheaper *York* design in February 1926, the British were ready to commit fully to building only smaller cruisers; the one nagging concern was the disadvantageous position in which this would put the Royal Navy if other navies did not follow suit. In an attempt to devise a strategy that would 'encourage' the Americans and Japanese, in particular, to build only smaller cruisers in the future, the Admiralty Board, in December 1926, proposed that a hard limit on cruiser tonnage be imposed and the 5:5:3 ratio agreed upon at Washington for capital ship tonnage between the three countries be applied to cruisers in such a manner that the construction of 'treaty maximum' cruisers would be limited, if not halted entirely, and only the construction of smaller cruisers, preferably armed with 6in guns, would be allowed.[37]

When Kellogg's invitation arrived in London, the British accepted eagerly. Having so recently presented a broad proposal to the League commission, the Admiralty still needed to fill in many details. With regard to cruisers, the British intended to propose that the displacement limit should be lowered to 7500 tons and the maximum gun calibre to 6in after an agreed-upon number of 'treaty maximum' cruisers had been completed. The Admiralty reiterated its long-standing desire for seventy cruisers – twenty-five for fleet work and forty-five for trade protection – while 'calculating' that, by the same formula, the United States needed a total of forty-seven cruisers and Japan twenty-one. With astonishingly clear foresight, the Admiralty acknowledged that the Americans and Japanese might make 'special claims' that would require some upward adjustment to the numbers they would be allocated in the British proposal.[38]

Perhaps even more incredible than the hubris involved in presuming to decide how many cruisers other nations needed – it was, after all, not much different in principle from what Hughes had done at Washington – was the decision, first proposed by Beatty, that the entire plan be kept secret until the conference began, so that it could be sprung on the assembled delegates with the same dramatic effect as Hughes' initial proposal had at Washington. As will be seen, this turned out to be a very bad idea.

The American opening position, worked out primarily by the conference delegation's naval experts, Rear Admirals Hilary P Jones and Andrew T Long, could be stated simply; while anticipating quite accurately that the British would attempt to negotiate a superior position in regard to cruiser numbers, the Americans intended to propose that the same 5:5:3 ratio that British and Japanese had accepted at Washington for capital ships should be applied to all lesser warship categories, forgetting how utterly this simple formula had failed to satisfy either nation five years earlier. As far as the Americans were concerned, parity between the United States and Royal Navies in cruisers, as in all other types of ships, was the only possible

The man the British blamed more than any other for the failure of the Geneva Conference of 1927 was then-Rear Admiral Hilary P Jones, USN, who was one of the technical advisors to the American head of delegation Ambassador Hugh S Gibson. Jones is seen in this image as a Vice Admiral – a temporary rank he held because he was serving as CinC US Fleet – on USS *Pennsylvania* (BB38) in 1923. (NARA)

basis for an agreement. Before the two Rear Admirals left for London in March, the General Board had worked out an acceptable quantitative limit for cruiser tonnage, understanding that the British would certainly have their own limits in mind, proposing a limit of between 250,000–300,000 tons for the Americans and British. (In practical terms, this would limit both navies to between twenty-five and thirty 'treaty maximum' cruisers.) It was well understood in Washington that this proposal had little chance of being acceptable in London.[39]

The other main player at the table in Geneva, of course, would be Japan, but neither the Americans or British were terribly concerned about the position of Tokyo going into the conference. The Japanese had proved to be susceptible to pressure at Washington, and the belief among the Western 'Powers' was that they would, albeit reluctantly, accept a similar secondary-power status again in Geneva. In fact, the Japanese delegation, led by former Navy Minister Admiral Saito Makoto, had been tasked primarily with addressing the still-irksome 60 per cent ratio they had been pressured into accepting at Washington. Their opening position was to propose an almost total cessation of new naval construction programmes, but, failing that, they then favoured an overall tonnage-based (quantitative) limitation system over an individual ship displacement-based (qualitative) limitation system, bringing them closer to the American than the British position.[40]

The gathering of the delegates began with the American delegation, led by Ambassador Hugh S Gibson, passing through London.[41] Rear Admiral Jones took advantage of the opportunity to pay a courtesy call at Whitehall, where he met the naval side of the British delegation; that delegation would be led by First Lord Bridgeman, with Deputy Chief of the Naval Staff Vice Admiral Frederick L Field as the lead naval expert. In only the briefest of visits, Jones made it clear to the Lords of the Admiralty that the Americans would never accept a position of less than equality with any other navy in any category of warship.

Geneva in mid-June 1927 proved to unseasonably hot and humid, the oppressive weather broken only by occasional thunderstorms. In the days before air-conditioning, it was hardly the most ideal conditions for a conference in which, from the beginning, it became clear there was little, if any, common ground for negotiation. The atmosphere leading up to the beginning of the conference, at least publicly, was cordial and optimistic, but that did not last long.[42] The opening session, which was held on 20 June, was led off by Gibson, as the Americans had called the conference. This brief, 45-minute session saw each of the three participants state their basic positions.

Gibson's opening address was short and well-received. The same cannot be said for the remarks by Bridgeman, leading the British delegation. Clearly, Beatty's desire to surprise the conference with Britain's opening proposition had succeeded, perhaps too well. The reaction among the Americans present appeared to be not pleasant surprise, but genuine shock and dismay.[43] The particular issues that raised the Americans' ire were Proposals Nos 7 and 8 (out of nine) from Bridgeman's opening statement. The first of these endorsed the 5:5:3 ratio of the Washington Treaty for 'treaty maximum' cruisers, the number of which that would be allowed was to be determined. (It was understood that the British wanted that number to be no larger than the number already built or building.) The second proposed restricting any future cruisers to the 7500-ton and 6in main-battery gun limits preferred by the Royal Navy. The American reaction was a point-by-point rejection of Bridgeman's proposals. The Americans had no interest in smaller cruisers. The United States did not have a world-wide network of naval bases comparable to that possessed by the British Empire, one that could support the use of smaller, shorter-ranging cruisers. Nor did the Americans see the logic behind reducing the main-battery gun calibre. (To the British, the main function of the smaller trade defence cruisers would be to protect convoys against the predations of enemy auxiliary cruisers – potentially numerous armed merchant conversions – which were unlikely to be armed with anything larger than a few 6in guns.) To the Americans, there was no point in going to the great effort of gaining Congressional funding for building a cruiser, and then arming it with anything less than the maximum possible weaponry. But the real irritant to the Americans was the issue of quantitative versus qualitative restriction; nowhere in Bridgeman's proposal was a limit on total cruiser tonnage mentioned. The Americans wanted a hard limit on total cruiser tonnage; their opening position was that the Americans and British should agree to a limit between 250,000 tons and 300,000 tons. The British were reluctant to address the issue of total tonnage-by-type, preferring to limit tonnage-by-ship. Reconciling the two approaches would be difficult, if not impossible.

The Japanese opening position was in some ways the most radical, because it proposed 'freezing' the fleets of the three nations at their currently authorised levels.[44] This position was driven largely by internal economic considerations; the Japanese economy had been suffering a serious downturn, and reaching an agreement with Great Britain and the United States that allowed the government to avoid new expenditures on naval construction was very much to be desired.

The opening session ended with the decision to set up a technical committee, to be chaired by Bridgeman, which would attempt to work out some sort of compromise on categories and limits. When that committee met on 5 July, Jones offered a significant concession, proposing to increase the total tonnage limit for cruisers for the Americans and British to 400,000 tons, with the added tonnage beyond 250,000 tons to be restricted to cruisers of smaller displacement, as long as the maximum gun calibre remained unchanged.[45] (Jones made it clear that he personally considered 400,000 tons to be far beyond the needs of the

United States Navy and hoped that the conference would settle on a figure closer to 300,000 tons.) The British reacted negatively, believing both that the total tonnage was still far too low to meet their needs – Bridgeman explained in a press conference that the Royal Navy needed 470,000 tons of cruisers – and that any cruisers built after the construction of large cruisers was halted should be restricted to 6in-gun main batteries. He made the point that a 6in-armed cruiser could only be seen as defensive rather than larger cruisers that he claimed were only designed for aggression.[46] Bridgeman went so far as to label Jones' proposal an 'ultimatum'.[47]

The British began working behind the scenes to undermine Jones' position. Bridgeman went first to Gibson, who seemed amenable to finding common ground, but would not order Jones to alter the American position.[48] The British Ambassador to the United States was roused from his 'Summer embassy' in Manchester, NH, to call on Kellogg in Washington, DC the next day, though to little avail. Despite official reticence to say anything substantive on record, it was clear to all that the two met to discuss the apparent deadlock in Geneva. Kellogg is believed to have told the Ambassador that 400,000 tons was as far as the Americans were willing to go in terms of aggregate cruiser tonnage, and was regarded in Washington as considerably in excess of the actual cruiser needs of either country. Further, Kellogg was reported as having emphasised that Japan's economic situation, which was forcing that nation to look for ways to limit sharply naval expenditures, had to be factored into any discussion of naval arms limitation. He is believed to have stated his belief that the Japanese delegation in Geneva would offer strenuous objection to the enlarged cruiser programme which the British experts had proposed.[49]

Indeed, Admiral Saito had made it clear on 6 July that the Japanese strongly favoured the lowest limitation figure that had been offered, the 250,000-ton lower limit first proposed by the Americans for themselves and the British, which implied acceptance of a 150,000-ton limit for Japan. His exact words were that 'it might be impossible for us to go home with a treaty agreeing to such cruiser figures as the British have submitted'.[50] There is no question that this turn of events was not to the liking of the British delegation, who clearly were hoping that the traditional Anglo-Japanese friendship and the growing tension in the Pacific would work in their favour. The Britons' disappointment was profound; they were described as receiving Admiral Saito's statement as if they had been physically assaulted. After the meeting, Bridgeman was seen driving away in his car, saying he needed a long drive in the fresh air to clear his mind.[51]

The next day brought new proposals from the Americans and Japanese as they scrambled to salvage what certainly appeared to be a failing conference. Jones presented a modified version of the 400,000-ton cruiser tonnage limit idea he had presented two days earlier. In this version, the United States and Great Britain would be limited to eighteen 'treaty maximum' cruisers – a number the Americans said the British would reach when they completed the ships then authorised – after that all cruisers built up to an aggregate tonnage of 400,000 tons would be to a maximum of 7500 tons displacement while retaining a maximum 8in main-battery gun calibre.[52] To the Americans, this was a major concession, lowering the number of 'treaty maximum' cruisers they were proposing to acquire by seven, from twenty-five to eighteen – albeit only eight of these were as yet authorised or funded by Congress. This new proposal, apparently made at Gibson's urging, was a good-faith effort on the part of the Americans to find a formula the British could accept without abandoning tonnage limits, which the Americans would not do. However, to the British, who remained focused on their goal of seventy cruisers overall, with smaller, more lightly-armed light cruisers making up the majority of that number, the American 'concession' was little more than window-dressing, because it would have limited the United States to forty-eight cruisers and the Royal Navy, theoretically, to a similar number.

The actual count would have been much more complex for the British because the Royal Navy retained thirty-nine pre-war, war-built or war-designed light cruisers of between 3700–5400 tons, although a number of those were 'war-weary' and about to be discarded; twenty-two of them, however, would survive to see service in the Second World War. Both sides spent a good deal of effort calculating what the other side had or needed when they could have just asked, but, given the state of Anglo-American relations at this point, it is likely that neither side would have trusted the answer they received. Indeed, so rancorous and petty were the relations, between Bridgeman and the Americans in particular, that the head of the British delegation gave vent publicly to rumours that had been circulating in Geneva about an American 'big navy' lobbyist, in the pay of the steel industry, who was supposedly in Geneva to undermine efforts at reaching agreement.[53] Bridgeman's public comments clearly irritated Gibson, his most useful friend in the American delegation. When Bridgeman asked what American steel and manufacturing interests would benefit from naval contracts, Gibson replied that it was certainly not 'the amalgamated needle workers or leather combines' that built warships for any nation.[54] Of course, what made the British complaints about the purported activities of the American lobbyist so absurd was that, assuming the lobbyist was really working to push for greater tonnage allocations, this should all have been in line with British interests, at least in terms of their position on cruiser construction.

The Japanese, fearful of the consequences of returning from Geneva with nothing to show for their efforts to redress the lingering displeasure at the outcome of the Washington Conference, tried again to find a formula that both lowered naval expenditures and gave them at least a marginal increase in allocation. Saito proposed a 450,000-ton limit for Great Britain and the United States in aggregate tonnage of cruisers and destroyers, with 300,000 tons for Japan.[55] At the same time he asked for an increase in the Japanese allocation of submarine tonnage, claiming they were needed for defensive purposes. The fact that these proposals would have increased the Japanese ratios (for auxiliary surface combatants) from 60 per cent to 66.67 per cent guaranteed American opposition to this proposal and the relatively low combined total assured British rejection.[56]

Needless to say, the British were not happy with either set of proposals put forth on 7 July. As much as they disliked the whole idea of quantitative limits, they finally accepted that in order to have any chance at an agreement they would have to produce a plan with limits they could accept. Bridgeman asked Gibson, as conference chairman, to call for a second plenary session of all delegates on Monday, 11 July, at which he intended to present a new British proposal that would be put together over the weekend.[57]

In the meanwhile, the conference came close to collapse as tempers flared at a technical committee meeting on Saturday, 9 July. British delegate Robert Cecil, in the midst of a discussion of the cruiser problem, responding to a point made by Rear Admiral Jones, is reported to have banged his fist on the table and to have exclaimed 'This is perfect nonsense!'[58] While that may seem to be a mild statement by 21st-century standards, when abrasive dialogue is increasingly accepted as normal, in the context of diplomatic discourse in 1927 it was absolutely shocking. Gibson, who was apparently still upset from remarks made earlier in the session by Cecil, is reported to have risen to his feet at this point and to have demanded a retraction from Cecil, stating that otherwise he would be obliged to leave. Cecil withdrew the remark.[59] This account, from a wire service report, was apparently a description of what had become a fairly typical interaction between the American and British delegations, who seemed, by this point, barely able to tolerate each other's presence. The frayed nerves on everyone's part were clearly evident.

While not the leader of the British delegation at Geneva in 1927, certainly the most combative was Robert Cecil, a career diplomat and strong supporter of 'collective security' as represented by the League of Nations. He is seen here in a portrait taken in 1915. (LOC/BNS)

A major impasse having been reached, the British asked that the plenary session planned for 11 July be postponed. A new British proposal was rapidly generated and presented informally that Monday. It was complex and, in a first for a British proposal, included a definite quantitative limit on tonnage. The British proposal called for 'treaty maximum' cruisers to be capped at twelve each for the United States and Great Britain and eight for Japan, giving the Japanese the ratio they desired in that category of warships. An aggregate total of 'auxiliary surface combatants' would be set at 550,000 tons (350,000 tons of cruisers) for the Americans and British and 320,000 tons (210,000 tons of cruisers) for the Japanese, which would give that nation 58 per cent of the tonnage of the 'major Powers', a figure certain to be unacceptable to Tokyo. All cruisers beyond the designated number of 'treaty maximum' cruisers would be limited to a displacement of 6000 tons and 6in maximum main-battery gun calibre, both figures certain to displease the Americans, who undoubtedly would find such a ship too small and too weakly-armed for their needs.[60]

When the delayed plenary session convened on Thursday, 14 July, the same three chief delegates, plus Admiral Jellicoe, spoke. That did not, however, mean that the interchanges were at all cordial. Gibson led off, stating his great desire that an agreement should be reached for the greater good of mankind and repeating that the Americans remained committed to a basic principle of quantitative limit by type. Bridgeman followed, changing the tone to one of recrimination, claiming that the 'conference atmosphere is being vitiated by gross misrepresentation of the British case,' and later in his remarks returning to the point, stating 'every atom of partial information has been dragged from its context in order to create friction and ill-will'.[61] There was absolutely no doubt in anyone's mind who Bridgeman thought was the guilty party. Gibson shot back, making it clear that the Americans believed they had been forthcoming in attempting to find the middle ground, and that it was now up to the Japanese and British, as the holders of the extreme positions, to craft a compromise. The implication was that the Americans would accept that compromise position, if it could be reached. Gibson's exact words were:

> We feel that we are in such close agreement with the Japanese delegation with respect to total tonnage limitation and types of the cruiser class that we could easily find a basis of agreement with them.
>
> But that is not enough. All three of us must be in agreement.
>
> If some basis can be found which is mutually acceptable to the British and Japanese delegations, I feel sure that it will be possible for the American delegation to make the agreement complete.[62]

Bridgeman's reaction to the prospect was far from enthusiastic; at the conclusion of Gibson's later remarks, he was reportedly overheard stating to one of his fellow delegates, 'He has passed the baby on for us to hold.'[63]

The following day seemed to be one in which all parties tried hard to avoid saying anything publicly that might worsen the already fraught situation. Gibson was seen playing golf, while Bridgeman and Saito made news in that they did not meet with each other, but British and Japanese 'experts' in fact did confer and began attempting to cobble together a compromise position.[64] By Saturday, 16 July, rumours were running rampant in Geneva that the British and Japanese were having difficulty reaching agreement, and, should they fail to do so by the end of the day on Monday, that Gibson was planning on calling another plenary session to introduce his own new compromise proposal, which would cap cruiser tonnage at 300,000 tons (with 180,000 tons for the Japanese) and a limit of eighteen 'treaty maximum' cruisers (twelve for the Japanese).[65] It was similar to the original American proposal except for the lower number of maximum-sized heavy cruisers. As an incentive for the Japanese to accept this proposal, the rumours said that the Americans intended to offer them the possibility of negotiating an increase in their allocation of cruisers to 200,000 tons.

On that Sunday evening, Ishii Kikujiro, a former Japanese Foreign Minister and delegate, met with Gibson to bring him up to date on progress in the Anglo-Japanese negotiations.[66] While not all issues had been decided, considerable agreement had been reached. The general terms agreed upon by the two nations included a limit of 500,000 tons of 'surface auxiliaries' for the United States and Great Britain, with an additional 25 per cent of that number in overage vessels not counted against that total which could be retained in service, thus effectively allowing 625,000 tons in total. Of the 500,000-ton figure, approximately 300,000 tons would be allocated to cruisers, of which twelve would be allowed to be 'treaty maximum' size and the remainder smaller. Issues still to be determined included the exact ratio of Japan's allocation in each of the categories – it was understood that Japan was seeking parity in submarine tonnage – and whether smaller cruisers would be restricted to mounting 6in guns as the maximum main battery.[67]

By Monday, even more details emerged. The British stated that general agreement was reached on terms much as Ishii had disclosed and that, further, the Japanese had accepted a limit of eight 'treaty maximum' cruisers.[68] While the British further stated that no specific proposal had been agreed upon, and that they, the British, still were considering whether the overall totals and the specific apportioning of ships within those totals were acceptable, the Japanese were claiming that a firm agreement had been reached and sent to Tokyo for approval. On that same day, Admirals Beatty and Jellicoe reported to the Prime Minister and Foreign Secretary in London on the progress so far in the negotiations with the Japanese.[69] It was at this point that wires appear to have gotten crossed; the message delivered by the admirals was apparently enough to convince Baldwin and the Foreign Secretary Austen Chamberlain that the Geneva delegation was giving away too much to the Japanese in order to strike a deal.

It was clear that what Beatty and Jellicoe told Baldwin was unsettling, because Robert Cecil was recalled to London on the evening of Tuesday, 19 July and Bridgeman early the next morning.[70] Bridgeman was to have been accompanied back to London by his senior naval expert, Vice Admiral Field, but the latter was suffering from one of his chronic bouts of intestinal distress and he remained in Geneva. (Indeed, Field's health had deteriorated to the point that when the chief delegates returned to Geneva, Field was replaced by Rear Admiral Alfred 'Dudley' Pound.) The recall to London was done so hurriedly that it was announced to the American and Japanese delegations by telephone after the fact. The reason given to Gibson for this dramatic move, was that the British Cabinet required 'elucidation' concerning the negotiations with the Japanese.

The British delegation remained in London for almost a week. Back in Geneva, it was reported on Wednesday, 20 July, that Tokyo had approved an agreement with the British that included a 500,000-ton limit on 'surface auxiliaries' for the United States and Great Britain and 325,000 tons (64 per cent) for Japan, with all three nations being allowed 60,000 tons of submarines. The number of 'treaty maximum' cruisers would be limited at 12-12-8, and all subsequent cruisers would be limited to 7500 tons and a 6in maximum main-battery gun calibre.[71] It is impossible to determine, at this remove, how accurate a rendition of any Anglo-Japanese agreement this was. Judging from how the Cabinet reacted and what Bridgeman actually proposed on his return from London, it likely was reasonably close to correct.

Assuming for the moment that the proposal just described was an accurate portrayal of the plan worked out by the British and Japanese, it was a 'non-starter' from the American point-of-view – because of the small number of 'treaty maximum' cruisers and the main-battery gun limit for the follow-on cruisers and also because of the proposed parity in submarine tonnage. The British worked over the weekend to cobble together a public relations offensive to make the case that the impending failure of the Geneva Conference was not their fault. This included an address in the House of Lords by the

Lord Privy Seal, James Gascoyne-Cecil (older brother of Robert Cecil), on 27 July laying out the British government's final defence of its position on cruisers.[72]

> . . . His Majesty's Government, while urging the special difficulties due to Britain's geographical position, are far from claiming the least right to dictate any small cruiser policy to other Powers. They accept the general principles which, as they understand them, underlie the President's policy that no maritime Power should maintain a larger navy than is required for its own security.
>
> To translate this into figures is . . . far more difficult in the case of small cruisers than in the case of the larger types of surface vessels. . . . Two nations each possessing a hundred thousand tons of battleships may be regarded without serious error as being (so far) equal in fighting power. No such statement can reasonably be made about two nations one of which has ten cruisers of 10,000 tons, while the other has twenty cruisers of 5,000 tons. It all depends upon circumstances; though naval experts would probably agree that, if it came to fighting, the more numerous but smaller vessels would stand but a poor chance against their more powerful but less numerous opponents. If so, the country which for any reason was obliged to distribute its available tonnage among smaller units would be at a permanent disadvantage compared with one which was able to adopt a different scheme. There would be nominal parity but real inequality.
>
> This is, of course, merely an illustration. But it suffices to explain why, in the opinion of His Majesty's Government, no provisions open to this kind of criticism should be given the international authority already possessed by those parts of the Treaty of Washington which deal with strength and numbers. In the opinion of His Majesty's Government there need be no difficulty in arriving at a temporary arrangement about the immediate future of cruiser building. But the British Empire cannot be asked to give to any such temporary arrangement the appearance of an immutable principle, which might be treated as a precedent. Any other course would inevitably be interpreted in the future as involving the formal surrender by the British Empire of maritime equality . . .[73]

This was an altogether incredible statement from beginning to end, at least from the American point of view. All naval planning is done with a potential adversary (or adversaries) in mind; since at least 1922, all American naval planning had been aimed at Japan as the primary (and for all intents, sole) potential enemy, which explains the insistence on the large cruisers needed to cross the expanses of the Pacific and survive damage far from supporting bases. It is clear from the statement quoted above, that the British planners, despite repeated assurances that they could imagine no case in which they would find themselves at war with America, seemed to be extremely concerned about exactly that eventuality. Their next most likely potential adversary would be the Japanese; against Japan, the British would be better served by large cruisers similar to those advocated by the Americans, because they would likely face similar strategic challenges fighting a war halfway around the world. The large number of smaller cruisers for trade protection they sought were best suited for fighting a war against France or Italy, nations with small navies that looked towards a strategy of *guerre de course* if forced to fight a dominant naval power like Great Britain. The fact that all of these nations had been allies in the First World War seemed not to impact the Royal Navy's thinking, because relations with all of them had cooled considerably since that war. Despite Gascoyne-Cecil's protestations at the beginning of the passage cited above that the British did not claim the 'right to dictate any small cruiser policy to other Powers', to the Americans, that was exactly what they appeared to be doing, especially after Bridgeman's return from London on Thursday, 28 July.

The British clearly wanted the best of all worlds, namely the freedom to build a navy that could defeat a *guerre de course*, while assuring themselves that no-one else (meaning the United States or Japan) was allowed to build a navy that could defeat it in a more conventional war. Of course, what made this position so totally absurd was that a simple glance at recent history showed that the biggest threat to Great Britain's vital seaborne lifelines came not from raiding cruisers (be they AMCs or regular warships), but rather from submarines. The dramatic defeat of the U-boat offensive in the First World War – by the adoption of the convoy system and the deployment of adequate numbers of escort vessels – led the Royal Navy to overlook the existential danger presented by rapidly-improving submarine types and to over-value the threat of surface raiders.

The ultimate British proposal, presented on the afternoon of 28 July, was for 590,000 tons of all auxiliary craft, including submarines, for the United States and Great Britain, and 385,000 tons for Japan.[74] (This would give the Japanese a 65 per cent ratio in aggregate tonnage.) Bridgeman proposed three categories of cruisers: 'treaty maximum' cruisers, to which the frequently-mentioned 12-12-8 limit would be applied; a 'catch-all' category of existing relatively-new somewhat-smaller cruisers, such as the *Hawkins*, *Emerald*s and *York*, the *Furutaka*s and *Aoba*s, and the *Omaha*s; and, finally, all future new cruisers beyond those allocated to the already-outlined sub-types; these would be limited to 6000 tons and 6in main-battery guns. (The British, noting that the 'catch-all' sub-type put the Americans at a disadvantage, would allow them to construct a small number of compensatory vessels.) The proposal then went on to specify that up to 25 per cent additional tonnage in 'overage' vessels – vessels older than the age limits for each type stated in the proposal – could be retained in commission by each nation; this, of course, was a proviso that almost exclusively benefitted the Royal Navy, at least as far as cruisers were concerned.

The reaction to this proposal was predictable. The Japanese were reported to be resigned to the failure of the conference because of the wide gap between the British and American positions on cruisers.[75] One report stated that Gibson was already preparing an address assigning blame for the failure of the conference. A busy weekend of diplomatic activity led Gibson to delay the next plenary session, although it was not revealed why he did so.[76] By Monday, it was clear that, if there was to be any hope for a compromise that might save the conference, it would have to be crafted by the Japanese. The Japanese delegation spent most of the day meeting among themselves, after which Ishii met with Bridgeman on into the evening, all without any obvious signs of progress. Saito and Ishii presented their plan separately to Gibson and Bridgeman on Tuesday.[77] This plan, labelled a 'status quo' proposal that attempted to be minimally disruptive of each nation's current plans, was apparently intentionally ambiguous on a number of points so as to avoid immediate rejection by either side. For 'treaty maximum' cruisers, the proposal followed the standard 12-12-8 limit, but later in the same section, stated that each nation would be allowed to complete its currently 'authorised' building programme. Beyond the number of allowable 'treaty maximum' cruisers, the displacement of any cruisers would be limited to 8000 tons. The thorny issue of maximum main-battery gun calibre was left for later discussion. It was not clear in this proposal how *York* and a second planned 'B' cruiser would count against these totals, as they would be smaller than 'treaty maximum', but larger than 8000 tons. Depending on who was counting and how generous they were with the numbers, the total aggregate cruiser tonnage allowed Great Britain under this proposal would be over 460,000 tons or under 400,000 tons.

A final face-to-face meeting between the three delegations, with Bridgeman and Cecil for the British, Saito and Ishii for the Japanese and Gibson for the Americans, took place in the afternoon on Wednesday, 3 August, to make one last attempt at compromise, but it was doomed from the start by mistrust and misunderstanding between the British and Americans.[78] Gibson started the meeting by explaining that the Americans did not understand exactly how the British interpreted the word 'authorised', which was critical to the Japanese proposal. (In America and Japan, 'authorisation' came by legislative act; at the time of the Geneva Conference, both nations had eight cruisers so authorised, meaning the Americans would be allowed some 'catching-up' under the Japanese plan. The British system was far more complex, at least to the outside observer. Neither the Americans nor Japanese understood exactly how many cruisers of what size were 'authorised' to be built in Great Britain, nor did they know what body did the 'authorising'. Was it the Birkenhead Committee, the Cabinet or Parliament?) When Gibson asked the British to explain what they understood the term to mean, the response from Cecil was unhelpful. Asked if the British intended to build all ships allowed by the Birkenhead Committee report, Bridgeman replied in the affirmative. When Gibson stated that this would allow them in excess of 450,000 tons of cruisers, Bridgeman's response was that the British preferred not to negotiate in terms of aggregate tonnage.

This effectively brought negotiations to an end. Gibson asked the two other delegations if they had any further proposals. When they replied negatively – Ishii's response almost inaudible – Gibson began discussion of arrangements for the plenary session the following afternoon, at which he suggested each delegation might make a brief final statement and a joint communique would be issued. Even at this point, the British and Americans could not see eye-to-eye. When Gibson stated his wish that the final statements be 'moderate' in tone, Cecil objected on the grounds that the British would not allow for any 'suppression of speech'.[79]

In the end, the final session was anti-climactic, with no fireworks or acrimony.[80] Bridgeman thanked Gibson for his patience and apologised for his own occasional lapses of temper, and then broadly restated Britain's position. Saito laid out Japan's repeated attempts to find common ground between the opposing sides and expressed his nation's regret at the failure to find a way to reduce arms expenditures. Gibson was the most outspoken in his final remarks, but he did, in this author's opinion, an excellent job of summing up the cause of the failure to reach agreement, when he stated:

> The British delegation in its proposals sought to secure agreement to limit very strictly the number of the larger type of cruisers with 8-inch guns and to limit all other construction to small size cruisers armed with 6-inch guns, a type of ship of relatively small use to us because of its lack of cruising radius and protection.[81]

As convincing as Gibson was, at least to an American audience, the British remained certain that the lion's share of the blame for the failure of the conference was due to American intransigence. As recently as the 1960s, when Roskill wrote his masterly *Naval Policy Between the Wars*, he put the onus for the conference's failure squarely on Rear Admiral Jones, and by extension, the General Board of the United States Navy, for so inflexibly refusing to agree to be limited to building only smaller, more lightly-armed cruisers. As Roskill put it:

> Thus although it would certainly be unfair to place the whole responsibility for the débâcle of 1927 on [the General Board], it does seem fair to attribute it mainly to American mishandling of the initiative and excessive rigidity in negotiation.[82]

The greatest lesson both sides drew from the experience was that a framework for agreement should exist before a conference of this importance convenes. It should not be assumed that simply because all sides agree that disarmament is a good idea and saving money on arms expenditures is of general benefit, that an agreement on how to accomplish these goals will be easy to achieve. The hard work of pounding out the rough shape of an agreement acceptable to the major parties needs to be accomplished well before the flags are unfurled and the trumpets sounded.

The Aftermath of Failure: *Exeter*, the *Surrey* and *Leander* Classes

The 1927 Royal Navy Estimates were to have included funding for one 'A' cruiser and two 'B' cruisers, but they fully anticipated having to revise those plans depending on the outcome of the Geneva Conference.[83] The outcome they least expected, and were least prepared for, was total failure; the Admiralty was left scrambling amidst the political backlash. The eventual outcome was that on 16 November 1927, Bridgeman asked Parliament for only a single repeat *York*, which was funded.[84] Only minor modifications were made in the earlier design. Perhaps the most significant change was in response to concern about the stability of the *York* design due to the narrowness of her hull and the height of her bridge structure; while the hull of HMS *Exeter* (68), as the new ship was named, had the same length as *York*'s, it was a foot broader. (It is worth noting that a small difference in beam can make a big difference in stability in otherwise similar designs.) During the design phase, *Exeter* was intended to carry two catapults like *York*, one on 'B' turret and one aft of the after funnel, but before the design was fixed, the 'B' turret catapult was deleted and two fixed catapults set to launch aircraft forward at a 45° angle from aft of the after funnel were planned, although they would not be fitted at the time of her completion. The deletion of the 'B' turret catapult allowed the adoption of a lower bridge structure, which also contributed to increased stability. The bridge was given angled sides that improved airflow around the structure, going a long way towards solving the problem of trapped funnel smoke; this became the model of Royal Navy cruiser bridge designs going

Another attempt to solve the problem of fitting aircraft facilities into ships that lacked adequate space was the plan adopted in *Exeter*, as seen here in this undated image. Just as seen before on *Norfolk* and *Sussex*, *Exeter* had the extensible catapults, but unlike those larger ships, she did not have room for a rotating catapult on the centreline. Instead, she had two fixed catapults, set at an angle so aircraft could be launched forward on either side. In this view, she has a pair of Supermarine Walruses with their wings folded back. (NHHC)

After the *Norfolk* class – and the failure of the Geneva Conference – the Royal Navy made a sincere, if inevitably futile, effort to lead the world to build smaller cruisers, by building first HMS *York* (90) and then *Exeter* (68), seen here as built, with one fewer main-battery turret and displacing approximately 17 per cent less than a 'treaty maximum' cruiser. She is shown here during the relatively brief period between her completion in 1931 and the installation of her catapults in the space between her second funnel and her after superstructure. Notice the somewhat lower bridge structure with angled sides and the trunking of the forward uptakes into (what would have been) the middle funnel, all in a mostly-successful attempt to resolve the problems of funnel smoke getting trapped behind the forward superstructure. (NHHC)

forward. Their different bridge shapes and the adoption of vertical rather than raked funnels in *Exeter* allow the two 'B' cruisers to be readily distinguished.

This design was approved by the Admiralty Board on 1 March 1928 and *Exeter*'s keel was laid down at Devonport on 1 August of that same year. Not long after her completion, the two catapults were installed and her two single 2pdr pompoms were removed. Besides those changes, she began the Second World War essentially unmodified.

The Royal Navy had been discussing design options for further 'A' cruisers even while arguing against such ships at the Geneva Conference. On 21 July 1927, even while that conference was staggering towards its eventual demise, Admiral Beatty, back in London, in one of his final acts as First Sea Lord, approved sketch designs of an improved-*Norfolk* – actually it was perhaps better described as an enlarged *Exeter* – that would have sacrificed some speed to gain incrementally-improved protection.[85] Money for two of these ships – to be named HMS *Surrey* and *Northumberland* – was included in the 1928 Naval Estimates and construction would have begun in the second half of 1929, but Stanley Baldwin's Conservative government was voted out of power in June 1929, being replaced by Ramsay MacDonald leading a Labour government that was even less amenable to supporting large naval expenditures. Among the first acts of the MacDonald government would be the temporary suspension of construction on all ships in the 1928 programme which had not yet been laid down.[86] This included the two *Surreys*.

With Beatty's retirement at the end of July 1927, the Royal Navy underwent a critical change in leadership. The new First Sea Lord was Admiral Charles E Madden, chosen in part in the hope of mending the on-going feud between the Beatty and Jellicoe 'factions' in the fleet. (Madden had served as chief-of-staff to Jellicoe and then second-in-command to Beatty, and had gotten along well with both.) The first planning Madden could influence was for the 1929 building programme. Assuming there were two 'A' cruisers as well as *Exeter* 'in the pipeline', thought turned to what kind of cruiser the Royal Navy most wanted and needed next.

Even though the Birkenhead Committee plan should have allowed three 'A' cruisers in the 1928 programme, only two were funded – the *Surreys* – which left considerable range for disagreement in the Admiralty about what the third cruiser should look like, when the funds became available. Bridgeman argued strongly that, having lobbied so strenuously at Geneva for smaller, 'defensive' cruisers, Great Britain was diplomatically 'obligated' to pursue that type of cruiser in the future.[87] Others, such as Field, were staunch partisans of the 'A' cruisers, and Vice Admiral A E M 'Ernle' Chatfield, Third Sea Lord and Controller of the Navy, in charge of procurement and thus very influential in the matter of ship design, was similarly opposed to 6in-gunned cruisers. Field and Chatfield were so strongly opposed to arming cruisers with the smaller main-battery gun that they cobbled together a plan for a 7000-ton ship armed with four 8in guns. After much discussion, the board decided to ask also for three 8400-ton cruisers armed with six 8in guns in the 1928 programme, but this ran into opposition from Churchill at the Treasury and the Admiralty withdrew the request.

After the change in government in 1929 and the cancellation of the *Surreys*, Bridgeman's long tenure as First Lord came to an end; he was replaced by Albert V Alexander, a career Labour politician. Alexander took the post vowing to support MacDonald's calls for further disarmament, in part by reducing future shipbuilding by the Royal Navy. Even before Bridgeman's departure, Madden had called for comments from the fleet on the types of cruisers needed to carry out fleet support and trade protection duties. In what was apparently something of a shock to the Admiralty Board, the fleet officers made it clear that large cruisers were not considered ideal for most fleet support functions.[88] Most fleet officers preferred the smaller and more manoeuvrable 'C' and 'D' class cruisers for tasks such as defence against destroyer attack and shadowing enemy formations. Larger cruisers might be better for tasks that required greater range and firepower, such as scouting and trade protection, but the higher rate of fire of the 6in gun was considered better suited for fleet support functions. Further, the consensus of opinion was that, if a new small cruiser was to have six or fewer 6in guns, it should carry them in single mounts; only if it were to carry eight or more main-battery guns would twin mounts be seen as the better arrangement.

With this information to work with, in December 1928, Madden asked Lillicrap for five sketch designs for small cruisers with main batteries ranging from five 5.5in guns to eight 6in guns.[89] This led to a staff requirement drawn up as follows:

Staff Requirement for Small Cruiser: Dec 1928

Displacement (std):	approx 6000 tons
Speed:	30.5 knots min @ deep load
Range:	7000nm @ 16 knots
Protection (side):	Immune to 6in gunfire beyond 16,500yd & 4.7in gunfire beyond 9000yd
Protection (horiz):	Immune to 6in gunfire inside 13,000yd & 4.7in gunfire at all ranges
Armament (main):	To be determined, 5.5in or 6in main battery
Armament (AA):	4 x 4in/45 QF Mk V (4 x 1); 8 x 0.50in/62 (2 x 4)
Armament (torp):	8 (10) x 21in (2 x 4 (5))
Aircraft:	To be determined, one catapult[90]

DNC, who was now William Berry, submitted the five sketch designs to the Admiralty Board on 23 January 1929. The board rejected the two designs with single-mount guns as being too lightly armed, and, from among the three remaining choices, liked best the one with four twin mounts. Although there were advantages to the one design with six 6in guns in single mounts – the board liked the dispersal of the mounts and their small size, which they believed enhanced survivability, and the high rate of initial fire, at least until ready-use rounds were exhausted – the higher sustained rate of fire offered by the design with four twin 6in mounts ultimately made that the most attractive choice. An interim sketch plan based on this option prepared in May was projected to have a standard displacement of 6500 tons, a length of 535ft at the waterline and, with a power plant that produced 60,000shp, would provide the desired 30.5 knots.

This sketch design was approved by the board on 3 June 1929. DNC did not like the internal arrangement of the power plant, with one large and one small boiler room; the design was recast with three equal-sized fire rooms, which provided better internal subdivision, but required 13ft additional length and appropriate additions to the beam and draft to maintain hull strength and hydrodynamic efficiency. After the board added another half-inch of armour to the main-battery magazine's protection, the displacement reached 7000 tons and needed added power to maintain the desired speed. This design, submitted in October 1929, was approved on 20 November. With further tweaking, including the adoption of a bulbous bow that improved hull efficiency at higher speeds, the design was approved again on 9 January 1930.

The 1929 building programme was originally intended to include one *Surrey* class 'A' cruiser and two of this new type, called 'O' cruisers. But the success of the First London Conference (see next chapter) in restricting the construction of large cruisers and the pressure of the looming economic downturn led the programme to be reduced to a single 'O' cruiser, HMS *Leander* (75); she would be laid down on 8 September 1930 at Devonport with the following specifications:

With the *Leander* class, the Royal Navy completed its commitment to building smaller cruisers armed with a smaller main battery. HMS *Achilles* (70), seen here on 26 February 1938, was flagship of the New Zealand Division – the Royal New Zealand Navy was not formed officially until October 1941 – and flies the pennant of the division's Rear Admiral. She has the single DCT and HADT forward that characterised this class, and the single funnel that made them unique among Royal Navy cruisers built in the twentieth century. With the adoption of the 6in/50 Mk XXIII in twin turrets, the Royal Navy abandoned the unsuccessful 8in/50 Mk VIII that armed their preceding post-war cruisers. The catapult carried was a new, lightweight model. (SLV/AGC)

'O' Cruiser: HMS Leander

Displacement (std):	7178 tons[91]
Length (oa):	554ft 3in
Beam (max):	55ft 2in
Draft (mean):	19ft 11in (deep)
Power plant:	72,000shp; Parsons geared turbines driving four shafts; six Admiralty three-drum water-tube boilers
Speed:	32.5 knots (std); 31 knots (deep)
Range (designed):	8000nm @ 12 knots; 1745 tons oil fuel
Protection (side):	3in NCA external belt armour on 1in Ducol (in way of engineering spaces only; one deck higher in way of firerooms to protect uptakes); 3.5in NCA (side plating in armoured box citadel around main-battery magazines)[92]
Protection (horiz):	1.25in Ducol (over engineering spaces at Middle Deck level); 2in–1in Ducol (crown of armoured box citadel over main-battery magazines)
Armament (main):	8 x 6in/50 Mk XXIII (4 x 2 – two forward and two aft)
Armament (AA):	4 x 4in/45 QF Mk V (4 x 1); 12 x 0.50in/62 (3 x 4)
Armament (torp):	8 x 21in (2 x 4)
Aircraft:	1, one catapult[93]

Leander was the lead ship of a class of five (eight, if three near-sisters built for or transferred to the RAN are included). She was commissioned without her catapult and aircraft, and also without her High-Angle Director Tower (HADT), which was to be mounted on a pedestal aft of her DCT on her forward superstructure; both would be fitted within months. The catapult was a lightweight model, intended to launch only smaller fighter-reconnaissance floatplanes, although these ships regularly carried the Supermarine Walrus, by no means a small aircraft. The three near-sisters differed primarily in being given a unit-system power plant – they had four rather than six boilers, which allowed them to have two rather than three fire rooms – that alternated boiler rooms and engine rooms, requiring two, widely-separated funnels. One of the three, HMAS *Sydney* (D48) was built for the Australians; the other two served briefly in the Royal Navy before they were also transferred to RAN service before war broke out. Of the five original *Leanders*, two served extensive time with the New Zealanders. HMS *Achilles* (70) joined the New Zealand

Division in 1936 and transferred to the Royal New Zealand Navy (RNZN) when that was officially stood up on 1 October 1941; *Leander* joined the New Zealand Division in 1937 and remained with the RNZN. They both served with the RNZN for the duration of the Second World War.

These were generally well-liked ships, handling well in most weathers; the only complaint registered by her first commanding officer was the narrowness of her bridge, which, he said, limited protected forward vision.[94] The most significant change made in these ships was the replacement of the single 4in Mk V mounts with twin 4in Mk XVI mounts; this was done in all the *Leander*s in 1937.

As seen in 1939, HMAS *Hobart* (D63) was one of three modified-*Leander*s; one was completed specifically for the Australians, the other two initially served in the Royal Navy, but transferred to the RAN in 1938–9. *Hobart* had spent her first two years as HMS *Apollo* before she transferred. The modified-*Leander*s differed from the originals primarily in the number and arrangement of boilers; with two fewer boilers arranged in a unit system that placed the forward engine room between the two fire rooms, these ships were (theoretically, at least) more survivable. The power plant rearrangement was signified by the reversion to a two-funnel profile. (SLV/AGC)

Slow as Molasses: Business-as-Usual on the Potomac

With the six ships of the *Northampton* class all to be laid down in 1928, the US Navy had no further hulls of this type authorised by Congress and had to face once again the daunting task of convincing a reluctant legislature to approve and fund any cruisers. The failure of the Geneva Conference only seemed to strengthen the already strong hand of those in Congress who wanted to reduce military spending to a bare minimum. Yet there remained enough sentiment in the legislature in favour of continuing to seek parity with the Royal Navy that the General Board was encouraged to present a full construction programme to Congress for FY1928. The '71 Ship Bill' was introduced into the House of Representatives on 14 December 1927; this bill called for four consecutive five-year programmes which would, in total, authorise the construction of twenty-five 'treaty maximum' cruisers, five aircraft carriers and forty-one ships of other types.[95] However, it did not get very far in the solidly-Republican Congress, which refused to commit to such a long-term construction programme. On 28 February 1928, a substitute bill was introduced, which became known as the 'Fifteen-Cruiser Bill', because it called for the construction of fifteen cruisers and one aircraft carrier, all to be completed within a span of six years.[96] Congress did not move on the legislation for a full year, but it was eventually passed in virtually unchanged form on 13 February 1929 and signed within hours by Coolidge.[97] It was passed with the understanding that Congress would fund the first five of the cruisers and the aircraft carrier immediately and then five more cruisers in each of the two following fiscal years.

The initial five cruisers built under this new authorisation were to have been essentially repeat *Northampton*s, although, through the use of light metals in non-structural elements and through greater use of welding in the construction process, it was hoped to save at least 215 tons which could be applied to increased protection, particularly to the magazines and the ammunition train.[98] However, by this time, *Salt Lake City* was approaching completion and it was realised for the first time that the first-generation American 'treaty maximum' cruisers were at least 900 tons under their target displacement. This was like a gift from heaven; suddenly, the Navy's designers had the freedom to add some serious armour protection in way of the magazines and engineering plant. But there was a problem. Contracts for the first five cruisers, authorised in 1929 – CL32–CL36 – had already been let, so the design changes allowed by the extra tonnage were initially intended to be applied only beginning with the FY1930 ships (CL37–CL41).

Changes to the five FY1929 ships would be limited to working in more protection in selected areas, improvements that could be achieved without major redesign, mainly in the form of thicker deck armour and somewhat better protection around the main-battery magazines, but otherwise, very little could be done. Concerned that the bulbous underwater bow form of the previous classes might cause 'pounding' – excessive pitching when heading at high speed into a seaway – this design eliminated the forefoot bulge; the hull was lengthened

When the 'Fifteen-Cruiser Bill' passed Congress in 1929, it came with money to start building five of those cruisers immediately. However, it was at just this time that the US Navy discovered how seriously underweight their first 'treaty maximum' cruisers really were, which offered the rare opportunity to add protection to the previously lightly-armoured *Northampton* class design. Before they had learned of the earlier cruisers' underweight condition, the Americans had planned on building five improved *Northampton*s, which would have been slightly longer to compensate for the deletion of the bulbous forefoot, and had let contracts for those ships. When they learned of the underweight condition, they were able to delay three of the contracts (those let to government yards), but could not prevent the construction of the two being built at private yards, the two-ship *Portland* class. One of these, USS *Indianapolis* (CA35), is seen here on 31 May 1934. They were given some extra protection, particularly to the magazines and decks, and larger forward superstructures so they could serve as fleet flagships. (NARA)

by 10ft to compensate for the lost buoyancy forward. Other differences included adding four more single 5in/25 DP guns into the secondary battery for a total of eight. The most obvious physical difference was a larger bridge structure, particularly in the case of USS *Indianapolis* (CL35), which was fitted out to serve as a fleet flagship.

The revised design for the FY1930 ships came together quickly and the Navy realised that some, at least, of the FY1929 ships could in fact be built to the new, improved standard. Of the five FY1929 contracts, two had gone to private yards and three to navy yards; the navy yard contracts could be put on hold while the new design was being finalised, but the same was not possible with USS *Portland* (CL33), laid down on 17 February 1930 at Bethlehem Steel Co, Quincy, MA, or *Indianapolis*, laid down 31 March 1930 at New York Shipbuilding.

The laying-down of the three FY1929 ships ordered from government yards was delayed for six months, during which time the redesign was completed.[99] The ships that emerged from this process were radically different in design philosophy and appearance from *Portland* and *Indianapolis*. Their hulls were shorter, with lower freeboard and a more noticeable sheer line, and the clipper bow of the first two was replaced with a simpler raked bow. While retaining the same power plant as the previous classes, the shorter hull forced the abandonment of the unit system arrangement in favour of a more conventional set-up, as indicated by the more closely-spaced funnels. (Because of the closely-spaced funnels, the aircraft arrangements were moved aft of the second funnel; the hangar, which had been located at the base of the after funnel in preceding classes, now became the lower level of a large after superstructure.) The internal arrangements were further altered by lowering the main-battery magazines, which in the preceding classes had been raised some distance above the double bottom to protect against mine damage, causing their crowns to project well above the waterline; lowering the magazines to bring them entirely below the waterline greatly increased their protection against gunfire at the cost of some increased vulnerability to underwater explosions.[100] (The shorter hull and lowered magazines also cost almost 200 tons of fuel oil stowage, which impacted the planned endurance of 10,000nm at 15 knots.) The level of armour protection all around, for the engineering spaces and barbettes in particular, was increased significantly. They also would, for the first time in American 'treaty maximum' cruisers, have fully-armoured main-battery turrets, which were also significantly smaller than the gunhouses carried by previous classes.[101] The other major changes included the deletion of torpedo tubes and the adoption of a much more compact tower forward superstructure without a tripod foremast. In part this was because these ships were the first to be fitted with the massive (and extremely heavy) new Mk 28 DP directors, which required a stable platform.

These three ships, starting with USS *New Orleans* (CL32), would have the following specifications:

New Orleans Class

Displacement (std):	10,000 tons (design); 11,515 tons (full load)
Length (oa):	588ft
Beam (wl):	61ft 9in
Draft (mean):	22ft 9in (full load)
Power plant:	107,000shp; Parsons geared turbines driving four shafts; eight Babcock & Wilcox boilers
Speed:	32.7 knots (design)
Range (designed):	10,000nm @ 15 knots; 2160 tons oil fuel
Protection (side):	5in–3.25in Class B external belt on 0.75in STS backing (in way of engineering spaces); 4in–3in Class B external belt (in way of main-battery magazines)[102]
Protection (horiz):	2.25in STS (over engineering spaces and main-battery magazines)
Armament (main):	9 x 8in/55 Mk 9 (3 x 3 – two forward and one aft)

Armament (AA):	8 x 5in/25 Mk 10 (8 x 1); 8 x 0.50in/90 M2 (8 x 1)
Aircraft:	4, two catapults[103]

The first of these three to be started would be USS *Astoria* (CL34), laid down on 1 September 1930 at Puget Sound Navy Yard. These ships were generally well-liked in the fleet, but they were often unfavourably compared to the *Northamptons* and *Portlands*. Among the complaints registered against them were that they were more cramped internally than their beamier predecessors and that they tended to roll more in a seaway, making them less satisfactory gun platforms. They also were criticised for their endurance being less than that of the preceding classes.[104] No major alterations were made to these ships before the outbreak of the Second World War.

Four more ships would be built to basically the same design as *New Orleans*. The next five cruisers in the series, CA37–CA41, were funded in FY1930 as planned. The only changes intended in these ships were due to the availability of a lightweight 8in/55 main-battery gun – the Mk 12, which replaced the Mk 9, which weighed 17.1 tons per barrel vs 30 tons – allowing an even more compact turret to be designed, with separate sleeves for each gun and a smaller barbette, with 15in less inner diameter, which in turn allowed 1.5in thicker barbette armour, to a maximum of 6.5in. The first two of this series – USS *Tuscaloosa* (CA37) and *San Francisco* (CA38) – were laid down shortly after their near-sisters in 1931.

The three ships of the FY1929 group that were delayed, were built to a new design that was radically-different from the *Portlands*. The ships of the *New Orleans* class were over 20ft shorter, had smaller, better-protected main-battery turrets, more closely-spaced funnels – which forced the relocation of the aircraft-handling facilities to abaft the second funnel – and overall much better protection. In this image, which shows USS *Minneapolis* (CA36) on 23 August 1935, the upgraded fire-control suite is visible; from the bow, besides the rangefinder enclosed in the aft end of each turret, there is: the navigation rangefinder in a shallow 'dish' in front of the pilot house, a Mk 31 main-battery director above and behind on the pilot house roof and, on its own pedestal, the large, boxy Mk 28 HA director with a canvas cover. (NARA)

A gap of over two years intervened before the next ship in the series, USS *Quincy* (CA39), was laid down. The reason for the delay was due to the 1930 London Treaty, which, as shall be seen in the next chapter, limited the United States, once the fifteenth American 'treaty maximum' cruiser was under construction, not to lay down another until 1933 and then only one per year for two more years.[105] It was convenient that this limitation suited the parsimony of the Republican-dominated Congress, strongly influenced by the effects of the Great Depression, which reached its nadir in 1932–3.[106]

The laying-down of *Quincy* on 15 November 1933, fittingly enough at the Bethlehem Steel yard in Quincy, MA, was the first major ship start in the United States in 26 months. *Quincy* was to have differed from her sisters in one major feature; the intervening years had impressed on the General Board the necessity of better anti-aircraft protection, and they insisted that the 1933 cruiser carry a pair of the newly-designed 1.1in/75 quadruple-mounts.[107] Since there was no longer any weight margin to allow for these large and heavy mounts (approximately 5 tons per mount, not counting mount foundation, magazine space, munitions, splinter shielding, crew, etc.), considerable effort was made to move around internal elements in the design to save some weight. The forward main-battery turrets were moved closer together by 8ft; this required the superfiring Turret No 2 to be raised by 6in and the forward main-battery magazine to be made shorter and broader, which pushed the magazine armour out to the shell plating for the first time. Emergency electrical power, which up to this point in American cruiser design had been provided by storage batteries, was to be supplied by diesel generators. The size (and weight) of the forward superstruc-

Rather than forego the chance to build the 'treaty maximum' cruiser permitted for 1934, the Americans opted to start a repeat-*Quincy*, with the basic arrangement of the later *New Orleans* class cruisers, but with the smaller forward superstructure and the more closely-grouped forward battery introduced with USS *Quincy* (CA39). This image shows the resulting ship, USS *Vincennes* (CA44), sitting for her portrait during her acceptance trials off Rockland, ME, 12 January 1937. Note that she has Mk 31 and Mk 28 directors aft in a similar arrangement to those carried forward. (NARA)

ture was reduced, as was the thickness of the main-battery barbettes, which were to be 5.5in thick. After all this rearrangement, *Quincy* was completed without the 1.1in mounts. (Most American 'treaty maximum' cruisers had four 1.1in mounts added in 1941 following the recommendations of the King Board, convened in June 1940 under leadership of then-Vice Admiral Ernest J King.)

The Americans would have liked to move on to an entirely new design of 'treaty maximum' cruiser, one incorporating the benefits gained from working up the design of the new large light cruisers allowed by the London Treaty of 1930 (see next chapter), but it was obvious that the new design would not be ready for at least a year and the window of opportunity to lay down the 1934 'treaty maximum' cruiser would have expired by then. Rather than forego that ship, the Americans opted to build a repeat-*Quincy*; USS *Vincennes* (CA44) was laid down at Bethlehem, Quincy, on 2 January 1934.

Much Talk, but No Action in Tokyo

The failure in Geneva probably had a more profound impact in Tokyo that in any other capital. Suffering equally from severe economic pressure, from the long-standing desire to improve their strength ratio in important warship categories and, at the same time, having to address the expansionist policies pushed by ambitious *bakuryo* – junior-level staff officers taking boldly (sometimes violently) aggressive positions which their superiors felt obliged to accommodate – the Imperial Navy struggled to find a naval programme that satisfied all parties. The Naval General Staff responded by appointing a committee on 15 October 1927 under the leadership of Vice Admiral Nomura Kichisaburo, Vice Chief-of-Staff, with the charge to establish the navy's current and near-future requirements given the debacle at Geneva and the 'Fifteen-Cruiser Bill' being considered (but not yet passed) by the US Congress.[108] The committee report, delivered on 6 August 1928, stated that, in order to maintain a satisfactory ratio of tonnage compared the Americans in the all-important category of 'treaty maximum' cruisers – which would require having twelve large cruisers in commission by 1936 – the Imperial Navy had to replace six of its ageing pre-war light cruisers with at least five large cruisers. This number was proposed by the Navy Ministry in a draft shipbuilding plan drawn up in March 1929 for submission to the Diet; after discussion with the Finance Ministry in May, the request was reduced to four 'treaty maximum' cruisers (as part of a 91-unit shipbuilding programme). However, before the Diet could act on this request, the invitation to the First London Conference was received and all shipbuilding plans were put on hold.

Old and New in France: Finishing the *Suffrens*, Trying Some New Ideas

The *Marine Nationale*, having laid down *Suffern* and *Colbert* in successive budget years 1925 and 1926, continued in the following two years to fund two more 'treaty maximum' cruisers to basically the same design. Having watched how other nations interpreted the definition of standard displacement, the STCN concluded that they had been overly strict in their inclusion of certain consumables, such as munitions, food and drinking water, in the calculation of the displacement, and that as much as 245 tons more were available, which could be 'invested' in restoring some of the power reduced to save weight in the earlier ships in the class.[109] The naval staff considered this proposal and rejected it, because it would have required a major redesign, but instead requested a change that was nearly as disruptive. In the place of the relatively-shallow external armour belt of *Suffren* and *Colbert*, the third cruiser in the class would have a deeper and marginally thicker armoured citadel well inboard from the shell plating, with a liquid-filled cell in-between. Other than these changes, the specifications of this new ship closely resembled those of *Colbert*.

The third ship in the French *Suffren* class was *Foch*, seen soon after completion, She can be readily identified by her wide-set tripod foremast that was supposed to carry not only her bi-level main-battery DCT, but also two HA directors on the wing platforms just below it. She has a GL 810 monoplane reconnaissance floatplane on her near catapult between her funnels. (NHHC)

The most distinctive external feature of this third half-sister of *Suffren*, given the name *Foch*, was her foremast, which was a wide-spaced tripod supporting a large foretop surmounted by a pair of HA directors and large main-battery director. *Foch* was laid down at Brest on 21 June 1928, two months after the launch of *Colbert*. Few, if any, modifications were made to her before the outbreak of the Second World War.

Towards the end of 1927, the French learned of the Italian decision to begin construction on the first four '*Condottieri*' type light cruisers in early 1928. This strongly influenced the decision on whether to proceed with a fourth *Suffren* and what characteristics that ship would possess.[110] Hearing that the '*Condottieri*' would be armed with a potent high-velocity, long-ranging 152mm/53 main-battery gun, the staff specified that the next large cruiser be up-armoured to protect the ship against this gun at the longer ranges, beyond 19,700yd, at which gunnery was to be expected in future battles.[111] Given

The last ship in the four-ship class was *Dupleix*, which is seen at Toulon in 1935. She returned to a more conventional foremast arrangement, with the main-battery DCT at the top, a searchlight platform with a range clock behind it just below, and the HA directors carried much lower, on separate pedestals, in way of the forward funnel. She has a 16ft 5in trainable coincidence rangefinder in an armoured hood on turret II and a similarly-sized tactical rangefinder on her conning tower. (Bougault)

that there was very little weight margin available – some savings could be gained by simplifying the forward superstructure, using more welding and light metals in the upperworks and adopting twin-mountings for the 90mm/50 AA guns – the added thickness to the armoured *caisson* was relatively modest. (Side bulkheads increased from 2.125in to 2.36in and armoured decks from 0.71in–0.79in to 1.18in.[112])

In this form, approval for this ship was included in a combined 1928–9 *tranche*, and she was laid down at Brest on 14 November 1929. She would be launched in October 1930 with the name *Dupleix*. Reverting to a conventional tripod foremast, *Dupleix* resembled *Colbert* fairly closely, the twin-mounted secondary battery being one of her few distinguishing characteristics.

The *Marine Nationale* briefly toyed with the idea of developing a follow-on to *Dupleix* with yet thicker armour for more effective protection against the main-battery of the '*Condottieri*' type light cruisers on which the Italians seemed to be concentrating, bringing the inner edge of the immune zone' down to 16,400yd, but that would require an additional 400 tons of armour, which could only be compensated for by reducing the armament or the size of the power plant.[113] Neither of those alternatives were acceptable to the naval staff; in fact, it was the staff's intent to introduce a larger 100mm/45 twin mount as a DP secondary battery to replace the 90mm/50. The STCN was aware that the internal *caisson* style of armour protection used in the *Suffren*s was inefficient in terms of structural weight, and that an external armour belt would save significant displacement, and urged the staff to allow them to generate an entirely new design with better protection, without sacrificing armament or speed.

This scheme was approved in mid-1928, spurred on by news from Rome that the Italians had authorised the construction of two new 'treaty maximum' cruisers with impressive characteristics that combined speed, firepower and protection. (What the French did not know – and could not have known at this time – was that the Italians achieved this success by exceeding the 10,000-ton standard displacement limit, as will be seen below.) Well aware that weight needed to be saved by all possible means in order to increase protection, the STCN started with the idea that propulsion technology had advanced to the point that substantial weight could be saved by adopting higher steam pressure without having to accept significantly lower power or speed. Increasing the working pressure of the system by 25 per cent (from 285psi to 355psi) allowed almost the same power (84,000shp) at a saving of 700 tons. There was discussion of reducing the three-shaft arrangement of the *Suffrens*, which was very unpopular for a number of reasons, to a two-shaft layout, but this was rejected out of concern that it would overload the propeller shafts, and, in the end, a four-shaft design was approved despite the fact that this required a broader hull form with greater water resistance.

The broader hull form, coupled with the earlier decision to adopt a more traditional armour scheme with an external armour belt and deck arrangement, allowed the space to fit a two-layer torpedo protective scheme backed by a 1.57in-thick torpedo bulkhead and another splinter bulkhead inside that for the length of the engineering spaces. For the first time in French post-war cruisers, the protective scheme employed armour steel, an 80kg NC plate, built up to 4.33in in the side strake, and the same material was used for the first time in the main-battery turrets and barbettes. Given the substantial torpedo protective system, it was considered safe to forego the unit-system layout of the power plant; this, in turn, allowed the engineering spaces, and the entire hull, to be made 25ft shorter, further saving armour weight which could be used to add to the belt and deck protection. A benefit of abandoning the unit system was that the exhaust gasses from all five boilers could be fed to a single funnel, which made arranging the aviation facilities and ship's boats on the main deck easier. As a further weight saving measure, this new design had no forecastle deck. In part to compensate for the lack of a forecastle deck, the hull was to be given considerable sheer forward and more flare at the bow. Another distinguishing feature was the adoption, in common with many other navies at this time, of a tower bridge structure in the place of a tripod foremast, to provide a more stable platform for the multiple main-battery and AA directors that needed placement as far above the waterline as practicable. In this form, with 93 per cent of the power of the *Suffren*s, the new ship would have a designed top speed of 31 knots, one knot slower than the earlier class.

Monies for this new ship, with which the naval staff was quite pleased, were included in the 1930 programme. Unlike all previous French post-war cruisers, which were named after famous sailors or administrators, this new ship was to be named *Algérie* to commemorate the centenary of the French colonisation of that North African territory. She was laid down on 19 March 1931 at Brest with the following specifications:

Algérie

Displacement (std):	10,000 tons
Length (oa):	610ft 11in
Beam:	65ft 7in
Draft (maximum):	20ft 7in
Power plant:	84,000shp; Rateau-Bretagne geared turbines driving four shafts; five Indret small-tube boilers (operating @ 384psi)
Speed:	31 knots (designed)
Range (designed):	8000nm @ 15 knots; 3140 tons oil fuel
Protection (side):	4.33in NC (in way of engineering spaces and main-battery magazines); 1in NC (steering compartment)
Protection (horiz):	3.15in–1.18in NC (over main-battery magazines and engineering spaces); 0.71in NC (over steering compartment)
Protection (torp):	Two-layer 'sandwich' with 1.57in torpedo bulkhead (in way of engineering spaces)
Armament (main):	8 x 203mm/50 Mle 1924 (4 x 2 – two forward and two aft)
Armament (AA):	12 x 100mm/45 Mle 1930 (6 x 2); 4 x 37mm/50 Mle 1925 (4 x 1); 16 x 13.2mm/76 Hotchkiss MG Mle 1931 (4 x 4)
Armament (torp):	6 x 550mm Mle 1923D (2 x 3); 3 reloads
Aircraft:	2 (2 x GL 812 HY); one trainable compressed-air catapult[114]

After her commissioning in October 1934, very little was done to modernise *Algérie* before the outbreak of the Second World War. At the beginning of 1937, the 16ft 5in coincidence rangefinder in the main-battery DCT atop her forward superstructure was replaced by a 26ft 3in stereoscopic model, and a larger funnel cowling was fitted to protect the bridge from smoke.[115] Further incremental upgrades included the addition of power controls for the DP guns and the installation of a 26ft 3in stereoscopic rangefinder on the roof of Turret III. In general, *Algérie* was well-liked in the *Marine Nationale*, and was considered by many to be one of the best 'treaty maximum' cruisers in any navy; the only complaints were that the amount of weight carried high above the waterline led to a high metacentre with its characteristic rapid roll period.

Despite these developments in the lineage of French 'treaty maximum' cruisers, there had been a somewhat parallel thread of development which saw the design and construction of the unarmoured large minelayer *Pluton*, laid down in 1928 (see Chapter 9). As a follow-on to *Pluton* and in a delayed direct response to the initial '*Condottieri*' of the Italians, STCN was directed in December 1928 to develop a design for another large minelayer, but one with much more distinctly cruiser-like features. (The French had decided that, rather than build further specialised minelayers, all future light warships would have the capability to be fitted with mine rails.[116]) The general specifications given to STCN were:

Croiseur Mouilleur de Mines[117]

Displacement (std):	5980 tons
Length (oa):	580ft
Power plant:	102,000shp
Speed:	34 knots (designed)
Range (designed):	3000nm @ 18 knots
Armament (main):	152mm/55 Mle 1930[118]

(Note the new 152mm/55 main-battery specified in anticipation of a gun calibre restriction at the next disarmament conference that would make the 155mm/50 fitted in the *Duguay-Trouin* class unavailable; in the event, the language in the First London Treaty was set so that sub-category (*b*) cruisers were allowed 6.1in guns specifically to include the *Duguay-Trouin* class retroactively.) Compared to the design process in most other nations, this design was rapidly rendered and approved with virtually no modifications. Almost the only change was in the designation of the ship, which, when she was laid down in August 1931, was designated as a *Croiseur de 2e classe* in keeping with London Treaty classifications. Only one ship of this design was built.

Reacting to the Italian '*Condottieri*' and to the restrictions imposed by the First London Treaty, even though the French did not agree to Part III of that treaty which contained the cruiser restrictions, the *Marine Nationale* built *Emile Bertin* to be small, fast and well-armed at the cost of protection, much like their Italian counterparts. To save space and weight, they opted for triple turrets for the 152mm/55 Mle 1930 main-battery gun. In this view dated 28 October 1938 near Toulon, note the 'neutrality stripes' – bands of blue-white-and-red (from the bow) painted on Turret II to mark the ship as French while participating in the so-called 'Non-Intervention Patrol' off the coast of Spain during that country's civil war – and the unusually widely-separated funnels. (NHHC)

Emile Bertin

Displacement (std):	5886 tons
Length (oa):	580ft 8in
Beam:	52ft 6in
Draft (maximum):	21ft 8in
Power plant:	102,000shp; Parsons geared turbines driving four shafts; five Penhoët small-tube boilers (operating @ 384psi)
Speed:	34 knots (designed)
Range (designed):	6000nm @ 15 knots; 1338 tons oil fuel
Protection (side):	1.18in 60kg plate (in way of main-battery magazines)
Protection (horiz):	0.79in mild steel (over main-battery magazines and engineering spaces)
Armament (main):	9 x 152mm/55 Mle 1930 (3 x 3 – two forward and one aft)
Armament (AA):	4 x 90mm/50 Mle 1926 HA (1 x 2 & 2 x 1); 4 x 37mm/50 Mle 1925 (4 x 1)
Armament (torp):	6 x 550mm Mle 1923D (2 x 3)
Aircraft:	2 (2 x GL 812 HY); one trainable compressed-air catapult[119]

She easily exceeded her designed speed during her acceptance trials, which were carried out in rough weather; in an average of three speed runs, she logged over 39 knots and sustained over 36 knots for eight hours. Her main battery proved to be troublesome, with numerous teething problems with the loading mechanisms and safety interlocks, but these were gradually worked out and had been resolved by the time the Second World War began. As was the case with a number of ships built at this time, her construction proved to be too light, which revealed itself when salvo-fire trials were attempted. Her hull had to be strengthened in 1935 to allow full use of her main battery. Other than this, *Emile Bertin* was little modified before the outbreak of war. The single 37mm AA mounts were replaced by an equal number of Mle 1933 twin mounts and four twin 13.2mm Mle 1929 mounts were added in late 1939; other than that she entered the war relatively unchanged.

In this view, crewmen on *Emile Bertin* train on the twin 90mm/50 Mle 1926 HA mount sited on the after shelter deck. This twin mount was introduced in *Dupleix* and was a well-regarded weapon, firing a large enough shell (20.96lb) at a high-enough sustained rate of fire (12–15rpm) to act as a barrage fire weapon. Unfortunately, in *Emile Bertin*, the ammunition supply from the magazine was inadequate to sustain that rate of fire. (Compare this image to that taken on *Bande Nere* seen above; it certainly seems as if the French *matelots* took their training more seriously, wearing anti-flash hoods and safety gloves, or, perhaps, it was merely the presence of the dark-suited officers causing the more serious air.) In the background, the rear of the after main-battery turret can be seen, with its integral 26ft 3in OPL stereoscopic rangefinder. (NHHC)

Hyperactivity on the Tiber: The *Zara* Class, *Bolzano* and more '*Condottieri*'

The decision to lay down the first four '*Condottieri*' type large scouts in no way signalled that Rome had lost interest in building 'treaty maximum' cruisers. Indeed, quite the opposite was true; with only ageing battleships to constitute a battle line, the naval staff began to look elsewhere for ships to form the core of the future *Regia Marina*. Starting from the *Trento* class design, which was already by 1927 understood to be too lightly-protected to stand up to anything larger than an enemy destroyer, a set of requirements was drawn up for MARICOMINAV that defined a ship that resembled the *Trento*s in armament – minus the torpedo tubes, which would not be needed by a ship designed for long-range gunnery – but otherwise traded speed for protection. Where the *Trento*s had a four-shaft power plant fed by twelve boilers, the new design would have two shafts and eight boilers, albeit more modern ones that could provide 80 per cent the power of the *Trentos*' engineering plant. The reduction in the number of boilers by one-third would allow the elimination of one of three fire rooms, with a significant reduction in hull length and of the area that would need armour protection. With that weight savings in mind, the instructions given MARICOMINAV were to provide 7.87in belt armour and a speed of 32 knots while maintaining much the same armament as the *Trento* class.[120]

Even with the shortened hull and advances in boiler technology, it proved impossible for MARICOMINAV to meet the staff requirements and come even close to the 10,000-ton displacement target. As previously noted, the *Trento*s exceeded the Washington Treaty limit by approximately 500 tons, and the Italians had no serious qualms about going even further over the limit, but there were practical limits imposed by the laws of hydrodynamics that were much more rigid than the quibbles of politicians. MARICOMINAV could not design a ship with the protection desired by the naval staff and the envisaged reduced power plant, and at the same time provide acceptable speed and stability. Only by

Natural enemies meet at Naples (Napoli) in 1935. To the left is the Italian 'treaty maximum' cruiser RN *Zara*, built with greater protection in a hull almost 100ft shorter than the *Trento*s and 4 knots slower. What was gained was a far more balanced design, which, despite all efforts, exceeded the Washington Treaty limits by more than 1000 tons. In this image, *Zara* is missing one of her DCTs; the auxiliary main-battery director that should be located in the tub directly abaft the second funnel is not present. To the right in this image are the Italians' nemesis, a squadron of six *Vauquelin* class *contre-torpilleurs* of the *Marine Nationale*. (NHHC)

reducing the planned belt armour thickness by 25 per cent, to 5.9in, and accepting a designed top speed of 31 knots, could a satisfactory design be generated, with a projected standard displacement of 11,500 tons. As much as the naval staff may have wanted a faster and better-protected ship, they realised this was the best they could expect and still pay lip-service to the Washington Treaty. This design was approved towards the end of 1928 and the first two ships of this class – the *Zara* class – were funded in the 1928–9 building programme. The specifications to which they were built are as follows:

Zara Class

Displacement (std):	10,000 tons (design); 11,500 tons (actual)[121]
Length (oa):	557ft 2in
Beam (wl):	62ft 10in
Draft (mean):	21ft 11in (deep)
Power plant:	95,000shp (design); 118,000shp (trials); Parsons geared turbines driving two shafts; eight Thornycroft (or Yarrow) boilers
Speed:	31 knots (design); 33 knots (trials)
Range (designed):	5400nm @ 16 knots; 2362 tons oil fuel
Protection (side):	5.9in–3.94in TC external belt (in way of main-battery magazines and engineering spaces)[122]
Protection (horiz):	2.76in–0.79in CN/AER (Main Deck over main-battery magazines and engineering spaces)[123]
Armament (main):	8 x 203mm/53 Mod 1927 (4 x 2 – two forward and two aft)
Armament (AA):	16 x 100mm/47 Mod 1924 (8 x 2); 4 x 40mm/39 Vickers-Terni (4 x 1); 8 x 13.2mm machine guns (4 x 2)
Aircraft:	3 (3 x IMAM Ro.43); one catapult (fixed in forecastle)[124]

In this form, two ships were laid down in 1929. RN *Fiume* was started at STT, Trieste, on 29 April; RN *Zara* was laid down at OTO, Muggiano (La Spezia), on 4 July. *Zara*, however was the first to be completed, on 20 October 1931. Two more of this class would be built, both at OTO, Livorno. RN *Gorizia* was ordered in the 1929–30 programme; she differed very little from the first two in the class, having a somewhat taller forward funnel. The fourth in the class, RN *Pola*, was funded

The *Regia Marina* routinely emblazoned the main-battery turrets of their major warships with emblems, names or patriotic slogans. In this view of the after turrets of *Zara*, it can be seen that turret No 3 has the fascist emblem, the bundled *fasces* (a bound bundle of wooden rods symbolising the power of the lictor to enforce law) and axe, while turret No 4 carries the word '*Tenacemente*' ('Tenaciously'). Note that the auxiliary main-battery DCT, missing in the last image, is seen here just above turret No 3. (NHHC)

in the 1930–1 programme. She could be visually distinguished by a built-up structure connecting her bridge and forward funnel that was used for accommodation and office space to allow her to serve as a fleet flagship.

With the *Zara* class, the *Regia Marina* introduced a new model main-battery gun, the Ansaldo 203mm/53 Mod 1927. This gun was longer and could be fired more rapidly than the 203mm/50 Mod 1924 carried in the *Trentos*, but they were mounted in a similar fashion, in a common cradle and too close together. Again, this caused dispersion problems during salvo firing, which were resolved in a similar fashion. Very few changes were made to these ships prior to the outbreak of the Second World War. One visible change was the replacement of the after pair of twin 100mm/47 mounts by four 37mm/54 Mod 1932 twin-mount water-cooled AA guns. The single greatest problem with the *Zaras*' design, indeed with all the early Italian post-war cruiser designs up to and including the *Zaras*, was one whose seriously did not become apparent until the outbreak of war. Italian cruisers up to and including the *Zara* class were found to have insufficiently redundant electrical systems, making them liable to 'single-point failure' of their electrical systems if they suffered underwater damage such as a hit by a torpedo.[125]

Like the French, the Italians would build one more 'treaty maximum' cruiser to a unique design, quite unlike the class of four cruisers that had immediately preceded her. But there were distinct differences between *Algérie* and RN *Bolzano*. The former was an attempt to improve on all previous cruiser designs, and succeeded in producing what is generally considered the best French inter-war cruiser. *Bolzano*, on the other hand, was a much more curious design, with a much less obvious reason for existing. Prior Italian planning had called for two three-ship cruiser divisions, but delays in plans to build new battleships, or reconstruct her four surviving ageing dreadnoughts, meant that *Pola* would likely be pressed into duty as a fleet flagship for many years after her entry into service in 1932, and thus would not be available to take her place in one of those divisions. This led to the addition of another 'treaty maximum' cruiser to the 1929–30 building programme. It does not, however, explain the decision to design this ship to a wholly-different set of characteristics than those developed for the *Zara* class.

That different set of characteristics was, in many ways, anachronistic, but not totally illogical. The two *Trentos* presented the *Regia Marina* with a tactical conundrum; any way the six Italian cruisers – two *Trentos* and four *Zaras* – were divided into two three-ship divisions, one or both *Trentos* would end up in formation with a *Zara*, which was significantly better protected but was 4 knots slower at high speed. But the *Regia Marina* was well-aware that for the *Trentos* to survive in combat with anything larger than an enemy destroyer, they would need to utilise every bit of speed they possessed. The Italians had a number of options here to address this dilemma; they could have, for example, abandoned the strict adherence to the tactical deployment of cruisers in three-ship divisions. (When war broke out, they

A similar view of *Zara*'s sister RN *Pola* showing her rear main-battery turrets. In this case, turret No 4 carries the fascist symbology while Turret No 3 has the motto *'Ardisco ad Ogni Impresa'*. This means 'I dare to attempt any task'. This phrase is famous for its association with the early Renaissance epic poem *Orlando Furioso*. (NHHC)

Zara introduced a new main-battery gun, the Ansaldo 203mm/53 Mod 1927; despite being longer and, theoretically, faster-firing than the similar gun fitted in the *Trentos*, it suffered from the same problems of shell dispersion during salvo fire due to the barrels being too close together. This problem was addressed in the same manner as before, by reducing shell weight and muzzle velocity and by adding in a delay circuit, so that the shells in a salvo did not leave the muzzles at exactly the same moment. Note the separate liner with its visible rifling inside the outer 'A'-tube of the gun. A naval rifle's rifling had a limited lifespan before wear led to reduced muzzle velocity and accuracy; these liners were designed to be replaceable without requiring the removal of the gun from the turret. (NHHC)

were forced to be more flexible in deploying cruisers, though they still preferred the three-ship division.) Regardless, the desire to provide a third ship with characteristics similar to the *Trentos*' won sufficient support to be approved by the staff and be included in the building programme.

The design criteria given to MARICOMINAV were rather straightforward. They were to start from the *Trento* design, but add in as many of the desirable features of the *Zaras* as possible without sacrificing speed. For example, *Bolzano* was to carry the newer model main-battery gun and follow *Pola*'s hull form with her forecastle deck and built-up superstructure between her bridge and forward funnel. The use of more efficient and powerful boilers allowed the same power – 150,000shp – generated by the *Trentos*' power plant to be supplied by ten instead of twelve boilers. However, this saving in internal volume was not used to reduce the length of the ship; in fact, *Bolzano* was, within inches, the same length as the *Trentos*. All that length was needed, both to allow the ship to move efficiently through the water, as she was designed to match the 36-knot designed top speed of the *Trentos*, and because the decision had been made to move the aircraft-handling facilities, including the catapult, from the forecastle, where they had been located in all previous Italian post-war cruisers, to a position between the funnels. This eminently sensible decision, which permitted the mounting of a rotating catapult and removed the aircraft storage from a very undesirable location ahead of the forward main-battery turrets, did force the internal trunking of funnel gasses to the after funnel to be extended, as the distance between funnels was increased in this ship.[126] With these alterations, the specifications for RN *Bolzano* were set, as follows:

Bolzano

Displacement (std):	10,000 tons (design); 11,065 tons (actual)
Length (oa):	646ft
Beam (wl):	67ft 7in
Draft (mean):	17ft 4in (deep)
Power plant:	150,000shp (design); 173,700shp (trials); Parsons geared turbines driving four shafts; ten boilers
Speed:	36 knots (design); 36.8 knots (trials)
Range (designed):	4432nm @ 16 knots; 2224 tons oil fuel
Protection (side):	2.76in CN external belt (in way of main-battery magazines and engineering spaces)
Protection (horiz):	1.97in–0.79in CN/AER (Main Deck over main-battery magazines and engineering spaces)
Armament (main):	8 x 203mm/53 Mod 1927 (4 x 2 – two forward and two aft)
Armament (AA):	16 x 100mm/47 Mod 1924 (8 x 2); 4 x 40mm/39 Vickers-Terni (4 x 1); 8 x 13.2mm machine guns (4 x 2)
Armament (torp):	4 x 533mm (2 x 2)
Aircraft:	3 (3 x IMAM Ro.43); one catapult (rotating, amidships)[127]

Note that *Bolzano* had exactly the same original armament suite as the *Zaras*, except that the fixed torpedo tubes carried in the *Trentos* were repeated here again. She was laid down at the Ansaldo yard, Genova-Sestri Ponente, on 11 June 1930. Any changes made to *Bolzano* before the outbreak of the Second World War parallel those made to the *Zaras*.

The first four of the '*Condottieri*' type large scouts were laid down in 1928, three at Ansaldo, Genova, and one at Cantiere di Castellammare di Stabia (CCS), Napoli. (The latter was, until 1939, a government-owned shipyard; the scout-cruiser built there, *Giovanni delle Bande Nere*, was always considered less well-finished than the Ansaldo-built ships in the class.[128]) None of these four were well-liked in the fleet for a number of reasons. They were considered poor sea boats, lacking in stability, due to a number of factors including the extremely light construction of the hull, the tall masts and forward superstructure with main- and secondary-battery directors carried high above the centre of buoyancy and the marked degree of tumblehome amidships which aggravated any tendency to roll. This last factor also reduced the area of the crew's berthing spaces in the middle and upper decks, making them very cramped internally. (The tumblehome was likely designed into these ships in an attempt to provide a constant roll rate as the draft of the ships changed with changing loading;[129] whether successful or not, as will be seen below, it was an unpopular feature and was eliminated in the next class of '*Condottieri*'.)

RN *Bolzano* is seen from the starboard quarter with the ship dressed and the crew manning the rails. Note the extension of the forward superstructure to enclose the forward funnel. A similar extension had been designed for *Pola*; the intent was to provide for staff accommodations and facilities, allowing these ships to serve as flagships. *Bolzano*'s turret No 4 carried the elaborate motto *'A Magnifica Impresa Intenta Ho l'Amo'*, which translates 'My spirit is engaged in a great task'. Note that with *Bolzano*, the *Regia Marina* finally moved the aviation facilities from the forecastle to a more conventional position between the funnels. (NHHC)

Well before these first '*Condottieri*' were completed, the designers at MARICOMINAV suspected they would suffer some of the problems they eventual did manifest, and, with authorisation to proceed with two more similar ships in the 1929–30 programme, set about resolving the issues. The second group of '*Condottieri*' were essentially repeats of the first four in terms of hull dimensions, but a great many detail changes were made. One of the most important, though least visible, was the adoption of vertical hull sides in the place of the tumblehome, which improved stability and, at the same time, increased crew berthing space, improving habitability. Other changes included designing a smaller forward superstructure with fewer fire-control directors mounted lower. The smaller forward superstructure was achieved by moving the aviation facilities from the forecastle to abaft the after funnel, where it was mounted at a fixed 23° angle towards the starboard side, making the hangar space at the lowest level of the forward superstructure unnecessary. The armament fit was similar except that the new ships carried a pair of 40mm/39 Vickers-Terni single-mount AA guns in the place of the four 37mm/54 twin mounts in the original series.

Other than those differences, the second group of '*Condottieri*' were much the same as the first group and would serve with them interchangeably before and during the war. The first of two ships of this group, RN *Armando Diaz*, was laid down at OTO, Muggiano, on 28 July 1930. Both would enter service in 1933. The only known modifications made before the outbreak of war were the removal of the 40mm mounts in 1938, which were replaced by four 20mm/65 Breda twin-mount AA guns.

RN *Armando Diaz*, one of the second group of '*Condottieri*', stopped in at Melbourne in September 1934 while on a round-the-world training cruise. She has a pair of CANT 25 seaplanes on the fixed catapult set at an angle to starboard aft of the second funnel, a far better location for aircraft facilities than on the forecastle, where they had been placed in the first group of '*Condottieri*'. Each of *Diaz*'s turrets had the name of a battle, a famous Italian victory, over the door in the turret's side. (SLV/AGC)

Chapter 7

Treaty Cruisers – The 'Big Babies': 1930–1936

The failure at Geneva did not mean an end to diplomatic activities aimed at limiting the construction of cruisers. If anything, it ratcheted up the pressure on the Preparatory Commission of the League of Nations Disarmament Conference, the meetings of which had stumbled to a halt in the spring of 1927 when invitations to the Geneva Conference went out. Neither did it represent the nadir of Anglo-American relations in the inter-war years; that would come as a result of further mistrust and misunderstandings resulting from the resumption of work by the Preparatory Commission in March 1928.[1] Apparently, during the course of informal discussions between the French and British delegations at that commission's meetings in June, a French officer, identified only as Captain Deleuze, is reported to have approached the leading British naval delegate, Vice Admiral William A H Kelly, with an informal proposal that pleased the Admiralty very much.[2]

Deleuze reportedly proposed a regulatory programme for warships with only four broad 'qualitative' categories: capital ships, aircraft carriers, submarines and then a catch-all category for surface warships mounting main-battery guns of 6in calibre and smaller. According to Deleuze's proposal, as understood by Kelly and transmitted back to First Sea Lord Madden, the first three categories would be regulated by numeric limits to be negotiated; the last category would be unlimited, each nation allowed to build the smaller warships it needed in the quantities required. This was indeed to the liking of the British. Grouping together 8in-gunned cruisers with battleships and battlecruisers as regulatable 'offensive weapons', while allowing smaller warships, including 6in-gunned cruisers, to be unregulated, fully vindicated the position the British had taken at the Geneva Conference.

The British took up this proposal with enthusiasm; on 26 June, their Ambassador in Paris was instructed to approach French Foreign Minister Briand, expressing Britain's strong support of the Deleuze proposal. There was only one problem; Briand was unaware of the proposal and had no interest in it. To make matters worse, word of the discussions between the governments was leaked to the press and immediately aroused American suspicions of an Anglo-French naval alliance. At the same time that the world was celebrating the signing of the Kellogg-Briand Pact in Paris on 27 August 1928 – a toothless declaration renouncing war as a means of resolving international disputes – the British government was attempting to denounce as false a letter from Austen Chamberlain to Briand that was circulating in the United States and Canada purporting to describe the details of just such an alliance.[3] Right or wrong, the Americans saw this as a sly attempt by the British to resurrect the formula that had been rejected a year earlier. British attempts to deflect American criticism by claiming that the ideas had originally been French only seemed to make matters worse. Very few in the United States would have had any kind thoughts regarding the British in the waning days of 1928. The Anglo-American relationship would improve; it could hardly get any worse.

In the spring of 1929, with a new President taking office in Washington DC, there was a feeling that perhaps a corner had been turned. Herbert Hoover, while also a Republican like his two immediate predecessors, was a man of very different background and experience. For one thing, he was not a career politician. He had been a successful and wealthy mining engineer, working around the world. The outbreak of war in 1914 found him in London, where, on his own initiative (and often with his own money), he set to work helping Americans stranded by the conflict, and then stayed on to help organise food relief for Belgium, an activity he led with great success for two years. Using his neutral status as leverage, he maintained good relations with officials on both sides in that country, and managed a distribution network independent of any government that, at its peak, fed more than 10 million people daily. Hugh Gibson, who was Secretary at the American Legation in Brussels when war broke out, was recruited to work on Hoover's Commission for Relief in Belgium from its inception in October 1914; he described Hoover as a 'wonder', having nothing but admiration for his ability to accomplish seemingly impossible tasks in remarkably little time.[4]

After America joined the war in 1917, Hoover lobbied Wilson to set up a central authority to manage food distribution in the United States; Wilson was receptive to Hoover's suggestion and put him in charge of the newly-created US Food Administration, which, after the war, became the American Relief Administration, managing food aid to Central and Eastern Europe. He had hoped to gain the Republican presidential nomination in 1920; when that did not materialise, he served as Commerce Secretary under Harding and Coolidge with great distinction, until winning the presidential nomination in 1928 and the election that November.

As President, Hoover had the great misfortune to serve at a time when the world's economies collapsed starting in October 1929. As a social progressive, but a strict economic conservative,

Hoover was the model of a breed of politician that once was not uncommon in the United States, but would be virtually impossible to find today; unfortunately, he was ill-equipped to deal with the market downturn which, in turn, led to stagnation in the entire economy. It would, however, take over a year for the full impact of the Great Depression to be understood, and another year or more after that for its greatest depth to be reached;[5] this was still in the future when the Preparatory Commission met for the eighth time in April 1929. Despite the failure of the United States to join the League of Nations, the Americans remained fully engaged in most League activities, and therefore it was not out of place that Gibson, as the primary American representative, took his turn to address the issues facing the Preparatory Commission. He started by restating that America had little interest in the land armaments side of the discussions, and that it was really only the naval armaments issues that concerned the United States.[6] He went on to reiterate the Americans' commitment to quantitative limitation as the correct approach to the naval arms limitation problem:

> The American Government has found no reason for modifying its view that the simplest, fairest and most practical method is that of limitation by tonnage by categories – a method which has been given practical and satisfactory application in the Washington Treaty. While it is realised that this does not constitute an exact and scientific gauge of strategic strength, we have nevertheless found that it constitutes a method which has the advantage of simplicity and of affording to each Power the freedom to utilise its tonnage within the limitation of each category according to its special needs.[7]

Gibson made sure he did not cut off any paths to possible compromise with the British, and also made early mention of the development of a conversion formula – what the Americans would call a 'yardstick' – whereby, using a ship's age and displacement (and, optionally, gun calibre), its 'value' compared to other ships could be established, setting up the potential for ships to be 'traded' between categories. He reiterated America's willingness to be flexible in reaching a disarmament agreement, as long as it truly involved a reduction of armaments.

> My Government is disposed to give full and friendly consideration to any supplementary methods of limitation which may be calculated to make our proposals, . . . or any other, acceptable to other Powers, and, if such a course appears desirable, my Government will be prepared to give consideration to a method of estimating equivalent naval values which takes account of other factors than displacement tonnage alone.[8]

Gibson's words were met with general approbation, both in Geneva and, more importantly, in London.[9] Ramsay MacDonald, the Labour Party leader who formed his second government at the beginning of June, shared Hoover's great desire to reduce defence expenditures. Adding to the sense that a fresh start was taking place in Anglo-American relations was the arrival in London of a new American ambassador, the former Vice President during the previous administration, Charles G Dawes. Indeed, MacDonald and Dawes proved congenial to one another; their initial discussions led to a very positive response by the British to Gibson's overtures in Geneva and discussion of the possibility of a meeting between the two new leaders. (It is not totally clear when the idea of a face-to-face meeting between Hoover and the British Prime Minister had its origins; it appears to have originated even before the change of government in Great Britain in June 1929.) On 11 June – five days after MacDonald took office – the American Chargé, Ray Atherton reported on rumours buzzing around London:

The dominant personality in British politics at end of the late 1920s and through the mid-1930s, the man with whom every American who came to London had to deal, was J Ramsay MacDonald, the Labour Prime Minister who firmly believed that arms reduction, particularly given the global economic downturn that he and all other world leaders were facing, was a necessity. (LOC/BNS)

> In usually well-informed circles it was rumored that Mr. Baldwin had been assured unofficially that the Prime Minister would be welcome should he proceed to Washington to discuss naval disarmament with the President and Mr. Mackenzie King in September.[10] That the same unofficial assurances from Washington have been extended to Mr. MacDonald and that upon his arrival in London General Dawes will convey to Mr. MacDonald an official invitation, is the rumor at present.[11] The latter has said 'If Mr. Hoover invites me to Washington, I shall go,' according to the London newspapers.[12]

When Dawes arrived, he in fact attempted to cool MacDonald's ardour for an immediate meeting with Hoover, pointing out several potential negatives in meeting the President before the basics of an agreement had been hammered out, including inviting misunderstanding among the general public of both nations regarding which had gotten the better of the deal. MacDonald agreed to postpone his visit, at least temporarily.[13]

The Japanese were actively following these developments. Dawes was acquainted with the Japanese ambassador in London, Matsudaira Tsuneo, from previous contact in the United States, and kept him well informed of the progress of talks with the British.[14] This was reinforced on 20 June by a report from Tokyo, in which the American Chargé there stated that the Japanese Prime Minister, Tanaka Giichi, 'was prepared to support any measures looking to further reduction of armaments; that the country wanted peace and lessened expenditure for war purposes.'[15] Nonetheless, their ambassador in Washington reminded the newly-installed Secretary of State Henry L Stimson that 'Japanese opinion was very sensitive on the question of the 5-5-3 ratio; that this had been agreed to as to capital ships but when it came to auxiliary vessels we would find their public opinion very keen'.[16]

Clearly, the impetus towards another naval disarmament conference was building. Conferring in London on 25 June, Dawes and Gibson drafted a lengthy message to Washington in which they detailed their arguments for why such a conference should be called at the invitation of the British rather than the Americans, primarily because they believed Great Britain had better leverage in persuading the French to join in the discussions, in anticipation of renewed resistance from Paris to limitations of cruisers or submarines.[17] MacDonald was receptive to the idea of Great Britain initiating the pending disarmament conference, especially if it were to be hosted in London.[18] Indeed, MacDonald seemed eager to send invitations immediately, thinking this would be for a 'preliminary' gathering of diplomats to precede the main 'technical' conference.

> Apparently MacDonald is exploring the possibility of coming into the conference after consulting with us and making some very general public proposal to the effect the Government of Great Britain is disposed to scrap certain construction, to abandon its present building program, and to contribute such further concessions as are possible and allow us an opportunity to reply in like manner, thus liquidating our problem but without resorting to the use of the yardstick at any time.[19]

The Americans once again felt it necessary to restrain MacDonald's enthusiasm, explaining their belief that the conference should not be called until the technical issues had been largely, if not entirely, worked out in private, multilateral diplomacy. It was suggested that Washington send a naval officer to London with the technical knowledge and authority to meet a counterpart from the Admiralty and they proceed together to Brussels (to sit down with Gibson) to negotiate the elusive 'yardstick' that would allow an equivalence to be drawn between the Royal Navy's multiple, older light cruisers and (presumably) some number of newer American cruisers of sizes yet to be determined.[20] The Americans were perfectly willing to hold all preliminary discussions in London (or Brussels), but, claiming proprietary rights to the idea of calling this next naval disarmament conference, withheld a decision as to where it would be held.[21]

The hectic pace of Anglo-American negotiations now slowed just a bit; MacDonald stated he needed to consult his Cabinet before responding to the latest American proposals. Then, on 8 July, a letter from MacDonald was delivered to Dawes outlining nine points of presumed or proposed agreement which the Prime Minister wished confirmed by the Americans, of which he thought some, if not all, should be announced to the world in a joint communiqué. Starting with basic points, such as mutual acceptance of the Kellogg-Briand Pact of August 1928 and parity between the United States and Great Britain as foundational bases, MacDonald stated that 'the object of negotiations must be reduction in existing armaments'.[22] With his third point, MacDonald got down to the more substantive parts of his letter:

> 3. We adopt the United States proposal that parity should be measured by an agreed 'yardstick' which enables the slightly different values in our respective national needs to be reduced to equality.[23]

He then went on to endorse Dawes' suggestion that an American and British naval expert meet to work out the details of that yardstick, with the American expert to make the initial proposal.

> 5. I think it would expedite matters if your officer would take with him a proposal which your people are prepared to make as to the 'stick' in all fairness to us.
> 6. When we agree as to the 'stick' we can proceed as to its application and so far as I can see little trouble will arise about this between us. If it does its cause has certainly not been evident to me yet.[24]

Here is a man taking pains to make sure his reader knows how much he desires an agreement be reached between the two sides. He went on to indicate that, while his eagerness for the anticipated naval conference, and for the meeting with Hoover that would precede it, may have been somewhat restrained by Dawes, it had not been daunted in any serious fashion, nor had the American caveats regarding the possible location of any conference made much impression on MacDonald:

> 8. We should also decide when the moment had come for the general conference to meet in London, when I should go to Washington, and when the final conference of ratification should take place. My own view is that if you got your officer over at once you and I would soon settle the preliminaries and the other conferences would follow.[25]

The American response, coming on 11 July, was generally agreeable, but more muted in tone than MacDonald's enthusiastic note. Stimson asked Dawes to remind MacDonald that 'the expression "slightly different values in our respective national needs" refers to characteristics of combatant ships but does not refer to reasonable equality of total combat strength'.[26] Stimson was clearly trying to alert MacDonald that the Americans believed a large gap still remained between the cruiser numbers in the two nations' fleets that needed to be addressed.

Further, Stimson wanted to make it clear that the Americans were viewing the proposed 'yardstick' quite differently than MacDonald was. The Prime Minister appeared to be thinking of its use as a tool to allow the Royal Navy to justify the construction (or retention) of numerous smaller 6in-gunned cruisers offset by a small number of American 'treaty maximum' cruisers. Clearly, the Americans were thinking of it more as a way to allow an orderly (and strictly controlled) transfer of tonnage between entirely different categories of ships, something that would be appealing to at least some of the other Contracting Powers.

In terms of exactly what the 'yardstick' might be, Stimson allowed the following speculation:

> F. We suggest that in measuring relative combatant strength of ships we should consider the elements of such a yardstick to be
>
> (*a*) Displacement.
> (*b*) Guns.
> (*c*) Age.
>
> Our general view is that protection, speed, habitability, etc., are entirely relative to the other factors and do not require special consideration.
>
> G. We suggest that that these factors may deserve different weight for different categories.
>
> H. It is not expected that any yardstick will be a mathematical nicety. . . .[27]

Thus, the Americans made clear that, in their minds, the 'yardstick' would never be a single, simple 'magic' formula, as MacDonald seemed to imagine it would be. Nonetheless, they offered; if MacDonald agreed, 'we could at once send a naval expert if it is desired or we could mutually exchange views upon the weight to be given factors mentioned in F with hope of early decision'.[28]

The 'problem', on MacDonald's end of this debate, was that pressure was building for major developments; the 'rumors' to which Atherton had alluded back in early June had, if anything, grown in urgency. In an attempt to move the process forward, MacDonald wrote a note for Dawes to pass along to Stimson:

> In view of our conversations I have just decided to slow down our preparations for laying the keels of the two cruisers in my naval program of 1928-29.[29] I hope they

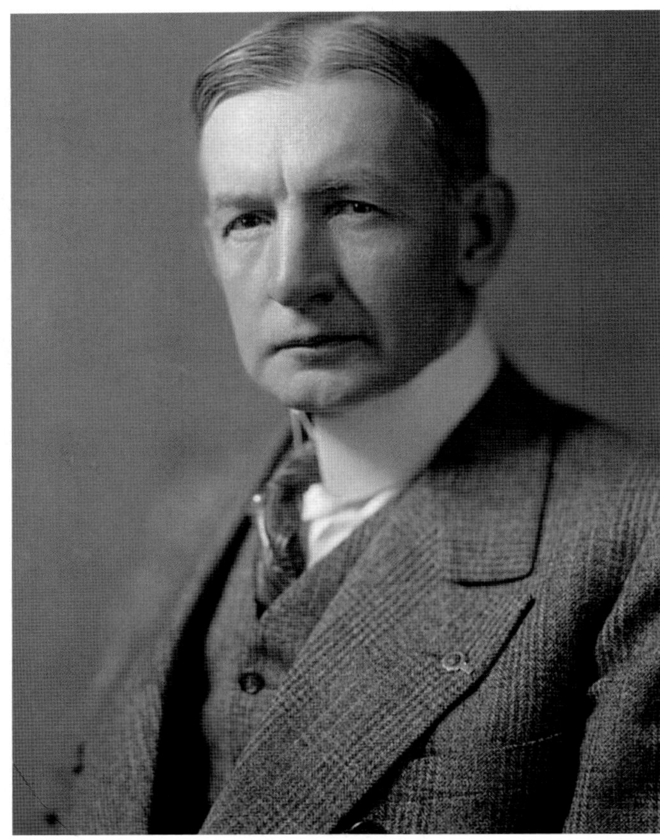

A true polymath, American Ambassador to the Court of St James Charles G Dawes was more than up to the task of dealing with MacDonald. He and the British Prime Minister formed a close personal bond that went a long way towards assuring the success of the First London Conference. (LOC/HEC)

> need never be built. Might I presume to remark that if a corresponding step could be taken on your side it would have a fine effect. I must announce this in a week or two before the House rises and a simultaneous statement of your plans would enable me to get this through without an attack on the ground that I have done something without any response.[30]

The Americans were immediately forthcoming, telling Dawes to assure MacDonald of their support for his intent to delay the construction of the *Surreys*:

> (2) We can cooperate with the Prime Minister's suggestion that there be a slow-down in construction. The United States has completed, or ready for early launching, eight of the new type . . . cruisers; there are two more under contract in private shipyards; in Government yards . . . there are three undertaken for construction . . . The United States can reciprocate upon Mr. MacDonald's announcement by a statement that we have slowed down our preparation for laying the keels of the three cruisers which have been undertaken by the Government yards . . .[31]

Of course, there was more than a bit of disingenuousness in Stimson's response since the option to delay the three government-built FY1929 cruisers was already being mooted (although the decision to use the FY1930 cruiser design for the three government-built FY1929 ships appears to have been made no earlier than November 1929, four months after these interchanges).[32] MacDonald was extremely pleased with this support and told Dawes to expect a formal written response within a few days. This arrived on 18 July; in it, MacDonald stated his agreement with all the points Stimson made in his message of 12 July.

MacDonald's letter becomes interesting, however, at the point at which he responded to an assertion made by Stimson regarding the number of 'new type' cruisers the Royal Navy possessed or planned to build. The American claim was that the British had fourteen of these ships in service and ten more building or authorised:

> These figures have been taken apparently from an out-of-date white paper.[33] Since then alterations have been made and the position today is: number built and building, fifteen; number projected, three—these three include the two I have slowed down.[34]

He then repeated his offer regarding the *Surreys*:

> . . . I have slowed up the preparations for laying down the two cruisers included in the 1928 program and have done so not merely for the purpose of lengthening out the time for the completion of that program but in the hope that it is the first step towards a reduction.[35]

With this statement, the negotiations over cruiser tonnage – the stubborn stumbling block that doomed the Geneva Conference – finally began to get serious. Stimson replied:

> The nub of our difficulties lies here . . . Both countries are now attempting to make a new beginning on the basis of the principle of cruiser parity. . . . the fundamental practical question to be settled is at what time and at what tonnage is parity to be determined. In settling that question, it is most important our actual tonnage situation is mutually understood. In this connection we are in some doubt whether we are fully aware of Great Britain's position . . .[36]

This was a major concession by Stimson, admitting that the Americans were largely ignorant of the details of the Royal Navy's building programmes, present or future. He could have pointed out that the British had multiple opportunities over the preceding few years to enlighten their erstwhile ally and had failed to do so, but he was diplomatic enough not to mention that fact. He then went on to outline the American understanding of the current and future British cruiser construction programmes. Stimson listed fourteen 'new type' cruisers believed to be in service: the four *Hawkins* class colonial cruisers completed between 1918 and 1925; the seven *Kent* class and three of the four *London* class 'treaty maximum' cruisers. He then listed seven cruisers under construction; these included the fourth *London* class cruiser, the two *Norfolk*s, *York* and *Exeter*, and the two *Surrey*s. Stimson then listed three unnamed further cruisers as authorised, but not yet laid down.

Now Stimson started on the always dangerous 'black art' of calculating tonnage based on these numbers:

> This brings the total of large cruisers to twenty-four of an aggregate tonnage of about 231,800. Is it to be our understanding that Great Britain is in a position to stop the building of eight of the ships included in the above figures and thereby to reduce to 160,000 tons the total large cruiser tonnage?[37]

These numbers may at first glance appear to have been conjured from thin air, but there is some thread of logic behind them. The first tonnage total Stimson gave (231,800 tons) can be arrived at only by assuming the Americans believed that the eight ships MacDonald would stop building were of various types that would have a mean displacement of approximately 8975 tons each; removing them from the equation would leave the Royal Navy with sixteen 'new type' cruisers – the four *Hawkins*, seven *Kent*s, four *London*s and one *Norfolk* – with an approximate total displacement of 160,000 tons. The 'magic number' sixteen derived from MacDonald's own statement of 18 July when he said Great Britain had fifteen large cruisers built or building and three more 'projected', of which he was willing to sacrifice two. From this, Stimson took sixteen to be a number with which the British could live. (Of course, the major disconnect here was the inclusion by the Americans of the four *Hawkins* class cruisers in the count that MacDonald gave; MacDonald's count of fifteen built or building in fact excluded the *Hawkins* class, instead comprising the *Kent*s (seven), *London*s (four), *Norfolk*s (two), *York* and *Exeter*, none of which were on his chopping block.)

Stimson continued with his logic, flaws and all. Adding in the existing war-built light cruisers, Stimson concluded that the Royal Navy's cruiser fleet had an aggregate total of approximately 402,800 tons. He then briefly stated the American numbers: twenty-three 'treaty maximum' cruisers building or authorised for 230,000 tons and the ten *Omaha*s for 70,500 tons, making for a total he rounded down to 300,000 tons. He then laid out the crux of the matter:

> We are anxious . . . to effect a reduction of our authorized program . . . ; how far this can go, however, is dependent on how far the British Government itself is willing to go in limiting its own cruiser class. It is impossible to develop a yardstick which would bridge the difference between 300,000 tons and a tonnage of 402,888 [*sic*]. Still less would it be possible to bridge a greater difference which might result from a scaling down of our program as now authorized. . . .[38]

This message seems to have finally pricked the bubble of optimism that MacDonald had maintained concerning the issues leading up to a naval disarmament agreement. On 23 July, Dawes sat down with MacDonald at 10 Downing Street and read through the entirety of Stimson's long message, part of which the Prime Minister had seen the day before. Then MacDonald handed Dawes a note he had written quite early that morning:

> I have been thinking over the despatch you showed me yesterday and though I have not yet had it (I am writing this early in the morning when only the birds are up and they even are sleepy) to study, it is clear that it raises a problem which we have assumed was smaller than it appears to be. We have been waiting for the 'yardstick', but the despatch of yesterday says that the gap between us is too wide for a yardstick to span. So we must examine it and I must get advice and guidance.
>
> I propose, if it meets your convenience, to stay in town till we settle something. This week finds me full of concerns till the House rises. Would it be possible for us to meet on Monday morning to go into the whole matter of this tonnage of cruisers and go at it until we agree on how we stand.[39] If Mr. Gibson could be with us, I would bring Mr. Alexander, the First Lord (Civil), and a day or two ought to see the end of our preliminary conversations. Then, I shall go on a holiday![40]

Part of what kept MacDonald busy the rest of that week was an address he made to the Commons the next day. As a courtesy rarely extended by one head of state to a representative of another, MacDonald offered Dawes an advance look at the text he intended to deliver, with the intent that he would forward it to Stimson and Hoover.[41] This was greeted positively in Washington, as were the remarks MacDonald delivered on 24 July. It was in this address that MacDonald announced publicly the suspension of all work on the two *Surrey*s, although they were not yet officially cancelled.

The following day, MacDonald addressed a long letter to Dawes, sober in mood, that clearly reflected his disappointment that goodwill alone would not suffice to resolve the cruiser 'problem'. With the written equivalent of a weary sigh, he stated:

> My dear General: I was hoping that we might have been able to proceed with a yardstick examination and test in accordance with the lines of our conversations, but the despatch you handed to me yesterday raises the whole question of tonnage in its old absolute form. A failure to escape from this led to a breakdown of the Naval Conference at Geneva.[42]

While not coming out and blaming the Americans, and their insistence on quantitative rather than qualitative limits, for the failure at Geneva and the gloom that MacDonald now saw descending on the present negotiations, it certainly was the implication in the first lines of the Prime Minister's note. He conceded:

> . . . but I see that the figures of absolute tonnage upon which your people have been working do appear to be a formidable obstacle and I am anxious to remove these and any other difficulties which lie in our way.
>
> . . . In the course of the conversation over the despatch which deals with the ingredients of the 'yardstick,' I also referred to the variety of ship included in the cruiser category and I shall now state what information I have gathered since I saw you yesterday . . .
>
> Large cruisers: We have 22, not 24, built and projected, the total tonnage being 216,200 not 231,000. . . .[43]

To get to this number, MacDonald had to include the four ships in the *Hawkins* class, along with the two *Surrey*s and one additional authorised large cruiser from the 1929 Building Programme, but he immediately tried to explain why the *Hawkins* should not be in this category:

> The relative values of classes in the cruiser categories raise details which can best be discussed and settled over a table . . . But in this note I point out by way of illustration that the *Hawkins* group laid down for war purposes in 1916 cannot either in their present condition as ships or in their

> armament of seven 7.5 inch guns, hand-worked and throwing a projectile of 200 pounds instead of 250 pounds, really be valued on displacement tonnage alone. We regard them as being nearer to the modern six-inch cruiser than to its eight-inch companion. This is preeminently a case for the yardstick. . . .[44]

With that argument made, he then turned to his large fleet of light cruisers, where, again, he took pains to point out that numbers could be deceiving:

> Smaller cruisers: Of these we have 40 classed as six-inch with a tonnage of 179,270. But here again we really need a yardstick because the tonnage value requires to be adjusted. I am told for instance that your *Omaha* class, of which you have 10 carries 120 six-inch guns and are of a total tonnage of 70,500. They cannot be compared to our 'C' class of which we have 24 carrying 109 six-inch guns and of a tonnage of 100,250. Here again is a case for an examination round a table not of service experts in command but of statesmen . . .[45]

Here MacDonald chose his case for comparison very carefully, selecting the oldest and smallest of the Royal Navy's remaining light cruisers to compare to the only light cruisers in service in the United States Navy, which did happen to be bigger and better armed. A much fairer comparison would have been between the *Omahas* and the eight *Danaes* and two *Emeralds*. The Prime Minister then summarised the picture as he saw it:

> To sum up I give you a table as I have received it in reply to inquiries I have made since I have had your despatch.
>
> > Eight-inch cruisers: British 15 ships, 146,800 tons; 3 projected, 30,000; total 176,800. United
> > States 13 building, 130,000; 10 projected, 100,000; total 230,000.
> > 7.5-inch cruisers: Great Britain, *Hawkins* class 4, 29,400. United States none.
> > Six-inch cruisers: Great Britain 40, 179,270. United States 10, 70,500.[46]

MacDonald was careful not to give grand totals when citing the comparative tonnages, which would have hardly supported his argument that the gaps were such as could be bridged by reasonable men with a good 'yardstick'. The raw numbers he listed, which were basically accurate, gave the British an aggregate tonnage advantage in cruisers of 385,470 tons to 300,500 tons, or 28 per cent greater tonnage of cruisers, assuming all projected ships were built. Counting only ships actually built and building, the British advantage was far greater – 355,470 tons to 200,500 tons, a 77 per cent advantage – all without taking into account the still standing British goal of reaching seventy cruisers – eight more than MacDonald listed as built, building or projected – or the stated American desire to reduce their projected building programme. Nonetheless, what is significant here, and seemed at the time to have slipped past unnoticed, was the tacit British acceptance of continued American construction of 'treaty maximum' cruisers, one of the issues that had caused the deadlock at Geneva in 1927.

The Americans reacted generally favourably to this approach by the British. The critical meeting on 29 July with MacDonald and his new First Lord Alexander, was coming up in just four days. In a lengthy cable, the American representatives were told to inform the British that they proposed a comprehensive programme which defined five categories of warships and agreed to reduce the number of destroyers and submarines the US Navy had in commission to match the Royal Navy's totals. The United States accepted the idea of the use of a yardstick formula within warship categories, along with agreeing, tentatively, with MacDonald's notion that a tonnage limit was the proper end point of these negotiations rather than a start line. They even agreed to hold the upcoming conference in London.

When Dawes, accompanied by Gibson, sat down with MacDonald and Alexander on Monday, 29 July, they presented the position contained in Stimson's cable, expecting a warm reception, given the lengths to which the Americans had gone to meet British desires. What they received from the Prime Minister was a prepared proposal that, while it offered some reduction from the position the British had taken at Geneva two years earlier, was far from what the Americans had been expecting. MacDonald stated that this was an entirely personal proposal that he had not yet presented to the Admiralty:

> General agreement as to cruisers:
> 1. The British Government would be satisfied with a large cruiser strength of 15 and would agree to the American Government building up to 18.
> 2. The British Government would ask for an equivalent (to be measured by the yardstick) in six-inch cruisers so that their total in that class should be 45.
> 3. As regards the *Hawkins* (or *Effingham*) group of 4 cruisers, an agreement will be come to that for the purposes of classification they shall, during their lifetime, be counted amongst the six-inch class and then be replaced by ordinary six-inch ships. . . ,
> 4. In order to arrive at parity the United States may construct up to 10 six-inch-gun ships.[47]

Dawes, in his report to Stimson, attempted to 'spin' this proposal by MacDonald as best he could, emphasising that the 'best possible spirit' was exhibited by the British at the meeting, but there was little he could do to disguise the fact that the Prime Minister was asking the Americans to accept twenty-three ships – ten *Omahas*, three authorised, but not-yet-funded, 'treaty maximum' cruisers and ten 6in-armed cruisers that were not authorised, planned or desired – as being the functional equivalent of forty-five cruisers of various sizes and ages, all by waving a 'yardstick' as if it were a magic wand. So disappointing was this offer to the Americans that it almost passed without notice that the total number of cruisers MacDonald was proposing for the Royal Navy was sixty and not seventy.

By the next morning, MacDonald must have realised that he was still asking too much of the Americans, because he sent Dawes a follow-on note that included:

> I should also like to let you know that although I agreed yesterday to the figures of 15 and 45 as my program of cruiser building I am going now to work to find out whether I cannot reduce both these figures but certainly the second one if we can get an agreement from Japan, France and Italy. So if there is any objection from America that the total reduction involved in our agreement of yesterday is a little disappointing please let it remain where it is because I think if we can extend our agreement to other powers I can offer you a still better arrangement.[48]

This was a case of 'too little, too late' on MacDonald's part. Before his note of 30 July begging for American patience could be received, the reaction to his proposal of the previous day had begun; to state that the Americans were displeased would put it mildly. On 31 July, Stimson sent the following to Dawes:

> Insurmountable obstacles to agreement are apparently presented by the tentative program proposed by Mr. MacDonald for the following reasons:
>
> (1) The principle of decrease in naval armament is totally abdicated.
> (2) The principle of parity and equality between the navies of Great Britain and the United States, the crux of which rest in the cruiser class, is abandoned.[49]

So irate was Simpson that he could not resist sending another cable to Dawes barely two hours after the first, in which he ranted:

> It is very difficult to tell you how keenly disappointed we are over the proposal made by the Prime Minister. We prefer no agreement in preference to his proposal, as we now see the situation.[50]

In the first of the telegrams sent to Dawes on 31 July, Stimson went into grim detail, ton-by-ton, explaining why the Americans were so disappointed by the Prime Minister's proposal. The Americans' mathematics came up with 'about' 376,226 tons in cruisers for the Royal Navy, while they would have 180,000 tons in 'treaty maximum' cruisers and 70,500 tons in the *Omaha* class for a total 250,500 tons for the United States Navy. The General Board insisted they had no need for or interest in building the ten 6in-armed cruisers MacDonald offered in his proposal.

MacDonald had no useful response to offer Stimson except a rather vague warning that if he were to offer greater unilateral reduction in cruiser strength, he would likely encounter such resistance in Parliament as to threaten his continued tenure as Prime Minister. Gibson came to MacDonald's defence in a lengthy cable, noting MacDonald's newness as Prime Minister and stating that there had been the implication, if not the outright statement, by the Prime Minister and First Lord, that there was some flexibility in the British intent to limit the Americans to eighteen 'treaty maximum' cruisers.[51]

What really prevented this from being the start of another Anglo-American deadlock was the presence of very different characters at the top of both governments and the very strong desire for a positive outcome to these negotiations on both sides of the Atlantic. In particular, the solid working relationship established by MacDonald and Dawes proved critical. They met again on 6 August – MacDonald coming back to London from his home in Scotland – and began with Dawes and Gibson pressing the British on the issue of how many 'treaty maximum' cruisers the Americans would be allowed to build under any final agreement. The British response was sobering (and cleverly crafted):

> Mr. MacDonald replied in a most definite manner that so far as the United States and Great Britain are concerned he would have no hesitation in complying and that he would not feel obliged to modify his naval building program no matter how many of these larger vessels were built by the United States, but he called our attention to the fact that neither Great Britain nor the United States could show the same indifference to the building of such cruisers by other nations and that, when the negotiations had reached the point where the five naval powers would be participating, it is quite apparent that Japan would desire to base the ratio of her cruiser strength on that of the navy of whichever country should have the greatest number of cruisers of the 10,000 ton, 8-inch-gun type.[52]

By 'playing the Japan card', MacDonald caught the Americans by surprise and hit them in their most vulnerable spot. However much Washington hated the thought of the British gaining any sort of advantage, the prospect of the Japanese being able to profit from an American misstep would be even more galling.

On 8 August, the Prime Minister wrote to Dawes from Scotland with a new proposal that went further than any previous offer by the British. Specifically, he proposed as follows:

> 4. I have been working at a scheme which would make British figures in 1936 the standard of parity. Then without replacement in the meanwhile we should have fifteen 8-inch and thirty-four 6-inch ships, a total of forty-nine. . . . That position is reached by the ordinary operations of scrapping, . . . , as a business proposition I would propose to scrap each year one cruiser which I would not otherwise scrap and replace it by a scheme of building which would leave us with fifty cruisers and no more.[53]

This seems to have been the break that finally led to the possibility of an agreement. Stimson replied on the 15th, stating up-front:

> In general we regard his letter as highly important and if we now correctly understand his position we think we see daylight and that it makes great progress toward agreement.[54]

Nonetheless, the cable went on for five more pages, parsing MacDonald's complex scheme and niggling many details, but the entire spirit of the negotiating process had clearly shifted to a more positive note.

Events at this point conspired to slow the process for a while. Gibson, in Brussels, developed a medical condition requiring surgery and was unavailable for some time, while the normal slowing of government activity in Washington in August, when the city becomes uninhabitable, took many major players out of the loop.[55] The Japanese also chose this point to insert themselves into the discussion, their ambassadors in Washington and London making near-simultaneous visits to the State Department and Foreign Ministry (with a courtesy visit to Dawes to reinforce the message).[56] The messages were simple; Dawes in London recorded one version of the message:

> This afternoon the Japanese Ambassador called on me and told me he was under instruction from his Government to say that it was most sympathetic to the idea of reduction as touching all categories. Mr. Matsudaira also stated that the Japanese Government would ask for a readjustment of the percentages of naval strength to a 10-10-7 basis.[57]

Furthermore, despite all the goodwill spread about, the hard central 'core' of the cruiser problem still remained – the differing perceptions between the two sides of the relative 'value' of some of the older, smaller cruisers in each other's fleets. On 23 August, Dawes received a letter from MacDonald in which he complained that the British public would 'turn and rend us' if he accepted as parity a deal that gave the Americans twenty-three 8in-gunned cruisers and ten *Omahas* as against the Royal Navy's fifteen large cruisers and thirty-five smaller ones.[58] The persistent disconnect arose from the British seeing the ten *Omahas* as much more powerful than their own war-built light cruisers, while treating their four *Hawkins* class colonial cruisers as functionally equal to their other small cruisers; from the American point of view, the counting-up of ships looked entirely different, with the four *Hawkins* class cruisers being seen as very nearly equal to 'treaty maximum' cruisers and the two *Emeralds* as equal to two of the *Omahas*.[59] This went a long way towards explaining the inability of the two sides agreeing to what constituted parity.

On 28 August, the Americans tried again to ask Dawes to appeal to MacDonald's sense of reason:

> There is no objection on our part to Great Britain's placing the point of parity in cruisers at fifty units if that is consistent with 330,000 tons total displacement.[60]

In an amplifying cable, sent later that same day, Stimson, as part of a listing of all the points he believed had been agreed between the two sides, explained how the 'magic number' of 330,000 tons in aggregate displacement for the Royal Navy cruiser force was arrived at:

> (11) A reduction of British cruiser strength shall be made by December 31, 1936, to fifty units whose total displacement shall not exceed a standard tonnage of 330,000. Fifteen of these fifty units shall be 8-inch cruisers with an aggregate standard tonnage of 146,800. There shall be four 7.5-inch gun cruisers, with an aggregate tonnage of 39,426, and there shall be thirty-one 6-inch gun cruisers with an aggregate tonnage of 143,774, of which, prior to 1936, not more than seven armed with 6-inch guns are to be constructed.[61]

In the same cable, Stimson asked Dawes to suggest to MacDonald that perhaps it would be better to defer the 'prolonged and highly technical mathematical discussions' about the yardstick until the actual five-power conference was convened.[62] His reasoning had to do with the need to share any preliminary conclusions with the other nations and the inevitability of public disclosure that would likely lead to 'violent press controversy' which would 'becloud all of the much more important matters' already agreed and 'render far more difficult a final agreement' in the subsequent conference. In yet a third cable sent the same day, Stimson instructed Dawes to communicate to MacDonald what he hoped would be a 'deal clincher', hinting at a further 'discount' over and above the 30,000-ton displacement advantage the Americans were already offering the British, the reduction of the United States Navy's cruiser programme by at least one, and possibly more than one, of its 'treaty maximum' cruisers.[63]

If the Americans had hoped that this would bring the two sides to agreement, they were to be disappointed again.[64] There were two points on which MacDonald found himself unable to agree with Stimson's proposal. One was the aggregate total of 330,000 tons cruiser tonnage the Americans calculated the Royal Navy would possess at the end of 1936. He corrected that to 339,000 tons; the Royal Navy, he stated, would not retain the four *Hawkins* class cruisers, and of the extant light cruisers, would keep only eleven of the 'C' class. Fourteen of the oldest, 'weariest' light cruisers would be replaced by 'O' cruisers, such as *Leander*, with an optimistically projected standard displacement of 6500 tons each. (This author is baffled as to why it took the British until the end of August to reveal these final details of their building plans for cruisers to the ally and partner with whom they had been talking on a daily basis for nearly three months, making the negotiating process much more difficult and frustrating in the process.)

The other point of disagreement was a replay of the 'Japan card':

> I should like to explain . . . the result of our very thorough examination of the American proposal that for our fifteen 8-inch cruisers you should have twenty-three. The ratio 5-5-3.5 which Japan asks for would mean in relation to the twenty-three Japan could build sixteen which would be one of a superiority over us. If you fixed your 8-inch cruisers at twenty, the ratio would mean that Japan could build fourteen. I am perfectly certain that the Dominions would reject any agreement on that basis. If on the other hand you made it eighteen for you, Japan could build 12.6 which would be thirteen. In order to get a settlement, we might get Japan to accept twelve and to that we would agree.[65]

He went on to argue that even if the Japanese accepted the original Washington ratio (5-5-3) for cruisers, that still would allow them fourteen if the Americans built twenty-three, and he was sure the stubborn Dominions would not accept the Japanese having more than twelve. The American response was exasperation once again. While greeting MacDonald's stated intent to dispose of the *Hawkins* class cruisers, Stimson bemoaned the attempt to reduce the number of 'treaty maximum' cruisers the Americans could build – 'the type to which our Navy is now committed' – stating it presented 'a problem which to us frankly seems extremely difficult if not insoluble'.[66]

MacDonald sensed he had pushed the Americans about as far as he could, but he could not resist another try at getting them to relent on demanding so many large cruisers. On 9 September, he sent Dawes yet another letter pleading his case:

> 4. I wonder if I might venture to make a suggestion to you regarding the numbers of 8-inch ships which you say you are bound to build? . . . If insisted upon I am unable to see any way out of the deadlock. I notice, however, . . . the very reasonable point is made that must you have ships capable of operating within a large radius.
>
> Could you not build ships that would satisfy the radius requirement and at the same time get me out of my difficulties in relation to other powers; for instance, would it be feasible for you to build say five 10,000 ton cruisers carrying 6-inch guns that would enable you to have the eighteen 8-inch cruisers, which I understood originally was satisfactory to you, and at the same time enable you to use effectively the tonnage which you say you require in order to enable you to satisfy your people that you have secured parity with us?[67]

This note from MacDonald was, as far as this author has been able to discover, the origin of the idea of the 6in-armed 'treaty maximum' cruiser, the 'Big Babies' for which this chapter is named. Despite the somewhat condescending tone taken by the Prime Minister, it was not really a bad idea, though on further analysis, it is easy to see that it did not really address the problem MacDonald was hoping to resolve, namely his concern that that excessive American construction of 'treaty maximum' cruisers would allow the Japanese to build more large cruisers than could be matched by British building programmes. It simply shifted the threat from one type of cruiser to another; whatever ships the Americans were allowed to build, the Japanese would expect to be able to build their allowable ratio of similar types.

The Americans were not immediately receptive to MacDonald's idea. The morning after receiving the Prime Minister's note, Hoover convened a meeting at the White House with Stimson, his Navy Secretary, Charles F Adams III, and the General Board, with the intent of determining what would constitute parity in cruisers.[68] The meeting was not an easy one; the General Board resisted accepting any form of smaller cruiser or cruiser with less than maximum armament, but finally relented under pressure from the President and the Secretary of State:

> 1. We have now spent the past week in most earnest consideration of the Prime Minister's proposed British cruiser fleet of 339,000 displacement tons . . .
> 2. Our Naval Board reports to us this morning that in an endeavor to meet the British proposals just as closely as they can they will for this purpose accept as representing parity with such a program, after taking into account both the age and gun factors, an American fleet comprising 21 8-inch 10,000 ton cruisers – that is 210,000 tons; 10 of the *Omaha* class – 70,000 tons; and 5 new cruisers of about 7,000 tons 6-inch class – about 35,000 tons, making a total of about 315,000 tons.[69]

This was altogether a strange proposal, given how strongly the Americans had held out against earlier British proposals that would have mandated a reduction in allowable cruiser size below 10,000 tons. Now, it seemed, the Americans were willing to give up two of their authorised 'treaty maximum' cruisers, building instead a number of additional light cruisers similar in size to the *Omahas*. While this was certainly not what MacDonald expected to hear – and hardly what he wanted to hear – it was obvious to him that it was the best he was going to get in the short term, and he declared himself able to accept this offer from the Americans, clearing the way for his planned meeting with Hoover.

Nonetheless, on the 23rd, MacDonald sent along a rambling note full of complaints about how he believed that the Americans had only to worry about their standing relative to Great Britain, while the British had to worry about relations with the rest of Europe and, indeed, the entire world. He even claimed that were it not for those worries, the British would have no interest in the parity debate.

> This parity business is of Satan himself. . . . Opinion in the United States demands it and the Senate will accept nothing which does not look like it. On my side I am not interested in it at all. I give it to you with both hands heaped and running down. When I am forced to scrutinize your program which you say embodies it, I turn from you altogether and have to think of things which, but for my importunities, you would not think much about, viz, the fleets of other nations.[70]

This really was a startling statement for the head of one friendly state to make to another, particularly heads of states about to meet to discuss an important international agreement. It sounds more like a schoolteacher lecturing a slow-learning student, a tone the British took frequently with the Americans during this period, much to Washington's irritation. He continued his lesson:

> Therefore, although in our talks with each other, we assume that the discussion takes place between us two, that is really not the case. There are shadowy entities between us. A spirit photograph would show you unaccompanied, but round me would be the ghost of the other nations. In its ultimate, the parity we are trying to devise is one between you and the rest of the world in relation to the British position in it. If the appearance of parity is to be obtained, neither of us can get away from the fact that the standard must be fixed by British needs.[71]

By the standards of diplomatic interchange, MacDonald, in that last statement, came close to a major *faux pas*, speaking what he believed to be the unvarnished truth with no trace of gloss or guile. It is, of course, a given that every nation negotiates with its own interests in mind and attempts to get as much as possible while conceding only as much as necessary, but it is rare indeed to see that stated so forthrightly. What made MacDonald's tone doubly inappropriate was the fact that the same day that his letter arrived in Washington, 24 September 1929, Stimson was meeting with the Japanese Ambassador, Debuchi Katsuji, going over that nation's concerns about the upcoming conference in considerable detail.[72] These concerns included whether the Japanese delegates would be allowed enough time to travel to the conference venue – the closing of the Trans-Siberian Railway had made travel to London much slower from Japan – and ongoing fears that the British and Americans had reached a deal that would presented to the Japanese as a *fait accompli*. Stimson was quite open with Debuchi, giving him the broad outlines of the then-current state of the Anglo-American negotiations. The ambassador reiterated Japan's desire to see real reductions in naval armament levels; after laying out Japan's current cruiser strength – eight 'treaty maximum' cruisers built or building, plus the four 7100-ton cruisers of the *Furutaka* and *Aoba* classes – he stated that if the Americans built eighteen 'treaty maximum' cruisers, the Japanese would feel obliged to build two more for a total of ten, while if the Americans built twenty-one, the Japanese would build four more for a total of twelve. But, he said, if the Americans would reduce their building programme to fifteen and the British to twelve, the Japanese would build no more 'treaty maximum' cruisers. In regard to the Japanese desire for a 70 per cent ratio of cruiser tonnage, Stimson told Debuchi that the United States was committed to maintaining the ratios established by the Washington Treaty.

MacDonald sailed from Southampton on 28 September 1929; significantly, his party included no-one from the Admiralty. Between 4 and 10 October, the President and Prime Minister met on a daily basis. Hoover suggested an age-based yardstick that permit cruisers that were more than 20 years old to be 'discounted' as much as half of their displacement.[73] He also repeated the American offer to lower the number of 'treaty maximum' cruisers built, building and planned to eighteen as long as the British met him 'at least half way'. There was no further breakthrough on the cruiser issue, but both men concluded that they were close enough to an agreement, and that the pressure for an agreement was such, that it was time to start the process of convening the long-awaited conference. Invitations went out from London on 7 October, the conference to convene at the beginning of the third week in January 1930.[74]

The Italians responded favourably on 14 October. Ten days later, their ambassador in Washington, Giacomo de Martino, met with Assistant Secretary of State Castle and laid out Italy's position regarding the upcoming conference.[75] That position was simply that Italy must have parity with France, that Italy depended as much or more than France on overseas trade for her sustenance, which counterbalanced any French arguments about needing a larger fleet due to having two widely separated coasts and having more and more distant colonies.

The French also responded positively on 16 October. Gibson met in Paris on 29 October with the French League of Nations chief delegate, René Massigli, who laid out France's position at the impending conference.[76] That position was that:

> . . . Anglo-American difficulties were not as hard to solve as those between France and Italy, inasmuch as the latter was worked up to a high degree of nationalistic feeling and was insistent on parity with France, while France was just as determined that Italy should not be granted parity. France's position, he explained, was based on the fact that the Italian forces were concentrated in the Mediterranean, while the French navy was spread all over the world; ship for ship parity would amount to giving the Italians manifest superiority.[77]

As pessimistic as Massigli was regarding the possibility of an agreement being reached between France and Italy, he was even more emphatic in his concern that British and Americans would, once they had hammered out a mutually satisfactory naval agreement in London, lose interest in the disarmament process.

Gibson did his best to assure Massigli of American intentions to continue pursuing general disarmament regardless of the outcome in London, but it was clear that the Frenchman was unconvinced. (For what it is worth, Massigli's fears about the future of the League of Nations' general disarmament process were well-founded, although it is unlikely that the outcome of the London Conference prejudiced that process in any fashion.) Beyond these points, the French position included a strong preference for a plan that included the ability to transfer tonnage between categories of ship types, an idea they had introduced in Geneva at the Preparatory Commission meetings as early as April 1927 and which had received American support.[78] The French also wanted a 'Mediterranean Agreement' to come out of this conference. Ultimately, the French wanted what amounted to a guarantee from the British and Americans that they would come to France's aid in the event of war with her eastern neighbours. (Neither the British or Americans were inclined to give the French such a guarantee.)

With this less-than-optimistic establishment of the French position, the delegations gathered after the turn of the year in London. Even in Great Britain and America there was less than solid unanimity of support behind the delegates preparing for the conference. When the Admiralty found out that MacDonald had agreed to a limit of fifty cruisers for the Royal Navy, there was loud protest; as late as 13 December, the Admiralty Board informed the Prime Minister that they still strongly recommended the same seventy-cruiser force they had supported two years earlier.[79] Admiral Jellicoe, who was once again asked to represent New Zealand at the conference, strongly supported the Admiralty position. On 15 January, the First Sea Lord, Madden, delivered what amounted to an ultimatum to the Prime Minister, in which he stated that he could only agree to a fifty-cruiser fleet if other nations agreed to a similar reduction in their cruiser forces and if the oldest cruisers were replaced at a rate of three each year.[80] MacDonald acknowledged receipt of Madden's note, but nothing more. At the last cabinet meeting before conference began, the fifty-cruiser limit was approved.

In the United States, the General Board was similarly irate at Hoover's willingness to sacrifice Congressionally-authorised cruisers; they stated on 7 January that they could approve lowering the American cruiser force to twenty-one 'treaty maximum' cruisers if the Royal Navy would agree to an aggregate 280,500-ton cruiser limit and similarly agree to eighteen American cruisers if the British agreed to a 250,500-ton total.[81] Like Madden's, their views were noted and filed away. As recently as 19 December, when Stimson met with the head of the Japanese delegation, Wakatsuki Reijiro, a former Prime Minister, who had stopped in Washington on his way to London, he repeated the American position on cruiser strength, which was that the United States 'demanded' twenty-one 10,000-ton cruisers.[82] Yet, before the American delegation left Washington in early January, the negotiating position agreed between Hoover and Stimson, who would lead the delegation, was that the United States would accept a limit of eighteen 'treaty maximum' cruisers.[83]

Once the London Naval Conference of 1930, generally referred to as the First London Conference, actually got underway, the process of negotiating an agreement went relatively smoothly, at least compared to Geneva three years earlier. The conference began with an opening address delivered by King George V in the Royal Gallery of the House of Lords on 21 January. The next two days saw the first working sessions, with addresses by MacDonald, who was voted chairman of the conference, by André Tardieu, the *Président du Conseil* (Prime Minister) of France and head of the French delegation, and by Dino Grandi, Minister of Foreign Affairs and head of the Italian delegation. None of the addresses included startling proposals. MacDonald laid out a general outline of the work to be done; he described the five categories of warships that were to be discussed and proposed that the cruiser category be sub-divided into more heavily-armed cruisers defined by their 8in main battery and more lightly-armed cruisers with a main battery of less than 6.1in calibre. Tardieu stated that France, based on purely mathematical analysis of the length of her coastlines and the size of her colonial empire, required a navy approximately two-thirds the strength of the Royal Navy.[84] (This would resolve itself over the coming days into a demand for ten 'treaty maximum' cruisers. The impetus for this demand was the laying down in Germany of an armoured ship of a new type tentatively named Ersatz-*Preussen*, which alarmed the *Marine Nationale*.[85]) Grandi's remarks were short and simple, stating that Italy 'will reduce her armaments to any level, no matter how low, provided that level is not exceeded by that of any other European Continental power'.[86] There could be no doubt in anyone's mind that this meant France. The main accomplishment of these sessions was the establishment of a heads-of-delegation committee, that would meet regularly and have the primary responsibility for deciding what issues were to be discussed, resolving those issues and deciding when further full plenary sessions needed to be called.

The first meeting of this committee occurred on 27 January, and was spent deciding whether the Italians or French should present their arguments first – it was finally decided to follow alphabetical order.[87] The following day the committee decided that an Experts Committee was needed to advise the heads-of-delegations on technical matters; this committee was set up by a plenary session on the 30th. The first issue submitted to this committee was the loaded question of whether limitation should be by global tonnage or by categories, and if by categories, whether any transfer of tonnage between categories was to be allowed. (The British and Americans were in total agreement on this issue and the Japanese were willing to go along hoping to earn their goodwill; the French desire for relatively free transfer of tonnage between categories was voted down.)[88]

The Americans had maintained a very low profile at the beginning of the conference; Stimson made no presentation at the opening public session and the whole delegation tried to keep as quiet as possible. In part this was because there was not yet total agreement among all the members of the delegation as to what that position should be. Finally, on 4 February, a proposal that met the approval of (almost) the entire delegation, including the leading naval representative, Commander-in-Chief of the US Fleet Admiral William V Pratt (but, predictably, not that of now-retired Rear Admiral Hilary P Jones), was generated and cabled to Washington for the President's approval. When details began to appear in the press, it was hurriedly made public two days later. Essentially it laid out a fully-detailed programme of tonnage allocation for the three main Powers for all five categories, starting with cruisers, because that was clearly the most contentious part. The tentative plan for cruisers gave preferred allocations for the United States, Great Britain and Japan, with alternate allocations in case the Americans opted for fewer 'treaty maximum' cruisers or the British for more. The preferred allocations were:

For United States:

Total tons		*Type*
180,000	18	10,000 tons carrying guns of 8-inch calibre
70,500	10	Existing *Omahas*
76,500	..	New cruisers carrying guns not exceeding 6-inch calibre
327,000	..	Total

For Great Britain:

110,000	11	10,000 [ton] cruisers now completed carrying 8-inch guns
20,000	2	10,000 ton cruisers now building carrying 8-inch guns
16,800	2	8,400 ton cruisers now building carrying 8-inch guns
91,000	14	New cruisers mounting 6-inch guns
101,200	21	Existing cruisers mounting 6-inch guns
339,000	..	Total

For Japan:

28,400	4	7,100 ton cruisers carrying 8-inch guns
40,000	4	10,000 ton cruisers now completed carrying 8-inch guns
40,000	4	10,000 ton cruisers now building carrying 8-inch guns
81,445	17	Cruisers carrying guns not exceeding 6-inch calibre
8,800	..	Existing or new cruisers carrying guns not exceeding 6-inch calibre
198,655	..	Total[89]

These were very nearly the allocations included in the final treaty. What is of interest is that although the Americans allocated for themselves 76,500 tons for new construction of 6in-gunned cruisers, no number of hulls is designated. This is because there was at this point no consensus in the General Board, or indeed elsewhere in the United States Navy, as to the best size for such a cruiser (see below). On 9 February, the British delegation recorded their positive reaction to the American proposal, asking only that the Americans reduce their cruiser tonnage to 320,000 tons.[90] (While 7000 tons lower than the figure proposed in the tentative plan, this was still 5000 tons higher than the total tonnage proposed by the Americans in September and, thus, should not have been difficult to accept.)

Nonetheless, there was no rapid resolution to the issues facing the conference. In part this was due to the instability of French governments between the wars; Tardieu, who had become Prime Minister only in November 1929, was voted out on 21 February 1930 and had to return to Paris. Ten days later, he was voted back in again and soon returned to London, but his hold on power and control of policy was always shaky. The Japanese were also in the midst of parliamentary elections, which distracted their delegation at critical moments. The French and Japanese attempted to hold out for their desired larger allocations of tonnage, particularly in the cruiser category, but neither the Americans nor British were inclined to grant their wishes.

Agreements were gradually worked out between the various nations involved. The Americans, bowing to pressure from the British, agreed to a compromise, splitting the difference between their original plan and the British proposal, agreeing on 27 February to an aggregate cruiser total of 323,500 tons.[91] The Japanese governing party, having won a significant majority in the recent elections, felt strong enough to agree to some concessions in London in order to get an agreement; accepting that American resistance would not yield on the question of the number of 8in-gunned cruisers Japan would be allowed – the Americans made limiting the Japanese to twelve such ships a condition of their accepting a limit of eighteen – the Japanese did get a 70 per cent allocation (compared to the American limit) of 6in-gunned cruisers and the Americans agreed to stretch out the start of construction of the last three of their allocated 'treaty maximum' cruisers over a three-year-span.[92] The first of the three – *Quincy* – could not be laid down until 1933, with the remaining two to follow in the next two years.

This agreement with the Japanese came only after a threat, made on 12 March, to conclude a two-power treaty between the Americans and British caused Wakatsuki to rein in dissenting members of his delegation and accept the American offer. There was some last-minute haggling over the allocation of 6in-gunned cruisers – the Americans offered 98,415 tons, the Japanese asked for 108,000 tons, the two sides compromised at 100,450 tons, which was exactly 70 per cent of the American allocation. (The Japanese were also allocated 70 per cent of the American and British totals in destroyer tonnage and parity in submarines.) Nonetheless, Wakatsuki needed approval from Tokyo for this compromises he had reached, approval that was not given until 2 April. No amount of threats or cajoling could bring the French to accept the number of cruisers the British, in particular, were willing to allow them. (The French demanded ten 'treaty maximum' cruisers, which was five more than they had built or building; MacDonald told Stimson that at the end of February he had offered them a maximum of seven.[93]) With the French unwilling to come to an agreement, the Italians had no level upon which they could seek parity, so they also were unable to come to an agreement on tonnage allocations for auxiliary warships.

So the London Conference of 1930 ground slowly to a somewhat unsatisfying conclusion. The first two parts of the resulting treaty, which mainly had to do with clarifying a few ambiguities in the Washington Treaty and listing exactly which ships could be retained for training or target use, were signed by all five Contracting Powers. The third part, the one which listed the tonnage allocations for cruisers, destroyers and submarines, which had only been defined for Great Britain, the United States and Japan, was only signed by those three nations. This somewhat unusual signing ceremony took place on 22 April 1930.

It is difficult to say whether any nation 'won' or 'lost', or even if the whole treaty process can be said to have served a useful function in the short or long term. The 'battleship holiday' was extended for five more years, which pleased budget-minded politicians, especially given the increasing impact of the Great Depression. Certainly, the British were pleased that the Americans had agreed to be limited to eighteen 'treaty maximum' cruisers and the Japanese to twelve, both major goals coming into the conference. They were less happy that had been unable to convince the other Contracting Powers to agree to lower the maximum size of cruisers, but the idea simply had insufficient support outside Great Britain. The Japanese were not pleased at their inability to gain a 70 per cent ratio across-the-board, but they did get some of what they wanted. Nonetheless, ultra-nationalist *bakuryo* back home seized on the failure as an anti-government rallying cry; in November, Prime Minister Hamaguchi Osachi was seriously wounded in an assassination attempt. He never fully recovered, and was replaced the following year by Wakatsuki. Opinion in America was divided concerning the treaty. Most of the public was pleased with the apparent movement towards disarmament, but within the Navy there was considerable displeasure with the sacrifice of at least three 'treaty maximum' cruisers, to be replaced by 6in-gunned cruisers of uncertain value. All of that displeasure was focused on Admiral Pratt, who had been the strongest supporter among the 'naval experts' of the compromise agreement with the British. The criticism reached the point that Pratt offered to resign, but was talked out of it by Navy Secretary Adams.[94] In September 1930, he was appointed CNO.

The Firstborn: The *Mogami* Class

The Japanese were the first to react to the restrictions established by the First London Conference. Within the Japanese allocation of 208,850 tons of cruisers outlined in Part III, Article 16 of the First London Treaty, 108,400 tons were assigned to the sub-category (*a*) 8in-gunned cruisers, of which the Japanese already had their permitted twelve built or building. Of sub-category (*b*) cruisers, those armed with 6.1in or smaller guns, the Japanese were allocated 100,450 tons and had 98,415 tons of existing cruisers that fitted this description in commission as of April 1930.[95] However, four of these cruisers were officially 'overage' in terms of the 16- or 20-year life spans allotted to cruisers in Annex I of Article 13 of the treaty and three more would become 'overage' by 1936.[96] In a special clause inserted into the treaty, Japan was allowed to replace the light cruiser *Tama* with new construction to be completed in 1936 (Article 20(*b*)). Additionally, Article 19 allowed all of the Contracting Powers to lay down replacements for cruisers that would become 'overage' between 1937 and 1939 also for completion in 1936. Between all these provisions and caveats, the Japanese calculated that they would be able to construct almost 51,000 tons of sub-category (*b*) cruisers for completion in 1936.[97]

To accomplish this construction, a staff group led by Admiral Nagano Osami, vice chief of the Naval General Staff, put together a two-stage building programme comprising 117 ships; the first stage, to be completed by December 1936, was to comprise seventy-six ships, including four cruisers, each of 8500 tons.[98] This plan was approved by the Navy Minister, Admiral Abo Kiyokazu, and presented to Prime Minister Hamaguchi on 7 October 1930, but was rejected as being too expensive. A modified programme of fifty-nine ships submitted at the same time met the same fate. The Finance Minister took the Navy's second, reduced proposal, and pared it down further, to twenty-five ships – although it still included the four cruisers – and won Cabinet approval. The Navy objected so strenuously to this drastic reduction in its building plans that a compromise was reached, and, on 9 November, a plan – still including the four cruisers – now totalling thirty-seven ships, was presented to the Diet, where it was approved. The official name of this programme was the 1931 Auxiliary Vessels Replenishment Programme, later shortened to the First Replenishment Programme, popularly known as the Circle-One Programme.

The staff requirements for the new cruisers, delivered to the Basic Design sub-section of the Navy Technical Department, still commanded by Constructor Captain Fujimoto, were not much different than those for the preceding class of 'A' class cruisers, except for the main battery:

8500-ton 'B' Class Cruiser

Displacement (std):	8500 tons
Speed:	37 knots (designed)
Range (designed):	8000nm @ 14 knots
Protection (designed):	Immunity against 8in gunfire in way of magazines; immunity against 6.1in gunfire in way of engineering spaces
Armament (main):	15 x 15.5cm/60 3rd Year Type (5 x 3 – three forward (third turret superfiring) and two aft)
Armament (AA):	4 x 12.7cm/40 (4 x 1); 2 x 40mm/60 '*HI*' Type (2 x 1)
Armament (torp):	12 x 61cm (4 x 3); 12 reloads
Aircraft:	3[99]

One important feature that the Naval General Staff made clear to Fujimoto was that the design should allow for the simple replacement of the triple 15.5cm main-battery turrets with twin 20cm turrets, as mounted in the 'A' class cruisers of the *Myoko* and *Takao* classes. The Japanese already anticipated a point in the not-too-distant future, well within the anticipated lifetime of these ships, when the treaty system would expire (or Japan would withdraw from the system) and the artificial restriction on cruiser main-battery armament would no longer apply.

Try as he might, Fujimoto was unable to develop a design that met the staff requirements and stayed within the intended target displacement of 8500 tons. When he reported his final draft of Basic Design C-37 to the Naval General Staff in the summer of 1931, it had a legend standard displacement of 9500 tons, despite the extensive use of welding in the place of riveting throughout the hull and the reduction of the power plant from twelve boilers to ten, which allowed the elimination of the after funnel and the shortening of the hull (compared to the *Takaos*) by 15ft. (One reason why the design was so much heavier than the original target displacement, despite all of Fujimoto's efforts at weight savings, was the insistence by the staff that the same 'castle-like' superstructure be fitted as in the preceding class.) This design was approved, and funding for the first two ships of the *Mogami* class was included in FY1931. *Mogami* was laid down on 27 October 1931 at Kure Navy Yard; *Mikuma* was started on 24 December 1931 at Mitsubishi, Nagasaki. The third and fourth of the class, *Suzuya* and *Kumano*, were funded one each in the next two fiscal years and laid down in December 1933 and April 1934.

Mogami and *Mikuma* were launched in March and May 1934 respectively, but at that point their stories get more complicated. The *Tomozuru* Incident in March of that year, which caused a fleet-wide re-examination of the stability of all ships, led to the work on these two cruisers being delayed. The most obvious and immediate correction that could be made was the replacement of the massive forward bridge structure with a much smaller one. In November 1934, Constructor Captain Fukuda Keiji, who replaced Fujimoto, oversaw the construction and testing of a full-scale wooden model of a seven-level bridge structure on *Mogami* at Kure.[100] This

This image shows the first of the 'treaty maximum' light cruisers engendered by the curious compromises reached by the First London Treaty. It shows *Mogami* not too long after her acceptance trials in March 1935. At the time of those trials, she had not yet received her second, after pair of 12.7cm/40 Type 89 mounts or her catapults and aircraft. In this view, the aviation facilities have been added, but not the after HA guns. She still mounts the triple 15.5cm/60 main-battery turrets that would be replaced by twin turrets for 20cm/50s. (NARA)

reduced-size bridge was approved and was fitted to *Mogami* and *Mikuma* and, in slightly-modified form, to the two later ships in the class. The reduction in size in the bridge structure alone saved 101 tons. Other changes included substitution of a smaller foremast and reductions in the after superstructures, saving an additional 14 tons of weight above the waterline. *Suzuya* and *Kumano*, which had not yet been launched, were altered even more dramatically; the height of their upper and superstructure decks was reduced and the width of the superstructure deck decreased by 4ft 7in. These two ships had their boilers further reduced from ten to eight, but retained the same hull form; the length saved in the engineering spaces was used to lengthen the forward main-battery magazines. All ships in the class had extra pumping equipment added to allow compartments in the double bottom to be rapidly flooded with seawater to increase stability when the ships were in light condition. One change made at this time which added topweight was the decision to carry four twin 12.7cm/40 AA mounts in the place of the planned single mounts.[101]

Despite all this effort, when *Mogami* ran her full-power trials in March 1935, the results were disastrous. While her stability proved to be acceptable, due to the weight reductions made in 1934, the strain on the welded longitudinal framing and shell plating of her hull, both aft near her screws and forward near her bow, caused distortion that sprang plates and caused fuel leaks. Even worse, because the fore- and aft-ends of the superstructure deck were physically attached to the barbettes of main-battery turrets Nos 3 and 4, the roller paths of both turrets were distorted, rendering them unusable.[102] *Mogami* was docked and repairs were made to patch up the leaks; she was commissioned in July 1935 and *Mikuma* in August. However, both ships were with the Fourth Fleet when it encountered the full force of a typhoon in September and both had further hull damage, including sprung hull plating, mainly forward. This time, the pair were taken out of service and placed in reserve while a technical board was convened to examine the issues revealed in this so-called 'Fourth Fleet Incident'. To confirm the problem, *Suzuya*, which was just then, in November 1935, undergoing her full-power trials, was taken in hand and docked to examine her hull for defects. The same kind of hull distortion and failed welds found in her two sister were seen in *Suzuya* as well; all three ships were scheduled for major reconstruction, while *Kumano*, not yet launched, was altered on the ways. The changes were extensive. Essentially, the entire external shell of the ships was replaced. At the ends, the welded Ducol steel plating was replaced by welded mild steel; for the middle 80 per cent of their length Ducol steel was retained, but was riveted rather than welded. A second thickness of Ducol plating was added for strength on either side of the keel and also high up on the ships' sides, in way of the upper and superstructure decks. The connection between the superstructure deck and barbettes of the adjacent turrets was severed, so that distortion in the hull would not affect the turrets. Finally, a bulge was added to

Looking forward from the bridge over the forecastle on *Kumano* in March 1936, the three forward main-battery turrets can be seen. Details of the turret roofs, showing the various projections for the gun captain's periscope – the cylindrical structure between the left and centre guns – and for the layers' (right) and trainers' (left) glasses – between the guns forward. The tall hood in the left rear of the turret roof was for an exercise aiming device. Note the antenna tower on turret No 3. (NHHC)

compensate for the additional weight, increasing the beam by 8ft 3in in *Mogami* and *Mikuma*, and by 7ft 2in in the later two. These rebuilds were completed for *Mikuma* and *Suzuya* only in October 1937 and for *Mogami* in February 1938.[103] *Kumano* was completed with all these changes already in place in October 1937.

In this definitive form, the specifications of the *Mogami*s (1938) were:

'B' Class Cruisers: Mogami Class

Displacement (std):	9500 tons (designed); 11,200 tons (actual)
Length (oa):	658ft 2in
Beam (max):	67ft 3in (*Mogami* & *Mikuma*); 66ft 3in (*Suzuya* & *Kumano*)
Draft (mean):	20ft (actual)
Power plant:	152,000shp; Kanpon geared turbines driving four shafts; ten Kanpon three-drum water-tube boilers (eight in *Suzuya* & *Kumano*)
Speed:	37 knots (designed); 35 knots (after reconstruction)
Range (designed):	8000nm @ 14 knots; 2280 tons oil fuel
Range (actual):	7000–7500nm @ 14 knots; 2215 tons oil fuel

Protection (side): 4in NVNC–1in CNC 20° slope (from sloped armoured deck to double bottom in way of engineering spaces); 5.5in–1in NVNC (from Lower Deck in way of main-battery magazines)[104]
Protection (horiz): 1.38in CNC (horizontal), 2.36in CNC (sloping over engineering spaces at Middle Deck level); 1.57in CNC (over magazines at Lower Deck level)
Protection (torp): Lower strake of side armour belt acted as torpedo bulkhead; two unarmoured bulges outside of belt armour with max width of 5ft; inner splinter bulkhead of thin HTS from armoured deck to double bottom
Armament (main): 15 x 15.5cm/60 3rd Year Type (5 x 3 – three forward (third turret superfiring) and two aft)
Armament (AA): 8 x 12.7cm/40 Type 89 (4 x 2); 8 x 25mm/60 Type 96 (4 x 2); 4 x 13mm/76 Type 93 (2 x 2)
Armament (torp): 12 x 61cm (4 x 3); 12 reloads
Aircraft: 3 (1 x Kawanishi E7K2 Type 94 No 2 and 2 x Nakajima E8N Type 95 reconnaissance seaplanes), two catapults[105]

Although significantly more compact in design, and comprising three fewer levels, the fire-control suite installed in the *Mogamis* was basically the same as in the preceding *Takao* class. The topmost level was a Type 95 director fire-control tower enclosing 4.72in objective lens sighting binoculars and a Type 14 main-battery director (*hoiban*). Below that was a Type 94 main-battery rangefinder tower with a 19.7ft duplex rangefinder capable of 360° rotation. The next level down, the compass bridge, contained a Type 13 *sokutekiban* and associated equipment.

An interesting detail view of the port side of the funnel on *Mikuma*, as seen in August 1938, with two white stripes indicating she was the second unit of *Sentai* 7. Note how forward and after uptakes are separate with separate caps; they appear to be trunked together by the expedient of plating over the gap with a thin sheet of steel. There are four exhaust pipes, probably from auxiliary generators or other motors, that follow the curve of the forward funnel. One pipe, that runs up to a whistle head, is vertical. The crewman in the image shows that the system of hand and foot rails is designed to allow easy access to the exterior of the funnel. (NHHC)

When the Japanese announced their decision to withdraw from the treaty regime starting in 1936, planning began for the re-gunning of the *Mogamis* with 20cm/50 3rd Year Type 2 main-battery guns similar to those in the *Myokos* and *Takaos*.[106] The process proved slower than expected, both because the *Mogamis* were otherwise occupied fixing their stability and hull strength problems, and because the original design, despite taking this re-gunning into consideration, in fact required the development of a modified turret because the roller path – where the turret rotated on top of the barbette – was 27in greater in diameter in the *Mogamis* than in the preceding class. The turret that was adopted, derived from the Model E_1 developed for *Maya*, the last of the *Takaos*, was known as the *Mogami* Model (or the Modified Model E_2).[107] The original designers of the *Mogamis* had not taken the longer length of the 20cm gun into consideration when designing the ships; when the new turrets and main-battery guns were fitted in 1939–40, it was found that the gun barrels of No 2 turret forward could not be fully lowered when facing forward because they would hit the after end of No 1 turret.

The *Mogamis* were popular ships. They incorporated habitability features that were new in Japanese warships, including steel-pipe bunks in crew quarters replacing the traditional hammocks, increased air conditioning and ventilation in living spaces, increased refrigerated food storage and even scuttlebutts providing cold drinking water in crew spaces.[108] All of these were vast improvements over any preceding cruiser class in the Imperial Japanese Navy.

Two additional cruisers, similar to *Kumano*, were ordered as part of the 1942 Special Estimates.[109] The first was laid down at Kure in April 1942 and launched in May 1943, with the name *Ibuki*. The hull was towed to Sasebo, where conversion to a light aircraft carrier was begun. That work was never completed.

Change of Course on the Potomac: The *Brooklyn* Class

Regardless of whether the General Board, or the US Navy as a whole, had wanted 6in-armed cruisers, these were the cruisers they were permitted to build. The issue facing the Board, as had been the case with the Japanese and British, was how to maximise the use of the available tonnage. The Americans had been allocated eighteen sub-category (*a*) 'treaty maximum' cruisers, which were all accounted for between those built or building, and those authorised by the 'Fifteen-Cruiser Bill'.

Much more complex was the issue of what to do with the tonnage allocation of sub-category (*b*) cruisers allowed by the treaty. The First London Treaty allocated 143,500 tons of cruisers armed with 6.1in or smaller guns to the Americans. The ten *Omaha*s displaced 70,500 tons; that left the United States Navy 73,000 tons of 6in-gunned cruisers to be built. Almost the only point that was in agreement across the fleet communities was that they should not simply be down-scaled versions of the preceding 'treaty maximum' cruisers, not even the most recent *New Orleans* class design. The common opinion was that all of these designs were less than optimal in such critical areas as aircraft handling; the movement of those facilities from between the funnels to abaft the after funnel in the *New Orleans* class was seen as an improvement, but not an ideal solution.[110] Additionally, designers in BuC&R believed significantly more weight could be saved in the ships' hulls by the use of longitudinal framing. BuOrd offered up a new main-battery gun, the 6in/47 Mark 16 firing an equally new 'super heavy' AP shell weighing 130lb (compared to the 105lb AP shell fired by the 6in/53 Mark 12 main battery of the *Omaha*s) as a semi-fixed round, meaning that while the shell and powder charge were separate, the powder was contained within a brass cartridge case plugged with cork, so that a sustained rate of 8–10 rpm per barrel (theoretically) could be maintained with hand loading.[111]

Starting from these bases, the General Board in the autumn of 1930 asked Preliminary Design for a 'spectrum' study – meaning they wanted a series of sketch designs that explored a broad range of displacement, armament, speed and protection options. In November, six sketch designs were delivered ranging in displacement from 6000 tons to 10,000 tons and in main-battery size from six to fifteen; all had a top speed of 32.5 knots.[112] The largest, most heavily-armed variant was considered a straight-up replacement for a 'treaty maximum' cruiser with similar striking power, protection and range; the smallest would be a very well-protected but weakly-armed scout. At this point, Admiral Pratt, newly-appointed CNO, weighed in, stating his preference for a 'flight-deck cruiser', a hybrid cruiser-aircraft carrier that would carry a small air group for scouting and spoiling attacks. He generally came down in favour of the smaller, better-armed but less well-protected designs in the middle of the 'spectrum', ships in the 7000–8000-ton range, as these would allow more hulls to be procured within the tonnage allocation, while still providing useful warships. The General Board showed a strong preference for a larger design – a 9600-ton ship mounting twelve main-battery guns in four triple turrets and providing protection on the same scale as the *New Orleans* class and a 10,000nm endurance – but Congress seemed to have the same fascination as Pratt did with the idea of a flight-deck cruiser, and, when no request for this ship type was forthcoming from the Navy Department, refused to allocate any funding for cruisers in FY1932.

Very little changed until mid-1931, when, influenced by reports of the *Zara*s, *Algérie* and, most significantly, *Mogami*, the General Board reiterated their preference for a large, relatively well-protected and well-armed gun-only cruiser; based on a recommendation from the Naval War College, this ship would not carry torpedoes as these were seen as presenting a serious liability in a gun battle. This was approved by Secretary Adams on 17 June 1931, but again ran into solid opposition in Congress and the regular FY1933 budget again included only monies for the construction of the long-planned *Quincy*. However, the process of planning for the next

In the spring of 1939, a World's Fair was opened in New York City; one of the celebrations surrounding the opening ceremonies was a naval review held in July. The US Navy sent five of their newest cruisers, led by USS *Brooklyn* (CL40), seen here moored midstream in the Hudson River, with four sister-ships in trail. Given similar design challenges, American and Japanese designers came up with very similar results; both nations chose flush-decked ships carrying fifteen 6in guns in the main battery in five triple turrets. Where the designs differed was the American decision to move the aviation facilities right aft into a capacious quarterdeck, leaving a shorter central 'citadel' of magazines and power plant to protect with armour, and the fact that the Americans had no plans to replace the 6in/47 Mk 16 main-battery guns with a larger calibre. (NHHC)

American cruisers continued. It was at this point that Preliminary Design suggested that one way to solve the problem of how to site the needed medium and light AA guns with clear arcs of fire without interference with aircraft-handling facilities would be to move those facilities right aft and move the hangar below decks in the fantail.[113] The iterative design process continued through 1932, with the design now looking at variants of 10,000-ton cruisers with between twelve and sixteen main-battery guns and differing levels of protection. Late in the year, a change of command occurred at the Preliminary Design section – Captain Van Keuren replaced Captain H S Howard – which seemed to re-energise the process. Official announcement in Japan in February 1933 of the general specifications of the *Mogamis*, including the fact that they would mount fifteen 15.5cm guns, further focused the design process.

However, it was the actions of the new President, Franklin D Roosevelt (FDR), and the passage of the National Industrial Recovery Act (NIRA) in June 1933, that finally broke the logjam. One side-effect of the Great Depression was a thorough shake-up of the political landscape in the United States; the 1932 presidential election saw a complete swing of power towards FDR and the 'New Deal' Democrats, who promoted a platform of government spending to remedy the economic downturn.[114] FDR pushed through many infrastructure projects that had a profound effect on the nation, putting people to work and helping develop large sections of rural America, projects such as the Tennessee Valley Authority and the various Works Projects Administration and Civilian Conservation Corps activities. An integral part of the New Deal programme was the build-up of the American armed forces in terms of manpower and equipment, both as a means to counter unemployment and as a way to strengthen national defence in the face of rising belligerence overseas.

Not the least because FDR had been Assistant Secretary of the Navy earlier in his career, he felt strongly that shipbuilding was a necessary part of this economic and military revival. Indeed, so strongly did Roosevelt feel on this subject that, on 16 June 1933, the same day that the enabling legislation, NIRA, was signed into law, the President issued an executive order allocating funds for the two highest-priority items in that bill – $400 million to the states for highway construction and $238 million to the Navy for shipbuilding.[115] NIRA money paid for thirty-two new warships, which included the first four of the nascent 6in-gunned cruisers (CL40–CL43).[116]

With the pressure of money on the table, it was now up the General Board to finalise the specifications of this new light cruiser. On 10 March, anticipating that this funding would be coming, Van Keuren ordered the development of nine further sketch designs, all at maximum displacement, trading off armament arrangements in triple and quadruple turrets against different levels of protection.[117] Some used the 588ft hull of the *New Orleans* class, others a longer hull which required less power to reach the desired 32.5 knots, but would require more weight of armour over their greater length. The General Board came out in preference of the scheme that most closely resembled the *Mogami* design, with fifteen main-battery guns in five triple turrets – BuOrd remained generally opposed to the idea of quadruple turrets. On 11 April, the board formally endorsed this scheme, despite the fact that it provided no immunity against 8in shellfire. Admiral Pratt signed off on the plans on 25 April 1933 and the new Navy Secretary, Claude A Swanson, followed suit the same day. The specifications for the new class, named for the lead ship, USS *Brooklyn* (CL40), were as follows:

Brooklyn Class

Displacement (std):	10,000 tons (design); 11,581 tons (full load)
Length (oa):	608ft 4in
Beam (wl):	61ft 7.25in
Draft (mean):	22ft 9in (full load)
Power plant:	100,000shp; Parsons geared turbines driving four shafts; eight Babcock & Wilcox boilers
Speed:	32.5 knots (design); 33.7 knots (actual)
Range (designed):	10,000nm @ 15 knots; 2207 tons oil fuel
Range (actual):	7260nm @ 15 knots; 1982 tons oil fuel
Protection (side):	5in–3.25in STS external belt on 0.625in STS backing (in way of engineering spaces); 4.7in–3in STS external belt (in way of main-battery magazines)
Protection (horiz):	2in STS (over engineering spaces and main-battery magazines)
Armament (main):	15 x 6in/47 Mk 16 (5 x 3 – three forward (middle turret superfiring) and two aft)
Armament (AA):	8 x 5in/25 Mk 10 (8 x 1); 8 x 0.50in/90 M2 (8 x 1)
Aircraft:	4, two catapults[118]

The most immediately distinctive feature in the appearance of the *Brooklyns* was their flush-decked hull with a high, boxy-looking fantail housing the large aircraft hangar. Fire control was provided by systems that were advanced for the day. Main-battery fire control utilised a Mk 34 director, which at first was equipped only with spotting glasses, only later being retrofitted with an 18ft-basis rangefinder.[119] It contained a cross-levelling periscope and an auxiliary rangekeeper in case the connection with the primary below-decks Ford Rangekeeper in the Plotting Room was lost. Below and ahead of the main-battery director was a new Mk 33 DP fire-control director. Designed with an open top, to aid in the spotting of aircraft, it proved difficult to operate in cold or inclement weather and during refits these were often enclosed. (The Mk 33 was a tachymetric

Above: This image of the midships section of *Brooklyn*, taken at the same time as the previous photograph, shows closely-spaced funnels – confirming the fact that she did not have a split-type engineering plant – the four single 5in/25 Mk 10 DP mounts – canvas covered here – and the fire-control suite on her forward superstructure similar, but not identical, to that seen on *Minneapolis*, and arranged differently. The arrangement here was somewhat awkward, with the new Mk 34 main-battery director (not yet fitted with a rangefinder) aft of and above the large Mk 33 DP director for the 5in battery (not yet fitted with a roof, so covered with canvas against inclement weather). The tactical rangefinder is below, in front of the pilot house. (NHHC)

Below: The last two ships of the *Brooklyn* class formed a separate sub-class, because their superstructure was redesigned with air defence in mind. As can be seen in this image of USS *St Louis* (CL49) dated 4 June 1941, the after superstructure has been moved up closer to the second funnel to create better arcs of fire for the AA battery. The eight single 5in/25 mounts have been replaced by four twin 5in/38 gunhouses, the latter a far superior heavy AA weapon. The Mk 34 DCT now is equipped with an integral rangefinder and the Mk 33 DP directors have been given permanent covers. It was not noticeable, because the spacing of the funnels did not change, but this sub-class re-introduced the unit system of alternating fire and engine rooms to the power plant. An indication that the US Navy felt war approaching can be seen in the fact that *St Louis* wears an Ms 1 Dark Gray system camouflage scheme, in which the entire ship, except for pole masts, were painted Dark Gray (5-D), with an elaborate Ms 5 false bow wave painted in white. (NARA)

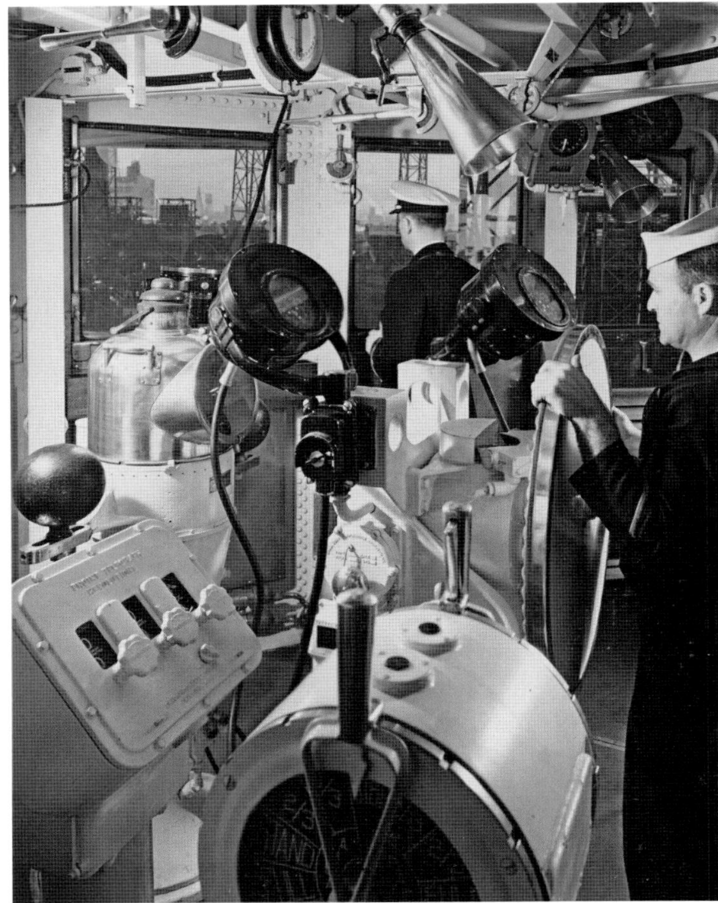

Above: In an obviously staged photograph, an officer gazes out from the command bridge of *Brooklyn*, 18 January 1938, over the cranes and other structures of a dockyard. In the foreground, a helmsman poses, both hands on the very modern-looking, solid metal wheel, staring intently at the compass repeater in front of him, but the engine room telegraph at the bottom is at 'STOP' and the engine revolutions display at the left shows all zeros. If the ship were actually underway, there would be more personnel on the bridge, with more work to do. (NHHC)

fire-control director, equipped with a novel analogue computer that calculated the future position of targets based on real-time changes in range, altitude and bearing.)

The *Brooklyns* were well liked in the fleet, being considered excellent gun platforms. Their construction, much like the *Mogamis*, proved to be too light; one of the original group of four, USS *Savannah* (CL42), encountered a gale in the English Channel in 1938 that caused significant structural damage. Even more distressing, the same ship, while in harbour at San Pedro, California, ran over her anchor cable, slicing through her bow. Three more identical sisters (CL46–CL48), were funded by the Vinson-Trammell Act of 1934 and followed immediately after the first four. Two more would be built to a somewhat modified design. USS *St Louis* (CL49) and *Helena* (CL50) would have a different arrangement of their power plants – they reverted to a unit system of alternating fire rooms and engine rooms – although the funnel spacing remained the same. Their after superstructure was built up closer to the after funnel to allow better arcs of fire for the AA battery; in the place of the eight single 5in/25 mounts, they carried four twin 5in/38 mounts in enclosed gunhouses. The nine ships of this class all entered service in 1938–9.

Testing the Extremes: The *Arethusa* and *Southampton* Classes

The Royal Navy's problems after the signing of the First London Treaty combined aspects of the different issues facing both the Japanese and Americans. As related in the last chapter, the Royal Navy was already committed to the construction of smaller than 'treaty maximum' cruisers armed with 6in guns, as evidenced by the decision to follow *York* and *Exeter* with the *Leander* class and the sacrifice of the *Surreys* on the altar of parity (and economy). It is clear the British expected (or at least hoped) that the rest of the world would see the clear and obvious logic of the Royal Navy's example – smaller and less expensive cruisers that could be produced in greater numbers – and voluntarily follow their lead. Regardless, it is no surprise that, once the dust had settled after the conclusion of the London Conference, the ship that the Royal Navy began to look at to fill out their fifty-cruiser fleet, as the war-built 'C' class light cruisers were retired, was even smaller than the *Leanders*.

The First London Treaty allocated 146,800 tons of sub-category (*a*) 8in-gunned cruiser to the United Kingdom and the Commonwealth nations; this would cover the thirteen cruisers of the *Kent*, *London* and *Norfolk* classes and the two 'one-offs', *York* and *Exeter*. In sub-category (*b*), the Royal Navy was allocated 192,200 tons, of which approximately 91,000 tons could comprise new or replacement ships to be completed before the end of 1936.[120] In terms of numbers, having accepted a cap of fifty cruisers and of fifteen sub-category (*a*) cruisers, the Royal Navy could thus have thirty-five sub-category (*b*) cruisers in commission; including *Leander* from the 1929 programme and the three further *Leanders* in the 1930 programme, the Admiralty figured that 91,000 tons needed to be divided among fourteen ships. They therefore planned on building three cruisers per year in each of the following three programme years and hoped the Australians would pitch in for the fourteenth hull. If the available tonnage (c91,000 tons) were divided by fourteen, each ship should displace 6500 tons, but the *Leanders* were bigger, displacing almost 7200 tons. In order to stay within the constraints of the London Treaty, therefore, at least some of the remaining cruisers had to be significantly smaller.

The idea of a 6in-gunned cruiser smaller than *Leander* had been mooted regularly; in July 1929, then-First Sea Lord Madden asked the ACNS to investigate the practicality of a ship that would be roughly a replacement for a 'D' class light cruiser, displacing approximately 4500 tons, armed with two triple 6in main-battery turrets, little or no side armour protection and a speed of 30 knots. While this particular design study led nowhere, it was the beginning of a series of similar studies, based on the belief that a small cruiser in the 4500–5000-ton range could be better defined by starting from a similarly-sized basis, such as the 'D' class, than by attempting to downsize a larger ship, such as *Leander*, even if that ship was a newer design.[121] Design work on a version with a displacement of 4200 tons mounting three twin turrets began in August 1930. A draft design was presented to the Admiralty Board by DNC on 23 October. This was criticised as being poorly subdivided internally and underpowered, so Lillicrap was told to proceed to a 'definitive' design on the basis of a ship with protection similar to the *Leanders* and a speed of 32 knots.[122] His instructions were that this ship should not displace more than 5000 tons. This sketch received board approval on 31 March 1931.

Despite this approval, there was significant unhappiness with this design, particularly with how cramped they would be internally. Certain alterations were adopted, such as the deletion of the second, after DCT, but this had minimal impact on the cramping problem. More serious was the strong push by the Engineering Department to rearrange the power plant by moving one of the three fire rooms between the engine rooms in order to reduce the chance that one hit could leave the ship without power.[123] (This same urging at roughly the same time led to the change in the arrangement in the power plants in the three modified-*Leanders*.) According to Lillicrap's quick calculations, this change would add 20ft to the length of the ship and raise the displacement to 5500 tons.[124] The Admiralty Board reacted strongly to this increase, stating that at this displacement, the number of cruisers that could be procured would be adversely affected, and sent Lillicrap back to the drawing board with instructions to bring back a design for a ship with a maximum displacement of 5180 tons.

This proved to be a very difficult task. The designs offered to the board by Lillicrap were poorly received as being badly cramped and under-powered. Even going to higher-pressure boilers, which allowed the number to be reduced from six to four, saving valuable space in the hull, was illusory, because the higher pressure boilers were larger and heavier and, critically, more costly in terms of fuel to operate, so that it became necessary to include a small auxiliary boiler in the design to provide power when the ships were in port. Finally, on 4 January 1932, the Admiralty Board accepted that Lillicrap was faced with an impossible task and offered him relief in the form of permission to raise acceptable displacement to 5500 tons. This design received board approval on 14 January 1932 and one ship to this design was included in the 1931–2 Building Programme. This ship was HMS *Arethusa* (26), which was laid down on 25 January 1933, the year-long delay between Board approval and construction start was due to budgetary issues directly related to the Great Depression. The specifications of the *Arethusa* class, of which four would be built, were:

Intermediate Cruiser: HMS Arethusa

Displacement (std):	5419 tons[125]
Length (oa):	506ft
Beam (max):	51ft
Draft (mean):	17ft 10in (deep)
Power plant:	64,000shp; Parsons geared turbines driving four shafts; four Admiralty three-drum water-tube boilers
Speed:	32.25 knots (std); 30.75 knots (deep)
Range (designed):	6500nm @ 16 knots; 1127 tons oil fuel
Protection (side):	2.25in NCA external belt armour (in way of engineering spaces only); 3.5in NCA (side plating in armoured box citadel around main-battery magazines)
Protection (horiz):	1in Ducol (over engineering spaces at Middle Deck level); 2in–1in Ducol (crown of armoured box citadel over main-battery magazines)
Armament (main):	6 x 6in/50 Mk XXIII (3 x 2 – two forward and one aft)
Armament (AA):	4 x 4in/45 QF Mk V (4 x 1)
Armament (torp):	6 x 21in (2 x 3)
Aircraft:	1, one catapult[126]

These ships were built to prove a point about how small a modern cruiser could be and still be effective, and, it was hoped, to set a precedent that would be followed by other nations. As such, they failed on several different levels. Even before they were approved, one of the basic design assumptions of the *Leander* and *Arethusa* classes, that they would mount their main battery in twin turrets, was called into question. In August 1930, the Ordnance Department was asked to begin development of a triple turret for the 6in/50 Mk XXIII gun.[127] It had been hoped that this might be ready to be fitted into the classes then being designed, but the gestation period proved to be lengthy. The Royal Navy's gunnery school, HMS *Excellent*, a vital link in the process, did not approve the idea until 1932 and working drawings were not approved until April 1933. This turret was an unusual design by any standard. The centre gun was set back from the two outer guns by 30in; this was variously described as a way to save space in the turret – the guns could be mounted closer together without the loading crews interfering with each other – or as a means to reduce salvo dispersion; it was effective at the former, less so at the latter.[128] Eventually, a delay circuit had to be introduced for the centre barrel to resolve dispersion problems. Another unusual 'feature' was that the powder hoist

Even smaller than the *Leander*s, the Royal Navy's *Arethusa* class was designed to explore how small a cruiser could be made and still be useful in terms of range and armament. This class was exemplified by the name-ship, HMS *Arethusa* (26), seen here leaving the Charleston Navy Yard after an eight-month-long repair and refit on 11 December 1943. This was followed by four more months of work at Chatham before she rejoined the fleet in time for the D-Day operations. The most obvious difference from the modified *Leander*s, caused by being 1100 tons lighter and more than 50ft shorter, was the loss of one main-battery turret; the *Arethusa*s had only one 6in turret aft. In this image, she carries a typical mid-war radar suite – one that would be further upgraded at Chatham; she has Type 281 air-search antennas at her mastheads, a Type 285 DP fire-control antenna on each HADT fore-and-aft and a Type 284 main-battery fire-control antenna on her big DCT forward. (USN via David Doyle)

brought the propellant charges up outside the turret ring to one deck below the turret; they were then handed into the barbette and manually passed up into the turret. In part because of the staggered arrangement of the gun barrels, the triple turret allowed a maximum elevation of 45°, compared to 60° for the twin turret. This put an end to any idea, however illusory, of using the main battery for AA fire.

By mid-1933 it had become obvious that no other nation intended to follow Great Britain's lead in building smaller cruisers; the Japanese had formally announced their intent to build the *Mogamis*, the Americans seemed to be following suit with the *Brooklyns* and even the French were building light cruisers 500 tons bigger than the *Leanders* (see below). Facing the reality of the utter failure of the 1932 general disarmament conference in Geneva, in which many in Britain had placed considered hope for relief from a potential 'arms race' in cruiser construction, and clearly aggressive noises coming from Japan – war in China began with the invasion of Manchuria in September 1931 – and Germany – Hitler was appointed Chancellor of Germany on 30 January 1933 – the Admiralty Board was forced to look at building cruisers with an eye towards facing much larger enemy counterparts.

The League of Nations Conference for the Reduction and Limitation of Armaments had finally convened in Geneva in February 1932. The British again proposed limiting cruiser displacement to a maximum of 8000 tons and main battery to 6in; the Americans, again represented by Hugh Gibson, seemed now inclined to accept the gun calibre limitation, but still resisted the attempt to restrict the size of cruisers.[129] On 22 June, Gibson presented a sweeping proposal crafted by Hoover that called for a one-third reduction of all armaments of all types, with only minor exceptions. In part this was in response to a proposal by the Germans that, since they were limited to a 100,000-man army and 10,000-ton ships by the Versailles Treaty, that all nations should scale back to the same level. The conference adjourned for the summer no closer to a general agreement than when it had started, and although it re-convened in the Fall, there was little movement from any of the participants. As stasis is an unnatural state unsustainable for any period of time, it was inevitable that, in the absence of progress, the talks would begin to fail. On 14 October 1933, Hitler announced that Germany was withdrawing from the League of Nations and, at the same time, from the Geneva Conference. The talks sputtered on until May 1934.

In mid-1932, Controller had asked DNC for sketch designs of a 7500-ton enlarged *Leander* with either nine main-battery guns (three triple turrets) or ten (two twin turrets and two triple turrets). Nothing further came of those designs, but a year later, DNC was asked to revisit the ten-gun sketch, this time with four triple turrets, compensating for the added weight in armament by reducing the top speed to 30 knots.[130] DNC reported that this could be achieved at a minimum displacement of 7800 tons. The Board was not pleased with this design, finding it too slow, and DNC was asked to develop a range of choices that would carry the desired twelve main-battery guns at better speeds without sacrificing protection. Obviously, these would have to be longer ships with greater displacement. In September, the board was offered three choices that offered a combination of box protection around the main-battery magazines and an external belt in way of the engineering plant, which would have a unit arrangement. The sketches varied in displacement between a low of 8625 tons and a high of 9600 tons. The Admiralty chose to follow-up on the middle sketch, a 600ft long ship with an estimated speed of 31.75 knots and a displacement of 8740 tons.[131]

As a detailed design was developed, the original two-shaft power plant was replaced with a four-shaft unit producing 7000shp more, which allowed hull length to be reduced to 584ft, which would allow the ship to be docked at more facilities. Displacement rose to a projected 9000 tons. Final drawings for HMS *Southampton* (83) were approved on 8 March 1934. Her specifications were:

Southampton Class

Displacement (std):	8947 tons[132]
Length (oa):	591ft 6in
Beam (max):	61ft 8in
Draft (mean):	20ft 4in (deep)
Power plant:	75,000shp; Parsons geared turbines driving four shafts; four Admiralty three-drum water-tube boilers
Speed:	32.25 knots (std); 30.75 knots (deep)
Range (designed):	8900nm @ 16 knots; 1943 tons oil fuel
Protection (side):	4.5in CA external belt armour (in way of engineering spaces only); 4.5in CA (side plating in armoured box citadel around main-battery magazines)[133]
Protection (horiz):	1.25in Ducol (over engineering spaces at Middle Deck level); 1in Ducol (crown of armoured box citadel over main-battery magazines)
Armament (main):	12 x 6in/50 Mk XXIII (4 x 3 – two forward and two aft)
Armament (AA):	8 x 4in/45 QF Mk XVI HA (4 x 2); 8 x 2pdr pompom (2 x 4)
Armament (torp):	6 x 21in (2 x 3)
Aircraft:	3, one fixed athwartships catapult[134]

Southampton was the lead ship of a class of five; the first two were funded in the 1933–4 building programme (along with the third *Arethusa*) and the remaining three in the following programme along with the last of the preceding class. All five were completed in 1937 and were essentially unchanged when war broke out in 1939.

Large boxy hangars provided protected storage for two aircraft just forward of the catapult on either side of the forward funnel. That catapult was a novel feature, a fixed

After the diminutive *Arethusas*, the Royal Navy followed with the significantly larger *Southamptons*, almost 75 per cent bigger in terms of displacement. That extra tonnage bought 85ft in length and one more main-battery turret, but the major advance in this class was the move to triple turrets, which allowed HMS *Birmingham* (19), seen here at completion in 1937, to carry twelve 6in/50 Mk XXIII guns. The centre gun in this new Mk XXII turret was set back 30in to save space in the turret and reduce salvo dispersion, at least in theory.

athwartships model that saved valuable deck space since it did not have to rotate and could handle the heaviest aircraft. The need for improved fire control, and reported problems in *Leander* with gun smoke interference with the DCT atop the bridge, led to these ships being given a taller and longer bridge structure, with the DCT set well back, and in the case of the 1934–5 programme ships, a more rounded and aerodynamically-shaped bridge face. All of them had at least two HADTs, mounted on either side of the bridge atop the hangar, indicating the increased concern about the possibility of simultaneous air attack from multiple directions. Indeed, the later three had a third HADT on the after superstructure.

Three more almost identical cruisers came along in the 1935 programme, differing only in being somewhat beamier and having a slightly thicker armoured deck over the engineering spaces. To compensate for the extra weight and added hydrodynamic resistance, the three ships of the *Gloucester* class had 7500shp additional power which gave them a marginally higher top speed. They were all completed in 1938 and 1939. Two enlarged *Gloucesters* were included in the 1936 programme; these carried their after main-battery turrets one deck higher, had the box protection of the main-battery magazines replaced by extension of the armour belt and a further thickening of the armoured deck to 3in over the magazines and 2in over the engineering spaces. The hull was lengthened by 22ft, which allowed the two ships of the *Edinburgh* class to reach 32.5 knots on 2500shp less power. Intended originally to mount quadruple main-battery turrets, these two ships instead mounted an improved triple turret with better armour protection. The ammunition supply was redesigned to allow both powder and shell to arrive in the turret directly from the magazines.

During the negotiations related to the Second London Treaty, covered in the next chapter, the Americans were told that the *Gloucesters* and *Edinburghs* were 9000-ton ships, like the *Southamptons*.[135] These statements were, at a minimum, convenient oversimplifications, if not utter deceptions. It was known, even at the time of their laying down, that the designed displacement of the *Gloucesters* was 9400 tons and of the *Edinburghs* was 10,000 tons. The actual displacement of the *Edinburghs* on completion was 10,550 tons.[136] Both ships of the *Edinburgh* class were laid down in late 1936 and entered service in 1939. In order to avoid violating the 'building holiday' on 10,000-ton cruisers imposed by the Second London Treaty, set to begin 1 January 1937, their laying-down was timed precisely; HMS *Edinburgh* (16) was laid down at Swan Hunter, Wallsend, Tyne, on 30 December 1936, beating the deadline by a day.

Of course, the problem with building larger cruisers was that fewer could be built within the tonnage restrictions agreed to in the First London Treaty. In the autumn of 1934, the First Sea Lord, which post was now filled by 'Ernle' Chatfield, faced up to the issue by proposing to the Admiralty Board that the retirement of war-built light cruisers be stopped and that £2 million be added to upcoming Naval Estimates to be used for maintenance and upkeep of these older ships.[137] In fact, when Great Britain went to war in 1939, thirteen 'C' class light cruisers plus one earlier *Birmingham* class light cruiser – HMAS *Adelaide* – were still in active service as were all the surviving 'D' class, *Emerald* class and *Hawkins* class cruisers, a total of fourteen additional older cruisers that predated the *Kent* class.

Leading Onward: More '*Condottieri*'

The Italians honestly had expected little from the London Conference in 1930 and their expectations were met. Thus, in the aftermath of the conference, there was no need for major revisiting of naval planning. Nonetheless, the *Stato Maggiore* did take this opportunity to look over their current building programme, that included the four *Zaras*, the one-off *Bolzano* and the six ships of the first two groups of '*Condottieri*'. In general, the staff was satisfied with the ships under construction and development, except the opinion was expressed that the '*Condottieri*' developed to date had sacrificed too much to gain gunpower and speed.

The early '*Condottieri*' had been the pet project of Chief of the Naval Staff Admiral Alfredo Acton, who retired at the end of 1927 in the wake of a scandal related to an anti-Fascist labour action that delayed the launch of *Trento*. His replacement, Admiral Ernesto Burzagli, favoured a more balanced design that added protection and size. The general specifications were set by the time the 1930/31 building programme was approved in April 1930. The task of completing the design was assigned by MARICOMINAV to Colonel (GN) Umberto Pugliese in October 1930.[138] His primary innovation was the reduced bridge structure described below.

Pugliese's design, based directly on the preceding *Armando Diaz*, differed mainly in more than doubling the thickness of the main armour belt, from 0.94in AER to 2.36in CN, maintaining this thickness for the full length of the belt, in way of the magazines and engineering spaces. Between the increased thickness, the consistent thickness and the greater ballistic resistance of CN compared to AER, the net increase in protection against short-to-medium-range gunfire in this design was more like three- or four-fold. An increase this dramatic in protection without any significant sacrifice in armament or speed – in fact, power was increased 11,000shp, which raised the top speed by a half-knot – had to have an impact on displacement, and it did; the two ships of the *Montecuccoli* group displaced over 2000 tons more than the *Cadornas*, were 42ft longer and 4ft beamier. Further adding to that increase was the switch from a fixed catapult to one that could rotate over a limited arc, moved from abaft the after funnel to between the funnels. The only major attempt to save weight was a reduced bridge structure; the large 'traditional' multi-level superstructure and 'quadripod' foremast gave way to a simplified conical structure with one rather than two main-battery directors and no foremast *per se*. This structure did save weight at the cost of a somewhat cramped upper bridge. The specifications of the *Montecuccoli* group were:

The third group of *'Condottieri'*, such as RN *Raimondo Montecuccoli* seen at Melbourne in 1938, increased protection and introduced a rotating catapult between the funnels, all of which added weight and required a larger power plant to maintain the high speed expected of the type. The only concession made by the designer, Colonel (GN) Umberto Pugliese, was to reduce the size of the bridge, coming up with this sleek, rounded (and cramped) design, sacrificing the auxiliary DCT carried lower on the forward superstructure in the preceding classes. (SLV/AGC)

'Condottieri' Type – 3rd Group

Displacement (std):	7405 tons
Length (oa):	597ft 9in
Beam (wl):	54ft 6in
Draft (mean):	19ft 8in (deep)
Power plant:	106,000shp (design); Belluzzo geared turbines driving two shafts; six Yarrow boilers
Speed:	37 knots (design)
Range (designed):	4200nm @ 18 knots; 1297 tons oil fuel
Protection (side):	2.36in CN shell plating with 0.98in AER splinter bulkhead inboard (in way of engineering spaces) and 1.18in AER splinter bulkhead (in way of main-battery magazines)
Protection (horiz):	1.18in AER (Upper Deck over main-battery magazines and engineering spaces)
Armament (main):	8 x 152mm/53 Mod 1929 (4 x 2 – two forward and two aft)
Armament (AA):	6 x 100mm/47 Mod 1927 (3 x 2); 8 x 37mm/54 Mod 1932 (4 x 2); 8 x 13.2mm/75.7 Breda machine guns (4 x 2)
Armament (torp):	4 x 533mm (2 x 2)
Aircraft:	2 (2 x Ro.43 reconnaissance floatplanes); one catapult[139]

The two ships of this group – the first was laid down on 10 April 1931 at CRDA, Trieste, and would be named *Muzio Attendolo*, but her sister *Raimondo Montecuccoli* would be launched and enter service first – were well-liked in the fleet, being less cramped internally and, with a raked and flared bow

and longer forecastle were drier in rough weather. Being launched in 1935, they were essentially unchanged before war broke out in 1939.

Indeed, the design of the *Montecuccoli*s was so well-liked by the *Stato Maggiore* that when it came time to consider the pair of follow-ons funded for the following fiscal year, it was an easy decision to order two repeat hulls, with 'minor' improvements. Those minor changes included:

1. A further increase in the thickness of the armour belt to 2.76in, the splinter bulkhead to 1.38in and the armoured deck to the same thickness. This percentage of displacement devoted to protection increased by 3 per cent.[140] This increased protection still did not provide an adequate immune zone against 8in gunfire.
2. To compensate for the weight of the added armour, power was increased by 4000shp. The internal arrangement of boilers was changed somewhat, reflected externally by the after funnel, which in this pair of '*Condottieri*', was longer, the same length as the forefunnel. Overall length was increased by 15ft 5in and beam by just under 3ft. The net effect of these changes was an increase in displacement of 912 tons and a decrease in top speed of a half-knot.
3. While the conical tower bridge remained the same height, the top level, just below the main-battery director, was encircled by an open observation platform, indicative of the fact that this pair was intended to serve as squadron flagships. This also served to relieve the cramping of the upper bridge space to an extent.
4. There were only minor changes in armament; the twin torpedo tubes on each side in the preceding group were replaced by triple mounts.

The first of the pair, *Emanuele Filiberto Duca d'Aosta*, was laid down at OTO, Livorno, on 29 October 1932. (The second was named for a seventeenth-eighteenth century general who fought the Turks and the French for the Austrians, *Eugenio di Savoia*, who, curiously, happens to have given his name to another cruiser built by another nation – also not Austria – as will be seen in a later chapter.)

One more two-ship group of '*Condottieri*' would be built. These were reconceived in many ways to respond to the French light cruisers of the *La Galissonnière* class (see below) and indeed to stand up in a straight-up fight with any French cruisers. They were to be given a new main-battery gun that had a somewhat longer barrel and was designed from the

With the fifth and final class of '*Condottieri*' to be completed, the *Regia Marina* opted for an almost conventional light cruiser design, with improved protection, accepting a decrease in speed as the price to be paid. This image shows RN *Giuseppe Garibaldi* in 1938, with her new model 152mm/55 Mod 1934 main-battery guns arranged in twin and triple turrets; this gun was designed to be individually-sleeved and operate at a lower muzzle velocity, thus avoiding the worst of the salvo-dispersion problems from the outset. The crowding issues in the command spaces were resolved by adding an annular ring around the forward superstructure at the navigation bridge level. (NHHC)

outset to have a lower muzzle velocity than the 152mm/53 Mod 1929 fitted in the earlier *Condottieri*, and further the mounts in their turrets would be individually sleeved, allowing them to be elevated separately. These changes was intended to address the issues that had nagged the earlier groups: salvo dispersion, an issue already largely resolved by the use of reduced powder charges and delay circuits, and the risk that both guns in a common cradle could be disabled by damage to one of the guns. Two more main-battery guns were carried, as turrets No 1 and No 4 were now triple mounts.

The entire theory of the armour protection of these ships was reconsidered; in the place of the 2.76in external belt of the preceding pair, these two had an external belt of 1.18in NCV intended as an 'uncapping' layer to remove the armoured caps from APC shells and then an internal belt of 3.94in TC angled inward at 12°, the lower part of which was curved so that it joined the external shell below the waterline. This was topped by a 1.57in armoured deck. The boilers were re-arranged, allowing the two funnels to be placed close to each other and two limited-rotation catapults carried, angled outward towards the bow, immediately aft. Of course, all these changes added weight. The two ships were approximately 1000 tons heavier than the preceding group, and, although the hull was within a few inches of being the same length, beam was increased by 4ft 7in. While the fire rooms were re-arranged – a larger number of smaller boilers were fitted, which, with the increased beam that allowed them to be arranged two abreast, made for shorter fire rooms – total power output was reduced to 100,000shp and top speed to 34 knots (31 knots in service).

'Condottieri' Type – 5th Group

Displacement (std):	9155 tons (*Garibaldi*); 9592 tons (*Abruzzi*)[141]
Length (oa):	613ft 6in
Beam (wl):	62ft
Draft (mean):	22ft 4in (deep)
Power plant:	100,000shp (design); Parsons geared turbines driving two shafts; eight Yarrow boilers
Speed:	34 knots (design)
Range (designed):	5360nm @ 14 knots; 1700 tons oil fuel
Protection (side):	1.18in POV shell plating/decapping layer with 3.94in TC concave belt inboard (in way of engineering spaces and main-battery magazines)
Protection (horiz):	1.57in POV (Upper Deck over main-battery magazines and engineering spaces)
Armament (main):	10 x 152mm/55 Mod 1934 (2 x 3 – turrets Nos 1&4, one forward and one aft; 2 x 2 – turrets Nos 2&3, one forward and one aft)
Armament (AA):	8 x 100mm/47 Mod 1927 (4 x 2); 8 x 37mm/54 Mod 1932 (4 x 2); 8 x 13.2mm/75.7 Breda machine guns (4 x 2)
Armament (torp):	6 x 533mm (2 x 3)
Aircraft:	2 (2 x Ro.43 reconnaissance floatplanes); two catapults[142]

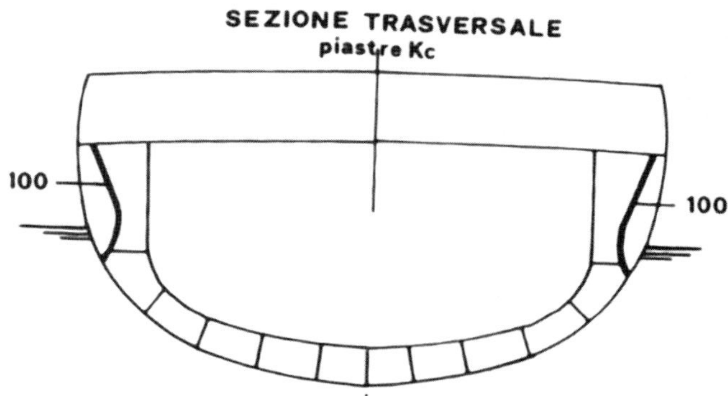

The unusual arrangement of the armour belt in the *Abruzzi* class of *'Condottieri'* is shown in this cross-section drawing. The shell plating was 1.18in (30mm) of POV – *Piastro Omogenee Nichel-Cromo-Vanadio* – Homogeneous Nickel-Chromium-Vanadium Plate – while the elaborately curved layer that combined an armour belt and a torpedo protective system, was 3.94in (100mm) of TC – Terni Cemented – Variable-Face-Thickness Armour. (Franco Gay via Enrico Cernuschi)

The first of the class was given the rather cumbersome name *Luigi di Savoia Duca degli Abruzzi*, who happened to be a first cousin of the King, and was laid down on 28 December 1933 at OTO, Muggiano at La Spezia; her name was most often shortened to just *Abruzzi*. The second received the more manageable name of *Giuseppe Garibaldi*. Both were completed in December 1937 and were unaltered before the outbreak of war. Plans were made to construct two more '*Condottieri*' to an even larger design in the 1939 programme, but in the event, construction was never begun.

Delayed Reaction: the *La Galissonnière* Class

After the First London Conference, it is fair to state that Italy was little influenced by the treaty process in deciding its naval programmes. The French still had hopes for the League of Nations disarmament discussions, but as the Geneva Conference of 1932 stretched on with little sign of positive result, the French too began to look to their own concerns and their own balance of power, particularly in the Mediterranean. In 1931, the French had laid down their best 'treaty maximum' cruiser yet, *Algérie*, and the cruiser-minelayer

In an attempt to build a ship generally similar to *Emile Bertin*, but better-protected, the *Marine Nationale* produced the *La Galissonnière* class, the lead ship of which is seen here in 1937. While only slightly longer, they were substantially broader, which made them more stable and popular ships in which to serve. One noticeable difference from *Bertin* was movement of the catapult from between the funnels to the roof of turret III. This was a new extensible model, much like that used by the Royal Navy. Note the hangar now in the place of the former after superstructure. The aircraft parked on the hangar roof is one of the GL 810-series. Note also the 26ft 3in OPL stereoscopic rangefinder in the main-battery DCT on her foretop. (NHHC)

Emile Bertin, but this was not considered to be a sufficient response to the Italian programme of the preceding two years that had included two *Zara*s, *Bolzano* and the second and third groups of '*Condottieri*'. Between June 1930 and July 1931, the *Marine Nationale*, looking over not only the Italian programme but also what the Royal Navy was building with the *Leander* class, laid out the specifications for a new class of light cruisers that would be able to stand up to these potential adversaries.

STCN was instructed to develop a ship as close to *Algérie* in protection as possible, but otherwise generally resembling *Emile Bertin* in most other characteristics except that speed could be sacrificed as needed to keep displacement down to approximately 7600 tons. A top speed of 31 knots at normal displacement was desired.[143] STCN soon reported back that the desired characteristics, in particular the requested level of protection, could not be achieved at a displacement less than 8850 tons. Only by considerable reduction in the level of protection, even with the reduced power plant cut back to two shafts, could the designed displacement be achieved. The resulting specifications, tentatively approved in time to lay down the first pair of such ships in December 1931, so that they would be a *fait accompli* before the start of the Geneva Conference, were as follows:

La Galissonnière Class

Displacement (std):	7600 tons
Length (oa):	588ft 11in
Beam:	57ft 4in
Draft (maximum):	17ft 7in
Power plant:	84,000shp; Parsons/Rateau-Bretagne geared turbines driving two shafts; four Indret small-tube boilers (operating @ 384psi)
Speed:	31 knots (designed)
Range (designed):	7000nm @ 12 knots; 1544 tons oil fuel
Protection (side):	4.13in NC (in way of engineering spaces and main-battery magazines)
Protection (horiz):	1.5in NC (over main-battery magazines and engineering spaces)
Armament (main):	9 x 152mm/55 Mle 1930 (3 x 3 – two forward and one aft)
Armament (AA):	8 x 90mm/50 Mle 1926 HA (4 x 2); 8 x 13.2mm/76 Mle 1929 (4 x 2)
Armament (torp):	4 x 550mm Mle 1923D (2 x 2)
Aircraft:	2–3 (Loire 130); one compressed-air catapult fixed on turret III[144]

STCN and the staff at the lead yard, Arsenal de Brest, were overwhelmed by the amount of work suddenly dropped on them by the *Marine Nationale* after so many 'lean' years, that the laying down of *La Galissonnière* at Brest and *Jean de Vienne* at Lorient was basically a token gesture; serious work did not begin on either ship for at least another year, and, in the case of *Jean de Vienne*, the ship would not be launched until July

Another ship that attended the naval review held to celebrate the New York World's Fair in July 1939 was *Georges Leygues*, one of the later ships in the *La Galissonnière* class. The location at which this image was taken can identified quite precisely by the presence of the Statue of Liberty visible between the funnels. These ships were originally intended to carry four aircraft – the Loire 130 models, two of which are seen here – two in the hangars and one each on the hangar roof turntable and catapult, but it was found that the aircraft stored on the catapult suffered from excessive vibration and they were soon landed. Note in this starboard side view, there are crests visible on the main-battery turrets. She is flying the flag of Rear Admiral René-Émile Godfroy. (NHHC)

1935 or completed until October 1937. Four more of the class were ordered in 1932 and built at private yards; they were all completed in the final months of 1937.

These ships had an intricate and novel system of aircraft handling. Hangar space for two of the large Loire 130 seaplanes made up the after superstructure, which was surmounted by the mainmast flanked by a pair of aircraft handling cranes. A telescoping catapult was fixed to the roof of the after main-battery turret and a landing mat could be extended from the transom stern, that, in theory at least, would allow the recovery of aircraft over the stern, using a separate crane, while the ship steamed at 10–15 knots. The basic idea worked, but there were practical issues with the system, such as the risk of flooding the landing mat compartment in rough weather and the inability to dry out the mat once it got wet, which led to the system being removed from all ships in the class in 1941–2.

This image shows a close-up of the quarterdeck of *Georges Leygues* in New York City, tied up at the French Lines dock in Manhattan with a sister-ship alongside. The sister-ship is certainly *Gloire*, which was also in New York at this time. Note the trainable 26ft 3in OPL stereoscopic rangefinder embedded into the rear of turret III and the size of the Loire 130 floatplane on the catapult. It appears that some ceremony of importance is just ending, as a pair of top-hatted dignitaries are headed towards the brow. (NHHC)

Chapter 8

Treaty Cruisers – The Last of the Type: 1934–1938

The day of the 'treaty maximum' cruiser was clearly coming to an end, because the treaty process was increasingly seen, even by its most ardent supporters, as having reached if not a dead end then a point of diminishing returns. The slow death of the League of Nations disarmament process was, in and of itself, not the critical factor. It seems only the French had serious hopes for that part of the treaty scheme, and even they could not have been too surprised that it yielded nothing resembling the general arms reduction and security guarantees they so desperately desired. Nevertheless, it appeared that most nations had lost interest in building the 10,000-ton, 8in-gunned cruiser that the Washington Treaty had defined and that had, briefly, been the default standard of cruiser development.

A Grown-Up Baby: Washington Runs Out the String

The First London Treaty had allowed the Americans to finish building their allocated eighteen 'treaty maximum' cruisers one per year, laying them down in 1933–5. The first in that series, *Quincy*, was being built to a modified *New Orleans* class design and the second, *Vincennes*, was as well, because the new design the General Board would have preferred was not ready in time. The ship the board wanted was an up-armoured and up-gunned version of the *Brooklyn* class light cruiser. None of that class had even been laid down yet when the specifications of the 1935 'treaty maximum' cruiser were being defined, but the expectations for the type were high and there was no doubt among members of the General Board that a relatively straightforward conversion of the *Brooklyn* class design was the correct approach.

On 13 March 1934, a joint initiative by BuC&R and the Bureau of Engineering (BuEng) formally proposed that the 1935 cruiser employ the *Brooklyn* class hull modified to mount three triple 8in-gun turrets.[1] The anticipated advantages of using the *Brooklyn* hull, as opposed to the *New Orleans* hull, were numerous. They included:

- The longer, stronger flush-decked hull would be more seaworthy and capacious, allowing better crew accommodation;
- The longer hull also would restore the fuel capacity lost in the *New Orleans* class and be more hydrodynamically efficient, giving better speed and endurance at lower power;
- Moving the aircraft-handling facilities aft into the broad quarterdeck allowed for a more compact (and therefore lighter weight) superstructure and better arcs of fire for the AA battery.

The proposition met no objections and obtained General Board approval on 19 March. The only delay in final approval of the specifications was due to efforts by BuOrd to address salvo-dispersion issues similar to those that had plagued most other nations.[2] The simple fact was that the 8in gun, firing a relatively lightweight shell at high velocity to gain the long range that all nations required, invited shell interference between the closely-spaced barrels of the main-battery turrets. The United States Navy tried multiple expedients to address the issue. A shorter shell reduced salvo dispersion, but had much inferior armour penetration. Firing split-salvos, with the outer guns of the triple turrets firing while the middle gun was loading and then vice-versa, would resolve the dispersion issue entirely, but would slow the rate of fire by 10–15 per cent. A redesigned turret with bore separation increased from 45in to 72in promised to reduce salvo dispersion by 15–20 per cent without requiring split salvos, but the issue there was that this would require a larger turret with a greater ring diameter and consequently heavier barbettes, all of which impacted the ability to provide armour protection over the rest of the ship. So contentious was the issue that, in October 1934, the technical bureau recommended that design work be stopped until the problem could be resolved. It took three

The heavy cruiser version of the *Brooklyn* class light cruisers was USS *Wichita* (CA45), seen here in war-games markings before the war. They shared the same hull design, which allowed the General Board to substitute three triple 8in/55 turrets for the five 6in/47 turrets of the earlier class. The process was complex, because the larger gun required larger turrets with barbettes of greater diameter and weight, but clever design resolved the problems. In the place of the eight 5in/25s of the *Brooklyns*, *Wichita* carried eight of the more capable 5in/38s, also in single-mounts, but four of them were given gunhouses for weather and splinter protection. (NARA)

months, but the resolution turned out to be a combination of clever compromises. The bore separation between barrels was set at 67in, which did require a larger turret and a larger turret ring; in order to reduce the weight increase from the resulting larger barbettes, the barbettes were made conical in section, narrowing top to bottom.[3] This actually allowed them to provide enhanced protection without any additional weight penalty. Still, the new turret was 64 tons heavier than the old one (314 tons v 250 tons). Nonetheless, the weight savings was sufficient that the designers were able to work in enhanced protection throughout the ship. The specifications at the time of the laying down of USS *Wichita* (CA45) were:

USS Wichita

Displacement (std):	10,000 tons (design); 13,015 tons (full load)
Length (oa):	608ft 4in
Beam (wl):	61ft 9.75in
Draft (mean):	23ft 9in (full load)
Power plant:	100,000shp; Parsons geared turbines driving four shafts; eight Babcock & Wilcox boilers
Speed:	33 knots (design); 33.7 knots (actual)
Range (designed):	10,000nm @ 15 knots; 1984 tons oil fuel
Range (actual):	6660nm @ 15 knots; 2044 tons oil fuel
Protection (side):	6in–4in Class A external belt on 0.625in STS backing (in way of engineering spaces and main-battery magazines)
Protection (horiz):	2.25in STS (over engineering spaces and main-battery magazines)
Armament (main):	9 x 8in/55 Mk 12 (3 x 3 – two forward and one aft)
Armament (AA):	8 x 5in/25 Mk 10 (8 x 1); 8 x 0.50in/90 M2 (8 x 1)
Aircraft:	4, two catapults[4]

While the hull was under construction, but before the ship was launched, considerable discussion went into the adequacy of the 5in/25 as the primary AA defence weapon. A new gun – the 5in/38 Mk 12 – developed as the DP main battery for the first new class of American destroyers to be designed since the 'four pipers', became available in 1934 and showed great promise as a superior secondary-battery weapon. It had an absolute altitude ceiling 10,000ft beyond that of the older gun and its effective range was easily twice as great. The only downside was that each single mount weighed nearly half again as much (33,500lb v 23,270lb). So great, however, were the perceived advantages of the new weapon, that the General Board authorised the replacement of the eight 5in/25s by six 5in/38s, four in enclosed, splinter-shielded mounts and two in open mounts. The decision whether to mount the two other guns (as open mounts) was deferred. After her initial inclining trials, which showed that *Wichita* would be marginally stable in lightly-loaded condition, the decision was made to add the two remaining 5in/38 mounts, and to remedy the stability problem by shipping 200 tons of pig iron in her double bottom and developing ballasting instructions that required filling emptied fuel tanks with sea water up to waterline level. Her fire-direction suite was identical to that of the *Brooklyn* class. *Wichita* commissioned in February 1939 and was unaltered, beyond the addition of the two AA mounts, before the war began in Europe.

The Ultimate Scout: The *Tone* Class

The Japanese Naval General Staff, now led by Prince Fushimi Hiroyasu, second cousin to Hirohito, developed a follow-on to the Circle-One Programme of 1930, delivering their proposals to the Navy Minister, Admiral Osumi Mineo, in June 1933.[5] This programme called for, among other construction, the building of two additional cruisers similar in size to the *Mogami*s. The requirements given to the Basic Design subsection of the Navy Technical Department were generally quite similar to those for the preceding class:

8450-ton 'B' Class Cruiser

Displacement (std):	8450 tons
Speed:	36 knots (designed)
Range (designed):	10,000nm @ 18 knots
Protection (designed):	Immunity against 8in gunfire in way of magazines; immunity against 6.1in gunfire in way of engineering spaces
Armament (main):	15 x 15.5cm/60 3rd Year Type (5 x 3 – three forward (third turret superfiring) and two aft)
Armament (AA):	8 x 12.7cm/40 (4 x 2); 12 x 25mm/60 Type 96 (4 x 3)
Armament (torp):	12 x 61cm (4 x 3); 12 reloads
Aircraft:	4[6]

The target displacement was slightly smaller and the designed top speed was one knot lower, but the endurance was to be increased as was the AA battery and the number of embarked aircraft. Those changes in requirements were driven by the evolving air-search doctrine of the Japanese fleet. As was the case with the other navies developing carrier air forces – the Royal Navy and the United States Navy – the early to mid-1930s was a period of rapidly evolving doctrines, as forces were deployed in increasingly realistic training exercises. Japanese carrier tactical doctrine developed in a unique manner, in many ways remarkably different from that developed by the other two navies. One of the most interesting aspects of that doctrine was the emphasis on the use of long-range, shore-based aircraft and floatplanes carried by cruisers to carry out most, if not all, search functions, allowing the carrier air groups to concentrate on attack and defence once enemy forces were located. The increased range,

AA battery and aircraft stowage, bought at the cost of a knot of top speed, were all intended to produce a pair of ships better suited to the role of fleet scout.

The design that was approved in 1934 as Basic Design C-38 was developed by Constructor Captain Fukuda. It was essentially a repeat *Mogami*. They were funded by the Second Replenishment Programme, also known as the Circle-Two Programme, approved in October 1933. The first of the pair, *Tone*, was laid down at Mitsubishi, Nagasaki, on 1 December 1934; the second, *Chikuma*, was laid down at the same yard on 1 October 1935. Construction was halted towards the end of 1935, first by the decision to redesign the hulls in a fashion similar to that done with *Suzuya* and *Kumano*, to increase strength and stability. While this redesign was in progress, the Naval General Staff decided to revisit the entire idea of a cruiser intended to support the fleet's search requirements. In 1936, it was decided that these two ships should be redesignated 'scouting cruisers' (*sakuteki junyokan*) and modified to carry a mix of long-range seaplanes for fleet reconnaissance and short-range aircraft for spotting and anti-submarine patrol. The number of aircraft would be increased to six, or even eight. Since any conceivable arrangement of aircraft storage space and catapults would be insufficient to fit all of the needed aircraft-handling facilities amidships, it was decided that these would be moved aft to the quarterdeck; further study showed that even with only six aircraft there was no way to store all of the aircraft out of the way of muzzle blast from the after turrets in a *Mogami*-like arrangement, so the decision was made to move all of the main-battery turrets forward. Then, simple calculations showed that it would be impossible to fit five main-battery turrets forward of the bridge; four would be the most that could be accommodated. Even after the decision was made to mount twin 20cm/50 turrets – Model E_3 turrets similar to the E_1 turrets installed in the *Takao* class cruiser *Maya* – still only four main-battery turrets could be fitted into the forecastle. These ships had been completed to the point where their lower main-battery barbettes were finished up to the level of the armoured deck; the barbettes at that level were the same 18ft 8.4in diameter as in the *Mogami* class. But, rather than use the modified turrets later adopted for the *Mogami*s, which incorporated a larger turret race, the designers chose to adopt an inverted conical section for the barbette above the armoured deck that reduced the diameter of the barbette to the original 16ft 4.8in of the E_1 turrets.

The resemblance of the Japanese 'A' class scouting cruisers of the *Tone* class to the preceding *Mogami*s is most visible in their mid-sections, between the forward superstructure and the end of their shelter deck aft of the mainmast and catapults, especially as seen here in this image of *Tone* in 1942. They had similar bridge structures, funnels, heavy AA batteries and after superstructures. Where they differed radically was in the forecastle, where the *Tone*s had four twin 8in/50 turrets and right aft, where they had an open quarterdeck, intended to store as many as eight reconnaissance aircraft. (NHHC)

As a direct result of the decision to move all the main-battery turrets forward, Fukuda was able to give the main-battery magazines of the *Tone*s somewhat thicker armour protection: 5.71in NVNC plate at a 20° incline tapering down to 2.165in where it ended in the double bottom. The engineering spaces were protected by a belt of 3.94in NVNC, also at a 20° incline, tapering down to 1.34in Ducol steel where it met the shell plating. Horizontal armour was generally similar to that of the *Mogami*s, although it was distributed somewhat differently. The bridge structure and fire control suite was basically the same as in the *Mogami*s, as well. One difference was the adoption of an updated Type 94 main-battery director (*hoiban*).[7] (The *Mogami*s had their main-battery directors upgraded to this model during their lengthy reconstructions.) Below decks, they had an updated Type 92 Mod 1 fire-control computer that made the inclinometer (*sokutekiban*) installation unnecessary in their compass bridge. (The *Mogami*s had this same computer upgrade installed, and the *sokutekiban*s removed, during their reconstructions.)

The 'as-built' specifications of the *Tone*s were:

'A' Class Scouting Cruisers: Tone Cass

Displacement (std):	11,215 tons
Length (oa):	661ft 1in
Beam (max):	60ft 8in
Draft (mean):	21ft 3in
Power plant:	152,000shp; Kanpon geared turbines driving four shafts; eight Kanpon three-drum water-tube boilers
Speed:	35 knots
Range (designed):	12,000nm @ 14 knots; 2690 tons oil fuel
Protection (side):	3.94in NVNC–1.34in Ducol 20° slope (from sloped armoured deck to double

	bottom in way of engineering spaces); 5.71in–2.165in NVNC (from Lower Deck in way of main-battery magazines)
Protection (horiz):	1.22in CNC (horizontal), 2.56in CNC (sloping over engineering spaces at Middle Deck level); 2.2in CNC (over magazines at lower deck level)
Protection (torp):	Lower strake of side armour belt acted as torpedo bulkhead; inner splinter bulkhead of thin HTS from armoured deck to double bottom
Armament (main):	8 x 20cm/50 3rd Year Type 2 (4 x 2 – all forward (second turret superfiring)
Armament (AA):	8 x 12.7cm/40 Type 89 (4 x 2); 12 x 25mm/60 Type 96 (6 x 2)
Armament (torp):	12 x 61cm (4 x 3); 12 reloads
Aircraft:	5 (3 x Kawanishi E7K2 Type 94 No.2 and 2 x Nakajima E8N Type 95 reconnaissance seaplanes), two catapults[8]

Both ships were in commission by 1939. Note that in practice they seem to have never carried more than five aircraft.

Last Tango in London: The Run-Up to the Second London Conference of 1935

Knowing that another in the series of naval disarmament conferences was due in 1935, the Americans began discussing among themselves what positions to take at such a conference as early as late 1933, when Norman H Davis, FDR's chosen arms negotiator, met with the United States Navy's General Board to gather their opinions.[9] (Davis was a financier and philanthropist who had entered government service as an advisor to the Treasury Department during the First World War; he had no particular naval expertise.) The Board took the position that a reduction in fleet strength was acceptable if a general agreement could be reached. The President's position was that the United States should continue on a programme of building up to the maximum numbers permitted by treaty provisions, until lower figures were negotiated.

Attitudes in London and Tokyo were hardening well in advance of the impending conference. The American Ambassador to Japan, Joseph C Grew, reported on 26 July 1933 that the Japanese saw themselves as the 'defender of peace in the Far East', and that their navy existed only for self-defence.[10] Grew's words summed up the American attitude towards the Japanese intent to 'protect' Asia from outside interference: 'Self-defence is of course legitimate, even if to the Japanese mind it entails seizing foreign territory and bombarding distant foreign cities.' This reeks of righteous rectitude, completely ignoring the fact that the Japanese were fully aware of the history of American treatment of Latin American nations, such as Honduras, which had been invaded

President Roosevelt's lead negotiator at the Second London Conference was Norman H Davis, a financier and philanthropist with no specific naval experience. Despite that, Davis proved to be well suited by temperament to the task of negotiating a treaty in an increasingly bleak international atmosphere.

by the Americans no fewer than seven times between 1903 and 1925, or Nicaragua and Haiti, both of which were occupied by American troops at the time Grew was writing his dispatch.[11] The Americans would justify these actions as necessary to stabilise an inherently unstable region; the Japanese saw their position in Asia as completely analogous. This impacted the naval debate insofar as, Grew stated, the Japanese believed that 'peace was threatened by the construction of any foreign navy which might challenge Japan's position . . . in the Far East'. The crux of his warning to the new Secretary of State, Cordell Hull, was:

> Behind all this agitation over American naval plans, and probably constituting the reason for accusing America of starting an armament race, is the determination of the Japanese to better their relative standing at the next naval conference. The 5-5-3 ratio has always been a sore spot in the Japanese consciousness, which is given to attach importance to evidence of national distinction.[12]

If that warning was not clear enough, more were to follow.

The British, meanwhile, made known their unhappiness

with American construction of the large *Brooklyn* class light cruisers in an *aide-mémoire* delivered to Hull by the British Chargé in Washington on 14 September 1933.[13] In it, the British complained that Stimson had told them in February 1930 that the United States had no interest in building 10,000-ton cruisers armed with 6in guns.[14] The British note then went on to observe that the American change of position on the subject was undoubtedly caused by the Japanese decision to build the *Mogami*s and *Tone*s. It then warned: 'We are in fact witnessing the first steps in competitive building in a new type in which His Majesty's Government will be compelled to follow suit. The effect of this on future British total tonnage requirements will be obvious.'[15] This was, of course, more than a little disingenuous on the part of the British. Design work on the approximately 9000-ton *Southampton* class had been underway for over a year and work was underway at the Admiralty, under the guidance of 'Ernle' Chatfield, preparing a detailed analysis of the Royal Navy's strategic requirements.[16] Harkening back to the days of the 'Two Power Standard', when, as recently as 1912, Great Britain had an established policy of maintaining a fleet a strong as that of any two rival powers, Chatfield noted that the British now needed to maintain a fleet in the Far East able to protect its interests there (against the implicit threat from Japan) and at the same time be prepared to face any potential rival in the Atlantic or Mediterranean.[17] Of particular import to this narrative were the findings of that analysis regarding cruisers; the report called for a fleet of seventy cruisers, comprised of the fifteen 8in-gunned cruisers allocated by the First London Treaty, a planned ten *Southampton*-type large light cruisers and forty-five smaller light cruisers, all of post-war design. This would, according to the Chatfield analysis, bring the total cruiser tonnage of the Royal Navy to 562,000 tons, dramatically up from the 339,000 tons allocated by treaty.

Chatfield submitted this report for Cabinet review in March 1934. At that time, he took the position that he preferred no agreement on cruiser levels at the forthcoming conference to acceptance of anything less than seventy.[18] He got significant push-back from the Cabinet, which argued that this would simply drive the Americans to build more and bigger cruisers of their own. Bolton M Eyres-Monsell, the First Lord of the Admiralty since 1931, tried to hold out against MacDonald, but eventually accepted a compromise under which the British would present the Americans a proposal for a British fleet of sixty modern cruisers and ten 'over-age' ships (more than 20 years old), with a 'fall back' position of fifty and twenty of each category.[19]

At the same time that Chatfield produced this strategic analysis, Norman Davis arrived in London to begin discussions with his British counterparts; these talks were brief and perfunctory – Davis was on his way to Sweden to deal with another issue – and it was agreed that more formal discussions would be held in London in June. It is clear that Davis was not advised of the contents of Chatfield's report in April. At the same time, the British also invited the three other Contracting Parties from the Washington Treaty to send representatives to London for similar one-on-one preliminary discussions.

Soon after the beginning of the new year, Ambassador Grew reiterated his warnings about the Japanese insistence on a change in ratios of allocated tonnage at the next disarmament conference.[20] He spoke of repeated references in the Japanese press to an impending 'crisis of 1935–36', which was understood to be an inflection point at which Japan would either rise to major power status or begin a process of decline. He presented a sampler of statements by the leadership of the Imperial Navy. Admiral Kato Kanji, head of the Supreme Military Council, was quoted as saying:

> In view of the changes that have taken place in international relations, Japan at the next Naval conference must secure at all costs a revision of the existing naval treaties for the purpose of perfecting her national defence. Such an opportunity may never come again if we miss it in 1935. Precisely speaking, we must insist on equality of armaments which is the prerogative of every independent nation.[21]

Vice Admiral Takahashi Sankichi, vice chief of the Naval General Staff and an important and vocal supporter of Kato's nationalistic Fleet Faction (as opposed to the more moderate Treaty Faction), stated openly: 'We are going to the 1935 conference with a demand for parity. If our demand is rejected, we shall return home.'[22] This time, the warning could hardly have been clearer or more accurate.

On 24 May, FDR called a meeting with some of the men who would join Davis in London for the preliminary discussions with the British on naval disarmament, in an attempt to establish the American position in those talks:

> [FDR] thought that this Government should have some very simple platform on which to stand which would show our desire to cooperate in world naval disarmament; his thought was that we should be willing to reduce our naval force by 25%, provided others did the same, keeping, I believe, the present ratio; . . . first by scrapping certain obsolete ships without replacement; second by a willingness to reduce by 25% our total treaty allowance by tonnage and by number. . . .[23]

This round of discussions between the United States and Great Britain began with a rather formal session at 10 Downing Street on 18 June 1934. Attending for the British were: MacDonald, still the Prime Minster; Eyres-Monsell; Vice Admiral Charles J C Little, Deputy Chief of the Naval Staff; and Robert L Craigie, a Foreign Office naval expert. On the American side were: Davis; Robert W Bingham, the

American Ambassador in London; Ray Atherton, Counsellor to the Embassy; and Admiral Richard H Leigh, current head of the US Navy's General Board.[24] Those initial talks went smoothly, with the British reporting that the Japanese and Italians had responded favourably to the invitations for preliminary discussions.

The Japanese Ambassador stated that a high-ranking officer was being sent from Tokyo, to arrive in October.[25] Given the length of time it would take for this man to conduct his negotiations, return to Japan and for the formal conference delegation to be assembled, briefed and dispatched to London, Matsudaira requested that the beginning of the conference, tentatively scheduled for January 1935, be moved back until April of that year. It was widely reported in London that an 'unofficial' announcement had been made in Tokyo the preceding day detailing the Japanese position at the upcoming conference. The essence of this position was that Japan wanted the Americans and British to agree to parity with Japan, and that this parity was to be achieved by the two other powers reducing their fleets to the size of Japan's.[26] Thereafter, fleet size would be determined on the basis of equality of aggregate tonnage.

On 20 June, the British finally 'lifted their skirts' a bit and MacDonald informed the Americans that 'he was sorry to have to say that the situation confronting the British Government . . . is very different and much more serious than when the London Treaty was signed, necessitating an increase in cruiser tonnage'.[27] The American response was to 'express surprise and regret' to learn of the intended increases and that they believed 'it would be a great shock to public opinion if the forthcoming Naval Conference were to result in substantial increases'. At this session, however, MacDonald only spoke in generalities; it was not until the next day, at a meeting of naval experts attended by Little and Craigie for the British and by Leigh, Atherton and two others for the Americans, that the British revealed the specifics of Chatfield's report. As revealed by Little, the British position was that they intended to develop a cruiser fleet, much as described in the report, comprising the fifteen 8in-gun cruisers allowed by the London Treaty, ten 10,000-ton 6in-gun cruisers (of the *Southampton* and derivative classes) and then 250,000 tons 'to be utilised in ships not over 7,000 tons'.[28] On top of these sixty ships, Little went to explain that:

> Also [his emphasis] 10 over-age cruisers to be retained and to be replaced successively by other cruisers as they in turn become over-age; thus cruisers becoming over-age are (1) replaced by new cruisers built, (2) not scrapped but retained while still older ships are scrapped.[29]

As shocking as this planned increase was to the Americans, both because of its size and its complete unexpectedness – the Americans had come to London expecting to discuss how much tonnage would be reduced, not to be faced with a massive proposed increase in cruiser tonnage – the British were once again utterly uncomprehending of the American perplexity.[30] The British felt strongly that American opposition to Japanese insistence on parity, which the British shared equally, and the demands of FDR's pro-employment ship-building programme, made them immune from any fundamental objections the Americans might have to their demands for increased cruiser tonnage. Therefore the British were more than a little surprised when the Americans left the meeting on 20 June *sine die* (with no scheduled date to reconvene), saying that they needed time to consider the Chatfield plan. The full American reaction was summed up the next day by Davis:

> Bingham and I feel that the program proposed by the British at the meeting of experts yesterday is so unacceptable from our point of view that we should tell the British we think it inadvisable to enter upon technical discussions on such a basis.[31]

Three days later, after further thought, he was even more emphatic:

> The position taken by the British is so completely different from what they indicated it would be . . . last April, and so unacceptable from our point of view as a basis for a treaty, that we have all come to the conclusion after full consideration that we should tell MacDonald frankly that the possibility of agreement . . . is so remote, that we feel it would serve no useful purpose to continue further with the discussions . . .[32]

Except for some informal meeting between Admirals Leigh and Little, who had established a good working relationship, the Anglo-American discussions did end for the moment, as the attention of the British shifted elsewhere. The last offer the Americans put on the table came directly from FDR on 27 June; in it he directed Davis to propose that the Washington and London treaties be extended for a minimum of ten years, during which period the navies of the Contracting Powers were to be reduced by 20 per cent.[33] This proposal received no formal reply before talks were suspended.

The Japanese were in no rush to return to the conference table, as their experiences at earlier disarmament conferences had been anything but positive. Grew in Tokyo reported that Captain Shimomura of the American Section of the Naval General Staff had come by the embassy on 22 June to request a visa to visit the United States. The purpose of his visit was to discuss naval disarmament matters with the new CNO, Admiral William H Standley and other high ranking American naval officers. He told the American naval attaché the following:

> Captain Shimomura stated positively and firmly that no Japanese delegates who signed a treaty agreeing to the

> present ratio could return to Japan and live and that no government which had so agreed could survive. If the United States insists in the preliminary conversations on maintaining the present ratio it would be of no use to hold the conference next year. This has now become a national issue in Japan. If parity with the United States and England is conceded in principle he did not believe that Japan would build up to it.[34]

To reiterate that final point made by Shimomura, which Grew considered critically important, he went on to emphasise:

> The Naval Attaché gathered from the conversation that the principle of parity with the United States is all important and believes that if such a concession could be worked out Japan would accept approximately her present tonnage with the right to build whatever types she desires within that tonnage.[35]

It is impossible to tell, at this remove, whether Grew and the naval attaché, Captain Fred F Rogers, were correct in their assessment of Japanese intentions, because the British and Americans were not inclined to allow the Japanese even token parity.

As promised by Matsudaira, the Japanese 'high ranking officer' arrived in London on 16 October, having taken the eastbound route that took him across the Pacific to Seattle, by train to New York and then by steamer to Southampton. He was Rear Admiral Yamamoto Isoroku – he would be promoted to Vice Admiral during the time he was in London – a man uniquely qualified for this mission by dint of two tours of duty in the United States, which had left him with a working knowledge of the English language and a profound respect for American industrial strength.[36] Yamamoto had been reluctant to take the mission to London, because he knew that the Japanese position was certain to be rejected by the Western Powers and that the almost inevitable consequence – Japanese withdrawal from the treaty regime – would be a diplomatic disaster for his country, but he eventually accepted the job because he believed that he stood a better chance than any other naval officer of making the Japanese position understood by the British and Americans.[37]

Yamamoto was given no flexibility in the proposal he was to present to the British and Americans. It was essentially as had been reported in the London newspapers in mid-June, but included additional features guaranteed to increase the chances of its rejection. Under the rubric 'Common Upper Limit', the plan Yamamoto presented started with the proposal that the three main 'Powers' – Great Britain, the United States and Japan – should achieve parity by reducing the tonnage of the fleets of the British and Americans to match levels allocated to the Japanese. The plan then further proposed the abolition (or dramatic reduction) of all 'offensive' warship types; the list of warship types the Japanese considered 'offensive' included battleships, battlecruisers, aircraft carriers and 8in-gunned cruisers.[38] The British, which Yamamoto approached first, only agreed with the abolition of 'heavy cruisers', as 8in-gunned cruisers were now commonly called. They expressed some interest in discussing reductions in both the size and numbers of capital ships and aircraft carriers, but found themselves frustrated by what they claimed was a deliberate vagueness on Yamamoto's part, an unwillingness to discuss details or to modify any part of the Japanese proposal.[39]

Both the Americans and British seemed to have a hard time understanding the essence of the Japanese proposal (or were just acting that way to avoid directly responding to Yamamoto). On the same day that Yamamoto arrived in London, Grew spelled out the Japanese proposal in simple terms:

> . . . Japan intends at London to propose the abolition of the existing agreements and their replacement by a simple agreement fixing a maximum global tonnage for the United States, Great Britain and Japan; that if such a proposal is accepted Japan hopes that the United States and Great Britain would conclude a 'gentleman's agreement' with Japan not to increase their naval forces beyond reasonable limits necessary for the defense of each. Japan would declare the tonnage she believes necessary for her own defense and would wish the others to do the same.
> 4. Failing an agreement of this kind Japan would have no other recourse after denouncing the existing agreements than to seek by other means, such as non-aggression pacts, to discourage if not prevent a naval armament race.[40]

Yamamoto essentially repeated the Japanese position, as laid out by Grew in the first paragraph of the above quote, in more-or-less the same words, every time he met with the British or the Americans. For this, he was criticised for his 'rigidity' and blamed for diminishing the chances of reaching an agreement.[41] This went on for most of a month, until, running out of patience, MacDonald informed Yamamoto on 6 November that Great Britain formally rejected the Japanese proposal.[42] The Americans were somewhat more patient, but no more flexible or understanding of the Japanese position. An anecdote told about Yamamoto's interactions with the Americans, quite possibly apocryphal, but illustrative nonetheless, recounts how, when told by one of the American delegates that the American 'five' – referring to the Washington Treaty ratios – was no threat to the Japanese 'three', Yamamoto is reported to have replied that, in the same spirit, the Americans should understand that a Japanese 'five' would present no threat to them.[43]

The British could come up with no better response than to offer the Japanese some baubles that gave the outward appearance of equality:

> Simon said he hoped that when the Japanese find that neither one of us will agree to the fundamental changes which their proposals would involve they might become more reasonable and perhaps be satisfied with a general statement of the equality of sovereign rights, et cetera, in a preamble to a treaty, and then in the body of the treaty, fix the respective relative limits, which would hold approximately to the existing ratios.[44]

As demeaning as this sounds to modern ears, this was a serious proposal that the British actually made to Yamamoto at the same time that MacDonald formally reject the Japanese proposal.[45] Yamamoto did not dignify it with a response.

The Americans should have known better. They, at least, knew from Grew's insightful cables that Yamamoto was simply following his government's instructions to the letter and that he had absolutely no 'wiggle room' to accommodate the British or Americans, even had he wanted to. What is equally clear is that British and Americans had no intention of budging from the ratios negotiated at the Washington and London Conferences, even though they understood full well this was strengthening the militarists in Japan and pushing that nation onto a path that might well make war in the Pacific inevitable. It is interesting to speculate what might have happened had the Anglo-Americans offered the Japanese something like a better ratio (or even, heaven forfend, actual parity).[46] It might have been a futile gesture, simply another example of the appeasement that was about to be displayed by the British in its most craven and futile form, or perhaps not.

The best the British could come up with, in the face of what they considered to be Yamamoto's intransigence, was a policy they described as a 'middle course', somewhere between simple continuation of the existing treaties – which the Japanese had made abundantly clear was unacceptable to them – and allowing the treaties to lapse with no replacement. This 'middle course' was always a rather fuzzy construct, but perhaps its best definition came out of an extended meeting between the British and Americans on 14 November.

> 1. An agreement on programs, if possible;
> 2. An agreement which would preserve out of the wreck non-fortification of bases;
> 3. An agreement which would preserve qualitative limitation;
> 4. An agreement which would preserve the provision for notification to be given of the laying down of new ships.[47]

The American position was that, following a Japanese denunciation of the Washington Treaty – fully expected to happen at the end of the year – with immediate negotiations on a new agreement, would seem like rewarding the Japanese for what the Americans considered to be 'bad behavior'.[48] Yamamoto, in the meanwhile, made it clear that the Japanese had no interest in qualitative limitation, rejecting the idea as counter to his nation's interests:

> If there is a failure to bring about quantitative limitations along the lines we have proposed, it will be necessary for to work out our national defence through the construction of the types that are most fitted to our own conditions and that, at the same time would be the most economical.
>
> I do not think actual types have been considered, so nobody knows whether they will take the form of the German pocket battleship. But if the leading powers refuse to reduce their huge navies, we cannot be left behind. As huge navies cost money, the only way open to us would be the development of types relatively low in cost. We have no intention of engaging in a naval race by building large quantities of the types possessed by others.[49]

Despite the clear failure of the preliminary discussions to achieve any worthwhile result, other than to drive the Americans and British somewhat closer together in their mutual antipathy to Japan's proposals, the discussions stumbled along for another month. Indeed, the closer it came to the end of the year, the less inclined the Americans were to even talk to Yamamoto, in order not to give him any 'excuse' for the denunciation that everyone knew was coming.[50] (The Americans were aware that the Japanese were uncomfortable with taking the onus of denunciation entirely on their own. At the end of November, they approached the French, asking them if they wanted to join Japan in abrogating the treaty; they believed the French had as much reason to hate the Washington Treaty as they did. However, the strategy backfired; the French announced publicly that, while they sympathised with the position of the Japanese, they would not join her in denouncing the treaty.[51] The Japanese also approached the Italians, with a similar lack of success.)

On this note, the Americans packed up and left London for the holidays on 20 December, after a brief (and utterly inconclusive) tri-partite meeting in MacDonald's offices the day before.[52] MacDonald left town the next day for his Scottish home. Yamamoto stayed on in London, not departing until 28 January 1935.[53]

Caving In: Britain Invites Germany to the Dance

The German navy, still officially the *Reichsmarine*, began design studies for a 10,000-ton cruiser in February 1934, while still bound by the Versailles Treaty and legally unable to build such a ship. However, Adolf Hitler had been appointed Chancellor the previous January and had been granted essentially dictatorial powers by the Enabling Act of 23 March 1933; from that point on, compliance with the Versailles Treaty was no longer a major factor in German military planning. The specifications given the design bureau by the naval staff, led by Admiral Erich J A Raeder, called for a ship that could stand up against *Algérie* offensively and defensively, was faster than the French battlecruiser *Dunkerque* (which had a top speed of 29.5 knots) and the range to sortie into the Atlantic for commerce destruction.[54] The choice of main-battery calibre was left open, but Raeder made his preference for 20.3cm guns known and this calibre was the only one seriously considered. The choice of propulsion system was much more contentious; options ranging from diesel-only (as in the *Panzerschiffe*), to mixed diesel-and-steam (used with varying success in all but one of the *Reichsmarine*'s light cruisers), to conventional steam propulsion, to high-pressure steam propulsion and even to turbo-electric propulsion (the latter two both in use for some time in commercial applications and pioneered in naval service by the United States Navy). The first two options were rejected because of previous negative experiences with those power-plant types and turbo-electric because there was no strong advocacy for the system within the German naval community. In the end, a high-pressure steam turbine system was selected as combining the needed power with the lowest weight and space requirements.

The design came together quickly under the leadership of Senior Naval Architect Hermann Burckhardt. Orders for the first two were placed at Deutsche Werke, Kiel, and Blohm und Voss, Hamburg on 30 October 1934, but the design was far from ready, nor were the Germans ready to make public the fact that they were building heavy cruisers. Despite the many activities going on in Germany that skirted or openly violated the provisions of Part V of the Versailles Treaty – the part that specifically limited Germany's armaments – many of which predated the Nazi's rise to power, Hitler was not prepared to openly challenge the former Allies.

It is known that when Hitler first met Raeder, the *Chef der Marineleitung* described to the new Chancellor the navy he wanted to build, with a target of naval parity with France. Hitler responded that Germany deserved a grander fleet, one built up to a one-third ratio of Royal Navy tonnage in each category of warship, not realising that the fleet Raeder was proposing would actually be somewhat larger, at least 35 per cent of the Royal Navy's totals.[55] Hitler appeared not to understand or care particularly about the few percentage points difference between one-third and 35 per cent, but finally agreed to promote the larger figure because he thought it made for better political posturing. It is not entirely clear when this 'desire' (or 'demand', depending on Hitler's mood) was first officially made known to the British. It is known that in November 1934, he made passing reference to it during a rambling interview with the British Ambassador, Eric C E Phipps.[56] Again, during an 'informal' visit to Germany by R Clifford Allen in January 1935, a prominent pacifist and Labour politician, a meeting with Hitler was arranged, during which the German desire for a naval agreement with Great Britain based on a 35 per cent ratio was raised.[57]

The former Western Allies were scrambling to figure how to limit the danger of an obviously resurgent, rearming Germany. In July 1934, during Anglo-French preliminary discussions, the subject of Germany's rearmament was discussed and the two sides agreed on allowing Germany levels of naval armaments that, while they exceeded the number and size of ships defined in the Versailles Treaty, were still small.[58] By the time they met again at the beginning of February 1935, the urgency to reach a deal that might restrain German rearmament had ratcheted up. After a weekend of meetings between MacDonald and French *Premier* Pierre Laval, a joint Anglo-French communiqué was issued in London on 3 February stating, quite openly, that Britain and France were ready to accede to the dismemberment of the Versailles Treaty:

> The British and French Ministers . . . have agreed that neither Germany nor any other power whose armaments have been defined by the peace treaties is entitled by unilateral action to modify these obligations.
>
> But they are further agreed that nothing could contribute more to the restoration of confidence and the prospects of peace among nations than a general settlement freely negotiated between Germany and the other powers. . . .
>
> . . . this settlement would establish agreements regarding armaments generally, which in the case of Germany would replace the provisions of Part V of the Treaty of Versailles at present limiting arms and armed forces in Germany. . . The French Government and the Government of the United Kingdom trust that the other governments concerned may share these views.[59]

It is hard to imagine that this incredible communiqué was greeted with any enthusiasm in any of the capitals of the 'other governments' potentially impacted, such as Brussels, Prague or Warsaw. Indeed, it is hard to understand why the French signed on to this complete surrender to Germany's unilateral renunciation of its obligations under the Versailles Treaty, except the French were undoubtedly in great fear of the consequences of parting ways with their ally and potentially facing a resurgent Germany alone. Events were soon to make this fear palpable.

Hitler, with a conman's instinct for sensing a weakness in a mark, realised that the British were susceptible to being pressed into making further concessions. Foreign Secretary Simon had planned on meeting Hitler in Berlin at the beginning of March, but Hitler had other plans. Hitler took his time with the German reply to the Anglo-French communiqué, not replying until 15 February and then keeping the reply deliberately vague except on one point. One of a conman's basic ploys, when faced with multiple marks, especially when one (e.g., France) is more suspicious than the other (e.g., Britain), is to attempt to deal with them separately. After a lengthy statement full of flowery language proclaiming Germany's commitment to negotiations aimed at securing European peace and stability, the reply then made its central point:

> Before the German Government participates in such negotiations, it believes it is desirable to clear up a series of basic preliminary questions by means of individual discussions with the governments concerned.
>
> It would therefore welcome it if after the preliminary Franco-British discussions, the British Government were first to declare its readiness . . . to enter into a direct exchange of views with the German Government.[60]

Then, employing yet another basic huckster's ploy, Hitler 'caught a cold', forcing Simon to postpone his trip to Berlin.[61] (A proximate 'cause' of Hitler's ill health was quite likely the release of a white paper in London on 4 March proposing substantial increases in defence spending in large part due to a perception of an increased threat from Germany.[62]) On 9 March, the Germans announced that Hitler had largely recovered from his illness, but was, nonetheless, retiring to Berchtesgaden to finish recuperating, and that Simon's visit to Berlin had been rescheduled for the end of the month.[63] And then, in a carefully-timed *coup-de-théâtre*, on 11 March, the Germans announced the existence of the *Luftwaffe* (German Air Force), which had been an open secret for some time. This was followed on 16 March by the announcement that universal conscription was being instituted and a standing army initially of 324,000 men was to be created.[64] This, however, was not the most important event in Berlin that day for the purposes of this narrative; on that same day, Hitler met with Phipps, who reported that Germany 'insisted on' equality with France in all military forms, but that relative to England, 'only sought 33%' of the Royal Navy's effective strength.[65] The American Chargé, who was reporting this conversation to Secretary Hull, made it clear that the 'Foreign Office understands no reference was made to naval strengths in conversations with French and therefore asks the above be regarded as strictly confidential'.[66] Hitler's ploy had succeeded; he had convinced the British to negotiate a naval convention separately and secretly, which was entirely to his advantage.

The British indeed were put in a terrible position, having agreed to a visit by Simon to Berlin on 24 March, at which it was planned that he would propose to Hitler that the French and British would agree to the abrogation of Part V of the Versailles Treaty on the condition that Germany rejoined the League of Nations and that they would come to London for discussions on a binding naval agreement, beginning soon after Easter (which in 1935 was on 21 April).[67] After a day of meetings and consultation with the French on the 17th, the British generated a protest note which was delivered to the German Foreign Ministry by Phipps.[68] In that note, after starting by protesting Germany's recent unilateral actions violating the Versailles Treaty, the note proceeded to remind the Germans that the French and British had offered to renegotiate the relevant parts of that treaty and ended by meekly proclaiming that the British were 'most unwilling to abandon any opportunity which the arranged visit might afford of promoting a general understanding', but felt 'bound to call the attention of the German Government' to the joint communiqué of 3 February and stated that 'they wish to be assured that the German Government still desire the visit to take place within the scope and for the purposes previously agreed'.[69]

The 'Western Democracies' would have other chances over the next four years to restrain Hitler, but, with all the wisdom of hindsight, it is possible to speculate that this may have been their best chance to do so, had they been able to muster the resolve. Clearly, however, when faced with the option of confronting Hitler, which brought the chance of war, or hoping that his behaviour could be controlled by conventional diplomacy, the erstwhile allies were all too willing to choose the approach that seemed to offer less proximate risk. It is easy to look back and shake one's head at what appears to be abject surrender in the face of Hitler's bluster, but, at the time, these politicians and military leaders felt keenly both the dread their populations shared about the possibility of another war so soon after the end of the last one and their own lack of preparedness for another conflict after years of scrimping on defence spending. Still, it is not possible to read the British note of 18 March without embarrassment. One can only imagine the smug satisfaction with which Hitler ordered his Foreign Minister, Constantin von Neurath, to respond that Germany still very much wanted Simon to come to Berlin on the 24th.

The story of the naval negotiations from this point onward is much less complicated. Simon went to Berlin as scheduled and invited the Germans to send a negotiating team to London in April. This was delayed somewhat by the Stresa meetings between MacDonald, Laval and Mussolini, which began on 11 April 1935 on Lago Maggiore, ending on 14 April with a flowery, but toothless, declaration of support for Austrian independence, the integrity of the Locarno Treaty (which had guaranteed the borders of some of Germany's neighbours after the First World War) and for the negotiated (as opposed to unilateral) revision of the Versailles Treaty restrictions on Germany's armaments. (It would be the last time Mussolini would line up with the former allies against Germany.)

Yet, even while MacDonald was at Stresa, Robert Craigie, who was now head of the American Department at the Foreign Office and the lead British negotiator for naval disarmament, urged his government to move ahead rapidly with the talks with Germany, asking only that, before the negotiations began, the Germans provide a detailed description of their planned building programme.[70] On 12 April, the British naval attaché in Berlin was informed that the German 1935 building programme included two enlarged *Panzerschiffe* (which became *Scharnhorst* and *Gneisenau*), two large cruisers (see below) and sixteen destroyers. (The construction of submarines by the Germans was not confirmed to the attaché until 25 April; when this information was confirmed by Simon in the Commons on the 29th, the Germans reacted angrily, claiming that it had not been meant for public disclosure.[71]) MacDonald attempted to patch over the dispute. In a long address to Parliament on 2 May, he listed at length all the steps Great Britain had taken attempting to draw Germany into the negotiation process and all the unilateral steps the Germans had recently taken violating the Versailles Treaty, and then went on to state: 'We recognise, with great regret, that circumstances have changed, but the general purpose of the Declaration [of 3 February] still remains the objective of immediate British foreign policy.'[72] Hitler, however, was not to be so easily mollified. MacDonald said in his remarks on 2 May that he expected the talks with Germany to begin in mid-May, but the Germans stalled. When a conman has his con set up and the hook is baited, nothing makes the mark more eager to bite than to slow things down.

The League of Nations had passed a unanimous resolution on 17 April, the language of which mirrored the 3 February Anglo-French communiqué condemning Germany's unilateral acts, at the same time, setting up a committee to study what types of economic sanctions might prevent a repetition.[73] Hitler's response was further to delay sending his negotiators to London. Instead, he let matters hang unresolved until 21 May, when he addressed the *Reichstag*, as was his wont when he had major announcements to make. As also was his wont, his rambling speech went on for hours, making MacDonald's address to the Commons on 17 April pale in comparison. Only parts of this screed covered foreign policy, which Hitler broke down into thirteen numbered points, only one of which, the eighth, was of specific interest to this narrative:

> The limitation of the German Navy to 35 per cent of the strength of the British Navy is still 15 per cent lower than the total tonnage of the French fleet. Inasmuch as different press commentaries express the opinion this demand is only a beginning, and it would be raised if Germany possessed colonies, the German Government declares in a binding manner: This demand is final and lasting for Germany.[74]

From this point onward, the naval negotiations between Great Britain and Germany went very quickly. Hitler understood instinctually, once the mark is presented the final deal, do not give him the time to reconsider his decision.

The Germans named a special Ambassador Extraordinary and Plenipotentiary, Joachim von Ribbentrop, a former wine salesman fluent in French and English, to head the small delegation they sent to London. Ribbentrop arrived in London in time for the first meeting to take place on 4 June. When Ribbentrop and his naval advisor, Rear Admiral Karlgeorg Schuster, sat down with Simon and his negotiating team, the British were in for a rude shock. Ribbentrop announced that acceptance of the 35 per cent ratio for the German Navy was a prerequisite for further discussions.[75] This could not have come at worse time for the British, as it demanded a firm

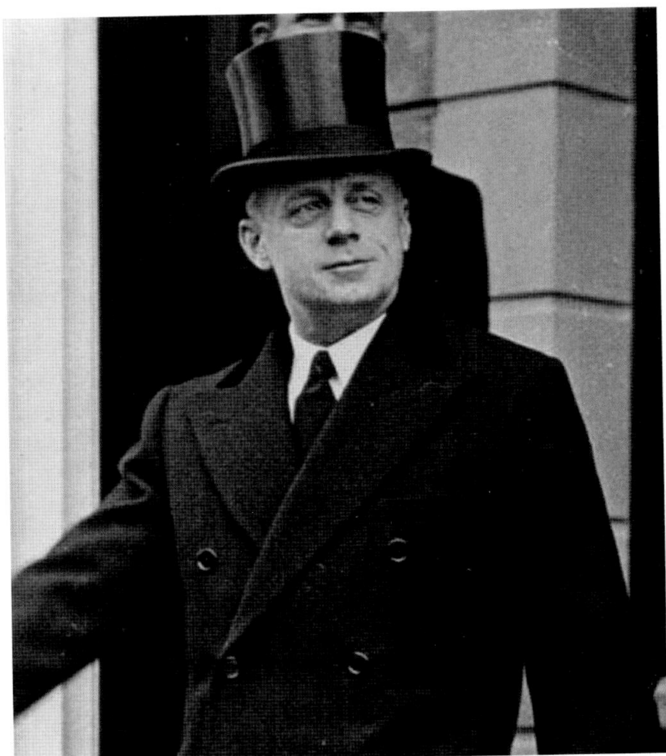

The man Hitler would send to London to 'seal the deal' on the naval agreement he had so masterfully stage-managed from Berlin was Joachim von Ribbentrop, a former wine merchant and one of the few Nazis with any experience in dealings beyond the borders of Germany. This image shows him in London in 1936, a year after the signing of the Anglo-German Naval Agreement, when he was appointed German Ambassador to the United Kingdom.

decision from the top leadership of the nation and, at this precise moment, that leadership was in flux. MacDonald's second National Government was under increasing pressure to resign because of lack of support within the Labour Party. Unable to reach a decision, the Cabinet passed the issue on to the Naval Conference (Ministerial) Committee (NCM), which comprised only the relevant subset of ministers.

Discussions continued the next day between Ribbentrop and Schuster for the Germans, and Craigie and Little for the British. The Germans were all sweet reasonableness, stating that the 35 per cent ratio would satisfy them, regardless of construction by the Russians or French, that they would accept limitation by category rather than by global tonnage and that they would abide by any qualitative limits and notification rules that came out of future disarmament conferences. Even after all this, the NCM, which met on the morning of the 6th, was concerned about Hitler's trustworthiness. The Naval Staff declared themselves ready to accept the 35 per cent ratio immediately, fearing that any delay might allow the Germans to increase their demand.[76] Simon accepted the German offer at face value. Samuel J G Hoare, who held the office of Secretary of State for India, was worried about the French reaction, but had no other concerns. Only Chatfield raised the issue of whether the British understood what the Germans meant by a 35 per cent ratio. Despite this concern, the NCM voted to accept the German 'offer' and, at the same time, to inform the other naval powers of the status of the negotiations. Stanley Baldwin, who was Lord President of the Council, and Eyres-Monsell, convinced the committee to inform the French only that the British intended to accept to German offer.[77] The next day, Baldwin and MacDonald switched offices, while Hoare replaced Simon at the Foreign Office; it made no difference as far as the Germans were concerned.

That same day, 7 June, Craigie sat down with Bingham; he showed the American Ambassador a secret *aide-mémoire* that had been sent to the French, Italian and Japanese governments. In it, the British laid out what the Germans had offered and agreed to up to that point and said that the British had concluded that the offer 'should be accepted'.[78] They asked for 'observations' from those governments 'in the course of the next few days'. Craigie then informed Bingham: 'As a matter of tactics the British delayed immediate formal acceptance but regardless of what the views of continental naval powers may be it is understood the British have given informal acceptance to the Germans.'[79]

The rest was mere formality. The Germans wanted a clause that would allow them to transfer tonnage between categories, to which the British objected, but agreed to language that accepted the principle of transfer, with the details to be negotiated on a case-by-case basis.[80] On 18 June, Hoare formally accepted the 35 per cent ratio, with the Germans allowed 45 per cent of the British tonnage of submarines (and the right to build up to 100 per cent of the Royal Navy's total if, in Germany's opinion, it became necessary). In this form, the agreement was signed that same day.

Although the agreement was signed on the 18th, the German delegation did not leave London for four more days because the British had been in such a rush to conclude this business that some loose ends remained to be tied up. The most important of these, which was the subject of a meeting on 20 June, was the German building programme between 1935 and 1942. (Astonishingly, these matters were only raised by the British after they had signed the agreement.) The programme the Germans revealed would bring them up to the full 35 per cent allowed by the agreement; among the long list of capital ships, aircraft carriers and submarines, were included eighteen cruisers of undefined size. When they heard the scope of this construction programme, the British delegates were clearly taken aback.[81] Craigie and Little asked the Germans if the rate of construction could not be slowed so as not to 'shock' other powers. The Germans did not respond to this request.

The British clearly knew that they had a serious problem on their hands in explaining their actions to their European allies. The French were irate; René Massigli, now assistant director of political affairs at the Quai d'Orsay, delivered the formal response on the same day as the agreement was signed, in which the French made it clear that they were 'indignant at the way in which the British, in what had been understood to be merely exploratory conversations, had come to a definite understanding with the Germans'.[82] The reaction from the Italians was hardly milder, but the most upset were the Soviets, who had considerable investment at this time in collective security, particularly with the French. The chief architect of Soviet foreign policy in the 1930s was People's Commissar of Foreign Affairs Maxim M Litvinov. His reaction to the Anglo-German Naval Agreement, as recorded by American Ambassador to the Soviet Union, William C Bullitt, was to label the British 'blacklegs'; he predicted it would be 'disastrous not only in Europe, but in the Far East'.[83] Bullitt said Litvinov believed:

> . . . that Hitler may only be restrained by a 'chain' of states armed to opposed Germany. Litvinov is convinced that England has now broken this 'chain' and that the defection of Italy and other states is likely to follow.
>
> The most serious concern of the Soviet Government, however, is with regard to the effect on Japan of the Anglo-German naval agreement. The Russians point out that the construction of the new German fleet will make it necessary for England to retain the greater part of her naval forces in the North Sea, that she will have to diminish her forces in the Mediterranean, and that it will be absolutely impossible for her to send a fleet to Singapore.[84]

Time would prove the remarkable accuracy of these predictions. Efforts were made then and later to defend the British decision to agree unilaterally to Hitler's demands. Reference is made to an Admiralty Plans Division study made in May 1935, which demonstrated that the Royal Navy in 1942 would be stronger than the combined fleets of Japan and Germany, thus allowing the British to maintain a 'two-power standard' much as they had at the end of the nineteenth century.[85] (Of course, this overlooked the fact that this standard generally pre-supposed that the two powers would both be European; it failed to take into account the case in which the powers were half-a-world apart.) More recently, the argument has been made that the naval agreement encouraged Germany to build a 'balanced' fleet rather than a fleet skewed towards commerce-raiding, as was proposed by some in the *Kriegsmarine*, who endorsed the construction of a *Kreuzerkrieg* force more designed for commerce raiding as opposed to conventional naval warfare.[86] It is difficult to give much credence to this argument, however, as most of the German naval leadership, from Raeder on down, were veterans of the *Hochseeflotte* and remembered fondly the dreadnoughts and battlecruisers of the Imperial German Navy.

It would, of course, be naïve to state that had the British followed some other course, that the result in the end would have been better in terms of containing Hitler. What can be said is that it could hardly have been worse.

On 6 July, the Germans publicly revealed their naval building programme that included two heavy cruisers identified as Ersatz-*Hamburg* and Ersatz-*Berlin*.[87] That same day, the keel of the first of what would be five heavy cruisers in the class was laid down at Hamburg; her specifications were:

Ersatz-Hamburg Class

Displacement (std):	14,050 tons (design); 14,247 tons (actual)
Length (oa):	665ft 4in
Beam (wl):	69ft 10in
Draft (mean):	19ft (design); 25ft 11in (deep)
Power plant:	132,000shp; Blohm u. Voss geared turbines driving three shafts; twelve La Mont single-ended water-tube boilers
Speed:	32 knots (design); 32.5 knots (actual)
Range:	6500nm @ 17 knots; 3050 tons oil fuel
Protection (side):	3.15in Wh external belt (in way of main-battery magazines and engineering spaces)[88]
Protection (torp):	0.79in Ww vertical bulkhead (inboard of external belt)[89]
Protection (horiz):	1.97in Wh (sloping armoured deck – *Böschung*); 1.18in Wh (flat Upper Deck over main-battery magazines and engineering spaces)
Armament (main):	8 x 20.3cm/60 SK C/34 (4 x 2 – two forward and two aft)
Armament (AA):	12 x 10.5cm/65 Flak C/33 (6 x 2); 12 x 3.7cm/83 SK C/30 (6 x 2); 8 x 2cm/65 C/30 (8 x 1)
Armament (torp):	12 x 53.3cm (4 x 3)
Aircraft:	3 (3 x Ar196 reconnaissance floatplane); one catapult[90]

Well before the signing of the naval agreement, the Germans were working on the design of a heavy cruiser that broke all the Versailles Treaty restrictions that had hobbled all previous post-war German designs. Designated Ersatz-*Hamburg*, because of the old cruiser she was intended to replace, the first of these big, powerful cruisers was laid down within weeks of the signing of the Anglo-German Naval Agreement. When she entered service in April 1939, now named *Admiral Hipper*, she had the straight stem seen here and, not visible in this image, no funnel cap. (NARA)

It did not take long for experience to show that *Hipper*'s straight stem was a poor design choice, causing her to be very wet forward and the lack of a funnel cap led to problems with smoke interference with bridge positions. In November 1939, she re-entered the Blohm u Voss yard where she had been built and had a more raked bow and a funnel cap added. At the same time, she received a FuMO 22 radar, whose large rectangular antenna was affixed to the front face of the bi-level DCT atop her tower foremast. It was in this form that she is seen here, surrounded by ice in Kiel Bay in late January 1940, during one of the coldest winters on record.

Hipper's slightly younger sister, *Blücher*, was just as unlucky as the armoured cruiser by that name completed not long before the First World War. She can readily be distinguished from *Hipper* by her far more raked bow. She was lost on her first operation; she was sent up Oslofjord to deliver 900 troops to occupy the Norwegian capital, but at the Drøbak Narrows she was shelled and torpedoed and capsized there. Sources differ as to the number of casualties that resulted from the sinking, between approximately 300 to over 1000. (NARA)

When Ersatz-*Hamburg* was launched on 6 February 1937, she was given the name *Admiral Hipper*. This ship had a straight stem with almost no rake; her sister, *Blücher*, completed only five months later, had a raked and flared 'clipper'-type bow and a large funnel cap, but was otherwise similar. Within two months of her commissioning in April 1939, *Hipper*'s straight stem with minimal flare was deemed a serious flaw and she was taken in hand for modification. She emerged from this refit in September 1939 with a more raked and flared bow (though not as markedly so as *Blücher*'s) and also with a prominent funnel cap.

Three more cruisers of similar design were laid down, two in 1936 and one a year later. Only one would be completed; *Prinz Eugen*, commissioned in August 1940, was named after the same person as the Italian *Eugenio di Savoia*. All of the *Hipper* class would suffer from problems with their engineering plants; despite their reputation as engineers, the Germans failed to master the intricacies of high-pressure steam propulsion in the 1930s.

In 1940, while Germany and Soviet Russia were still allied as a result of the Non-Aggression Pact signed in 1939, the incomplete *Hipper* class cruiser *Lützow* was sold to Russia as partial payment for the raw materials the Soviets were shipping to Germany. She is seen here being towed from the Deschimag (AG Weser) yard in Bremen to Leningrad (St Petersburg). Note the prominent anti-torpedo bulge, most of which would be submerged at normal loading. She was renamed *Petropavlovsk* by the Russians, but was little advanced from the condition seen here when the Germans invaded in 1941. The guns in the forward main-battery turret were used in the defence of Leningrad until she was sunk in April 1942. Raised again and renamed *Tallinn*, she was used briefly to help drive the Germans away from the city and then remained in Soviet service as a training hulk and barracks ship until scrapped in the late 1950s.

A Cold Winter on the Thames: The Second London Naval Conference 1935–1936

The Americans, in September 1935, began another round of preliminary discussions in London. The British again pressed for lower limits on cruiser size and main-battery armament, which again the Americans resisted.[91] Despite American advice that, under the circumstances calling the next disarmament conference would be counter-productive, on 23 October, the British Cabinet decided to issue invitations to a multi-national conference to begin on 2 December, which date was immediately pushed back to 5 December. The American delegation, again led by Davis, joined by the new CNO, Admiral William H Standley, was given general instructions to attempt to negotiate a reduction in overall levels of tonnage, while defending the integrity of the existing treaties and maintaining a preference for quantitative over qualitative limits.[92] Given all that, the Americans understood that, with British plans to increase their cruiser fleet to seventy ships and Japanese insistence on parity, the United States would have to approach the conference with multiple 'fall-back' options. The

Americans were prepared to accept a treaty without Japan, but not one solely with the British. They would accept an agreement with increased cruiser tonnage if some tonnage in other categories was sacrificed. They would even accept a treaty without quantitative limits at all, if that was the best available deal. The one caveat FDR insisted on was an 'escape clause', which could be invoked if another power was building excessively in any category.[93]

The Japanese made it clear that their position had not changed from that expressed a year earlier by Yamamoto. The instructions given to their delegation, led by Admiral Nagano Osami, were that he was to accept nothing short of parity with the United States, but that he had flexibility to adjust the level of the Common Upper Limit in dealings with other nations, particularly if this served to drive a wedge between the British and Americans. The Japanese did approach the French and Italians with an eye towards gaining their co-operation in this endeavour, but both responded negatively and reported as much to the British.[94]

The British position was relatively simple. While they would have liked to advocate the total banning of 8in-gunned sub-category (*a*) cruisers, they understood the Americans would object, so their position was to include them in the mix, but to urge that no more be built.[95] Sub-category (*b*) cruisers would be limited to 6in guns and 7600 tons standard displacement. Finally, all signatories were to keep each other informed by annual advanced disclosure of their building programmes.

The conference actually began on 9 December with remarkably little fanfare. The lack of pomp and ceremony was in part due to a sombre mood in London due the failing health of King George V – he would die on 20 January 1936 – and in part due to low expectation of a positive result by all participants. As usual, the initial plenary session was followed by several meetings of a heads-of-delegations committee, known as the First Committee, that met the next day. It was at the first three of these meetings that Nagano spelled out the Japanese proposal for a 'Common Upper Limit'. This proposal included the abolition of capital ships, aircraft carriers and even heavy cruisers as 'offensive' weapons, and the reduction of the American and British fleets to the same tonnage levels as the Japanese. At one point in late December, the Japanese approached the British with a proposal that they – the Japanese and British – should recognise each other's need for a higher common tonnage limit than was required by the Americans.[96] Whatever other issues the British and Americans may have with each other in these discussions, and they were many, they did not include the question of how to react to the Japanese proposal; the British politely declined Nagano's attempt to split them apart on this issue.

Only adding to the delay and confusion at this time was the holiday season, which always slowed business in Western capitals, and the replacement of Hoare as British Foreign Secretary by Anthony Eden on 22 December. Nagano, following instructions received from Tokyo, told Eden that the Japanese would not discuss any other issues, such as the advance disclosure greatly desired by the British, unless their Common Upper Limit proposal was accepted.[97] The British appeared to be eager to find some alternative that would allow the Japanese to accept some form of agreement short of the Common Upper Limit. Craigie stated that he believed that while the Japanese naval faction wanted to bring the issue to a head as quickly as possible, the Japanese Foreign Office still had hopes of prolonging the conference and that the British believed a consultation pact or even a non-aggression pact might be worked out with Japan that might maintain the *status quo*. Davis, for the Americans, stated that such agreements would be seen as essentially meaningless and impossible to explain to the Senate, which would have to ratify them. Without American help in attempting to placate the Japanese, the issue of the Common Upper Limit came up for debate at the First Committee on 15 January; when no other nation supported the Japanese proposal, Nagano announced his nation's withdrawal from the conference.[98] Two observers remained behind, but Nagano left immediately for Tokyo.

With the departure of the Japanese, the business of the conference proceeded relatively smoothly, but there was not much chance that matters of substance would be decided. The British wanted very much to invite the Germans and Soviets to join the talks, but the French were insistent that the Germans not be included.[99] The pain from the Anglo-German Naval Agreement was still far too raw. Sitting down at the same table with the Germans would signal acceptance of that agreement, which the French were not yet willing to do.[100]

A sub-committee under Craigie's leadership was set up to work out the advance disclosure scheme. The Italians offered a proposal at the first meeting of this body that was eventually adopted essentially unchanged. The gist of the proposal was that each nation would announce its annual building programme no later than 1 May of any year, that no ship so announced would be laid down before 1 October of that year, and that no announced programme was to be exceeded.

Another sub-committee under Chatfield was set up to establish qualitative limits for all warship categories. (The Americans had accepted by now that any hope of obtaining a treaty with quantitative limitation had faded; no other nation had any interest in reducing the size of their fleet.) Nonetheless, the same old disagreements between the Americans and British based on different perceived needs resurfaced. On 23 January, Chatfield and Standley met and restated the old positions: 'In opening the cruiser discussion Chatfield said they will build 25 or more of smaller type in next 5 or 6 years. It is of great importance to them that their cruisers should not be individually outmatched by larger vessels.'[101]

Once again, as they had at Geneva, the British wanted to build the ships they needed and they wanted, at the same time, to write the rules so that no-one else built ships that were bigger or better-armed that the ships they were building.

> Quantitative limitation is gone forever [Chatfield] said. In regard to qualitative limits for cruisers Standley said that it was essential that the new treaty provide for both category A cruisers and 10,000-ton category B cruisers. Also that we could not agree never to build any more 10,000-ton cruisers as these categories are necessary when replacements become due and to enable us if necessary to reply to Japanese building in these types . . . The British are apparently ready to [agree to?] retention of these types provided that a 5- or 6-year building holiday commencing January 1, 1937, is agreed to.[102] . . .
>
> The reason for fixing the length of the building holiday at 6 years instead of a shorter period, say 3 years, was because a nation might delay all cruiser construction for a short period in order subsequently to build the larger types, whereas if it were for 6 years every nation would have to undertake some cruiser construction and would therefore become committed to the smaller type.[103]

Ultimately, the Americans stated their willingness to forego building any more 'treaty maximum' cruisers for a defined period, whether 8in-gunned or 6in-gunned, and agreed to the British desire to build only smaller cruisers, unless the Japanese forced their hand. This was a major concession and went a long way toward prevent a repeat of the deadlock that occurred at Geneva, but still, there were details to be hammered out.

> The first category A replacement cruiser in any navy is due to be laid down by Japan in 1943.[104] The British suggest that the termination of the 10,000-ton cruiser building holiday in both subcategories might therefore logically be fixed as January 1, 1943. Admiral Standley suggested that we must consider a building holiday in big cruisers as provided in the British plan until January 1, 1942. . . .
>
> Summarizing as to cruisers, the British proposal is an agreement for all powers after January 1, 1937, not to build for a period 6 years any more 8-inch gun cruisers nor any more 6-inch gun cruisers over 8,000 tons.[105]

Davis concluded that part of his lengthy cable to Hull by stating 'an expression of the Department's views as to the acceptability of the British proposal is desired'.[106] Davis made it clear in a follow-up cable that, while he supported Standley and believed the British proposal should be accepted, no formal reply had been made.[107] This situation continued for several more days, as the British developed a shifting definition of a new category of ships they called 'light surface vessels', which, after a few rounds of discussion and refinement, ended up having three sub-categories, the first two of which looked exactly like sub-category (*a*) and sub-category (*b*) from the First London Treaty. Finally, on 6 February, the air had cleared sufficiently, that Washington was able to send the following to Davis:

> Upon the basis of the information and the conditions in the above . . . , the Navy and the State Departments agree that you may proceed with the discussion of a holiday for a period of 5 or 6 years in building Category A or 10,000-ton Category B cruisers with the reservation that there is no agreement, expressed or implied, either to abolish these types or continue the holiday period beyond 5 or 6 years. . . .
>
> When the foregoing was brought to the attention of the President he approved it. However he asked that your attention and that of Admiral Standley should be called to the fact that by this agreement we would revert in new cruiser construction to 6-inch gun cruisers of less than 8,000 tons displacement.[108]

With this concession by the Americans, the biggest obstacle to reaching an agreement was removed. The remaining issue was whether either the French or Italians could be persuaded to sign on. This was critical, because FDR insisted that he would not approve a bilateral Anglo-American treaty, which he saw as pointless in serving the purposes of arms control. The French were persuaded to agree to sign on the resulting treaty, despite the fact that its provisions did not impact them in any significant manner. The Italians had their own issues. After the invasion of Ethiopia (Abyssinia) in October 1935, the British and French had been instrumental in organising League of Nations economic sanctions against Italy in November, which, as so often is the case, only angered Mussolini without in any way restraining him. When word was made public in December that Hoare and French Foreign Minister Laval had been negotiating a treaty with the Italians and Ethiopians that would give Mussolini most of Ethiopia, Hoare was forced to resign. Nonetheless, the economic sanctions remained, and the Italians, upset at what they considered to be British hypocrisy, refused to sign the Second London Treaty, despite having materially contributed to its development.[109] The resulting treaty was signed by the United States, Great Britain and France on 25 March 1936. What little impact it had on the development of cruisers in the world's fleets will be described in the next chapter.

Chapter 9

True Babies – London's Offspring and Other (Mostly) Small Cruisers: 1936–1941

In the 1930s, and in at least one case into the 1940s, many of the nations followed here built much smaller cruisers. In some cases, this was because it was mandated (or endorsed) by the Second London Treaty. In some cases, it was because some navies had discovered that 'traditional' fleet work, such as scouting and the leading of and protection against attacks by destroyer flotillas, could be done better by a smaller cruiser. In some cases, it was to act as a training ship for midshipmen or technical apprentices. In some cases, it was simply as an attempt to economise. In some cases, it was because these ships were being seen as fulfilling an entirely new role for cruisers, that of anti-aircraft escort. In most cases, it was some combination of the above reasons.

Small by Design: The *Dido* Class

The origin of the Royal Navy's *Dido* class precedes the Second London Treaty by two-and-a-half years. In August 1933, the First Sea Lord, Admiral Chatfield, queried his major fleet commanders about whether they would support the development of a cruiser smaller than the *Leander*s (c7000 tons) and *Arethusa*s (c5250 tons) to replace the ageing First World War-vintage 'C' class cruisers.[1] The responses were generally favourable regarding a small cruiser, particularly one intended to lead in flotilla attack and defence. A year later, he asked DNC to produce a series of designs for a cruiser in the 4500–5000-ton range; the resulting sketch designs varied widely in size, armament, speed and protection, sharing only a 6in main battery. (As an added fillip, DNC threw in a sketch for a smaller ship, armed with a 4.7in main battery, which caught the attention of the Naval Staff and was rapidly developed into the 'Tribal' class large destroyers, the first of which were ordered in the 1935 building programme.) Of the sketch designs DNC produced in August 1934, the one that garnered the most favourable reaction (design Q) had five single 6in mounts, four 4in AA guns, protection similar to the *Southampton*s, and a projected speed of 33 knots in a hull with a displacement of 5000 tons.

In April 1935, after much internal discussion over the need for a small cruiser given that the 'Tribals' were then being ordered, two further sketch designs were proffered, one similar to design Q, but with less protection to reduce the displacement to 4500 tons, and the other with twin 4.7in/45 mounts for the main battery as carried by the 'Tribals'.[2] This second variant would displace 200 tons more. DNC offered the option of mounting a planned 5.1in/50 gun, which was considered to be the largest gun that could be 'manhandled' in a seaway. When this gun's development was abandoned when it was determined that, at 108lb, the fixed rounds were too heavy, the decision was made to proceed instead with the development of the 5.25in/50 QF Mk I, which fired separate rounds.[3] In November 1935, the Naval Staff decided to delay the final decisions concerning the design of the new small cruiser until this new gun was available.[4]

With that decision, the basic design of the *Dido* class was fixed. DNC produced a pair of alternative designs in January 1936; both alternatives carried five twin 5.25in mounts, differing primarily in the arrangement of the power plant. In April, Chatfield ordered DNC to proceed with detailed design

The small cruisers of the Royal Navy's *Dido* class were originally conceived as flotilla leaders, not as the anti-aircraft cruisers they were often thought to be. The mistake is perhaps understandable given that their main battery was the 5.25in/50 Mk I in twin gunhouses, similar to those used as the DP secondary battery on the Royal Navy's new capital ships. It seems as if no two of the eleven ships in this class carried exactly the same gunnery outfit; in part this was because the British shipbuilding industry, suddenly inundated with orders in 1937 after more than a dozen lean years, could not produce enough of the 5.25in mounts. Intended to carry five of these mounts on the centreline, three forward and two aft, only six had the full set; most of the rest had four. One of those completed with only four main-battery gunhouses was HMS *Phoebe* (43), seen here in June 1943. She was completed with a 4in/45 Mk V in 'Q' position (the upper forward superfiring position). On 23 October 1942, she had been torpedoed off the coast of the Congo; from January until June 1943, she was repaired at the New York Navy Yard, where she received three quadruple 40mm/56 Bofors mounts, including one in 'Q' position. The 5.25in mount in 'A' position has been moved to 'B' position and the 'A' position blanked off in this image. When she returned to England, *Phoebe* had a spare 5.25in mount installed in 'A' position; other ships in the class that had been completed with five such mounts were having their 'Q' mount removed at this time to allow for the addition of more light AA weapons. (NARA)

Two of the ships in the *Dido* class, including HMS *Charybdis* (88), seen here in 1942, carried no 5.25in mounts at all. These were completed with eight 4.5in/45 Mk III guns in twin mounts, two forward and two aft. This was an excellent weapon, but the all-up round proved to be too heavy to be manhandled in rough weather; later marks went to separate rounds.

of the alternative with a unit machinery arrangement and a projected displacement of 5100 tons. It would be a mistake to believe that this ship was designed to be an anti-aircraft cruiser; despite the intent to use the 5.25in/50 as a DP gun, it proved to be a poor AA weapon for a number of reasons. (The Royal Navy was in the process of introducing into service a true DP weapon for use in its aircraft carriers and modernised capital ships, the 4.5in/45 QF Mk I, but this weapon was rejected as the main-battery weapon of the planned fleet-support cruisers because it was thought that it would fire too light a shell to be effective stopping an enemy destroyer attack.[5]) For one thing, the original twin mount envisaged for the 5.25in/50 was an open mount, so that when firing at aircraft targets, it was assumed that only one mount forward and aft would be able to fire, any others would be unservable due to blast effects to the other gun crews. Additionally, with a maximum train and elevation rate of 10°/second, the 5.25in gun could not track a modern high-speed aircraft. Even if it could have tracked the targets, the rate of fire of 7–8rpm was too slow to be effective.[6] Before construction began, DNC was informed that a long-trunk Between Deck (BD) twin mount was available for the 5.25in gun; this mount, while somewhat heavier, had the advantage of being fully enclosed, thus allowing all mounts to engage HA targets simultaneously, and also lowered the magazines below the waterline, allowing some reduction in armour without loss of protection, but was quite cramped internally. With this change, the design was finalised in February 1937, and funding for five of the class were included in the 1936–7 building programme. The specifications to which these ships were intended to be built are as follows; as will be seen, circumstances caused some considerable variation, particularly in the main-battery size and arrangement:

Dido Class

Displacement (std):	5600 tons; 6850 tons (deep)
Length (oa):	512ft
Beam (max):	50ft 6in
Draft (mean):	16ft 10in (actual)
Power plant:	62,000shp; Parsons geared turbines driving four shafts; four Admiralty three-drum water-tube boilers
Speed:	32.25 knots (std); 30.75 knots (deep)
Range (designed):	5500nm @ 16 knots; 1100 tons oil fuel
Protection (side):	3in NCA (in way of engineering spaces only)
Protection (horiz):	1in Ducol (over engineering spaces at Middle Deck level); 2in NCA (crown of main-battery magazines)
Armament (main):	10 x 5.25in/50 Mk I (5 x 2 – three forward and two aft)
Armament (AA):	8 x 2pdr Mk VIII pompom (2 x 4)
Armament (torp):	6 x 21in (2 x 3)[7]

Eventually, eleven *Dido*s were built to essentially the original design – the five in the 1936–7 programme, two the following year, three in the 1938–9 programme and one of six small cruisers in the 1939 Emergency Programme (five were

The Royal Navy liked the idea of the *Dido*s and followed them up with an order for five more before any of the original eleven had entered service. The follow-on ships were almost identical; their funnels were vertical rather than raked and they all carried only four 5.25in gunhouses. In this view of the midsection of HMNZS *Bellona* (63), taken in April 1947, she looks essentially as she did at the end of the war. The fact that she never was, in the minds of the Sea Lords, intended to act solely as an anti-aircraft cruiser can be seen from the fact that she has, atop her bridge, both a conventional DCT and an HADT. (SLV/AGC)

completed to a slightly modified design, known as the *Bellona* class) – but, due to short supply of the 5.25in/50 turrets, which were also needed as the secondary battery of the *King George V* class battleships, only six were delivered with all five main-battery turrets. Three, including *Dido*, were completed with only four main-battery turrets, and two had four 4.5in/45 QF Mk III twin turrets as their main battery. The five *Bellona*s were designed from the beginning to carry only four main-battery turrets.

These ships, as befitted their derivation as flotilla leaders, had separate dedicated LA and AA directors in the primary control positions forward, the idea being they might be called on to engage surface and aerial targets simultaneously. The LA DCT was sited atop the bridge, feeding data to an AFCT Mk VI* located in the transmitting station below decks.[8] Above and abaft the DCT, on a stub mast, was an HADT connected to a High-Angle Calculating Table Mk IV*, co-located in the transmitting station. A combined LA/HA DCT was sited on the after superstructure.

HMS *Dido* (37) was not the first of the class to be laid down or completed. The first to be laid down was HMS *Naiad* (93), whose keel was laid at Hawthorne Leslie, Tyneside, on 26 August 1937; the first to complete was HMS *Bonaventure* (31) at Scotts, Greenock, on 24 May 1940.

Small as Required: The *Atlanta* Class

Unlike the British, the Americans had no pre-existing desire to build smaller cruisers. However, a number of factors pushed the US Navy in that direction. One was the Vinson-Trammell Act, passed by the US Congress in 1934, which authorised the construction of 'underage' naval strength up to the maximum limit allowed by treaty.[9] Another was the Second London Treaty of 1936, which established the limits at which cruisers would be considered 'overage'.[10] Additionally, that treaty set the gun calibre and displacement limit for cruisers at 6.1in guns and 8000 tons. Following those rules, the US Navy, once it completed the cruisers authorised in 1929 and funded by the Vinson-Trammell Act, would not be able to build any more cruisers until the *Omaha*s reached 'overage', which, for the first two, would occur in 1939. The remaining eight *Omaha*s, laid down later, would not reach 'overage' until 1943–5. Given the rules for ship replacement written into the First London Treaty, replacement ships of cruiser size could be laid down three years before the planned replacement date.[11] With only minimal fudging of the rules, the General Board was able to justify the replacement of the first two *Omaha*s by the last two *Brooklyn*s, which were laid down in late December 1936. (The United States could get away with laying down this final pair of 10,000-ton light cruisers because the Second London Treaty did not come into effect until 1 January 1937.[12] They would fit within the tonnage limit defined in the First London Treaty for sub-category (*b*) after subtracting the first two *Omaha*s, if one squinted at the numbers. Regardless, the Second London Treaty effectively removed all aggregate tonnage limitations.) However, when the time came to begin replacing the remaining *Omaha*s, no such juggling, no matter how tempting, would be permissible. They would each be limited to 8000 tons standard displacement.

Faced with the problem of defining a useful cruiser within the limits defined in the Second London Treaty, in July 1936 the General Board turned to the various bureaux and fleet elements, seeking their opinions.[13] As might be expected, the range of opinions varied considerably, ranging all the way from an 8000-ton version of a *Brooklyn* class general-purpose cruiser to a smaller one in the 4000 tons–5000 tons range intended specifically as a flotilla leader. Attempting to draw a single set of characteristics from the wide range of responses, in December 1936, the CNO, Standley, recommended that ten new cruisers of between 5000 tons–7000 tons be constructed. The General Board asked Preliminary Design to generate a 'spectrum series' of sketch designs between 3500 tons and 8000 tons for comparison purposes.

The set of sketch designs delivered in January 1937 fell into three fairly distinct groups: 1) a destroyer-leader-type of 3000–3500 tons with a speed of 36 knots; 2) a light general-purpose cruiser of 5000–5500 tons with a speed of 34.5 knots; and 3) a larger general-purpose cruiser of 7500–8000 tons with a speed of 33 knots.[14] One feature all the designs shared was a main battery of 6in/47 guns and a secondary battery of 5in/38 guns. The reaction of the General Board was that this combination, although it had been approved for the last two *Brooklyn*s – four twin 5in/38 gunhouses replacing the eight single 5in/25s of the seven earlier ships – was undesirable. The characteristics of the two weapons were too similar; the new, smaller cruiser should be armed with a single-sized main battery of DP mountings of one calibre or the other. (Of course, the DP single-mountings for the 5in/38 already existed at this point and the twin mountings were under development for the two final *Brooklyn*s, while any DP mountings for the 6in/47 existed only as design studies.)

In mid-June 1937, the General Board convened a hearing to debate the merits and practicalities of the various options.[15] The CNO's representative strongly supported the alternative that mounted the twin 5in/38 mounts, but his opinion was far from universally approved. Another day of discussion led to narrowing the choice down to two alternatives: one armed with four twin 6in/47 mounts on a displacement of approximately 6500 tons, the other with seven twin 5in/38 mounts on about 5500 tons. While both ships had their advocates, the former seemed to be favoured by more in the fleet and by a majority of the General Board until a board meeting in September, when the head of BuOrd revealed that not only did no design for a DP 6in/47 mount exist, but that there was little, if any, chance that the design for such a mount could be ready in time for the ships to be laid down as planned.

With the choice of main battery simplified, Preliminary Design returned to the task of designing the new, small cruiser, producing a pair of sketch designs for ships of approximate 6000 tons, a speed in the range of 32.5–34 knots, an armour belt for the magazines and engineering spaces providing an immune zone against destroyer weapons from 6000–16,000yd, endurance of 9000nm at 15 knots and AA armament comprising three quadruple 1.1in/75 mounts and eight 0.50cal MGs. They differed in that one had a main battery of eight twin 5in/38 mounts in gunhouses with splinter protection 1.25in thick, while the other had only four main-battery mounts with 4in armour protection. As much as the extra protection for the gun crews may have been desirable, the variant with the up-armoured gunhouses was not pursued further. The sketch design with eight twin main-battery mounts was approved by the new CNO, Admiral William D Leahy, on 2 March 1938 with a few minor revisions – the 0.50cal MGs and fuel for 500nm of steaming were sacrificed to allow the shipping of a pair of triple 21in torpedo tubes with one set of reloads.[16] In essentially this form, the first four *Atlanta* class light cruisers were ordered on 25 April 1939, to the following specifications:

Atlanta Class

Displacement (std):	6000 tons (design); 8340 tons (full load)
Length (oa):	541ft 6in
Beam (wl):	53ft 2in
Draft (mean):	20ft 6in (full load)
Power plant:	75,000shp; Westinghouse geared turbines driving two shafts; four Babcock & Wilcox boilers
Speed:	32.5 knots (design); 33.67 knots (actual)
Range (designed):	8500nm @ 15 knots; 1360 tons oil fuel
Range (actual):	7530nm @ 15 knots; 1578 tons oil fuel
Protection (side):	3.75in–1.8in STS external belt (in way of engineering spaces and main-battery magazines)
Protection (horiz):	1.25in STS (over engineering spaces and main-battery magazines)
Armament (main):	16 x 5in/38 Mk 12 (8 x 2 – three forward, three aft and two abreast after superstructure)
Armament (AA):	16 x 1.1in/75 Mk 1 (4 x 4); 8 x 20mm/70 Mk 2 (8 x 1)
Armament (torp):	8 x 21in (4 x 2)[17]

The Americans built a class of ships that were in some ways similar to the *Dido*s, yet were also quite different. The lead ship of the class, USS *Atlanta* (CL51), is seen here from USS *Tangier* (AV8) on 25 October 1942, just a few weeks before her loss off Guadalcanal. Like the *Dido*s, the *Atlanta*s had a DP gun as their main battery; in this case it was the excellent 5in/38 Mk 12 in eight dual gunhouses. To direct those guns she has two Mk 37 DP directors, each topped by an antenna for the FD (Mk 4) fire-control radar. On her foremast, she has the antenna for an SC air-search radar. As with the other early members of the class, *Atlanta* was completed with four 1.1in/75 quadruple mounts. Note the rather 'un-American' knuckle at the bow; the *Atlantas* were among the only US Navy cruisers to exhibit this 'feature' – it would reappear on a few classes of American ships after the war, as will be seen. (NARA)

After the first four *Atlantas*, seven more followed armed with two fewer main-battery gunhouses, the two waist mounts being sacrificed to allow more medium and light AA guns to be shipped. This 18 September 1944 image of USS *Flint* (CL97) was made by the builder, Bethlehem, San Francisco, and was annotated with the radars (SC, SG, Mk 12 and Mk 22), jammers (BK and BL) and IFF (Mk 3) called out. (NHHC)

Rumours persisted that these ships were intended to reach 40 knots, which was in fact never the case. The lead yard, Federal Shipbuilding and Drydock Co, Kearny, NJ, specialised in building destroyers, using the firm of Gibbs & Cox to provide the expertise in high-temperature, high-pressure steam engineering. (The power plant of the *Atlantas* employed steam at 850°F at 665psi, certainly greater heat and pressure than had been employed in any cruiser to date.) The decision had been made to substitute 40mm/56 Mk 1 Bofors twin mounts for the 1.1in/75 mounts, but these were not yet available, and the first ships in this class were completed with the originally-planned 1.1in mounts. The triple torpedo tubes were replaced by quadruple tubes without reloads when the latter became available. The first ship in the class to be laid down was actually USS *San Diego* (CL53) at Bethlehem, Quincy, on 27 March 1940. All of the first four were commissioned in the early months of 1942. A second group of four to the same design were ordered from Bethlehem, San Francisco, on 9 September 1940. Three more ordered in 1943 from Federal, Kearny completed the series. All seven of the later ships substituted a greatly-increased medium and light AA fit for the two 5in gunhouses flanking the after superstructure. The last three were built to a somewhat modified design, generated in 1942, intended to reduce topweight issues caused by the proliferation of light and medium AA guns and their directors; not only were the two 'waist' main-battery mounts deleted,

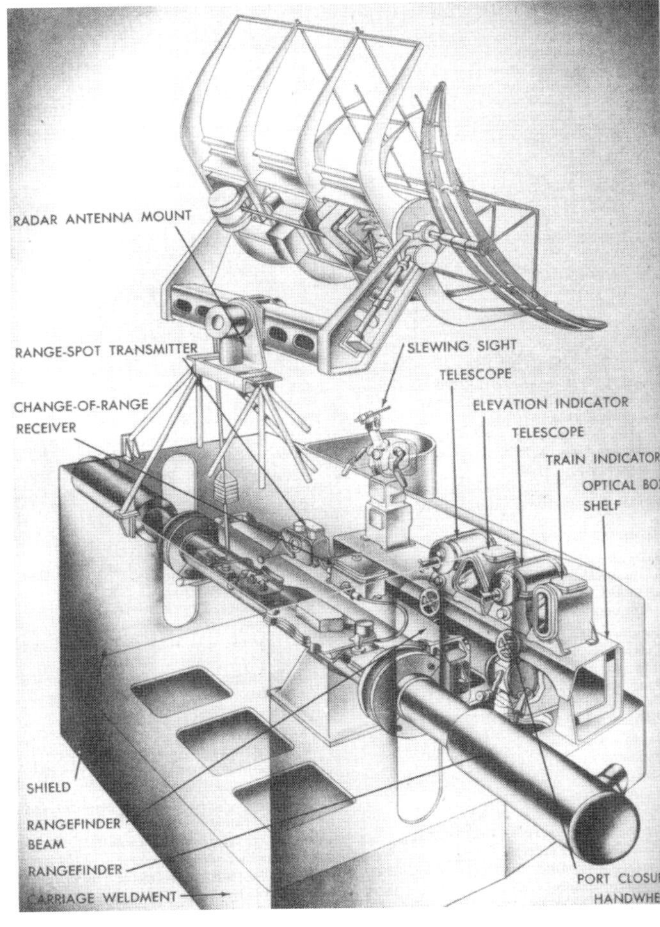

One thing that distinguished the *Atlantas* from the *Didos* was the use of a single DP fire-control director for the main battery. The Mk 37 DP director integrated an optical rangefinder and a fire-control radar; in this diagram from the 1950 version of the NAVPERS 16116 Manual of Naval Gunnery, the internal workings of the director are shown, as well as Mk 12 and Mk 22 antennas mounted above it. (The Mk 22 is the narrow 'orange peel' antenna used for height-finding to the right of the main two-lobe Mk 12.) The director captain keeps the target in sight with the 'Slewing Sight'. All data generated by the radars, rangefinder and telescopes were fed to the Mk 1 computer below decks. (USN)

The last three ships of the *Atlanta* class form a distinctive sub-class, completed with mounts Nos 2 and 5 at the Main Deck level and a smaller superstructure. One of this series, USS *Spokane* (CL120), is seen at launch from the Federal Shipbuilding and Drydock Co, Kearny, NJ, on 22 September 1945. (NHHC)

but mounts No 2 and 5 were lowered to Main Deck level and mounts No 3 and 4 to the 01 level. Additionally, a lower and smaller forward bridge structure was introduced.

It must be noted that these ships, like the *Dido*s, were not designed to be anti-aircraft cruisers, despite often being described as such. In fact, their fire-control set-up suited them for the anti-aircraft role; they had the well-regarded Mk 37 DP director fore-and-aft. These were connected to a Mk 1 computer with its associated stable element located in the plotting room, which generated fire-control solutions. From the beginning, they carried radar – initially an FD (Mk 4) fire-control set – on each director. One sign that these ships were not seen as anti-aircraft cruisers by the US Navy, at least not at first, was the fact that they were completed with a sonar outfit and depth-charge rails and throwers. The latter were removed soon after the first units were completed when it was realised that these ships would never be used to hunt submarines.[18]A unique feature of these ships was their forward hull form, which incorporated a very British-looking 'knuckle' in the place of a more typical flared bow form. They were among the few American cruisers to have this bow form.

Suitably Small: '*Les Bébés Français*' and Other Minelayers

During the late World War, extensive minefields had been laid off the north-western coast of France that had a dramatic, some might say decisive, effect on the outcome of the war. This led the Germans to develop a pair of 'fast minelayers', the cruiser-sized *Brummer* class, which were reputed to have much higher speed than they actually could achieve. After the war, the British responded by building a much larger – 6740 tons standard v 4385 tons design displacement – purpose-built minelayer named HMS *Adventure* (27), which was laid down in November 1922. The French felt the need to reciprocate and drew up a design for their own dedicated cruiser-minelayer – originally classified just as a *mouilleur de mines de surface*, but later reclassified as a *croiseur mouilleur de mines* – as part of the 1925 *tranche*.[19] There was remarkably little debate or dissention in the development of the design, which was to mount a main battery of two 203mm/50 in single mounts, a secondary battery of four single 75mm/50 Mle 1922 HA guns and four single 37mm/50 Mle 1925 HA guns, plus room for 220–270 mines, depending on the type carried, or 1000 troops. Due to overload at French shipyards, this ship, *Pluton*, could not be laid down for three years, until April 1928, during which time it was decided to replace the large main-battery guns and the larger of her secondary-battery guns with four 138.6mm/40 Mle 1923 single-mount guns, a gun which was intended for LA fire only, but, because it had a relatively high trunnion to permit higher elevations, it proved difficult to load at lower elevation angles and generally had a lower rate of fire than intended.[20] To provide an adequate AA battery, the number of 37mm/50 single mounts was increased to ten. The specifications of *Pluton*, as built, were as follows:

Pluton

Displacement (std):	5300 tons (design)
Length (oa):	500ft 4in
Beam:	51ft 2in
Draft (maximum):	17ft
Power plant:	57,000shp; Breguet geared turbines driving two shafts; four du Temple small-tube boilers
Speed:	30 knots (designed)
Range (designed):	4500nm @ 14 knots; 1200 tons oil fuel
Armament (main):	4 x 138.6mm/40 Mle 1923 (4 x 1 – two forward and two aft)
Armament (AA):	10 x 37mm/50 Mle 1925 HA (10 x 1)
Armament (mines):	220–250 Sautter-Harlé H5/270 Breguet B4 mines[21]

Note the total lack of armour. Almost immediately after her completion at Lorient in January 1932, it was decided to convert *Pluton* to a gunnery training ship; this required that she mount the most current fire-control equipment, which

Reminiscent of the cruiser-sized minelayers built by the Germans during the First World War, *Pluton* was designed by the *Marine Nationale* as a large, fast minelayer for use in a Mediterranean war against the Italians. This image shows her during her trials, still with her original main battery of four single 138.6mm/40 Mle 1923 guns. Soon after entering service she was converted into a gunnery training ship and her armament was suitably altered. (Courtesy of John Jordan)

The purpose-built training cruiser *Jeanne d'Arc* joined the *Marine Nationale* in 1931; she is seen here on one of her regular training cruises that took her around the world, off San Diego, CA, 8 December 1934. Note the oversized main-battery turrets; these were essentially the same turrets as on the *Duguay-Trouin* class, but made wider to allow room for the several extra instructor/officers who were to observe and train the cadets who would be manning the guns. (NHHC)

required the replacement of her light foremast with a heavier mast to carry a HA director. An LA director was mounted on her bridge structure. She had four single 75mm/50 Mle 1924 HA guns fitted and six twin 13.2mm/76 Hotchkiss MGs, so that her trainees could practise on the full range of then-current French HA weapons. Eight of the 37mm mounts were removed in an only partially-successful attempt to counter excessive topweight due to all the added weaponry. She remained in essentially this form until 1939, when she was converted back into a minelayer, most of the extra fire-control equipment was landed, and she was in this form when she was lost at Casablanca soon after the war began due to mishandling of fused mines.

Since 1912, the *Marine Nationale* had a training ship for officer cadets and apprentice engineers named *Jeanne d'Arc*. The first training ship with that name, actually the fourth French warship to carry it, had been an armoured cruiser launched in 1899, which had been employed as a training ship before the First World War, had been converted back to a fully functional warship for the duration, but then reverted to her training role after the war. By the late 1920s, however, the old ship was showing her age and the *Marine Nationale* decide to construct a purpose-built training ship that could both provide cadets and apprentices experience with up-to-date equipment and could also be a useful asset in the event of war.[22] This ship, given the elaborate description *croiseur école d'application des enseignes de vaisseau*, was funded in the 1926 *tranche*, but, like *Pluton*, was not started immediately.

The initial proposal from the *État-major* was for a ship smaller and slower than *Pluton*, but that was rejected by the French legislature as being of no value in wartime. The naval staff responded with a revised proposal for a ship of approximately 6500 tons, with gun armament similar to the *Duguay-Trouin* class, a speed of 25 knots and endurance in the range of 6000nm. This ship, given the name *Jeanne d'Arc*, was approved and a contract placed with AC St-Nazaire-Penhoët, with the following specifications:

Jeanne d'Arc

Displacement (std):	6496 tons (design)
Length (oa):	557ft 9in
Beam:	58ft
Draft (maximum):	21ft
Power plant:	32,500shp; Parsons geared turbines driving two shafts; four du Temple small-tube boilers
Speed:	25 knots (designed)
Range (designed):	6670nm @ 11 knots; 1400 tons oil fuel
Protection (side):	0.79in 60kg steel (in way of main-battery magazines)
Armament (main):	8 x 155mm/50 Mle 1920 (4 x 2 – two forward and two aft)
Armament (AA):	4 x 75mm/60 Mle 1924 HA (4 x 1); 2 x 37mm/50 Mle 1925 HA (2 x 1)
Armament (torp):	2 x 550mm Mle 1923D (2 x 1)
Aircraft:	2 (CAMS 37); two compressed-air catapults[23]

Although the specifications called for two aircraft and two catapults to be carried between the after funnel and the mainmast, the catapults were never fitted. The aircraft were carried through 1940, but they had to be hoisted by crane into and out of the water; after that date they were landed. *Jeanne d'Arc* had two long shelter decks aft of her forward superstructure to accommodate 156 trainees, giving her an appearance that some said made her look like a cruise liner. Her four main-battery turrets were functionally identical to those in the *Duguay-Trouin* class, but were made physically larger to allow room for instructors as well as officer-trainees and guncrew. The fire-control outfit, as was the case with *Pluton*, was regularly updated to reflect the state-of-the-art in French naval technology.

The Royal Navy built their own fast cruiser-minelayers for much the same reasons as did the French. The *Abdiel* class were as often as not used as fast transports in the Mediterranean or Indian Ocean as they were as minelayers, their speed of close to 40 knots making them attractive for the role despite their lack of armour. For that reason, they were often in harm's way, and three of the six in the class were lost in the war. One of the survivors, HMS *Manxman* (I70), is seen here on 29 March 1946. (SLV/AGC)

As part of the 1938 building programme, the Royal Navy included four fast minelayers. Similar in concept to *Adventure*, but 20 per cent smaller and significantly faster, they were designed for nocturnal operations off enemy coasts. As such, the *Abdiel* class minelayers stretched the lower edge of the definition of the cruiser classification at a standard displacement of 2650 tons and a main battery of six 4in/45 guns. These four, and the two additional sisters laid down in 1941 as part of the War Emergency programme, are included for the sake of completeness; nonetheless, these ships fought hard during the war, proving to be valuable as fast transports due to their top speed, which approached 40 knots in trials condition and 38 knots full load. Three of the original four were lost in the Mediterranean. Without armour, speed was their only protection; it often wasn't enough when operating in narrow waters.

Small Again: The '*Capitani Romani*' Class

In the on-going development of the '*Condottieri*', the Italians had built ships that became increasingly like 'conventional' light cruisers. In 1935, the decision was made by the *Stato Maggiore della Marina* to revert to smaller, faster 'oceanic scouts' (*esploratori oceanici*) largely in reaction to the continued French construction of ever-larger *contre-torpilleurs*, particularly the 2569-ton *Le Fantasque* class of 1933–4, followed by the *Mogador* class laid down in 1936–7. These large super-destroyers were armed with a powerful new 138.6mm/50 gun. MARICOMINAV was directed to develop a design for an Italian counterpart, the work being turned over to General (GN) Umberto Pugliese and Ignazio Alfano.[24] They started from the design of the large destroyer *Tashkent*, that had been ordered in September 1935 from OTO, Livorno by the Soviet government. OTO was also the lead yard for this class of 'oceanic scouts' which shared a number of characteristics with *Tashkent*. They both had large, lightly-constructed hulls, mixing longitudinal and traditional laterally-framed construction, although the new design had a flush-deck hull with a long amidships deckhouse. Armament was to be eight 135mm/45 Mod 1938 in twin turrets, with six of a new 65mm/64 DP gun as the secondary battery. They were to be fitted with a power plant capable of generating 110,000shp, which would give them a top speed of 40 knots. Pugliese and Alfano made every

The Italian influence on Soviet Russian naval design dates from the 1930s, when the fascist regime was one of the few that would sell arms and related materials to the communist state. One form this took was the large destroyer *Tashkent*, ordered from the OTO yard at Livorno to the basic design shown here dated 8 February 1935. This ship was to be armed with six 130mm/50 B13 Pattern 1936 guns in twin mounts of Russian manufacture. She was ordered in September 1935 and delivered in February 1939 to the Soviet Black Sea Fleet, armed with a provisional armament of 130mm/55s in single mounts because the twin mounts were not ready yet. The designed main battery (although not in the planned DP gunhouses) was fitted in 1941. She was nicknamed the 'Blue Cruiser' because of the Italian standard blue-grey colour in which she was painted. Damaged early in the German invasion of the Soviet Union, she sank at Novorossisk in July 1942. (via Enrico Cernuschi)

Comparing this profile view of RN *Attilio Regolo*, seen in 1942, to the design of *Tashkent* makes the lineal descent obvious. The small cruisers of the *'Capitani Romani'* class displaced 800 tons more than *Tashkent* on a hull of very similar length. The extra tonnage was spent providing a fourth twin turret (mounting 135mm/45 Mod 1938 guns) and greater breadth for better stability. Only four of the twelve ships of this class were completed; one (*San Marco*, ex-*Giulio Germanico*) was scuttled incomplete in 1943 and not finished until 1956. (USMM via Enrico Cernuschi)

effort to meet the target displacement of 3400 tons, but even after sacrificing all armour protection (excepting only some splinter protection for the bridge and gunhouses) and replacing the 65mm/64 guns, the development of which was more than a year behind schedule, with eight 37mm/54 RM 1939s, they exceeded their planned target by approximately 350 tons. (They missed their target displacement despite the deletion from the design of the floatplane and aircraft-handling crane originally planned for these ships.[25]) Nonetheless, the design was received enthusiastically and twelve ships to this design were ordered as part of the 1939 building programme. All were to be named after military leaders of the Roman period, which gave the class its name, the '*Capitani Romani*'. They were built to the following specifications:

'Capitani Romani' Class

Displacement (std):	3686 tons
Length (oa):	468ft 9in
Beam (wl):	47ft 3in
Draft (mean):	16ft (deep)
Power plant:	110,000shp (design); Beluzzo SR/Parsons geared turbines driving two shafts; four Thornycroft boilers
Speed:	40 knots (design)
Range (designed):	4300nm @ 17 knots; 1400 tons oil fuel
Armament (main):	8 x 135mm/45 Mod 1938 (4 x 2 – two forward and two aft)
Armament (AA):	8 x 37mm/54 RM 1939 (8 x 1); 8 x 20mm/70 RM 1935 Scotti-Isotta Fraschini machine guns (4 x 2)
Armament (torp):	8 x 533mm (2 x 4)[26]

Eleven of these twelve ships were laid down in September and October of 1939 – one, RN *Giulio Germanico*, was laid down at Castellammare di Stabia yard in April of that year in an attempt to boost the local economy – but the exigencies of war meant that only eight were launched and just three were actually commissioned into the *Regia Marina*. (When the Italians found, to their dismay, that the defeat of France and the subsequent conquest of Greece did not end their involvement in the Second World War, but rather they found themselves mired down in an open-ended war in Russia, the decision was made to lower the priority on the completion of the '*Capitani Romani*'.) The first to be completed was RN *Attilio Regolo*, at OTO, Livorno, on 14 May 1942. For a brief period in the summer of 1943, the three '*Capitani Romani*' in service operated with the '*Condottiero*' RN *Luigi Cadorna* as a fast minelaying and raiding squadron operating out of Taranto.

Perfectly Small: The *Katori*, *Agano* and *Oyodo* Classes

Like the French, the Imperial Japanese Navy had been using ageing armoured cruisers, three of them, as training ships for their officer cadets.[27] The plan was to scrap these old ships in the mid-1930s, replacing them with three *Kuma* class light cruisers, which the First London Treaty had earmarked for retirement when the latest *Mogami* class cruisers were completed. However, when the Japanese denounced the treaty regime at the end of 1934, it was decided to retain the old 5500-ton light cruisers as 'heavy torpedo-equipped ships', which raised the issue of replacing the old armoured cruisers all over again. The issue was given additional urgency when one of those old cruisers, *Asama*, was badly damaged in October 1935. The Naval Staff finally acted in 1937, adding the request for three purpose-built training cruisers to the May 1937 budget; funding for two ships was included in the 1938 building programme. A third ship was included in the large Fourth Replenishment Programme of 1939, the so-called 'Circle-4 Programme'. A fourth was funded as part of the 1941 building programme. The staff requirements for these ships outlined a standard displacement of 5800 tons, a top speed of 18 knots and accommodations for 375 midshipmen or trainees from specialist branches, such as engineering. The task of designing these ships was handed off to Lieutenant Commander Ozono Daisuke of the Fourth Section of the Navy Technical Department, under Fukuda's supervision.

The Japanese also built a class of training cruisers, with the intent that they should become area fleet flagships in time of war. The high freeboard of the class-leader *Katori*, seen here at Shanghai in September 1940, shows how they could provide ample accommodations for a fleet command staff. (She was obviously being employed in this role already at this time, as evidenced by the Vice Admiral's pennant flying from the mainmast.) In their training role, they were provided with the most up-to-date fire-control suite in the Imperial Japanese Navy. (NHHC)

Their design carried markings that indicated the Japanese considered these ships to be auxiliaries, rather than cruiser-class warships, but the Americans always classed them as cruisers and they are included here for that reason. Their specifications at the time of their construction were:

Training Cruisers: Katori Class

Displacement (std):	5890 tons
Length (oa):	405ft 2in
Beam (max):	52ft 4in
Draft (mean):	18ft 10in
Power plant:	8000shp; Kanpon geared turbines driving two shafts; three Kanpon three-drum water-tube boilers; two Kanpon No 22 Mod 10 4-cycle 10-cyl 1800shp diesels (one diesel geared to each shaft)
Speed:	18 knots (designed)
Range (designed):	9900nm @ 12 knots; 600 tons oil fuel
Range (actual):	7000–7500nm @ 14 knots; 2215 tons oil fuel
Armament (main):	4 x 14cm/50 Type 3 (2 x 2 – one forward and one aft)
Armament (AA):	4 x 12.7cm/40 Type 89 (2 x 2); 4 x 25mm/60 Type 96 (2 x 2)
Armament (torp):	4 x 53.3cm Type 93 (2 x 2); 4 reloads
Aircraft:	1 (1 x Kawanishi E7K2 Type 94 No.2 reconnaissance seaplane), one catapult[28]

The first two ships in the *Katori* class were laid down in August and October 1938 at Mitsubishi, Yokohama, the other two in 1940 and 1941. The first three were completed, the last of the three, *Kashii*, just before the war began. The fourth was cancelled when the war began and was broken up on the stocks. It was planned from their inception, in the event of war, that these ships would be employed as area fleet flagships, for which they would be well suited given their spacious accommodation. This is, in fact, how they were employed when the war in the Pacific began; for example, Vice Admiral Inoue Shigeyoshi, who commanded the Japanese 4th Fleet during the Coral Sea Campaign in 1942, did so, in part, from his flagship *Kashima*, the second of the *Katori* class training cruisers.

As had been the case with *Jeanne d'Arc*, the Japanese intended to equip these ships with the most up-to-date fire-control suite, so that the officer trainees would gain experience with modern equipment. They were fitted with a Type 94 LA fire-control installation, which comprised a Type 94 director (*hoiban*) atop the pilot house and a Type 94 computer (*shagekiban*) in the transmitting station below decks.[29] The director housed five men, three of whom (the control officer, trainer, pointer/layer and cross-leveller) had binoculars with 12cm or 4.5cm objective lenses.[30] The 14ft 9in rangefinder for the main battery was located abaft and above the director in a separate housing. The Type 94 computer was a semitachymetric device, meaning it had partial ability to develop predictive solutions based on automatic data input. Bearing and cross-level data were transmitted automatically from the director – later marks of the computer added a stable vertical element that obviated the need for cross-level data from the director and, in fact, sent cross-level information back to the director in the form of a match-needle pointer – and the computer gained own-ship data from the gyrocompass and pitometer log. A range plot was used to visually establish range rate using a light shining through a rotatable slit; after lining up the light with the trace on the range plot, the angle of rotation of the slit corresponded to the range rate. Gun

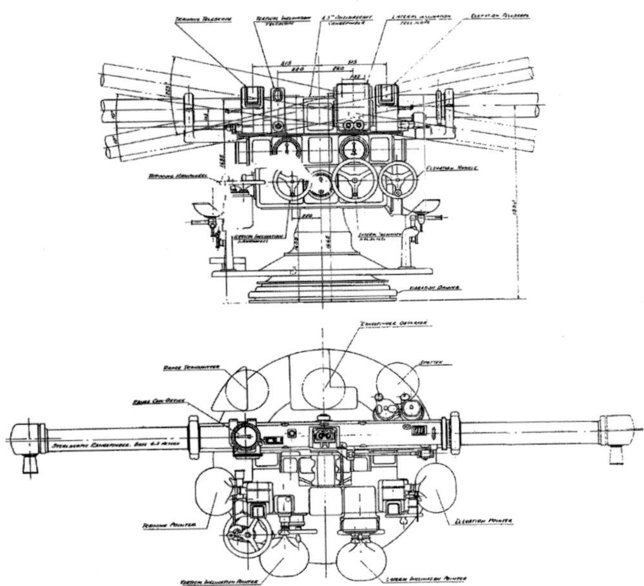

On top of her after superstructure, *Katori* had a Type 94 HA director (*koshaki*) with its incorporated 14ft 9in stabilised stereoscopic rangefinder. As is clear from this diagram, taken from one of the post-war reports made by the US Navy's Technical Mission to Japan sent to evaluate Japanese naval technology, this director required seven men to operate. Three were in back of the rangefinder: the spotter, who identified and tracked targets; the rangefinder operator (observer) and the range transmitter, who passed the range information to the Type 94 HA computer (*kosha shagekiban*) below decks; and four were in front: men who controlled handwheels that allowed the target's azimuth (training angle), elevation and angles of travel split into vertical and horizontal components to be entered. (USN)

bearing and elevation solutions were transmitted directly to the gun turrets.

In the *Katori* class, a Type 94 HA fire-control installation was sited atop the after superstructure. This comprised a Type 94 HA director (*koshaki*), which incorporated a 14ft 9in stereoscopic rangefinder, and a Type 94 HA computer (*kosha shagekiban*) in the transmitting station.[31] The director was manned by seven men, making it very cramped; it automatically supplied the computer with range, training angle, elevation angle and target inclination. The computer supplied the gun mounts with an aiming solution, including training angle, elevation angle and fuse setting for the shells. This equipment was made by the Nippon Optical Co (*Nippon Kogaku Kogyo Kaisha*), the predecessor of the current Nikon Corp.

The Circle-4 Programme of 1939 also included the funds for four ships described as 'destroyer-squadron flagships'.[32] The origin of this requirement goes back to April 1936, when the Naval General Staff, freed from the constraints of the disarmament treaties, proposed a major multi-year naval building programme that included thirteen 6000-ton flagship cruisers for destroyer and submarine squadrons, though none were to be ordered until the second phase of the programme, starting in 1939.[33] In the meanwhile, four 5500-ton light cruisers of the *Nagara* and *Sendai* classes were designated as provisional destroyer squadron leaders and were modified with expanded accommodations for the command staff, upgraded communications facilities and improved night-fighting capabilities (better searchlights and torpedo batteries). These changes did not prove totally satisfactory. Since their conversion had added significant displacement, the modified 5500-ton cruisers were found to be too slow, too short-legged and too cramped; they were generally under-armed compared to the latest American destroyers and in any weather proved to be poor sea boats.[34] Thus, when the time came to prepare a design for a purpose-built destroyer flagship for inclusion in the Circle-4 Programme, the Naval Staff was ready with a defined set of requirements, as in the following specifications:

Destroyer Flagships – Requirements of 27 Nov 1937

Displacement (std):	5000 tons
Speed:	36 knots
Range (designed):	7000nm @ 18 knots
Protection (side):	3.94in NVNC (in way of engineering spaces)
Armament (main):	6 x 15.5cm/60 3rd Year Type (2 x 3 – one forward and one aft)
Armament (AA):	8 x 8cm/60 Type 98 (4 x 2); 6 x 25mm/60 Type 96 (3 x 2)
Armament (torp):	8 x 61cm (2 x 4); 8 reloads
Aircraft:	1, one catapult[35]

As was so frequently the case with such sets of staff requirements, these were wildly unrealistic, and the initial sketch designs presented by the Fourth Section in March 1938 replaced the main battery with three twin 15cm/50 41st Year Type mounts in thinly-protected gunhouses, reduced the number of 8cm mounts to two, lowered the steaming radius by 1000nm and cut the armour protection roughly in half – while extending it to cover the main-battery magazines – and still could not bring the displacement down to less than approximately 6500 tons.[36]

When the authorisation for these ships was approved in March 1939 as part of the Circle-4 Programme, the design responsibility was turned over to Constructor Lieutenant Commander Ozono. As had been the case with the *Katoris*, he chose a relatively conventional hull form, a flush-deck hull without the sinuous weather deck favoured in earlier Japanese cruiser designs. The definitive design was presented to the Naval Staff on 13 October, with the following specifications:

'B' Class Cruisers: Agano Class

Displacement (std):	6652 tons
Length (oa):	571ft 2in

Beam (max):	49ft 10in
Draft (mean):	18ft 6in
Power plant:	100,000shp; Kanpon geared turbines driving four shafts; six Kanpon three-drum water-tube boilers
Speed:	35 knots
Range (designed):	6000nm @ 18 knots; 1420 tons oil fuel
Protection (side):	2.36in CNC external belt (in way of engineering spaces); 2.17in CNC internal box (in way of main-battery magazines)
Protection (horiz):	0.79in CNC (over engineering spaces and magazines)
Armament (main):	6 x 15cm/50 Type 41 (3 x 2 – two forward and one aft)
Armament (AA):	4 x 8cm/60 Type 98 (2 x 2); 6 x 25mm/60 Type 96 (2 x 3); 4 x 13mm/76 Type 93 (2 x 2)
Armament (torp):	8 x 61cm (4 x 2); 8 reloads
Aircraft:	2 (2 x Aichi E13A1 Type 0 reconnaissance seaplanes), one catapult[37]

The *Agano* class flotilla leaders were excellent small light cruisers which had the misfortune of being built too late and in too small numbers to impact the Japanese naval war in any manner. Thrown into battle against long odds, the first three were lost to submarine or carrier air attack, having had no chance to act in their designed capacity of leading Japanese destroyer forces in night attacks against the American fleet. Only the last one completed, *Sakawa*, survived the war and that only because she entered service so late that there was little fighting left for the Imperial Navy to do. She is seen here after the war, being disarmed; one of her quadruple Type 93 torpedo tube mounts is being off-loaded to a lighter. Her radars are marked in the image: the Mk 2 Mod 2 Kai 4 surface-search 'horn' antennas on either side of the bridge are marked '1'; the large 'mattress' antenna of the Type 2 Mk 2 Mod 1 air-search set is marked '2'. (NHHC)

The plan was to build four *Aganos*, the first two of which were to be laid down at Kure Navy Yard, the third at Yokosuka Navy Yard and the fourth at Mitsubishi, Nagasaki, all in early 1940. However, the workload at both government and private shipyards at this time was such that only the one ship assigned to the Yokosuka yard was built where it was intended, and that one was not laid down until September 1941. The remaining three were all built at the Sasebo Navy Yard, the first, *Agano*, being laid down on 18 June 1940. The other two were built at Sasebo on the same slip as *Agano*, each following as the preceding was launched. They had the same fire-control set-up as described for the *Katoris*. The first three would be war losses; only the last to be completed – *Sakawa*, which was commissioned on 30 November 1944 – would survive the war, only to be sunk in the Crossroads nuclear tests after the war.

The April 1936 staff requirement which established the need for the destroyer flagships that eventually became the *Agano* class light cruisers also included a requirement for similarly-sized and equipped flagships for the Imperial Navy's submarine squadrons. Two purpose-built submarine depot ships were constructed in the mid-1920s, which served well, but by the mid-1930s they were deemed to be too slow to perform their intended support functions with the new long-ranging high-speed submarines coming into service. While it was initially presumed that the destroyer and submarine squadron flagship tasks could be carried out by the same class of ships, it soon became obvious that the submarine flagship had special requirements not applicable to a destroyer flagship, including greater range, greater search capability, but less need for a powerful main battery. The following requirements were developed for the Fourth Section:

Submarine Flagships – Requirements of mid-1938

Displacement (std):	5000 tons
Speed:	36 knots
Range (designed):	10,000nm @ 18 knots
Protection (side):	Unspecified
Armament (main):	8 x 12.7cm/40 Type 89 (4 x 2)
Armament (AA):	18 x 25mm/60 Type 96 (9 x 2)
Armament (torp):	Desirable
Aircraft:	6–8 long-range, high-speed reconnaissance aircraft, 1–2 catapults[38]

As was the case with the *Aganos*, these requirements proved to be no more achievable within the target displacement. The sketch design that was submitted to the Naval General Staff on 8 September 1938 was for a ship of 6600 tons with no torpedo tubes, two large catapults on the quarterdeck and six aircraft (four in a hangar just forward of the quarterdeck and two on the catapults). The staff criticised several aspects of this design; specifically, they thought the twin catapults aft would interfere with each other and suggested one catapult instead, sited aft of a larger hangar capable of housing all six aircraft,

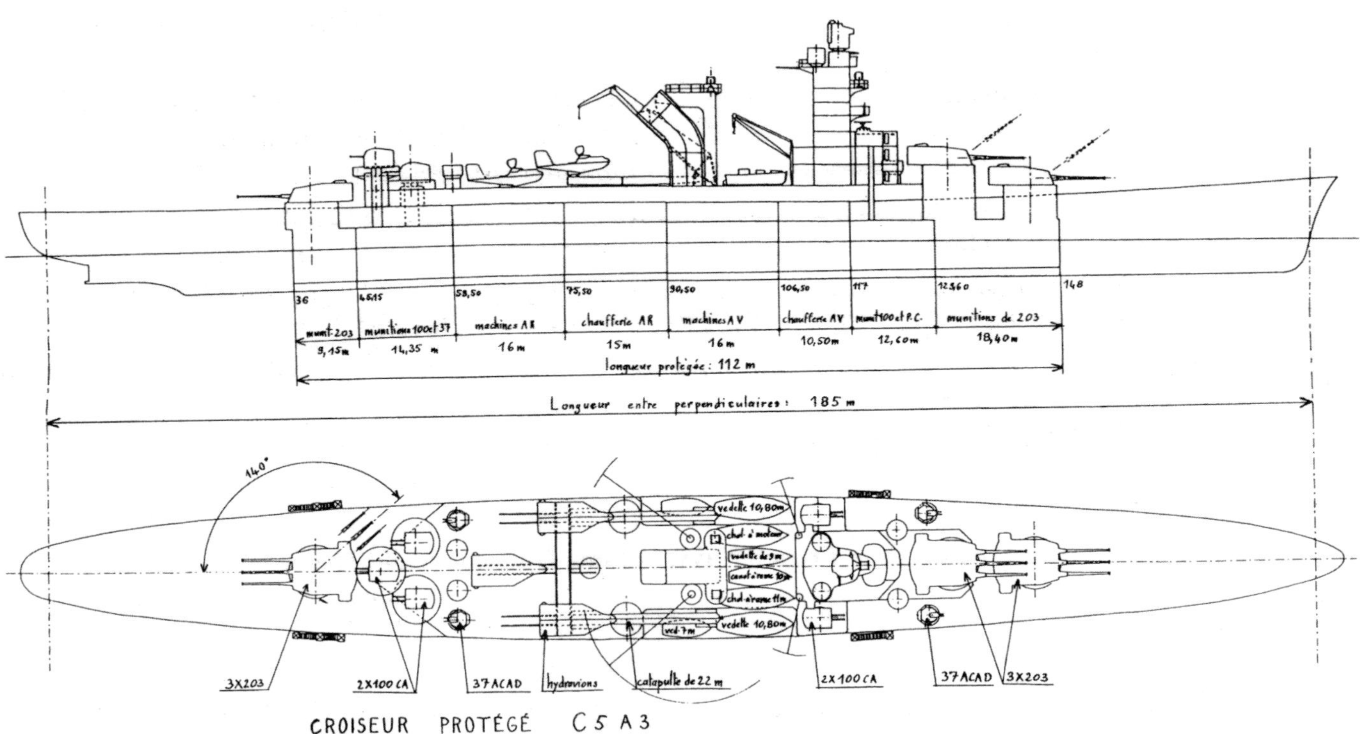

The French plan for a follow-on to their last 'treaty maximum' cruiser, *Algérie*, came in two variants. The design sketch shown here was for the 'C5 A3', where the 'C5' indicated this would follow *Algérie*, which had been 'C4' in the French numbering sequence, and the 'A3' indicated it was to carry three aircraft (*avions*). The armament would have been nine 203mm guns in the main battery, with ten 100mm and eight 37mm as medium and light HA guns. (Moulin/Marines:Guerre/*Warship International*)

and they thought the 12.7cm guns too small to defend these ships against enemy cruisers or destroyers and recommended mounting a pair of the triple 15.5cm/60 3rd Year Type turrets being removed from the *Mogami* class cruisers in their place. Their primary AA battery was to be the new 10cm/65 Type 98 in four twin-mounts; this was easily the best AA weapon the Japanese had developed to date, power-operated, with a high rate of fire and a 28.67lb HE shell massive enough to bring down a large, fast-moving aircraft.[39] In this basic form, two ships of this type were included in the Circle-4 Programme of 1939, the first being ordered from the Kure Navy Yard in December 1939 with the following specifications:

'C' Class Cruisers: Oyodo Class

Displacement (std):	8164 tons
Length (oa):	630ft 3in
Beam (max):	54ft 6in
Draft (mean):	19ft 6in
Power plant:	110,000shp; Kanpon geared turbines driving four shafts; six Kanpon three-drum water-tube boilers
Speed:	35 knots
Range (designed):	8700nm @ 18 knots; 2445 tons oil fuel
Range (actual):	10,315nm @ 18 knots
Protection (side):	2.36in CNC external belt (in way of engineering spaces); 2.95–1.18in CNC internal box (in way of main-battery magazine)
Protection (horiz):	1.18in–1.10in CNC (over engineering spaces); 1.97in–1.10 CNC (over magazine)
Armament (main):	6 x 15.5cm/60 3rd Year Type (2 x 3 – two forward)
Armament (AA):	8 x 10cm/65 Type 98 (4 x 2); 18 x 25mm/60 Type 96 (6 x 3)
Aircraft:	6 (6 x Kawanishi E15K1 Type 2 high-speed reconnaissance seaplanes), one catapult[40]

Due to the same backlog of work that slowed the construction of the *Aganos*, *Oyodo* was not laid down until 14 February 1941, with the second ship of the class to follow as soon as the first was launched. In the event, the second ship was cancelled at the outbreak of war, but construction on *Oyodo* continued, and she was commissioned in February 1943. The E15K1 high-speed reconnaissance seaplane that was supposed to comprise her air unit had a long and troubled development, eventually being produced in small numbers, but never

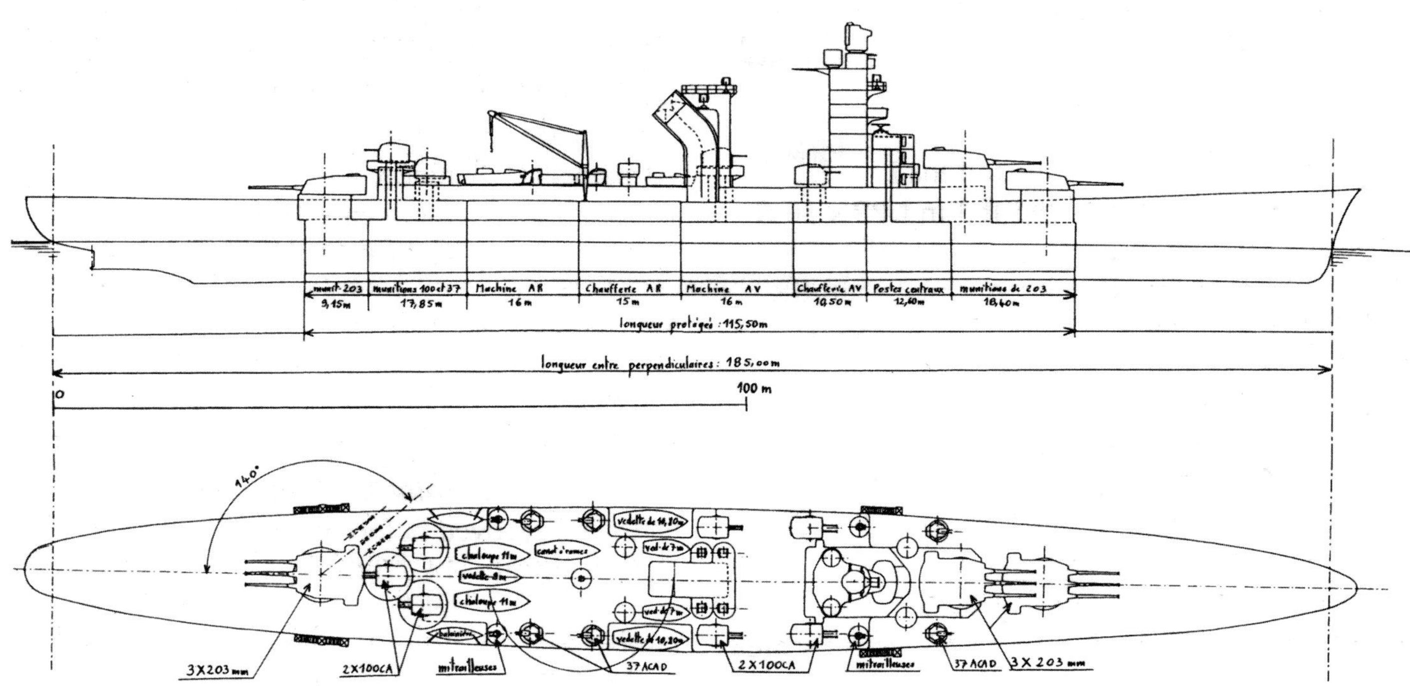

An alternative plan would have been a similar ship with no aircraft – hence the name 'C5 SA1', where 'SA' stood for *'sans aviation'* ('without aircraft'). The weight savings allowed two more mounts of both the 100mm and 37mm guns to be carried as well as some lighter machine guns (*mitrailleuses*). None of the 'C5' designs got past the planning stage before France fell to the Germans in 1940. (Moulin/Marines:Guerre/*Warship International*)

operated from *Oyodo*. When she entered service, she carried Aichi E13A1 Type 0 reconnaissance seaplanes, codenamed 'Jakes', never more than two at a time. Her fire-control installation was the same as the *Katori*s and *Agano*s.

Oyodo was one of the first Japanese warships to receive radar, having a Type 21 air-search set with its mattress antenna installed on the front of the forward rangefinder tower soon after her commissioning.[41] During a March 1944 refit, she received a Type 22 surface-search set, with its characteristic 'twin-horn' antennas, upgraded to add fire-control capability in an October 1944 yard period at Yokosuka. A Type 13 air-search set, with its 'ladder' antenna mounted on her mainmast, was added at the same time. The role for which she had been designed was already overtaken by events; she spent most of the war as an anti-aircraft escort for the Japanese carrier forces, a role for which she was reasonably well suited, given the quality and quantity of her AA armament.

Grand Plans on the Seine: C5 and *St-Louis*

Knowing that the existing treaties might well have expired when the time came replace their first post-First World War cruisers, and knowing equally that the replacement process could take up to six years, the French began thinking about unrestricted cruiser designs in 1939.[42] This process did not get very far before the start of the Second World War brought all such future musings to a halt, but before that happened, the STCN had generated a number of interesting designs. Some were basically follow-ons to the 'treaty-maximum' *Algérie* design, known as 'C4' in the French nomenclature; the follow-on designs were given various 'C5' designations. These all would have had the same main battery as *Algérie* and somewhat improved protection, but differed in their AA batteries; all featured a new power-operated, remote-controlled 37mm ACAD gun which the French believed showed great promise. The 'C5 A3' variant was basically similar to *Algérie*, while a 'C5 SA1' variant was proposed – 'SA' for *sans aviation* (without aircraft) – using the weight saved by deleting aircraft-handling facilities to further bolster the AA battery. One final sketch design was generated in May 1940 for a cruiser unlimited by treaty restrictions that would carry both aviation facilities and the upgraded AA battery of 'C5 SA1'; this was dubbed *St-Louis* after a decommissioned battleship it was intended to replace.

Chapter 10

Mass Production: 1935–1944

The British, as much as they may be faulted for the role they played in the sad episode that led up to the Anglo-German Naval Agreement of 1935, must at the same time be given credit for being the first nation (among the 'Western Democracies') to see clearly the approach of war in the mid-1930s and to do their best to prepare for it.

Chatfield's Vision: The 'Colony' Class

The Chatfield Report of March 1934, which accurately predicted the need for Great Britain to prepare for combat in both European waters and the Far East, and concluded that the Royal Navy would not only need a force of seventy cruisers – twenty more than they were allocated by the First London Treaty – but also that preferably at least sixty of those should be of modern, post-war construction.[1] By the time the ink had dried on the Second London Treaty in March 1936, and work was well underway on the *Dido* class, Chatfield's thoughts had turned towards the next cruiser design, the logical successor to the *Southampton* series of large cruisers, but tailored to fit within the 'qualitative' limits of that treaty. Unlike the *Dido*s, which grew out of a requirement to replace the Royal Navy's oldest and smallest light cruisers, this next design would be the closest approximation to a general-purpose cruiser that could be conjured within the confines of 8000 tons.

Having realised sooner than any other of the 'Western Democracies' that another war was coming to Europe, the British began planning for a greatly-expanded cruiser fleet as early as 1934; unfortunately, they did not have the ability to start on this project until 1938 and, even then, the numbers they could build were far short of the numbers they needed. Five hulls were laid down in the 1937 Building Programme and four more the following year. One of this latter group was HMNZS *Gambia* (48), representative of the 'Colony' class, the primary Royal Navy wartime production cruiser design, as seen here in Australia, sometime between September 1943 and March 1946. Judging from the radars she is carrying, it is likely towards the end of this period; she has Type 281 air-search antennas at her mastheads, a Type 285 DP fire-control antenna on each HADT fore-and-aft and a Type 284 main-battery fire-control antenna on her big DCT forward. Above her after HADT, she has a pair of Type 283 'barrage fire control' radar antennas, intended to allow the use of the main-battery 6in guns as an AA barrage weapon, despite the fact that the guns could not elevate past 45°. (SLV/AGC)

Needless to say, it proved to be extremely difficult to fit the various attributes of a *Southampton*, not to mention the later, even larger *Gloucester*s or *Edinburgh*s, into a ship displacing more than a thousand fewer tons. Various sketch designs were generated by DNC during 1936, the work falling to Constructor W G John, who tried out various combinations of armament – some had three quadruple turrets, some just three triple turrets, although the Naval Staff strongly preferred retaining the four triple turrets of the *Southampton*s – and various compensatory adjustments of protection and speed.[2] Some proposals were offered in July 1936 that mounted as many as seven twin 5.25in/50 turrets – a sort of enlarged *Dido* – but these alternatives did not generate much support. More popular were two options with a 6in/50 main battery, one with three quadruple turrets, somewhat less protection than the *Southampton*s (3.5in belt armour and 2in deck armour) and a speed of approximately 30 knots, the other similar but with ten main-battery guns divided between two twin turrets and two triple turrets, a longer hull and a half-knot less speed.

In September 1936, the Third Sea Lord, Rear Admiral Reginald Henderson, requested a Naval Staff conference to settle the matter. As Controller, Henderson had as much influence on future designs as anyone in the Royal Navy, with the possible exception of Chatfield, and he actually favoured the proposal with seven twin 5.25in/50 turrets, because he believed the four twin 4in/45 HA guns proposed for the other designs to be inadequate AA armament. He rejected the proposal with quadruple turrets outright, because the Ordnance Department stated that it would take at least six months to produce a working design for such a turret. In October, with the staff no closer to a decision, Henderson requested two new sketch designs from John, one with four triple 6in/50 turrets and one with seven twin 5.25in/50 turrets. The former would be three-quarters of a knot slower, because of greater displacement, and retained the weak medium AA armament, of which Henderson disapproved, but nonetheless was chosen by the Naval Staff because it was believed it would stand up to potential Japanese opponents better than a ship armed with a lighter main-battery weapon.

As design work progressed on this selected alternative, problems arose, mainly having to do with displacement. In November 1936, John estimated this ship would displace 8360 tons, just barely within the 5 per cent 'allowance' the constructors were given over the 8000-ton treaty limit. To make matters worse, stability calculations soon showed that the originally planned beam of 59ft 6in would not be sufficient to assure stability and an adequate metacentre; increasing the beam by a foot would increase the metacentre from a dangerously low 1.9 to a somewhat better 2.34.[3] This added width drove the displacement above the acceptable margin; the only way to bring it down again was to further reduce armour protection. By thinning the armoured trunks below the turrets and the magazine crowns, and slightly reducing the power plant – to one that provide a half-knot less top speed – John was able to keep displacement at a barely acceptable level. This design was submitted on 22 December and approved by the Admiralty Board on 14 January 1937, with the request that DNC look into improving the accommodation for the crew, which was considered to be excessively cramped.

That should have been the end of the design process, but in April the Controller again raised the question of how much displacement could be saved by shortening the ship or, alternatively, deleting one of the two planned DCTs, one of the four main-battery turrets, the aircraft-handling facilities or torpedoes, or by further reducing armour protection. John produced another series of sketch designs; Henderson approved an option that sacrificed a half-inch of belt armour and carried no torpedo tubes (but reserved space so they might be mounted in the event of war). Chatfield signed off on this design in May; the entire Admiralty Board was unhappy about the loss of armour protection and decided to restore it to 3.5in, but reluctantly accepted the deletion of the torpedo tubes and a top speed of 32 knots. The after DCT was deleted, replaced by a control position atop 'X' turret. Accommodation space was increased by adding a foot-and-a-half of width, to 62ft, and shortening the engineering spaces and store rooms;

A sister to *Gambia*, HMS *Bermuda* (52), is seen on 5 September 1946. What is immediately obvious are the greatly-upgraded electronics; the radars carried by *Bermuda*, as evidenced by the antennas on her mastheads and superstructure, are a generation newer than *Gambia*'s. The only ones that appear to be the same are the Type 285s on her HADTs and the Type 283s. The 'double cheese' radar antenna on her main-battery DCT is for a Type 274 fire-control set. Above that is the dish for the antenna for the Type 277 surface-search set. At the head of her foremast, she had the 'stabilised cheese' antenna for the Type 293 target designator, which operated in conjunction with the Type 281B air-search set on her mainmast. She appears to have the vertical dipoles of the Type 243 IFF atop her mainmast and also mounted forward of the foremast just under the Type 293 antenna. On her bridge face, she has a pair of Type 283 'barrage fire control' radar antennas, each in its own tub. (SLV/AGC)

speed was maintained by adopting a transom stern, which gives the hull the hydrodynamic characteristics of a longer ship. In this form, the design was re-approved by the Board on 8 July 1937. Detailed design drawings were signed off in November, with a calculated standard displacement of 8170 tons; the actual displacement when these ships completed would be significantly higher, but by then treaty limits would be irrelevant. The 'as built' specifications of these 'Colony' class cruisers were as follows:

'Colony' Class

Displacement (std):	8170 tons (calculated); 8530 tons (deep)
Length (oa):	555ft 6in
Beam (max):	62ft
Draft (mean):	19ft 10in (actual)
Power plant:	80,000shp; Parsons geared turbines driving four shafts; four Admiralty three-drum water-tube boilers
Speed:	32.25 knots (trials); 31 knots (actual) [4]
Range (designed):	8000nm @ 16 knots; 1700 tons oil fuel
Protection (side):	3.5in–3.25in NCA (in way of engineering spaces and main-battery magazines)
Protection (horiz):	2in NCA (over engineering spaces and main-battery magazines)
Armament (main):	12 x 6in/50 Mk XXIII (4 x 3 – two forward and two aft)
Armament (AA):	8 x 4in/45 QF Mk XVI HA (4 x 2); 8 x 2pdr Mk VIII pompom (2 x 4)
Armament (torp):	6 x 21in (2 x 3)
Aircraft:	2; one catapult[5]

The first five of the class were included in the 1937/38 Building Programme. They were ordered in December 1937 and the first, HMS *Nigeria* (60), was laid down at Vickers-Armstrongs, Tyne, on 8 February 1938. The first to enter service was HMS *Fiji* (58) on 17 May 1940. Four more were ordered the following year to the same design. Four more were to follow in the 1939/40 programme, but after the war broke out, it was decided to replace two of them with the final *Dido* and the five *Bellona*s.

Two of the class – *Fiji* and *Kenya* (14) – were completed without aircraft facilities, and the remainder had theirs removed by the end of 1944. As topweight due to ever-increasing AA weapons, directors and sensors continued to accumulate, stability increasingly suffered; The last three ships of the class – *Uganda* (66), *Ceylon* (30) and *Newfoundland* (59) – were completed with only 'Y' turret aft in the main battery. By the end of the war, four of the earlier ships – *Bermuda* (52), *Jamaica* (44), *Mauritius* (80) and *Kenya* – had their 'X' turret removed.

Two follow-on classes of very similar design were built during the war by the Royal Navy. They followed the modified 'Colony' design in that they mounted only three main-battery turrets, and they added another foot in beam to enhance stability; otherwise their basic design was the same as the 'Colonies'. Three ships were authorised in the 1941 Building Programme and two were completed during the war; the

Laid down mid-war, HMCS *Ontario* (53), is seen here in 1951 with a new pennant number assigned by the RCN. She was one of two ships of the *Swiftsure* class, follow-ons to the 'Colonies'. The differences at completion were primarily that *Ontario* was built with only three main-battery turrets – she never had a turret in 'X' position – no aviation facilities, heavier AA armament and a foot greater beam. Since the end of the war, her light AA battery has been reduced and the 2pdr pom-poms with which she was originally outfitted replaced by 40mm Bofors quadruple mounts. The tubs for the pair of Type 283 'barrage fire control' radar antennas on her bridge face appear to be empty now. Otherwise, her radars appear to be quite similar to those seen on *Bermuda*, except that the Type 277 surface-search antenna has been replaced by the Type 277Q with clipped sides, allowing enhanced height-finding capability, and the antennas on her HADTs – aft and abreast her forward funnel – are the centimetric Type 275. (SLV/AGC)

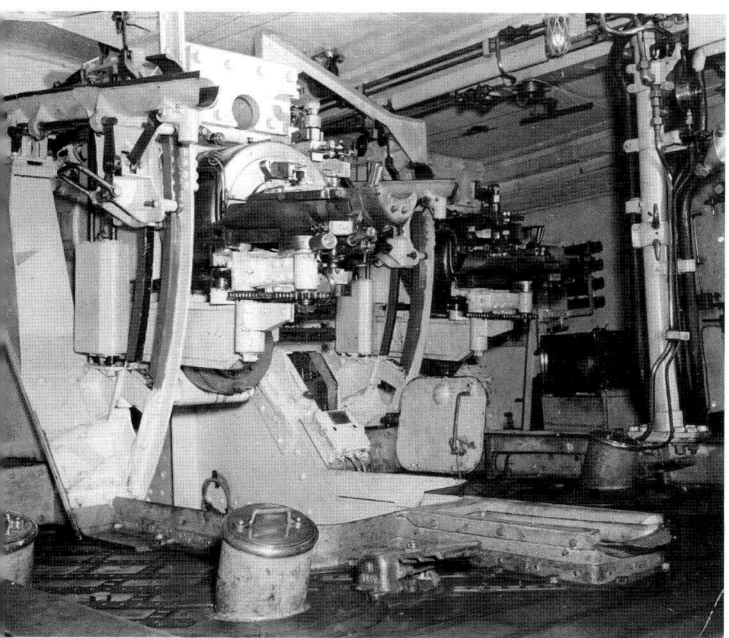

A view of the interior of 'Y' turret on *Ontario*, showing the centre and right gun breech ends. This shows clearly how far back the centre gun was set compared to the wing guns. The loading tray in the upper centre of the image would swing behind the open breech when the breech block was opened to the right. Shells came up the shell hoist and were tipped into the intermediate tray in the upper left and then into the loading tray, which was swung behind the open breech and rammed in. Meanwhile, the 'cordite member' would have retrieved a powder charge in its safety container from the powder hoist – the covered tube in the bottom foreground – removed it from the container and handed it to the 'cordite loader' who placed it on the loading tray for manual ramming behind the shell. (Ken Johnson Collection)

second of those was transferred to the Royal Canadian Navy after launch and renamed HMCS *Ontario* (53). The third of that group was never started. Five more were ordered in the 1941 and 1942 Supplementary Programmes. Of those, only one was completed as designed, HMS *Superb* (25), which was given a beam another foot wider (64ft) to offset continually rising topweight. Of the remaining four, one was cancelled and three were completed in the late 1950s–early 1960s as heavily-modified light cruisers with DP twin automatic 6in/50 QF Mk N5 turrets fore-and-aft. Two would be taken in hand in the mid-1960s and converted into helicopter-cruisers, in which role they would serve on into the late 1970s.

Cheaper by the Dozens: The *Cleveland* Class

Even after the September 1937 decision to arm the *Atlantas* with a main battery of 5in/38 guns, the idea of a light cruiser with a main battery of DP 6in guns did not die away in the US Navy. On 20 February 1939, the General Board agreed to a set of characteristics for a ship of 8000 tons with five twin 6in/47 DP turrets, the first two of which, CL55 and CL56, were to be ordered in FY1940.[6] Interestingly, the main criticism of this design came in May from the President, who thought it was under-armed and expressed concern that this ship would be unable to stand up against the German *Panzerschiffe*, which carried six 28cm/52 guns. This was especially true since the tightness of this design, necessary to stay within the 8000-ton limit, required that its armour was nowhere thicker than 3in.

The incoming CNO, Admiral Harold R Stark, backed by the General Board, stood up to the President. Facing a 15 September deadline, by which time contract specifications would need to be issued for ships in FY1940, the CNO looked across the Atlantic for salvation. At the outbreak of war in Europe, the British had indefinitely suspended their participation in the treaty regime and Stark jumped on this as an opportunity to solve the problem. (Great Britain suspended its participation in the treaty regime on 3 September 1939; the United States followed suit exactly one month later.) He was firm in his disapproval of the ten-gun 8000-ton option, seeing it as under-armed and pointless to construct. With no time to develop a new design for a larger cruiser, Stark turned to the design of the last two *Brooklyns*, sometimes referred to as the *Helenas*, which differed from their predecessors in mounting their secondary battery in four twin 5in/38 gunhouses. On 2 October 1939, Stark proposed that CL55–CL56 follow the same basic design, substituting two more secondary-battery mounts for one of *Helena*'s forward main-battery turrets. In record time, this proposal was accepted and contracts let with New York Shipbuilding Corp for both ships.

Two significant design changes occurred between this point and the completion of the first ships of the class in mid-1942. One came early, around the time the ships were laid down. Responding to concerns that these ships would be seriously overweight and potentially unstable – there was already discussion about whether permanent added ballast would be required – the lead contractor came up with a clever solution. New York Shipbuilding proposed realigning the ships' main external armour belt, which had in the *Brooklyn* class sloped inward from top to bottom at 2°, to slope outward at 6°. This would give the ships a small amount of tumblehome; while leaving the beam at Main Deck level the same, it would increase the beam at the waterline by approximately 2.5ft. The net effect would be a significant increase in buoyancy and would resolve stability concerns, at least for the moment. This was fortuitous, because the demands for additional topweight would not cease. The King Board of June 1940 recommended that every US Navy warship of sufficient size mount at least four quadruple 1.1in/75 mounts. This added significant topweight, as these mounts weighed 10,500lb each. In the event, these ships never carried this mount, as experience soon showed it to be an overly-complex and unreliable weapon; therefore in mid-1941 BuOrd ordered the quadruple 1.1in mounts replaced by twin 40mm/56 Bofors mounts of similar weight. The specifications to which the first ships of the class were to be built were as follows:

Cleveland Class

Displacement (std):	10,000 tons (design); 14,131 tons (full load)[7]
Length (oa):	608ft 4in
Beam (wl):	64ft 4in
Draft (mean):	24ft 6in (full load)
Power plant:	100,000shp; General Electric geared turbines driving four shafts; four Babcock & Wilcox boilers
Speed:	32.5 knots (design); 32.3 knots (actual)
Range (designed):	11,000nm @ 15 knots; 2100 tons oil fuel
Range (actual):	8640nm @ 15 knots; 2184 tons oil fuel
Protection (side):	5in STS (in way of engineering spaces); 3.25in–1.25in STS external belt (in way of main-battery magazines)
Protection (horiz):	2in STS (over engineering spaces and main-battery magazines)
Armament (main):	12 x 6in/47 Mk 16 (4 x 3 – two forward and two aft)
Armament (AA):	12 x 5in/38 Mk 12 (6 x 2); 8 x 40mm/56 Bofors Mk 2 (4 x 2); 10 x 20mm/70 Oerlikon Mk 2 (10 x 1)
Aircraft:	4, two catapults[8]

The first of the class to be laid down, launched and completed

American war production began in earnest with the *Cleveland* class light cruisers which were essentially follow-ons to the *St Louis* sub-class of the *Brooklyn* class, with No 3 main-battery turret sacrificed to allow the number of 5in/38 twin mounts to be increased to six and the medium and light AA fits to be similarly increased. Even the sacrifice of a main-battery turret was not enough to compensate for this added weight in the AA battery, so these ships were given a noticeable degree of tumblehome to add beam and stability. This view shows USS *Birmingham* (CL62), the sixth of the class to commission, running her trials on 20 February 1943. In all, fifty-two would be ordered and twenty-nine would be completed as gun cruisers, making it, by far, the biggest class of cruisers ever built. Note the awkward arrangement of surface and HA directors atop her superstructures carried over from the *Brooklyn* class; the designers attempted to prevent blockage of the main-battery DCT, with its FH (Mk 8) radar, by the FD (Mk 4) antenna on the Mk 37 DP director by raising the FD antenna on tall supports. (NARA)

This image shows the same ship, *Birmingham*, right after the end of the war. She wears a freshly-painted Ms 21 overall Navy Blue (5-N) system – that became common in the Pacific at the end of the war because it was the most effective against observation from the air – now with much larger hull numbers painted on in white, a concession to peacetime relaxation of rules. Her electronics suite, as evidenced by the antennas she carries, is much updated from 1943. The most obvious difference is replacement of the FD antennas on her Mk 37 DP directors with the Mk 12/22 pairs, which were much too heavy to carry on the tall supports; to allow the main-battery Mk 34 directors and their Mk 13 radar antennas to see above the Mk 37s and their antennas, the forward Mk 34 was raised while the after Mk 37 was lowered. On her foremast she has an SK air-search antenna with an SG surface-search antenna on the short pole above it. On her mainmast, she has a SM-1 fighter-control radar antenna with a TDY jamming system antenna above it. (SLV/AGC)

was USS *Cleveland* (CL55), which commissioned on 15 June 1942. What Admiral Stark could not have foretold when he proposed that two FY1940 cruisers be more-or-less simple repeats of the *Brooklyn* class was that this new class would join a navy at war, or that by the time *Cleveland* joined the US Navy, she would have twenty-two sister-ships in various stages of construction or that, before all was said and done, a total of fifty-two would be ordered to this design, making it by far the largest class of cruisers ever ordered. By no means would all of these be built. Thirteen of those would be cancelled towards the end of the war and a fourteenth broken up on the building slip; additionally, nine of those hulls would be converted to light aircraft carriers. That left twenty-nine that were completed as light cruisers, making it still by far the largest class of cruisers ever built. Only the first one, *Cleveland*, carried exactly the weapons fit described in the above specifications. By the time the second ship in the series came along, USS *Columbia* (CL56), it had been decided that the standard light AA fit should be two quadruple 40mm/56 Bofors along with two twin mounts, and it only increased from there.

Fire control was provided for the main battery by a pair of Mk 34 directors fore-and-aft, each topped by an FC (Mk 3) antenna. High-angle fire control was provided by a pair of Mk 37 directors, each with its associated FD (Mk 4) radar antenna on a particularly tall support to allow line-of-sight clearance for the main-battery directors, which, curiously, were mounted above the HA directors. An SC air-search radar was carried on the mainmast and an SG microwave surface-search set on the foremast. All of these radars would be upgraded on later-built or refitted ships, and multiple smaller directors for the AA battery would proliferate in the superstructure, only adding to the topweight issues.

Starting with the FY1942 ships, BuShips (the successor bureau created by merging BuC&R and BuEng in June 1940) began the first of several major design changes to the *Cleveland* class. Experience at Pearl Harbor had shown that the enclosed command bridge, then standard in US Navy warships, did not allow the captain and his officers adequate 'situational awareness' of the sky above his ship.[9] The response was to develop a new design for an open bridge above an enclosed and armoured (by 1.25in STS) command platform, replacing the conning tower. (The deletion of the conning tower was necessitated by the switch from light metals to steel in the construction of the superstructure; as war production ramped up, particularly of aircraft, the supply of aluminium for shipbuilding became very tight.) Later, starting in 1943, the size of the forward superstructure was further reduced and the problem of interference between the LA and HA directors resolved by switching their positions. As had been the case with the *Atlantas*, this class had a significant design update in 1942, intended similarly to reduce topweight and clear arcs of fire for the AA battery. In the end, only two ships, USS *Fargo* (CL106) and *Huntington* (CL107), were completed to this revised design, which trunked the two funnels into one larger one and generally reduced the height and length of the superstructure. They would not enter service until after the war.

Two of the last *Clevelands*, including USS *Huntington* (CL107) seen here on 12 April 1947, were built to a modified design with a reduced superstructure and the two funnels trunked into one to save topweight and improve the arcs of fire of the AA battery. (NARA)

In general, the *Cleveland* class must be considered a mixed success. From the beginning, they were limited by being built on *Brooklyn* class hulls, which condemned them to a constant battle against overweight and stability problems that proved impossible to overcome. Nonetheless, they fought well throughout the war and, once peacetime allowed some of their AA weaponry and aircraft facilities, and the crew that served them, to be removed, they served well in peacetime. Still, they were not as well-liked in the fleet as the more capacious *Baltimores*, and with few exceptions, they disappeared from the US Navy fairly rapidly after the war.

Any discussion of US Navy ship design in this period must include mention of the introduction by BuOrd, first mooted in December 1939, of the so-called 'superheavy' armour-piercing shells which were introduced with the wartime production ships of the *Cleveland* and *Baltimore* classes.[10] The increase in weight of these shells was significant; for example, the 'superheavy' 8in AP Mk 21 round weighed 335lb compared to 260lb for the previous standard AP Mk 19. The impact of the introduction of these shells, which had significantly better ability to penetrate armour, was minimal on the *Cleveland* and *Baltimore* classes. As much as the designers of these ships may have wanted to follow the 'rule of thumb' that a warship should be protected to resist its own guns within a reasonable immune zone, both of these were limited by displacement considerations and retained the protective schemes of their predecessor classes essentially unchanged. In the case of the wartime-designed classes described later in this chapter,

An idea that would not die, the promise of a ship carrying automatic DP 6in guns lured the Americans into ordering four ships of the *Worcester* class, of which only two were actually built. The twin 6in/47 DP Mk 16 mount, being much heavier than the 5in/38 mounts in the later *Atlantas*, required a cruiser 8000 tons heavier and 130ft longer to accommodate six main-battery turrets. The 6in DP gun never lived up to its expectations, never achieving the 12rpm it was designed to fire and proving to be prone to regular failures. Neither USS *Worcester* (CL144), seen here in June 1950, or her sister, remained in service more than ten years. (NHHC)

the *Worcester* and *Des Moines* classes, which were less constrained, there still was a limit to the extent that armour could be increased and still retain the size and speed needed in a cruiser. In both of those classes, the vertical protection remained unchanged from the *Cleveland* and *Baltimore* classes, but the horizontal protection was significantly increased, by more than 50 per cent, acknowledging the greater threat presented by bombs.

Even after committing to building the *Cleveland* class in record numbers, the idea of a light cruiser armed with a main battery of DP 6in guns did not go away in the US Navy. More importantly, BuOrd never stopped working on the twin 6in/47 DP mount. Enthusiasm for the idea waxed and waned during the war as, initially, there was great fear of high-altitude bombing of warships, which was soon shown to be greatly exaggerated, but was revived with added impetus by the introduction of radio-controlled glide bombs, such as the Fritz-X by the Germans in 1943.[11]

Design studies for the ship that eventually became USS *Worcester* (CL144) began in May 1941, with a request from the General Board for a series of sketch designs for a ship mounting twelve 6in DP guns and protected by a thick armoured deck (but, interestingly, no side armour). These designs, which were reviewed in July, came out much larger and heavier than the Board expected, at 14,000 tons nearly as massive as the 8in-gunned *Baltimore* class cruisers, and even then were less well protected than the board had envisaged. There followed almost two years of back-and-forth between the General Board and Preliminary Design as they attempted to define a platform for the DP mount. These designs ranged in size between 12,200 tons and 14,200 tons and carried between eight and twelve main-battery guns, but the biggest issue in the board's opinion was protection, as war experience showed the need for greater survivability in cruiser-sized ships. In May 1943, a threat arose to the whole idea of a 6in-armed DP cruiser, when BuOrd announced the imminent availability of an automatic version of the 8in/55 gun in triple mounts. This gun would be able to fire at three times the rate of the standard 8in/55 (10rpm v 3–4rpm) as opposed to the predicted rate of 12rpm for the automatic 6in/47 twin mount, and like the 6in mount, be able to load at any elevation angle; the only advantage the 6in gun would have was that its planned maximum elevation was in excess of 75°, while the 8in mount would elevate only to slightly more than 40°. (It is not clear from the available documentation the extent to which the board considered the 8in/55 RF Mk 16 to be a DP weapon, but there is some evidence pointing in that direction. One piece is that the HC rounds provided for this weapon could be fitted with a mechanically-timed (MT) fuze, in which configuration, they were referred to as AAC rounds.[12] Another is that the fire-control director associated with this gun, the Mk 54, was described in the 1950 update of the US Navy instruction manual for gunnery as differing 'from the Mark 34 in having more complete provisions for control of the main battery against aircraft'.[13])

This new gun immediately appealed to the General Board; the only complaint generally heard against the new *Baltimore* class heavy cruisers (see below) was that their 8in/55 main battery fired too slowly. In August 1943, a meeting was called to discuss the 'competing' designs for 6in-armed and 8in-armed cruisers with automatic main-battery weapons. With a decision looming on if and when to order the next group of cruisers in the *Cleveland* and *Baltimore* series – these would be CA139–CA142 and CL143–CL149 – BuShips argued in favour of the anti-aircraft cruiser armed with the 6in gun, but was firmly overruled by the board, which recommended to Admiral Ernest J King, CNO since March 1942, that the full series of cruisers with hull numbers 139 through 149 be ordered as heavy cruisers armed with the 8in/55 RF Mk 16 gun. This was not to be, not because King did not approve – in fact, he endorsed the Board proposal – but because BuOrd announced that they would be unable to supply enough of the 8in mountings in time. BuOrd proposed that only three of the seven hulls that had originally been planned as light cruisers – CL143, CL148 and CL149 – be ordered as heavy cruisers; the remaining four – CL144–CL147 – should be ordered as light cruisers armed with the new twin DP mount. Given the pressure for a decision to be made if new designs were to be ready for ships to be laid down in 1945, and given also the realisation by the General Board that the War in the Pacific, at the end of 1943, was clearly swinging in the favour of the Allies and that the days of unlimited budgets were drawing to an end, King and the board acceded to BuOrd's proposal and four very large light cruisers, armed with six twin 6in/47 DP Mk 16 turrets were ordered to the last of the Preliminary Design sketch designs. This design was protected in a manner much the same as the *Clevelands*, with 5in belt armour, although it did have stronger horizontal protection, with a 1in Main Deck and a 3.5in armoured deck at Second Deck level. This ship grew almost 70ft in length, compared to the *Clevelands*; as designed, it was supposed to displace 13,800 tons, but the turrets continued to gain weight as they were developed, and by the time the first two of the ships were actually laid down in 1945, the standard displacement had increased to 14,700 ton.

There is more than a little suspicion that BuOrd's claimed inability to supply a sufficient number of turrets to complete the entire 1945 series as 8in-armed cruisers was more than a little 'convenient', in that BuOrd greatly desired to see the 6in DP mount, on which it had worked sporadically since 1936, actually go to sea.[14] In the end only the first two ships in the class – USS *Worcester* (CL144) and *Roanoke* (CL145) – were laid down; both were completed, though not until 1948. The main-battery DP gun system, the whole reason for the existence of these ships, never lived up to expectations. It proved to be fragile, prone to breakdowns, and never achieved the rate of fire for which it was designed. Both ships were decommissioned after only ten years of service.

Wichita Unchained: The *Baltimore* Class

Unlike the *Cleveland* class, the development of the *Baltimore* class, the US Navy's war-production heavy cruisers, was never hindered by being tied to an existing hull. While the design owed a great deal to *Wichita*, it was not restrained in any way by the treaty limits that had restricted that ship's size. Immediately after the acceptance of Admiral Stark's proposal to proceed with the development of the first two *Clevelands* at the beginning of October 1939, the General Board asked for sketch designs of a new heavy cruiser, similar in most respects to the just-defined *Clevelands*, but armed with a larger main battery.[15] Preliminary Design responded on 3 November

Above and below: The story of the American war-production heavy cruisers, the *Baltimore* class, was much different from that of the *Clevelands*. In the first place, no attempt was made to start the design of the *Baltimores* from a *Brooklyn* class hull, despite a superficial resemblance due to the high freeboard and flush deck. The *Baltimores*, such as USS *Boston* (CA69), the second in the class to be completed, seen in these two views taken during her full power trials run on 22 October 1943, also looked a great deal like the *Clevelands*, except for having one fewer main-battery turret, but they were 63ft longer and displaced 2700 tons more. They carried the same number of 5in/38 twin mounts, but from the beginning carried almost double the number of 40mm barrels. Also, from the beginning they had the FH radar for their main battery and a better arrangement of their fire-control directors, with the HA directors sited above the main-battery DCTs. (NHHC)

with two designs, one for a 12in-gunned ship that evolved into the *Alaska* class, the other mounted nine 8in/55 guns in triple turrets like *Wichita* and twelve 5in/38s in twin gunhouses like the *Clevelands*. Armour protection was to be similar to *Wichita*'s, with a 6in belt of Class A armour. Hull length would increase to 640ft overall, despite the fact that this would limit the number of dry docks the ship could use. Steam pressure and temperature would increase to 600psi and 850°F. On 15 December 1939, the General Board accepted this design, with a few minor revisions: the fire rooms were each to be divided in two to aid survivability and power was to be increased to 120,000shp, because the ships' length had now increased again by 15ft. The estimated displacement figures kept increasing as the design went through the approval process, reaching 13,600 tons before the first ships were ordered from Bethlehem, Quincy, to the following specifications on 1 July 1940:

Baltimore Class

Displacement (std):	13,600 tons (design); 17,031 tons (full load)[16]
Length (oa):	673ft 5in
Beam (wl):	70ft 10in
Draft (mean):	24ft (full load)
Power plant:	120,000shp; General Electric geared turbines driving four shafts; four Babcock & Wilcox boilers
Speed:	33 knots (design); 33 knots (actual)
Range (designed):	10,000nm @ 15 knots; 2343 tons oil fuel
Range (actual):	7900nm @ 15 knots
Protection (side):	6in–4in Class A external belt (in way of engineering spaces); 3in–2in STS external belt (in way of main-battery magazines)
Protection (horiz):	2.5in STS (over engineering spaces and main-battery magazines)
Armament (main):	9 x 8in/55 Mk 12 (3 x 3 – two forward and one aft)
Armament (AA):	12 x 5in/38 Mk 12 (6 x 2); 48 x 40mm/56 Bofors Mk 2 (12 x 4); 26 x 20mm/70 Oerlikon Mk 2 (26 x 1)
Aircraft:	4, two catapults[17]

The first of the class, USS *Baltimore* (CA68), was laid down on 26 May 1941 and commissioned in April 1943. A total of twenty-five of this class were ordered, of which seventeen were completed as heavy cruisers, six were cancelled, one was completed as a command ship and one was re-ordered as a *Des Moines* class cruiser (see below). Their fire-control set-up was essentially the same as that of the *Cleveland* class, except that from the beginning, the HA Mk 37 directors were sited above the LA Mk 34 directors.

Just as the *Atlanta* and *Cleveland* classes had 1942 redesigns with the intent of reducing topweight and the size of the superstructure, the same was done with the *Baltimore* class, even before the first of the class had entered service. In a similar manner, the two funnels were trunked into one and the superstructure was redesigned to be lower and more compact to allow better arcs of fire for the AA battery. However, delays in the redesign process, caused by overload at BuShips, meant that only the last four ships in the class to be started (those laid down in 1944) were built to this design, and one of those was diverted to be completed as a 'command light cruiser'.

Much of the story of the last class of American heavy cruisers was told above, starting with the May 1943 announcement of the impending availability of an automatic version of the 8in/55 triple mount. Having decided to build the remaining twelve authorised cruisers – hull numbers CA139–CA142 and CL143–CL149, plus CA134 – armed with the new gun mount – that number almost immediately reduced to eight by the decision to build four *Worcester*s – the issue then became what that ship would look like, or more to the point, given the experience with the *Cleveland* and *Baltimore* classes, how to keep the size of this ship from ballooning out of control. The first sketch designs came up with a ship displacing 16,500 tons.[18] Considerable effort was put into reducing this number by limiting crew size and splinter protection, but the revelation of German glide bombs off Salerno raised all new concerns that led to the introduction of four 2.5in STS transverse bulkheads intended to make it harder for a single large weapon like a Fritz-X or a Japanese 'Long Lance' torpedo to sink one of these ships. Ultimately, between that added protection and incremental weight growth in the 8in/55 RF Mk 16 gun mounts, these ships grew to a standard displacement of 17,225 tons and a full-load displacement of close to 21,000 tons with a hull 716ft 6in in overall length.

In the end, only four ships of the *Des Moines* class were ordered and only three completed, all in 1948–9. Unlike the *Worcester*s, however, these ships were considered to be successful, mainly because the 8in/55 RF Mk 16 worked well. One of them, USS *Newport News* (CA148), suffered a turret explosion in 1972 caused by the explosion of a shell in the

As had happened with the *Atlantas* and *Clevelands*, the last four *Baltimores* were redesigned with a more compact superstructure to allow better siting of the AA battery; only three were actually completed in this configuration, including USS *Albany* (CA123), seen here on 19 January 1947. Note that in this redesign, the main-battery DCTs have been returned to the higher siting. (NHHC)

As well as pursuing an automatic 6in gun, which equipped the *Worcester* class light cruisers, the Americans developed the automatic 8in/55 RF Mk 16 and built three ships in the *Des Moines* class carrying this more successful weapon. This image gives an idea of the size of the gun turrets required to mount this weapon and of the ships to carry these turrets, compared to a standard war-production *Baltimore* class heavy cruiser. In this photograph taken 26 November 1966, *Boston*, now converted to the first American guided-missile cruiser and designated 'CAG1', is on the left – her two forward gun turrets with three 8in/55 Mk 12s remain as before – while on the right is USS *Newport News* (CA148), which was equipped with larger turrets mounting the 8in/55 RF Mk 16 and was very nearly 3000 tons heavier and 43ft longer. (USN)

middle barrel of turret No 2 while conducting a shore bombardment off Vietnam; the cause of the explosion was not related to the automatic loading system. The only complaint against the ships of the *Des Moines* class was their expense, both to build and to operate, which was calculated to be approximately three times that of a *Baltimore* class cruiser, while gaining a ship that could fire approximately three times faster. At first glance that would seem to be something of a 'wash', but spreading one's weapons over three platforms that could be separated by considerable distance gave a survivability advantage to three *Baltimore*s compared to one *Des Moines*.

A brief mention must be made of the largest cruisers ever built, the large heavy cruisers of the *Alaska* class. (Of course, there can be an argument made that the German battlecruisers of the *Scharnhorst* class were bigger, but while those two ships actually carried a smaller main-battery gun than the *Alaska*s, all their other characteristics, in particular their armour protection and general hull form, were on a capital ship scale, not on a cruiser scale. Other larger cruisers were planned, such as the Japanese B-65 project or the Soviet *Kronshtadt* class, but were either never started or, in the case of the Russian cruisers, never advanced much past being laid down.) The origin of the *Alaska* class goes back to March 1938, when the General Board asked BuC&R for sketch designs for a 'cruiser killer', a ship that would well-armed enough and fast enough to track down and defeat any of the world's cruisers. The idea received a further boost when, in reviewing early design options for the *Cleveland* class in May 1939, the President expressed the strong desire for a ship that could stand up to the German *Panzerschiffe*. Further impetus came from knowledge gained from intelligence about the *Scharnhorst*s and about Japanese plans for the B-65 class large cruisers. The final impetus came from Vice Admiral King, who at this time was Commander, Aircraft, Battle Force, expressing concern about whether the US Navy would have enough large cruisers and battleships to escort adequately the anticipated number of carrier and invasion task groups that were envisaged. With a new 12in/50 gun under development by BuOrd intended to fire a new 'superheavy' 1140lb AP round, the General Board had the option to develop a large cruiser with protection more than sufficient to take on any existing cruiser (but not, significantly, a battleship). By the time the decisive meeting of the General Board was held in mid-July 1939, King had become a member of the board, perhaps its most influential member, and the decision was made to recommend proceeding with the design and production of a cruiser of 27,500 tons with a speed of 33 knots, belt armour between 10.1in–7.7in and a main battery of eight 12in/50 guns. One point the board made in its instructions to BuC&R regarding the design was that with a maximum range more than 20 per cent greater than that of an 8in-gunned cruiser, this ship would have to carry its main-battery fire-control directors farther above the waterline than any cruiser yet designed for the US Navy. In this form, the ship characteristics were approved by Admiral Stark and FDR.

Before the first of the ships of the *Alaska* class were laid down in December 1941, the armour belt had been thinned to 9in–5in of Class A armour in order to increase the main battery to nine guns in three triple turrets. The displacement rose to 29,779 tons before USS *Alaska* (CB1) was commissioned in June 1944. Six ships in this class were authorised

The Americans built one class of super-heavy cruisers, sometimes dubbed 'battlecruisers', like the German *Scharnhorst*s or the French *Dunkerque*s, but the two ships of the *Alaska* class that were completed were truly just overgrown heavy cruisers, despite their nine 12in/50 guns and their rather battleship-looking tower foremasts. The lead ship of the class, USS *Alaska* (CB1), is seen here on 8 August 1944, soon after her commissioning. Built in part to counter rumoured Japanese ships of similar characteristics that never materialised, they were ships without a natural role in the fleet and they were both decommissioned in 1947. (NARA)

and three actually laid down, but only two were completed. They proved to be ships with no natural role to play and the two that did join the fleet were laid up soon after the war as being too expensive to keep in active status.

Not To Be Forgotten: Soviet Resurgence

The Soviet Union began worrying about naval defence of its coastal frontiers after its internal integrity was assured by the end of the prolonged Civil War. To restore a shipbuilding industry would take some effort, which was included in the first of the Five-Year Plans, which strongly emphasised re-establishment of the steel industry and the various machine tool factories needed to support shipbuilding. The first plan, which ran 1928–33, included only limited shipbuilding, but saw much effort put into restoring the navy yards at Leningrad (St Petersburg), Nikolayev (Mykolaiv) and Komsomolsk-on-Amur. The second plan, which began in 1933, included four cruisers, two to be built at Leningrad's Ordzhonikidze Yard and two at Nikolayev's Marti (South) Yard.[19] The plans for these ships were prepared with considerable 'assistance' from Ansaldo, Genova, and many features of these ships strongly resembled Italian cruisers from this period. The first two were laid down, one each at Leningrad and Nikolayev, in October 1935. They were both completed before Russia was invaded

The Soviets, much like FDR, saw warship building as doubly beneficial, both as a way to encourage the development of industrial infrastructure and at the same time bolster national defence. Towards that end, the Russians planned to build the seventeen-ship *Chapayev* class of light cruisers in their third Five-Year Plan starting in 1938, but, in the event, only seven were started before the German invasion and only five survived the war to be completed in 1949–50. Because considerable design support came from the Italian Ansaldo yard, it is not surprising that there was some clear external resemblance to the later classes of *'Condottieri'*, as can be seen here in this image of *Komsomolets* (ex-*Chkalov*), seen in the Baltic in 1969. She remained in commission until 1981. (NHHC)

by the Germans in 1941, during which war they saw limited action, but both survived. They had an unusual main battery of nine 180mm/57 in three triple turrets, a calibre midway between the 6in and 8in guns carried by most light or heavy cruisers. The second pair, again one at each yard, were similar, but somewhat larger and better protected, laid down in 1936 and completed in 1940–1; they also survived the war. A third pair, authorised under the third Five-Year Plan, were laid down in 1939 at the Komsomolsk Yard and were completed in 1943–4. All six, the *Kirov* class, served in the post-war Soviet Navy, at least two of them into the 1970s.

A massive further class of seventeen true light cruisers, armed with a main battery of twelve 152mm/57 B-38 guns in four triple turrets was authorised in the third Five-Year Plan. Eleven ships were actually ordered in 1939 – six for the Baltic Fleet, four for the Black Sea Fleet and one for the Pacific Fleet. Only seven – three at Leningrad and four at Nikolayev – had actually been started before the German invasion in 1941. These seven – the *Chapayev* class – had all been laid down between 1939 and 1940, but only four of the ships, two of those being built at Leningrad and two at Nikolayev, were launched before war engulfed the Soviet Union; the two launched at the Ukrainian port were towed to safety to Poti (P'ot'i) in Georgia in the eastern Black Sea to prevent their capture when Nikolayev fell to the Germans. In the event, two more incomplete hulls of this class were captured by the Germans and scrapped. The remaining incomplete hull, at the Ordzhonikidze Yard at Leningrad, was not launched until 1948. These five ships in the class were all completed in 1949–50 with the following specifications:

Chapayev Class

Displacement (std):	11,300 tons; 15,000 tons (full load)
Length (pp):	659ft 5in
Beam (wl):	64ft 8in
Draft (mean):	21ft
Power plant:	130,000shp; geared turbines driving two shafts; six water-tube boilers
Speed:	33.5 knots
Range:	7000nm @ 19 knots; 3200 tons oil fuel
Protection (side):	3.94in
Protection (horiz):	1.97in
Armament (main):	12 x 152mm/57 B-38 (4 x 3 – two forward and two aft)
Armament (AA):	8 x 100mm/56 Model 34 (4 x 2); 24 x 37mm/67 (12 x 2)
Armament (torp):	6 x 533mm (2 x 3)[20]

In external appearance and in many details, these ships bore a strong resemblance to the later groups of '*Condottieri*' built by the Italians, which is not coincidental, because considerable design support before the war came, as with the *Kirov* class, from Ansaldo. Most of these ships did not last long in service. Two were decommissioned after only ten years, another after fifteen years. One, *Komsomolets* (ex-*Chkalov*), the one that was not launched until 1948, remained in commission until 1981.

Another view of *Komsomolets*, this time focusing on her forward superstructure, shows details of her bridge, which has the compact conical structure introduced by Pugliese with the *Montecuccoli* class, topped by an enlarged navigation and command bridge structure and then by a massive bi-level DCT with a pair of 32ft 10in rangefinders. Turrets Nos 2 and 3 had radomes for a SHTAT-5 ('Egg Cup') range-only fire-control radar. She had a Zalp-M2 ('Top Bow') surface-search/fire-control radar on a foremast platform above the DCT and a FUT-N ('Slim Net') air search radar above that. (NHHC)

As part of Stalin's post-war plan to build a 'Blue Water' navy capable of protecting Russia's four widely-separated coastlines, the Soviet Navy was to be massively expanded around a core of aircraft carriers and battlecruisers, protected by light cruisers, destroyers and submarines. One of the key elements of this plan was the planned construction of no less than forty modified-*Chapayev* class cruisers. The ships of the *Sverdlov* class were sufficiently similar to the preceding class, with the same main-battery armament, power plant and armour scheme, as to be assigned the same 'project' number by the Soviet Navy; they differed in being lengthened by 33ft, which increased fuel stowage and thus range by 2000nm, allowed better underwater protection and an increased AA battery. The original order was for thirty ships in this class, but after Stalin's death in 1953, support for the programme at the top of the political system waned. The order was soon cut to twenty-one ships: nine from the Baltic Yard, Leningrad; four from the Admiralty Yard,

The *Chapayev* class was followed after the war by the *Sverdlov* class, enough like their predecessors that they shared a project number. The original plans called for forty to be built, but the numbers steadily dwindled, until eventually fourteen were completed, of which *Admiral Nevsky*, seen here in the Atlantic on 26 October 1983, was one. The big 100mm/70 AA mounts along her side had 'Egg Cup' radomes just like main-battery turrets No 2 and 3. (USN)

Leningrad; four from Marti (South), Nikolayev; and four from the Sevmash Yard, Severodvinsk (White Sea). The first fourteen hulls were laid down to the original design – six, three, three and two from the yards listed above – after which the remaining seven were to be built to a design modified to be more resistant to nuclear contamination, but this group was never completed. In the end, therefore, fourteen *Sverdlovs* were built, still a significant number and a tremendous expenditure of national resources on a ship type that by 1953, when the last of these was being laid down, was clearly obsolescent. Some attempts were made to convert them into missile cruisers, generally without success. Several were converted into command ships with greater success; these served into the late 1980s and a few cases until 1990.

Two of the *Sverdlov* class cruisers, including *Zhdanov*, seen here on 10 July 1983, were converted into command ships, with their No 3 main-battery turret replaced by a large accommodation and control space. (USN)

Chapter 11

The Test of Battle, Part 2: 1939–1945

Cruisers were ubiquitous throughout the Second World War, both because, as the largest gun-armed warship that could be built under the treaty regime, they were the most available large combatant in most navies, and because, having been designed for the roles of fleet escort and trade warfare/protection, they were present at most of the critical moments when combat ensued. This gives the author looking to select some exemplary engagements to illustrate how well (or poorly) these cruisers fought a large number from which to choose. Nor is it necessary to attempt to search out only gunfire engagements to illustrate cruiser combat, because cruisers were designed from the beginning not just as gun platforms, but also to carry torpedoes and, even if they did not specifically have DP main batteries, they often found themselves cast in the role of anti-aircraft escorts for carriers or convoys.

From this rich array of possible engagements to describe, the author has chosen three. They were chosen not because they are the best known, quite the opposite; with one exception, the incidents chosen are among the less well-covered in the war. None were decisive, but each in its own way illustrates some of the strengths and weaknesses of the ships described in this book and, thus, serves the author's purpose in selecting them.

An Unhappy Christmas: Convoy WS 5A – 25 December 1940

The 'WS' series of convoys were critical to Great Britain's conduct of the Second World War. It may have been apocryphal, but many believe that 'WS' stood for 'Winston Specials', indicating these convoys were organised at the highest level of the British government. What is demonstrably true is that each one carried a precious cargo, generally troop reinforcements to the Middle or Far East. That was true for WS 5A, the slow section of which formed up in the Irish Sea on 18 December 1940 with ships from Liverpool, Glasgow and Belfast, heading south towards Freetown, Sierra Leone; it comprised nineteen ships, of which eight carried transport and support equipment and the rest carried troops, more than 14,000 in total, for the defence of Egypt and India.[1] (Two of the cargo ships from the slow section suffered defects and returned.) Given the importance of the mission and the precious nature of the cargo, the convoy was given an impressive escort that included the old aircraft carrier HMS *Argus* (I49), the cruiser *Bonaventure*, seven destroyers, a sloop and four 'Flower' class corvettes.[2] When the fast section of five ships sailed two days later, their escort included another old aircraft carrier, HMS *Furious* (47), and the cruiser *Naiad* (93). Because the fast section would be steaming four knots faster than the slow section (15 knots v 11 knots), it was expected that the two sections would join up well before they reached the latitude of Cape Finisterre, the north-western point of Spain. (The two aircraft carriers were not actually as impressive an escort as it might have seemed on paper. *Argus* had aboard six Fairey Swordfish of No 821X Sqdn earmarked for delivery to Gibraltar and two other Swordfish of No 825 Sqdn for self-defence; *Furious* carried forty RAF Hawker Hurricanes, mostly crated, in her hangar and on her flight deck, for delivery to Takoradi, and six Blackburn Skuas of No 801 Sqdn for self-defence.) On 24 December, the cruiser HMS *Berwick* (65) one of the first-generation Royal Navy 'treaty maximum' cruisers came out from Gibraltar, and *Dunedin* (D93) from Portsmouth, to relieve *Naiad* in WS 5A's escort. The plan then was for *Argus* and *Bonaventure* to detach to deliver the former's aircraft to Gibraltar in preparation for Operation 'Excess', a plan to run supplies in to Malta.[3] This detachment was scheduled to take place on 26 December, but definitely not before *Berwick* and *Dunedin* joined.

The Christmas Day encounter in 1940 off the north-west corner of Spain included *Berwick*, on the British side, one of the oldest of the Royal Navy's 'treaty maximum' cruisers. This image shows her in 1942, similar in most ways to how she looked at that battle. One difference was the camouflage – in December 1940, she was painted in overall medium grey, a scheme she wore very briefly only during this one month; she did not received the elaborate disruptive pattern seen here until she was docked for repairs at Portsmouth after the Christmas Day engagement. She also would not yet have had the gun tubs on 'B' and 'X' turrets. (via Ken Macpherson)

To oppose this convoy, which was headed to the Middle East with stops at Freetown, Cape Town and Durban en route to Suez, the Germans had U-boats and, towards the end of December 1940, two major warships at sea in the Atlantic. After the defeat of France in June 1940, Hitler hoped he could lure the British, who were now without major allies, into an armistice, and, as part of that process, he temporarily restrained his fleet from overt action. This was not so difficult to arrange, as the *Kriegsmarine* had suffered terrible losses in the Norwegian campaign; the new heavy cruiser *Blücher* and two of the 'K' class light cruisers were sunk and the *Panzerschiff Lützow* and both battlecruisers – *Scharnhorst* and *Gneisenau* – had been damaged and put out of action for an extended time. That left only the heavy cruiser *Admiral Hipper* capable of immediate deployment.

The other major Royal Navy unit involved in the Christmas Day engagement in 1940 was HMS *Bonaventure* (31), one of the *Dido* class small light cruisers. As can be seen in this unfortunately poor-quality view forward over her open navigation bridge looking towards her forecastle, she had all three of her forward 5.25in/50 main-battery gunhouses, one of the small number of *Dido*s to carry all three forward mounts as designed. The open bridge was a standard feature in Royal Navy designs that was gradually adopted by the Americans as they came to realise that the command watch needed constant, uninterrupted 360° situational awareness of the seas around and the skies above a ship. *Bonaventure* survived the Christmas Day engagement undamaged (by the enemy), only to be sunk by an Italian submarine three months later off Sollum (As Sallum), Egypt. (via Ken Macpherson)

When time passed and the British showed no signs of negotiating peace, political restraints were loosened and plans made for the resumption of raiding into the Atlantic by the only active German surface unit. *Hipper*, which on 24 September was ready after completing a month-long yard period at Wilhelmshaven, slipped into the North Sea and headed towards Norway.[4] The plan was that she would make a sweep north around the British Isles, refuelling near Greenland, then, after preying on the transatlantic convoys, head into St-Nazaire, where fuel and supplies would be waiting. That, however, failed to take into account the fragile nature of *Hipper*'s power plant. Off Stavanger a cooling pump failed and she had to put into Kristiansand for emergency repairs. Leaving there again on 27 September, serious vibrations in the starboard turbine were noted; unable to identify the cause of these, the ship continued north around the Norwegian coast, but the next day, again near Stavanger, an oil feed line into the turbine broke off and the spillage caught fire. Before the fire could be controlled, all three engines had to be shut down – the port and starboard turbines were in the same engine room and the middle turbine suffered an unrelated failure – and the ship was left drifting in the North Sea for four hours before power could be restored to the port turbine and *Hipper* could make her way back to Kiel. She ended up back at the Blohm u Voss yard at Hamburg, where she had been built; repairs took until 28 October. In the meanwhile, the *Panzerschiff Admiral Scheer* completed an extended refit and departed Gotenhaven (Gdansk) for what would be an extended raid into the North and South Atlantic that would last into the following year.

Hipper worked up in the Baltic for most of November, arriving at Brunsbüttel on 28 November and departing for the north-around route again two days later, on an operation grandly named *Nordseetour* (North Sea Tour). She refuelled for several days south-east of Jan Mayen Island, waiting for bad weather to cover her passage through the Denmark Strait. This came on 5 December with the approach of a typical North Atlantic storm front, which covered *Hipper*'s passage between Greenland and Iceland the next day. She refuelled from another prepositioned oiler south of Greenland and then searched for two weeks without success for successive eastbound and westbound Halifax convoys, refuelling again on 16 and 20 December. She then swept eastward and back westward across the north-south track taken by the 'SL' convoys, again without success. Finally, early on 24 December, running low on fuel again, she turned eastward again. By this time, there was concern once again about the state of her power plant, so she shaped a course towards France. She was heading for Brest, but swinging well to the south, intending to enter the Bay of Biscay along the northern coast of Spain to stay well clear of snoopers flying from British bases. Up till now, *Hipper*'s patrol had been an utter failure; she had not sighted a single enemy vessel. This was about to change.

By the evening of 24 December, *Hipper* was making her way eastward into the increasing gloom when, at 16.48, approximately 20 minutes before sunset, her FuMO 22 radar, which operated at the 80cm wavelength and could detect large surface targets at 13nm, reported multiple targets to the east. Very quickly, Captain Wilhelm Meisel realised he had stumbled upon a convoy, the kind for which he had been searching since leaving Germany a month earlier. When he saw that the convoy seemed unaware of his presence, he decided to wait out the long, misty night, falling into a trailing position in the convoy's wake.[5] *Hipper* remained in that position, undetected by the convoy or its escorts, until first light the next morning.

At 07.08 on Christmas morning, lookouts in *Hipper* were able to identify a three-funnelled cruiser in the escort of the convoy she had been tracking through the night.[6] Meisel ordered torpedo tubes readied to fire at this ship, identified as a heavy cruiser, but delayed as more ships came into view in the growing light.[7] The heavy cruiser, *Berwick*, was 3nm ahead of the convoy; *Bonaventure* and the corvette HMS *Clematis* (K36) were on the starboard side, from which *Hipper* was approaching. Finally, at 07.39, *Hipper* opened fire at *Berwick* with her main battery of eight 20.3cm/60 guns. As far as can be ascertained, this was the first inkling anyone with the convoy had of *Hipper*'s presence. Fortunately, *Berwick*, as was the case with all the ships of WS 5A, was at dawn Action Stations, with all crew at their weapons, and she reacted quickly, firing back at *Hipper* within two minutes and getting off a message to the Admiralty, reporting the presence of a *Deutschland* class *Panzerschiff* bearing 290°, distance 12nm. (The misidentification of *Hipper* as one of the *Deutschlands* is perhaps understandable given that the British were well aware that *Scheer* was loose in the Atlantic – although her exact position was unknown, the Admiralty had noted the presence of an enemy 'raider' near Ascension Island the day before.[8] Nothing in the Admiralty War Diaries indicates any knowledge that *Hipper* was in the North Atlantic, a situation no doubt abetted by the fact that she had not seen, or been seen by, any ship other than her oilers since leaving Germany.)

The protagonist at the Christmas Day engagement in 1940 was *Admiral Hipper*, seen here as she appeared at Brest at the end of the sortie the Germans codenamed *Nordseetour*. The camouflage scheme in which she is painted was chosen specifically to mimic that used on the British battleship HMS *Revenge* (06).

The action that followed was sporadic, confusing (both for the participants and historians), inconclusive and unsatisfying. It was most of the above because the weather was hardly conducive for a sea battle; while the sea was calm and the wind light, thick patches of mist regularly disrupted visibility and even *Hipper*'s FuMO 22 radar was insufficiently precise for fire control when visual contact was lost. A message from *Furious* reporting the action to the Admiralty stated that visibility was often limited to a half-mile.[9] Other ships in the escort reacted quickly. *Clematis*, armed with a single 4in/45 gun forward and capable of 16 knots on a good day, swung around towards *Hipper*, but the enemy was soon lost to sight and she returned to the convoy. *Bonaventure*, one of the *Didos* completed with only four main-battery turrets, likewise turned towards *Hipper* and was soon dodging shell splashes while chasing the enemy. This immediately showed up a weakness of the early *Didos*, indeed of many of the 'treaty cruisers' of many of the nations covered here; due to excessive flexing of her forecastle during the extreme manoeuvres involved in salvo-chasing, caused by the lightness of her construction, her 'A' turret jammed in train and was unusable after that.[10] For that reason, and the poor visibility, *Bonaventure* neither hit nor was hit in her 24-minute-long engagement with *Hipper*.

While this was going on, between 07.39 and 08.56, *Hipper* and *Berwick* intermittently exchanged fire when they could see each other. During one of the periods when *Berwick* was not visible, *Hipper* opened fire on several ships of the convoy that were briefly visible and was able to damage the cargo ship *Arabistan* and the troop transport *Empire Trooper*, the latter

seriously enough that she had to be escorted to Ponta Delgada in the Azores for emergency repairs with sixteen of her embarked soldiers killed. At 08.05, *Hipper* scored a hit on *Berwick*'s 'X' turret, killing four of the Royal Marines manning it, seriously wounding another and putting it out of action. At 08.08, *Berwick* was hit again, this time below the waterline below 'B' turret, causing some flooding and putting that turret out of action as well. *Berwick* was hit at least two more times, possibly more, because she reported a shell passing through her forward boiler room without exploding, a 4in AA gun destroyed and her middle funnel holed. She claimed one hit on *Hipper*, but this did not occur. The latter, under explicit orders to avoid combat with enemy warships, slipped away into the murk towards the west-north-west at approximately 09.15.

This could hardly be considered a good day for any of the cruisers involved. *Hipper* fired 185 main-battery rounds and 113 secondary-battery rounds, and obtained four or five hits on *Berwick* and an unknown, but very small, number on the two merchantmen, a hit rate below 3 per cent. This has to be seen as somewhat disappointing, given the relatively short ranges, often down to 8000yd, at which this battle was fought, though mitigated a bit by the poor visibility. Nonetheless, it was better than the Royal Navy's rate. *Berwick*'s fire was terrible, scoring not a single hit. *Hipper*'s crew reported that *Berwick*'s fire was consistently falling well short; after the battle, *Hipper*'s deck was littered with spent shell fragments which had fallen harmlessly. Further, this battle exposed a serious flaw in the design of the *Dido* class; the lightly-constructed forecastle was strengthened in those ships still under construction and in earlier ships when they were refitted; in the meanwhile, captains were advised to avoid violent manoeuvres, particularly during heavy weather.

Both main protagonists headed to the nearest dockyard – *Hipper* to Brest and *Berwick* to Gibraltar. *Hipper*'s stay at the French port was relatively brief; she arrived on 27 December and departed again on 1 February on another commerce raid. *Berwick* stayed at Gibraltar only long enough to get her underwater damage patched up. She departed for Portsmouth on 5 January 1941, and upon arrival was docked there for permanent repairs and refit. In May she transferred to Rosyth where her refit continued, rejoining the fleet on 15 October at Scapa Flow, after an absence of nine-and-a-half months.

The commanding officer of the Allied forces at the Battle of Savo Island was Rear Admiral Victor A C Crutchley, RN, succeeding the ill-starred John Crace as RACAS (Rear Admiral Commanding Australian Squadron). Crutchley, for all his personal bravery, was no luckier than Crace. The disposition he chose for the Allied forces off Guadalcanal on the night of 8 August 1942 was unfortunate, made doubly so by his decision to take his flagship HMAS *Australia* (D84) with him when he was called to a command conference by Rear Admiral Richmond K Turner. (AWM)

Unprepared for the Present: Savo Island – 9 August 1942

The night was stifling, airless, unnaturally dark; the men were exhausted, having been, in many cases, on alert with hardly any time off for two days. However, neither nature nor the enemy were in any mood to give them a break.

Two days before, on 7 August 1942, they had steamed into Savo Sound, a reef-bound strait that separates the Florida Islands (Nggela Islands) from Guadalcanal, a body of water that would soon become famous by another name. There they had supported the landings of US Marines on Tulagi, where the Japanese had established a seaplane base in May, and at Lunga Point on Guadalcanal, where there was a construction crew close to completing work on a dirt airstrip. The decision to invade these islands, despite the stated 'Europe First' strategy adopted when America entered the Second World War after the Pearl Harbor attack, came on 2 July 1942, which actually was two days before aerial reconnaissance detected the work on the airfield on Guadalcanal.[11] There is much about the whole affair that was impromptu, so much so that many of the participants in Operation 'Watchtower' dubbed it Operation 'Shoestring'.

Nowhere was this more apparent than in the naval support

for the operation, which had been hastily organised and whose leadership was complex and often uncoordinated. The landings themselves were the responsibility of COMPHIB-SOPAC (Commander, Amphibious Forces South Pacific) Rear Admiral Richmond K Turner, but the fire support and local defence was commanded by Rear Admiral Victor A C Crutchley, RN, who had succeeded Rear Admiral John G Crace as RACAS (Rear Admiral Commanding Australian Squadron) after the Battle of the Coral Sea. (For the purposes of carrying out these landings, the naval forces carrying and supporting the Marines were organised as TF62, with the defence forces organised as task groups under Turner's overall command.) To confuse matters further, the air support for the landings was even more fragmented, with some coming from land-based assets in Australia – both American and Australian – and also flying from bases on New Caledonia (*Nouvelle-Calédonie*), Espiritu Santo, Ndeni (Nendö, also known as Santa Cruz Island) and Fiji, but the most significant air support came from three US Navy aircraft carriers in Vice Admiral Frank J Fletcher's TF61. Fletcher had commanded US naval forces at the Coral Sea and again at Midway, emerging victorious both times, but not without some criticism of his leadership for being overly cautious and for displaying more concern for the fuel state of his ships than for pursuing the enemy. By virtue of rank, Fletcher was the senior officer in support of the Guadalcanal landings; the question was how long would he stay in support of those landings.

It turned out that was a valid concern. Even before the landings, Fletcher made it known that he intended to stay in support range of the shore only a brief time and, on 8 August, the day after the landings, he told Vice Admiral Robert L Ghormley, COMSOPAC (Commander, South Pacific Area) that he intended to withdraw immediately.[12] This decision left Turner and Crutchley with a serious problem and, after the sun had set that day, Turner called a command conference on his flagship off Lunga Point to discuss how to handle the situation. This, in turn, disturbed Crutchley's carefully-considered defensive plan for protecting the only partially-unloaded transports gathered off Tulagi and Lunga Point.

Crutchley was aware that there was a threat from the direction of Rabaul. What he did not know was how great a threat or when he could expect that threat to materialise. Six unidentified Japanese ships were reported in St George Channel outside Rabaul at 12.31 on the 7th by USAAF aircraft, a not unusual or particularly alarming bit of news which reached Turner late that night.[13] The American submarine USS *S-38* (SS143), patrolling off the southern exit from St George Channel sighted Japanese warships later that day, at 20.00, and reported 'two destroyers and three larger ships of unknown type' moving at high speed towards the south-east.[14] This was somewhat more interesting, but not terribly unexpected so close off a major Japanese base and still a long way away – the point where *S-38* sighted the Japanese force was approximately 550nm from Tulagi. Turner ordered enhanced air patrols of the sea lanes to the north-west of the landing zones, in particular of the passage down the New Georgia Sound between the eastern and western 'chains' of the central Solomons, a channel soon to be dubbed 'The Slot' by the Americans.

The flagship of Vice Admiral Mikawa Gunichi at the Battle of Savo Island was *Chokai*, seen here off China in 1938. In this view, *Chokai* appears much as she would have at Savo Island; she and her sister *Maya* had been scheduled for reconstruction, with bulges added to compensate for an even larger superstructure and increased AA armament, but war began before this work could be carried out. She still has her single 12cm/45 heavy HA guns on her shelter deck. (NHHC)

The force that the submarine sighted was one that most definitely should have concerned Crutchley. When news of the 'Watchtower' landings reached Vice Admiral Mikawa Gunichi, commander of the Japanese 8th Fleet based at

Seen at high speed during a training exercise in 1940, *Kako* shows the most obvious signs of the extensive reconstruction she underwent in 1936–7, the replacement of her six single main-battery gunhouses with three twin turrets. The reduction in the number of gun mounts and replacement of her broader after funnel by a much narrower one give her a very unusual silhouette, especially with her forward turrets turned away, so that the 20cm/50 guns are not visible. *Kako* fought well at Savo Island, hitting USS *Chicago* (CA29) with a torpedo and *Vincennes* with gunfire, but she was not allowed to enjoy her success for long, being torpedoed and sunk the next day. (NHHC)

Rabaul, he acted immediately. The force under his immediate command at Rabaul was small; he had just the two old light cruisers *Tenryu* and *Yubari*. However, at Kavieng, at the other end of the archipelago, five heavy cruisers – the four pre-'treaty maximum' cruisers of *Sentai* 6 (*Furutaka*, *Kako*, *Aoba* and *Kinugasa*) and the newer *Chokai*, plus the destroyer *Yunagi* – were just leaving port; Mikawa ordered them immediately redirected towards Rabaul. where they would be sighted by the USAAF aircraft in St George Channel, and then, now joined by his two cruisers, sighted again by *S-38*. They were indeed moving at a good clip towards the south-east, but would soon thereafter turn to the east on a course that would take them north of Buka Island before they would turn south-east again. They made that turn at 02.00 on 8 August and then headed along the eastern side of Bougainville Island before turning again, at approximately 06.25, to a course of due south that would take them into the Bougainville Strait and the northern entrance of The Slot. At this point, Mikawa had each of his heavy cruisers launch a scout aircraft to search a wide arc ahead, looking for the location of Allied forces off Guadalcanal and any support forces lurking nearby.

At 10.28 and again at 11.01 on the 8th, a pair of Australian Hudsons, flying from Milne Bay, Papua New Guinea, sighted Mikawa's force soon after the scout planes were launched.[15] This critical information took a long time to reach the interested parties off Guadalcanal; Crutchley did not receive the first report until after 18.30 and the second after 22.00, but it was flawed in other ways as well. The Australian intelligence summary for 9 August gave the following report:

> (vi) BUKA-BOUGAINVILLE AREA – Allied aircraft on recce 8/8 observed numerous small groups of enemy vessels N. and W. of Bougainville and Buka Is. The minimum total of enemy shipping in the area is considered to be 6 cruisers (including probably 3 heavy) 5 destroyers, 2 possible seaplane tenders, 4 gunboats, 1 or more submarines, 6 merchant vessels.[16]

The ways in which this report was unhelpful are almost too many to mention. The location mentioned here was well to the north and west of the actual sightings, and the inclusion of two 'possible seaplane tenders' was enough to throw off everyone's expectations on the Allied side. Apparently, both the 'on-site' commanders and the Allied intelligence staff in Australia interpreted the possible presence of the seaplane tenders as indicating that this movement was part of an expected Japanese scheme to set up an advanced seaplane base at Rekata Bay on the north-west coast of Santa Isabel Island. Critically, it did not give solid enough warning to the on-site commanders to prepare better for the assault that was coming.

Because that was exactly what was coming, an assault on the Allied landing forces off Guadalcanal and Tulagi and on any ships defending them. Once Mikawa had recovered his scout aircraft at approximately noon – they reported the Allied naval presence in Savo Sound with reasonable accuracy – he formed up his force in battle order and started down the Bougainville Strait at 24 knots. His force was drawn up in a single line ahead, with his flagship *Chokai* in front, followed in order by *Aoba*, *Kako*, *Kinugasa*, *Furutaka*, *Tenryu*, *Yubari* and *Yunagi*. His battle order, issued at 16.40, was simply to enter Savo Sound after dark through the southern passage between Savo Island and Guadalcanal, attack any shipping found off Lunga Point with torpedoes, turn north and attack shipping off Tulagi with guns and torpedoes and then retire at high speed through the northern passage, so as to be as far as possible from the scene and the risk of air attack by Fletcher's carriers by daylight.[17]

Crutchley, thus, may not have had any certainty that enemy forces were approaching as the sun sank over the rugged backbone of Guadalcanal on 8 August, but he knew he had to deploy his ships to defend the landing forces just in case. The forces that Crutchley had to deploy for the defence of the landing beaches were not inconsiderable. He had his own TF44 – the former ANZAC Squadron that was the core of Australian naval defence – re-numbered TG62.6 for Operation 'Watchtower', which comprised *Australia*, *Canberra*, *Hobart* (D63), USS *Chicago* (CA29), *Helm* (DD388), *Bagley* (DD386), *Patterson* (DD392) and *Jarvis* (DD393). Crutchley also had command of TF62's attached support group, which comprised USS *Vincennes*, *Quincy*, *Astoria*, *San Juan* (CL54), *Blue* (DD387), *Ralph Talbot* (DD390), *Wilson* (DD408), *Monssen* (DD436) and *Buchanan* (DD484). Crutchley's problem was how to organise these forces to defend the landing beaches on the night of 8/9 August.

The plan that Crutchley devised was complex because his problem was complex. Savo Sound had a narrow entrance to the east – actually three channels of which only the middle one, Sealark Channel, was deep enough for easy navigation. It was unlikely, but not impossible, that the Japanese would approach from that direction, and it would have been foolhardy to discount it entirely. To the north-west, the entrance was much broader and divided in two by Savo Island; the southern half of that entrance was approximately 7nm wide, the northern half was somewhat broader at just over 10nm. As these entrances pointed in the direction of the closest major Japanese naval base at Rabaul, it was easy for Crutchley to presume that the greater threat lay in this direction. Part of the problem was that the eastern and north-western entrances were separated by 25nm, making it difficult, but not necessarily impossible, to cover all the entrances with a unified force. No doubt Crutchley had to consider the possibility, however remote, that a Japanese attack might materialise from both ends of the sound at the same time.

Whatever his reasoning may have been, Crutchley decided to divide his forces into three task groups, each assigned a discrete role.

TG62.3 – Comprised of *Vincennes* (Captain Frederick L Riefkohl), commanding, *Quincy* and *Astoria* following in line, with *Helm* on *Vincennes'* port bow and *Wilson* to starboard. This group's assigned sector was the northern half of the north-western entrance into the sound. Riefkohl had his formation cutting a square centred just south of a line between Savo Island and the western tip of Florida Island (Ngella Sule), at 10 knots, 600yd between ships, turning 90° to port every half-hour. Detached, but technically part of TG62.3, were two more destroyers – *Blue* and *Ralph Talbot* – which were on picket duty west of the two north-western entrances to Savo Sound. Both destroyers carried SC radars, which were air-search sets with some limited surface-search capability – they might have the ability to detect a large surface target at 10nm in ideal conditions. They also had Mk 4 (FD) fire-control radars on their DP directors, but those would be of limited use in a search capacity unless they were pointed at a previously-identified target. Unfortunately, the conditions were far from ideal on the night of 8/9 August 1942, with scattered rain squalls and nearby land masses, both of which interfered with radar reception, especially in the hands of inexperienced operators such as were to be found on Crutchley's ships this night. Each of these destroyers was assigned the task of patrolling back-and-forth across its assigned half of the north-western entrances – *Blue* in the south and *Talbot* in the north. Besides these two destroyers, each of the four American heavy cruisers were equipped with an air-search radar and a fire-control radar for their main-battery guns.[18]

TG62.4 – Comprising *San Juan*, *Hobart*, *Monssen* and *Buchanan*, commanded by Rear Admiral Norman Scott in *San Juan*. Their assignment was covering the eastern entrance into Savo Sound. As such, they would miss the action this night, probably to their great good fortune. (Curiously, *San Juan*, which was an *Atlanta* class light cruiser, was the only one of the Allied ships equipped with the excellent new SG (Sail George) microwave surface-search radar set.)

TG62.6 – Including Crutchley's flagship *Australia*, *Canberra* and *Chicago*, in line ahead, with *Patterson* on *Australia*'s port bow and *Bagley* to starboard. These were ships that had served together, in some cases for many months, as part of the former ANZAC Squadron, later re-designated TF44. Crutchley had them on a back-and-forth patrol line south-east of Savo Island, 600yd apart, steaming roughly north-west to south-east at 12 knots, reversing course every hour, covering the southern half of the north-western entrance into Savo Sound

The Allies had one more warship, the destroyer *Jarvis*, which had been damaged in a Japanese air attack earlier on the 8th and was making her way westward through the southern half of the north-western entrance into Savo Sound while this night's action developed.

This disposition has been severely criticised, primarily because it split a strong force into weaker sub-units that could be (and, under the circumstances, were) overwhelmed individually.[19] But the biggest problems Crutchley's cruisers faced this night were not caused by his disposition of forces. One was his absence from the scene when the enemy struck; as mentioned above, he was called to a command conference with Turner and left TG62.6 in *Australia* to head towards Lunga Point, missing the battle that developed in his absence. He left Captain Howard Bode in *Chicago* in tactical command of TG62.6, but assigned no-one to assume his overall command responsibility while he was absent. No effort was made to move *Chicago* into the lead of this now-shortened line; apparently Bode believed Crutchley would be back before he would have to make any command decisions. Another problem was a particularly unfortunately timed and placed heavy rain squall that moved south-east off Savo Island directly between the two western cruiser groups, blocking their view of each other just as Mikawa was approaching from the north-west.

Finally, there was the fact that, at this point in August 1942, the Japanese were simply better equipped and better trained for night fighting. They practised night manoeuvres regularly, so that they were second-nature to officers and men. Their ships were equipped with better weapons for night fighting, particularly the excellent Type 93 24in torpedo, which had range and speed totally unexpected by the Allied forces at this point in the war.[20] The Japanese went so far as to test their sailors for low-light visual acuity and to post those seamen with good night-vision as lookouts. This in part accounts for the fact that lookouts in *Chokai* sighted *Blue* at 00.54 on 9 August at a range of well over 11,000yd, while the latter was steaming away on the south-west leg of her patrol line; the Japanese force, heading south-east at 26 knots, turned briefly a few degrees to port to give *Blue* a wider berth, but then turned back south-east at 01.05, undetected by the picket destroyer. Shortly, with Savo Island in sight, *Chokai* swung further south and then back eastward. At 01.34, lookouts sighted a single destroyer only 3000yd to the north on an opposite heading and Mikawa ordered a spread of torpedoes fired; this ship, the independently-operating *Jarvis*, soon disappeared into the night, unharmed in any way. At approximately 01.36, lookouts in *Chokai* caught sight of TG62.6 almost dead ahead, range 12,500yd. At 01.40, Mikawa started to bring his line around to port so that his ships could, in turn, launch torpedoes at the enemy force which continued to approach, apparently unaware of his presence. In fact, it was not until three minutes later that lookouts in *Patterson*, off *Canberra*'s port bow, sighted the enemy and sounded the alarm. The range at that time was down to 5000yd.

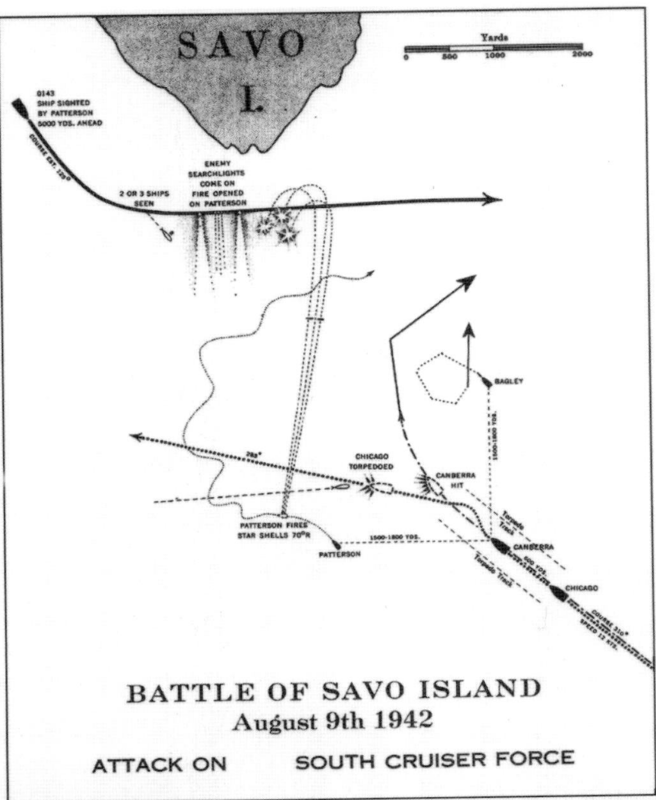

This chart is one of two developed by the US Navy in an attempt to understand what happened in the night action at Savo Island, 8/9 August 1942. Given the fact that it was drawn up not long after the end of the war, based on action reports and interrogation of Japanese survivors, it is surprisingly accurate. Only the direction from which the torpedo came that hit *Chicago*'s bow is noticeably incorrect; *Chicago* was hit in her starboard bow (as will be clearly seen in a later image). All the torpedoes seen by the southern cruiser group came from the north-west, even those that passed on the port side. (USN)

The battle that ensued will not be described in any detail here; this engagement has been recounted many times by other authors.[21] Suffice it to say that of the five heavy cruisers in the two north-western task groups, four were sunk and the fifth damaged by Japanese gunfire and torpedoes. What makes the Battle of Savo Island potentially interesting to this narrative is not the strategy or tactics involved, but the damage and in particular the sinkings – why and how five Allied heavy cruisers were knocked out of action, and four of them sunk, in a remarkably short period of time and with relative ease, by a Japanese force that was, at least on paper, somewhat inferior in fighting qualities. Was it entirely a matter of how the ships were fought or was there something in their design that predisposed them to sink that night? Would better designed or built ships have survived? In the case of the one cruiser that survived, was it because she was hit less frequently or in less vital areas, or perhaps because she was just luckier, or was there some other reason? To look at these questions, it is best to examine the fates of these ships individually:

HMAS *Canberra* – Leading the southern line of two cruisers, *Canberra* was the initial target for the three cruisers at the head of the Japanese line. While precision is impossible, various sources state that she was hit by approximately twenty-four 20cm and 12.7cm shells within two minutes, and that these hits were sufficient to jam 'A' turret in train and also disabled 'X' turret, to disable her power plant, mortally wound her captain and destroy her radio facilities, leaving her without power or means of communication.[22] What is known with certainty is that *Canberra* was unable to fire her main-battery guns before she lost all power and the ability to do so. It is also believed with some degree of assurance that she was struck by at least one and possibly two torpedoes, most likely on her starboard side, which, since she had turned to starboard before losing power, was facing away from the enemy. What is also known is that the destroyer *Bagley*, which had been on *Canberra*'s starboard bow at the beginning of the action, began a sharp turn to port (towards *Canberra*) as soon as action commenced, hoping to unmask her starboard torpedo tubes. This, however, did not give her enough time to arm the torpedoes, so she continued the turn through another 180° until, with her port side facing the enemy, four torpedoes were fired. Two were heard to hit, but no Japanese ship was hit by torpedoes during the battle. Even an American official history accepts the likelihood that *Canberra* was hit by *Bagley*'s torpedoes.[23]

The proximate cause of the loss of *Canberra* was fire and the inability to contain the fires due to their extent and the loss of power, with the resulting loss of water pressure. The 'art' of fire-fighting in a ship rests chiefly in the ability of the crew to establish lines of containment that can prevent the fire's spread and allow it to be beaten back compartment-by-compartment. This, however, depends on many factors working in the crews' favour, which include an adequate supply of water (or other fire-fighting chemicals).[24] Design factors, such as the arrangement of the power plant or the redundancy of the cross-connections of the fire mains, could (and did in many cases) have an influence on the ability of a crew to fight fires and were improved in later classes of cruisers in the US and Royal Navies, but were less advanced in the classes that fought at Savo Island.

Having decided that the transports and other support craft would have to withdraw in the morning, Turner ordered that any ship that could not raise steam by 06.30 was to be scuttled, which sealed *Canberra*'s fate. It simply is not possible to say whether she could have been saved had more time been available, nor is it possible to state that she would have been saveable had she not been hit by

Canberra is seen here steaming across Ironbottom Sound on 7 August 1942, with Tulagi and the Florida (Nggela) Islands in the background. Invasion transports, with multiple landing craft around them, lie in between. *Canberra* and *Australia* were sister-ships and looked a great deal alike, but there were detail differences that allow the two to be distinguished; for one thing, *Australia*'s mainmast at this time was noticeably shorter than her foremast, while *Canberra*'s masts were approximately the same height; also, *Australia* had a taller and more prominent searchlight platform forward of the HADT on her after control platform. (NARA)

This image was taken at approximately 06.00 on 9 August 1942. It shows *Canberra* in distress, afire and listing noticeably to starboard, the side that would have been away from the Japanese during the engagement (and towards USS *Bagley* (DD386)). Both 'B' and 'X' turrets are hard over to port, obviously jammed in that position when the ship lost power. Two other American destroyers were here attempting to help out; at *Canberra*'s near bow was USS *Blue* (DD387) – the southern picket destroyer in the pre-battle disposition – with USS *Patterson* (DD392) approaching from the right. Note that both *Blue* and *Patterson* have SC radar antennas on the mastheads and FD antennas on the front face of their DP directors. *Canberra* would be deemed unsalvageable and scuttled shortly after 08.00. (NARA)

torpedoes, whatever their source. What is known is that she proved difficult to sink when the time came to scuttle her. One American destroyer put over 200 5in rounds and four torpedoes into her without finishing the job; it took a fifth torpedo from a second destroyer to sink her at 08.00 on 9 August. There were 193 casualties among her crew, including eighty-four dead or missing.

USS *Chicago* – Although designated temporary flagship of TG62.6, *Chicago* was at the end of the two-ship line and, if anything, was even less prepared for the onslaught about to overtake it. Her captain had retired to his stateroom for some needed rest. Most ships were in a form of 'relaxed' Condition I, that allowed some men a chance to grab some sleep while keeping all weapons and stations manned. Lookouts in *Chicago* had seen 'orange flashes' ahead, noted in the log at 01.42, which were almost certainly the firing charges of Japanese torpedo tubes going off – according to Japanese records, torpedoes had been fired at the southern force as early as 01.40, but all times must be taken as approximations, given the rush of events and the inaccuracy of clocks – followed almost immediately by the illumination of aircraft flares and flashes of gunfire from the leading Japanese cruisers. As Bode rushed to the bridge he ordered star shells fired, but, in keeping with American luck this night, these failed to detonate. A lookout sighted a torpedo track to starboard, causing Bode to order a hard turn to port, but seconds later, tracks were sighted to port and the turn order was reversed. Moments later, at 01.47, a single torpedo hit *Chicago*'s starboard forefoot. (Several sources positively identify *Kako*, third in the Japanese line, as firing the torpedo that hit *Chicago*.[25]) Fortunately for *Chicago*, the torpedo hit right forward, so the damage, while locally serious, was isolated and never threatened the ship's buoyancy. The shock of the hit did temporarily knock out forward main-battery fire control.

With targets visible straight ahead, *Chicago* continued off to the west-north-west, briefly engaging the ships at the end of the Japanese line, firing twenty-five rounds from her forward guns; she seems to have achieved one hit with her secondary battery on *Tenryu* that killed twenty-three men and wounded another twenty-one. The destroyer *Yunagi*, apparently suffering a navigation equipment failure, remained south of Savo Island, luring *Chicago* further west. Before exiting the battle, *Chicago* received a hit from the starboard that damaged one leg of her

Chicago is seen here on 20 December 1942 at Mare Island Navy Yard after completion of repairs and a minor refit following the damage she received at the Battle of Savo Island. For all intents, she looks the same as she did at that battle. Her electronics suite has been partially upgraded: a CXAM air-search antenna at the top of her foremast; two Mk 3 (FC) antennas for main-battery fire control, one on the foretop and the other aft just above turret No 3; an SG surface-search antenna on a platform midway down the top part of the forward leg of her foremast and two Mk 4 (FD) antennas for AA fire control, one on each of her HA directors. (NARA)

foremast and detonated in way of her forward funnel, killing two men and wounding another twenty-one. She continued on towards the west while the battle quickly moved away to the north. Bode was faulted for not following after Mikawa and for not sending warning messages reporting his encounter with the Japanese. It is perhaps understandable, given the damage to his ship, that Captain Bode chose not to dash off into the night after the enemy. His decision not to alert the other forces as to the enemy's presence may be, perhaps, due to an assumption on his part that, by this time, everyone in the area knew the Japanese were there, and the last thing anyone needed was more radio chatter.

Chicago's survival this night was clearly due to the fact that she received just the two hits, neither of them serious enough to endanger the ship or her ability to move or defend herself. Bode's decision to steer away from the action was sharply criticised after the fact, but it no doubt was a factor in *Chicago*'s survival.

USS *Vincennes* – By the time the Japanese force encountered the northern cruiser force (TG62.3), it had split into two parallel columns. The effect of this was devastating for the American cruisers, which got caught in a crossfire, with four Japanese cruisers, led by *Chokai*, to the east, and the other three to the west. Coming through the dense squall that had moved between the two Allied western task groups, the Japanese launched torpedoes at approximately 01.48 and, continuing to close, turned on searchlights and opened fire with devastating effect at 01.55.[26] Within a minute, gunfire had hit the bridge, the antenna trunk, the battle lookout position in the after superstructure called 'Battle II', the carpenter shop and the hangar in *Vincennes*, starting intense fires in the latter two compartments. In another minute, hits on Sky Forward and Sky Aft caused further serious casualties, particularly as the latter blew the after Mk 33 DP director overboard. Captain Riefkohl ordered speed increased and a turn to port, but neither had time to be effective; by 02.00, a hard right turn was ordered as the enemy fire was becoming even more intense. By this time, attempts at controlling the spreading fires were becoming increasingly futile as all fire main risers had been destroyed. Intense fires in the movie locker and cane

As the chart of the action of the southern cruiser group showed, *Chicago* was torpedoed and continued on, away from the action. Unlike in the chart, as this image showing the ship's crew working to cut away the damaged shell plating on 9 August 1942, the torpedo did not hit from the port bow, but rather from the starboard, causing the torn sheet steel seen here, bent off to port. Fortunately for *Chicago*, this hit, which was the worst damage she received in this battle, was low and right forward, and never threatened her survival. (NARA)

fender storage burned out of control. At approximately 02.00, a torpedo (or a 20cm AP shell) struck *Vincennes*' port side in way of No 1 fire room, flooding that compartment.[27] At approximately 02.05, while again making a hard turn to port, her pilot house was destroyed, caused a temporary loss of steering control. By the time steering control had been restored through the after control station, all power had been lost due to abandoning of the engine rooms because they were filling with toxic fumes from the fires amidships. Turret No 2 had been disabled by a shell that penetrated the face plate at 02.09, which, although it did not explode, nonetheless ignited all the powder charges in the gun room. Earlier in the action, the barbette of turret No 1 had been hit, jamming that turret in train. Finally, at 02.15, the Japanese cruisers, now heading north-westward away from the area, shut off their searchlights and ceased firing. *Vincennes*, with an increasing list to port, drifted to a stop with only one main-battery turret and one secondary-battery gun still functioning.

In all, *Vincennes* had been hit by fifty-seven known shell hits (almost certainly more than that) and at least one torpedo (in way of turret No 2). Captain Riefkohl held off issuing the order to abandon ship for fifteen minutes after the action died down, but, by 02.30, it was quite clear that there was no possibility of saving the ship and the order was given. That proved to be timely, as twenty minutes later, at 02.50, *Vincennes* capsized to port and slid bow-first under the surface approximately a mile north-east of Savo Island. There is no mystery as to why she sank and

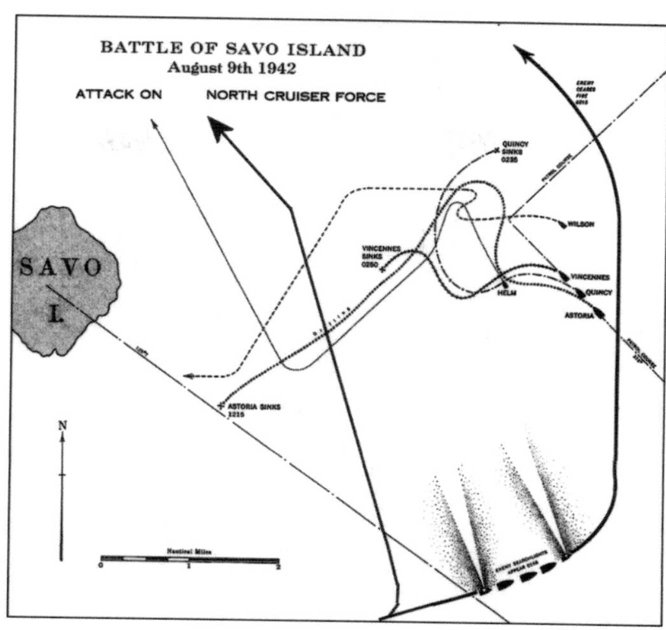

This chart shows the tracks of the northern cruiser group at the Battle of Savo Island reasonable well (except that *Vincennes* sank further to the west), the Japanese groups less so. It does show how the Japanese line split, though not the disorganisation with which it split, nor does it show that *Chokai* split from the eastern Japanese cruiser group, manoeuvring independently and not rejoining until they were well north of Savo Island. It shows quite well how the American formation fragmented under Mikawa's attack, each of the three cruisers in the northern group writhing in its own death agony. (USN)

The line of three cruisers in the northern group was led by *Vincennes*, the newest of the cruisers at Savo Island. Her radar suite appears to include an SC radar at her foremast head and FC antennas on her main-battery directors, as seen in this image taken at Pearl Harbor in May 1942. She wears a complex Ms 12 Mod Graded System camouflage of Sea Blue (5-S) at the waterline, with lighter patches of Ocean Gray (5-O) above that on her hull and up into the superstructure, and then patches of even lighter Haze Gray (5-H) breaking up the Ocean Gray on the superstructure. (NARA)

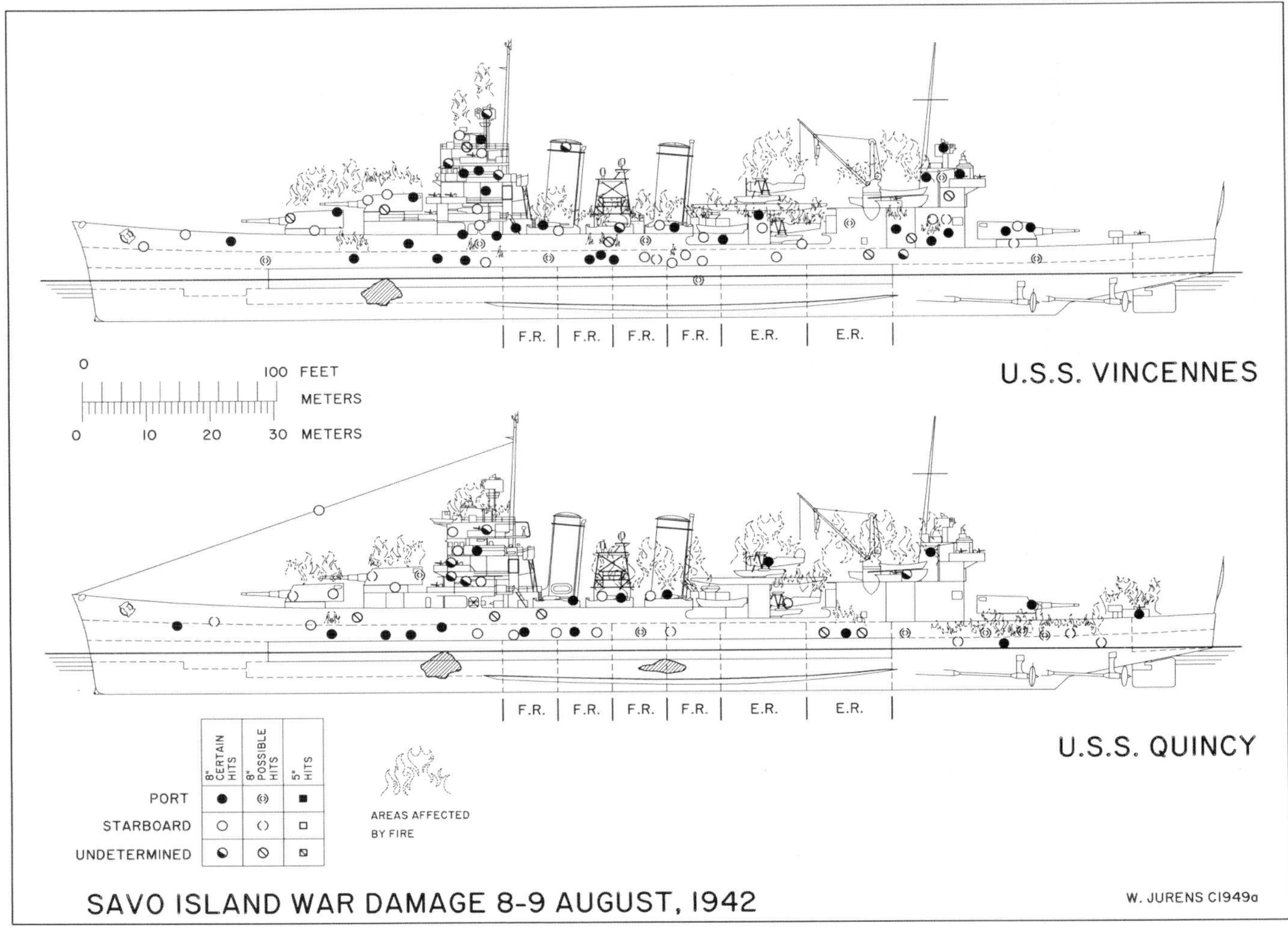

It is not possible to look at this diagram of the damage done to *Vincennes* and *Quincy* by Mikawa's cruisers, derived from a chart included in the War Damage Report generated in June 1943 from the best evidence then available, and believe that either ship could have survived. It shows dozens of documented gunfire hits with many more probable hits and also torpedo hits, all of which occurred in a period of twenty minutes. No ship of this size could be expected to survive this amount of punishment. (William Jurens)

no question that any ship of her size, even one with better protection, would likely have succumbed to the battering that she took. Three hundred and thirty-two men died in *Vincennes*, with another 258 wounded.

USS *Quincy* – The first hit on *Quincy* came only moments after she was illuminated at 01.55, striking a 1.1in mount right aft on her fantail.[28] Moments later she followed *Vincennes* as that ship turned to port and then, after getting off two salvos from her main battery, she swung around hard to starboard, during which manoeuvre she was hit repeatedly from both sides by 20cm and 12.7cm rounds. Battle II, turret No 3, the 1.1in clipping room at the base of her foremast and her bridge were all hit at this time, in some cases repeatedly. At the beginning of this turn, *Quincy* was hit by two torpedoes in her port side; one hit in way of her IC (interior communications) room just aft of turret No 2, the other at the bulkhead between fire rooms No 3 and No 4, flooding both compartments and reducing power immediately by half. A 20cm AP shell penetrated turret No 2, where it detonated in the gun room, setting off all exposed powder charges, gutting the turret and leaving it 'burning like a torch'.[29] At the same time, turret No 1 was disabled by hits in the upper powder room and on the shell deck below that, which left it burning as well. The bridge was hit hard, killing most of the personnel there, including the captain, and destroying steering control, leaving the ship steaming a random course until power was lost at about 02.15. Without officers to exercise command, some of the crew began abandoning ship shortly thereafter; the remaining officers began ordering

Also sporting Ms 12 Mod camouflage, although a somewhat less complicated version, is *Quincy*, seen at New York City on 23 May 1942, with the newly-commissioned escort aircraft carrier HMS *Biter* (D97), whose conversion from SS *Rio Parana* had just been completed at the Atlantic Basin yard in Brooklyn, in the background. *Quincy* appears to have the same radar set-up as *Vincennes* had; *Biter* appears to have a Type 279 antenna (half of the two antenna set is visible) on her foremast and a Perspex 'lantern' for a Type 271 surface-search radar antenna on her small bridge. (NARA)

the remaining crew to follow suit at approximately 02.35. This was none too soon, as the ship's port list rapidly increased to the point that, sometime before 02.40, she rolled over and sank bow first approximately two miles east of the point where *Vincennes* would sink.

Quincy sustained thirty-six known shell hits, plus an unknown number of additional hits that were not recorded. The fact that she took even less time to sink than *Vincennes*, despite having received far fewer shell hits, is certainly attributable to the massive damage caused by the two torpedo hits on her port side and the widespread fires that prevented any meaningful attempt at damage control. No ship of her size could have survived this amount of damage. Even without the torpedo hits, her survival would have unlikely; an examination of the gunfire damage diagram attached to the War Damage Report shows a concentration of hits near the waterline just above her narrow armour strake that would likely have, over a short period of time, led to flooding as severe as that caused by the two torpedoes, which were the proximate cause of her sinking. Because of the hurried and ad hoc nature of her abandonment, *Quincy*'s losses were the highest among the Allied cruisers at Savo Sound this night; 370 men were killed and a further 167 were wounded.

USS *Astoria* – As the third ship in the northern line, *Astoria* was spared any torpedo damage and seemed to receive somewhat less attention from the Japanese, not that this spared her from sharing the fate of her two sisters.[30] The first three salvos fired at *Astoria* by the Japanese after she was illuminated at 01.55 missed forward, From the fourth, one shell hit well forward, starting a fire in her paint locker. The fifth salvo hit with devastating accuracy, setting fire to the boats on her boat deck just abaft the after funnel and hitting the hangar where three aircraft were stored, starting an intense fire there. Another shell hit the aftermost 5in/25 mount on the port side, in way of the after funnel, setting off the ready-use rounds stored there and destroying the ventilation blower serving No 3 fire room. Three shells from the sixth salvo hit turret No 1 in the barbette and face plate, disabling the turret and killing the entire gun crew. From this point on, shells landed more rapidly and the accounting of their order and placement becomes less complete. At some point just before 02.00, a shell penetrated No 1 fire room and detonated inside, killing or wounding most of the work force. By 02.00, the entire amidships section of the ship at the Upper Deck level was afire and flames was spreading on the two decks below this.

The heaviest shellfire hit *Astoria* over the next six minutes, between 02.00 and 02.06. The forward engine room was abandoned at approximately 02.02 when it began to fill with toxic smoke, reducing the ship's speed to 9 knots. Most of the remaining compartments in the engineering plant were abandoned in turn as they became untenable due to heat and smoke – No 4 fire room at 02.09, No 3 fire room at 02.11, the after engine room at 02.15 – leaving the ship with no power as it drifted to a stop about a mile south-east of Savo Island with a 2–3° list to port. At the same time, the captain ordered the bridge abandoned because ammunition on the 1.1in clipping room in the lower superstructure began cooking off.

With the amidships section now completely ablaze, most of the surviving crew assembled on the forecastle under the command of Captain William G Greenman, while on the fantail, a smaller group was led by the

Executive Officer. Both officers organised bucket brigades, and the group at the bow rigged a gasoline-powered handy-billy portable pump, and began to make some limited progress against the fires. (Neither group of survivors had communication with the other or even knew of the other's existence.) At approximately 03.00, the groups at the bow and stern independently decided to flood the magazines as a preventative measure; however, the 5in magazines could not be flooded because the controls could not be reached. At about 04.00, the destroyer *Bagley* came alongside the forecastle and took off the men there; at first light, *Bagley* returned and took the wounded off the stern.

With dawn came hope. The large rain squall had passed over the ship at 03.30 and had reduced the fires somewhat and some had burned themselves out.[31] The main remaining fire was in the wardroom area below the forward superstructure. Led by Greenman, a salvage party of 325 men (including those able-bodied men remaining on the fantail) came back aboard in an attempt to save the ship. It was found that both engine rooms and No 4 fire room could be occupied and work began attempting to raise steam. Meanwhile, at about 07.00, USS *Hopkins* (DMS13) attempted to take the ship under tow, with only limited success. At about 09.00, *Wilson* approached the forward section and began streaming water on the fire there. Both efforts were abandoned at about 10.00, when both *Hopkins* and *Wilson* were called away. Small explosions forward had been occurring for some time, explosions caused by fire reaching individual 5in rounds in the hoists. Finally, at 11.30, a major explosion was heard (and felt), which was certainly the forward 5in magazine going off; it must have blown out a section of the shell plating under the forward superstructure, because the list to port, which had been slowly increasing to approximately 10°, now rapidly increased to 15° with no indication that the increase would stop. The destroyer *Buchanan*, which was approaching with the intent of helping fight *Astoria*'s fires, now stood by to rescue her remaining crew. Shortly after 12.00, Greenman ordered the salvage crew off the ship; at approximately 12.15, she capsized to port and slipped under stern first. Two hundred and sixteen of her officers and men died in her; another 186 were wounded.

Astoria, because she was not torpedoed, gives the 'purest' example of the survivability of her generation of 'treaty maximum' cruisers. Still, the fact that she suffered thirty-four known shell hits, plus some unknown number of unrecorded hits – the official US Navy account states that she was hit 'at least 65' times – would have likely overwhelmed even a far more modern, better-protected ship of her size.[32] (The reader should remember that when treaty restrictions were lifted, the US Navy built heavy cruisers that were significant larger – 14,470 tons in the case of the *Baltimore* class or 17,255 tons for the *Des Moines* class compared to 10,136 tons for the *New Orleans* class – and that none of those newer, larger ships were ever tested the way that *Astoria* or her sisters were at the Battle of Savo Island.)

USS *Astoria* (CA34), one of the first group of *New Orleans* class cruisers, is seen here exercising near Pearl Harbor on 8 July 1942. It is not possible to tell from this image whether she is painted in an Ms 11 Sea Blue (5-S) system or the recently-authorised Ms 21 Navy Blue (5-N) system. Navy Blue was darker than Sea Blue, but they would be difficult to distinguish in this light, especially if recently painted, before the blue pigment faded. (NARA)

Still, some points should be considered regarding these designs. One is that none of the four cruisers lost had a unit-system engineering plant. It is possible, at least in the case of the three cruisers that were torpedoed, that their chances of survival might have been enhanced had they had this design feature. Another is that none, at least among the American cruisers, had yet benefited from the hard lessons taught by the war about reducing the amount of flammable material aboard ships. Addressing the case of *Astoria* directly, the analysts at BuShips made the following observation:

> Fires (particularly the one in the wardroom country) were the direct cause of the loss of ASTORIA. Excess equipment, paint on bulkheads, records, and so forth in officers' spaces and in ship's offices provided fuel for a fire which gradually worked downward exploding ammunition in the 5" hoists. From there the heat of the fire eventually reached and exploded the unflooded 5" magazine. This blew a hole in the ship's side below the waterline. The flooding which resulted caused the ship to capsize 45 minutes later.[33]

Unstated is the question of whether, had there been less

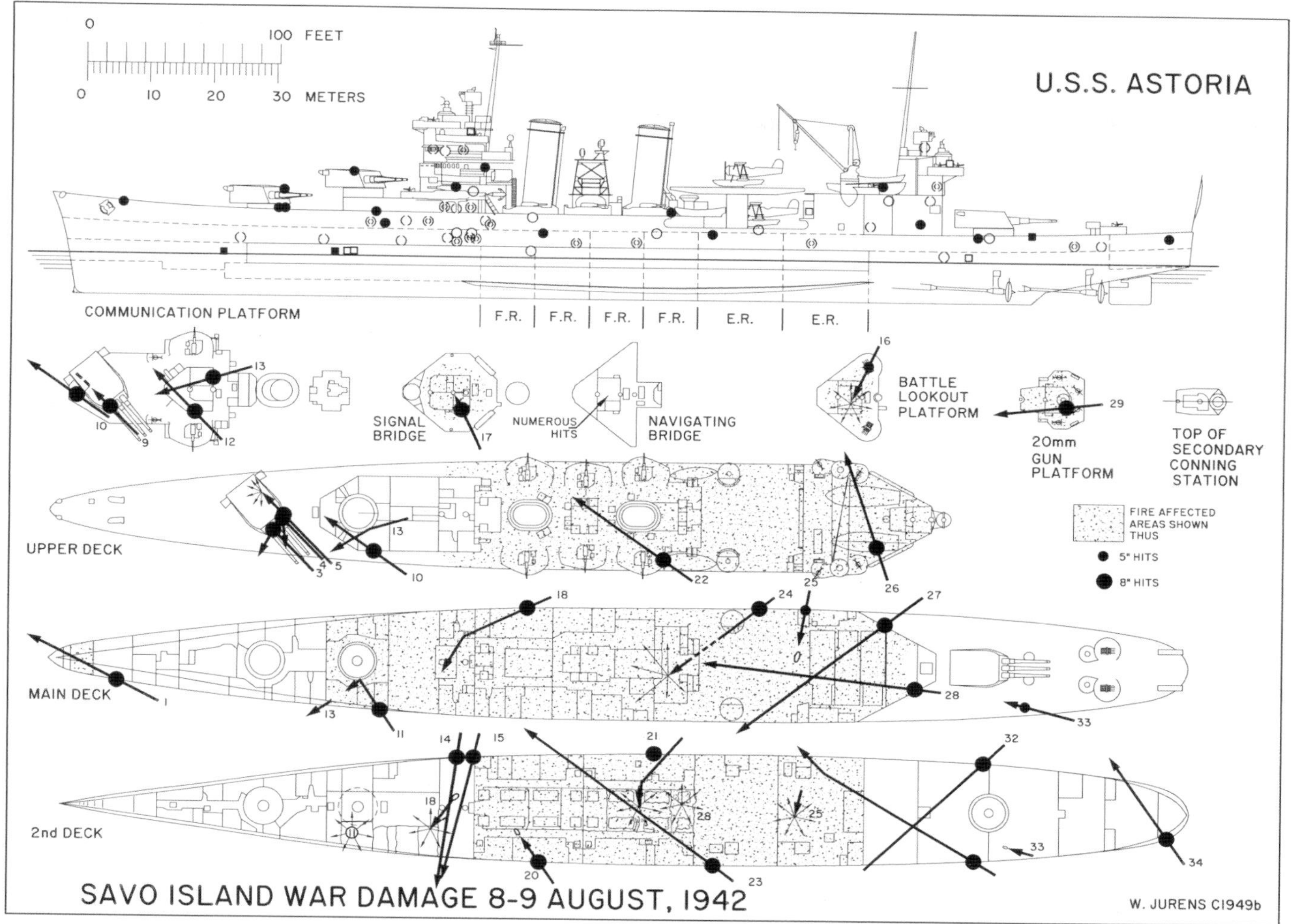

This diagram shows, in almost surgical detail, the destruction of *Astoria*, entirely by shellfire, and details the spread of the fires that eventually doomed her. Even without being hit by torpedoes, shellfire had damaged her hull to the extent that she had taken on a 10° list to port before the explosion of her 5in magazine that opened up her hull. (William Jurens)

flammable material in the ship, the fires might have been contained in time to prevent *Astoria*'s loss. That is impossible to answer in any definitive manner, but it is a possibility. It is interesting to speculate whether a later *Baltimore* class heavy cruiser, which were physically larger and structurally stronger, might have stood a better chance of survival, but it would be just speculation because none of the *Baltimores* were ever punished to this extent.

Not directly related to this battle, but nonetheless relevant, is the fate of *Kako*, third in Mikawa's line. Expecting an air attack at first light, the Japanese had been making speed north up 'The Slot', but when the morning passed with no interference from Allied aircraft, Mikawa allowed the four older cruisers of *Sentai* 6 to proceed alone up to Kavieng, while he took the rest of his force to Rabaul.[34] At dawn the next morning, 10 August, off the north-eastern coast of New Ireland, another old American submarine was waiting. At 07.50, Lieutenant Commander John R Moore, commanding USS *S-44* (SS155) spotted a line of four enemy warships approaching on a track that would bring them to a closest point 900yd away. He waited patiently until he had an optimal set-up on the last of the line and launched four torpedoes at 08.06, then took his boat deep in anticipation of a depth-charge attack. He heard all four torpedoes explode a few minutes later, but that assured him of nothing, because torpedoes often exploded at the end of their runs. However, not long after that, he heard an enormous rumbling sound, far larger than the detonation of a torpedo's warhead, which gave him confidence that he had sunk his target.

What he had heard earlier was three of the four torpedoes hitting *Kako*. The first hit well forward, in way of No 1 turret;

the damage twisted the ship's structure such as to open the whole bow section to the sea and might well have been enough to sink *Kako*, but two more torpedoes hit, one in way of the forward main-battery magazines and the other opened the forward fire room to the sea. The torpedoes hit at 08.08; *Kako* rapidly took on a list to starboard that brought the lowest row of scuttles on that side underwater and accelerated the flooding. By 08.15, she had rolled on her side and slipped bow-first into the Pacific, her boilers exploding as she sank, which explained the loud rumbling sound Moore heard. Sixty-eight of her officers and men were lost in the sinking.

Kako never stood a chance. Almost one-third smaller than the four Allied cruisers lost the day before, she simply could not absorb the kind of damage she sustained, with the resulting loss of buoyancy caused by the three torpedoes. No hull of her size, no matter how designed, would likely have done much better.

The question must be asked, why did the Allies, specifically the Americans, who had radar on all of the cruisers lost in this battle, fare so poorly against ships without this technology. The answer is complex. First and foremost was the fact that Japanese, as already mentioned, had trained repeatedly in night manoeuvres and had both equipment and doctrine better suited for night warfare than the Allies at this stage of the war. During this period of night battles in the Solomons, they regularly sighted Allied formations at greater distances and minutes earlier than they were detected by radar-equipped Allied ships. Some of this was due to the inexperience of American radar operators, who had difficulty operating their equipment effectively in an environment with multiple nearby land masses and constantly moving and changing squall lines, which confused the radar returns. (The reader must remember that these first-generation radars such as the CXAM, SC and FC used 'A' type oscilloscope displays, not the PPI 'God's-eye-view' display that was introduced with the next-generation of radars, such as the SG in *San Juan*. The oscilloscopic display required a highly-trained operator to distinguish a meaningful return from 'noise', even without the added difficulty of the interference caused by land masses and weather.) With their excellent torpedoes, their well-coordinated use of aerial flares dropped by floatplanes and their highly-trained crews, the Japanese had a distinct advantage in these night engagements, not offset until a combination of better radars and better training balanced the scales.

This battle was chosen for description here because it was hoped it might offer an opportunity to examine the survivability of a cross-section of early-to-middle 'modern cruisers' – *Kako* preceded the treaty regime, *Canberra* was one of the *Kent* class of the first-generation of 'treaty maximum' cruisers, *Chicago* was one of the *Northampton*s and the other three were from the *New Orleans* class, all mid-generation 'treaty maximum' cruisers. However, it turns out to have been less than successful than anticipated, because the damage received by the five cruisers that sank would likely have been enough to sink a ship designed without treaty limitations, and the one that survived did so because its buoyancy was never severely threatened. It would take another weapon, in another kind of battle, to test fairly the mettle of a 'modern cruiser'.

Because of the devastation wrought this night and more than a dozen other nights, Savo Sound would go down in history – and in such august geographic authorities as the *Times Atlas* – as 'Iron Bottom Sound'.[35] Before the war had moved off to the north, at least forty-four ships from both sides would be sunk within the confines of this appropriately renamed embayment.[36]

Savannah Meets the Future: Salerno – 11 September 1943

Savannah has already been mentioned in these pages (see Chapter 7), as an example of the lightness of the construction of the *Brooklyn* class light cruisers built by the US Navy in response to the Japanese *Mogamis* and the restrictions imposed by the First London Treaty. So has the Fritz-X, the large – 3086.5lb (1400kg) – AP radio-controlled glide bomb developed by the Germans and first deployed in response to the Allied landings at Salerno in September 1943. They would meet off the Italian coast with interesting, indeed, one might say, surprising results.

When German Do 217K-2s of III./KG100 entered into the airspace over the Allied landing beaches at Salerno off the southern Italian coast, they were at such high altitude as to cause no particular alarm. The aircraft that dropped the Fritz-X that hit *Savannah* was actually tracked by one of the cruiser's Mk 33 DP directors as it approached at 18,700ft; the FD (Mk 4) radar associated with that director was able to track the aircraft but was not able to detect the glide bomb as it was released or as it fell. This was not the first encounter by the Allies with this weapon; Fritz-X glide bombs had been dropped without success for the first time on 21 July. On 9 September, two days before this hazy morning off the Italian coast, they had been used with quite different results to sink the Italian battleship RN *Roma* as she was on her way to Malta to surrender.

The Fritz-X was not a guided missile, in the sense that it was not propelled by anything but gravity and the forward momentum of the launching aircraft, but it was guided, in the sense that it had a tail unit with movable fins that allowed a bombardier in the control aircraft to alter its ballistic trajectory to a limited extent in the pitch and yaw axes (the bomb's course and, to a greater extent, its range could be altered). A flare in the bomb's tail was ignited when it was dropped to aid the bombardier in tracking its path, which left a highly-visible smoke trail and led to the mistaken belief at the time that it was rocket-propelled. Guidance was by a radio link, which proved to be the weapon's 'Achilles heel', because the Allies very quickly learned that this link could be jammed, but, on 11 September 1943, that was still some time in the future.

The first inkling anyone in *Savannah* had that they were the target of a Fritz-X was when it struck turret No 3 in a nearly vertical dive, very nearly on the centreline, approximately a yard from the front edge of the turret roof.[37] The time was 09.44. Fourteen minutes earlier, the fighter director for the fleet operating off Salerno had called out an intruder warning; a dozen German fighters were approaching at high speed. *Savannah*, which had been stopped among the invasion fleet, was ordered ahead at 10 knots and material condition 'ABLE' was set.[38] At 09.41, speed was increased to 15 knots, but the crowded roadstead prevented any manoeuvring. The approaching bomber was seen, as was the smoke trail left by the flare in the tail of the Fritz-X, but was misinterpreted as the 'death spiral' of a downed enemy aircraft. None of this alerted *Savannah* to her imminent danger and the impact of the Fritz-X on turret No 3 was utterly unexpected. The approach and impact of the bomb were reported as being virtually noiseless; survivors close to the point of impact reported a 'whooshing' sound as the bomb struck, but the jolt was strong enough to knock men off their feet on the bridge.[39]

The bomb penetrated the 2in STS roof plate of the turret, passed through the turret into the barbette, glanced off the roller path, which put it on a more vertical trajectory, through the Third Deck (1in STS) and the First Platform (2in STS) before detonating just above the Second Platform in the 6in handling room. The resulting explosion of 594lb of RDX-like high-energy explosive blew out the Second Platform decking for a radius of 15ft, demolishing the bulkheads of the handling room on all sides, blew a hole in the ship's bottom plating just to the port of the centreline approximately 17ft long and a seam of similar length was ripped open between the lower strake of belt armour and the shell plating on the port side adjacent to turret No 3.[40] Explosive gases vented upwards through the turret, killing anyone not already dead in the barbette and gunhouse, and starting a stubborn fire that took several hours to put out. They also vented through the holes in the hull and up the outside of the hull of the ship. Most seriously, they blew out closed watertight doors in otherwise intact transverse bulkheads at the Second Platform level in an area extending more than 50ft along the length of the ship. This damage allowed smoke and gases to move rapidly into the magazines and handling rooms under turrets Nos 2 and 1, and then up into the turrets themselves. The smoke was highly toxic, containing nitrous oxide and carbon monoxide. All the men from turret No 2 were removed within thirty minutes, but except for five who escaped quickly, the rest succumbed to the fumes.[41] Most of the men from turret No 1 were able to escape with their lives.

The extensive damage caused by the bomb's detonation did have one beneficial side effect. Not surprisingly, the detonation of such a high-order explosive in the midst of a ship's magazine spaces – adjacent to the compartment where the bomb exploded were a 6in powder magazine, a 6in shell room, a 40mm magazine, two 5in handling rooms and four 5in magazines, all of which were exposed to the explosion by the destruction of the intervening bulkheads – resulted in fires

The Fritz-X that hit USS *Savannah* (CL42) was not seen and barely heard before it slammed into turret No 3 on 11 September 1943 off Salerno. One of the reasons for *Savannah*'s survival can be seen in this image taken seconds later, capturing the huge cloud of explosive gases thrown up both inside the ship and outside her hull, indicating a significant percentage of the energy of the detonation escaped downward and out of the ship, appearing here as a dark plume compared to the lighter-coloured smoke rising from inside the ship. (NHHC)

In a desperate race against time to save the men in turret No 2 – the armoured hatch, which hangs down here, had an inner cover which failed to stay open, trapping all but five men inside – the rescue crew is pulling bodies out of the turret. None of the trapped men could be revived, despite the fact that all were removed within thirty minutes. Note the letter 'Z' marked on the hatch cover; this indicated that this cover was to remain closed when the ship was at General Quarters except in emergencies. (NARA)

in those spaces and the destruction of powder cases and the burning of powder. This might have led very rapidly to a magazine explosion, but this was prevented by the equally rapid inrush of seawater through the hole punched in the shell plated by the explosive gases venting downward, largely because the 2in-thick STS of the First Platform contained the damage, to a great extent, below that deck. This immediately quenched any fire below that deck.

Within minutes of the bomb's detonation, the full extent of the damage to *Savannah* became apparent. The ship flooded above the Third Deck to a depth of 18in in the damaged area; as the ship slowed this flooding increased, reaching a depth of 4ft.[42] Draft forward increased from 22ft 3in to approximately 34ft, and the ship took on an 8° list to port. A serious fire was burning in turret No 3, while small fires fuelled by debris from the life rafts stored on that turret's roof were burning on the Main Deck. All electrical power was lost immediately upon bomb impact – mainly caused by short-circuits that tripped all main distribution boards – except for that supplied by an emergency diesel-powered generator, which kicked in as designed and powered the emergency battle lanterns.[43] Most internal communications were lost. Water pressure on the fire mains dropped to almost nothing. Steam pressure to the ship's engines was falling rapidly – No 1 fire room filled with smoke and had to be temporarily abandoned, its boilers shut down, while the feed water supply to the boilers in No 2 fire room and the fuel supply to those in Nos 3 and 4 were failing for lack of power.

This list of problems seems long and dire, but the stoutness of the ship and the excellence of her crew brought the situation under control in a remarkably short period of time. Firstly, and most importantly, the flooding reached its maximum extent in the first five minutes.[44] Within one minute, the after emergency fire pump was started, and within four minutes, normal 80lb water pressure was available at fire plugs adjacent to turret No 3. This was augmented by five gasoline-power handy-billies, which pumped water through hoses equipped with fog nozzles that were particularly effective in containing fires fed by chemicals. Water was directed into the turret through the hole in the roof, the rear door and the muzzles of the guns. The fire was contained within 15 minutes, although it would not be entirely extinguished for two hours. At 10.08, twenty-four minutes after the bomb hit, a secondary explosion occurred in turret No 3, caused by the 'cooking off' of two 6in HC shells; the explosion was described as 'low-order', but it was strong enough to knock down men on the turret roof manning the fire hose. No-one was injured by this explosion.

Electric power was restored by a process of isolating the damaged circuits that were short-circuiting the switchboards.[45] Within eight minutes, two turbo-generators were back on line and power had been restored to the after half of the ship. With 16 minutes, power was restored to the entire vessel excepting only the damaged areas. The restoration of steam power had proceeded even before the restoration of electric power. At the

Crewmen play a hose into the hole in the roof of turret No 3 of *Savannah* while, in the background, small dramas are being played out. Almost all of the crew of turret No 2 was killed by toxic gases from the explosion and the burning of powder charges. A few men escaped through the armoured hatch that can be seen hanging down below the floater net basket on the near side of the turret below the rangefinder hood. Several men are being worked on by corpsmen to the left of the turret; another, beyond help, has been wrapped in a blanket to the right. (NARA)

time of the hit, six of the eight boilers were on line and the other two were on 15-minutes' notice. When the bomb hit, the electric-powered fuel pumps in Nos 3 and 4 fire rooms stopped, but the engineers immediately started the steam-powered back-up pumps and within three minutes the fires were relit under the four boilers in those two compartments. Within six minutes, two of the boilers were cut in on the main steam lines and the engine rooms had sufficient pressure to restart the turbo-pumps supplying water pressure to the fire mains and to power the main turbines. By 10.05, the process of moving oil fuel to tanks on the starboard side to correct the list to port was started.

By this point, *Savannah*'s survival was essentially assured. She moved to shallower water where she anchored at 11.08; two salvage tugs came alongside to take off casualties and to attempt to pump out some of the water forward. This attempt was unsuccessful. It was found that four men were trapped alive in Radio III, a compartment on First Platform, starboard side, under the forward superstructure.[46] Damage to adjacent compartments was such that it was impossible to get to the men. However, once the area was cleared of smoke, the compartment's ventilation system was started and was found to be delivering good air, so the most immediate concern about the men's survival was relieved. An electric power circuit was jury-rigged, allowing the men light and the ability to operate a fan. The trapped men tied a piece of thread to some

By 18.00 on the day of the attack, just over eight hours after the bomb hit, *Savannah* was underway towards Malta under her own power. This photo was probably taken the next day, as it took her until 19.00 that day to reach Valletta. Draft forward had increased by almost 12ft, making the calm seas she was facing a very fortunate state. (USN)

toilet tissue which was carried up the ventilation duct; this allowed a two-way pull-line to be established, after which food and water were supplied to them. *Savannah* departed for Malta at 18.00 that evening, reaching Valletta harbour at 19.00 the next day after an uneventful passage. Once at Malta, the men were cut out of the compartment where they had been trapped for sixty hours. One hundred and ninety-seven men died in *Savannah* because of this attack and another fifteen received wounds classified as serious.

It took a week to relieve *Savannah* of enough weight forward to reduce her draft to the point that she could enter the dry dock at Malta. Once there, temporary repairs were made that allowed her to head for Philadelphia, where she entered the navy yard there for permanent repairs that include the addition of a bulge to address topweight issues and the replacement of her eight single 5in/25 secondary-battery guns by four twin 5in/38 gunhouses, bringing them up to a standard close to the *St Louis* sub-class. The intent was that all seven of the original *Brooklyn*s were to receive this modification, but, besides *Savannah*, only USS *Honolulu* (CL48) did. The war ended before the others could be so modified.

The discussion by the designers at BuShips brought up a few interesting points. One was that no practical thickness of deck armour could prevent a weapon the size and mass of a Fritz-X from penetrating and damaging a ship of *Savannah*'s size.[47] The 2in-thick First Platform was noted as being quite effective in limiting the upward spread of damage caused the explosion, which was almost entirely beneficial.[48] This, however, brought up the most serious defect found by BuShips, which was the repeated failure of watertight doors in transverse bulkheads in instances when the bulkhead had otherwise held.[49] This happened in at least four cases. It was a primary cause of both the spread of smoke and gas into turrets Nos 1 and 2, with its concomitant loss of life, and in the flooding of otherwise intact compartments forward of the detonation site. The solution to this problem was to eliminate, as much as possible, any openings in transverse bulkheads below the Second Deck, and, where that was not possible, to install watertight doors of similar blast-resistance as the bulkheads in which they were located.

Any analysis of this incident must look at the factors that allowed *Savannah* to survive while *Roma* was destroyed. (At least two other warships were hit by Fritz-Xs: HMS *Uganda* (66) on 13 September 1943 and *Warspite* (03) on 16 September. The Fritz-X hit *Uganda*, a 'Colony' class light cruiser, amidships and passed entirely through the ship, penetrating seven decks and passing out through her keel, before exploding beneath her hull. Three of her four engineering spaces were flooded, but she stayed afloat and was towed to Malta for temporary repairs. *Warspite* was targeted by three Fritz-Xs, one of which hit and two near-missed; the one that hit passed through her mid-section and exploded just under one of her fire rooms, opening it to the sea and led to the flooding of five of her six fire rooms. Another exploded close enough to gash her starboard side bulge. She was towed to Malta for temporary repairs; never fully repaired, she did provide fire support for the Normandy landings.[50])

Roma was hit by two Fritz-Xs, while *Savannah* was hit by only one; that certainly was one factor in their differing fates. The first hit on *Roma* was much like those on *Uganda* and *Warspite*, hitting in the engineering spaces and detonating just under the ship, flooding large parts of the ship's mid-section, but was (probably) not sufficient to be fatal to the ship. The second detonated in the forward engine room, the explosion blowing through the forward fire rooms and setting off the adjacent main-battery magazine, which led to the ship breaking in two and sinking. It is most likely that *Roma* would have sunk had the first hit not occurred. She sank from the second hit, precisely because the explosive energy was mostly, if not entirely, contained within her hull, leading to the magazine explosion. Had she been more lightly-constructed,

like *Savannah*, at least some of the explosive energy might have escaped the hull and perhaps not reached her magazines. Would she, under those circumstances, have survived, or would the first hit then have become a more decisive factor in determining her survival? This question may be interesting to contemplate, but is impossible to answer.

Flipping that line of inquiry around, the question becomes, were *Savannah* more robustly-constructed, such that all of her bomb's energy were contained within her hull and no inrush of sea water occurred to quench the fires in her magazines, could she have survived? Then, again, it is pertinent to ask whether she would have survived a hit in the mid-section any better than *Uganda*? And, of course, it is obligatory to ask, could she have survived two hits, such as were inflicted on *Roma*? Any answer to any of these questions is pure speculation. It is possible that *Savannah* would have survived a mid-section hit somewhat better than *Uganda* because she was a bigger ship (though, interestingly, *Uganda* actually had a slightly broader beam that might have aided her survival). It is certainly doubtful that *Savannah* would have steamed away from an amidships hit under her own power, if she survived at all. Two hits, placed like those that hit *Roma*, would have almost certainly doomed her. *Savannah* survived because she was well-designed and well-built, because she had a good, experienced crew that reacted well when tested and because she was lucky. It is quite possible that last factor was the most important.

The most direct reason why *Savannah* survived was probably the blown-out strake of hull shell plating seen here at the Valletta dry dock. The massive explosion of 594lb of high-energy explosive was largely contained in an upward direction by the 2in of STS of the First Platform, forcing the gases fore-and-aft and downward, where this damage occurred. The start of the port side bilge keel can be seen to right on the damaged strake. The bright 'streak' on the upper right side of this image is a staple that held the photograph in place in the original damage report, later helped by a strip of cellophane tape, the traces of which can be seen at the left. (NARA)

Chapter 12

The More Things Change . . . : 1946 –

By the end of the Second World War, the role of sea power had changed more profoundly than anyone could have imagined before 1945, and the changes have continued. The cruiser, with traditional tasking such as scouting or trade protection/predation, became anachronistic rather rapidly, although the role of fleet protection did not fade away, nor did the newer role of shore bombardment, however much their parameters may have changed. They continue to this day, albeit often with vastly different weapons than in the past. The question becomes, are all (or indeed any) of the ships called 'cruiser' in the post-Second World War era really in fact cruisers by any commonly understood definition, and, conversely, should not some ships called by some other names more appropriately be called cruisers.

This chapter has no pretensions to being an in-depth survey of cruiser development since 1945. It will skim the surface, making mention of the high points that stand out, noting the numerous conversions of war-built or war-designed ships to play roles more fitting for late twentieth and even twenty-first century naval structures, as well as the small number of newly-designed cruiser types. The coverage will be by nation, with little, if any, attempt to compare the fighting qualities of these ships, as they were, for the most part, not designed with the thought of fighting each other foremost in their designers' minds.

The United States

Logically enough, no navy ended the Second World War with more cruisers that the US Navy, because no nation had built so many. But even had the Americans desired to keep so many cruisers in commission, the post-war demobilisation and the shrinkage in military budgets would have forced a drastic reduction. The first ships to be disposed of were the oldest. All of the surviving pre-war cruisers and even the earliest *Cleveland* class light cruisers – all of those laid down before 1943 and many later ones – were decommissioned by the end of 1947. Even those *Cleveland*s that survived this first round of decommissionings were mostly caught up in a second wave that occurred in 1949 and 1950, leaving only a few in service and only one – USS *Manchester* (CL83), the last to be launched – remained a 'gun cruiser' in continuous commission through the end of the Korean War. (Interestingly, six of the surviving *Brooklyn* class light cruisers – the ones not reconstructed like *Savannah* – were all sold to South American countries, where they served, in one case, until 1992. One, ex-USS *Phoenix* (CL46) became the Argentinian ARA *General Belgrano*, famous for being sunk by the Royal Navy nuclear submarine

Boston, now converted to the US Navy's first guided-missile cruiser designated 'CAG1', in an image dated 21 January 1956, only a few months after her recommissioning. Her forward half has not been radically altered, although she had been given a more compact forward superstructure somewhat similar to that designed for the later *Baltimore*s, along with the single large funnel, but pushed quite far forward to make room for two twin-arm Terrier SAM launchers, their large magazines (for 144 missiles) and the necessary target-acquisition and guidance radars. Everything about the conversion of *Boston* and her sister *Canberra* (CAG2, ex-CA70) was rushed and improvised, but the results were successful and the ships remained in service as missile cruisers until 1968. (USN)

HMS *Conqueror* (S48) during the Falklands War. *Belgrano* was hit by two Mk 8 torpedoes with 805lb Torpex warheads. One hit well forward, blowing off her bow, but was not fatal; the other hit at the after end of the engineering spaces, causing extensive flooding and was the proximate cause of her sinking. Over 330 men died in the sinking, most of those in the explosion which occurred in an area that included crew berthing and recreational spaces.) Two of the last three of the *Atlanta* class, which were not commissioned until 1946, often described as a separate sub-class because of the topweight-reduction features (see Chapter 9), were retained in largely unchanged condition until being retired after serving through the Korean War.

Six *Clevelands* were earmarked for conversion to guided-missile cruisers. They were not the first to be so converted; that 'honour' went to a pair of *Baltimore* class heavy cruisers (see below). Like those two earlier conversions, the six converted *Clevelands* retained their gun armament forward (although four of them were further modified to become fleet flagships, sacrificing turret No 2 to make room for a longer forward superstructure). The two after main-battery turrets made way for a single twin-rail missile launcher and its associated loading equipment and magazine. Half of the conversions were fitted with RIM-2 Terrier medium-range surface-to-air missiles (SAMs) and half with RIM-8 Talos missiles, the latter having longer range, but were much larger and required two radars rather than one for target acquisition and guidance. For that reason, Talos missiles equipped only the three converted *Clevelands* and four later ships. All of the converted *Clevelands* served through to the end of the 1960s; the last, USS *Oklahoma City* (CLG5, ex-CL91) was not decommissioned until 1979.

The *Baltimore* class heavy cruisers had very different fates post-war than the *Clevelands*, being highly popular ships with the space to accept some 'mission-growth'. Most were decommissioned soon after the end of the war, but seven remained in commission as gun-armed cruisers. One, whose construction had been halted soon after being laid down in August 1944, was completed as a fleet flagship armed with four 5in/54 RF guns. (This was USS *Northampton* (CLC1, ex-CA125).) Two, USS *Boston* (CA69) and *Canberra* (CA70), were taken out of reserve in 1952 and converted to guided-missile cruisers, the first to be so converted, with a pair of twin-rail launchers for Terriers aft replacing turret No 3. They were re-designated CAG1 and CAG2. Later, three more *Baltimores* were designated for far more extensive conversions; two of these were in active commission and one came from reserve. These ships, starting with USS *Albany* (CG10, ex-CA123), were razed down to the Main Deck, all of their existing gun armament was removed, and their superstructures and funnels replaced by tall, lightweight structures intended to carry the numerous sensor and guidance radars required by the missile armament, which comprised two twin-rail

The heavy cruiser *Albany* (CG10, ex-CA123) was one of three war-built hulls given a far more extensive conversion than *Boston*. She received twin-arm Talos SAM launchers fore-and-aft, each with a fifty-two missile magazine – the Talos was quite a bit larger than the Terrier – and the paired SPG-49 guidance radars each launcher required, which in turn required an extremely tall bridge structure to give the ship's command bridge visibility. Towering above the bridge were two 'macks' (combination masts and 'stacks'), carrying search and target-acquisition radars. Short-range defence was provided by a pair of twin-arm Tartar SAM launchers, one on either side of the forward superstructure, a box-launcher for ASROC ASW missiles and a pair of open 5in/38 mounts in way of the after 'mack'. The Tartar was essentially a Terrier without a booster, intended to provide close-in air defence. (NHHC)

launchers for Talos missiles and two twin-rail launchers for RIM-24 Tartar missiles (which were Terriers without the booster stage, making them short-range missiles). Once in service, the lack of gun armament was seen as a serious deficiency in these ships and they were retrofitted with a pair of single 5in/38 mounts for defence against slow-moving aircraft and small boats. Two of these ships served until 1980.

The late-war designs built around the automated 6in and 8in guns remained in commission after the war, but, as mentioned above, their fate was directly related to the success of their gun systems. The two *Worcesters*, armed with the troublesome 6in/47 DP mount, served through the Korean War, but were retired not too long after. The three *Des Moines* class, armed with a more successful main-battery weapon, lasted somewhat longer, but the day of the all-gun cruiser was over. The last such in the US Navy, USS *Newport News* (CA148), was decommissioned in 1975.

Brief mention must be made of the last ship the US Navy designed as a cruiser, USS *Long Beach* (CGN9, ex-CLGN160).[1] The idea for *Long Beach* originated with the planning for the first nuclear-powered aircraft carriers, which would require equally long-legged escort vessels. *Long Beach* emerged as a ship approximately the size of the *Worcesters*, but armed much like the later *Baltimore* conversions, except she had Terriers in the place of Tartars. Like those ships, she was later fitted with a pair of 5in/38 guns for self-defence. Her search radars were the flat-panel phased-array AN/SPS-32/33, at that time a highly-experimental system that evolved into the very successful AN/SPY-1 radar and Aegis combat system mounted on the *Ticonderoga* class guided-missile cruisers and *Arleigh Burke* class destroyers. Authorised in FY1957, she commissioned in 1961 and served on into the 1990s, her missile armament being updated to comprise RIM-67 Standard missiles in the place of the Terriers, a pair of box launchers for BGM-109 Tomahawks replacing the Talos launcher aft, two Phalanx CIWS (Close-In Weapon System) mounts supplementing the 5in guns for defence against anti-ship missiles and two RGM-84 Harpoon anti-ship missile box launchers further bolstering the defence against surface attack. In this configuration, she served on until her retirement in 1995. (The main reason for the decommissioning of what was still a fairly young and capable warship was the perceived reduction in threat with the end of the Cold War and the high cost, in terms of crew, to man such a large and complex ship; she had a complement of 1160 officers and men, compared to the approximately 280 officers and men required to man a *Burke* class guided-missile destroyer which mounts a similar sensor and weapons suite.)

It is somewhat misleading to state, as is often claimed, that *Long Beach* was the US Navy's first (and last) post-Second World War 'true' cruiser to be built, that all the rest were ships originally conceived as other types, renamed as cruisers for lack of a better name. Consider, for example, the case of USS *Norfolk* (DL1, ex-CLK1). This was the first new warship authorised for the US Navy after the Second World War, laid down in September 1949, built on a hull nearly identical in dimensions, though not in design, to that of the *Atlanta* class light cruisers. *Norfolk* was intended to be the first of a new type of anti-submarine light cruiser with a full suite of detection and destruction resources such as could not be possibly fit into a destroyer-sized platform; *Norfolk* had a standard displacement of 5600 tons v 2616 tons for the late-war *Gearing* class destroyers. *Norfolk*'s size made her 'cruiser-like', but her (almost complete) lack of armour and her light armament – her main battery was four 3in/50 twin mounts and a full suite of anti-submarine weapons – made her seem more 'destroyer-like', leading to the invention of a new warship category for the US Navy, the 'destroyer leader', which accounted for the change in designator from 'CLK1' to 'DL1', and *Norfolk* indeed led destroyer flotillas for much of her early career, which at one time was a frequent use for small cruisers.[2] Four more destroyer leaders were authorised at the same time, but they were a very different type ship, more like large destroyers.[3] This ship category was considered to be awkward and not necessarily appropriate given the different ship types included under this rubric; the US Navy changed the designation to 'frigate', but this was no less confusing, because it differed dramatically from the usage of that term by most of the rest of the world's navies (particularly the Royal Navy),

Designed to provide air-defence escort for USS *Enterprise* (CVAN65), the US Navy's first nuclear aircraft carrier, USS *Long Beach* (CGN9), seen here near Hawai'i on 9 May 1973, was a nuclear-powered cruiser-sized ship with an air-defence battery roughly equivalent to *Albany*'s, but with the superior SPS-32/33 search and acquisition radar with its phased-array antennas mounted on all four sides of the large square forward superstructure. She carried a pair of Terrier launchers forward and a single Talos launcher aft. The original plans called for her to carry Regulus or Polaris nuclear-armed missiles, but this never materialised. Note the return of the British-style 'knuckle' in the hull forward, but it is there for a very different reason; notice that it starts somewhat back from the bow, because it is there to accommodate the width of the forward missile magazine, not to reduce bow flare forward. (USN)

which used 'frigate' to designate a smaller escort ship, not a larger one.

Beginning in FY1958, the US Navy was authorised to build ships with the type designator 'DLG' or 'DLGN' (standing for 'guided-missile frigate' or 'nuclear guided-missile frigate'), in a series that would extend from USS *Leahy* (DLG16) – laid down in December 1959 – to USS *Mississippi* (DLGN40) – laid down in February 1975. Each would be re-designated as 'cruisers' when the use of the term 'frigate' simply became too confusing; 'DLG's became 'CGs' and 'DLGNs' became 'CGNs'. One further ship in this series, USS *Arkansas* (CGN41), was redesignated before she was laid down. All of these ships have been decommissioned, the last two in July 1999.

As more nuclear-powered aircraft carriers were laid down, starting with USS *Nimitz* (CVAN68) in 1968, the need was felt for more nuclear-powered air-defence escorts, but not as big or expensive as *Long Beach*. This image shows USS *Virginia* (CGN38, ex-DLGN38), lead-ship of a four-ship class laid down in 1972. This image is undated, but is clearly from relatively early in her career, before she was fitted with Harpoon anti-ship missile canisters ahead of her bridge. Her forward missile launcher is for Standard SAM missiles; the aft launcher can fire Standard or ASROC missiles. The guns are lightweight 5in/54 Mk 45 fully-automatic mounts. These large nuclear-powered missile cruisers introduced the use of Kevlar armour, as the biggest threat facing ships now was not high-velocity point projectiles, but rather high-mass missiles with the ability to spread damaging debris and burning propellant over a wide area. (USN)

After the *Virginia* class, the US Navy built no more nuclear-powered surface escorts for its aircraft carriers. The cost of nuclear-powered ships compared to those powered by newly-available gas-turbine power plants made it clear that nuclear power was an unaffordable luxury in cruiser-sized ships. Along with efficient turbine power plants, by the late-1970s, the miniaturisation of electronics made phased-array antenna technology available in a ship just a little more than a third the size of *Long Beach*. Hence, the *Ticonderoga* class guided-missile cruisers, built on the hull of *Spruance* class destroyers, carrying the SPY-1A radar linked to the Aegis Combat System; USS *Anzio* (CG68) is seen here on 2 July 2016. The first five of the class, armed with twin-arm missile launchers, have been retired; the rest, carrying their missiles in VLS pods totalling 122 cells will begin a phased retirement in 2020. (USN)

A final series of missile cruisers was brought about by the proposal made in 1975 to mate the Aegis system with the hull of the existing *Spruance* class destroyers.[4] In all twenty-seven of these ships were built. The first four initially retained their 'DDG' destroyer designations associated with the *Spruance* class when authorised, but these were changed to 'CG' guided-missile cruiser designations before they were laid down. The first five had twin-rail missile launchers fore-and-aft, after which these ships were fitted with vertical launch system (VLS) cells that significantly increased flexibility in weapons deployment. Those first five have been decommissioned (in 2004–5); as of 2017, the two oldest of the VLS-armed *Ticonderoga* class cruisers were scheduled to be decommissioned in 2020, with nine more to follow over the next five years.[5]

The US Navy is building a three-ship class of very large (15,742-ton) destroyers with guns that were originally designed specifically for land attack. These ships, the survivors of a planned class of thirty-two ships, repeatedly trimmed back because of serious cost overruns, among other issues, are now ships without a credible mission, because the 155mm/62 Mk 51 Advanced Gun System is a weapon without munitions. (The intended munition, a guided ballistic round capable of reaching 60nm, became so expensive that the programme was cancelled.) What makes these three ships of any interest to this discussion is their size and the reported intent of the US Navy to retask these ships as surface-warfare assets – making them sound much like traditional cruisers.[6] Yet, these three ships of the *Zumwalt* class paradoxically retain guided-missile destroyer designations.

Officially classed as destroyers, but displacing more than 15,700 tons and 610ft long, the ships of the *Zumwalt* class probably should be classified as cruisers. The roles they were designed for and for which they are now intended are both very 'cruiser-like'. They were built around a pair of 155mm/62 Mk 51 guns, seen on her forecastle in their protective housings in this view of the lead ship of the class, USS *Zumwalt* (DDG1000), taken from *Monsoor* (DDG1001) on 7 December 2018, intended to make them land-attack platforms. Unfortunately, the guns are inoperative since the munitions have proven to be prohibitively expensive. The ships are reportedly being retasked as surface warfare assets at the centre of an experimental unit of unmanned surface vessels. Note the raised blast shields for the eighty Peripheral VLS cells that line the edge of their capacious quarterdeck. (USN

Soviet Russia

After the cancellation of the remaining *Sverdlov* class all-gun light cruisers, the Soviet Navy looked to a more modern approach to sea power projection, beginning in 1956 to develop the specifications for a ship, originally defined as a destroyer, but redefined as guided-missile cruisers soon after the first was laid down.[7] With this ship, the Russians attempted to fit a massive offensive and defensive battery into an incredibly small hull; the four ships of the 'Kynda' class displaced 4400 tons, but carried two four-tube launchers for the large SS-N-3b 'Shaddock' anti-ship missile (with a full set of reloads), a two-rail launcher for the SA-N-1A 'Goa' SAM (with twenty-four missiles), two twin 76.2mm/59 AK-726 gun mounts, two anti-submarine rocket mounts and two triple 533mm torpedo tubes.[8] It is small wonder they turned out to be top-heavy and, instead of the planned class of ten ships, only four were built and further orders were cancelled in favour of the larger 'Kresta I' class. These ships were laid down in 1960–1, commissioned in 1962–5 and, despite their continuing struggle with topweight, remained in service well into the 1990s, in one case until 2002.

At 6000 tons standard displacement, the 'Kresta I' class addressed the most immediate problem of the 'Kynda' class, namely the attempt to cram too much weaponry into too small a hull. In this class, one of the quadruple 'Shaddock' launchers was sacrificed and the other replaced by two twin launchers with no reloads. (The intent had been to replace the 'Shaddocks' with a more modern anti-ship missile, but they were not ready in time.) Two twin-rail launchers were carried

The Soviets began their post-war cruiser programme in earnest with the 'Kynda' class of 1960, a class of four small (4400-ton) guided-missile cruisers whose primary weapons system was the SS-N-3b (P-35) 'Shaddock' anti-ship missile in its massive quadruple launchers fore-and-aft. They also had a twin-arm launcher forward for SA-N-1A (M-1 Volna) 'Goa' SAMs (with twenty-four missiles) and two twin 76.2mm/59 gun mounts aft. This image shows *Grozniy* late in her career on 11 August 1986. Four 30mm/54 AO-18 'Gatling' guns have been added, two per side in way of the forward funnel. (DoD)

for the 'Goa' SAMs, the number of torpedo tubes was increased to ten and two helicopters were carried aft to help guide the anti-ship missiles. The intent had been to build this ship in large numbers, but the decision was made, after four were ordered, to switch the emphasis of this design to anti-submarine warfare; the resulting design, known as the 'Kresta II' class, is quite correctly not considered a cruiser and is not included here. The same is true for the even larger ships of the 'Kara' class. The four 'Kresta Is' all served well into the 1990s.

The Russians returned to building ships they considered to be cruisers with the truly massive, nuclear-powered *Kirov* class multi-purpose cruisers built around a series of advanced missile systems, most served from vertical launch systems embedded in the long forecastle. The design dates from the early 1970s, when Soviet military doctrine was focused on protecting the strategic deterrent represented by the nation's ballistic missile submarines. The *Kirovs* were intended to counter what was seen as the biggest threat to that deterrent, the US Navy's carrier battle groups. To that end, they carried twenty launchers for the P-700 Granit (SS-N-19 'Shipwreck') anti-ship cruise missile, the long-delayed 'Shaddock' replacement. To protect the ships from the inevitable attack from the air and underwater, they were equipped with various numbers of 4K33 Osa-M (SA-N-4 'Gecko'), S-300F Fort (SA-N-6 'Grumble'), 3M95 Kinshal (SA-N-9 'Gauntlet'), URPK-5 Metel (SS-N-14 'Silex'), RPK-2 Vyuga (SS-N-15 'Starfish') or S-300FM (SA-N-20 'Gargoyle') missiles, the combinations varying because the four ships in this class were laid down over a span of twelve years, between 1974 and 1986, and completed between 1980 and 1998. At approximately 24,300 tons standard displacement and with a length of 827ft, they are the largest surface combatants currently in any fleet, but the Russians have had a hard time keeping them operational. It is believed that only one is currently in commission, the last one to be launched, *Pyotr Velikiy*. A second ship, *Admiral Nakhimov* (ex-*Kalinin*) has been under intermittent refit at Sevmash since 2006, with a current announced completion date of 2021–2. The other two are out of commission and reportedly in poor condition.

On 15 April 2011, US Navy CNO, Admiral Gary Roughead, paid an official visit to the Russian Northern Fleet base at Severomorsk, where he posed here for a portrait on the long foredeck of the cruiser *Pyotr Velikiy* between the ship's captain and a Russian rear admiral. In the foreground are two cells for the ship's SAMs; behind them are the twenty cells for the 'Shipwreck' anti-ship missiles. The huge double radar antennas at the foremast head are the 'Top Pair' which comprise a MR-600 Voskhod ('Top Sail') frequency-scanning air-search radar, facing forward, and a MR-500 Kliver ('Big Net') long-range air-search set, facing away. (DoD)

Above and below: Easily the largest post-war cruisers laid down by any nation, the Russian *Kirov* class nuclear-powered guided-missile cruisers were designed to lead Russian task groups in countering American carrier strike groups. They are loaded to the gills with missiles. Their primary offensive weapon is the SS-N-19 (P-700 Granit) 'Shipwreck' anti-ship cruise missile, carried in twenty VLS cells. The rest of the impressive missile and gun armament is defensive, consisting – in these views of *Pyotr Velikiy* taken near Brest on 7 May 2014 – of ninety-six SA-N-20 (S-300FM) 'Gargoyle' SAMs in twelve VLS cells ahead of the 'Shipwrecks' and 128 SA-N-9 (3M95 Kinshal) 'Gauntlet' SAMs in VLS cells in her slightly-raised forecastle and aft along the sides of her quarterdeck. Trailing the Russian behemoth is the air-defence destroyer HMS *Dragon* (D35). (MoD)

Laid down in 1978, but still the epitome of Russian surface naval power, the guided-missile cruiser *Marshal Ustinov* is seen here transiting the English Channel on 15 November 2018. Her primary armament is sixteen SS-N-12 (P-500 Bazalt/P-1000 Vulkan) 'Sandbox' supersonic anti-ship cruise missiles in the massive tubes alongside her forward superstructure and eight octuple vertical launchers for the SA-N-6 (S-300F Fort) 'Grumble' SAMs. The red stars on the 'Sandbox' tubes mark her status as a 'Guards' cruiser, a special honour intended to single out a unit that has shown particular bravery in battle or efficiency in training. On her foremast is the Fregat-MA ('Top Plate') planar-array electronically-scanned search and targeting radar; on her mainmast is the larger MR-650 Podberiozovik-ET2 long-range three-dimensional search radar. (MoD)

As impressive as the *Kirov*s were on paper, they were exorbitantly expensive and the Russians knew a more reasonably-priced alternative was needed if more than a few ships were to be deployed. The result was the *Slava* class large guided-missile cruisers, which were developed in the late 1970s. Conventionally-powered with gas turbines and more reasonably-sized at 9800 tons, ten ships of this class were planned, but in the end only five were laid down before the collapse of the Soviet Union and then only three of those were completed. The main weapons system around which they were built is the P-500 Bazalt/P-1000 Vulkan (SS-N-12 'Sandbox') supersonic anti-ship cruise missile, of which sixteen are carried. For self-defence, there are sixty-four SA-N-6s in eight octuple launchers and forty SA-N-4s in two circular silos aft. At least two of these ships, *Marshal Ustinov* (ex-*Slava*) with the Northern Fleet and *Varyag* (ex-*Chervona Ukraina*) in the Mediterranean, remain active.

The Russians built three classes of aircraft-handling ships that they called cruisers, but which really stretch the definition of the type to (and beyond) the limit. The *Moskva* class of two ships was designed for anti-submarine work, primarily with helicopters. Their after half was given over to a large flight deck, but her forward part bristled with three twin-rail missile launchers and a pair of anti-submarine rocket launchers. The *Kiev* class, of four ships, was designed to carry vertical/short-takeoff-and-landing (VSTOL) aircraft as well as helicopters. They had a through flight deck angled to port. The *Tbilisi* class of two ships had a complete flight deck. The last of these were not true cruisers in the sense defined in this narrative.

Great Britain

At the end of the Second World War, the British, like the Americans, found themselves in a world without major threats, besides what the ever-prescient Churchill saw looming beyond what he dubbed the 'Iron Curtain'. Unlike the Americans, the British faced that future with an economy devastated by a war that had drained the nation's resources very nearly to the breaking point. It took all the resources that could be mustered to complete the three suspended *Swiftsure* class light cruisers whose construction was halted at the end of the war. All three were completed between 1959 and 1961. The most interesting feature of these ships was the incorporation of the new 6in/50 QF N5 twin mounts in their two main-battery turrets. This gun, like the American attempt at an automatic 6in gun, was only a partial success; it appears to have achieved somewhat better reliability that the American 6in/47 DP Mk 16, but all accounts report the very high levels

Laid down in 1941, launched in 1945, but not completed until 1959 to a much revised design, HMS *Tiger* (C20), seen here in April 1965, was an attempt to make a gun cruiser for an age in which gun cruisers were no longer relevant. One of the class was completed in 1945 to a design quite similar to *Ontario*, but of the other three launched in 1944–5, construction was stopped and not resumed again until 1954. Above the weather deck, very little of the original design remained. The two twin main-battery turrets held 6in/50 QF N5s, which proved to be reliable, but only if given a very high level of skilled maintenance. The gun in 'B' position (and also on either side of the after funnel) was an automatic twin mount for the 3in/70 QF N1, which was similarly found to be reliable and effective if satisfactorily maintained. These ships were successful and well-liked in the fleet, but had no natural mission in a post-war fleet, except as command and control ships, and so, starting in 1965, two of the three were taken in hand for conversion to that role. (MoD)

When *Tiger* emerged from her reconstruction in 1972, she had a large boxy hangar for two helicopters replacing her after superstructure and a raised flight deck aft of that. Her funnels had been heightened to help smoke clear the massive structures aft. She is seen her from USS *Iowa* (BB61) at Portsmouth on 21 August 1986. (USN)

After the war, the *Marine Nationale* was faced with the mass obsolescence of most, if not all, of the ships they had built pre-war. This included the training cruiser *Jeanne d'Arc*, which had been completed in 1931. When this ship approached thirty years of age, it was decided to replace her with another training ship that similarly would have a useful role in wartime; the resulting ship was an innovative design that proved to be a prototype for several other nations' helicopter-cruisers, with more-or-less conventional armament and superstructure forward, and a hangar and large flight deck aft. Forward, *Jeanne d'Arc*, seen on 4 July 1986 at New York City, carried just a pair of 100mm/55 Mle 1953 guns and six canisters for Exocet MM38 anti-ship missiles. (DoD)

of constant maintenance required to keep these guns working. One ship, HMS *Lion* (C34) (ex-*Defence*), remained a gun cruiser for her entire career, but was in commission for just twelve years. Her two sisters, HMS *Tiger* (C20) and *Blake* (C99), were taken in hand for conversion to helicopter-cruisers within a few years of completion. The conversion involved replacing their after ends with a hangar and flight deck, leaving only the forward main-battery turret. In this configuration, *Blake* and *Tiger* remained in service until 1979.

The three light aircraft carriers of the *Invincible* class, laid down beginning in 1973, were sometimes classed as cruisers – the *Jane's* of that year labelled them as 'Through Deck Cruisers' – but for the same reasons given for excluding the Russian *Tbilisi*s from this discussion, the *Invincible*s will be politely ignored.

France

Just before the outbreak of the Second World War, the *Marine Nationale* was planning a class of three light cruisers armed with a main battery of DP 152mm/55 guns in triple mounts. These ships were to be incrementally bigger than the ships of the *La Galissonnière* class, somewhat faster and more lightly armoured, but otherwise generally similar. A distinctive visual difference would have been the single funnel, compared to the earlier class's two funnels. Three ships in this class were authorised, the first in the 1937 *tranche*, but was not laid down at Lorient until August 1939, and little progress had been made before war broke out and construction sputtered to a stop when France surrendered in June 1940, with work approximately 28 per cent complete.[9] (The other two ships had not been laid down.) The Germans allowed work to continue at a slow pace with the idea that the slipway might be freed up. Little progress was made, but, at the end of the war, it was found that considerable material had actually been assembled and concealed from the Germans, so that construction began again soon after the end of hostilities and the ship was launched in September 1946 with the original intended name – *De Grasse*. However, here matters stood for some time, as there was no consensus regarding how to proceed. So the hull, complete up to the Main Deck, sat at Lorient while discussion continued regarding two competing designs – one not too different from the original design and one with twin 127mm DP mounts as the main battery.

Ultimately, the financial constraints of post-war France made these exercises academic until the end of the 1940s, when the infusion of American military assistance funds opened up the opportunity to proceed again with the completion of *De Grasse*. In January 1951, the decision was made to complete the ship as an anti-aircraft cruiser, armed with eight twin 127mm/54 Mle 48 mounts – this was a French-designed gun firing American-made 5in rounds – and ten twin 57mm/60 Mle 51 HA mounts.[10] Thus configured, she was completed at Brest in August 1955. She served in this form until 1965, when she was converted into a command ship, which involved the removal of some of her after gun mounts and the addition of accommodation spaces. She served as the flagship of the fleet in the Pacific managing the

French nuclear tests, which role she fulfilled until decommissioned in 1973.

Based on exactly the same armament scheme as developed for *De Grasse*, STCN developed a design for a new anti-aircraft cruiser of slightly smaller dimensions, to be built from the keel up at Brest. Laid down in 1953 and completed in 1958, *Colbert* served in this configuration until 1970, when she was taken in hand for a major reconstruction as a guided-missile cruiser. She emerged with a completely different armament and sensor suite. Aft she carried a twin-rail launcher for the Masurca Mk 2 SAM and four tubes carrying MM-38 Exocet anti-ship missiles; forward she mounted two 100mm/55 Mle 68. In this configuration she served until decommissioned in 1991.

The French built a 'helicopter cruiser', named *Jeanne d'Arc*, laid down in 1959. Like the *Moskvas*, which she preceded by almost 20 years, she had a broad aircraft platform comprising the after half of the ship. Unlike the *Moskvas*, *Jeanne d'Arc* was, as were her recent predecessors with same name, also a training ship, serving this role, training classes of French midshipmen until 2010.

Italy

In 1957, the *Marina Militare*, the post-war successor to the *Regia Marina*, began the reconstruction of *Giuseppe Garibaldi*, one of the four '*Condottieri*' that remained in Italian service after the war.[11] This was a major rebuild, much like how the US Navy rebuilt *Albany* and her two sisters. The two after main-battery turrets were deleted, replaced by a twin-rail Terrier launcher and four vertical silos for the American-made UGM-27 Polaris submarine-launched ballistic missile.[12] The two forward main-battery turrets were replaced by twin mountings for the 135mm/45 Mod 1938 guns carried on the '*Capitani Romani*', but in a new DP mount originally planned for the two *Etna* class light cruisers, ordered in 1938 by Thailand from the CRDA yard, requisitioned by the *Regia Marina* in 1942, but never completed. In this form, she rejoined the fleet in 1961. The Polaris missile battery was tested once, successfully, using a dummy missile, but when the ship became operational, it was without missiles, the Americans having cooled on the idea of deploying nuclear-tipped ballistic missiles in mixed-manned surface ships. (The Italians responded by developing a Polaris-like missile of their own, dubbed *Alfa*, which got as far as several test firings in 1973–5 before the Italians signed up to the Nuclear Non-Proliferation Agreement and scrapped the programme.) *Garibaldi* was decommissioned in 1972.

In 1953, Italy began development of a series of multi-purpose warships that, in a manner analogous to the US Navy's, were designated first as 'guided-missile frigates' (DLGs) and later as 'guided-missile cruisers'. The two classes built by the Italians were quite similar in design and intent, with twin-rail Terrier launchers and eight OTO-Melara 76mm/62 guns forward, anti-submarine torpedo tubes and a hangar and landing platform aft for helicopters. The two-ship *Andrea Doria* class was laid down in 1958 and served until decommissioned in the late 1980s. The following *Vittorio Veneto*, laid down in 1965, had a larger helicopter deck and hangar,

The four scout cruisers of the *'Capitani Romani'* class that were completed – three before the Italian surrender and one long afterward – all served long post-war careers. Two were handed over to the French was reparations and served in the *Marine Nationale* until stricken in the early-1960s; the other two remained in the post-war *Marina Militare*. *San Giorgio*, seen here at New York City at the Bicentennial celebrations held on 4 July 1976, had been commissioned into the *Regia Marina* in June 1943 as RN *Pompeo Magno*. By this time, she has been significantly reconstructed. Her power plant has been replaced by a CODAG (Combined Diesel and Gas) unit; she has American 5in/38 twin-mounts in positions Nos 1 and 4, an Italian-made Menon triple ASW mortar in No 2 position and a single 76mm/62 MMI made by OTO-Melara in No 3 position. In this configuration, she served as a training ship until 1980. (NARA)

Built with American missiles and electronics, but with Italian guns, the guided-missile cruiser *Andrea Doria* was commissioned in 1964. She has one twin-arm launcher for the Terrier SAM along with its associated radars: an SPS-39 on a mainmast platform for hemispheric search using FRESCAN (frequency scanning), an SPS-12 air-search antenna on a foremast platform and the two SPG-55Bs on her pilot house and in front of her bridge for missile guidance. She had eight of the same 76mm/62 MMI single-mount guns as seen on *San Giorgio*. (USMM via Cernuschi)

making her in many ways similar to the *Moskvas*. A planned sister-ship was to be recast as a through-deck cruiser, but inter-service rivalry between the post-war Italian Navy and Air Force – one that had its origins before the Second World War with the so-called 'Balbo Law' of 1931 that gave the *Regia Aeronautica* control over all aviation assets, a situation not unlike the British Royal Navy and Royal Air Force before the war – caused the plan to be dropped at this time, but it would not go away.

The idea was indeed revived in 1975, in the form of a small aircraft carrier designed to handle VSTOL aircraft and helicopters, like the *Invincibles* and *Tbilisis*, which was laid down in 1981, and was given the name *Giuseppe Garibaldi*. For the administrative and legal reasons alluded to above, it was given the type designation '*incrociatore tuttoponte*', literally an 'all-deck cruiser'.[13]

The Netherlands

A nation that has not been mentioned in this narrative, not because they did not build cruisers, but because they built them and used them, for the most part, for peaceful patrolling, is the Netherlands. Even during the Second World War, when their country was rapidly overrun by the Germans in the spring of 1940, their navy was little involved; their cruisers were doing what they always did, patrolling the islands of the Netherlands East Indies (NEI), the role for which they had been designed. It was only after war broke out in the Pacific that Dutch cruisers found themselves at war and, sadly, suffered for it. The old cruiser *Java* and the newer *De Ruyter* were both sunk by Japanese torpedoes at the Battle of the Java Sea on 27 February 1942. Two small scout cruisers were under construction in the Netherlands in the late 1930s. One, *Tromp*, was completed and actually left for the NEI; the other, *Jacob van Heemskerck*, was incomplete, but able to steam to England before the Germans over-ran the Netherlands. Both survived the war and served until the late 1950s.

After the war, the Dutch were able to revive their ship-building industry, in part, by continuing work on two larger cruisers that had been designed and laid down just before the war began. The original design was for a ship of 8350 tons carrying ten 15cm/53 guns designed by the Swedish firm Bofors. Work on one of the ships had proceeded to the point that the Germans had her launched in December 1944 to clear the slip. This ship, named *De Zeven Provincien*, was renamed *De Ruyter* when work began again in 1947. The other, tentatively named *Eendracht*, was given the name *De Zeven Provincien* when she was launched in 1950. Both were completed as gun cruisers, with an updated version of the Bofors gun, now a 15.2cm/53 Model 1942, in four twin turrets. In a refit between 1962 and 1964, *De Zeven Provincien* had her two after turrets removed and replaced by a Terrier missile system. Lack of funds prevented the plan to make the same modification to *De Ruyter* from being carried out. In 1971, Chile bought the Swedish cruiser *Göta Lejon*; not to be outdone, Peru negotiated the purchase of *De Ruyter* in 1973, renaming her BAP *Almirante Grau*.[14] (In 1976, *De Zeven Provincien* was also purchased by Peruvians and, after a refit that saw the removal of the Terrier missile system, was commissioned as BAP *Aquirre*. She served the Peruvian Navy until decommissioned in 1999.) BAP *Almirante Grau* had a major modernisation between 1985 and 1988 that saw, among upgrades, the addition of launchers for eight Otomat Mk 2 anti-ship missiles, but she retained her entire main battery. In this form, she served until decommissioned in 2017, the last gun cruiser in the world's navies.

Afterword

The cruiser, as a type, evolved to fulfil a set of needs for navies that, for the most part, can now be addressed without requiring specialised warships. Scouting, certainly, can be performed in the twenty-first century far better by satellite and airborne platforms than by any ship. Submarines can interdict trade far better than any surface platform. The resurgence of small-scale near-shore piracy requires types of ships quite different from cruisers to lead suppression efforts. But some of the tasking that fell to the cruisers described in this book can still best be addressed by a platform that is not submerged and is not the primary target. Whether that platform is called a large destroyer or a small cruiser, it would ideally mount an array of sensors sufficient to give complete 'situational awareness' even if satellite communications are disrupted, be armed with an array of weapons capable of defending itself and other ships around it from threats under, on and above the sea's surface and of attacking those threats in turn and be survivable enough to accept some damage and continue functioning. Whether this is a single hull of 'traditional' cruiser size or a central 'control' ship with a 'swarm' of semi- (or fully-) autonomous unmanned platforms surrounding it or some other networked entity remains to be seen, but if it performs the functions traditionally assigned to a cruiser, it deserves the name.

Peru's BAP *Almirante Grau* (CLM-81, ex-*De Ruyter*) was the last gun cruiser to serve in the world's navies, seen here after a 1996 refit. She was decommissioned on 26 September 2017. She served no practical purpose at this point, other than to carry her nation's colours proudly and look majestic. (USN)

Notes

A Note on Nomenclature and Units, etc

[1] The USN began assigning hull numbers to ships around 1890. A few American ships mentioned in this text pre-date this period and had no hull number assigned.
[2] The RN used several different pennant number schemes prior to the primary period of interest of this study and again after that period, but the only pennant numbers given here will be those in use during the Second World War.

List of Abbreviations/Acronyms

[1] *Kriegsmarine* – literally 'war navy' – was the official name of the German navy only from 1935 through the end of the Second World War. Until the surrender of Imperial Germany in 1918, the German navy was called the *Kaiserliche Marine* ('Imperial Navy') and then until 1935, the *Reichsmarine* (another way of saying 'imperial navy', as in 'navy of the empire', in the sense of 'national navy').

Introduction

[1] To be precise, that apology came at the end of Chapter 7 in that book: Robert C Stern, *The Battleship Holiday: The Naval Treaties and Capital Ship Design* (Barnsley: Seaforth Publishing, 2017), p 139.
[2] For the purposes of this book, the adjective 'modern' is understood to refer to that period after the end of the First World War.
[3] The literature of the time used the terms 'locomotive torpedo' and 'automotive torpedo' interchangeably to refer to the early Whitehead and other self-propelled torpedoes developed in the 1860s. They were called 'locomotive' or 'automotive' to distinguish them from 'spar torpedoes', which were simply explosive charges mounted at the end of a long pole (or spar), or static mines, which at this time were called 'torpedoes'. When, during the American Civil War Battle of Mobile Bay, Rear Admiral David Farragut was quoted as saying: 'Damn the torpedoes, full speed ahead' (or similar words), the 'torpedoes' to which he was referring were static mines.
[4] William Hovgaard, *Modern History of Warships: Comprising a Discussion of Present Standpoint and Recent War Experiences* (London: E & F N Spon Ltd, 1920), pp 175–6. Seagoing breastwork monitors began being built without sailing rigs in 1869; as late as 1886, reputable naval architects recommended sails to augment the steam engines in cruising ships, both to extend the range of the ships and to add speed on top of that provided by steam engines.
[5] Robert C Stern, *Destroyer Battles: Epics of Naval Close Combat* (Barnsley: Seaforth Publishing, 2008), pp 15–18; Juan del Campo, *Britons and Peruvians Fight at Sea*, 4 August 2004.
[6] Hovgaard, *Modern History of Warships*, p 203; Roger Chesneau and Eugene M Kolesnik (eds), *Conway's All the World's Fighting Ships 1860-1905* (London: Conway Maritime Press, 1979), p 186. She was named for Grand Duke Konstantin Nikolayevich, the brother of Tsar Alexander II, who commanded the Imperial Russian Navy, with the rank of General-Admiral, from 1853 through 1881, during which time he built it into the third largest navy in the world.
[7] The Bessemer process was the first to make inexpensive steel available in usable quantities, predating the Siemens-Martin process by about a decade, but the latter was easier to control and could be scaled up more easily, so that by 1895, the Siemens-Martin open hearth method had largely replaced Bessemer furnaces in Great Britain.
[8] Hovgaard, *Modern History of Warships*, pp 19 and 356–7.
[9] Ibid, pp 168–9; Chesneau and Kolesnik (eds), *Conway's All the World's Fighting Ships 1860-1905*, p 74. A barkentine rig is a three-masted rig in which only the foremast is square-rigged.
[10] Norman Friedman, *British Cruisers of the Victorian Era* (Barnsley: Seaforth Publishing, 2012), pp 116–25.
[11] Hovgaard, *Modern History of Warships*, pp 58–60; Chesneau and Kolesnik (eds), *Conway's All the World's Fighting Ships 1860-1905*, p 341.
[12] For instance, the *Regia Marina*'s *Regina Elena* class battleships were well ahead of their time when laid down in 1901–3, but were obsolescent when completed in 1907–8, cf., Stern, *The Battleship Holiday*, pp 21–2.
[13] Norman Friedman, *U.S. Cruisers: An Illustrated Design History* (Annapolis, MD: Naval Institute Press, 1984), p 41.
[14] Hovgaard, *Modern History of Warships*, pp 174–6. In way of the engineering spaces, the cork in the cofferdam was replaced by coal.
[15] *Idzumi* is a dated transliteration of the kanji (和泉), now commonly rendered '*Izumi*'. It is the name of a province near Osaka.
[16] David C Evans and Mark R Peattie, *Kaigun: Strategy, Tactics and Technology in the Imperial Japanese Navy, 1887-1941* (Annapolis, MD: Naval Institute Press, 1997), pp 14–15. White served as Barnaby's Deputy Director of Naval Construction (DNC) at the Admiralty until April 1883, when he replaced Rendel at Armstrong; he stayed there until 1 August 1885, when he returned to the RN as DNC upon Barnaby's retirement. Rendel joined the Admiralty as Civil Lord when he left Armstrong. This was clearly an early example of what would come to be called the 'revolving door' between government and industry, a practice very much frowned upon in the United States. In Great Britain at this time it was considered not only acceptable but beneficial.
[17] Friedman, *British Cruisers of the Victorian Era*, p 140.
[18] A more modern transliteration using the *pinyin* system would render these names *Zhiyuen* and *Jingyuen*.
[19] *Yoshino* was designed by Phillip Watts, who succeeded White at Armstrong when the latter returned to the Admiralty in 1885.
[20] William Oliver Stevens and Allan Westcott, *A History of Sea Power* (Garden City, NY: Doubleday, Doran & Co., Inc., 1944), p 268.
[21] HMS *Scout* (1580 tons) was laid down in January 1884, the prototype in the Royal Navy of a torpedo cruiser, which were to evolve into third class cruisers, useful for leading destroyer flotillas and at foreign stations where docking facilities were limited.
[22] K D McBride, 'Re: HMS *Kent* (1914-1915) (W.I. No. 1, 1998)', *Warship International* No 4 (1998), p 334.
[23] Ibid.
[24] Friedman, *British Cruisers of the Victorian Era*, p 146. What made matters worse was that the *Orlando*s were delivered seriously overweight, so that the top of the 5.5ft tall armour belt, instead of being 3.5ft above the waterline at full load, was 2ft underwater.
[25] Chesneau and Kolesnik (eds), *Conway's All the World's Fighting Ships 1860-1905*, p 66.
[26] '*Rurik*' really should be rendered '*Riurik*' in English, as this more closely approaches the pronunciation of the Cyrillic 'Рюрик', however, the former version is by far the more common rendition.
[27] Friedman, *British Cruisers of the Victorian Era*, p 226n7.
[28] Ibid, pp 221 and 229–30.
[29] Ibid, pp 231–3.

Chapter 1: Cruisers in all Sizes and Shapes – A First Glimpse of the Future: 1897–1914

[1] Nathan Okun, *Table of Metallurgical Properties of Naval Armor and Construction Materials*, http://www.navweaps.com/index_nathan/metalprpsept2009.php#Average_'Mild/Medium'_Construction_Steel_and_Armor, 26 September 2009. Until 1890, only Schneider had the capability to make steel plate of this thickness.

[2] Palliser shot was a pointed, cylindrical cast-iron shot with a small cavity for an optional bursting charge introduced into British service in 1867. The nose of the shot was chilled during casting to harden it. The chilled casting technique was derived from Gruson's, as detailed later.

[3] Erwin F Sieche, 'Austria-Hungary's *Monarch* class coast defence ships', *Warship International* No 3 (1999), p 223. Charles Cammell & Co was one of the predecessor companies of present-day Cammell Laird.

[4] http://www.navweaps.com/index_nathan/metalprpsept2009.php#Average_'Compound'_Hard-Steel-Faced_Wrought_Iron_Armor. The hardening of iron/steel by selective quenching (rapid cooling) was not a new discovery; its use goes back in history to the swordsmiths and armourers of Damascus and Japan in medieval times and perhaps earlier.

[5] A Brinell Number is an expression of the hardness of a metal, with 100 being the hardness of wrought iron and a (theoretical) maximum hardness of 800. Any number greater than 650 is an approximation, as the hardness of the test sample approaches the hardness of the test apparatus.

[6] http://www.navweaps.com/index_nathan/metalprpsept2009.php Average_Nickel-Steel_Armor. Nickel works to harden steel by randomly replacing iron in steel crystals when the metal cools; the atoms are similar enough that this does not impact the normal properties of steel, but different enough as to resist the propagation of cracks along crystal boundaries.

[7] http://www.navweaps.com/index_nathan/metalprpsept2009.php#Average_Harveyized_Nickel-Steel_Armor.

[8] http://www.navweaps.com/index_nathan/metalprpsept2009.php#Average_Original_Krupp_Cemented_Armor_(KC_a/A). While initially just known as Krupp Cemented, this armour plate introduced in 1894 was renamed 'Krupp Cemented a/A' (Krupp Cemented old type) after Krupp AG began development of an improved cemented armour they called 'Krupp Cemented n/A' (Krupp Cemented new type) in the 1920s.

[9] Tests by the US Navy showed that for plates thicker than 5in, KC was approximately15 per cent more effective at stopping AP shot than an equivalent thickness of Harveyized nickel-steel, cf., *Naval Ordnance and Gunnery Manual*, US Navy, 1937, http://www.eugeneleeslover.com/ARMOR-CHAPTER-XII-A.html.

[10] http://www.navweaps.com/index_nathan/metalprpsept2009.php#Average_Harveyized_Nickel-Steel_Armor.

[11] Cf., *Naval Ordnance and Gunnery Manual*, US Navy, 1937, http://www.eugeneleeslover.com/USNAVY/CHAPTER-XIII-PAGE-1.html

[12] Holtzer steel was originally a proprietary product of Jacob Holtzer & Cie, Unieux, St-Étienne, France.

[13] Picric acid is a chemically-active compound that reacts strongly with the metal of shell casings, causing them to have a short 'shelf life'. For that reason, and because Lyddite-type explosives were still too shock-sensitive for consistent use in AP shells, countries began abandoning picric acid for the more stable TNT (trinitrotoluene) beginning with Germany in 1911. Unfortunately, the Royal Navy retained Lyddite through the First World War, cf., Stern, *The Battleship Holiday*, pp 110–11 and 110n8.

[14] McBride, 'Re: HMS Kent *(1914-1915)* (W.I. *No. 1, 1998*):', p 335.

[15] Friedman, *British Cruisers of the Victorian Era*, p 221.

[16] Hovgaard, *Modern History of Warships*, pp 206–7. The *Marine Nationale* had conducted a firing trial in 1886 using the old ironclad *Belliqueuse* during which it was concluded that 100mm steel plate armour would suffice to detonate HE shells outside the hull of a ship.

[17] Ibid, p 210.

[18] Cf., http://www.navweaps.com/Weapons/WNBR_6-45_mk7.php#gunnote4. This rate of fire was generally attainable only as long as ready-service rounds held out; after that, when rate-of-fire depended on rounds passed by hand up from magazines, it typically dropped to 2–3rpm, but with six guns sustaining even that slower rate, it posed a substantial threat.

[19] Friedman, *British Cruisers of the Victorian Era*, p 221.

[20] Hovgaard, *Modern History of Warships*, pp 207–8.

[21] The psychological burden of fighting without his ship's main-battery guns may, in part, explain the decision by *Colón*'s captain to beach and scuttle his ship in virtually undamaged condition on 3 July 1898.

[22] Chesneau and Kolesnik (eds), *Conway's All the World's Fighting Ships 1860-1905*, p 258. The first two of the class – *Gazelle* and *Niobe* – were lighter (2916 tons); the last three – *Frauenlob*, *Arcona* and *Undine* – were heavier (3130 tons).

[23] http://www.navweaps.com/Weapons/WNGER_41-40_skc00.php.

[24] Quadruple-expansion engines were designed and built, but were found to be not worth the weight of the added large cylinder and its linkages.

[25] Hansgeorg Jentschura, Dieter Jung and Peter Mickel, *Warships of the Imperial Japanese Navy, 1869-1945*, trans. Anthony Preston and J D Brown (London: Arms & Armour Press, 1977), p 103.

[26] Friedman, *U.S. Cruisers: An Illustrated Design History*, pp 67–70. When they were laid down, they were designated 'scout cruisers' and given the hull number CS1–CS3, but when the nomenclature of American cruisers was rationalised in 1920 and 1921, they were redesignated light cruisers (CL1–CL3).

[27] Hovgaard, *Modern History of Warships*, p 194, considers them as the beginning of the light cruiser series; others, such as Randal Gray (ed), *Conway's All the World's Fighting Ships 1906-1921* (London: Conway Maritime Press, 1985), p 51, give that honour to the *Bristol* class of the 1908–9 building programme.

[28] Metacentric height (GM), measured in feet, is one of several important measures of a ship's stability. Generally, the higher this number the better, except that when it gets too high, it can make a ship overly sensitive to wave action, causing it to have a rapid roll period, making it an unstable gun platform. On the other hand, a low GM causes a ship to 'wallow', lagging behind wave action and, in extreme cases, brings the risk of capsizing in rough weather.

[29] Eric Lacroix and Linton Wells III, *Japanese Cruisers of the Pacific War* (Annapolis, MD: Naval Institute Press, 1997), pp 7–10.

[30] This construction technique was called the Isherwood System in Great Britain, where it was patented in 1906 for use in merchant ships. However the idea for a longitudinal framing system had been around for at least 50 years.

[31] Norman Friedman, *British Cruisers: Two World Wars and After* (Barnsley: Seaforth Publishing, 2010), pp 26–9. The decision to add side armour came from the 1908 gunnery trials on the target ship HMS *Edinburgh* and another later series that showed that HE shells could be defeated by a thin strake of side armour, which, while it offered no benefit in stopping AP shells, in no way worsened the damage they caused.

[32] Simply put, an oil-fired power plant weighed less, took up less space and required many fewer men to run, while the space needed to store the fuel was less for any distance steamed. The only downsides to the switch from coal to oil were the loss of the protective effect of coal bunkers and the fact that, for most naval powers – the Americans

being the notable exception – cheap locally-available coal had to be replaced by expensive imported oil.
[33] Friedman, *British Cruisers of the Victorian Era*, pp 257–60.
[34] Ibid, pp 260–2.
[35] The only exception was Italy's *San Giorgio* class of 1905–7.
[36] Evans and Peattie, *Kaigun*, pp 60–4. The limiting factor was the slow development of an indigenous steel industry. It was not until 1901 that the first Japanese-made armour plate was produced and the first large, cruiser-sized warship to be laid down in Japan was the armoured cruiser (semi-battlecruiser) *Tsukuba*, at Kure on 14 January 1905.
[37] Lieutenant Commander Newton A McCully, USN, *The McCully Report: The Russo-Japanese War, 1904-05*, edited by Richard A von Doenhoff (Annapolis, MD: Naval Institute Press, 1977), pp 177–93. Almost all the account of the Ulsan engagement told here comes from this source; the rest is from Hovgaard, *Modern History of Warships*, pp 223–4 and Piotr Olender, *Russo-Japanese Naval War 1905, Vol. 2* (Petersfield: MMP, 2010), pp 38–50.
[38] According to Olender, *Russo-Japanese Naval War 1905, Vol. 2*, p 40n24, Japanese sources state the range had dropped to under 9200yd before they opened fire.
[39] This sounds like a form of stadiametric rangefinding, in which the observed distance between masts of a target is measured using the reticles in the telescope eyepiece and an estimated range is calculated (or looked up in a range table) based on a known distance between masts of a known target. It is a straightforward trigonometric calculation.
[40] McCully, *The McCully Report*, p 185.
[41] As late as the end of the First World War, the Royal Navy and most of the world's other navies used 'points' rather than degrees to communicate compass headings, a point being 11.25°, the compass ring being divided into 32 points.
[42] 'Battle of Ulsan,' *The Samurai Archives/SamuraiWiki*, last modified 31 August 2007, https://wiki.samurai-archives.com/index.php?title=Battle_of_Ulsan.
[43] Peter Brook, 'Armoured Cruiser versus Armoured Cruiser: Ulsan 14 August 1904' in Anthony Preston (ed), *Warship 2000-2001* (London: Conway Maritime Press, 2000), p 43.
[44] McCully, *The McCully Report*, pp 185–6.
[45] Funnels on a steam-powered warship, like the exhaust system in an automobile with an internal combustion engine, provide back-pressure necessary to the proper operation of the engine(s). Shooting holes in funnels, like getting a hole in a car's muffler, reduces back-pressure, harming the efficiency of the engine(s).
[46] Hovgaard, *Modern History of Warships*, p 224.
[47] McCully, *The McCully Report*, p 186.
[48] This hit analysis is from to Olender, *Russo-Japanese Naval War 1905, Vol 2*, p 47. That sources gives precise numbers, stating that Japanese fired 958 8in rounds and 4528 6in rounds. Similar precision, for obvious reasons, is not possible with the Russians, who are said to have fired 2000–2300 rounds of the two calibres combined.
[49] McCully, *The McCully Report*, p 192.
[50] Ibid, p 186.
[51] These numbers are from Olender, *Russo-Japanese Naval War 1905, Vol 2*, p 46. Other sources cite similar, but not identical, numbers.
[52] Sources differ considerably on the range at which action was initiated. Gray (ed), *Conway's All the World's Fighting Ships 1906-1921*, p 232, states fire was opened at 19,000yd. McCully, *The McCully Report*, p 141, states fire was opened at 14,000yd. In any case it was well beyond the useful range of the rangefinders.
[53] These were the Ansaldo-built *Kasuga* (ex-*Rivadavia*, ex-*Mitra*) and *Nisshin* (ex-*Mariano Moreno*, ex-*Roca*).
[54] Nicholas A Lambert, *Sir John Fisher's Naval Revolution* (Columbia, SC: University of South Carolina Press, 1999), p 107.
[55] Quoted in Jon T Sumida, *In Defense of Naval Supremacy: Finance, Technology, and British Naval Policy 1889-1914* (Milton Park: Routledge, 1993), pp 50–6.
[56] Also in that informal group was W H Gard, chief constructor of the Portsmouth Dockyard, who had worked with Fisher on many of his early ship design ideas.
[57] Admiral Reginald H S Bacon, RN, *The Life of Lord Fisher of Kilverstone: Admiral of the Fleet, Vol. 1* (Garden City, NY: Doubleday, Doran & Co., Inc., 1929), p 256.
[58] In particular, cf., Sumida, *In Defense of Naval Supremacy*, p 56.
[59] Lambert, *Sir John Fisher's Naval Revolution*, p 108.
[60] The curious reader can choose from multiple accounts, particularly of the performance of the British battlecruisers at Jutland, such as Stern, *The Battleship Holiday*, pp 48–57.
[61] Gary Staff, *German Battlecruisers of World War One: Their Design, Construction and Operations* (Annapolis, MD: Naval Institute Press, 2014), p 12.

Chapter 2: The Test of Battle, Part 1: 1914–1916
[1] Geoffrey Bennett, *Coronel and the Falklands* (Edinburgh: Berlinn Ltd, 2000), pp 69–70.
[2] Vincent P O'Hara and Leonard R Heinz, *Clash of Fleets: Naval Battles of the Great War, 1914-18* (Annapolis, MD: Naval Institute Press, 2017), pp 89–91.
[3] Bennett, *Coronel and the Falklands*, p 73.
[4] Port Stanley is now formally known as just 'Stanley'. It was, and is, the primary deep-water port in the Falklands.
[5] Bennett, *Coronel and the Falklands*, p 82.
[6] This was, in fact, not true. It seems that Cradock and even *Canopus*' own CO were being misinformed by the ship's Chief Engineer. *Canopus*' CO did not find out until 30 October that his ship was capable of maintaining 16.5 knots, and, for reasons that are hard to explain, he refrained from passing the information along to his superior. cf., Bennett, *Coronel and the Falklands*, pp 21–2.
[7] —, 'Monograph 1. – Operations Leading Up to the Battle of Coronel' in *Naval Staff Monographs, Vol. I* (Naval Staff, Training and Staff Duties Div., July 1919), p 34.
[8] Ibid, p 36.
[9] Much of this account is taken from —, 'Monograph 27. – The Battles of Coronel and the Falkland Islands' in *Naval Staff Monographs, Vol. IX* (Naval Staff, Training and Staff Duties Div., October 1923), pp 224–35, with additional material from O'Hara and Heinz, *Clash of Fleets*, pp 92–6 and Bennett, *Coronel and the Falklands*, pp 27–36.
[10] —, 'Monograph 27. – The Battles of Coronel and the Falkland Islands', p 301.
[11] http://www.navweaps.com/Weapons/WNBR_92-47_mk10.php.
[12] http://www.navweaps.com/Weapons/WNGER_827-40_skc95.php.
[13] There is disagreement among sources as to when *Monmouth* fell out of line. O'Hara and Heinz, *Clash of Fleets*, p 93, say it happened five minutes into the action, while Arthur J Marder, *From the Dreadnought to Scapa Flow, The Royal Navy in the Fisher Era 1904-1919, Vol. II, The War Years: To the Eve of Jutland 1914-1916* (Barnsley: Seaforth Publishing, 2013), p 114, puts it approximately a half-hour after the battle started. —, 'Monograph 27. – The Battles of Coronel and the Falkland Islands', p 230n5, offers two choices – *Glasgow*'s log stating *Monmouth* fell away at 18.44, approximately 11 minutes after Spee opened fire, while the German record states it occurred at 18.50.
[14] —, 'Monograph 27. – The Battles of Coronel and the Falkland Islands', p 232.

[15] Ibid, p 232n1.
[16] Ibid, p 233; Bennett, *Coronel and the Falklands*, p 33.
[17] Given the prevailing weather conditions of Force 6 wind and seas, it is perhaps not so curious after all that no survivors were heard.
[18] This is from *Glasgow*'s log quoted in Bennett, *Coronel and the Falklands*, p 32.
[19] Marder, *From the Dreadnought to Scapa Flow, Vol. II*, p 111. The CO of *Glasgow*, the future Rear Admiral John Luce, in remarks he wrote down in 1929, reported Cradock as saying just before the Coronel battle 'I will take care I do not suffer the same fate as poor Troubridge'. In the event, Troubridge was 'honourably acquitted' of all charges against him, but was never again given a seagoing command.
[20] Ibid, p 114, gives Spee's consumption of main-battery rounds in this action as precisely 42 per cent.
[21] —, 'Monograph 1. – Operations Leading Up to the Battle of Coronel', p 42.
[22] —, 'Monograph 27. – The Battles of Coronel and the Falkland Islands', p 229.
[23] Ibid, p 227, states that half of the crews of *Scharnhorst* and *Gneisenau* had rotated home in June 1914, but the remainder had been with the ships for three years. *Good Hope* and *Monmouth* had been recommissioned from reserve only months before the battle.
[24] Ibid, pp 227 and 234. This source describes the 6in AP shells fired by the British as 'obsolescent' and uses the same adjective to describe the fuses of the British 6in and 4in HE shells.
[25] Ibid, p 231n7, O'Hara and Heinz, *Clash of Fleets*, p 94 and Marder, *From the Dreadnought to Scapa Flow, Vol. II*, p 114.
[26] According to N J M Campbell, *Jutland: An Analysis of the Fighting* (London: Conway Maritime Press, 1986), pp 354–6, the best sustained shooting by a British ship or unit at Jutland was by HMS *Barham* and *Valiant*, which together achieved a hit rate of approximately 3.7 per cent. The best by a German ship was by SMS *Lützow*, which shot at a 5 per cent hit rate.
[27] —, 'Monograph 27. – The Battles of Coronel and the Falkland Islands', p 234.
[28] Marder, *From the Dreadnought to Scapa Flow, Vol. II*, p 123.
[29] The reader interested in this part of the battle can read any of the several excellent books on Jutland I used as source material that are listed in the bibliography, or the coverage specifically of the performance of the battlecruisers in Stern, *The Battleship Holiday*, pp 48–59.
[30] V E Tarrant, *Jutland: The German Perspective* (London: Arms & Armour Press, 1995), p 75.
[31] Ibid, p 115.
[32] John Brooks, *The Battle of Jutland* (Cambridge: Cambridge University Press, 2016), p 252.
[33] Tarrant, *Jutland*, pp 111–12.
[34] Ibid, p 115.
[35] Brooks, *The Battle of Jutland*, p 253.
[36] William Schleihauf, 'The Dumaresq and the Dreyer: Part I', *Warship International* No 1 (2001), pp 8–11. The Mk V Dumaresq was being deployed in cruiser-sized ships as early as 1915. The site of installation depended on where space was available; in light cruisers it was often first installed in the conning tower because the control tops in Royal Navy light cruisers pre-Jutland were most often quite small.
[37] Gary Staff, *Skagerrak: The Battle of Jutland through German Eyes* (Barnsley: Pen & Sword Maritime, 2016), p 95, quotes *Pillau*'s log, which states that the *E-Uhr* was not of use in the engagement with *Chester* because the range-rate was constantly changing.
[38] —, *Handbook for Fire Control Instruments, 1914*, Admiralty, Gunnery Branch, G.01627/14, ADM/186/191, The National Archives, Kew, retrieved May 2018, pp 6–7.
[39] Ibid, pp 72. This is Appendix I, which lists the fire-control instruments for all capital ships and cruisers extant in 1914 (and would not have changed for these ships by 1916).
[40] Ibid.
[41] Ibid, p 66.
[42] These casualty figures are from Staff, *Skagerrak*, p 94. Other sources give other numbers, but in the same general range.
[43] Tarrant, *Jutland*, p 115, gives the range as 8000yd; Campbell, *Jutland*, p 112, gives it as 10,000yd. The 9000yd figure comes from Lieutenant Commander Holloway H Frost, USN, *Diagrammatic Study of the Battle of Jutland* (Washington, DC: U.S. Navy Office of Naval Intelligence, 1 December 1921), Fig 16.
[44] Specifically, for an account of 3BCS's action against Hipper's IAG, cf., Stern, *The Battleship Holiday*, pp 56–7.
[45] Captain Vincent B Molteno, RN, 'Narrative of HMS '*Warrior*'', in H W Fawcett and G W W Hooper (eds), *The Fighting at Jutland: The Personal Experiences of Forty-five Officers and Men of the British Fleet* (London: Hutchinson & Co Ltd, 1929), p 107. This is entirely consistent with Beatty's BCF being 20–25nm north-west of its reported position.
[46] This could only have been 1st LCS, led by Commodore E S Alexander-Sinclair in HMS *Galatea*, directly ahead of Beatty's four remaining battlecruisers. It is difficult to understand how Molteno could have described the sighting bearing to *Galatea* as being 'almost the same' as that to IIAG, as she would have appeared on a bearing at least 45° clockwise relative to IIAG from *Warrior*'s position at that time.
[47] Molteno, 'Narrative of HMS '*Warrior*' ', in Fawcett and Hooper (eds), *The Fighting at Jutland*, pp 107–8. 'Green 80' indicates 10° forward of the starboard beam, expressed as 80° off the starboard bow.
[48] Brooks, *The Battle of Jutland*, p 268.
[49] Molteno, 'Narrative of HMS '*Warrior*'', in Fawcett and Hooper (eds), *The Fighting at Jutland*, p 108. Frost, *Diagrammatic Study*, Fig 16, shows that fire was opened at 16,000yd, a figure corroborated in Campbell, *Jutland*, p 122. The 9.2in/47 and 9.2in/50 main-battery guns carried by *Defence* and *Warrior* had a theoretical maximum range of over 25,000yd, but, in practical terms, they were considered to have an 'effective range' of 13,000yd, cf., http://www.navweaps.com/Weapons/WNBR_92-50_mk11.php.
[50] Before the war, many cruisers were fitted with 'range drums' mounted on the fore-and-aft faces of the spotting tops that displayed the range to target using rolling numerical drums, but these proved very hard to read in practice and most had been removed by the time of Jutland. The more practical 'range dials' came into use after Jutland.
[51] Molteno, 'Narrative of HMS '*Warrior*'', in Fawcett and Hooper (eds), *The Fighting at Jutland*, p 108.
[52] Campbell, *Jutland*, p 395.
[53] Molteno is being more than a bit disingenuous here. Actually, Arbuthnot's two cruisers cut so closely in front of Beatty's line that, according to Campbell, *Jutland*, p 115, '*Lion*'s helm had to be put hard over, so that she swung under the *Warrior*'s stern and cleared her by only 200yds.'
[54] Molteno, 'Narrative of HMS '*Warrior*'', in Fawcett and Hooper (eds), *The Fighting at Jutland*, pp 108–9.
[55] Much of this part of the account comes from Brooks, *The Battle of Jutland*, pp 280–1.
[56] —, 'Narrative of HMS '*Yarmouth*', 3rd Light Cruiser Squadron' ', in Fawcett and Hooper (eds), *The Fighting at Jutland*, p 106.
[57] Jellicoe had made the critical decision to deploy to the left and, as his columns deployed into a line by turning in succession 90° to port, many of his battleships, particularly towards the rear of the line, found themselves able to see and open fire on Hipper's battlecruisers and the leading dreadnoughts of the HSF coming up from the south.
[58] —, 'Narrative of HMS '*Obedient*' of 12th Destroyer Flotilla', in

Fawcett and Hooper (eds), *The Fighting at Jutland*, pp 105–6.
[59] This sounds suspiciously like a *Gabel* ('fork'), which was German practice while initially finding the range to a target. In this system, the shells in a half-salvo were spread over 800m in range, with 200m separation between shells, with rapid up and down adjustments in an attempt to find a straddle of the target in minimal time.
[60] —, 'Narrative of HMS '*Neptune*', 6th battleship from the rear of the line', in Fawcett and Hooper (eds), *The Fighting at Jutland*, pp 106–7.
[61] —, 'Narrative of HMS '*Colossus*', Battleship', in ibid, p 106. For those unfamiliar with the expression, 'a Catherine wheel' originally referred to an ancient torture device associated with St Catherine of Alexandria, later applied to any spinning pyrotechnic display.
[62] —, 'Narrative of HMS '*Neptune*', 6th battleship from the rear of the line', in Fawcett and Hooper (eds), *The Fighting at Jutland*, p 107.
[63] These times and accounts are from Brooks, *The Battle of Jutland*, pp 260–1, 264–5, 291–4 and 302–3, and Campbell, *Jutland*, pp 205 and 395.
[64] These were, in approximate chronological order, HMS *Marlborough, Hercules, Agincourt, Barham, Iron Duke, Monarch, Colossus, Conqueror, Thunderer, Royal Oak, Superb, Canada, Bellerophon, Temeraire, Vanguard* and *Revenge*.

Chapter 3: War Production and the Gold Standard – The *Hawkins* Class and their Contemporaries: 1914–1922
[1] Friedman, *British Cruisers: Two World Wars and After*, pp 42–8.
[2] Ibid, pp 48–50.
[3] P C Jumonville, 'Question 36/44 (*W.I.* no. 4 (2008): 279-282). Bow "Knuckles"', *Warship International* No 4 (2009), p 333.
[4] Friedman, *British Cruisers: Two World Wars and After*, pp 54–5.
[5] Gray (ed), *Conway's All the World's Fighting Ships 1906-1921*, p 64. The German cruiser-minelayers the *Emeralds* were designed to counter were the *Brummer* class, which proved to be not nearly as fast as originally believed, having a top speed of 28 knots.
[6] These were the Italian RN *Taranto* (ex-*Straßburg* [*Magdeburg* class]) and *Bari* (ex-*Pillau* [*Pillau* class]).
[7] Friedman, *British Cruisers: Two World Wars and After*, pp 65–70.
[8] Gray (ed), *Conway's All the World's Fighting Ships 1906-1921*, p 63.
[9] Friedman, *British Cruisers: Two World Wars and After*, p 69.
[10] John Jordan and Jean Moulin, *French Cruisers: 1922-1956* (Barnsley: Seaforth Publishing, 2013), pp 24–5.
[11] Evans and Peattie, *Kaigun*, pp 175–6.
[12] Lacroix and Wells, *Japanese Cruisers*, pp 17–27.
[13] Lillian Ruth Nelson, '*The Naval Policy of the United States, 1919-1931*' (Master's Thesis, Loyola University Chicago, 1941), pp 8–9. This act authorised (but did not necessarily fund) the construction of a massive fleet of new ships of all sizes (see the next chapter for more details). Actual funding was provided for four battleships, four battlecruisers and four scout cruisers, a substantial commitment from the normally parsimonious US Congress.
[14] Friedman, *British Cruisers: Two World Wars and After*, pp 13–14.
[15] Friedman, *U.S. Cruisers: An Illustrated Design History*, pp 74–80.
[16] This Admiral Fletcher – he would be promoted to full admiral in March 1915 – a Medal of Honor recipient for actions at the Battle of Veracruz in 1914, was the uncle of Admiral Frank Jack Fletcher of Coral Sea and Midway fame, who also received a Medal of Honor for actions at the same battle.
[17] At this time, the US Navy's 6in/53 gun was only available as an open single mount, so fitting an additional gun mount on the forecastle was not considered, given the danger of blast from the four guns mounted at the corners of the forward superstructure.
[18] At the time of their laying down, these ships were considered scout cruisers, hence the 'CS' designation. Before launch, their classification was changed to light cruisers, with a 'CL' designator.
[19] —, *The Treaty of Peace with Germany (Treaty of Versailles)*, 1919 For. Rel. (Paris Peace Conference, XIII), pp 55, 740, 743; Senate document 51, 66th Congress, 1st session, pp 126.
[20] Gerhard Koop and Klaus-Peter Schmolke, *German Light Cruisers of World War II*, trans. Geoffrey Brooks (London: Greenhill Books, 2002), pp 9–12.

Chapter 4: The Washington Treaty and its Immediate Consequences: 1920–1922
[1] Nelson, '*Naval Policy*,' pp 8–9. The only new starts of capital ships from mid-1916 to the end of the war, besides those in the US, were the four 'Admiral' class battlecruisers in Britain and the two Japanese *Nagatos*.
[2] George W Baer, *One Hundred Years of Sea Power: The U.S. Navy, 1890-1990* (Stanford, California: Stanford University Press, 1996), p 83.
[3] The reader is invited to check out the account of the 'Naval Battle of Paris' and its immediate aftermath in Stern, *The Battleship Holiday*, pp 87–98.
[4] Add to this the terror that capital, in the form of the property-owning class in Britain, felt at the successful Bolshevik Revolution in Russia in 1917 and the subsequent spread of socialist agitation among labour movements throughout Europe.
[5] The rationing of sugar and butter continued into 1920. The wartime Ministry of Food, that managed the rationing system, was not disbanded until 1921.
[6] Joseph S Davis, 'The War Debt Settlements', *The Virginia Quarterly Review* Vol 4, No 1 (Winter 1928).
[7] Captain Stephen W Roskill, RN, *Naval Policy Between the Wars I: The Period of Anglo-American Antagonism, 1919-1929* (Barnsley: Seaforth Publishing, 2016), pp 22–3.
[8] The Monroe Doctrine, dating from 1823 and named for then-US President James Monroe, stated that any attempt by a European power to establish a new colony in the Western Hemisphere would be viewed as an 'unfriendly' act. It was a unilateral declaration made by the Americans, never agreed to formally by the British and other European states .
[9] In the first decades of the twentieth century, America was still a nation with large, only partially-integrated immigrant communities that still self-identified with their country of origin; the German and Irish immigrant communities were among the largest and most vocally anti-British.
[10] Roskill, *Naval Policy Between the Wars I*, p 23. One RN officer reported that an American mission had arrived at a Turkish port accompanied by representatives of the Standard Oil Co and National City Bank of New York. The presence of the oil company man, in particular, must have worried the British, who considered Middle Eastern oil to be their strategic monopoly.
[11] Davis, 'The War Debt Settlements'.
[12] Kevin C Murphy, 'Chapter Seven: America and the World – Progressives and the Foreign Policy of the 1920s, III. Disarming the World' in *Uphill All the Way: The Fortunes of Progressivism, 1919–1929* (2013).
[13] Arthur Lee is best known to the British public today for his great philanthropy; he co-founded the Courtauld Institute and donated his country home Chequers to become the country residence of British Prime Ministers in perpetuity. Lee was much more sympathetic to the American point of view than most in Britain; he had spent a large part of his early career posted in Canada and had married an American wife.
[14] 'Naval Equality a Peace Policy.' *The New York Times*, Vol. LXX, No. 23,117, 5 May 1921, p 16. In the original article, published in the

editorial page of the *Times* this day, the words 'excepted' and 'except' were reported in the place of the words 'accepted' and 'accept'. This was corrected the next day on p 12 in an editorial entitled 'Equal Navies and World Peace'. The quote here shows the corrected version.

[15] Lee's quote here is from Harold Sprout and Margaret Sprout, *Toward a New Order of Sea Power: American Naval Policy and the World Scene, 1918-1922* (Princeton, NJ: Princeton University Press, 1946), p 129.

[16] Ibid; Raymond Carl Gamble, 'Decline of the Dreadnought: Britain and the Washington Naval Conference, 1921-1922,' (PhD diss., University of Massachusetts, Amherst, MA, 1993), p 285n101 .

[17] The press release by Dr Iyenaga can be found in 'Says Japan Won't Provoke Conflict.' *The New York Times*, Vol. LXX, No. 23,101, 24 April 1921, p 29.

[18] Roskill, *Naval Policy Between the Wars I*, p 213.

[19] These were three *Weymouth* class, six *Chatham* class, three *Birmingham* class, six *Arethusa* class, six *Caroline* class, two *Calliope* class, four *Cambrian* class, two *Centaur* class, three *Caledon* class, five *Ceres* class, five *Capetown* class, eight *Danae* class and two *Hawkins* class.

[20] —, *Conference on the Limitation of Armament: Address of the President of the United States at the Opening of the Conference at Washington, November 12, 1921, together with the Address of Charles E. Hughes, Secretary of State of the United States and American Commissioner, also The Proposal of the United States for the Limitation of Naval Armament*, Senate Document No.77, 67th Congress, 1st Session, Government Printing Office, Washington, DC, 14 November 1921, p 14.

[21] Ibid.

[22] Ibid, pp 14–15.

[23] Sprout and Sprout, *Toward a New Order of Sea Power*, p 155.

[24] —, *Conference on the Limitation of Armament: Address of the President of the United States*, pp 24–7.

[25] Roskill, *Naval Policy Between the Wars I*, p 312.

[26] 'Britain Would End All Submarines.' *The New York Times*, Vol. LXXI, No. 23,307, 16 November 1921, pp 1 and 3; Sprout and Sprout, *Toward a New Order of Sea Power*, pp 162–4.

[27] Colonel Roosevelt was actually Theodore Roosevelt III, but was always called 'Teddy Junior'. He was the eldest son of President Theodore Roosevelt, who actually was Theodore Roosevelt, Jr. Curiously, Colonel Roosevelt, whose military career had included a reserve commission as a lieutenant colonel in the US Army during the First World War, was then serving as Assistant Secretary of the Navy, the same post held by his father in 1897–8 and by his cousin Franklin between 1913 and 1920.

[28] Sprout and Sprout, *Toward a New Order of Sea Power*, pp 162–4.

[29] 'Britain Would End All Submarines.' *The New York Times*, Vol. LXXI, No. 23,307, 16 November 1921, p 3; Stern, *The Battleship Holiday*, pp 103–4.

[30] This term 'Contracting Power' was used in diplomatic language, and in the Washington Treaty and subsequent disarmament treaties discussed here, to describe the nations that signed a treaty or other international agreement.

[31] Sprout and Sprout, *Toward a New Order of Sea Power*, p 210.

[32] 'Text of Session's Speeches.' *The New York Times*, Vol. LXXI, No. 23,307, 16 November 1921, p 2.

[33] 'Japan Gets Two-Day Delay on Far East Discussion.' *The New York Times*, Vol. LXXI, No. 23,309, 18 November 1921, p 1. In a separate press release made the same day, the Japanese reiterated their desire for a 70 per cent ratio, compared to the United States and Great Britain, in tonnage of capital ships and submarines.

[34] Sprout and Sprout, *Toward a New Order of Sea Power*, pp 188–9; 'France to Ask for Larger Navy.' *The New York Times*, Vol. LXXI, No. 23,313, 22 November 1921, pp 1–2.

[35] 'Concern Over French Navy Plan.' *The New York Times*, Vol. LXXI, No. 23,315, 24 November 1921, p 1.

[36] 'Navy Experts Defend Rival Claims.' *The New York Times*, Vol. LXXI, No. 23,314, 23 November 1921, p 1.

[37] —, *Conference on the Limitation of Armament, Washington, November 12, 1921-February 6, 1922* (Washington, DC: Government Printing Office, 1922), p 102.

[38] Roskill, *Naval Policy Between the Wars I*, p 325.

[39] —, *Conference on the Limitation of Armament, Washington, November 12, 1921-February 6, 1922*, pp 568–70. The French position was delivered by Albert Sarraut, Deputy Minister for the Colonies, who was now head of the delegation, Briand having departed for home to face a vote of no confidence in the *Chambre des députés*. It would bring to an end his sixth term as Prime Minister of France; he would serve in that position eleven times during his long career.

[40] Ibid, p 574.

[41] Sprout and Sprout, *Toward a New Order of Sea Power*, p 211. In particular, see the text of Lloyd George's instructions to Balfour quoted here.

[42] —, *Conference on the Limitation of Armament: Address of the President*, p 27.

[43] Roskill, *Naval Policy Between the Wars I*, p 325 states that the idea of a 10,000-ton displacement limit was included in a communication between the British delegation and the Admiralty dated 19 November 1921. Sprout and Sprout, *Toward a New Order of Sea Power*, pp 213–15 and Friedman, *U.S. Cruisers: An Illustrated Design History*, p 106, indicate that the US Navy had, since May 1918, been using the British *Hawkins* class as the standard to which any future American cruisers would be designed; these sources state that the qualitative limits proposed by Hughes had their origin in US Navy General Board specifications going back three years.

[44] —, *Conference on the Limitation of Armament*, p 578.

[45] Sprout and Sprout, *Toward a New Order of Sea Power*, p 215. In the afternoon session on 28 December, the French Admiral de Bon had expressed the opinion that limiting the calibre of the main battery of 'auxiliary surface combatant craft' to 8in should be sufficient, but that the 10,000-ton displacement limit was arbitrary and unnecessary, cf., —, *Conference on the Limitation of Armament*, pp 590–2.

[46] Jordan and Moulin, *French Cruisers*, pp 25–7. After the war, the French no longer referred to these small cruisers as 'scouts' (*éclaireurs*); by 1920, these were officially referred to simply as '8000-ton cruisers' (*croiseurs de 8000 tonnes*). I thank John Jordan for this clarification.

[47] These ships actually carried 1400 tons of oil fuel, but as often is the case, a percentage of the fuel could not normally be reached; only 1200 tons was considered usable. In all specification tables in this book, the fuel listed in the designed range line is the total fuel carried, while the fuel listed in the actual range line, if one is given, is the usable fuel quantity.

[48] Jordan and Moulin, *French Cruisers*, p 30; Roger Chesneau (ed), *Conway's All the World's Fighting Ships 1922-1946* (London: Conway Maritime Press, 1980), p 262. As originally designed, these ships were not intended to carry aircraft; the decision to add a catapult and two FBA 17s was made in 1926, when the ships were under construction.

[49] Jordan and Moulin, *French Cruisers*, pp 34–5. The rangefinder housings on the conning tower and between the funnels were not DCTs; they provided no direct control of the guns. The housings between the funnels proved to be unusable in action and were removed during the Second World War.

[50] Lacroix and Wells, *Japanese Cruisers*, p 49.

[51] In the rush to modernise and 'Westernise' after the Meiji Restoration, a number of family-owned industrial firms (*zaibatsu*)

prospered, in part due to the close relationship they developed with the government, particularly the military.

[52] The IJN, like most navies, reused ship names frequently. Japanese light cruisers were named after rivers. The name was reused for one of the 'A' class cruisers that were substituted for the five cancelled *Sendai*s, even though 'A' class cruisers were normally named after mountains, such as *Furutakayama*.

[53] Evans and Peattie, *Kaigun*, pp 224–5. The inclined armour in *Yubari* was unusual in one important aspect; most inclined armour was tilted inward at the bottom, so that a plunging shell would strike it at a more oblique angle. *Yubari*'s armour tilted outward at the bottom, exactly the opposite of normal practice. This must have been done for structural reasons, as it made no sense from a protective standpoint. One theory is that this might have been done to provide more space for fuel bunkerage in an otherwise very small ship.

[54] http://www.navweaps.com/index_nathan/metalprpsept2009.php#apanese_New_Vickers_Non-Cemented_%28NVNC%29_Armor. NVNC (New Vickers Non-Cemented) was a high-carbon homogeneous armour used in plates up to 12in thick.

[55] Lacroix and Wells, *Japanese Cruisers*, pp 798–800; Chesneau (ed), *Conway's All the World's Fighting Ships 1922-1946*, p 187.

[56] Lacroix and Wells, *Japanese Cruisers*, p 47.

[57] Evans and Peattie, *Kaigun*, pp 225–6.

[58] Armour protection is often defined in terms of an immune zone, an inner and outer range between which an armour scheme will theoretically protect against a specific enemy weapon; inside the inner range, a projectile will retain enough energy to penetrate the side armour, and beyond the outer range, a projectile will plunge at a steep-enough angle and high-enough velocity to penetrate the horizontal protection.

[59] Lacroix and Wells, *Japanese Cruisers*, pp 800–2; Chesneau (ed), *Conway's All the World's Fighting Ships 1922-1946*, p 187.

[60] Lacroix and Wells, *Japanese Cruisers*, pp 65–7.

[61] Ibid, p 68n19.

[62] It appears that the Type 11 change of range calculator was the predecessor to the Type 92 *shagekiban* fire-control table developed by Aichi Clock Co and introduced in 1932., cf., —, *Japanese Surface and General Fire Control*, O-31, U.S. Naval Technical Mission to Japan, January 1946.

[63] Lacroix and Wells, *Japanese Cruisers*, pp 69–70.

[64] Ibid, p 805. The catapults were not ready when these ships were commissioned in 1927; *Kinugasa* became the first IJN ship fitted with a catapult, a Kure Type 1, soon after commissioning.

[65] Ibid, pp 804–6; Chesneau (ed), *Conway's All the World's Fighting Ships 1922-1946*, p 188.

Chapter 5: Treaty Cruisers – The First Generation: 1922–1926

[1] Lacroix and Wells, *Japanese Cruisers*, p 51.

[2] John Jordan, *Warships after Washington: The Development of the Five Major Fleets 1922-1930* (Barnsley: Seaforth Publishing, 2011), p 109.

[3] Ibid.; Jordan and Moulin, *French Cruisers*, p 41.

[4] One last 'C' class light cruiser (HMS *Capetown* (D88)), two 'D' class light cruisers (HMS *Despatch* (D30) and *Diomede* (D92)), two 'E' class light cruisers (HMS *Emerald* (D66) and *Enterprise* (D52)) and two *Hawkins* class 'colonial' cruisers (HMS *Frobisher* (D81) and *Effingham* (D98)) were still under construction as of February 1922.

[5] Friedman, *British Cruisers: Two World Wars and After*, p 99.

[6] During this period, the Third Sea Lord was also the Controller of the Navy, responsible for procurement of ships and all other materiel, which put DNC and the Design Department under him.

[7] Friedman, *British Cruisers: Two World Wars and After*, p 104.

[8] Jordan, *Warships after Washington*, p 110; Roskill, *Naval Policy Between the Wars I*, p 352.

[9] Jordan, *Warships after Washington*, pp 125–6.

[10] Lacroix and Wells, *Japanese Cruisers*, p 82. The terms 'direct' and 'indirect' in referring to the protection standard are not common terminology. This author believes that the reference is to the angle at which the shell hits the side armour, a 'direct' hit being a perpendicular or near-perpendicular strike, while an 'indirect' hit is one at a greater angle, which would encounter a greater effective thickness of armour and have a greater likelihood of ricocheting off the armour plate rather than penetrating.

[11] Ibid, pp 82–3 and 114–16; http://www.navweaps.com/Weapons/WTJAP_PreWWII.php.

[12] Ibid, p 717. Interestingly, another source, Evans and Peattie, *Kaigun*, p 522, gives Hiraga's nickname as 'Yuzurazu', with the meaning 'inflexible'.

[13] Lacroix and Wells, *Japanese Cruisers*, pp 83–4.

[14] Ibid, pp 717–18.

[15] Ibid, pp 84–5; Evans and Peattie, *Kaigun*, p 228.

[16] Lacroix and Wells, *Japanese Cruisers*, pp 88–90; Evans and Peattie, *Kaigun*, p 229.

[17] Lacroix and Wells, *Japanese Cruisers*, pp 808–10; Chesneau (ed), *Conway's All the World's Fighting Ships 1922-1946*, p 188. At completion, the *Myoko*s carried only a single aircraft.

[18] Lacroix and Wells, *Japanese Cruisers*, pp 219–29.

[19] Ibid, pp 264. This complete installation was made in the *Myoko*s only over the course of this modernisation sequence and a second sequence in 1940–1.

[20] Jordan and Moulin, *French Cruisers*, p 41.

[21] Ibid, p 43. The French referred to these ships as light cruisers (*croiseurs légers*) until after the London Conference of 1930, which created a distinction between 8in-gunned heavy cruisers and light cruisers with 6in or smaller main batteries. The Americans did something similar, laying down and commissioning their first eight 'treaty maximum' cruisers as light cruisers (CL24–CL31), redesignating them as heavy cruisers (CA24–CA31) only on 1 July 1931.

[22] Ibid.

[23] Ibid, pp 43–4.

[24] Ibid, p 44; Chesneau (ed), *Conway's All the World's Fighting Ships 1922-1946*, p 263.

[25] Jordan and Moulin, *French Cruisers*, pp 49–50.

[26] Roskill, *Naval Policy Between the Wars I*, pp 332 and 350–1.

[27] Ibid. It should be noted that the First Sea Lord, Beatty, argued for smaller cruisers, but he was a lone voice at this time.

[28] Ibid, pp 412.

[29] Friedman, *British Cruisers: Two World Wars and After*, pp 99–100. The reference is to Lillicrap's design notebook on this date.

[30] Ibid, p 101.

[31] Ibid, p 103.

[32] Roskill, *Naval Policy Between the Wars I*, pp 411–12.

[33] Ibid, p 422.

[34] http://www.navweaps.com/index_nathan/metalprpsept2009.php#Average_Post-WWI_Extra-High-Strength_%22D%22_Silicon-Manganese_HT_Steels. Ducol, also known as 'D-Steel', was a high-strength, non-armour-grade steel used for all ship construction purposes and, in thicknesses up to 2in, as splinter shielding and for torpedo bulkheads. It was introduced in the early 1920s by David Colville & Sons, the Scottish steel works.

[35] Friedman, *British Cruisers: Two World Wars and After*, pp 391–2; Chesneau (ed), *Conway's All the World's Fighting Ships 1922-1946*, pp 26–7.

[36] Stern, *The Battleship Holiday*, p 74; Norman Friedman, *Naval Firepower: Battleship Guns and Gunnery in the Dreadnought Era* (Annapolis, MD: Naval Institute Press, 2008), p 123.

[37] Roskill, *Naval Policy Between the Wars I*, p 353; http://www.navweaps.com/Weapons/WNBR_75-45_mk6.php.
[38] There are good reasons why loading was limited to relatively shallow elevation angles. The shells and powder cases were tipped off their respective hoists into the loading tray and then rammed into the gun's breech by a hydraulic or chain rammer. The combined shell and powder charge for the 8in/50 Mk VIII weighed 322lb (256lb for the shell and 66lb for the powder charge); obviously, the steeper the angle of the gun, the greater the strain on the ramming mechanism.
[39] http://www.navweaps.com/Weapons/WNBR_8-50_mk8.php. To make matters worse, training was limited to 2°/second while the guns were loading.
[40] Roskill, *Naval Policy Between the Wars I*, p 353. This is saying something, because there was considerable dissatisfaction in the fleet with the 16in/45 Mk I gun developed in the same time frame for the 'G3' class and mounted in the *Nelson*s.
[41] Friedman, *U.S. Cruisers: An Illustrated Design History*, p 112.
[42] Ibid, p 113.
[43] Ibid, pp 115–16.
[44] Ibid. Note the lack of provision for aircraft, which the General Board did not consider important at this time.
[45] Edward S Miller, *War Plan Orange: The U.S. Strategy to Defeat Japan, 1897-1945* (Annapolis, MD: Naval Institute Press, 1991), pp 111–15.
[46] Ibid, pp 115–21.
[47] Ibid, p 123.
[48] Ibid, pp 125–31.
[49] The first American underway-replenishment trials were carried out under the command of Lieutenant Chester Nimitz on 28 May 1917, when he was able to refuel six destroyers crossing the Atlantic for operations in European waters.
[50] Sean Walsh, *A Historical Review of Cruiser Characteristics, Roles and Missions*, SFAC Report 9030-04-C1, Ser 05D /68 28 March 2005 (Washington, DC: NAVSEA 05D1, 31 December 2004).
[51] http://www.navweaps.com/Weapons/WNUS_8-55_mk9.php. A 260lb AP shell fired by this gun could (theoretically, when new) penetrate 4in Class A belt armour at any range inside 23,500yd and 1.5in horizontal armour at any range beyond 17,600yd. The maximum range of over 30,000yd was also very much a theoretical figure, because practical spotting of shell splashes at that range was problematic.
[52] Friedman, *U.S. Cruisers: An Illustrated Design History*, p 116.
[53] http://www.navweaps.com/index_nathan/metalprpsept2009.php#U.S._Carnegie_Corp._Special_Treatment_Steel_%28STS%29_Armor%2FConstruction_Steel. STS (Special Treatment Steel) was a high-nickel, homogenous armour-grade steel introduced in 1910 for use in thin armour plates; by 1930, it was being used by the Americans extensively as a basic warship steel, particularly for amidships hull construction above the waterline. It was essentially interchangeable with Class B armour in plates up to 5in thick.
[54] Friedman, *U.S. Cruisers: An Illustrated Design History*, p 471; Chesneau (ed), *Conway's All the World's Fighting Ships 1922-1946*, p 113.
[55] At 585ft 6in overall, they were by far the shortest first-generation 'treaty maximum' cruisers, some 41ft shorter than the French *Duquesne*s, the next shortest, and 83ft shorter than the *Myoko*s, the longest.
[56] The US Navy was careful to distinguish between turrets and gun mounts, even if both were topped by armoured gunhouses. A turret's understructure, meaning its shell and powder handling rooms and their associated hoists, rotated with the gunhouse, while some or all of those understructure elements did not rotate with the gunhouse in the case of a mount.
[57] The *Pensacola*s did not have a below-decks plotting room, cf., Friedman, *U.S. Cruisers: An Illustrated Design History*, p 333.
[58] Ibid, p 130. The extremely light construction of the earliest American 'treaty maximum' cruisers led to them being labelled 'tinclads', both for the paucity of their armour and the multiple structural problems revealed when the main-battery guns were fired or rough weather was encountered.
[59] Enrico Cernuschi, emails to the author, 9–19 July 2018. This influence was only increased by the fact that *Helgoland* and her sister *Saïda* came to Italy as war reparations in 1920, so the Italians had a chance to study them closely.
[60] The Italian naval engineering service (*Genio Navale*) was a branch of the naval service that, until 1968, assigned army-style ranks to its members, hence Rota held the rank of *Generale Ispettore del Genio Navale*, which was the equivalent of Vice Admiral in line officer ranking. Other GN ranks that will be mentioned in this narrative (along with their line officer rank equivalents) are: Captain (Lieutenant), Major (Lieutenant Commander) and Colonel (Captain).
[61] The two *San Giorgio*s had different engineering plants. The name ship had a VTE system producing 19,595ihp; her sister *San Marco* had a turbine system producing 23,000shp.
[62] All seven of the 'treaty maximum' cruisers built by the *Regia Marina* were given the names of cities in formerly Austro-Hungarian territory annexed to Italy after the First World War. Four of those cities, including both Trento and Trieste, remain Italian.
[63] There is disagreement among sources as to the actual standard displacement of the *Trento*s at completion. Chesneau, (ed), *Conway's All the World's Fighting Ships 1922-1946*, p 291, gives 10,344 tons for *Trento* (slightly less for *Trieste*). Enrico Cernuschi, Alessandro Gazzi and Michele Maria Gartani, *Sea Power: The Italian Way* (Rome: Ufficio Storico della Marina Militare, 2017), p 126, state that the target displacement was exceeded by 500 tons; most other sources agree.
[64] These were, of course, trials speeds in calm water and shallower water; actual maximum sustainable open ocean speeds were lower. By 1941, their machinery being in need of replacement, the highest sustained speed was 31 knots. The reader may assume similar results for all ships described in this book, namely that actual sustainable open water top speeds, all other factors being equal, were at least 10 per cent lower than trials speeds.
[65] Maurizio Brescia, *Mussolini's Navy: A Reference Guide to the Regia Marina 1930 – 1945* (Barnsley: Seaforth Publishing, 2012), pp 291–2; Chesneau (ed), *Conway's All the World's Fighting Ships 1922-1946*, p 113. Theoretically, three aircraft could be carried, two disassembled in the hangar and one on the catapult. During wartime service, only a single aircraft was carried, on the catapult.
[66] Friedman, *Naval Firepower*, pp 131–2. The Barr & Stroud 'Central Station Instrument Board', put on the export market in 1923, was roughly analogous in capabilities to the contemporaneous AFCT.
[67] http://www.navweaps.com/Weapons/WNIT_8-50_m1924.php; ibid, pp 266n22. The Italians were not the only ones to suffer from this problem; the *Pensacola* class (and most of the following American 'treaty maximum' heavy cruisers up through the *New Orleans* class) also had a common sleeve and close proximity, and likewise suffered from dispersion problems. To get an idea of how close together the barrels of the guns in the *Trento*s' turrets were, compare the 39.4in axis of their guns to the 84in axis of the guns in the twin turrets of the contemporary *Kent* class of the Royal Navy. The Royal Navy concluded that 14 calibres separation was required to prevent interference entirely between barrels when fired simultaneously, which, for a 203mm gun, would have required a 112in separation.
[68] Enrico Cernuschi, *Myths and Misinformation about the Italian Navy in WW2: A documented different point of view*, unpublished article,

2018. This remains a controversial issue with disagreement as to the cause of the problem and whether (and how) it was resolved.
[69] The Treaty of Versailles had not defined maximum gun calibres for the ship types allowed the post-war *Reichsmarine*; this was left for the NIACC to determine, and that body had made it clear in 1922 that 15cm was the largest gun the Germans could expect to be approved.
[70] Koop and Schmolke, *German Light Cruisers of World War II*, p 15. As a theoretical exercise, Ebrenburg calculated that if the entire 1220 tons of bunkerage was given over to diesel fuel, the range of this class would have been 18,000nm.
[71] M J Whitley, *Cruisers of World War Two: An International Encyclopedia* (Annapolis, MD: Naval Institute Press, 1995), p 51.
[72] This high-percentage nickel alloy steel, called *Qualität 420 Stahl* by Krupp, was used until the *Wotan*-series homogeneous armour steels became available later in the decade, cf., http://www.navweaps.com/index_nathan/metalprpsept2009.php#German_Krupp_%22High-%25%22_Nickel-Steel.
[73] Koop and Schmolke, *German Light Cruisers of World War II*, pp 14–15; Chesneau (ed), *Conway's All the World's Fighting Ships 1922-1946*, p 230. All were completed without aircraft facilities; catapults and other requisite aircraft-handling facilities were shipped briefly only in the mid-1930s.
[74] Koop and Schmolke, *German Light Cruisers of World War II*, p 109.

Chapter 6: Treaty Cruisers – Trying to Stem the Tide: 1926–1930
[1] Roskill, *Naval Policy Between the Wars I*, p 416.
[2] Ibid, pp 446–8.
[3] Ibid, p 450. The essence of the argument against building cruisers was that the Royal Navy had only one prospective rival in sight, namely Japan, and either the prospect of war with Japan was remote or it was pointless for the British to consider defending her Pacific possessions. Either way, the need for a major programme of cruiser construction was unsupportable.
[4] 'Settlement Reported on Cruiser Issue.' *The New York Times*, Vol. LXXIV, No. 24,652, 23 July 1925, p 4.
[5] Friedman, *British Cruisers: Two World Wars and After*, p 105.
[6] http://www.navweaps.com/Weapons/WNBR_8-50_mk8.php.
[7] Friedman, *British Cruisers: Two World Wars and After*, p. 108.
[8] The amount of topweight added during the modernisation of *London* stressed her lightly-built hull far beyond its designed limits. Her rejoining the fleet in 1941 was delayed by more than a month when her post-refit trials revealed these issues and steps were taken to reinforce the hull in places, cf., Chesneau (ed), *Conway's All the World's Fighting Ships 1922-1946*, p 27; http://www.naval-history.net/xGM-Chrono-06CA-HMS_London.htm.
[9] Friedman, *British Cruisers: Two World Wars and After*, p 108.
[10] Ibid, p 396; Chesneau (ed), *Conway's All the World's Fighting Ships 1922-1946*, p 28.
[11] Ibid, p 111.
[12] Ibid, p 113.
[13] Roskill, *Naval Policy Between the Wars I*, p 434.
[14] Whitley, *Cruisers of World War Two*, p 235.
[15] Friedman, *U.S. Cruisers: An Illustrated Design History*, p 126. The reader must remember that these discussions were taking place in 1926, long before it was realised how far under their permitted displacement the *Pensacola* class would be.
[16] Ibid, p 472; Chesneau (ed), *Conway's All the World's Fighting Ships 1922-1946*, p 114.
[17] Friedman, *Naval Firepower*, p 201.
[18] Japanese emperors have given names, used only during their lifetime, and posthumous names that are given to their 'era' and by extension to them after their death. The Meiji Emperor, whose given name was Mutsuhito, was succeeded by his only son, Yoshihito, whose posthumous name was Taisho; he, in turn, was succeeded by Hirohito, whose posthumous name was Showa.
[19] Lacroix and Wells, *Japanese Cruisers*, pp 117–18.
[20] Ibid, pp 133–5. It was soon found that in practice, elevation beyond 55° was not possible without putting undo strain on the elevation and recoil systems; the last of the four ships in this class, *Maya*, was given a modified turret design, the 'E_1' Model, in which elevation was limited to 55°.
[21] Ibid; Lacroix and Wells, *Japanese Cruisers*, p 137.
[22] Ibid, p 148. This 'actual' figure is an average of the four ships; the actual trials figures, run at approximately ⅔-trials displacement, which was more than 1500 tons greater than standard displacement, ranged from 35.0 knots for *Maya* to 35.6 knots for *Chokai*.
[23] Ibid, pp 813–16; Chesneau (ed), *Conway's All the World's Fighting Ships 1922-1946*, p 189. At the time of their commissioning, the *Takao*s embarked only two aircraft.
[24] Janusz Skulski, *The Heavy Cruiser Takao* (Annapolis, MD: Naval Institute Press, 1994), p 9.
[25] Lacroix and Wells, *Japanese Cruisers*, p 130.
[26] Ibid, p 129. It may seem counter-intuitive that a more heavily-loaded ship had a better metacentric height, but this can happen when a great deal of the overweight is above the waterline and the consumable loading is below.
[27] Jordan and Moulin, *French Cruisers*, p 51.
[28] French 60kg steel plate was a high-tensile-strength construction steel, similar in composition and use to British 'D' steel. I thank John Jordan for this clarification.
[29] Jordan and Moulin, *French Cruisers*, pp 58–60. The coal was primarily for protective purposes, but this design included two small mixed-fired (coal-or-oil) boilers intended to power the ship while cruising. The coal was something of a 'cheat' as far as calculating standard displacement was concerned, because fuel was not included in 'treaty displacement' calculations.
[30] Ibid, p 59; Chesneau (ed), *Conway's All the World's Fighting Ships 1922-1946*, p 263.
[31] Jordan, *Warships after Washington*, p 215.
[32] Much of this information was kindly supplied by Enrico Cernuschi in his comments.
[33] Brescia, *Mussolini's Navy*, pp 82–3; Jordan, *Warships after Washington*, p 206.
[34] Whitley, *Cruisers of World War Two*, p 129. AER (*Acciaio a Elevata Resistenza* – High Resistance Steel) similar to British 'D'-Steel, was used for thin plates.
[35] Chesneau (ed), *Conway's All the World's Fighting Ships 1922-1946*, p 293. Both aircraft could be carried in a hangar that occupied the entire lowest deck of the forward superstructure. After the outbreak of war, only one aircraft was normally carried, due to a shortage of qualified observers.
[36] Costanzo Ciano should not be confused with his son, Galeazzo Ciano, who served as the Foreign Minister of Italy between 1938 and 1943, and was widely considered to be the second most powerful person in the Fascist state before the fall of Mussolini.
[37] Roskill, *Naval Policy Between the Wars I*, p 499. The idea of the 5:5:3 ratio for cruisers was being promoted by three of the Sea Lords – Admirals Dreyer, Field and Chatfield – two of whom would become First Sea Lord in the 1930s, but notably not by the present First Sea Lord, which post was still held by Beatty until July 1927.
[38] Ibid, p 500.
[39] Ibid, p 502.
[40] Stern, *The Battleship Holiday*, p 132.
[41] Hugh S Gibson was an experienced American diplomat,

Ambassador to Belgium at the time of the Geneva Conference. He had no particular naval expertise, but had a reputation as a tough, fair-minded negotiator, earned by his work in Poland after the end of the First World War.
[42] 'Cards on Table Is Plan of Powers at Geneva Today.' *The New York Times*, Vol. LXXVI, No. 25,349, 19 June 1927, p 1.
[43] Ibid.
[44] 'Japan for Caution in Naval Changes.' *The New York Times*, Vol. LXXVI, No. 25,350, 20 June 1927, p 3.
[45] Roskill, *Naval Policy Between the Wars I*, p 505.
[46] 'Americans Propose Limit for Cruisers Nearer to Britain's.' *The New York Times*, Vol. LXXVI, No. 25,365, 6 July 1927, p 1.
[47] Roskill, *Naval Policy Between the Wars I*, p 506.
[48] Ibid.
[49] 'Unheralded Kellogg-Howard Conference in Capital Begets Theory Envoy Came to Save Naval Parley.' *The New York Times*, Vol. LXXVI, No. 25,366, 7 July 1927, p 1.
[50] 'Japan Intervenes in Geneva Deadlock, Urging Our 250,000-ton Cruiser Limit; Figure Impossible, Bridgeman Retorts.' *The New York Times*, Vol. LXXVI, No. 25,366, 7 July 1927, p 1.
[51] Ibid.
[52] 'New Cruiser Offer, 18 of 10,000 Tons, Made by Americans.' *The New York Times*, Vol. LXXVI, No. 25,367, 8 July 1927, p 1.
[53] Roskill, *Naval Policy Between the Wars I*, p 506. In this account, his name is given as William B Shearer.
[54] 'Japan Intervenes in Geneva Deadlock, Urging Our 250,000-ton Cruiser Limit; Figure Impossible, Bridgeman Retorts.' *The New York Times*, Vol. LXXVI, No. 25,366, 7 July 1927, pp 1 and 6.
[55] 'Japan Asks More Submarines.' *The New York Times*, Vol. LXXVI, No. 25,367, 8 July 1927, p 6.
[56] This author has never been a big fan of counterfactual history, but the temptation to speculate on what might have happened had the US shown even a bit more flexibility in dealing with the Japanese in the 1920s is undeniable. During this period, the ultra-nationalists who came to dominate the nation had not yet consolidated their power; there was still a chance for a moderate government to succeed if it could show any success in negotiating with the Western Powers as an equal.
[57] Roskill, *Naval Policy Between the Wars I*, p 507.
[58] Viscount Cecil of Chelwood, born Edward Algernon Robert Gascoyne-Cecil, known more commonly as Robert Cecil, was a British diplomat and fierce proponent of the League of Nations.
[59] 'Cecil Bangs Fist and Calls Our Stand 'Nonsense;' Withdraws Slight When Gibson Threatens to Quit.' *The New York Times*, Vol. LXXVI, No. 25,369, 10 July 1927, p 1.
[60] 'Naval Parley Halt While Capitals Act, Forecast in London.' *The New York Times*, Vol. LXXVI, No. 25,373, 14 July 1927, p 1; Roskill, *Naval Policy Between the Wars I*, p 506.
[61] 'Crisis at Geneva Persists After Full Session Fails to End Cruiser Deadlock.' *The New York Times*, Vol. LXXVI, No. 25,374, 15 July 1927, p 1.
[62] 'Big Cruiser Deal on 12-12-8 Basis Reported in Geneva.' *The New York Times*, Vol. LXXVI, No. 25,378, 19 July 1927, 1; Roskill, *Naval Policy Between the Wars I*, p 509. It certainly is ironic in retrospect to read the remarks of an American diplomat, using the closeness of the positions of his nation and the Japanese as leverage against the British.
[63] 'Crisis at Geneva Persists After Full Session Fails to End Cruiser Deadlock.' *The New York Times*, Vol. LXXVI, No. 25,374, 15 July 1927, p 1.
[64] 'Geneva Reattacks Navy Limit Problem.' *The New York Times*, Vol. LXXVI, No. 25,375, 16 July 1927, p 1.
[65] 'Gibson Makes Plans to End Futile Talk.' *The New York Times*, Vol. LXXVI, No. 25,376, 17 July 1927, p 1.
[66] Ishii was well-known to the Americans. He had negotiated the Lansing-Ishii Agreement in 1917 in a well-intended, but ultimately unsuccessful, attempt to settle differences between the US and Japan concerning China.
[67] 'New Plan Revives Hope.' *The New York Times*, Vol. LXXVI, No. 25,377, 18 July 1927, p 2.
[68] 'Big Cruiser Deal on 12-12-8 Basis Reported in Geneva.' *The New York Times*, Vol. LXXVI, No. 25,378, 19 July 1927, p 1.
[69] 'London More Hopeful.' *The New York Times*, Vol. LXXVI, No. 25,378, 19 July 1927, p 7.
[70] 'British Government Calls Geneva Delegates Home to Seek Cruiser Deal.' *The New York Times*, Vol. LXXVI, No. 25,379, 20 July 1927, p 1.
[71] 'Baldwin Tackling Geneva Problem.' *The New York Times*, Vol. LXXVI, No. 25,380, 21 July 1927, p 1.
[72] The Lord Privy Seal is a uniquely British office, currently appointed by the reigning monarch on the advice of the Prime Minister.
[73] https://api.parliament.uk/historic-hansard/lords/1927/jul/27/naval-disarmament-conference. According to 'Temporary Cruiser Deal Hinted by Chamberlain; Won't Do, Says Washington.' *The New York Times*, Vol. LXXVI, No. 25,387, 28 July 1927, pp 1–2, Austen Chamberlain gave the exact same address to the Commons the same day.
[74] Roskill, *Naval Policy Between the Wars I*, pp 511–12; 'Americans Flatly Reject New British Naval Plan; Failure of Parley Looms.' *The New York Times*, Vol. LXXVI, No. 25,388, 29 July 1927, pp 1 and 4; 'Washington Loses Hope of Agreement.' *The New York Times*, Vol. LXXVI, No. 25,388, 29 July 1927, p 4.
[75] 'Said to Be Britain's Last Word.' *The New York Times*, Vol. LXXVI, No. 25,388, 29 July 1927, p 4.
[76] 'Geneva Session Deferred to Middle of the Week amid an Air of Mystery.' *The New York Times*, Vol. LXXVI, No. 25,391, 1 August 1927, pp 1–2.
[77] 'Japanese Offer New Naval Plan.' *The New York Times*, Vol. LXXVI, No. 25,393, 3 August 1927, pp 1 and 6.
[78] 'Naval Parley Fails; Final Meeting Set for This Afternoon.' *The New York Times*, Vol. LXXVI, No. 25,394, 4 August 1927, pp 1 and 3.
[79] Ibid, p 3.
[80] 'Naval Parley End in No Agreement; Urges Direct Negotiations Continue; Hint of Another Call by Coolidge.' *The New York Times*, Vol. LXXVI, No. 25,395, 5 August 1927, pp 1–2.
[81] 'Gibson Declares British Puzzle Him.' *The New York Times*, Vol. LXXVI, No. 25,395, 5 August 1927, p 2.
[82] Roskill, *Naval Policy Between the Wars I*, p 516.
[83] Friedman, *British Cruisers: Two World Wars and After*, p 117.
[84] Roskill, *Naval Policy Between the Wars I*, pp 555–6.
[85] Friedman, *British Cruisers: Two World Wars and After*, pp 120–1.
[86] Roskill, *Naval Policy Between the Wars I*, p 565 gives the date as 27 June 1929. Chesneau (ed), *Conway's All the World's Fighting Ships 1922-1946*, p 29, gives the date as 14 January 1930, which must have been the date the official cancellation paperwork was signed.
[87] Roskill, *Naval Policy Between the Wars I*, p 555.
[88] Friedman, *British Cruisers: Two World Wars and After*, pp 144–5.
[89] Ibid, p 145.
[90] Ibid, pp 145–6.
[91] Ibid, p 153.
[92] http://www.navweaps.com/index_nathan/metalprpsept2009.php#Average_British_Post-1930_Non-Cemented_Armor_%28NCA%29, NCA was the successor to KNC in British shipbuilding starting in 1930; it was a high-Molybdenum-content homogeneous armour with excellent protective characteristics used in plates up to 4in thick.
[93] Friedman, *British Cruisers: Two World Wars and After*, p 397;

Chesneau (ed), *Conway's All the World's Fighting Ships 1922-1946*, p 30.
[94] Friedman, *British Cruisers: Two World Wars and After*, p 155.
[95] Roskill, *Naval Policy Between the Wars I*, p 554; '$725,000,000 Plan for Navy Presented.' *The New York Times*, Vol. LXXVII, No. 25,527, 15 December 1927, p 10.
[96] Roskill, *Naval Policy Between the Wars I*, p 555; 'Coolidge Insists There Is No Threat in Our Navy Plans.' *The New York Times*, Vol. LXXVII, No. 25,603, 29 February 1928, p 1.
[97] 'President Signs the Cruiser Bill.' *The New York Times*, Vol. LXXVIII, No. 25,954, 14 February 1929, p 1.
[98] Friedman, *U.S. Cruisers: An Illustrated Design History*, p 139.
[99] There was a political component in delaying the three government-built FY1929 cruisers, as will be explained in the next chapter.
[100] Friedman, *U.S. Cruisers: An Illustrated Design History*, p 141.
[101] These were true turrets, according to the definition of that term used by the USN, because they had a fully-rotating sub-structure.
[102] http://www.navweaps.com/index_nathan/metalprpsept2009.php#Average_U.S._WWII-Era_Class_%22B%22_Armor. American Class B armour was very similar in characteristics to STS and was often used interchangeably.
[103] Friedman, *U.S. Cruisers: An Illustrated Design History*, pp 473–4; Chesneau (ed), *Conway's All the World's Fighting Ships 1922-1946*, p 115.
[104] Whitley, *Cruisers of World War Two*, p 244.
[105] —, *Limitation and Reduction of Naval Armament (London Naval Treaty)*. The article in question is Article 18 in Part III that was agreed to by only the Americans, British and Japanese.
[106] —, *Message of the President of the United States Transmitting the Budget for the Service of the Fiscal Year Ending June 30 1933* (Washington, DC: Government Printing Office, 1931), p xv.
[107] Friedman, *U.S. Cruisers: An Illustrated Design History*, p 148.
[108] Evans and Peattie, *Kaigun*, pp 234–7; Lacroix and Wells, *Japanese Cruisers*, pp 155–7. Nomura is best known to history as the Japanese Ambassador to the United States at the time of the Pearl Harbor attack, which put him in the unfortunate position of having to deliver the final Japanese note to Secretary of State Cordell Hull after that attack had already begun.
[109] Jordan and Moulin, *French Cruisers*, pp 69–71.
[110] Ibid, pp 77–81.
[111] http://www.navweaps.com/Weapons/WNIT_6-53_m1926.php. The French were correct in believing that Italian doctrine emphasised long-range gunfire, and that the 152mm/53 Mod 1926, when introduced, had a maximum range of over 31,000yd, but, like the larger 203mm/50 mounted in the *Trento* class, this gun in the '*Condottieri*' suffered dispersion problems that were resolved by adopting a lighter (104.7lb) AP shell and a reduced charge for a maximum range of 24,700yd.
[112] Jordan and Moulin, *French Cruisers*, p 72.
[113] Ibid, p82.
[114] Ibid, p 110; Chesneau (ed), *Conway's All the World's Fighting Ships 1922-1946*, p 264.
[115] Jordan and Moulin, *French Cruisers*, pp 118–20.
[116] Ibid, p 96.
[117] '*Mouilleur de mines*' translates as 'minelayer'.
[118] Jordan and Moulin, *French Cruisers*, p 96.
[119] Ibid, p 99; Chesneau (ed), *Conway's All the World's Fighting Ships 1922-1946*, p 265.
[120] Jordan, *Warships after Washington*, p 144.
[121] Again, there is no agreement between sources as to the actual standard displacement of these ships, made worse by the fact that no two of the four seems to have had the same displacement. The reported displacements, according to Chesneau (ed), *Conway's All the World's Fighting Ships 1922-1946*, p 292, varied between 11,326 tons for *Fiume* and 11,712 tons for *Gorizia*. This latter figure for *Gorizia* comes from the Royal Navy, which had a chance to examine her at close quarters when she was dry-docked at Gibraltar in August 1936 after suffering a gasoline explosion in her bow.
[122] TC stands for 'Terni Cemented', the Italian post-First World War version of KC plate. It rated very highly in post-war testing, comparing favourably with American Class A plate. Cf., http://www.navweaps.com/index_nathan/metalprpsept2009.php#Italian_Post-1930_Terni_Cemented_KC-Type_Variable-Face-Thickness_Armor.
[123] CN was a Chromium-Nickel steel homogeneous armour plate used by the Italians for thin armour plates. Sometimes vanadium would be added for additional strength, which was then called POV (*Piastre Omogenee Nichel-Cromo-Vanadio* – Homogeneous Nickel-Chromium-Vanadium Plates), http://www.navweaps.com/index_nathan/metal-prpsept2009.php#Italian_%22Piastro_Omogenee_Nichel-Cromo-Vanadio%22_%28NCV%29_Light_Armor. These armours were used interchangeably.
[124] Brescia, *Mussolini's Navy*, p 76; Chesneau (ed), *Conway's All the World's Fighting Ships 1922-1946*, p 292.
[125] I thank Enrico Cernuschi for this information, passed along in several emails dated October 2018 quoting from the —, 'R.N. Gorizia Relazione sugli inconvenienti dovuti al mare grosso nella missione del 22-23 marzo c.a. (1942)' in the *Gorizia* File in the Archivio dell'Ufficio Storico della Marina Militare, Rome, 1942.
[126] Not only was the catapult relocated, but the type of catapult was changed to a more powerful, compressed-air-driven type, replacing the older explosive-charge type.
[127] Brescia, *Mussolini's Navy*, p 80; Chesneau (ed), *Conway's All the World's Fighting Ships 1922-1946*, p 293.
[128] Brescia, *Mussolini's Navy*, p 82. She was nicknamed '*Brande Nere*' in the fleet, which means, 'black hammock', because the level of interior finish in this ship was so comparatively poor.
[129] I thank Bill Jurens for pointing this out.

Chapter 7: Treaty Cruisers – The 'Big Babies': 1930–1936

[1] After halting while the Geneva Conference was meeting, the Preparatory Commission met again briefly at the end of November 1927 and then formally reconvened on 15 March 1928.
[2] Roskill, *Naval Policy Between the Wars I*, pp 546–7.
[3] 'Naval Deal Letter Called a Forgery.' *The New York Times*, Vol. LXXVII, No. 23,783, 27 August 1927, p 15.
[4] Hugh Gibson, *A Journal from Our Legation in Belgium* (Garden City, NY: Doubleday, Page & Co, 1917), p 282.
[5] As a fiscal conservative, Hoover reacted to the decline in tax revenues by sharply increasing taxes in 1932 to avoid deficit spending, which only exacerbated the already severe economic contraction.
[6] —, *Documents of the Preparatory Commission for the Disarmament Conference Entrusted with the Preparation for the Conference for the Reduction and Limitation of Armaments – Series VIII – Minutes of the Sixth Session (First Part) of the Preparatory Commission for the Disarmament Conference*, Series of League of Nations Publications, IX. DISARMAMENT 1929, IX, p 3 (Geneva, Switzerland: League of Nations Publications, 25 May 1929), pp 56–8.
[7] Ibid, p 56.
[8] Ibid, p 57.
[9] —, *Papers Related to the Foreign Relations of the United States – 1929* (in Three Volumes) Volume I (Washington, DC: Government Printing Office, 1943), 500.A15/887, Gibson to Stimson, 22 April 1929, No.13, pp 96–7. Gibson cabled Stimson relating how pleased he was at the reaction to his address and also his concern that it 'has

already given rise to a degree of optimism that may be difficult to sustain.'

[10] William Lyon Mackenzie King was a long-time Prime Minister of Canada.

[11] Dawes rose to the rank of Brigadier General in the US Army in the First World War and was often referred to as General Dawes thereafter as a courtesy. He won the Nobel Peace Prize in 1925 for his work on the Dawes Plan, which stabilised the German post-war economy. He was also a self-taught musician who wrote a melody, which, when words were added in the 1950s, became a No 1 popular hit in the US and UK. He has the distinction of being the only person to have won a Nobel Prize, held national elected office in the American government and written a No 1 hit song.

[12] —, *Papers Related to the Foreign Relations of the United States – 1929*, (in Three Volumes) Volume I (Washington, DC: Government Printing Office, 1943), 500.A15a3/7:Telegram, Atherton to Stimson, 11 June 1929, No.154, pp 116–17.

[13] Ibid, 500.A15a3/10:Telegram, Dawes to Stimson, 17 June 1929, No. 158, pp 117–19. See also, Annette B Dunlap, *Charles Gates Dawes: A Life* (Evanston, IL: Northwestern University Press, 2016), p 225.

[14] Ibid. Dawes reported that he visited Matsudaira on 17 June and that the Japanese ambassador 'approved heartily of all the suggestions' presented by the Americans in London and Geneva.

[15] —, *Papers Related to the Foreign Relations of the United States – 1929*, Vol I, 500.A15a3/12:Telegam, Neville to Stimson, 20 June 1929, No.65, p 130.

[16] Ibid, 500.A15a3/8, Stimson to Neville, 24 June 1929, No.573, p 132. This message records a conversation between Stimson and the Japanese ambassador Debuchi Katsuji.

[17] Ibid, 500.A15a3/25:Telegram, Dawes and Gibson to Stimson, 25 June 1929, No.168, pp 132–5.

[18] Ibid, 500.A15a3/26:Telegram, Dawes and Gibson to Stimson, 25 June 1929, No.169, pp 135–6.

[19] Ibid, 500.A15a3/28:Telegram, Dawes to Stimson, 26 June 1929, No.171, pp 136–7.

[20] Ibid, 500.A15a3/37:Telegram, Dawes to Stimson, 28 June 1929, No.175, pp 139–40.

[21] Ibid, 500.A15a3/26:Telegram, Stimson to Dawes, 27 June 1929, No.160, pp 137–8.

[22] Ibid, 500.A15a3/50:Telegram, Dawes to Stimson, 9 July 1929, No.179, pp 140–1. This quote is from MacDonald's point No.2. Dawes reproduced MacDonald's letter of 8 July in its entirety in this cable to Stimson.

[23] Ibid. Only a career politician such as MacDonald could have described the wide gap that still separated American and British targets for cruiser construction as 'slightly different values in our respective national needs'.

[24] Ibid.

[25] Ibid.

[26] Ibid,

[27] Ibid, 500.A15a3/50:Telegram, Stimson to Dawes, 11 July 1929, No.174, pp 141–3.

[28] Ibid.

[29] These were *Surrey* and *Northumberland.*

[30] —, *Papers Related to the Foreign Relations of the United States – 1929*, Vol I, 500.A15a3/50:Telegram, Stimson to Dawes, 11 July 1929, No.174, pp 141–3. For American readers, the word 'rise' in reference to Parliament means to adjourn the legislative session.

[31] Ibid, 500.A15a3/61:Telegram, Stimson to Dawes, 12 July 1929, No.177, p 147.

[32] Friedman, *U.S. Cruisers: An Illustrated Design History*, p 142.

[33] This reference presumably is to the Naval Programme (Birkenhead) Committee White Paper of 27 July 1925 which was the subject of heated discussion (and miscommunication) at Geneva (see preceding chapter).

[34] Ibid, 500.A15a3/70:Telegram, Dawes to Stimson, 18 July 1929, No.197, p 148.

[35] Ibid.

[36] Ibid, 500.A15a3/70:Telegram, Stimson to Dawes, 21 July 1929, No.182, pp 149–52.

[37] Ibid.

[38] Ibid.

[39] 23 July 1929 was a Tuesday, so MacDonald was proposing a meeting on 29 July.

[40] —, *Papers Related to the Foreign Relations of the United States – 1929*, Vol I, 500.A15a3/76:Telegram, Dawes to Stimson, 23 July 1929, No.202, pp 156–8.

[41] Ibid, 500.A15a3/75:Telegram, Dawes to Stimson, 22 July 1929, No.201, pp 153–5.

[42] Ibid, 500.A15a3/79:Telegram, Dawes to Stimson, 25 July 1929, No.204, pp 159–61.

[43] Ibid.

[44] Ibid.

[45] Ibid.

[46] Ibid.

[47] Ibid, 500.A15a3/86:Telegram, Dawes to Stimson, 29 July 1929, No.209, pp 164–6.

[48] Ibid, 500.A15a3/92:Telegram, Dawes to Stimson, 30 July 1929, No.211, p 166.

[49] Ibid, 500.A15a3/92:Telegram, Stimson to Dawes, 31 July 1929, No.195, pp 167–8.

[50] Ibid, 500.A15a3/92:Telegram, Stimson to Dawes, 31 July 1929, No.196, pp 168–70.

[51] Ibid, 500.A15a3/105:Telegram, Dawes to Stimson, 4 August 1929, No.220, pp 176–81. The Gibson letter was contained in this Dawes cable and somewhat emended in Ibid, 500.A15a3/105:Telegram, Dawes to Stimson, 5 August 1929, No.221, p 181.

[52] Ibid, 500.A15a3/109:Telegram, Dawes to Stimson, 6 August 1929, No.223, pp 183–5.

[53] Ibid, 500.A15a3/113:Telegram, Dawes to Stimson, 9 August 1929, No.228, pp 186–8.

[54] Ibid, 500.A15a3/113:Telegram, Stimson to Dawes, 15 August 1929, No.217, pp 190–5.

[55] Ibid, 500.A15a3/115:Telegram, Dawes to Stimson, 12 August 1929, No.235, p 189.

[56] Ibid, 500.A15a3/117:Telegram, Castle to Cotton, 12 August 1929, unnumbered, pp 188–9. William R Castle, Jr was the Assistant Secretary of State, and Joseph P Cotton was an Under Secretary of State, both acting in Stimson's absence. Also see, ibid, 500.A15a3/115:Telegram, Dawes to Stimson, 12 August 1929, No.235, p 189.

[57] Ibid, 500.A15a3/115:Telegram, Dawes to Stimson, 12 August 1929, No.235, p 189.

[58] Ibid, 500.A15a3/130:Telegram, Dawes to Stimson, 24 August 1929, No.242, pp 196–201.

[59] Ibid, 500.A15a3/135:Telegram, Stimson to Dawes, 28 August 1929, No.224, pp 203–7.

[60] Ibid.

[61] Ibid, 500.A15a3/130:Telegram, Stimson to Dawes, 28 August 1929, No.225, pp 207–9.

[62] Ibid.

[63] Ibid, 500.A15a3/130:Telegram, Stimson to Dawes, 28 August 1929, No.226, pp 209–10.

[64] Ibid, 500.A15a3/148:Telegram, Dawes to Stimson, 31 August 1929, No.255, pp 214–16.
[65] Ibid, 500.A15a3/146:Telegram, Dawes to Stimson, 31 August 1929, No.242, pp 213–14.
[66] Ibid, 500.A15a3/150:Telegram, Stimson to Dawes, 3 September 1929, No.237, pp 217–18.
[67] Ibid, 500.A15a3/162:Telegram, Dawes to Stimson, 10 September 1929, No.266, pp 220–2.
[68] Charles F Adams III was the scion of the Adams family that included two American Presidents, one his great-grandfather, the other his great-great-grandfather.
[69] —, *Papers Related to the Foreign Relations of the United States – 1929*, Vol I, 500.A15a3/162:Telegram, Stimson to Dawes, 11 September 1929, No.242, pp 222–3.
[70] Ibid, 500.A15a3/197:Telegram, Dawes to Stimson, 24 September 1929, No.281, pp 253–6.
[71] Ibid.
[72] Ibid, 500.A15a3/215, Memorandum by the Secretary of State of a Conversation with the Japanese Ambassador (Debuchi), 24 September 1929, unnumbered, pp 257–9.
[73] Roskill, *Naval Policy Between the Wars II*, pp 46 and 46n1.
[74] —, *Papers Related to the Foreign Relations of the United States – 1929*, Vol I, 500.A15a3/233, The Identic [*sic*] British Notes Delivered to the French, Italian, and Japanese Ambassadors in Great Britain, October 7, 1929, unnumbered, pp 263–5.
[75] Ibid, Memorandum by the Assistant Secretary of State (Castle) of a Conversation With the Italian Ambassador (De Martino), October 24, 1929, unnumbered, pp 269–70. See also, Roskill, *Naval Policy Between the Wars II*, p 50.
[76] Ibid, 500.A15a3/322:Telegram, Gibson to Stimson, 29 October 1929, No.84, pp 270–2.
[77] Ibid.
[78] Ibid, 500.A15a3/407:Telegram, Stimson to Dawes, 18 November 1929, No.299, pp 281–3.
[79] Roskill, *Naval Policy Between the Wars II*, pp 52–3.
[80] Ibid, p 53.
[81] Ibid.
[82] —, *Papers Related to the Foreign Relations of the United States – 1929*, Vol I, 500.A15a3/550, The Department of State to the Japanese Embassy, December 26, 1929, unnumbered, pp 307–13.
[83] Roskill, *Naval Policy Between the Wars II*, p 55.
[84] 'Stimson Presents No Detailed Offer.' *The New York Times*, Vol. LXXIX, No. 26,298, 24 January 1930, pp 1–2. Interestingly, the *Times* report, in several places, has Tardieu stating that France needed a fleet one-third the size of Great Britain's, and other sources, such as Roskill, *Naval Policy Between the Wars II*, p 61, quite explicitly gives the figure as two-thirds, which does agree with the rest of Tardieu's statement.
[85] Ersatz-*Preussen*, so-named because she was intended to replace an old pre-dreadnought battleship named *Preussen*, was the first of three *Panzerschiffe* built by the *Reichsmarine* with at least a nod towards compliance with the Versailles Treaty limit of 10,000 tons standard displacement. She would be launched in 1931 and given the name *Deutschland*.
[86] 'Stimson Presents No Detailed Offer.' *The New York Times*, Vol. LXXIX, No. 26,298, 24 January 1930, pp 1–2.
[87] —, *Papers Related to the Foreign Relations of the United States – 1930*, (in Three Volumes) Volume I (Washington, DC: Government Printing Office, 1945), 500.A15a3/649, Stimson to Acting Secretary of State, January 28, 1930, No.22, pp 10–11. Stimson colourfully stated: 'Three and a half hours were wasted in yesterday's meeting of the heads of the five delegations by debate between the French and Italians concerning whether the items proposed by one or the other should precede each on the informal agenda . . .'
[88] —, *Limitation and Reduction of Naval Armament (London Naval Treaty)*, Part III, Art. 17.
[89] —, *Papers Related to the Foreign Relations of the United States – 1930*, 500.A15a3/665, Stimson to Acting Secretary of State, February 4, 1930, No.35, pp 13–17.
[90] Roskill, *Naval Policy Between the Wars II*, p 56.
[91] Op.cit., 500.A15a3/718, Stimson to Acting Secretary of State, February 28, 1930, No.95, p 32.
[92] —, *Limitation and Reduction of Naval Armament (London Naval Treaty)*, Part III, Art. 16 and Art. 18. According to Roskill, *Naval Policy Between the Wars II*, p 64 there was an 'agreement' that the Japanese claimed the right to start replacing their smaller 8in-gunned cruisers of the *Furutaka* and *Aoba* classes in 1943 with 'treaty maximum' cruisers and that the United States claimed the right to object to this when the time came. No language to this effect appears in the First London Treaty.
[93] —, *Papers Related to the Foreign Relations of the United States – 1930*, 500.A15a3/731, Stimson to Acting Secretary of State, March 3, 1930, No.103, pp 36–9.
[94] Roskill, *Naval Policy Between the Wars II*, p 67.
[95] Lacroix and Wells, *Japanese Cruisers*, pp 430–1.
[96] —, *Limitation and Reduction of Naval Armament (London Naval Treaty)*. The four cruisers already 'overage' were *Tone*, *Yahagi*, *Hirato* and *Chikuma*; the three that would become 'overage' in 1935–6 were *Tenryu*, *Tatsuta* and *Kuma*.
[97] Lacroix and Wells, *Japanese Cruisers*, pp 430–1.
[98] Ibid. The actual available tonnage was slightly less than 51,000 tons, so the plan was for the construction of four cruisers of 8500 tons and then two more of slightly smaller displacement in the second phase.
[99] Ibid, p 437.
[100] Ibid, p 438.
[101] Ibid, p 439.
[102] Ibid, p 440.
[103] Ibid, pp 441–2.
[104] CNC is Copper Non-Cemented armour plate used for the lower, thinner strakes in way of the engineering spaces; http://www.navweaps.com/index_nathan/metalprpsept2009.php#Japanese_Copper_Non-Cemented_%28CNC%2C_CNC1%2C_%26amp%3B_CNC2%29_Armor. Nickel was in short supply in Japan, and it was found that in thin plates, up to 3in thick, a high percentage of nickel could be replaced by copper as a hardening additive in armour steel with no loss in toughness.
[105] Lacroix and Wells, *Japanese Cruisers*, pp 817–22; Chesneau (ed), *Conway's All the World's Fighting Ships 1922-1946*, p 190.
[106] The Japanese announced their intention to withdraw from the Washington Treaty on 29 December 1934, but that did not impact cruiser armament. It was the decision to abandon the Second London Conference on 15 January 1936 that was crucial in this narrative.
[107] http://www.navweaps.com/Weapons/WNJAP_8-50_3ns.php#mountnote6.1back.
[108] Lacroix and Wells, *Japanese Cruisers*, p 482.
[109] Ibid, pp 538–41.
[110] Friedman, *U.S. Cruisers: An Illustrated Design History*, p 183.
[111] http://www.navweaps.com/Weapons/WNUS_6-47_mk16.php.
[112] Friedman, *U.S. Cruisers: An Illustrated Design History*, pp 184–5.
[113] Ibid, p 189.
[114] The House of Representatives had swung Democratic at the beginning of 1932, but it took the November 1932 elections to change the Senate and Presidency, with the change not taking full effect until March 1933.

[115] —, *Executive Order 6174 on Public Works Administration*, June 16, 1933. The $238 million allocated by the President would be approximately $4.5 billion in today's dollars. However, the number of ships that money would buy, even in inflation-adjusted dollars, is dramatically diminished, due to many factors. The monies that FDR approved in his executive order would have bought more than twenty *Northampton* class cruisers or one modern attack submarine.
[116] Walsh, Senator David I, *The Decline and the Renaissance of the Navy, 1922-1944*, presented on 7 June 1944 (legislative day 9 May 1944) (Washington, DC: Government Printing Office, 1944).
[117] Friedman, *U.S. Cruisers: An Illustrated Design History*, p 195.
[118] Ibid, pp 474–5; Chesneau (ed), *Conway's All the World's Fighting Ships 1922-1946*, p 116.
[119] Friedman, *Naval Firepower*, p 202. Experience showed that a rangefinder mounted in a director atop a tower bridge suffered less vibration and had better visibility than turret rangefinders; by 1939, the process of retrofitting rangefinders into Mk 34 directors fleet-wide was complete.
[120] Friedman, *British Cruisers: Two World Wars and After*, pp 156–7.
[121] Ibid, p 157.
[122] Ibid, p 159.
[123] Ibid, p 161. As well intended as this decision was, it proved to be futile, because in ships of this size, the fire rooms were still large enough that if any two adjacent engineering spaces flooded, the ship could capsize.
[124] Ibid.
[125] Ibid, p 400; Chesneau (ed), *Conway's All the World's Fighting Ships 1922-1946*, p 31. This displacement figure is from Friedman; *Conway's* gives a lower figure: 5220–5270 tons.
[126] Friedman, *British Cruisers: Two World Wars and After*, p 400; Chesneau (ed), *Conway's All the World's Fighting Ships 1922-1946*, p 31.
[127] Friedman, *British Cruisers: Two World Wars and After*, p 172.
[128] http://www.navweaps.com/Weapons/WNBR_6-50_mk23.php.
[129] Roskill, *Naval Policy Between the Wars II*, pp 136–40.
[130] Friedman, *British Cruisers: Two World Wars and After*, p 173.
[131] Ibid, p 174.
[132] Ibid, p 401; Chesneau (ed), *Conway's All the World's Fighting Ships 1922-1946*, p 31. This displacement figure is from Friedman; *Conway's* gives a higher figure: 9100 tons.
[133] http://www.navweaps.com/index_nathan/metalprpsept2009.php#British_Post-1930_Cemented_Armor.
[134] Friedman, *British Cruisers: Two World Wars and After*, p 400; Chesneau (ed), *Conway's All the World's Fighting Ships 1922-1946*, p 31.
[135] —, *Foreign Relations of the United States, Diplomatic Papers, 1936 (In Five Volumes), Volume I – General, The British Commonwealth* (Washington, DC: Government Printing Office, 1953), 500.A15/635: Telegram, The Chairman of the American Delegation (Davis) to the Secretary of State, January 24, 1936, No.67, pp 44–8.
[136] Chesneau (ed), *Conway's All the World's Fighting Ships 1922-1946*, pp 32–3.
[137] Roskill, *Naval Policy Between the Wars II*, p 167.
[138] Brescia, *Mussolini's Navy*, p 90.
[139] Ibid, p 89; Chesneau (ed), *Conway's All the World's Fighting Ships 1922-1946*, p 295; Whitley, *Cruisers of World War Two*, p 134.
[140] Brescia, *Mussolini's Navy*, p 93.
[141] Ibid, p 96. Chesneau (ed), *Conway's All the World's Fighting Ships 1922-1946*, p 296, gives different, somewhat smaller figures for the two ships, but with about the same difference in tonnage. The difference is explained by the fact that the two ships, while having the same basic dimensions, had different underwater profiles; *Abruzzi's* hull was fuller, with a lower midship section coefficient, accounting for the difference in displacement.
[142] Brescia, *Mussolini's Navy*, p 96; Chesneau (ed), *Conway's All the World's Fighting Ships 1922-1946*, p 296; Whitley, *Cruisers of World War Two*, p 139.
[143] Jordan and Moulin, *French Cruisers*, pp 121–3.
[144] Ibid, p 124; Chesneau (ed), *Conway's All the World's Fighting Ships 1922-1946*, pp 265–6.

Chapter 8: Treaty Cruisers – The Last of the Type: 1934–1938
[1] Friedman, *U.S. Cruisers: An Illustrated Design History*, p 210.
[2] Ibid, pp 210–15.
[3] The 67in bore separation figure comes from http://www.navweaps.com/Weapons/WNUS_8-55_mk12-15.php. Friedman, *U.S. Cruisers: An Illustrated Design History*, p 214, gives the figure as 70in.
[4] Friedman, *U.S. Cruisers: An Illustrated Design History*, p 476; Chesneau (ed), *Conway's All the World's Fighting Ships 1922-1946*, p 117.
[5] Lacroix and Wells, *Japanese Cruisers*, pp 502–3.
[6] Ibid, p 502.
[7] Ibid, p 517.
[8] Ibid, pp 822–4; Chesneau (ed), *Conway's All the World's Fighting Ships 1922-1946*, p 190.
[9] Roskill, *Naval Policy Between the Wars II*, p 284.
[10] —, *Foreign Relations of the United States, Diplomatic Papers, 1933 (In Five Volumes), Volume I – General* (Washington, DC: Government Printing Office, 1950), 711.94/830, The Ambassador in Japan (Grew) to the Secretary of State, July 26, 1933, No.480, p 380.
[11] David Bergamini, *Japan's Imperial Conspiracy* (New York, NY: Simon & Schuster, Inc, 1972), p 12. The *Koa Domei* (Asia Development Society) flourished in Japan in the 1930s, with clandestine Imperial support, promoting Japanese conquest of Asia and exploitation of other Asian peoples.
[12] Ibid. It is simply astonishing, looking back on 1933 from eighty-plus years in the future, to see the incredulity of a man as intelligent as Ambassador Grew at the simple fact that the Japanese wanted to be treated as equals by the British and Americans, and that they should take offence when they were not so treated.
[13] —, *Foreign Relations of the United States, Diplomatic Papers, 1933*, 811.34/539, The British Embassy to the Department of State, September 14, 1933, unnumbered, pp 382–4.
[14] Stimson wrote a lengthy memorandum to Hull refuting the British claim that he had made such a statement, cf., —, *Foreign Relations of the United States, Diplomatic Papers, 1933*, 811.34/554, Memorandum by Mr. Henry L. Stimson, November 3, 1933, unnumbered, pp 389–95.
[15] Ibid, p 383.
[16] Roskill, *Naval Policy Between the Wars II*, pp 286–7.
[17] For a brief look at the history of the 'Two Power Standard', cf., Stern, *The Battleship Holiday*, pp 30 and 98.
[18] Roskill, *Naval Policy Between the Wars II*, p 288.
[19] Ibid, p 289.
[20] —, *Foreign Relations of the United States, Diplomatic Papers, 1934 (In Five Volumes), Volume I – General, The British Commonwealth* (Washington, DC: Government Printing Office, 1951), 500.A15A5/24, The Ambassador in Japan (Grew) to the Secretary of State, January 22, 1934, No.650, pp 217–20.
[21] Ibid, p 218.
[22] Ibid, p 219.
[23] —, *Foreign Relations of the United States, Diplomatic Papers, 1934*, 500.A15A5/58, Memorandum of the Under Secretary of State (Phillips), May 24, 1934, unnumbered, pp 237–8.
[24] 'Navy Talks Opened by U.S. and Britain; Tokyo Aims Feared.' *The New York Times*, Vol. LXXXIII, No. 27,905, 19 June 1934, p 1.

[25] —, *Foreign Relations of the United States, Diplomatic Papers, 1934*, 500.A15A5/101 : Telegram, The Ambassador in Great Britain (Bingham) to the Secretary of State, June 19, 1934, No.338, p 265.
[26] 'Navy Talks Opened by U.S. and Britain; Tokyo Aims Feared.' *The New York Times*, Vol. LXXXIII, No. 27,905, 19 June 1934, p 9.
[27] —, *Foreign Relations of the United States, Diplomatic Papers, 1934*, 500.A15A5/104 : Telegram, The Ambassador in Great Britain (Bingham) to the Secretary of State, June 21, 1934, No.343, pp 266–7.
[28] —, *Foreign Relations of the United States, Diplomatic Papers, 1934*, 500.A15A5/105 : Telegram, The Ambassador in Great Britain (Bingham) to the Secretary of State, June 22, 1934, No.344, pp 267–8. Simple math allows thirty-five 7000-ton ships in 250,000 tons aggregate displacement.
[29] Ibid, p 268.
[30] 'Big Navy Increase Sought by Britain; U.S. Approval Seen.' *The New York Times*, Vol. LXXXIII, No. 27,908, 22 June 1934, pp 1 and 8.
[31] —, *Foreign Relations of the United States, Diplomatic Papers, 1934*, 500.A15A5/106 : Telegram, The Ambassador in Great Britain (Bingham) to the Secretary of State, June 22, 1934, No.349, p 269.
[32] Ibid, 500.A15A5/109: Telegram, The Ambassador in Great Britain (Bingham) to the Secretary of State, June 25, 1934, No.352, pp 272–4.
[33] Roskill, *Naval Policy Between the Wars II*, p 290.
[34] —, *Foreign Relations of the United States, Diplomatic Papers, 1934*, 500.A15A5/107: Telegram, The Ambassador in Japan (Grew) to the Secretary of State, June 22, 1934, No.132, pp 270–1.
[35] Ibid, p 270.
[36] Hiroyuki Agawa, *The Reluctant Admiral: Yamamoto and the Imperial Navy*, trans. John Bester (New York, NY: Kodansha International USA, Ltd., 1979), p 21. Yamamoto almost always used an interpreter when in diplomatic meetings in London, but this was because it gave him extra time to think about the content of the conversations.
[37] Ibid, pp 20–1.
[38] Agawa, *The Reluctant Admiral*, pp 33–5; Roskill, *Naval Policy Between the Wars II*, p 295.
[39] Roskill, *Naval Policy Between the Wars II*, p 296.
[40] —, *Foreign Relations of the United States, Diplomatic Papers, 1934*, 500.A15A5/207: Telegram, The Ambassador in Japan (Grew) to the Secretary of State, October 17, 1934, No.230, pp 309–11.
[41] Roskill, *Naval Policy Between the Wars II*, p 296.
[42] Ibid, p 298.
[43] Agawa, *The Reluctant Admiral*, p 37.
[44] —, *Foreign Relations of the United States, Diplomatic Papers, 1934*, 500.A15A5/215: Telegram, The Chairman of the American Delegation (Davis) to the Secretary of State, October 25, 1934, No.9, p 312. John A Simon was the British Foreign Secretary.
[45] Roskill, *Naval Policy Between the Wars II*, p 296.
[46] —, *Foreign Relations of the United States, Diplomatic Papers, 1934*, 500.A15A5/229: Telegram, The Ambassador in Japan (Grew) to the Secretary of State, November 1, 1934, No.240, pp 322–3. In this cable, Grew reported on a meeting with Captain Shimomura, in which the possibility of Japan accepting a 90 per cent ratio compared to the Americans was raised by the Japanese.
[47] Ibid, 500.A15A5/287, Minutes of the Meeting Between British and American Delegations in the Prime Minister's Office at the House of Commons on November 14, 1934, 3 p.m., unnumbered, p 349. This list of objectives was enumerated by John Simon.
[48] Ibid, 500.A15A5/280a : Telegram, The Secretary of State to the Chairman of the American Delegation (Davis), November 22, 1934, No.34, pp 364–5.
[49] Yamamoto quoted in 'Japan Won't Limit Navy Ship's Types.' *The New York Times*, Vol. LXXXIV, No. 28,060, 21 November 1934, p 1.
[50] —, *Foreign Relations of the United States, Diplomatic Papers, 1934*, 500.A15A5/327½, President Roosevelt to the Secretary of State, December 7, 1934, unnumbered, pp 390–1.
[51] 'France Declines Japan's Naval Bid.' *The New York Times*, Vol. LXXXIV, No. 28,071, 2 December 1934, p 28.
[52] —, *Foreign Relations of the United States, Diplomatic Papers, 1934*, Minutes of a Meeting in the Prime Minister's Office at the House of Commons, December 19, 1934, 4 p.m., unnumbered, pp 402–3.
[53] Agawa, *The Reluctant Admiral*, p 48.
[54] Whitley, *Cruisers of World War Two*, p 58; Gerhard Koop and Klaus-Peter Schmolke, *Heavy Cruisers of the Admiral Hipper Class*, trans. Geoffrey Brooks (London: Greenhill Books, 2001), pp 8–9.
[55] D C Watt, 'The Anglo-German Naval Agreement: An Interim Judgment', *The Journal of Modern History* Vol 28, No 2 (Chicago, IL: The University of Chicago Press, June 1956), p 160; Joseph A Maiolo, *The Royal Navy and Nazi Germany, 1933-39: A Study in Appeasement and the Origins of the Second World War* (London: Palgrave Macmillan, 1998), pp 23–4.
[56] Maiolo, *The Royal Navy and Nazi Germany*, p 25.
[57] Watt, 'The Anglo-German Naval Agreement: An Interim Judgment', p 160.
[58] Roskill, *Naval Policy Between the Wars II*, p 292. The numbers discussed included, among others, five capital ships, seven light cruisers, one aircraft carrier and even 5000 tons of submarines.
[59] 'Franco-British Statement.' *The New York Times*, Vol. LXXXIV, No. 28,135, 4 February 1935, p 4.
[60] 'Reich's Reply to Note.' *The New York Times*, Vol. LXXXIV, No. 28,147, 16 February 1935, p 4.
[61] —, *Foreign Relations of the United States, Diplomatic Papers, 1935 (In Four Volumes), Volume I – General, The Near East and Africa* (Washington, DC: Government Printing Office, 1953), Memorandum by the Chargé in the United Kingdom (Atherton), March 5, 1935, unnumbered, pp 194–6.
[62] 'Britain to Increase Arms; Loss of Faith in Pacts Seen.' *The New York Times*, Vol. LXXXIV, No. 28,164, 5 March 1935, pp 1–2.
[63] 'Germany Renews Simon's Invitation.' *The New York Times*, Vol. LXXXIV, No. 28,169, 10 March 1935, p 1.
[64] 'Germany Creates Army of 500,000, Orders Conscription, Scraps Treaty; Entente Powers Confer on Action.' *The New York Times*, Vol. LXXXIV, No. 28,176, 17 March 1935, p 1. There were two articles under this main headline; this had the sub-headline: 'Blow to Peace Parley'.
[65] This conversation was reported in —, *Foreign Relations of the United States, Diplomatic Papers, 1935*, 862.20/742 : Telegram, The Chargé in the United Kingdom (Atherton) to the Secretary of State, March 19, 1935, No.121, pp 66–7. Note that Hitler had apparently forgotten his decision to raise the requested tonnage ratio from one-third to 35 per cent.
[66] Ibid, p 67.
[67] Ibid. See also 'Germany Creates Army of 500,000, Orders Conscription, Scraps Treaty; Entente Powers Confer on Action.' *The New York Times*, Vol. LXXXIV, No. 28,176, 17 March 1935, p 1, under the sub-headline: 'British Cabinet to Meet'.
[68] 'Text of British Note.' *The New York Times*, Vol. LXXXIV, No. 28,178, 19 March 1935, pp 1–2.
[69] Ibid, p 2.
[70] Maiolo, *The Royal Navy and Nazi Germany*, pp 32–3.
[71] https://api.parliament.uk/historic-hansard/commons/1935/apr/29/germany-submarine-orders.
[72] https://api.parliament.uk/historic-hansard/commons/1935/may/02/foreign-office.
[73] 'League Censures Germany, Moves to Apply Sanctions for Future

War Threats.' *The New York Times*, Vol. LXXXIV, No. 28,208, 18 April 1935, p 1.
[74] 'Textual Excerpts from Reichsfuehrer Hitler's Speech on German Armaments.' *The New York Times*, Vol. LXXXIV, No. 28,242, 22 May 1935, p 14.
[75] Maiolo, *The Royal Navy and Nazi Germany*, pp 35–6.
[76] Roskill, *Naval Policy Between the Wars II*, pp 303–4.
[77] Maiolo, *The Royal Navy and Nazi Germany*, pp 35–6.
[78] —, *Foreign Relations of the United States, Diplomatic Papers, 1935*, 500.A15A5/413 : Telegram, The Ambassador in France (Straus) to the Secretary of State, June 18, 1935, No.511, pp 165–6.
[79] Ibid, p 164.
[80] Roskill, *Naval Policy Between the Wars II*, p 305.
[81] Ibid, p 306.
[82] —, *Foreign Relations of the United States, Diplomatic Papers, 1935*, 862.34/127 : Telegram, The Ambassador in the United Kingdom (Bingham) to the Secretary of State, June 7, 1935, No.259, pp 163–4.
[83] —, *Foreign Relations of the United States, Diplomatic Papers, 1935*, 862.34/194 : Telegram, The Ambassador in the Soviet Union (Bullitt) to the Secretary of State, June 28, 1935, No.682, pp 168–9.
[84] Ibid.
[85] Maiolo, *The Royal Navy and Nazi Germany*, p 34; Stern, *The Battleship Holiday*, p 30.
[86] Maiolo, *The Royal Navy and Nazi Germany*, pp 66–72. The change from Weimar *Reichsmarine* to Nazi *Kriegsmarine* is difficult to pin down to an exact date, as Nazi insignia were being added to German ships all through 1934, but the official name change appears to have taken place on 1 June 1935, although the *Kriegsmarine* ensign with swastika was not adopted until 7 November 1935.
[87] 'Nazis Tell Powers Their Naval Plans.' *The New York Times*, Vol. LXXXIV, No. 28,288, 7 July 1935, p 8.
[88] http://www.navweaps.com/index_nathan/metalprpsept2009.php#%22Wotan_H%C3%A4rte%22_%28Wh%29. 'Wh' was *Wotan hart*, a homogeneous high-nickel, molybdenum-added homogeneous armour steel made by Krupp intended for plates less than 9in thick.
[89] http://www.navweaps.com/index_nathan/metalprpsept2009.php#%22Wotan_Weich%22_%28Ww%29. 'Ww' was *Wotan weich*, a 'softer', more ductile variant of Wotan steel intended for holding bulkheads.
[90] Whitley, *Cruisers of World War Two*, pp 57–8; Koop and Schmolke, *Heavy Cruisers of the Admiral Hipper Class*, pp 11–34; Chesneau (ed), *Conway's All the World's Fighting Ships 1922-1946*, p 228.
[91] Roskill, *Naval Policy Between the Wars II*, p 310.
[92] —, *Foreign Relations of the United States, Diplomatic Papers, 1935*, 500.A15A5/564, Memorandum by Mr. Noel H. Field of the Division of Western European Affairs of a Meeting Held November 19, 1935, at the Executive Office of the White House, November 23, 1935, unnumbered, pp 144–9.
[93] Ibid, p 149.
[94] —, *Foreign Relations of the United States, Diplomatic Papers, 1935*, 500.A15A5/598, Memorandum of Conversation at the Admiralty, London, Between Messrs. Norman H. Davis, William Phillips, and Admiral Standley for the United States, and Viscount Monsell, Admiral Sir Ernle Chatfield, and Mr. R. L. Craigie for the British Government, December 8, 1935, unnumbered, pp 156–8.
[95] Roskill, *Naval Policy Between the Wars II*, p 310.
[96] Ibid, p 315.
[97] —, *Foreign Relations of the United States, Diplomatic Papers, 1936*, 500.A15/601 : Telegram, The Chairman of the American Delegation (Davis) to the Secretary of State, January 8, 1936, No.38, pp 24–6.
[98] Roskill, *Naval Policy Between the Wars II*, p 316.
[99] —, *Foreign Relations of the United States, Diplomatic Papers, 1936*, 500.A15/632 : Telegram, The Chairman of the American Delegation (Davis) to the Secretary of State, January 23, 1936, No.64, pp 40–2.
[100] Roskill, *Naval Policy Between the Wars II*, p 318.
[101] —, *Foreign Relations of the United States, Diplomatic Papers, 1936*, 500.A15/635 : Telegram, The Chairman of the American Delegation (Davis) to the Secretary of State, January 24, 1936, No.67, pp 44–8.
[102] The '[agree to?]' in the quote is in the original, apparently an attempt to fill in an omission in the original message.
[103] —, *Foreign Relations of the United States, Diplomatic Papers, 1936*, 500.A15/635 : Telegram, The Chairman of the American Delegation (Davis) to the Secretary of State, January 24, 1936, No.67, p 45.
[104] According to Annex I of Part II of the First London Treaty, to which Japan was still technically bound, replacements for the cruisers *Furutaka* and *Kako* could be laid down in 1943.
[105] —, *Foreign Relations of the United States, Diplomatic Papers, 1936*, 500.A15/635 : Telegram, The Chairman of the American Delegation (Davis) to the Secretary of State, January 24, 1936, No.67, pp 45–6.
[106] Ibid, p 47.
[107] —, *Foreign Relations of the United States, Diplomatic Papers, 1936*, 500.A15/638 : Telegram, The Chairman of the American Delegation (Davis) to the Secretary of State, January 26, 1936, No.72, p 48.
[108] —, *Foreign Relations of the United States, Diplomatic Papers, 1936*, 500.A15/647 : Telegram, The Secretary of State to the Chairman of the American Delegation (Davis), February 6, 1936, No.33, pp 57–8.
[109] The Italians believed that the British, who still held the largest colonial empire, acquired at horrific cost in indigenous blood, and who only seventeen years earlier had turned troops loose on an unarmed crowd of Indians at Amritsar, killing or wounding over 1500, had little moral standing to condemn Italian actions in Ethiopia.

Chapter 9: True Babies – London's Offspring and Other (Mostly) Small Cruisers: 1936–1941
[1] Friedman, *British Cruisers: Two World Wars and After*, p 186.
[2] Ibid, p 189.
[3] http://www.navweaps.com/Weapons/WNBR_51-50_mk1.php; http://www.navweaps.com/Weapons/WNBR_525-50_mk1.php.
[4] Friedman, *British Cruisers: Two World Wars and After*, p 190.
[5] http://www.navweaps.com/Weapons/WNBR_45-45_mk1.php; http://www.navweaps.com/Weapons/WNBR_525-50_mk1.php. The difference in shell weight of an SAP round was 58.25lb v 80lb.
[6] To compare this performance with that of the American 5in/38 in the typical Mk 29 twin-base ring-mount, as fitted in the *Atlanta* class, the mount could train at 25°/second, elevate at 15°/second and fire at 15–22rpm.
[7] Friedman, *British Cruisers: Two World Wars and After*, p 402; Chesneau (ed), *Conway's All the World's Fighting Ships 1922-1946*, p 33.
[8] Friedman, *British Cruisers: Two World Wars and After*, p 191.
[9] —, *The Vinson-Trammell Act of 1934*, U.S. Congressional Record, 73d Congress, Sess. II, Chs. 94, 95, March 27, 1934, pp 503–5
[10] —, *Treaty for the Limitation of Naval Armament (Second London Naval Treaty)*, London, March 25, 1936, Part I, Art. 1 C & Part II, Art. 6 (1).
[11] —, *Limitation and Reduction of Naval Armament (London Naval Treaty)*, Part II, Art. 13, Annex I, Sect. I
[12] Op cit, Part V, Art. 30 (1).
[13] Friedman, *U.S. Cruisers: An Illustrated Design History*, pp 220–3.
[14] Ibid, pp 224–5.
[15] Ibid, pp 231–2.
[16] Ibid, p 233.
[17] Ibid, p 477; Chesneau (ed), *Conway's All the World's Fighting Ships 1922–1946*, p 118.

[18] Friedman, *U.S. Cruisers: An Illustrated Design History*, pp 238–9.
[19] Jordan and Moulin, *French Cruisers*, pp 83–4.
[20] http://www.navweaps.com/Weapons/WNFR_55-40_m1923.php.
[21] Jordan and Moulin, *French Cruisers*, p 85; Chesneau (ed), *Conway's All the World's Fighting Ships 1922-1946*, p 264.
[22] Jordan and Moulin, *French Cruisers*, pp 89–90.
[23] Ibid, p 93; Chesneau (ed), *Conway's All the World's Fighting Ships 1922-1946*, p 264.
[24] Brescia, *Mussolini's Navy*, p 100.
[25] While these ships were originally intended to carry a single aircraft, as they were seen as operating independently in the Atlantic or off East Africa, it never had been intended that they would mount a catapult. I thank Enrico Cernuschi for this insight.
[26] Brescia, *Mussolini's Navy*, p 100; Chesneau (ed), *Conway's All the World's Fighting Ships 1922-1946*, p 297; Whitley, *Cruisers of World War Two*, p 142; Elio Andò, 'Capitani Romani: Part 1 – Design and Construction', *Warship* No 7 (July 1978), p 150.
[27] Lacroix and Wells, *Japanese Cruisers*, pp 660–1. The three old cruisers were *Asama*, *Iwate* and *Yakumo*.
[28] Ibid, pp 833–5; Chesneau (ed), *Conway's All the World's Fighting Ships 1922-1946*, p 191.
[29] Lacroix and Wells, *Japanese Cruisers*, p 557.
[30] Ibid, pp 576–7; —, *Japanese Surface and General Fire Control*, O-31 (San Francisco, CA: U.S. Naval Technical Mission to Japan, January 1946), pp 17–18.
[31] Lacroix and Wells, *Japanese Cruisers*, pp 239–42; —, *Japanese Anti-Aircraft Fire Control*, O-30 (San Francisco, CA: U.S. Naval Technical Mission to Japan, January 1946), pp 13–17.
[32] Lacroix and Wells, *Japanese Cruisers*, p 556.
[33] Ibid, p 231.
[34] Ibid, pp 554–5.
[35] Ibid, pp 556.
[36] Ibid, pp 556–8.
[37] Ibid, pp 826–8; Chesneau (ed), *Conway's All the World's Fighting Ships 1922-1946*, p 191.
[38] Lacroix and Wells, *Japanese Cruisers*, p 612.
[39] http://www.navweaps.com/Weapons/WNJAP_39-65_t98.php.
[40] Lacroix and Wells, *Japanese Cruisers*, pp 831–3; Chesneau (ed), *Conway's All the World's Fighting Ships 1922-1946*, p 192.
[41] Lacroix and Wells, *Japanese Cruisers*, p 632.
[42] Jordan and Moulin, *French Cruisers*, pp 159–63.

Chapter 10: Mass Production: 1935–1944
[1] See Chapter 8.
[2] Friedman, *British Cruisers: Two World Wars and After*, pp 214–24.
[3] Ibid, p 220n18.
[4] In practice, these ships were never run at higher than approximately 72,500shp, which, in clean condition and in calm water, would drive them at 31 knots. Chesneau (ed), *Conway's All the World's Fighting Ships 1922-1946*, p 34, actually lists that power output as the 'official' figure for this class and its successors.
[5] Friedman, *British Cruisers: Two World Wars and After*, p 403; Chesneau (ed), *Conway's All the World's Fighting Ships 1922-1946*, p 34.
[6] Friedman, *U.S. Cruisers: An Illustrated Design History*, pp 244–7.
[7] These numbers are more than a little arbitrary. The design number applied only to the first pair, and even then there was only a sideways glance at the former treaty limit, with no serious attempt to hold to that limit. The figure given in Chesneau (ed), *Conway's All the World's Fighting Ships 1922-1946*, pp 119–20 for the standard displacement of USS *Biloxi* (CL80), laid down in July 1941, is 11,744 tons. Likewise, the full-load figure shown here is for *Biloxi*; no doubt later ships displaced more.
[8] Friedman, *U.S. Cruisers: An Illustrated Design History*, pp 479–80; Chesneau (ed), *Conway's All the World's Fighting Ships 1922-1946*, pp 119–20.
[9] Friedman, *U.S. Cruisers: An Illustrated Design History*, p 268.
[10] Ibid, pp 287; http://www.navweaps.com/Weapons/WNUS_6-47_mk16.php; http://www.navweaps.com/Weapons/WNUS_8-55_mk12-15.php.
[11] Ibid, pp 349–57; The Fritz-X, or more correctly, the PC 1400X, was a 1400kg (3086.5lb) AP glide bomb with limited pitch and yaw control; it required a guide aircraft to fly a steady course at an altitude of at least 13,000ft, which was beyond the effective slant range of the US 5in/38.
[12] http://www.navweaps.com/Weapons/WNUS_8-55_mk16.php.
[13] —, *Naval Ordnance and Gunnery*, NAVPERS 16116-B, Bureau of Naval Personnel, US Navy (Washington, DC: Government Printing Office, September 1950), p 438.
[14] Friedman, *U.S. Cruisers: An Illustrated Design History*, p 356.
[15] Ibid, pp 271–4.
[16] As with the *Cleveland*s, these numbers are snapshots of a moving target. The design number applies only to the first few ships; the figure for full-load displacement is from Chesneau (ed), *Conway's All the World's Fighting Ships 1922-1946*, pp 120–1 for an unidentified ship. It is likely that no two ships of this class had the same full load displacement.
[17] Friedman, *U.S. Cruisers: An Illustrated Design History*, pp 480–1; Chesneau (ed), *Conway's All the World's Fighting Ships 1922-1946*, pp 120–1.
[18] Friedman, *U.S. Cruisers: An Illustrated Design History*, pp 357–62.
[19] The Ordzhonikidze Yard was, at various times, also known as the Baltic Yard, Baltiysky Zayod and Shipyard 189.
[20] Chesneau (ed), *Conway's All the World's Fighting Ships 1922-1946*, p 328.

Chapter 11: The Test of Battle, Part 2: 1939–1945
[1] This information is from the entry for WS 5A in *Convoy Web*, http://www.convoyweb.org.uk/misc/index.html and —, *Admiralty War Diaries, 11/1/40 to 12/31/40* (Washington, DC: National Archives and Records Administration), pp 301–3, 340–2.
[2] —, *Admiralty War Diaries, 11/1/40 to 12/31/40*, p 327.
[3] —, *Admiralty War Diaries, 11/1/40 to 12/31/40*, pp 341–2.
[4] Much of the following comes from Koop and Schmolke, *Heavy Cruisers of the Admiral Hipper Class*, pp 46–7 and from Vincent P O'Hara, *The German Fleet at War, 1939*-1945 (Annapolis, MD: Naval Institute Press, 2004), pp 70–2. Also referenced was Captain Stephen W Roskill, RN, *The War at Sea, 1939-1945, Vol. I, The Defensive* (London: Her Majesty's Stationery Office, 1954), pp 291–2.
[5] It is clear from the actions of the escorts of WS 5A that at no point this night or the next morning was *Hipper* detected by any means other than visual sighting. This author has seen a poor-quality image of *Bonaventure* that appears to show Type 279 antennas at her mastheads, which would have been of little benefit because this was an air-search radar with very limited surface-search capability. Its presence is also confirmed in Derek Howse, *Radar at Sea: The Royal Navy in World War 2* (Annapolis, MD: Naval Institute Press, 1993), pp 41, 64. Other than that, he has been able to find no other information indicating the presence of radars among the convoy's escorts; the reader, however, should remember that the absence of evidence is not evidence of absence.
[6] The times given here are local time, time zone 'N', which was GMT ('Zulu') minus 1 hour. On 25 December 1940, the sun rose at 08.13, with the condition called 'civil twilight' at 07.40. (Civil twilight is defined as the point at which the centre of the sun is 6° below the

horizon; it is more practically defined as that point on a clear morning before sunrise at which outdoor activities may be carried on without artificial lighting.)

[7] One source, http://www.naval-history.net/xDKWW2-4012-25DEC02.htm, states that *Hipper* made an unsuccessful torpedo attack at 03.53, after which Meisel decide to wait until dawn.

[8] —, *Admiralty War Diaries, 11/1/40 to 12/31/40*, p 505.

[9] Ibid, p 520.

[10] http://www.navweaps.com/Weapons/WNBR_525-50_mk1.php.

[11] Samuel Eliot Morison, *History of United States Naval Operations in World War II, Vol. V: The Struggle for Guadalcanal, August 1942-February 1943* (Boston, MA: Little, Brown & Co, 1948), pp 12–14.

[12] Ibid, p 27; Richard B Frank, *Guadalcanal: The Definitive Account of the Landmark Battle* (New York, NY: Penguin Books, 1992), p 54. Cf., also John B Lundstrom, *Black Shoe Carrier Admiral: Frank Jack Fletcher at Coral Sea, Midway, and Guadalcanal* (Annapolis, MD: Naval Institute Press, 2006), pp 333–5.

[13] Morison, *United States Naval Operations, Vol. V*, pp 18–19.

[14] Ibid.; also cf., —, *Combined Operational Intelligence Centre (COIC) Naval Summaries, 1 August, 1942-31 August, 1942*, pp 64–5. The COIC entry was for 9 August and gives the time as 19.00 on the 7th; *S-38* should have been operating on the same time (Z+10) as COIC, which was located in Melbourne.

[15] The Lockheed Hudson was a small twin-engined bomber and reconnaissance aircraft derived from the Model 14 Super Electra airliner. They were used extensively by the Australians who liked their ruggedness, manoeuvrability and long range.

[16] —, *COIC Naval Summaries, 1 August, 1942-31 August, 1942*, p 65. The numeral 'six' for the number of cruisers sighted was pencilled in and the number 'five' crossed out.

[17] Morison, *United States Naval Operations, Vol. V*, p 20.

[18] *Chicago* had a CXAM air-search radar; the other three had less-effective SC sets. All four had FC fire-control radar for the main batteries.

[19] Morison, *United States Naval Operations, Vol. V*, pp 30, 30n14.

[20] The Americans took to calling this torpedo the 'Long Lance', a term never used by the Japanese.

[21] Among many, look at Morison, *United States Naval Operations, Vol. V*, pp 35–53; Frank, *Guadalcanal*, pp 102–17.

[22] Australian official accounts are understandably very imprecise. For example, —, *HMAS Canberra (I)*, http://www.navy.gov.au/hmas-canberra-i, simply states that she was hit more than twenty times.

[23] https://www.history.navy.mil/research/histories/ship-histories/danfs/b/bagley-iii.html.

[24] Depending on the fuel(s) feeding the fire, water may not be the optimal fire-fighting tool. For example, oil or avgas fires can actually be spread by water. Later in the war, additional tools would be available to aid in the fighting of shipboard fires, including chemical additives, such as a soy-based powder called Aer-O-Foam (or more generally called 'foamite' or 'navy bean soup'), which when mixed with water in specially-designed nozzles, produced a thick foam that would float on any liquid surface and act to smother a chemical fire, and 'fog nozzles' that turned a water stream into a fine mist that served to cool fires in confined spaces rapidly.

[25] Frank, *Guadalcanal*, p 106. Cf., also https://www.history.navy.mil/research/histories/ship-histories/danfs/c/chicago-ii.html.

[26] —, *U.S.S. Quincy (CA39), U.S.S. Astoria (CA34), U.S.S. Vincennes (CA44) Loss in Action, Battle of Savo Island, 9 August, 1942*, War Damage Report No. 29, Preliminary Design Branch, Bureau of Ships, Navy Department (Washington, DC: US Hydrographic Office, 21 June 1943), pp 5–6.

[27] Ibid, pp 15–16. In the discussion of the damage, the opinion was offered that, due to the relatively limited amount of damage caused by this hit, it may well have not been a torpedo, but rather a 'plunging' hit by a 20cm shell. Similarly, the post-action report by the captain stated that a torpedo struck fire room No 4, but the slow flooding that occurred, taking more than seven minutes, caused the authors of the War Damage Report to conclude that the 'agent' was a 20cm shell and not a torpedo.

[28] Ibid, pp 3–4.

[29] Ibid, p 3.

[30] Ibid, pp 1–3.

[31] The remainder of the story is supplemented by https://www.history.navy.mil/research/histories/ship-histories/danfs/a/astoria-ca-34-ii.html and by http://www.ussastoria.org/Iron_Bottom_Sound.html.

[32] https://www.history.navy.mil/research/histories/ship-histories/danfs/a/astoria-ca-34-ii.html.

[33] —, *U.S.S. Quincy (CA39), U.S.S. Astoria (CA34), U.S.S. Vincennes (CA44) Loss in Action, Battle of Savo Island, 9 August, 1942*, War Damage Report No. 29, p 18.

[34] The details from here are from http://www.combinedfleet.com/kako_t.htm.

[35] —, *The Times Comprehensive Atlas of the World, Thirteenth Edition, Reprinted with Changes* (London: Times Books, 2013), Plate 12.

[36] The exact number of ships to include depends on where you draw the lines limiting Savo Sound. I have chosen to be strict about it, drawing the lines from the western and northern tips of Savo Island to the western tips of Guadalcanal and the Florida Islands. This excludes several sinkings that are often included, such as *Hiei*, *Kirishima* and *Fubuki*.

[37] —, *U.S.S. Savannah (CL42) Bomb Damage, Gulf of Salerno, Italy, 11 September, 1943*, War Damage Report No. 44, Preliminary Design Branch, Bureau of Ships, Navy Department (Washington, DC: US Hydrographic Office, 15 June 1944), p 1.

[38] According to http://cv6.org/ship/logs/ops/ops_chap_43.htm, which reproduces parts of the pre-war Operations Manual of USS *Enterprise* (CV6), this material condition (called 'Afirm' in this document rather than 'Able', using an older version of the phonetic alphabet) is described as follows: 'Material Condition Afirm represents the maximum watertight integrity of the ship. Access and living conditions are secondary to the requirements of watertight and air-tight integrity.' This means that all doors, valves and fittings are closed, excepting only those marked as 'Class W', which must be kept open at all times (except in absolute emergencies), such as fire room ventilation ducting.

[39] —, *U.S.S. Savannah (CL42) Bomb Damage*, pp 4–5.

[40] RDX was the British name for a high-energy explosive developed in the 1930s for use in depth charges and armour-piercing shells, called 'hexogen' by the Germans.

[41] —, *U.S.S. Savannah (CL42) Bomb Damage*, p 7.

[42] Ibid. The shell plating hanging down from the hole torn in *Savannah*'s hull created a suction that drew water out while she was moving.

[43] Ibid, pp 5–6.

[44] Ibid, p 2.

[45] Ibid, pp 8–10.

[46] Ibid, p 8.

[47] Ibid, p 16.

[48] Ibid, p 17.

[49] Ibid, p 13.

[50] http://www.naval-history.net/xGM-Chrono-01BB-HMS_Warspite.htm; Stern, *The Battleship Holiday*, pp 212–13.

Chapter 12: The More Things Change . . . : 1946–

1 Captain John E Moore, RN (ed), *Jane's Fighting Ships, 1973-74* (New York, NY: McGraw-Hill Book Co, 1973), p 406.

2 Norman Friedman, *U.S. Destroyers: An Illustrated Design History* (Annapolis, MD: Naval Institute Press, 1982), pp 257–8.

3 Ibid, pp 243–4.

4 Ibid, pp 321–2.

5 https://www.executivegov.com/2017/10/report-navy-to-start-decommissioning-oldest-cruisers-in-2020/.

6 https://www.thedrive.com/the-war-zone/16695/the-navy-is-changing-its-plans-for-its-dumbed-down-zumwalts-and-their-ammoless-guns.

7 They were all originally given destroyer-style names; in Russian naval tradition, destroyers are given names in adjectival forms, where the adjectives describe admirable military qualities. The four ships in this class were originally to be named *Grozniy* (Formidable), *Steregushchiy* (Watchful), *Doblestniy* (Valorous) and *Soobrazitel'niy* (Shrewd). Cruiser names, on the other hand, do not follow any specific pattern in Russian practice; they can be named after people, places or previous ships.

8 Based on the same principle as the Allied Reporting System for Japanese aircraft that gave us the colourful names for such aircraft as the 'Zeke', 'Kate' and 'Val', widely used during the Second World War, adopted because the actual designation were complex and nearly-impossible for the average non-Japanese to remember, NATO developed a naming system for Russian weapons. Thus the system the Russians knew as the 'P-35 3M44 Progress' was known to NATO as the SS-N-3b 'Shaddock'.

9 Jordan and Moulin, *French Cruisers*, pp 145–9.

10 http://www.navweaps.com/Weapons/WNFR_5-54_m1948.php.

11 The other three were *Luigi Cadorna*, *Raimondo Montecuccoli* and *Luigi di Savoia Duca degli Abruzzi*. Of these, *Cadorna* was the oldest and did not last long before being retired; *Montecuccoli* served as a training ship until 1964; *Abruzzi* served until 1961.

12 Early in the Polaris programme, it was not certain that underwater launching of the missile would be practical, so, as a fall-back position and as a way of including NATO allies in America's nuclear deterrence plans, the idea of a 'Multilateral Force', based on Polaris missiles carried by NATO surface warships with mixed Allied-American crews controlling the missiles was conceived. The only actual realisation of this idea, before it became mired in political controversy, was the inclusion of the Polaris canisters in *Garibaldi*.

13 Once again, I must thank Enrico Cernuschi for this insight into the workings of the Italian Navy.

14 *Göta Lejon* was one of two Swedish *Tre Kronor* class light cruisers built during the Second World War. While well-built ships, their nation's neutrality meant that these ships and their predecessors had no influence on this narrative.

Sources

As readers are no doubt aware, given the research resources available at the beginning of the twenty-first century, many sources once available only at physical archives or from private individuals are now available in cyberspace. (A small percentage of these are available only online.) In these cases, I have given the hyperlink to the source rather than the more traditional publisher information. It is an unfortunate characteristic of such sources that they are sometimes more ephemeral than paper-and-ink sources. When the site that serves the pages is changed or ceases to exist, the effect can be as if every copy of a particular book has instantly vanished. All links listed here were active and available at the time this manuscript was written.

Primary/Official Sources

First off, the author wishes to acknowledge with profound gratitude the effort the British government has made putting the debates of the Houses of Parliament online as far back as 1803. They are not absolutely complete, having some gaps in frustrating places, but the coverage is still remarkable. This is of great value to any historian interested in the official actions of Great Britain since the time of Napoleon. They may be found at http://hansard.millbanksystems.com/commons/.

—, *Admiralty War Diaries, 11/1/40 to 12/31/40* (Washington, DC: National Archives and Records Administration).

—, *Combined Operational Intelligence Centre (COIC) Naval Summaries, 1 August, 1942-31 August, 1942*, http://www.navy.gov.au/sites/default/files/documents/01-31_Aug_1942.pdf.

—, *Conference on the Limitation of Armament: Address of the President of the United States at the Opening of the Conference at Washington, November 12, 1921, together with the Address of Charles E. Hughes, Secretary of State of the United States and American Commissioner, also The Proposal of the United States for the Limitation of Naval Armament*, Senate Document No.77, 67th Congress, 1st Session (Washington, DC: Government Printing Office, 14 November 1921).

—, *Conference on the Limitation of Armament, Washington, November 12, 1921-February 6, 1922* (Washington, DC: Government Printing Office, 1922), https://catalog.hathitrust.org/Record/001756221. (This is the full record of all discussions at the Washington Conference.)

—, *Documents of the Preparatory Commission for the Disarmament Conference Entrusted with the Preparation for the Conference for the Reduction and Limitation of Armaments – Series VIII – Minutes of the Sixth Session (First Part) of the Preparatory Commission for the Disarmament Conference*, Series of League of Nations Publications, IX. DISARMAMENT 1929, IX. 3 (Geneva, Switzerland: League of Nations Publications, 25 May 1929), http://digital.library.north-western.edu/league/le00305a.pdf.

—, *Executive Order 6174 on Public Works Administration*, 16 June 1933, http://www.presidency.ucsb.edu/ws/index.php?pid=14671. (This was the executive order signed by President Franklin Roosevelt authorising the release of $238 million for naval construction, among other expenditures.)

—, *Fire Control Installations*, Naval Postgraduate School, PGS 5, No. 178 (Annapolis, MD: US Naval Academy, 1934), http://www.ibiblio.org/hyperwar/USN/ref/FireControlInst/index.html#contents.

—, *Foreign Relations of the United States, Diplomatic Papers, 1933 (In Five Volumes), Volume I – General* (Washington, DC: Government Printing Office, 1950), https://images.library.wisc.edu/FRUS/EFacs/1933v01/reference/frus.frus1933v01.i0008.pdf.

—, *Foreign Relations of the United States, Diplomatic Papers, 1934 (In Five Volumes), Volume I – General, The British Commonwealth* (Washington, DC: Government Printing Office, 1951), https://images.library.wisc.edu/FRUS/EFacs/1934v01/reference/frus.frus1934v01.i0006.pdf.

—, *Foreign Relations of the United States, Diplomatic Papers, 1935 (In Four Volumes), Volume I – General, The Near East and Africa* (Washington, DC: Government Printing Office, 1953), https://images.library.wisc.edu/FRUS/EFacs/1935v01/reference/frus.frus1935v01.i0006.pdf.

—, *Foreign Relations of the United States, Diplomatic Papers, 1936 (In Five Volumes), Volume I – General, The British Commonwealth* (Washington, DC: Government Printing Office, 1953), https://images.library.wisc.edu/FRUS/EFacs/1936v01/reference/frus.frus1936v01.i0006.pdf.

—, *Handbook for Fire Control Instruments, 1914*, Admiralty, Gunnery Branch, G.01627/14, ADM/186/191 (Kew: The National Archives, retrieved May 2018).

—, *HMAS Canberra (I)*, http://www.navy.gov.au/hmas-canberra-i.

—, *Japanese Anti-Aircraft Fire Control*, O-30 (San Francisco, CA: U.S. Naval Technical Mission to Japan, January 1946), http://bulletpicker.com/pdf/USNTMJ-200E-30.pdf.

—, *Japanese Fire Control*, O-29 (San Francisco, CA: U.S. Naval Technical Mission to Japan, February 1946), http://bulletpicker.com/pdf/USNTMJ-200E-29.pdf.

—, *Japanese Projectiles General Types*, O-19 (San Francisco, CA: U.S. Naval Technical Mission to Japan, February 1946), http://bulletpicker.com/pdf/USNTMJ-200E-19.pdf.

—, *Japanese Surface and General Fire Control*, O-31 (San Francisco, CA: U.S. Naval Technical Mission to Japan, January 1946), http://bulletpicker.com/pdf/USNTMJ-200E-31.pdf.

—, *Limitation and Reduction of Naval Armament (London Naval Treaty)*, https://www.loc.gov/law/help/us-treaties/bevans/m-ust000002-1055.pdf. (The Treaty was signed in London, England, on 22 April 1930, and was registered by the League of Nations as No 2608 on 6 February 1931.)

—, *Message of the President of the United States Transmitting the Budget for the Service of the Fiscal Year Ending June 30 1933* (Washington, DC: Government Printing Office, 1931), https://fraser.stlouisfed.org/files/docs/publications/usbudget/usbudget_1933.pdf.

—, 'Monograph 1. – Operations Leading Up to the Battle of Coronel' in *Naval Staff Monographs, Vol. I* (London: Naval Staff, Training and Staff Duties Div., July 1919). (The nearly complete set of Royal Navy Staff Monographs covering the First World War has been put online at http://www.navy.gov.au/media-room/publications/world-war-i-naval-staff-monographs.)

—, 'Monograph 27. – The Battles of Coronel and the Falkland Islands' in *Naval Staff Monographs, Vol. IX* (London: Naval Staff, Training and Staff Duties Div., October 1923).

—, *Naval Ordnance and Gunnery*, NAVPERS 16116, Bureau of Naval Personnel, US Navy (Washington, DC: Government Printing Office, May 1944).

—, *Naval Ordnance and Gunnery*, NAVPERS 16116-B, Bureau of Naval Personnel, US Navy (Washington, DC: Government Printing Office, September 1950).

—, *Naval Ordnance and Gunnery Manual*, US Navy, 1937, http://www.eugeneleeslover.com/NAVAL-ORDNANCE-1937.html.

—, *Papers Related to the Foreign Relations of the United States – 1929* (in Three Volumes) Volume I (Washington, DC: Government Printing Office, 1943), https://images.library.wisc.edu/FRUS/EFacs/1929v01/reference/frus.frus1929v01.i0006.pdf.

—, *Papers Related to the Foreign Relations of the United States – 1930* (in Three Volumes) Volume I (Washington, DC: Government Printing Office, 1945), https://images.library.wisc.edu/FRUS/EFacs/1930v01/reference/frus.frus1930v01.i0007.pdf.

—, 'R.N. Gorizia Relazione sugli inconvenienti dovuti al mare grosso nella missione del 22-23 marzo c.a. (1942)' in the *Gorizia* File in the Archivio dell'Ufficio Storico della Marina Militare, Rome, 1942.

—, 'The Many Lives of Herbert O. Yardley' *Cryptologic Spectrum*, Vol. 11, No. 4, Fall 1981, pp 5–29 https://www.nsa.gov/news-features/declassified-documents/cryptologic-spectrum/assets/files/many_lives.pdf.

—, *The Russo-Japanese War Fully Illustrated, No. 1* (Tokyo, Japan: Kinkodo Publishing Co., 1904).

—, *The Treaty of Peace with Germany (Treaty of Versailles)*, 1919 For. Rel. (Paris Peace Conference, XIII) 55, 740, 743; Senate document 51, 66th Congress, 1st session.

—, *The Vinson-Trammell Act of 1934*, U.S. Congressional Record, 73d Congress, Sess. II, Chs. 94, 95, March 27, 1934, pp 503–5, http://legisworks.org/congress/73/publaw-135.pdf. (This piece of legislation actually had the following full title: AN ACT – To establish the composition of the United States Navy with respect to the categories of vessels limited by the treaties signed at Washington, February 6, 1922, and at London, April 22, 1930, at the limits prescribed by those treaties ; to authorise the construction of certain naval vessels ; and for other purposes.)

—, *Treaty for the Limitation of Naval Armament (Second London Naval Treaty)*, London, March 25, 1936, http://www.navweaps.com/index_tech/tech-089_London_Treaty_1936.htm.

—, *Treaty No. 609 – Treaty between the United States of America, the British Empire, France, Italy and Japan, for the Limitation of Naval Armament, Signed at Washington, February 6, 1922*. (The instruments of ratification were deposited at Washington, DC, on 17 August 1923, and the treaty was registered by the League of Nations as No. 609 on 16 April 1924.)

—, *U.S.S. Quincy (CA39), U.S.S. Astoria (CA34), U.S.S. Vincennes (CA44) Loss in Action, Battle of Savo Island, 9 August, 1942*, War Damage Report No. 29, Preliminary Design Branch, Bureau of Ships, Navy Department (Washington, DC: US Hydrographic Office, 21 June 1943).

—, *U.S.S. Savannah (CL42) Bomb Damage, Gulf of Salerno, Italy, 11 September, 1943*, War Damage Report No. 44, Preliminary Design Branch, Bureau of Ships, Navy Department (Washington, DC: US Hydrographic Office, 15 June 1944).

Cernuschi, Enrico, Alessandro Gazzi and Michele Maria Gaetani, *Sea Power: The Italian Way* (Rome, Italy: Ufficio Storico della Marina Militare, 2017).

Frost, Lieutenant Commander Holloway H, USN, *Diagrammatic Study of the Battle of Jutland* (Washington, DC: U.S. Navy Office of Naval Intelligence, 1 December 1921). (This may be found at https://babel.hathitrust.org/cgi/pt?id=loc.ark:/13960/t57d3bb83;view=1up;seq=1.)

Morison, Samuel Eliot, *History of United States Naval Operations in World War II, Vol. V: The Struggle for Guadalcanal, August 1942-February 1943* (Boston, MA: Little, Brown & Co, 1948).

Roskill, Captain Stephen W, RN, *The War at Sea, 1939-1945, Vol. I, The Defensive* (London: HMSO, 1954).

Walsh, Senator David I, *The Decline and the Renaissance of the Navy, 1922-1944*, presented on 7 June 1944 (legislative day 9 May 1944) (Washington, DC: Government Printing Office, 1944), https://www.ibiblio.org/pha/USN/77-2s202.html.

Walsh, Sean, *A Historical Review of Cruiser Characteristics, Roles and Missions*, SFAC Report 9030-04-C1, Ser 05D /68 28 March 2005 (Washington, DC: NAVSEA 05D1, 31 December 2004), http://www.navalmarinearchive.com/research/cruisers/cr_navsea.html#LinkTarget_8391.

First-hand Accounts by Participants

Bacon, Admiral Reginald H S, RN, *The Life of Lord Fisher of Kilverstone: Admiral of the Fleet, Vol. 1* (Garden City, NY: Doubleday, Doran & Co., Inc., 1929).

Fawcett, H W, and G W W Hooper (eds), *The Fighting at Jutland: The Personal Experiences of Forty-five Officers and Men of the British Fleet* (London: Hutchinson & Co Ltd, 1929).

Gibson, Hugh, *A Journal from Our Legation in Belgium* (Garden City, NY: Doubleday, Page & Co, 1917).

McCully, Newton A, Lieutenant Commander, USN, *The McCully Report: The Russo-Japanese War, 1904-05*, edited by Richard A von Doenhoff (Annapolis, MD: Naval Institute Press, 1977).

Secondary Sources (author/editor known)

Agawa, Hiroyuki, *The Reluctant Admiral: Yamamoto and the Imperial Navy*, trans. John Bester (New York, NY: Kodansha International USA, Ltd., 1979).

Andò, Elio, 'Capitani Romani: Part 1 – Design and Construction', *Warship* No 7 (July 1978), pp 146–57.

———, 'Capitani Romani: Part 2 Operational History', *Warship* No 8 (October 1978), pp 246–57.

Baer, George W, *One Hundred Years of Sea Power: The U.S. Navy, 1890-1990* (Stanford, California: Stanford University Press, 1996).

Bennett, Geoffrey, *Coronel and the Falklands* (Edinburgh: Berlinn Ltd, 2000).

Bergamini, David, *Japan's Imperial Conspiracy* (New York, NY: Simon & Schuster, Inc, 1972).

Bertin, L E, *Marine Boilers: Their Construction and Working Dealing More Especially with Tubulous Boilers*, trans. Leslie S Robertson (New York, NY: D Van Nordstrand Co, 1906).

Braisted, William R, 'On the General Board of the Navy, Admiral Hilary Jones, and Naval Arms Limitation, 1921-1931.' The Dwight D Eisenhower Lectures in War & Peace, No.4, Kansas State University, Manhattan, KS, 1991, https://web.archive.org/web/20120321225012/http://www.k-state.edu/history/specialevents/Eisenhowerlecture/eisenhower5.htm.

Brescia, Maurizio, *Mussolini's Navy: A Reference Guide to the Regia Marina 1930 – 1945* (Barnsley: Seaforth Publishing, 2012).

Brook, Peter, 'Armoured Cruiser versus Armoured Cruiser: Ulsan 14 August 1904', in *Warship 2000-2001*, edited by Anthony Preston (London: Conway Maritime Press, 2000), pp 34–47.

Brooks, John, *The Battle of Jutland* (Cambridge: Cambridge University Press, 2016).

Campbell, N J M, *Jutland: An Analysis of the Fighting* (London: Conway Maritime Press, 1986).

Cernuschi, Enrico, *Myths and Misinformation about the Italian Navy in WW2: A documented different point of view*, unpublished article, 2018.

Chesneau, Roger (ed), *Conway's All the World's Fighting Ships 1922-1946* (London: Conway Maritime Press, 1980).

———, and Eugene M Kolesnik (eds), *Conway's All the World's Fighting Ships 1860-1905* (London: Conway Maritime Press, 1979).

Davis, Joseph S, 'The War Debt Settlements.' *The Virginia Quarterly Review* Vol 4, No 1 (Winter 1928), https://www.vqronline.org/essay/war-debt-settlements.

del Campo, Juan, *Britons and Peruvians Fight at Sea*, https://web.archive.org/web/20040803142718/http://members.lycos.co.uk/Juan39/BATTLE_OF_PACOCHA.html, 4 August 2004.

Dunlap, Annette B, *Charles Gates Dawes: A Life* (Evanston, IL: Northwestern University Press, 2016).

Evans, David C, and Mark R Peattie, *Kaigun: Strategy, Tactics and Technology in the Imperial Japanese Navy, 1887-1941* (Annapolis, MD: Naval Institute Press, 1997).

Frank, Richard B, *Guadalcanal: The Definitive Account of the Landmark Battle* (New York, NY: Penguin Books, 1992).

Friedman, Norman, *British Cruisers of the Victorian Era* (Barnsley: Seaforth Publishing, 2012).

———, *British Cruisers: Two World Wars and After* (Barnsley: Seaforth Publishing, 2010).

———, *Naval Firepower: Battleship Guns and Gunnery in the Dreadnought Era* (Annapolis, MD: Naval Institute Press, 2008).

———, *U.S. Cruisers: An Illustrated Design History* (Annapolis, MD: Naval Institute Press, 1984).

———, *U.S. Destroyers: An Illustrated Design History* (Annapolis, MD: Naval Institute Press, 1982).

Frost, Commander Holloway H, USN, *The Battle of Jutland* (Annapolis, MD: Naval Institute Press, 1964).

Gamble, Raymond Carl, 'Decline of the Dreadnought: Britain and the Washington Naval Conference, 1921-1922.' PhD diss., University of Massachusetts, Amherst, MA, 1993.

Gardiner, Robert (ed), *Conway's All the World's Fighting Ships 1947-1995* (London: Conway Maritime Press, 1995).

Gray, Randal (ed), *Conway's All the World's Fighting Ships 1906-1921* (London: Conway Maritime Press, 1985).

Hovgaard, William, *Modern History of Warships: Comprising a Discussion of Present Standpoint and Recent War Experiences* (London: E. & F.N. Spon, Ltd, 1920).

Howse, Derek, *Radar at Sea: The Royal Navy in World War 2* (Annapolis, MD: Naval Institute Press, 1993).

Jentschura, Hansgeorg, Dieter Jung and Peter Mickel, *Warships of the Imperial Japanese Navy, 1869-1945*, trans. Anthony Preston and J D Brown (London: Arms & Armour Press, 1977).

Jordan, John, *Warships after Washington: The Development of the Five Major Fleets 1922-1930* (Barnsley: Seaforth Publishing, 2011).

——— and Jean Moulin, *French Cruisers: 1922-1956* (Barnsley: Seaforth Publishing, 2013).

Jumonville, P C, 'Question 36/44 (*W.I.* no. 4 (2008): 279–282). Bow "Knuckles".' *Warship International* No 4 (2009), p 333.

Koop, Gerhard and Klaus-Peter Schmolke, *German Light Cruisers of World War II*, trans. Geoffrey Brooks (London: Greenhill Books, 2002).

—, *Heavy Cruisers of the Admiral Hipper Class*, trans. Geoffrey Brooks (London: Greenhill Books, 2001).

Lacroix, Eric and Linton Wells III, *Japanese Cruisers of the Pacific War* (Annapolis, MD: Naval Institute Press, 1997).

Lambert, Nicholas A, *Sir John Fisher's Naval Revolution* (Columbia, SC: University of South Carolina Press, 1999).

Lundstrom, John B, *Black Shoe Carrier Admiral: Frank Jack Fletcher at Coral Sea, Midway, and Guadalcanal* (Annapolis, MD: Naval Institute Press, 2006).

Maiolo, Joseph A, *The Royal Navy and Nazi Germany, 1933-39: A Study in Appeasement and the Origins of the Second World War* (London: Palgrave Macmillan, 1998).

Marder, Arthur J, *From the Dreadnought to Scapa Flow, The Royal Navy in the Fisher Era 1904-1919, Vol. II, The War Years: To the Eve of Jutland 1914-1916* (Barnsley: Seaforth Publishing, 2013).

McBride, K D, 'Re: HMS Kent *(1914-1915)* (W.I. *No. 1, 1998*):.' *Warship International* No. 4 (1998), pp 334–41.

Milanovich, Kathrin, 'Armoured Cruisers of the Imperial Japanese Navy.' in *Warship 2014*, edited by John Jordan (London: Conway Maritime Press, 2014), pp 83–4.

Miller, Edward S, *War Plan Orange: The U.S. Strategy to Defeat Japan, 1897-1945* (Annapolis, MD: Naval Institute Press, 1991).

Moore, Captain John E, RN (ed), *Jane's Fighting Ships, 1973-74* (New York, NY: McGraw-Hill Book Co, 1973).

Murphy, Kevin C, 'Chapter Seven: America and the World – Progressives and the Foreign Policy of the 1920s, III. Disarming the World' in *Uphill All the Way: The Fortunes of Progressivism, 1919-1929* (2013), http://www.kevincmurphy.com/uatw-america-disarming.html.

Nelson, Lillian Ruth, '*The Naval Policy of the United States, 1919-1931*.' Master's Thesis, Loyola University Chicago, 1941, http://ecommons.luc.edu/luc_theses/294.

O'Hara, Vincent P, *The German Fleet at War, 1939-1945* (Annapolis, MD: Naval Institute Press, 2004).

——— and Leonard R Heinz, *Clash of Fleets: Naval Battles of the Great War, 1914-18* (Annapolis, MD: Naval Institute Press, 2017).

Okun, Nathan, *Table of Metallurgical Properties of Naval Armor and Construction Materials*, http://www.navweaps.com/index_nathan/metalprpsept2009.php, 26 September 2009.

Olender, Piotr, *Russo-Japanese Naval War 1905, Vol. 2* (Petersfield: MMP, 2010).

Perkins, Richard, *British Warship Recognition–The Perkins Identification Albums: Volume III: Cruisers 1865-1939, Part 1* (Barnsley: Seaforth Publishing, 2017).

———, *British Warship Recognition–The Perkins Identification Albums: Volume III: Cruisers 1865-1939, Part 2* (Barnsley: Seaforth Publishing, 2017).

Prados, John, *Combined Fleet Decoded: The Secret History of American Intelligence and the Japanese Navy in World War II* (Annapolis, MD: Naval Institute Press, 1995).

Raven, Alan, *Camouflage Volume One: Royal Navy 1939-1941* (New York, NY: WR Pres, Inc, 2000).

Roskill, Captain Stephen W, RN, *Naval Policy Between the Wars I: The Period of Anglo-American Antagonism, 1919-1929* (Barnsley: Seaforth Publishing, 2016).

———, *Naval Policy Between the Wars II: The Period of Reluctant Rearmament, 1930-1939* (Barnsley: Seaforth Publishing, 2016).

Saibene, Mark, 'The Redoutable', *Warship International* No 1 (1994), pp 15–45.

Schleihauf, William, 'The Dumaresq and the Dreyer: Part I', *Warship International* No 1 (2001), pp 6–29.

Sieche, Erwin F, 'Austria-Hungary's Monarch class coast defence ships', *Warship International* No 3 (1999), pp 220–60.
—, *German Naval Radar to 1945*, http://www.navweaps.com/Weapons/WNGER_Radar.php.
Skulski, Janusz, *The Heavy Cruiser Takao* (Annapolis, MD: Naval Institute Press, 1994).
Sprout, Harold and Margaret Sprout, *Toward a New Order of Sea Power: American Naval Policy and the World Scene, 1918-1922* (Princeton, NJ: Princeton University Press, 1946).
Staff, Gary, *German Battlecruisers of World War One: Their Design, Construction and Operations* (Annapolis, MD: Naval Institute Press, 2014).
————, *Skagerrak: The Battle of Jutland through German Eyes* (Barnsley: Pen & Sword Maritime, 2016).
Stern, Robert C, *Destroyer Battles: Epics of Naval Close Combat* (Barnsley: Seaforth Publishing, 2008).
————————, *The Battleship Holiday: The Naval Treaties and Capital Ship Design* (Barnsley: Seaforth Publishing, 2017).
Stevens, William Oliver, and Allan Westcott, *A History of Sea Power* (Garden City, NY: Doubleday, Doran & Co., Inc., 1944).
Stille, Mark, *Italian Cruisers of World War II* (Oxford: Osprey Publishing, 2018).
Sumida, Jon T, *In Defense of Naval Supremacy: Finance, Technology, and British Naval Policy 1889-1914* (Milton Park: Routledge, 1993).
Tarrant, V E, *Jutland: The German Perspective* (London: Arms & Armour Press, 1995).
Terzibaschitsch, Stefan, *Cruisers of the US Navy, 1922-1962* (Annapolis, MD: Naval Institute Press, 1984).
von Schütz, Julius, *Gruson's Chilled Cast-Iron Armour*, trans. Commander H H Grenfell, RN (London: Whitehead, Morris & Lowe, 1887).
Watt, D C, 'The Anglo-German Naval Agreement: An Interim Judgment.' *The Journal of Modern History* Vol 28, No 2 (Chicago, IL: The University of Chicago Press, June 1956), pp 155–75.
Whitley, M J, *Cruisers of World War Two: An International Encyclopedia* (Annapolis, MD: Naval Institute Press, 1995).
Wurl, William M, 'Admiral William S. Benson and the American Tradition of Sea Power,' MA thesis., Kent State University, 2009.

Secondary Sources (author/editor not identified):

—, 'Battle of Ulsan.' *The Samurai Archives/SamuraiWiki*. Last modified 31 August 2007. https://wiki.samurai-archives.com/index.php?title=Battle_of_Ulsan.
—, *The Times Comprehensive Atlas of the World, Thirteenth Edition, Reprinted with Changes* (London: Times Books, 2013).
—, 'Says Japan Won't Provoke Conflict.' *The New York Times*, Vol LXX, No 23,101, 24 April 1921, p 29.

Periodicals

Warship International, International Naval Research Organisation, PO Box 48, Holden, MA 01520, http://www.warship.org. (This quarterly journal is invaluable for any serious student of naval history.)

Indispensable Websites

These are sites I referenced constantly during the writing of this and many other books.

Convoy Web: Arnold Hague Convoy Database, http://www.convoyweb.org.uk/misc/index.html. (This is an immensely useful site cataloguing the convoys that sailed to and from Great Britain in the Second World War.)
Dictionary of American Naval Fighting Ships, http://www.history.navy.mil/danfs/index.html. (The entries in this immense effort vary considerably in detail and completeness. For the most part, though, it's an excellent first reference for any USN ship.)
NavWeaps: Naval Weapons, Naval Technology and Naval Reunions, http://www.navweaps.com/. (In indispensable site for information on the weapons carried by warships since the late nineteenth century and many related topics.)
Nihon Kaigun, http://www.combinedfleet.com/kaigun.htm. (This site covers the movements of most Japanese warships in the Second World War in great detail.)
World War 2 at Sea: SERVICE HISTORIES of 1,000 ROYAL and DOMINION NAVY WARSHIPS, including British Ships manned by Allied Navies, http://www.naval-history.net/xGM-aContents.htm. (A massively useful site for any interested in the Royal Navy in the Second World War.)
WW2 Timeline, http://ww2db.com/event/timeline/. (This useful chronology of the war combines a number of sources.)

Index

Ships, persons or locations shown in images or mentioned in captions are indicated in *italics*. For navy abbreviations, see the 'Abbreviations/Acronyms' section at the beginning of the book; for those nations whose navies are not so defined, nationality codes are used, see https://en.wikipedia.org/wiki/ISO_3166-1_alpha-2; for ship type designators, see https://www.history.navy.mil/research/histories/ship-histories/abbreviations.html. (It should be noted that, despite being quite comprehensive, the list of ship type designators at the abovementioned site does not include all the ship types described here, and some 'invention' was required. The reader should also note that the navy abbreviation 'KM' is used to designate all the successive German navies covered here. When two ships or classes in a navy share the same name and type, they are distinguished by the year in which they were laid down.) Items mentioned in ship's specifications in the text are not indexed.